UNSPOKEN ROME

Latin literature is a hotbed of holes and erasures. Its sensitivity to politics leaves it ripe for repression of all sorts of names, places and historical events, while its dense allusivity appears to hide interpretative clues in a network of texts that only the reader's consciousness can make present. This volume showcases innovative approaches to the field of Latin literature, all of which are refracted through this prism of absence, which functions as a fundamental generative force both for the hermeneutics and the ongoing literary aftermath of these texts. Reviewing and working with various influential approaches to textual absence, the contributors to *Unspoken Rome* treat these texts as silent types, listening out for what they do not say, and how they do not speak, whilst also tracing the ill-defined borders within which scholars and modern authors are legitimised to fill in the silences around which they are built.

TOM GEUE is Lecturer in Latin at the University of St Andrews. He is the author of *Juvenal and the Poetics of Anonymity* (Cambridge, 2017) and *Author Unknown: The Power of Anonymity in Ancient Rome* (2019). He is usually away from home.

ELENA GIUSTI is Associate Professor in Latin Language and Literature at the University of Warwick. She previously taught Classics at the Universities of Glasgow and Cambridge, where she was Research Fellow in Classics at St John's College. She is the author of *Carthage in Virgil's* Aeneid (Cambridge, 2018).

UNSPOKEN ROME

Absence in Latin Literature and its Reception

EDITED BY

TOM GEUE

University of St Andrews

ELENA GIUSTI

University of Warwick

Shaftesbury Road, Cambridge CB2 8EA, United Kingdom

One Liberty Plaza, 20th Floor, New York, NY 10006, USA

477 Williamstown Road, Port Melbourne, VIC 3207, Australia

314–321, 3rd Floor, Plot 3, Splendor Forum, Jasola District Centre, New Delhi – 110025, India

103 Penang Road, #05–06/07, Visioncrest Commercial, Singapore 238467

Cambridge University Press is part of Cambridge University Press & Assessment, a department of the University of Cambridge.

We share the University's mission to contribute to society through the pursuit of education, learning and research at the highest international levels of excellence.

www.cambridge.org
Information on this title: www.cambridge.org/9781108823319

DOI: 10.1017/9781108913843

© Cambridge University Press & Assessment 2021

This publication is in copyright. Subject to statutory exception and to the provisions of relevant collective licensing agreements, no reproduction of any part may take place without the written permission of Cambridge University Press & Assessment.

First published 2021
First paperback edition 2023

A catalogue record for this publication is available from the British Library

Library of Congress Cataloging-in-Publication data
NAMES: Geue, Tom, editor. | Giusti, Elena, editor.
TITLE: Unspoken Rome : absence in Latin literature and its reception / edited by Tom Geue, Elena Giusti.
DESCRIPTION: Cambridge, United Kingdom ; New York : Cambridge University Press, 2021. | Papers from a conference, entitled Unspeaking volumes: absence in Latin texts, held at the University of St. Andrews in June 2017. | Includes bibliographical references and index.
IDENTIFIERS: LCCN 2021017704 (print) | LCCN 2021017705 (ebook) | ISBN 9781108843041 (hardback) | ISBN 9781108823319 (paperback) | ISBN 9781108913843 (ebook)
SUBJECTS: LCSH: Latin literature – History and criticism – Congresses. | Absence in literature – Congresses. | BISAC: HISTORY / Ancient / General | HISTORY / Ancient / General | LCGFT: Conference papers and proceedings.
CLASSIFICATION: LCC PA6027 .U57 2021 (print) | LCC PA6027 (ebook) | DDC 870.9–dc23
LC record available at https://lccn.loc.gov/2021017704
LC ebook record available at https://lccn.loc.gov/2021017705

ISBN 978-1-108-84304-1 Hardback
ISBN 978-1-108-82331-9 Paperback

Cambridge University Press & Assessment has no responsibility for the persistence or accuracy of URLs for external or third-party internet websites referred to in this publication and does not guarantee that any content on such websites is, or will remain, accurate or appropriate.

Contents

List of Figures	page vii
Unspoken Rome: Acknowledgements	viii
List of Contributors	ix

    Introduction   1
    Tom Geue and Elena Giusti

PART I ABSENCE IN TEXT   17

1 Catullus' Sapphic *Lacuna*: A Palimpsest of Absences
    and Presences   19
    Ábel Tamás

2 Speaking *Aposiopeseis:* The (Generic) Sound of Silence in Statius'
    Thebaid   35
    Stefano Briguglio

3 Allegorical Absences: Virgil, Ovid, Prudentius and Claudian   47
    Philip Hardie

4 *Tamen apsentes prosunt pro praesentibus*: Proxied Absences
    and Roman Comedy   67
    Giuseppe Pezzini

5 Absence Left Wanting: The Groove in Ovid's *Remedia*   89
    Victoria Rimell

6 The Gaze on the Void: Hermeneutic Responses to Dido's First
    Appearance   109
    Viola Starnone

PART II ABSENCE IN CONTEXT — 123

7 Speaking Silence in Cicero's *Brutus* and Tacitus' *Dialogus de Oratoribus* — 125
  Kathrin Winter

8 *Et sine auctore notissimi uersus*: Unauthored Poetry and Rome's Authoritarian Turn — 142
  Barbara Del Giovane

9 Looking for the Emperor in Seneca's Letters — 165
  Catharine Edwards

10 Marcus Aurelius: Medi()ations Not Medi(c)ations — 185
  John Henderson

11 Lost in *Germania*: The Absence of History in Tacitus' Ethnography — 201
  James McNamara

12 Conspicuous Absence: Tacitus' *De Re Publica* — 219
  Ellen O'Gorman

PART III GOING BEYOND — 237

13 The Slave, Between Absence and Presence — 239
  William Fitzgerald

14 In Search of the Lost City: The Enduring Absence of Pompeii — 250
  Joanna Paul

15 *Omnibus umbra locis adero*: Elena Ferrante and the Poetics of Absence — 270
  Francesca Bellei

16 The Philology of Grief: Catullus 101 and Anne Carson's *Nox* — 289
  Erik Fredericksen

17 Absence, Metaphysically Speaking: From Reception to Instauration? — 307
  Duncan F. Kennedy

Afterword: Lights Out — 324
  Emily Gowers

Bibliography — 334
General Index — 364
Index Locorum — 375

Figures

14.1 Tom Price, *The Presence of Absence*. Photo: Jaroslav Moravec — page 263

14.2 Antony Gormley, *Untitled*, 2002. Bright mild steel blocks 25 x 25 x 50 mm. 17 11/16 x 74 7/16 x 20 7/8 in. (45 x 189 x 53 cm). © Antony Gormley. Photo © Stephen White Courtesy White Cube — 264

14.3 Allan McCollum, *The Dog from Pompei*, 1991, Polymer modified hydrocal, 53 x 53 x 53 cm each. Courtesy of the artist and Petzel, New York — 265

Unspoken Rome: Acknowledgements

The present volume is based on a conference held at the University of St Andrews in June 2017: *Unspeaking Volumes: Absence in Latin Texts*. We owe a great debt to the Department of Classics at the University of St Andrews, to the British Academy, to the Institute of Classical Studies in London and to the Classical Association for allowing us to hold the conference and for providing us with graduate bursaries. We are also grateful to all the participants in the audience at St Andrews, and especially to Nora Goldschmidt, Lydia Spielberg and Alexei Zadorojnyi for contributing papers that ended up being part of other projects. In the three-year gestation period of the volume, a number of cutting-edge theoretical projects have been published in Classics. We wish we could have taken them into consideration. Among these, we single out M. Formisano and C. S. Kraus (eds.) *Marginality, Canonicity, Passion* (2018, Oxford University Press), T. Rood, C. Atack and T. Phillips' *Anachronism and Antiquity* (2020, London Bloomsbury) and The Postclassicisms Collective, *Postclassicisms* (2020, University of Chicago Press). Finally, we would like to thank each other and our friends and families for keeping intellectual life buoyant in the wake of childbirth, childcare, break-up, parental illness and now, last but not least, a global pandemic splitting our hemispheres to make Giusti's day Geue's night. We remain firm friends despite the conditions of academia having other ideas. Solidarity to all our colleagues, casual and other, whose jobs are hanging in the balance, or who have lost them already. We write this in dark times for the University; we hope you're reading it in better ones.

Contributors

FRANCESCA BELLEI is a doctoral candidate in Comparative Literature at Harvard University.

STEFANO BRIGUGLIO is Research Fellow in Latin Language and Literature at the Università di Torino.

BARBARA DEL GIOVANE is Assistant Professor in Latin Literature at the Università degli Studi di Firenze.

CATHARINE EDWARDS is Professor of Classics and Ancient History at Birkbeck, University of London.

WILLIAM FITZGERALD is Professor of Latin Language and Literature at King's College London.

ERIK FREDERICKSEN holds a doctorate from Princeton University.

TOM GEUE is Lecturer in Latin at the University of St Andrews.

ELENA GIUSTI is Associate Professor in Latin Literature and Language at the University of Warwick.

EMILY GOWERS is Professor of Latin Literature at the University of Cambridge and a Fellow of St John's College.

PHILIP HARDIE is Senior Research Fellow and Honorary Professor of Latin Emeritus at Trinity College, Cambridge.

JOHN HENDERSON is Emeritus Professor of Classics at the University of Cambridge and a Fellow of King's College.

DUNCAN F. KENNEDY is Emeritus Professor of Latin Literature and the Theory of Criticism at the University of Bristol.

JAMES MCNAMARA is DAAD-Prime Postdoctoral Research Fellow at Universität Potsdam.

ELLEN O'GORMAN is Senior Lecturer in Classics and Director of the Institute for Greece, Rome and the Classical Tradition at the University of Bristol.

JOANNA PAUL is Senior Lecturer in Classical Studies at the Open University.

GIUSEPPE PEZZINI is Associate Professor of Latin Language and Literature at the University of Oxford and a Fellow of Corpus Christi College, Oxford.

VICTORIA RIMELL is Professor of Latin Language and Literature at the University of Warwick.

VIOLA STARNONE is Research Fellow at the Scuola Superiore Meridionale.

ÁBEL TAMÁS is Senior Lecturer in Latin and Comparative Literature at Eötvös Loránd University, Budapest.

KATHRIN WINTER is Lecturer in Latin at the Ruprecht-Karls-Universität Heidelberg.

Introduction
Tom Geue and Elena Giusti

Unspeaking Volumes

Classicists are nothing if not experts on absence. A large part of our day job is filling gaps and breaking silences, to make something of the textual wrecks and material ruins of our favourite lost world. The practices and conceptions of archaeology underpin the work of classical philologists and literary critics alike, as we deal with unfinished, unpreserved, unattributed, unrecognised texts and their equally unrecoverable contexts. The fragmentary state of antiquity, both as a whole and in its specific manifestations, is the recognisable feature of Classics as an academic discipline – so much so that the work of the critic and his or her positioning in hermeneutic, epistemological or aesthetic terms can never be disjoined from the perception of that unsatisfactory distance that keeps us separated from, and thus ever-desirous of, the unattainable and incomplete object of our study.

Our relationship of absence with respect to the classical past is twofold, since – as Duncan Kennedy via Joseph Brodsky points out in this volume – we are more absent to the ancient world than the ancient world is to us. As in the case of our reception of Pompeii (analysed here by Joanna Paul) or of our treatment of famous textual lacunae (in the chapters of Ábel Tamás and Erik Fredericksen), the promise of *our* reconstruction and restoration, combined with a Lacanian economy of desire as lack,[1] turns our longing for the lost classical world into a desire for survival, for the very essence of being – our necessary re-inscription into a story that did not initially involve us. And yet at the same time the gaps in our knowledge of both texts and contexts, and our role as readers and critics, allow the play of the texts to come into fruition in a continuous process of contestation and renewal of 'meaning'[2] – an

---
[1] See Lacan 2013.
[2] See Iser 1978: *passim* on narrative gaps as a central feature of literary texts and their 'plays' (on 'the play of the text' see Iser 1989).

incessant transformation of textual presence into absence, into presence-as-illusion, into further absence-becoming-presence – that forms what Victoria Rimell calls in this volume the 'groove' of our desire as pleasure and production in our encounters with the ancient literary world.[3]

Absence as a scholarly opportunity is by no means a special feature of Classics, but is quite frankly a common condition of academic practice as a whole. Much scholarly work, as well as academic careers, start with the promise of a gap that needs to be filled. And Greek and Latin textual and literary criticism, standing as it does on the shoulders of Aristarchus and his followers, has its own special 'gap-complex', a longing for Callimachean untrodden paths. In a field so old and 'done to death', the praise of 'it hasn't been done yet' is our holy grail. Most of our projects are framed in such a way as to sell the gap before anyone can mind it: an intertext that had escaped even the most comprehensive *Quellenforschungen*; a newly discovered lacuna in a text that has so far been regarded as sound; a hitherto unexplored methodological perspective, borrowed from some other academic field. In this academic model, as much as we may lament the maimed and incomplete status of our texts and sources, every lacuna becomes an opportunity, every lost source a blessing. But Classics is by no means the only academic field that has turned absence into profitable convenience. English literature in particular has long noticed how the model of the (Freudian) 'critic-as-archaeologist', who digs deep into the literary strata of the text in order to diagnose its unconscious pathologies, has given rise to a fever of neurotic 'interpretosis' whose basic hermeneutic principles are a struggle to counteract.[4] And silences waiting to be filled are no less detectable in contexts, since Marxist and suspicious readings are also predicated on the principle of unmasking invisible networks of power dynamics by attentively discovering clues that have been supposedly hidden in the unspoken undergrowth of literary texts.[5]

We editors of this volume have no intention of arguing against the importance of singling out the gaps in our knowledge of the discipline, nor do we seek to displace Freudian or suspicious readings in classical literature (which continue to be critical to the discipline)[6] – although we would like to

---

[3] On desire as production, against Lacan's conception of desire as lack, see Deleuze and Guattari 1983. As a companion piece to her chapter in this volume, see also Rimell 2019.
[4] See Felski 2015: 52–69; on 'interpretosis' as one of the two 'humankind's fundamental neuroses', see Deleuze and Guattari 1987: 133: 'the best interpretation … is an eminently significant silence'.
[5] See especially Ricoeur 1970, Jameson 1981.
[6] Especially since we have both made use of them in our most recent academic work (Geue 2018, Giusti 2018), just as some of the contributors to this volume do (Winter, Edwards, Del Giovane).

see a more self-critical deployment of them. Rather, we hope that the present collection of essays will serve Latin literary scholars in refocussing our attention towards our practices and responsibilities in handling textual absence. For if scholarly practice has long been devoted to reading ancient texts in view of their enigmatic qualities, whose mysteries it has often been the interpreters' work to enlighten, much can be said by and about the texts themselves once we start reading their lacunae as active producers of meaning rather than empty vessels waiting to be filled by speculation. At the same time, we would like our readers (here and now, and as they read) to reflect upon who gets to handle the rules of the game of filling these gaps, especially as regards Latin intertextual studies. For handling absence with care is more than a scholarly obligation. With the risk of revealing straightaway our debt to ideology critique, we wish to emphasise that complex academic power structures lie behind the regulations of who is allowed to distinguish meaningful against meaningless absences, tendentious against courageous arguments. The label of scholarly 'reconstruction' marks the most authoritative as well as the most criticised works in the field, but which reconstructions are stamped 'authoritative', and which criticised, has a lot to do with which institutions they come from. The hierarchies of our academic publications are defined in turn by a maze of conscious and subconscious academic biases and recognisable erasures of marginalised voices that we trust are facing a new wave of pressure and scrutiny, especially in the United States.[7] The most prestigious works of classical philology have all been in some way about overcoming absence, but only certain profiles have been allowed unlimited – and enduring – access to the game.

Based and building on a stimulating and cohesive conference held at the University of St Andrews in June 2017 (*Unspeaking Volumes: Absence in Latin Texts*),[8] the volume aims to showcase a mixture of old and new approaches to the field of Latin literary studies, all of which will be refracted through this prism of 'absence'. One of our major points is to show how absence functions as a fundamental 'generative' force both for the hermeneutics and the ongoing literary aftermath of Latin literature; in other words, the discipline of textual criticism cannot eventually be disjoined from the field of classical reception. Many of these texts' lacunae (broadly conceived) produce significant literary and political effects, but also supply the gaps that later receptions must mind or fill. In underscoring

---

[7] We think especially of the public-facing online journal *Eidolon* (https://eidolon.pub/), as well as organisations such as the *Women Classical Committee* (https://wcc-uk.blogs.sas.ac.uk/) or *Classics and Social Justice* (https://classicssocialjustice.wordpress.com/).
[8] See Giusti 2017b for the conference's chronicle.

and probing these various absences for their intrinsic qualities, and for the reception they produce, the book seeks to reflect upon and gesture towards some possible futures beyond the influential approaches to textual absence that are still dominant in Latin literary studies, especially intertextuality and new historicism. In other words, instead of Alessandro Barchiesi's landmark *Speaking Volumes* (2001), which takes Latin texts as garrulous creatures always talking to their companions in a holistic system of echoes and presences, *Unspoken Rome* treats them as silent types, listening out for what they do not say, and how they do not speak, while also tracing the ill-defined borders within which scholars and modern authors are legitimised to fill in the silences around which they are built.

The Game and Its Rules

While all ancient texts are buoyed and rocked by their own uplift of omission and amnesia, Rome in particular has left a literature that is a hotbed of holes and erasures. Its sensitivity to politics leaves it ripe for repression of all sorts of names, places, historical events, while its dense allusivity appears to hide political messages and interpretative clues in a network of texts that the reader's consciousness is suddenly allowed to make present. Its reception history, too, is often built upon the readers' desire to fill in these textual gaps. In all of these ways, the Latin corpus is remarkably energised by its own perforations.

Scholars of Latin literature have already come up with a formidable arsenal of ways to attack such absences. The generation of loosely post-structuralist critics tied to the 'New Latin' in the nineties and noughties was galvanised by Derrida's focus not just on absence as a theme, but as a general condition of writing *per se*. As Kennedy reminds us in his chapter, Derrida famously pitched the myth of writing in Plato's *Phaedrus* as one of the founding moments of Western phonocentrism, an ontological hierarchy bundling speech with presence, and writing – the unfathered, mute child unable to vouch for itself – with absence. That sense of writing as a substitute for something not there became the standard of a critical generation particularly enamoured of Ovid. To take a prominent example, Philip Hardie's *Ovid's Poetics of Illusion* (revisited by Hardie in this volume) made the Ovidian world into something marked all over by 'absent-presences',[9] the efforts through writing to 'conjure' things not there,

---

[9] Hardie 2002; Hardie's more recent magnum opus (2012) also engages with *Fama* as a kind of absent-presence personified, which he builds on in his chapter for the volume.

a game of tease with images that evaporate as soon as you fancy them caught. This was and is an indispensable and rewarding framework with which to read Latin poetry, a corpus of verse shot through with issues of image and fictiveness. Absence as writing/writing as absence has in fact been a critical point of reference across the board for Ovidian studies, especially concerning the epistolary mode, which makes special use of the paradoxes of writers and readers separated in space and time.[10] Moreover, Ovid was ripe for the silent treatment because of the way he tends, especially in the *Metamorphoses* and *Fasti*, to flag stories he won't tell, 'roads not taken'.[11] This poster-child of poetic self-consciousness became such a focal point for the textual turn of postmodern Latin also because he responded spectacularly well to certain modes of reading, and critical concepts, predicated on neat textuality: persona, genre, intratextuality, metapoetics.[12] The last of these – differently tackled in this volume by Stefano Briguglio, Giuseppe Pezzini and Victoria Rimell – could be figured as a kind of traumatised disavowal of the absent things 'outside' the text, in preference for explaining textual phenomena by reassuring reference to the terms of the text 'itself'; an inward turn as a coping mechanism, if you will. Ovid seemed born for this kind of clever and intricate 'explaining Homer from Homer' style of exposition, because his systems of metaphor and networks of self-reference are so elaborate, and so *there* at the critic's fingertips. Finally, in a very different sense, the holes of the Ovidian life and death have proved to be particularly fruitful 'generative' absences, whether they motivate obsessive speculations over the mystery of his exile,[13] or encourage Indiana Jones-style questing after his tomb.[14]

If deconstructing the absent-presence dichotomy of western metaphysics somehow became a game that Latin studies could play, especially with its totem toy-boy Ovid, its most common idiom could also be thought of as a form of tracking absent-presences: intertextuality. 'The presence of Virgil in Ovid' *vel sim.* is a type of formulation we read, write, speak and hear all the time. By that, we mean something like this: for every fleeting yet recognisable verbal echo tunnelling back to a textual predecessor, 'targeting' it perhaps, that text can be thought to suddenly *be there*, supplied largely from the competent reader's mind. But it is also, in obvious ways, *not there* – an absence which can only be glimpsed, then imagined. Intertextuality relies heavily on the reader or critic to import the

---

[10] On the textuality/epistolarity of the *Heroides*, see Farrell 1998, Spentzou 2003, Fulkerson 2005 and especially Kennedy 2002; for the exile poetry's use of absent-presence, see Hardie 2002.
[11] See Tarrant 2005. [12] See Orrells and Roynon 2019. [13] Thibault 1964.
[14] Trapp 1973; see also Goldschmidt 2018.

absent text to make meaning, but there is always among cautious classicists an anxiety over the proportions: how much is 'there' in the text? How much is 'not there'? How much of one text can another text 'bring with it'? Or, more to the point, how much can it 'leave behind'? This last question has been firing the intertextuality debate more and more lately, as scholars have started to move beyond the pinning of verbal echoes, and more towards other forms of 'interaction' – a form of which can be occlusion or silence with regard to an intertext, rather than direct engagement.[15] Stefano Briguglio in this volume shows us clearly how intertextual behaviour can be silent in form, and exclusive in purpose: in the case of Statius' *Thebaid*, it can be marshalled to block out certain genres and texts, while somehow still 'bringing them in' – aposiopesis as *praeteritio*. Francesca Bellei, too, gives us an example of intertextuality as silence – for Elena Ferrante, it is a way of pointing to 'what Virgil never said,' while her choice of authorial self-erasure that allows her to exist solely as textuality triggers a powerful inversion of the directionality source > target text of the kind long heralded by postmodern readers of Latin.[16]

A galvanising strand of recent scholarship in Latin studies that has also proved 'generative' for this project lies somewhere between intertextuality and reception studies (which by their nature overlap anyway): that is, the notion of the 'supplement'. Irene Peirano Garrison's work on Latin pseudepigrapha makes use of the framework of the 'creative supplement' to understand phenomena of literary fakes such as those of the *Appendix Vergiliana*; in that case, the career and poetry of Virgil leave certain gaps, hints and roads not taken, to be chased up by later authors trained in the art of writing as someone else.[17] Further down the centuries, Leah Whittington is writing on Renaissance continuations and supplements to fragmentary classical texts, which are a later version of the same basic readerly/writerly impulse to 'fill in the blanks'.[18] In this volume, Ábel Tamás' opening chapter very much works in this crystallising tradition, as he writes about the famous lacuna in Catullus 51 producing readerly responses and other sounds within its (not so) blank space – and how these lacunose poetics shuttle right back to the Sappho of which the poem stands as translation, as well as the previous poem in the collection (50), to which it stands as supplement. Tamás exploits the terminology of the supplement directly; Viola Starnone doesn't, but her chapter on the reception of

---

[15] König and Whitton 2018 devote a whole section to such a subset of intertextuality (see Section 3: 'Into the Silence', with chapters by Marchesi, Geue, Uden and Gibson).
[16] See Martindale 1993 and Fowler 2000.   [17] Peirano 2012.   [18] Whittington forthcoming.

Aeneas' absent gaze on Dido in their first meeting in *Aeneid* 1 could be seen as yet another way of thinking about the readerly desire to supplement absence, in the scholarly tradition's painful scouring for an erotically charged look that simply isn't there. Similarly, Philip Hardie's chapter on allegory and personification exposes Prudentius' and Claudian's attempts to transform the textual and conceptual gaps in Virgil's and Ovid's texts into potential vessels for the unspeakable par excellence – that which 'transcends the limits of human understanding'. In all these cases, the gaps are no defects, but they themselves become the productive and generative forces of both literature and scholarship.

One theoretical framework which has found a tight crossover with intertextuality in Latin studies – and is sensitive to absences by definition – is that of psychoanalysis. Freud's system always had a strong basis in literature; indeed, some have seen it as a form of literary interpretation itself. So it's unsurprising that scholars of Latin literature have made use of it. Ellen Oliensis and Alessandro Schiesaro are two practitioners of the method, doubling, no coincidence, as leading lights in Latin intertextual studies. Oliensis' 2009 book *Freud's Rome* showed us just how productive psychoanalysis can be at reading between the lines, or beyond the text, to the 'textual unconscious' lurking just offstage. But the critic-as-therapist model, which posits the text as a kind of repressed subject revealing snatches of underlying truth through slips, glitches and fissures, has come under its own interrogation from other recent work in literary studies: Rita Felski in particular has spotlighted the dangers of letting psychoanalysis 'take over literature by translating it into the categories of its own hermeneutic code'.[19] Although the work of psychoanalytically informed classicists such as Oliensis and Schiesaro remains judiciously modest, and would never seek to squeeze its objects of study exclusively into a single code, Felski's points resonate for Latin literature as much as for any other field of literature. When the patient is so silent, perhaps the method has to change; it may be no accident that the chapter in this volume which comes closest to Freudian-Lacanian psychoanalysis is also the one that seeks to move beyond it, inspired by Felski's warnings. Instead of understanding Ovidian desire in negative terms as lack or frustration, Victoria Rimell springs us forward, via Nancy, to show that the intervals are 'an integral part or stage in the undular *propulsion* of desire'. Absence is allowed to become truly crucial to desire in a productive and already fulfilling way, rather than something blocking the way of its consumption.

---

[19] Felski 2011: 226, explaining the argument of Felman 1982. See also Felski 2015.

Psychoanalytic critics understand repression as internalised, something the personified textual subject does to itself; but historicist scholars of Latin literature have been following the many forms of *external* repression visited on Latin texts for a long time now. Ever since Shadi Bartsch revolutionised the way we treat imperial literature by extending the insights of Frederick Ahl (locally, from Classics) and James C. Scott (globally, from anthropology),[20] we have become habituated to thinking with the modes of political domination which lead more or less directly to phenomena of censorship and self-censorship.[21] Texts directly engaged with power often present a 'public transcript', the face of ideological acceptability; but ancient authors, well-trained in the art of figured speech, could always gesture ever-so-gently to the subversive world of the hidden transcript down below, something that Catharine Edwards shows extensively in Seneca's attitudes to Nero in this volume. Whether the metaphors imply an ontological hierarchy (cf. Hardie) where the 'submerged' meaning is the real one (cf., say, Lyne 1987, *Further Voices in Vergil's Aeneid*); or whether they are more egalitarian, allowing a text to speak different languages to different audiences simultaneously (e.g. Bartsch's doublespeak, or strictly 'ambivalence'), the search for political valence has been as strong a wing of the 'hermeneutics of suspicion' in Latin studies as any. As with intertextuality, so with subversion: the attack from the reactionary wing has always been that these things are simply 'not there'; that we are imagining them; that they are not present *in the text*.

Newer historicisms in Latin studies have also perched themselves on the lookout for certain forms of absence. In this case, you could understand the search as a quest for absent contexts to supply and surround the inherently deficient text; to plug it back into the discursive and material realities of a world from which it stands oddly severed. Here Latin and its surging (mostly new) historicism have perhaps partly fallen into line with the current state of literary studies elsewhere, which are, as Joseph North has recently argued, completely dominated by the 'historicist-contextualist paradigm'.[22] Though North's account needs to be adjusted heavily to fit the idiosyncratic history and epistemological challenges of a discipline such as Classics – not to mention the fact that the actual workaday practice of a discipline happens a long way from the theoretical and methodological navel-gazing that takes place at its self-appointed 'vanguard' – it is undoubtedly true that much recent scholarship in the field would fancy

---

[20] Bartsch 1994, Ahl 1984, Scott 1990.   [21] On which, see Baltussen and Davis 2015.
[22] North 2017.

itself historicist or new historicist in some measure. At its most reductive – and here, of course, we caricature for clarity – such scholarship tends to treat literature as a subset of an overlapping and completely inter-communicative sphere of 'culture', operating synchronically; literature becomes a way of knowing, just another kind of 'evidence' to throw into the mix, and a means of 'diagnosing' culture. It is our conviction, however, that literature does its own thing in the cultural field, and creates epistemologies that are about logging the unknown and helping us feel what it's like to *not* know (as James McNamara shows in his chapter on *Germania*), as they are diagnostic tools to access a knowable world. New historicism has seen 'contexts' proliferate (even if they are often themselves highly 'textualised' contexts), but it has also often fallen short in ignoring contexts of reception; as per below, we editors believe this attention to reception should be a *sine qua non* of Latin now, as well as Latin next. In that sense, new historicism's quest to fill certain absences has come at the cost of creating others.

The chapters in our second section take these historicist and new historicist traditions in new directions. The important task of tracking imposed silences is still very much a priority, in the spirit of the most sophisticated political historicism. Catharine Edwards tackles *parrhesia* head on as she deals with Seneca's politically necessary strategy of talking about Nero by *not* talking about him. In Edwards' reading, Nero does enter Seneca's *Epistles* via oblique avatars and back-door channels, e.g. the dig at luxury building in 90, or the famous critique of Maecenas in 114. If Edwards handles a case of prose satire fudging its target, Barbara Del Giovane scrutinises an overlooked brand of poetry that covers up its *source*. She gives us a history of anonymous lampoons in the early Principate, which runs in tandem with imperial legislation trying to tie the slippery culprit down. At the same time, she shows us how the elite could appropriate the popular power of the anonymous for their own political ends; anonymity is not just a way of evading power, but also a means of exercising it. While both of these cases deal with power squeezing literature into certain shapes even as literature pushes back, John Henderson handles a case of a self-censoring emperor who is very good at not talking about himself by talking about himself; Marcus Aurelius cuts out a big chunk of his particular first person, and the cargo of history it inevitably shoulders, by refusing to talk politics, and holding tight to a stripped down philosophising self. We also have examples of a more cultural historicism, plugged into contemporary modes of making sense (or not) of the world. James McNamara shows how a text can make a dark world represent the epistemic shortcomings of a whole culture: for him, the vague rumours about Germania in *Germania* constitute 'small bright spots of knowledge amidst a vast expanse of thicket'. Ellen O'Gorman complements McNamara by homing in on embodied and embedded (lack of) knowledge in Tacitus' historical works: she understands Tacitus' Principate as a kind of impoverished sensory world compared with the 'lost plenitude' of the Republic, and ventures thought about the literary ways those lost senses might be brought back. If O'Gorman tracks a historical loss through Tacitean eyes, i.e. largely through the sense of sight, Kathrin Winter measures a similar distance between (the end of) Republic and Principate via *speech*. In Winter's reading, Tacitus' *Dialogus* folds out from the eloquent but circumscribed silences of Cicero's *Brutus* onto a world of failed speech acts, unanswered questions and broken promises – but the silence still generates a strange form of plenitude.

On the other hand, the volume draws inspiration from the other political forms of historicism, such as Marxist ideology critique, which both editors consider central to their own intellectual formation – and, for better or worse, perhaps a silent and unacknowledged presence in the recent history of Latin literary scholarship. These critical historicist readings look for the gaps or blips in the text which show the ideological contradictions of the societies under which they were produced. They have ways of making reluctant texts talk; as Rita Felski has spotlighted in her challenge to the approach, '[for the Marxist critic] even silences can be made to speak; that certain topics are not mentioned only confirms the ubiquitous denials and disavowals of capitalist ideology.'[23] Marxist critics often talk of a text's blind spots, but sometimes they can be a little insensitive to their own. Fitzgerald's chapter, a highly evolved form of ideology critique, moves us beyond this problem by paying heed to both the blind spots of the poem and the blinkers of the critic; he asks whether our own 'misreadings' can form part of the absent stratum of a text, what it doesn't or can't say about slavery. He also throws down an important challenge to historicist readers of Latin texts by hinting at the end not just towards what the texts don't talk about, but about what they *never* talk about – the free poor. That historically transcendent occlusion could well be the most shocking of all: 'Perhaps the most scandalously unspeaking volume is the one that does not speak of its own time.' Unlike the truly passed-over free poor, much has been made of slaves as the paradigmatic absent-presence of Latin literature. Giuseppe Pezzini twists on this

---

[23] Felski 2015: 99.

tradition by showing just how important slaves are to the dramatic and literary functions of comedy, precisely in their roles as proxies or substitutes; indeed, Pezzini's concept of proxiness becomes a fruitful way of thinking about the logic of substitution that is inherent to both literature and performance per se. As friction-causing proxies, slaves create the comedies in which they star.

We mentioned above that absence is particularly important for the 'supplementary' drive at the heart of reception; and (as we explain in more detail below) it is part of our self-imposed brief in this volume to integrate reception and other forms of classical scholarship more fully. Francesca Bellei's reading of Elena Ferrante pays homage to the generator of Elena Greco's text that is the absent muse Lila, who is herself pushed to write after the traumatic loss of her daughter Tina; the creative power of loss, the compensatory art that it generates, becomes Ferrante's redemptive swerve on the self-destructive Dido myth. The ghosts of reception are harnessed to productive ends. And indeed, absence itself has haunted recent trends in reception studies. As Joanna Paul points out, absence is fundamental to Billings' 'erotics of reception', which calls for as much attention to absence as presence. Answering the call, Paul takes us through a case study – or site study – in the charged absence that is Pompeii. As she guides us, we realise most of Pompeii's reception history is directly about what to do with a gaping void in the past, present and even future. Paul ends with Pompeii as a place that is good to think our impending apocalypse. Doomsday becomes a feature of Duncan Kennedy's chapter too. He uses Scheffler's thought experiment in *Death and the Afterlife* to resolve the Epicurean 'conundrum' of death as definitive full stop, and to show that, instead, we *are* meaningfully connected to the future through Latourian attachments, just as Horace from his *Epistles* vantage point, in a sense, is connected to us. In Kennedy's terms, we should no longer think of ourselves as atomised beings, isolated *points* of reception, but as relational *processes* over time. And that sense of reception as an extended, processual relationship also comes out loud and clear for Erik Fredericksen in his treatment of Anne Carson's *Nox* vis-à-vis Catullus 101. Carson's grief philology is the kind of endless, endlessly incomplete work that nicely bears out Kennedy's 'existential incompleteness of every thing'; the prolific meaning-making of *Nox* could be thought of as a creative application of Kennedy's call for 'instauration' over 'reception' – or, in the older words of Boeckh quoted by Fredericksen, 'the knowledge of what has been known'. In all these pieces of cutting-edge reception studies, the gap is the gift that keeps on giving.

Operational Absences

So much for the variety of approaches to textual absence with which the contributors to this volume engage, each in their own ways. For within this methodological heterodoxy we wish for the present volume to fulfil at least one common aim, namely to set aside a space for 'literature' proper in the fissures left open by these debates. Absence, we'd like to claim in this volume, is a specific domain of literature. Or, to put it differently, textual absence plays a crucial role in the very definition of what a 'literary' text is. Indeed, literary texts are always accompanied, in their readerly and literary receptions, by a plethora of further 'absent', unwritten scripts that follow the words on the page like their unspoken shadows. Paraphrases and intertexts are the most common examples of these, but the unspoken script of literature is obviously receptive to an open-ended list of possibilities. This script is not necessarily (although it can be) the one waiting to be dug up or discovered by the critic – rather, it takes the form of a veritable 'dialogue' with absence, paradoxical by its very nature (Kennedy), whether the missing piece is the author (Pezzini, Del Giovane, Henderson), the reader (Kennedy), the context (Edwards), the detail (Starnone), the meaning, the allo- that any text necessarily speaks (Hardie). More often than not, the lack evoked by literary texts, with its authorisation of a communication with absent, unavailable authors or readers (see especially Fredericksen and Kennedy, but also Tamás and Bellei) allows literature to showcase death as the unspeakable par excellence, to speak 'the other', or let it speak, without allowing it to become the fixed domain of either author or critic.

Our definition of textual absence comes close to what literary critics have more appropriately defined 'negativity'. Negativity is no negation, and especially no Freudian negation. It is also not the *sous rature* device of Heidegger and Derrida, nor the Heideggerian paradigm of the work of art as occurring in a double movement of disclosure and refusal. It does not imply – like negation does – that there is another, hidden text to be recovered or deconstructed below certain formulations. Rather, as Budick and Iser put it, it is a basic feature of all texts, an operational device:

> inevitable when we consider the implications, omissions, or cancellations that are necessarily part of any writing or speaking. These lacunae indicate that practically all formulations (written or spoken) contain a tacit dimension so that each manifest text has a kind of latent double. Thus, unlike negation, which must be distinguished from negativity, this inherent doubling in language defies verbalization. It forms the unwritten and unwritable – unsaid and unsayable – base of the utterance. But it does not therefore

negate the formulations of the text or saying. Rather, it conditions them through blanks and negations.[24]

Negativity 'can only be described in terms of its operations' as 'a process of transforming positions which gives dynamic presence to the absence of otherness'.[25] Many of the contributors in this volume, starting from Tamás on the absence of a line in Catullus 51 and ending with Kennedy on the absence of ourselves in Horace's *Epistles*, shift the focus onto how absence operates on and transforms the texts of Latin literature. Some of them home in closely on certain devices of textual absence: the poetic and generic power of aposiopesis (Briguglio), the evocative and illusory games of allegory (Hardie), the creation of the comic space at the hands of absentees (Pezzini), plenitude engendered by silence (Winter), the anxious undermining of self-promotion instigated by Marcus Aurelius' textual gaps (Henderson), anonymity as a feature of political resistance (Del Giovane), negation of history as affirmation of a new borderless narrative (McNamara), the space accorded to women's narrative after the Muse's defection (Bellei), incompleteness allowing for attachment (Kennedy). Others approach textual absence by reading it in terms of its generative power, a pulse prompting its readers and future authors to fill in the gaps left open in the models.[26] This path of 'generative absence' is followed by Starnone, Paul, Bellei and Fredericksen. All of these chapters encourage us to push beyond a conceptualisation of 'reception' studies which flattens works of literature into somewhat passive receivers of the (hierarchically more valuable) ancient texts. They instead force us to read 'reception' as operational negativity of both ancient and modern literature, and urge us to reflect productively upon what it means for us readers and critics to encounter the ancient texts in the shadow of that which we cannot unknow: their 'future perfect' literary histories.

The different approaches and topics showcased in this volume are by no means intended to be comprehensive of the ways in which Latin literary scholars can approach textual absence, but we believe that together they contain the germs of a shared desire to go beyond the model of the text as the enigmatic container of a hidden or erased truth that is the critic's task to discover. And yet beyond this general response to absence suggested by this

---

[24] Budick and Iser 1989: xii.
[25] Budick and Iser 1989: xii and xiv; cf. also Iser 1989: 335. Cf. also Adorno 1990 on negativity and Derrida 1976 on how absence/negativity plays a vital role in his notions of 'différance' and 'supplement'.
[26] On this type of generative absence in literature, see Kermode 1979.

volume's contributors there are no doubt a large number of omissions in terms of both topics and methods that we are inevitably guilty of excluding. We would like to turn some of these absences into a few quick sketches of possible future directions.

In the political/historical realm, the practice of *abolitio* (*damnatio memoriae*) is as obvious a missing piece as an erased name in a giant inscription; this is perhaps the greatest conspicuous absence in our volume, which doubles as the greatest force for conspicuous absence in Roman imperial culture. But we would like to see some future work on *damnatio memoriae* take account of the findings in this volume: could we understand the stricken records of *damnatio memoriae* as providing some kind of generative absence, rather than just another paradoxical absent-presence? Likewise, absence as a form of oblivion might add something to, or better, subtract something from, the accelerating industry of 'cultural memory' within Classics: how is collective memory sculpted by what a culture forgets, either concertedly or accidentally?

Further, there are a number of other areas where the lens of absence could produce fruitful results. Two papers that were originally part of the conference covered some more ground on the concept of the 'non-event' (*res non gestae,* in the formulation of Lydia Spielberg in her contribution on Tacitus' *Annals*), or 'non-act' (explored in Valerius Maximus by Alexei Zadorojnyi as historical characters' refusals to act), and its relation to counterfactual history and new historicist readings of ancient historical accounts. Viola Starnone in this volume provides a powerful example of how the surprising absence of an erotically charged detail such as Aeneas' gaze on Dido allows us to get a glimpse of a number of 'phantasmic', counterfactual *Aeneid*es stalking the shadows of the scene's reception history. In the future, similar analyses could expand, for example, to topoi like the *adunata*: how gaps in the narrative contribute to expressing things that could never happen, ways of marking out the possible with the impossible. There would also be space for more work on the many strategies of omission and compression across Latin literature; although some of our chapters certainly touch on omission (e.g. Winter), there are patent cases wherein the rhetoric of *praeteritio* is central to the text (e.g. Ovid's *Fasti*, or Velleius Paterculus) and its creation of a gigantic excluded world just on the other side of it. Most importantly, absences play a crucial role in certain (traditionally and still) marginalised areas of classical studies: feminist criticism (treated here in very different ways by Victoria Rimell and Francesca Bellei) as well as queer theory and critical race theory, both unrepresented in this volume. Other readers will spot yet more missing pieces. That is precisely our point, and our provocation.

We have subtitled this volume 'absence in Latin literature *and its reception*' out of a slightly polemical spirit. The challenge is very quiet, and needs some amplification here. Classics is used to factoring reception into its ambit now; but in many edited collections, especially companions, there is a chronological imperative that ends up inadvertently ghettoising reception in 'the reception section', putting it after the 'main classics bit', as if the strictures of time simply meant that reception could never quite measure up to the real thing. We think that is not good enough, and certainly no reflection of where we editors see Classics now, or where we want to see it going. This is why we have tried to integrate reception more fully into the very fabric of the volume; to diffuse it across it, from the very beginning (Tamás, Hardie, Starnone) to the very end (Paul, Bellei, Fredericksen, Kennedy), so that no one can mistake reception as being anything other than central, or better, the alpha and omega, of what we do and want done.

In this sense, we would also like the volume to hint at another path not taken within it. We have chosen to eschew chronology to help bring out some of the trans-temporal crosses and collisions which are now on the agendas of some of the most interesting work being produced in classical scholarship. Shane Butler's edited volume *Deep Classics* (2016), which reconceptualises classical reception as an almost 'heterotopic' encounter where spatial and temporal coordinates collapse in 'jarring juxtaposition of distant past and immediate presence'[27] shares with us a desire to overcome the implicitly hierarchical and too tight boundaries of 'reception' studies, although it does so by privileging presence in the form of epiphany rather than absence[28] – something that Nora Goldschmidt's chapter on Ovid's tomb, originally presented at *Unspeaking Volumes*, also makes painstakingly clear.[29] Similarly pioneering in its reconceptualisation of 'reception' studies is the most recent work produced on the encounter between the classical world and contemporary art: we think of Victoria Rimell's *The Closure of Space in Roman Poetics* (2015), which juxtaposes each reading of

---

[27] Butler (ed.) 2016: 4. Although Butler does not specifically acknowledge it, the language is that of Foucault's heterotopia (See Foucault and Miskowiec 1986: 25 on how they 'juxtapose in a single real place several spaces, several sites that are in themselves incompatible' and Foucault 1966 for textual heterotopias), a concept that, incomplete as it may be, is especially useful for thinking about the trans-spatial and trans-temporal operations of literary texts; see Giusti 2017a.
[28] See Butler (ed.) 2016: 4 on the 'awe-inspiring *presence* of the distant past', our emphasis.
[29] Goldschmidt 2018.

a Roman literary text with a discussion of a contemporary work of art; Brooke Holme's *Liquid Antiquity* (2017), with its 'wrinkle in time' temporality inspired by the work of philosopher Michael Serres; and Michael Squire's research project on 'Modern Classicisms', opened by the 2018 exhibition *The Classical Now*. With absence having been so long the realm of 'scholarly' literary critics (however one wants to take it), the innovative aspect of all these projects lies in their privileging of presence, of the epiphanic visuality of the work of art against the unspoken, hidden workings of the literary text.

What this volume attempts to do is to open up a trans-temporal and non-hierarchical conception of classical 'reception' without losing the specificity of literature and its reception as the domain of absence and negativity. In the future, we would like to see the unspoken of literature continue to play a role as classical studies expand in space and time. Following Butler's intuition, we believe that the concept of 'Deep Time' – that we could use beyond classical reception, to explore comparative literature and especially global ancient literature – still has a larger role to play in Classical Studies. In 2006, Wai Chee Dimock made Deep Time highlight in literature 'a set of longitudinal frames, at once projective and recessional, with input going both ways, and binding continents and millennia into many loops of relations, a densely interactive fabric'.[30] Although she applies the concept to American literature, it is meant to single out a specific domain for literature as a whole as 'the home of nonstandard space and time'.[31] This is a particularly refreshing reminder for us classicists and our kneejerk historicism; it is also an invitation to deterritorialise classical literature, expand our textual, contextual and theoretical horizons as we allow Latin and Greek literary texts to travel beyond the constraints of language and nation. We would like to see Latin literary studies clued in not just to the 'interdisciplinarity' of Latin and Greek, or Latin and material culture, or Latin and history, but turned into a field collapsing into and collaborating with the universe of world literatures. We hope for a trans-national and a trans-global Latin – not in terms of imperial conquest, but in terms of infinite freedom of movement. This project has reaffirmed for us that literature travels, and absence is a way of powering it through space and time. We are very happy with what will be said in the next pages to that end. But we also look forward to all the things that are yet to be spoken.

---

[30] Dimock 2006: 4–5.   [31] Dimock 2006: 5.

PART I
Absence in Text

CHAPTER I

Catullus' Sapphic Lacuna
A Palimpsest of Absences and Presences
Ábel Tamás*

Auch Absenz hinterläßt eine Spur, ihre Markierung heißt Schrift
'Absence too leaves a trace: its mark is called script'[1]

The Textual Absence That 'Must Be Supplied'

What do we talk about when we talk of textual absence? In my approach, significantly influenced by Hans Ulrich Gumbrecht's 'philosophy of presence',[2] textual absence is an *effect*, which is generated in the act of reading by something that the reader (whether rightly or not) attributes to the damaged or at least problematical condition of the *Textträger*. Textual absence, accordingly, is an event of the act of reading: a 'scar' – as Gumbrecht formulates with a 'dramatic emphasis'[3] – that forces the reader to focus on the material conditions of the text in question and, in a sense, to

---

* This chapter has benefited very much from other people's help. Above all, I would like to thank the manifold support I received from Elena Giusti and Tom Geue, who edited this volume with unbelievable intellectual energy. The way they read and commented on different versions of this text was extremely helpful. Heartfelt thanks are due to CUP's anonymous readers for their useful caveats. I'm also highly grateful to my colleagues in Hungary, András Kárpáti, Dániel Kiss and Attila Simon, for their invaluable comments, as well as Andrea Timár and Janka Kovács, who polished my English with a lot of care. Last but not least, I wish to thank warmly the participants of the conference in St Andrews for their excessively astute remarks. I use Mynors' text of Catullus (Mynors 1958) and Hutchinson's text of Sappho (Hutchinson 2001). The English translations of ancient texts are taken or adapted from the Loeb editions.

[1] Ernst 2001: 15.
[2] Cf. primarily Gumbrecht 1997, a chapter written for the volume on fragments in the book series 'Aporemata', later reprinted in Gumbrecht 2003: 9–23. In the *Aporemata* chapters that make up his *Büchlein* on philology, Gumbrecht applies his 'philosophy of presence' for the interpretation of the philological work, but without explaining the theory in any general sense. For this, see Gumbrecht 2004, where the author outlines the concept of the 'presence effect' that influences my approach throughout this chapter. See also Don Fowler's seminal essay on ruins, monuments, absence and the desire to fill the gaps (Fowler 2000b), which stands as a fundamental example for thinking of poetic texts as thematising their own 'philological' future.
[3] Gumbrecht 1997: 320.

start thinking both 'philologically' and 'aesthetically' about it. Consequently, this kind of textual absence connects aesthetics and philology in a very special way: the reader, if touched by this effect, feels obliged to distinguish between the hypothetical original and the particular copy they hold in their hands, and to wonder whether the latter is the correct representation of the former, while they also feel that this 'philological' problem is not entirely independent of the aesthetic experience they partake of while reading the text. Generally speaking, textual absence helps or urges us to take both the 'pastness' and the 'reproducibility' of a particular literary work into consideration, and to embed this material and at the same time sensual aspect in our aesthetic experience, which is, in fact, enriched by our sudden desire to fill in the 'gap' in our imagination. Consequently, textual absence is one of the most effective 'presence effects' that a literary work can generate. With regard to Wolfgang Ernst's insight quoted in the epigraph to this chapter, a real or imagined textual gap only reinforces what is implied in all written texts: that they necessarily testify to something that is entirely absent and for which, accordingly, we are hopelessly longing.

Textual absence is, of course, closely connected to fragmentarity, but it is not only fragmentarity that can generate the effect of textual absence: unfinishedness, whether intentional or not, can produce it just as well. As a matter of fact, this kind of effect is intentionally generated by every (not merely literary) work of art, which simulates being a fragment or being fragmentary. This, from the Romantic period onwards, is an established artistic device: that is, the embedding of the *Vergangenheit* in the sense of 'pastness' into the aesthetic effects of a work of art. This does not imply, however, that all fragmentary texts that survived from classical antiquity necessarily 'inherit' this effect or at least its potential: it is only a possibility one has to reckon with when thinking of texts endowed with textual gaps.

In Latin literature, the half-lines in Virgil's *Aeneid* represent an example in which the potential of textual absence is highly present.[4] Whether we regard them as depending upon the unfinishedness of Virgil's epic work, or else attribute them to the poet's intention, in view of the empirical fact that they really are half-lines, and that much philological debate is associated with them concerning the genesis of the *Aeneid*, we are almost forced to think of them in terms of textual absence. Reading the half-lines of the

---

[4] For a very balanced and concise view of Virgil's half-lines in the *Aeneid*, see O'Hara 2010: 99–100. Special thanks to William Fitzgerald and Elena Giusti, who encouraged me to take Virgil's half-lines into consideration.

Aeneid, we oscillate between a number of reader-responses to textual absence:

a) a romantic meditation on the passing away of even such an immortal poetic work as the *Aeneid* (this is the traditional sense associated with the ruins of antiquity);
b) a historicist curiosity regarding the emergence of these lines (in this case, we have to speculate on the 'absent' Virgil and Augustus, and the similarly 'absent' editorial activity of Varius and Tucca);
c) a philological instinct to fill in the gaps (even if in this case it is a taboo in modern classical philology, because of the biographical tradition testifying that the half-lines belong to the finished unfinished text of the *Aeneid*[5]);
d) an interpretative activity in its narrow sense where we embed the brokenness of these lines into their literary interpretation (this time, we necessarily apply a kind of 'poetics of absence').

For example, the half-line *infabricata fugae studio* ('[logs] unhewn, in their eagerness for flight', *Aen.* 4.4) can be interpreted as referring to both the 'unfinishedness' of the ships that the Trojans are building and, metapoetically, to the incompleteness of the half-line itself, and indeed of the whole *Aeneid*. And yet, a question emerges: who or what is alluding to the unfinishedness of the text? Virgil? Varius and Tucca? Or the unfinished text itself? Can a text that plays on its own unfinishedness still be called 'unfinished'? In my view, these are the possible meditative questions of a reader who is touched by the special effect that I call textual absence; or, more precisely, such questions make up the effect that I call textual absence. In this particular case, this effect may not be independent of the immediate context of the half-line in question, for this concerns the perception of the events by both the reader and Dido: the reader 'sees' (*cernas*, 401) the bustling of the Trojans from a distant perspective, just like Dido does (*cernenti*, 408) – and, in view of the simile of the Trojans as ants in this passage (*Aen.* 4.402–7), both perceive them as 'distant', i.e. distant in time and in space respectively.[6] Consequently, beyond the textual

---

[5] This was not a taboo in antiquity: cf. Conte 2016: 57–9 on ancient interpolations of Virgilian half-lines.
[6] Cf. Smith 2005: 112–13, emphasising the connection between Dido's gaze and the reader's, but without referring to their 'distant' character. For an intertextual and historical interpretation of this Virgilian 'deviant focalisation', implying the historical distance of the reader from the text, see Reed 2007: 99; for Dido's gaze as a 'sublime vision', see Hardie 2009: 163. The *locus classicus* of Lucretian 'distant views' is De Lacy 1964.

absence implied in the half line, the reader's absence from the text is also encoded in Virgil's gap. Textual absence, speaking as metaphysically as Duncan Kennedy in the close of the present volume, spells our absence from the ancient texts as well.

In what follows, I will discuss a particular textual absence, Catullus 51.8. This is the famous *lacuna* of the poet's 'translation' of Sappho's fr. 31, if you like, a possible forerunner of the Virgilian half-lines. According to James J. O'Hara, Virgil had no precedent in the use of half-lines, 'unless we are overly fond of the passage in Catullus 51 where that poet's notoriously flawed manuscripts have a missing short line right where the speaker says his voice breaks off when he looks at Lesbia'.[7] I think that Catullus' *lacuna* can be interpreted in a way that takes into account the *possibility* that Catullus, as an ancient representative of, say, Stéphane Mallarmé's poetics of absence, deliberately left this line empty. At this point, however, I have to emphasise that I do not intend to probe the historicity of Catullus' authorial intention. Maybe he did leave the line empty on purpose, but we cannot, and never will, be certain of it. Nevertheless, I suggest that we focus on how the effect of textual absence is generated by certain ambiguities present in the act of reading itself, and realise that the question regarding authorial intention is constitutive of these ambiguities. The reader of the *lacuna*, if touched by textual absence, is enjoined to ask whether it was Catullus' intention to leave a missing line – this question, together with the instinctive drive to 'fill in the gap', is part of the reader's aesthetic experience. In the absence of any testimony suggesting the authorial or editorial intentionality of the 'omission', it is not a taboo to fill in this gap, as is, in fact, documented by the thirty or so conjectural supplements that have been made in the poem's textual history.[8]

If we take the text as it appears in the critical editions, and set aside, for a while, the philological imperative of filling in the gap, we can say that Catullus, in poem 51.7–8, translates Sappho's fr. 31.7–8 ὥς με φώνησ' / οὐδὲν ἔτ' εἴκει ('my voice comes no more') as follows:

    nihil est super mi
    < ... >

---

[7] O'Hara 2010: 100. He interprets *Aen.* 3.340 *quem Tibi iam Troia?* ('Whom now, lo, when Troy…') as suggesting Andromache's trauma, which makes it impossible for her to speak Creusa's name. One could call this a 'Catullan absence effect' in the *Aeneid*.

[8] For the full apparatus, see Dániel Kiss's online repertory of conjectures on Catullus called 'Catullus Online' (Kiss 2013: www.catullusonline.org/).

That is, he translates it partly into a mere linguistic void, into pure silence, or else into an empty Adonic verse, making manifest the *nihil* included in the previous Sapphic verse. This *lacuna* – precisely because of its emptiness – draws our attention to the metrical structure of the Adonic itself, to its name and origin, and to the multiple significance of textual emptiness. The textual lack makes us desire the absent presence of the past, including that of Sappho herself and her resounding and breaking voice. Furthermore, it makes us meditate on the function of this void right in the middle of the poem. Is this empty Adonic verse an *aposiopesis*?[9] Or, literally, a *lacuna*? Although the rhetorical effect of the *aposiopesis* is at play here, I do not think that we should dismiss the term *lacuna* even if we were to assume that it is an intentional one. *Lacuna* usefully suggests that Catullus' line 51.8 is a philological matter from its inception. Let me imagine Catullus' first readers meeting with this empty line, conceding that it is, of course, a *Gedankenexperiment*. As soon as they read the empty line, if there was some indication, or if they realised the lack of an Adonic verse (in the case that the primary manuscript and its first copies, just like the medieval manuscripts, simply did not contain the 'lost' line, as if nothing were missing), either way they would *perform* with their own voice the break of the poet's voice which is only *described* by any of the supplements. Thus, in the moment they 'read' the textual absence with their breaking voice, they would feel obliged to blame Catullus or someone else for the omission and to demand or even insert a supplement. Accordingly, this linguistically empty line is a *lacuna* by all means, embedding a 'philological moment' into the acts of writing and reading. Because, as the philological imperative dictates, it 'must be supplied'.[10]

Sappho's Falling Silent, Literacy and the Sublime

Jesper Svenbro has analysed Sappho's fr. 31 in a way that makes it possible for the fragmentary poem – in which fragmentarity as such is also part of the play – to be read as an allegory of writing and reading.[11] The speaking 'I' is the writing Sappho herself; the male third person singular, the 'he' of the

---

[9] For *aposiopesis* as a poetic device in Latin literature, especially in Statius, see Briguglio in this volume.
[10] 'In an attractive irony of textual history, part of that crucial moment, all of v. 8, is lost from the (lost) archetype ('Veronensis') and must be supplied.' (Stevens 2013: 310, n. 19.) For his beautiful interpretation of the silence in Catullus 51, see 251–2.
[11] Svenbro 1993: 145–59. I quote some of Svenbro's most pregnant sentences, 155: 'Instead of writing, as in inscriptions, "I am Sappho's poem; you will read me," Sappho writes, "You are my poem; he will read you." The reader will breathe into the poem the ψυχή that Sappho breathed out there. In short, the reader will restore life, voice, sound, and meaning to the γραφή by making it "speak" and "laugh"

poem, is the eternal reader;[12] and as far as the female 'you' is concerned, she is nothing other than the written poem itself. In Svenbro's allegorical reading, the miniature drama is a tragedy consisting of the falling silent of the female writing self, who, having written down and fixed the poem, is immediately constructed as absent, and even dead, jealous of the meeting of her poem (the female 'you') and her reader ('he'). The poem is being reanimated again and again by the male reader as he reads it aloud and keeps it alive (this reader is a series of readers over centuries, of course), while the authorial voice is falling victim to the silencing effect of the intrusion of literacy into the sphere of lyric poetry. Although Svenbro does not explicitly mention the famous hiatus included in γλῶσσα †ἔαγε†, which has made the verb ἔαγε suspect in textual criticism, its 'voicelessness' fits his interpretation very well.[13] Instead of illustrating what Sappho says, it *performs* the breaking or almost dying of the poetic voice. One of the 'solutions' to the suspect line has been to assume the presence of a digamma as the first letter of ἔαγε, which is, in fact, as Yopie Prins writes, an odd solution, 'since the hiatus functions equivocally to mark both the absence and presence of a letter that used to be voiced: the digamma is a non-sound, a voiceless consonant representing something written or read but *not* heard.'[14] If we think of this Sapphic hiatus as performed by the reader who, for a short moment, becomes voiceless when reading the poem aloud, this could pose a challenge to Svenbro's reading, since the reader, according to his interpretation, is living and breathing 'in the poem the ψυχή that Sappho breathed out there'.[15]

If we imagine the reader as, for a short moment, being voiceless, how is it possible that he is the triumphant survivor whose liaison with the poem is seen by the poetess with jealous eyes? I would argue that this is the point where the anthropology of reading *à la* Svenbro could be connected with the aesthetic perspective suggested by Pseudo-Longinus, to whom we owe the survival of Sappho's poem. The author of *On the Sublime* presents fr. 31 as follows (*De subl.* 10.1–3):

---

each time that he reads it, since the present tense that is used, ὑπακούει "he listens" will always refer to the reading of the poem, at which the reader is the foremost listener. The present tense creates the possibility of an eternally renewable reference. In this perspective, not surprisingly does the reader take on the character of a god: although readers are mortal, the Reader is eternal. Sappho is jealous of that Reader, living in a future in which she will be dead.'

[12] This is why, exclusively in the context of Svenbro's interpretation, I will refer to the 'reader' with a male pronoun.
[13] Cf. O'Higgins 1990: 159; Greene 1999: 9; Prins 1999: 33–5.   [14] Prins 1999: 34.
[15] Svenbro 1993: 155.

Sappho, for instance, never fails to take the emotions incident to the passion of love from its attendant symptoms and from real life. And wherein does she show her excellence? In the skill with which she selects and combines the most striking and intense of those symptoms. [. . .] Is it not wonderful how she summons at the same time, soul, body, hearing, tongue, sight, skin, all as though they had wandered off apart from herself? She feels contradictory sensations, freezes, burns, raves, reasons, so that she displays not a single emotion, but a whole congeries of emotions. Lovers show all such symptoms, but what gives supreme merit to her art is, as I said, the skill with which she takes up the most striking and combines them into a single whole.[16]

Is it not possible, we might ask, that the sublime experience – of which the poem is an example in Pseudo-Longinus – is simultaneously a reading experience staged by the miniature drama of fr. 31? The successive readers are offered the paradoxical opportunity to witness the magnificent emotional earthquake of Sappho from both an external position and an internal one, which is due to the fact that the reading of the poem almost turns us, readers, into Sappho. By becoming Sappho, we experience her 'fragmentation' from both a safe and a dangerous position: by reanimating her voice, we have to share in the *pathos* of the poetess. In Svenbro's terms, the reader, when he is listening to the voice of the addressee/poem from a short distance, necessarily hears his own voice, which is the supplement, the continuation or the reanimator of the Sapphic 'I' due to the mechanism of the medium of the poem itself. Accordingly, the breaking of the voice is not only a symptom of Sappho's emotional concussion but can be interpreted also as a physical reaction to this sublime experience of reading.[17] To quote Yopie Prins, who combines Svenbro's allegorical reading with Pseudo-Longinus' interpretation as

---

[16] Translation by W. H. Fyfe (Loeb Classical Library).
[17] My reasoning in this paragraph has been inspired by Neil Hertz's reading of Pseudo-Longinus' interpretation of Sappho, which emphasises the fragmentation and disorganisation of the Sapphic experience (Hertz 1983); Gábor Bolonyai's analysis of the Longinian sublime as a simultaneity of different perspectives, esp. an external and an internal one as in the case of fr. 31 (Bolonyai 2007); as well as Ellen Greene's articles on Sappho fr. 31 and Catullus 51, which emphasise the fragmentation of the erotic self (Greene 1995, 1999, 2007). See also Porter 2016: 117–24, with an analysis of Pseudo-Longinus' reading of Sappho, where sublimity is interpreted as 'a theory of reading'. The fact that the poem fr. 31 is a fragment itself, in my view, enriches this picture with new colours: the fragmented poetic self is testified by a text that partakes in similar experiences, being the 'fragment', i.e. the kind of object which can be taken as a specific combination of absence and presence, an important generator of the sublime since early Romanticism (cf. Fetscher 2001: 561–2). As for Catullus' act of translation, we do not know whether Catullus knew Sappho's poem as a fragment or not. However, to quote one of Tom Geue's comments on the present chapter, 'even if Catullus wasn't translating a fragment, he was responding to a fragmentarity of voice and emotion that was kind of inherent in the original all along'.

much as I do: 'Not only does fragment 31 leave Sappho suspended in *ekstasis*, literally standing outside of a self, but the fragment leaves its reader in a suspended state as well. [. . .] In his reading of fragment 31, we see the shifting identifications that structure the Longinian sublime. The self-scattering in Sappho's fragment is transferred to the reader, who is also scattered in the process of reading it.'[18]

In his Lacanian book *A Voice and Nothing More*, the Slovene philosopher Mladen Dolar discusses the 'object voice' in a way which is highly useful for my investigation. Writing on the metaphysics of the voice, Dolar emphasises the difference between logocentrism and phonocentrism, mentioning 'a dimension of the voice which runs counter to self-transparency, sense, and presence: the voice against logos, the voice as the other logos, its radical alterity'.[19] According to Dolar, voice will lose its unproblematic connectedness to presence in the moment 'sense is eluded'. As he says, 'the object voice is a pivotal point precisely at the intersection of presence and absence', being 'a truncated presence built around a lack'.[20] I think this is how the Sapphic hiatus – an equivalent of a sigh or a breath – is made present in the act of reading. The reader, performing the hiatus, will be touched by a very special effect. Taking into consideration Gumbrecht's theory of presence and, especially, *Stimmung* ('mood', the German word being closely connected to *Stimme*, 'voice' and *stimmen*, 'to tune an instrument'), according to which lyric poetry, by intensifying the opportunity of *touching* inherent in the sound, is able to coordinate bodies with bodies so that they will touch each other in an almost physical way,[21] I assume that, in this particular case, it is precisely the special *Stimmung* of absence-and-presence which is being mediated. Through the hiatus, the reader feels bodily connected to Sappho's 'absence and presence'. Sappho's voice, silenced by the effect of writing, is being reanimated in the later acts of reading as a kind of 'truncated presence'. It is to her broken voice that we are intensively connected, 'being touched as if from inside'.[22]

---

[18] Prins 1999: 38. [19] Dolar 2006: 52. [20] Ibid.: 55.
[21] As for his view of lyric poetry, see most recently his lecture in Cambridge held on 13 May 2016 (www.crassh.cam.ac.uk/gallery/video/hans-ulrich-gumbrecht-why-prosody-and-rhythm-matter-in-poetry-and-in-the-hu). For his general concept of *Stimmung* and how this 'hidden potential' of literary texts can be revealed, see Gumbrecht 2012, esp. the introductory essay on pp. 1–20. For an interesting application of Gumbrecht's theory of presence and *Stimmung*, pointing out an epiphanic experience of the past which is presentified simultaneously as absence and presence by certain 'sounds' of literary texts, see Vásári 2012.
[22] Toni Morrison's words as quoted in Gumbrecht 2012: 4 as a 'definition' of *Stimmung*.

Catullus' Sapphic *Lacuna* and the Translator's Task

Once again: how does the 'absence and presence' of the Sapphic voice survive in the Catullan translation? In Catullus 51.7–9 we read: *nihil est super mi / < ... > / lingua sed torpet* ('no ... remains ..., but my tongue falters'). As for *lingua sed torpet*, this is the adaptation of γλῶσσα †ἔαγε† ('my tongue is broken', fr. 31.9), but we do not see the hiatus here. In the previous line, however, there is a more radical textual event: the equivalent of φώνησ' / οὐδὲν ἔτ' εἴκει sounds in the Catullan translation as follows: *nihil est super mi / < ... >*. Is it not possible to read it as a performative *lacuna* with the intention to make the reader fall silent? Or, more precisely, to break her voice as it is described in the next line? If we understand the *lacuna* in such a way, we can call this a material event of translation: after Catullus has caught sight of the original (*nam simul te, / Lesbia, aspexi, nihil est super mi / . . .*, 'for whenever I see you, Lesbia, at once no ... remains...', 51.6–8, with Lesbia as 'Sappho'), the energy of his translation dissipates into a *lacuna*.[23] On the material or corporeal surface of the text, a 'scar' emerges, a *uulnus* caused by Eros,[24] which makes present the experience of both poems – such as the absence of the Other, the fragmentation of the self and the breaking of the voice – and does so in a highly avant-garde way. Sappho's poem addresses both the survival and the lack of the survival of the poetic voice, viz. the paradoxical circumstance that the voice of Sappho is both being silenced and reanimated in the text. The text, being made to sound again and again, functions as an 'empty monument' of the mortal and immortal lyric voice.[25] Catullus' *lacuna*, in turn, may not be independent of the Sapphic origin of the name of the Adonic verse, the mourning lament ὦ τὸν Ἄδωνιν (fr. 168). Accordingly, the act of translation implied by the *lacuna* can be understood as the material building of this cenotaph – I repeat: the empty monument of mortal and immortal lyric voices – on the surface of the text, as an inscription of absence in the material texture of the translation. Through its wounding and fragmenting nature, this *lacuna*, which transmits the fragmentary character of the Sapphic poem, is permanently pointing to the enduring option of both the Sapphic and

---

[23] I owe this formulation to Tom Geue. For a brilliant interpretation of the translator's gaze and the elision in *Lesbia, aspexi*, which 'unites' the translator with the author of his source text, see Young 2015: 170.

[24] I'm highly grateful to Victoria Rimell for her phenomenal suggestion that Catullus' *lacuna* could be understood as a textual wound caused by Eros. This idea productively meets with Gumbrecht's 'scar'.

[25] Cf. Fowler 2000b: 196 (in the context of Ovid and Martial), and Hardie 2002: 96–7 (in the context of the epilogue of Ovid's *Metamorphoses*).

Catullan poems themselves getting lost or falling silent. The Sapphic voice addresses her own death; the translation, which would guarantee the survival of the voice, builds a cenotaph recording and archiving the absence – or 'truncated presence' – of the voice. I would say that the Catullan *lacuna* functions as a phonographic device: it records the silent sound of Greek lyric poetry. Silence, to be sure, is the only sound that can be recorded through the medium of writing.[26]

The original context of the Sapphic poetic performance is, of course, entirely missing from Catullus. The feeling of absence triggered by both the poem and its translation ('why is it the Other, and not me, who can experience you from a short distance?') is intertwined with an impersonal feeling of absence, namely the atmosphere of lost authenticity. The sonorous world of the Greek *melos* is lost forever; its reanimation in translation is part of a poetic performance that is entirely committed to writing.[27] The Catullan *lacuna* seems to be important even in that context: the cenotaph built to the broken Sapphic voice – as a literal implementation of 'silent writing', because it literally does not tell and does not contain anything, being both empty and material – has a highly paradoxical effect: as a locus of the sublime experience of fragmentarity, containing both the infinite and the nothing, it causes the broken Sapphic voice to sound in such a way that it turns absence into presence. Accordingly, the Sapphic *lacuna* can be seen as a radical gesture of the Catullan poetics which, through emphasising its own indebtedness to writing, permanently suggests its deprivation of the sonorous poetic voice.

Irrespective of whether contemporary readers have read the poem silently, aloud, or murmuring, when they faced the *lacuna* (if there was a *lacuna*), they had to stop for a moment, until they found a solution: they could implement the *lacuna* with any conventional sound of the metric structure, supplying the absent words with verbal or nonverbal forms of the

---

[26] Material events of translation are discussed in Mezei 2017, an analysis of Shakespeare's Sonnet 55 ('Not marble, nor the gilded monuments...') and its Hungarian translation by Lőrinc Szabó, where the translated poem is interpreted as a 'monument' which archives the survival of the lyric voice. For the genuine silence of the funerary monument and the writing (both of which: σῆμα) and for Theognis' 'voiceless stone', see Svenbro 1993: 8–25 and 16, respectively. The voice recording as a kind of technological immortalisation of the voice and the ghostly aspect of the technologically stored voice are addressed in Kittler 1986: 112–13. For a recent approach to ancient literature from the perspective of voice recording, see Butler 2015.

[27] In contemporary Catullan studies, the question of writing as a locus of poetic performance is omnipresent. Cf., e.g., Farrell 2009; Stroup 2010; Kennedy 2014. For example, Catullus 42 is a highly sophisticated poetic play with the opposition of his sonorous poetic voice and the silent writing as its medium, which makes the reader responsible for the reanimation of the Catullan voice and thus the poem itself (see above all Lowrie 2009: 36–8).

Adonic verse. Or they could fall silent. But even in this silence, there is the pulsation of the Adonic verse, the metrical rhythm itself, which, in this case, manifests its articulated musicality without the disturbing intrusion of language, in a pure form. If we understand *melos* as a unity of text, melody and rhythm, as Plato did (*Rep.* 398 c–d), then this *lacuna* helps us realise what kind of sounds we would be supposed to hear. The 'pure' Adonic verse helps us recall the illusory totality of *melos* in the act of reading: in this silence, we do not hear the melody, but we seem to hear the Lesbian *barbitos*, and, perhaps, the song too – or is this an illusion? In the axis of the poem, this *lacuna* makes the *melos* itself sound again, neither in Greek nor Latin, but in the universal language of lyric poetry. Accordingly, *lingua sed torpet* in the next line can be interpreted as follows: it is language itself, Greek or Latin, which breaks off here, and gives place to the universal and meaningless language of the lyric. The falling silent is, from this perspective, the kind of silence which is music itself and which makes music possible. In the axis of the first genuinely lyric poem of surviving Latin literature, this extraordinary 'presence effect' makes the lyric poetry sound *like* lyric poetry in Rome and, even in the epiphany of the breaking of the voice, it makes the sensual experience of the lyric past possible. If we listen to Catullus, through this acoustic channel of 'sublime historical experience',[28] we can hear real sounds and voices: the sigh and broken voice of Sappho in love; the sounds of the accompanying instruments of Greek poetic performances; the murmuring, scansion without language and rhythmic thrumming of a series of Catullan readers.

    The Catullan *lacuna* may be the place where – if 'the translator's task' *à la* Walter Benjamin is well performed – 'the echo of the original' is really awakened.[29] Immediately, it allows us to hear the sound of 'pure language', which is overrunning the original due to the act of translation itself, pointing to 'the predetermined, inaccessible domain where languages are reconciled and fulfilled'.[30] Based on Benjamin's famous parable, according to which the original and the translation 'must correspond to each other' 'just as fragments of a vessel',[31] I would suggest that the intentional fragmentarity of Catullus 51 – in the sense of *intentio translationis* – is not only the echo of the Sapphic fragmentarity or the performative recreation of the Sapphic falling silent in the material event of translation, but, additionally, it is something more fundamental, the re-radiating of 'pure

---

[28] This phrase is borrowed from the title of Ankersmit 2005.
[29] Benjamin 1997: 159. For Benjamin's famous essay on translation as a highly relevant text for contemporary media theory, see Krämer 2015: 117–25.
[30] Benjamin 1997: 157–8.   [31] Ibid.: 161.

language'[32] towards the Sapphic fragment in such a way that the speechlessness of language becomes manifest precisely in its emphatic fragmentarity. This is the falling silent of the particular languages of both the original and the translation, i.e. Greek and Latin, or, rather, their solemn *unio mystica* in the spirit of 'pure language'. The event of translation consisting of the fitting of the two 'fragments' is made special by the circumstance that, intentionally or not, both the original and the translation are fragments. While it is the end of Sappho's poem that is lost, the empty Adonic verse is located in the middle of Catullus' poem; as such, it has the nature of a linguistic 'abyss', such as that which, in Benjamin's essay, is represented by Hölderlin's translations of Sophocles, where 'meaning plunges from abyss to abyss until it threatens to become lost in the bottomless depths of language'.[33]

The abyss inscribed in the surface of the text, where the Sapphic-Catullan voice stands still and trembles, is, however, the redeemer of sublime experience. But what happens with the voice on the margin of the abyss? It breaks, of course, i.e. becomes fragmented. How should we imagine the fragmented voice? It is not only the case that it stops functioning. The voice continues to exist, but in a fragmented, unarticulated and desemanticised way. In this form, it is a radically material phenomenon: the debris of the sound, inscribed as a negative inscription on the material surface of the text. This is not far away from what we call *Rauschen*, or noise, the other side of communication, which is, on the one hand, the condition of the possibility of communication as such, and, on the other hand, an acoustic abyss, where we perceive things that are unperceivable: the aggregate of acoustic effects that, under normal circumstances, are eliminated by our auditory system, e.g. the Aristotelian continuous buzzing of our ears caused by the permanent motion of the air in them (*De an.* 420a). *Tintinant aures* ('my ears ring with inward humming', Cat. 51.11) can be read as an intensified version of this inaudible sound. If we like, this is the negative side of the music of the spheres, the symphony of the *cosmos*, which human ears cannot hear. In the *lacuna*, understood as a material

---

[32] Ibid.: 162.
[33] Ibid.: 164–5. Accordingly, the *lacuna* can be understood as a Catullan 'middle', i.e. 'a plunge into the abyss [...] from which there can be no escape to a place from which we can view the totality of a structure having a clearly delimited beginning and an ending'. (Hardie 2004a: 26, commenting on Don Fowler's first thoughts on middles in Latin poetry which, because of Fowler's early death, had no chance to be elaborated. I'm very grateful to Elena Giusti for having directed my attention to Philip Hardie's preface.)

inscription of *Rauschen* or even of the music of the spheres, we experience the recording of what cannot be recorded.[34]

As a surprising but intriguing parallel to our textual *lacuna* we may turn to the 1915 work of art by Kazimir Malevich entitled *Black Square*, which is intended to present (1) the so called *zaum*, 'a new language of sounds unrelated to meaning' in the form of a painting; (2) the apotheosis of the black colour absorbing the light, the medium of visibility; and (3) the zero point of painting which contains nothing and everything at the same time.[35] The fragmented material surface of this 'suprematist' work of art as we see it today was, of course, not the intention of Malevich. This patina, as a material inscription of the optical noise in the surface of the artwork, is, from a historicist perspective, an obstacle in the way of historical cognition only to be eliminated in order to have access (at least in our historical imagination) to the original condition of the work, understood as the authentic source of information. However, from the point of view of Malevich, including the optical realisation of the *zaum* in the form of a painting, we could legitimately ask: is this noise to be eliminated? Is this not a noise that is inherent in the authentic ontological mode of the *Black Square*?

Catullus, Calvus and the Supplementary Reading

I think that something very similar happens in Catullus 51. We will never know for sure, but it is at any rate possible that the *lacuna* of Catullus 51 was caused by an *error scribae*, and in the original, instead of the *lacuna*, the contemporary reader could read something that 'existed' in the form of words, perhaps a line identical with one of the later supplements – as, for example, the most popular *uocis in ore*. At the same time, this *lacuna*, if it is regarded as a *lacuna* in a pregnant sense of the word, as a *lacuna par excellence*, is a more organic part of the poem than any of the subsequent supplements. I am saying this without the intention of fetishising the manuscript tradition or of criticising the readers, copyists, humanists and philologists of the last 2000 years who have been continuously working on the emendation of classical texts, including Catullus' *oeuvre*. I am saying

---

[34] On *Rauschen* and the sublime, see Scharnowski 2001.
[35] On *Black Square* and Malevich's suprematism see, above all, the commentaries on the Tate Modern's home page: www.tate.org.uk/context-comment/articles/five-ways-look-Malevich-Black-Square (with the definition of the *zaum* as 'a new language of sounds unrelated to meaning', quoted above). For the avant-garde and the sublime in the context of emptiness, absence and silence, with the *Black Square* as an example, see Lyotard 2012.

this for an entirely different reason: because I regard this *lacuna* as an ancient version of the *Black Square*. The *zaum* of our *lacuna*, if taken seriously, condenses everything in itself that happened with/in/around this poem from its birth and beyond, already from its Sapphic model onwards, having its afterlife and survival in Catullus' translation. Paradoxically, Catullus 51 would be *incomplete* without this *lacuna*.

According to the fiction enacted in poem 50 – and this is something I suggest in accordance with many interpreters[36] – poem 51 with its Sapphic translation is nothing other than a literary present for Calvus, the friend. The poet friends have spent a textually inspired day together, in Calvus' place, where, in the framework of a private poetic competition, they have written various poems in various metrical forms. The fictional situation implies, on the one hand, that the outcomes of the competition have been again and again erased from Catullus' wax tablets on which they have fixed them (*in meis tabellis*, 50.2), and, on the other hand, that from time to time a given metric form has been indicated, in which, then, the poets composed their poems, supposedly in the form of a kind of *amoebaeum*, 'Wechselgesang'. As the poem goes on:

I came away from this so fired by your wit and fun, Licinius, that food did not ease my pain, nor sleep spread rest over my eyes, but restless and fevered I tossed about all over my bed, longing to see the dawn, that I might talk to you and be with you (*simulque ut essem*). But when my limbs were worn out with fatigue and lay half dead on my couch, I made this poem (*hoc ... poema*) for you, my sweet friend, that from it you might learn my suffering. (Cat. 50.7–17)

As several interpreters claim (and I agree with them),[37] *hoc poema* refers to the next poem, i.e. the translation, in the Catullan *liber*, which, at least here, mirrors the original polymetric collection. Accordingly, poem 50 is to be understood as a 'cover letter' of poem 51, storing the memory of sending the letter in the composition of the *liber* itself. Seen from this angle, poem 51 seems to be nothing other than the *in-absentia*-continuation of the poetic interplay performed by the poet friends the night before on the fluid medium of the wax tablets.[38] Can this continuation of the poetic

---

[36] E.g. Finamore 1984; Wray 2001: 97; Gaisser 2009: 138–44; Stroup 2010: 233; Young 2015: 120–2.
[37] For references, see the previous footnote.
[38] *Pace* Gaisser 2009: 142. To go one step further: as Lydia Spielberg suggests to me, *reddens mutua* (Cat. 51.6) can be understood as a metaphor for translation. If we accept this idea, poem 51 can be taken as a very natural continuation of what the two friends have done in the fictional world of poem 50: they have translated various love poems from Greek into Latin. At any rate, this is how Elizabeth Marie Young reads this Catullan 'drama of translation': 'When 50 is read this way, 51 becomes the triumphant endpoint in a contest between two authors who spent an ecstatically creative day translating Greek lyrics and elegies.' (Young 2015: 122.)

interplay be imagined as performed on a solid medium, i.e. on papyrus scroll? Or do we see a situation similar to that of poem 42, and, accordingly, does the message arrive to Calvus on Catullus' wax tablets mentioned in poem 50? And is what we read on papyrus, parchment, printed book, or digital media, the fixed version of the 'original' manuscript – the one that, perhaps, already contains the collaboration of Calvus? Is it not possible that Calvus is the supplementer No. 1? At least in Catullus' secret desires?

The required metrical form is Sapphic stanza. The task to perform is to translate Sappho's Φαίνεταί μοι into Latin. The aim is to get Calvus, personally, to knock on Catullus' door as soon as possible. The means of solution is to make a translation that not only presents Calvus with the poetic model of erotic and literary passion and of making-somebody-jealous or with the mirror games of absent and present *personae*, but that almost assumes his physical presence.[39] The role of the reader is, in this particular case, an eminently active or, more precisely, collaborative one. Is it not possible that the famous last stanza (the '*otium*-stanza'), with its disputed status in the poem, has to be understood as an imagined answer of Calvus or as an answer with which he has complemented the Catullan poem in the framework of the *in-absentia*-continuation of their private poetic competition?[40] And, in the same vein, is it not possible that the *lacuna* is the trace of an erasure performed by Calvus? Or that Catullus has left the line empty in order to allow Calvus to fill the gap? With his imagined or really sounding – or breaking – voice? Or with his bodily presence? Fragmentarity, at this point, can be read as the sign of a continuous dialogue: all readers enter the mirror game of voices and echoes that starts with Sappho and is here being exponentially multiplied.[41]

---

[39] For (illusory) presence, absence and desire in Catullus 50 and 51, see Hardie 2002: 50–4.

[40] As several interpreters suggest (see Fantuzzi and Hunter 2004: 472–4; Young 2015: 167–78; Hunter 2019: 51–5), poem 51 can be read as a 'metatranslation', reflecting on the act of translation performed by itself. Accordingly, *superare* (51.2) might be the trace of the literary *aemulatio* included in the desire for Romanising Sappho, and the self-addressing (and very 'Sapphic', cf. Hunter 2019: 54–5) last stanza can be read as a reflection of the *otium* which – according to poem 50 (*otiosi*, 50.1) – generated the process of literary *aemulatio* culminating in Catullus' translation of Sappho (cf. Fowler 2000a: 25). If poem 51's *ille* points back to Calvus as the next potential translator (Young 2015: 176), one might read the last stanza as Calvus' reflection on Catullus' overdone *otium* and the textual and erotic passions it implies. On Lesbia as the speaker of the last stanza (a mostly rejected idea of E. Kalinka), see Kőrizs 2004.

[41] Duncan Kennedy, albeit interpreting *hoc poema* (50.16) as referring to poem 50 itself, outlines a scenario that is highly interesting from my point of view. In the context of Genette's theory of paratextuality, he bases his reading of poem 50 on poem 14 (the latter written to Calvus, threatening him with a selection of bad poets), and poses the question of what the anxious Catullus does plan to do after he has written poem 50: 'A trip to the *librarii* as soon as they open (as in 14.17) to have these

Poems 50 and 51 can thus be read together with poem 101, the epigram in which, according to Erik Fredericksen in this volume, loss is 'reinscribed' many times.

Whatever the case may be regarding the emergence of the *lacuna*, line 51.8 testifies that the 'philological moment', consisting of the reader's desire to erase or to fill in, is an inherent part of the poem. The continuation of this gesture – which is both the gesture of Calvus as the primary reader and a philological gesture – is nothing but the whole *Über-* and *Fortleben* of the poem in its Benjaminian sense. The 'afterlife', 'survival' and 'continuing life'[42] of this poem is a series of sounds and silences echoing in the *lacuna* as an acoustic channel of textual tradition. In the *lacuna*, we can hear the whisper of parchments, the murmur of copyists, the scratching sound of the styluses, the noise of printing machines and the sighs of philologists. Accordingly, the *zaum* of the *lacuna* absorbs the known and unknown supplements of the *lacuna*, documented from the fifteenth century up to the present. Catullus' 'Black Square' condenses in itself – even retroactively, i.e. from Sappho onwards – a myriad of absences and presences: this *lacuna*, as a radical event of translation, manifests the *Fortleben* of the broken Sapphic voice in such an avant-garde way that it is impossible *per definitionem* to define its ideal form. The ideal form of Catullus 51 is variability itself: it generates its own future of multivocality. Catullus' empty Adonic verse is a genuine philological challenge: from the moment of its birth, this *lacuna* – *lacuna*? – is demanding from the absent Calvus and all his absent successors that they fill the gap with their broken voices, supplements and presences, and, accordingly, that they give themselves up to the sublime *zaum* of textual transmission. From its birth, this *lacuna* is a palimpsest of absences and presences.

---

poems – and now with the addition of poem 50 to form a preface – committed to a roll as an offering to Calvus?' (Kennedy 2014: 26). And how will Calvus react? 'Calvus may have been fine with some alcohol-fuelled poetic flirting (cf. *lusimus*, 50.2) with Catullus yesterday, but what will be his reaction in the cold and sober light of morning when he finds that slender "corpus" insinuated next to his own in a roll together?' (Kennedy 2014: 27). Although this is a highly different scenario from that which I have been outlining in this chapter with regard to the connection of poems 50 and 51 (since I assume the permanent erasure of the poems written by the two friends during the day, while Kennedy bases his reading on the assumption that they have been stored *in meis tabellis*), the two readings meet in the assumption of an 'anxious' desire for a *textual* presence of Calvus as being implied in poem 50, or in both 50 and 51, respectively.

[42] Benjamin 1997: 153.

CHAPTER 2

Speaking Aposiopeseis
The (Generic) Sound of Silence in Statius' Thebaid[*]

Stefano Briguglio

Commentators have always noticed Statius' predilection for *aposiopesis*, and they have variously tried to explain its narrative function. Very rarely, however, has this figure received a detailed analysis in its own right. In this chapter, after a brief introduction to *aposiopesis* and its definitions, I will examine some instances in which the trope contributes to the development of the epic plot. I shall then take a step further and argue that Statius uses *aposiopeseis* in the *Thebaid* to mark programmatic *loci* in which he stages a tension between epic and other literary genres, as well as providing reflections on his own role as an epic poet.

In his seminal study on silence as a means of communication, after a detailed analysis of several cases of *aposiopesis* in Latin poetry, Henri Bardon concludes that Statius is 'the master of silence', as he provides 'the most varied and richest range' of silent features.[1] Indeed, Statius' epics – the *Thebaid* and the *Achilleid* – offer the highest number of occurrences of *aposiopeseis* of all the Latin poets: twenty-six occurrences. While Virgil and Ovid[2] also explored the figure, there are no *aposiopeseis* in Catullus, Tibullus or Propertius. Nor do the other Flavian epicists appear to share Statius' predilection for the trope: there are few *aposiopeseis* in Silius Italicus and Valerius Flaccus combined.[3] Therefore, we can agree with Caspar von Barth, when he comments, at *Theb.* 3.87, that such 'interruptions or breaches' in the poetry (*interruptiones aut praeruptiones*) are emblematic of Statius, more than any of his predecessors (*ualde familiares sunt Papinio*

---

[*] I am grateful to Elena Giusti and Tom Geue, the editors of this volume, and to the participants at the *Unspeaking Volumes* conference (especially Stefano Cianciosi, Ludovico Pontiggia and Tommaso Spinelli) for their suggestions on how to improve this paper.
[1] Bardon 1943: 120: 'le maître des silences est Stace; il en présente la gamme la plus variée, la plus riche'.
[2] See e.g. *Aen.* 1.135; *Ecl.* 3.8–9 (with Cucchiarelli 2012 ad loc.); Hofmann-Szantyr 1965: 822–4; *EV s.v. aposiopesi* (but for the presence of *aposiopesis* in Ovid's *Metamorphoses*, see Barchiesi 2005: CLI).
[3] No more than three, according to Hofmann-Szantyr 1965: 824.

nostro, nec ulli ueterum magis); and indeed Barth also added, as an appendix to his commentary, an index entitled *abruptus sermo Papinii*.[4]

Aposiopesis: Some Definitions

But what exactly is *aposiopesis* or *reticentia* in Latin? According to Lausberg, '*reticentia* is the omission of the expression of an idea, made known by breaking off a sentence already begun, sometimes also explicitly confirmed afterwards'[5] – a definition that corresponds exactly with that of ancient rhetoricians. Following this, and taking into consideration the remarks of Licinia Ricottilli,[6] we can list three functions of *aposiopesis*:

a) it interrupts a sentence already begun (cf. e.g. *praecisio est, cum dictis quibusdam reliquum, quod coeptum est dici, relinquitur incoatum iudicium*, Rhet. Her. 4, 30, 41);[7]
b) it removes an element of the sentence (cf. e.g. *cum intra nos supprimimus ea, quae dicturi uidemur, quod aut turpia aut inuidiosa aut alioqui nobis grauia dictu sunt*, Aquila Rom. *de fig. sent.* §5 Halm);[8]
c) it marks the incompleteness of the sentence or thought[9] (cf. *ut ad alium sensum transeat, ideo abruptum et pendentem reliquit*, Serv. *ad Aen.* 1.135).[10]

Moreover, breaking off with an *aposiopesis* is especially pointed: it highlights how part of the meaning of the sentence lies in the 'unsaid'.[11] In colloquial language, *aposiopesis* is a common feature in Plautus and Terence, and in Cicero's letters and speeches: so we are not surprised to find few instances of it in Virgil's *Aeneid*, because it is a colloquial trope – and that is why one might be all the more surprised to find twenty-six occurrences in Statius' epics.

As I shall go on to argue, this impressive number of *aposiopeseis* in Statius' epics is both dictated by narrative choices and self-reflexive in its nature: there are several cases of strategic silences that I shall refer to as 'generic *aposiopeseis*'. Indeed, one of the most striking (and best-known)

---

[4] To be read with Berlincourt 2013: 394–6.   [5] Lausberg 1998: 394.   [6] Ricottilli 1984: 13–14.
[7] 'Aposiopesis occurs when something is said and then the rest of what the speaker had begun to say is left unfinished...' (trans. Caplan). See Calboli 1969 ad loc.
[8] 'When we inwardly let fall something we seem to be about to say, because it's shameful or hostile or otherwise because we find it heavy to say.'
[9] It is worth recalling the main difference between *aposiopesis* and the other tropes of omission (*Abbruchsformel*): the former does not aim at shortening a sentence; rather it highlights the importance of something that, for various reasons, cannot be said.
[10] 'In order to move to another thought, he has left the previous one broken and unfinished.'
[11] See Hofmann 1965: 53: 'Von der affektischen Ellipse unterscheidet sich die Aposiopese lediglich durch bewussten Selbstabbruch der Rede mit Schlusspause, die durch Gesten und Gebärden das Fehlende – Sätze und Satzteile – ersetzen lässt.'

aspects of Statius' epic poetry is his leaning towards literary inclusiveness. Following the pivotal legacy of Ovid's *Metamorphoses*, in his *Thebaid* Statius aims at summoning the entire literary tradition – the works and poetic contexts of his predecessors. In Laura Micozzi's words, 'if it is normally the tradition that contains the author, Statius reverses this axiom: it is the poem that incorporates the tradition'.[12] The project is ambitious and implies a reconsideration of the genre system in Latin poetry: the *Thebaid* would not be merely defined as an epic poem, but as an epic poem comprising of a range of literary genres, such as tragedy and elegy. By following the path laid out in Ovid's *Metamorphoses* and further developed in Lucan's *Bellum Ciuile*, Statius' poem is crossed by great tensions: his major challenge, as he presents a tragic myth in an epic form, is to deal with the 'foreign bodies' that enrich the plot but threaten the consistency of the poem's generic identity.[13]

I argue that one of the means that Statius uses to harness the 'generic' tensions of the *Thebaid*, while also highlighting them, is precisely *aposiopesis*. One could say that Statius appropriates a standard rhetorical device and turns it into a new means of communication, endowing it with metapoetic features.[14] Indeed, in the *Thebaid* there are several passages where this 'generic threat' could become a generic clash – passages that open a window on different texts and intertexts that would not be appropriate in an epic poem. Generic *aposiopesis* has, I believe, two purposes: i) it signals the limits of the epic form and breaks off possible deviation from the epic agenda; and ii) it highlights specific intertextual connections.

Generic *Aposiopesis*

A number of examples may illustrate the point. Book 8 opens with Pluto's complaint about the irruption of Amphiaraus into his kingdom; the god recalls the times when other heroes dared to descend into the Underworld, violating his realm. These were Hercules, Theseus, Pirithous and Orpheus (8.53–60):

---

[12] Micozzi 2015: 325 with further bibliography.
[13] This is the path followed by imperial epic poetry: see the seminal Barchiesi 2001b.
[14] In doing so, Statius develops previous, and especially Ovidian, experiments: see e.g. Ov. *Her.* 12.205–8 (with Bessone 1997 ad loc., and Hinds 1993: 40), where *aposiopesis* avoids a shift from elegy to tragedy: *quod uiuis, quod habes nuptam socerumque potentes,/ hoc ipsum, ingratus quod potes esse, meum est. / Quos equidem actutum – sed quid praedicere poenam / attinet? Ingentes parturit ira minas*, 'That you are alive, that you take to wife one who, with the father she brings you, is of kingly station, that you have the very power of being ingrate – you owe to me. Whom, hark you, I will straight – but what boots it to foretell your penalty? My ire is in travail with mighty threats' (trans. Showerman revised by Goold).

> ... me Pirithoi temerarius ardor
> temptat et audaci Theseus iuratus amico,
> me ferus Alcides tum cum custode remoto
> ferrea Cerbereae tacuerunt limina portae;
> Odrysiis etiam pudet (heu!) patuisse querelis
> Tartara: uidi egomet blanda inter carmina turpes
> Eumenidum lacrimas iterataque pensa Sororum;
> me quoque – sed durae melior uiolentia legis.

...Pirithous' reckless passion tries my patience and Theseus sworn to his audacious friend, and wild Alcides too, when the iron threshold of Cerberus's gate fell silent with its guardian removed. Even to Odrysian plaints (with shame I say it) was Tartarus opened up. I saw the Eumenides weeping disgraceful tears at the cozening song and the Sisters' threads respun. Me too – but the harsh law's violence took a better way.[15]

When Pluto is about to mention the tears that he shed as he was listening to Orpheus' song, *aposiopesis* breaks the speech off (8.60). Augoustakis notes that 'the *aposiopesis* interrupts the flow of the speech at the time when Pluto needs to maintain the appearance of the traditionally ἀμείλιχος (*Il.* 9.158) and *illacrimabilis* (Hor. *Carm.* 2.14.6)'.[16] Furthermore, *reticentia* points to the Ovidian tale in the *Metamorphoses*, according to which Orpheus made the Eumenides but not Pluto himself cry (*Eumenidum maduisse genas*, Ov. *Met.* 10.45).[17] Statius makes Pluto add a new revealing detail – one not suited to his account. Tears and lovers suit elegy, not epic, and threaten to change the nature of epos: when Pluto recalls the magic of Orpheus' love and song of despair (the prototype of the elegiac poet) and is about to become an elegiac character, he cuts his speech off, adding the coda *sed durae melior uiolentia legis* (8.60) – the *lex* of the Underworld, and (so to speak) the norm of epic poetry.[18]

Book 12 contains a similar example of generic *aposiopesis*, this time in relation to tragedy. When Argia meets Antigone on the battlefield, at night, the two women do not recognise each other and are afraid of each other. Antigone asks Argia who she is, and Polynices' wife reveals her

---

[15] All translations of the *Thebaid* are from Shackleton Bailey's edition (except 12.382–5, where I use Mozley's).
[16] Augoustakis 2016 ad loc.
[17] '...their cheeks [of the Eumenides] grew wet with tears...' (trans. Hill).
[18] For a real metamorphosis of Pluto we have to wait until Claudian's *De raptu Proserpinae*, where the god can blush (1.68–9) and is precisely described as *mitior* (2.307), after having tried to dry Proserpina's tears.

identity, suggesting they team up to bury the corpse. Antigone replies (12.382–5):

> 'mene igitur (pro fors ignara!) malorum,
> mene times? mea membra tenes, mea funera plangis.
> Cedo, tene, pudet, heu! pietas ignaua sororis!
> haec prior' – hic pariter lapsae iunctoque per ipsum
> amplexu miscent auidae lacrimasque comasque...

'It is me then whom you fear? – how blind is chance! – me, the partner of your woes? Mine are the limbs that you are holding, mine the corpse that you bewail. I yield. Take him, he is yours! Ah, shame! Ah, for the cowardly devotion of a sister! She came before me – !' Side by side they fall, and together embracing the same body they mingle greedily their tears and tresses...

In this case Statius stages a real challenge of *pietas*: a sister's love pitted against a wife's. Some scholars have noticed a revival of *furor* and *odium* in this scene,[19] while others have argued more persuasively for the novelty of Argia's epic *aristeia* and Antigone's Senecan heroism.[20] As scholars have emphasised, Antigone's high degree of self-consciousness stands out: she is aware of being a 'tragic successor' in a long tradition, starting with Sophocles' and Euripides' *Antigone*. The heroine knows that she has always looked for the corpse of Polynices, and that she has always paid the price for her heroic deed.[21] She is, to sum up, a tragic character placed in an epic poem. *Aposiopesis* marks a break here. Scholars have usually interpreted *prior* (385) as linking Statius' scene with Attic tragedies on Antigone:[22] the girl, who comes and buries the corpse, has arrived 'second'.[23] Interrupted speech here suggests epic 'belatedness', while also highlighting Statius' inclusion of (part of) a canonical *pièce* about Antigone in his poem. Argia is not present in Sophocles' tragedy and here she changes Antigone's pattern of behaviour. As Karla Pollmann writes,

---

[19] See Lovatt 1999: 136; Ganiban 2007: 210–12; *contra* see Manioti 2016 on the 'sisterhood' of Argia and Antigone.
[20] See Heslin 2008: 114–15; Bessone 2011: 210–12.
[21] Cf. also 12.331–2 *ubi incluta fama / Antigone?* (where [is] Antigone, renowned for fame?); 366–7 *'cuius' ait 'manes, aut quae temeraria quaeris / nocte mea?'* ('Whose body do you seek?' she says. 'And who are you that dare do it in *my* night?') and perhaps 351–2 *illam* (sc. *Antigone*) *nam tempore in omni / attendunt uigiles.* ('For all the time guards attend her [Antigone]'). For Antigone's (and others characters') self-consciousness in the *Thebaid*, see e.g. Hershkowitz 1998: 296; Hardie 1993: 36; Pollmann 2004 *ad* 12.366–7; Hardie 1993: 36; Feeney 1991: 341–3; Micozzi 2015.
[22] Shackleton Bailey 2003 punctuates the text differently, thus not reading the *aposiopesis* and interpreting *haec* as referring to *pietas* rather than Argia: *'pietas ignaua sororis! haec prior.'*, and translates: 'A sister's piety is but a poor thing. *This* has first place'; cf. Shackleton Bailey. *Contra*, see Lesueur 1994: 181 n. 31; Pollmann 2004 ad loc.; Bessone 2011: 211 n. 4.
[23] For a deeper survey on this topic, see Heslin 2008: 115–16.

'there is no evidence that Argia appeared in Euripides' lost play *Antigone*,[24] and it is debated whether the episode was modelled on Callimachus' *Aitia*.[25] The presence of Argia could be an innovation of Latin poetry, perhaps starting from Accius.[26] But even if Statius did draw the detail from Accius,[27] the unexpected meeting – and the *reticentia* – in *Thebaid* 12 reminds Antigone and the reader[28] that the scene is not exactly another *mise en scène* of a tragic play: there is no room for mere tragedy, but rather for a tragedy reworked according to epic standards.

Generic Aposiopesis and the Epic Tradition

So far, I have tried to show how in the *Thebaid aposiopesis* invokes parts of the literary tradition only to silence them, ruling out genres that would be inappropriate in the epic poem. In this context, *aposiopesis* is both an intertextual trope and a generic *rappel à l'ordre*. I am going to further develop this notion and consider whether the *reticentia* in the poem involves not only different genres (such as elegy and tragedy) but also the whole epic tradition. What does *aposiopesis* tell us about the relationship between Statius and his epic predecessors? A number of important things, I think, of which some examples follow.

Again in Book 12, Argia strives hard to find her husband's corpse, but darkness hinders her efforts; Juno, the goddess of marriage, decides to help her and asks the Moon to shed light on the battlefield (12.299–302):

---

[24] Pollmann 2004: 44; *ad* 12.349–408.
[25] According to Pfeiffer 1949, Massimilla 2010 and Harder 2012, Call. fr. 175.6 Pfeiffer (from *Aitia* 4?) may refer to Antigone and Argia together by Polynices' corpse, if we accept the reading ἅμα κεδνῆ[ι for ναμακεδνη; see also Schönberger 1965: 237.
[26] See Ribbeck 1875: 483–7; Aricò 1987: 206–12; Dangel 1995: 362.
[27] But see also Hyg. *Fab.* 72: *Antigona soror et Argia coniunx clam noctu Polynicis corpus sublatum in eadem pyra qua Eteocles sepultus est imposuerunt. Quae cum a custodibus deprehensae essent, Argia profugit, Antigona ad regem est perducta*, 'His sister Antigone and his wife Argia lifted Polynices' body secretly during the night, and placed it on the same pyre on which Eteocles had been cremated. When they were apprehended by the guards, Argia fled and Antigone was taken to the king' (trans. in Manioti 2016: 123).
[28] The meeting of Antigone and Argia is a good case study to reflect on the role of the reader, aware that we are dealing with a 'secondary poem', coming after a long literary tradition. Just when the reader imagines that the scene in *Thebaid* 12 will turn into another *Antigone*, *aposiopesis* intervenes and changes the expected context. For a similar narrative strategy, see also Ov. *Met.* 1.689–721, where Ovid does not make Mercury tell Argo the whole story of Pan and Syrinx; in this case, the use of indirect speech saves the reader from listening to the detailed description of a rape for the third time in Book 1 (see Barchiesi 2005: 224–5).

> 'da mihi poscenti munus breue, Cynthia, si quis
> est Iunonis honos; certe Iovis improba iussu
> ter noctem Herculeam ... – ueteres sed mitto querelas:
> en locus officio...'

I have a small favour to ask, Cynthia; grant it if you have any regard for Juno. To be sure, at Jove's bidding you tripled Hercules' night, shameless – but I leave old grudges aside. See, you have a chance to do me a service ...

Since Feeney's seminal study,[29] the metamorphosis of Juno has been included among the most striking innovations in Statius' *Thebaid*: haunted by revenge, the angry goddess of Virgil's *Aeneid* has turned into a mild *numen* and appears for the last time in the poem as Argia's helper. As Feeney writes, 'she refuses to follow up her resentment against the moon-goddess for her action on the night of Hercules' conception';[30] the *ueteres ... querelas* that she mentions (12.301) have, at this point, been set aside. Juno breaks her speech off, thus signalling a shift from the epic (mostly Virgilian) tradition. *Aeneid* 12 ends with a tormenting reconciliation: it was inevitable that Juno should give up and surrender to Jupiter's plans. *Thebaid* 12, instead, ends with a spontaneous *grand geste* by Juno; she only hints at Jupiter's adulterous adventures, and even pretends to reprimand the Moon (*improba*, 12.301), but eventually the goddess grants forgiveness. She does not conclude her customary complaints: it is not time to recall the main epic tradition on her *grauis ira* (Verg. *Aen.* 5.781) – not even, one might add, the prologue of Seneca's *Hercules Furens*, the manifesto of her bad relationship with Hercules.[31]

There is another episode in the poem in which *aposiopesis* highlights the place of the *Thebaid* in a generic tradition; it encompasses a major theme, namely Jupiter's behaviour, and the striking difference between the *Thebaid* and Ovid's *Metamorphoses* in its treatment. In Book 7, Bacchus begs Jupiter to spare Thebes, realising that his birthplace is about to be destroyed (which he mistakenly attributes to Juno's evil plans).[32] Jupiter reassures his son and starts a famous speech *de clementia*, imbued with sweetness, by boasting that his anger is at rest (*quies irarum*, 7.199) and his fires have been put aside (*iam torta reponam / fulmina*, 7.201–2): he

---

[29] Feeney 1991: 337–64; see also Ganiban 2007: 97–106; Pollmann 2004.
[30] Feeney 1991: 343; see also Pollmann *ad* 12.301.
[31] Sen. *Herc. f.* 1–124; for the double-night motive, see line 24 *in cuius ortus mundus impendit diem* ('this son for whose begetting the whole world lost a day', trans. Fitch), with Fitch ad loc.
[32] On Bacchus' (misleading) certainty that Juno is customarily taking revenge on him, see Ganiban 2007: 96–114.

punishes *inuitus* (7.203), 'against his will'.[33] Nevertheless, the Labdacidae's crimes are too great (7.207–14):

> Labdacios uero Pelopisque a stirpe nepotes
> tardum abolere mihi; scis ipse (ut crimina mittam
> Dorica) quam promptae superos incessere Thebae;
> te quoque – sed, quoniam uetus excidit ira, silebo.
> Non tamen aut patrio respersus sanguine Pentheus,
> aut matrem scelerasse toris aut crimine fratres
> progenuisse reus, lacero tua lustra repleuit
> funere: ubi hi fletus, ubi tunc ars tanta precandi?

But the progeny of Labdacus and Pelops it is high time for me to abolish from the root. You know yourself (to say nothing of Dorian offences) how prompt is Thebes to assail the High Ones. You too – but since the old anger is forgotten, I shall be mute. And yet Pentheus, who was not stained with his father's blood nor guilty of defiling his mother's bed or the crime of begetting brothers, filled your wilds with his lacerated corpse. Where were these tears then, where such elaborate entreaty?

This section of Jupiter's reply is awkward: the people Bacchus is begging mercy for are among the most evil on earth, as Bacchus himself should know. Jupiter stops talking just as he is about to recall Bacchus' anger. By mentioning Pentheus, against whom Bacchus had taken his bloody revenge, Jupiter is clearly referring to the cruelty of his son, now pleading for his father to spare the same city he once punished. The *aposiopesis* prevents a transition towards Books 3 and 4 of Ovid's *Metamorphoses*, where Bacchus' anger comes out in full. What follows the *aposiopesis* (*sed, quoniam <u>uetus</u> excidit <u>ira</u>, silebo*) tells us that we are in an up-to-date context, where there is no room for anger and revenge, *et pour cause*: this is Jupiter's *On mercy*. After showing his would-be mild epic status, Jupiter grants Bacchus' request, expressly avoiding taking his son's vengeful past into account. Ovid's epic makes him aware of such a past and also ensures that Bacchus is made aware of it. But this is not a summary of Ovid's Theban history: Bacchus' anger against Thebes is put to one side, and Jupiter does not wish to recall it. The balance of power has shifted, and the siding of the main divine characters has been slightly modified.

Another instance, drawn from Book 4, is even more revealing: in the second half of the book, Tiresias performs necromancy to foresee the outcome of the war. The meeting, or rather the clash, between the kingdoms of death and life is a gruesome version of Aeneas' *katabasis*,

---

[33] For a detailed analysis, see Smolenaars 1994 *ad* 7.193–226; Bessone 2011: 69–70.

filtered by Book 6 of Lucan's *Bellum Ciuile*. Like Erichtho, Tiresias has to deal with the dead: initially they refuse to obey, and the seer, helped by his daughter Manto, resorts to threatening them (4.500–18). These lines clearly allude to the Lucanian witch: Tiresias is her 'epic successor', in a context where belatedness, poetic self-consciousness and literary traditions are intertwined.[34] Tiresias explicitly quotes Erichtho at the end of his speech (4.514–8):

> '...scimus enim et quidquid dici noscique timetis
> et turbare Hecaten (ni te, Thymbraee, uererer)
> et triplicis mundi summum, quem scire nefastum.
> Illum – sed taceo: prohibet tranquilla senectus.
> Iamque ego uos...' – auide subicit Phoebeia Manto...

'...For I know whatever you fear spoken or known. I can harry Hecate, did I not respect you, Lord of Thymbra, him too, highest of the triple world, whom to know is blasphemy. Him – but I hold my peace: tranquil old age forbids. And now I –.' Eagerly Phoebus' Manto puts in her word...

Here we have two *aposiopeseis*:[35] the latter (*iamque ego uos* ...) is a quotation from Luc. 6.732, as scholars have pointed out.[36] Thus Erichtho had threatened the gods of the Underworld (using Neptune's very words in Verg. *Aen.* 1.135) at Luc. 6.732–4: *iam uos ego nomine uero / eliciam Stygiasque canes in luce superna / destituam.*[37] The first *aposiopesis*, where Tiresias boasts of his power, is more intriguing: if forced, he could frighten the gods, and even summon up the mightiest of them all – but just as he is about to utter the name, the seer stops talking. Erichtho too had threatened the Underworld with the unmentionable *ille*, but she managed to complete her speech (Luc. 6.744–9):

> ...paretis, an ille
> conpellandus erit, quo numquam terra uocato
> non concussa tremit, qui Gorgona cernit apertam
> uerberibusque suis trepidam castigat Erinyn,
> indespecta tenet uobis qui Tartara, cuius
> uos estis superi, Stygias qui peierat undas?

...Do you obey? Or to Him must I appeal, at whose name the shaken earth never fails to tremble, Him who can look uncovered Gorgon, who can chastise the

---

[34] See the precise allusions at 4.504–5; 508–10; 513; also Parkes 2012 *ad* 4.507–8: 'Erichtho is surely the figure we are meant to recall here'.
[35] See Frings 1991: 64–5.   [36] Parkes 2012 *ad* 4.517–8; Korenjak 1996 *ad* 6.732.
[37] 'Now by your real names I will call you, you Stygian she-dogs, and in this upper light maroon you' (quotations of the *Bellum Ciuile* are from S. Braund's translation).

cringing Erinys with her own lashes, Him who occupies a Tartarus to you unfathomable, Him in whose power are you upper gods, Him who by the waters of the Styx can falsely swear?

Lucan is a ghost haunting Flavian epic: as Marco Fucecchi argues, Erichtho is one of the favourite guises of this ghost in the *Thebaid*.[38] There are several *loci* where the *Thebaid* has to face this widespread literary memory ('*memoria diffusa*', as Laura Micozzi calls it)[39] and Tiresias, too, deals with the most popular witch in Latin poetry. Lucan performs a similar rite, quotes her very words and threatens the same gods. Statius prevents him from metamorphosing completely into a Lucanian character. The seer is another Erichtho (via Seneca's *Oedipus*), and the *Thebaid* follows the *Bellum Ciuile*, but in the end the shadow of the witch is cast thanks to an *aposiopesis*. The *tranquilla senectus* (*Theb.* 4.517) seems to be a suitable reply to Erichtho's evil frenzy. As a result, repetition is threatened,[40] but suddenly turned into difference. By avoiding such a fullscale identification, Statius does not merely echo a Lucanian *locus*, but offers his own point of view about the tradition of epic necromancy by playing a lead role, as he highlights his own position within this poetic *lignée*.

A final example can show us how Statius manages the norms and features of an epic poem: in a sense, this is a generic *aposiopesis* because it deals with a theoretical discussion on epic conventions.

In some cases, *reticentia* can just delay a major theme, without avoiding it completely. This is what happens, for instance, in Hypsipyle's speech in Book 4. After meeting Hypsipyle, Adrastus begs the woman to help him find a spring, as if she were a goddess. She humbly replies (4.776–81):

> 'diua quidem uobis, etsi caelestis origo est,
> unde ego? mortales utinam haud transgressa fuissem
> luctibus! altricem mandati cernitis orbam
> pignoris; at nostris an quis sinus, uberaque ulla,
> scit deus; et nobis regnum tamen et pater ingens –
> sed quid ego haec, fessosque optatis demoror undis?

How should I be a goddess for you, even though my origin be of heaven? Would that I had not transcended mortality by my sorrows! You see the bereaved foster mother of a child entrusted to my care. But heaven knows whether mine have bosom and breast – and yet I had a kingdom and a mighty father. But why do I talk and keep the weary from the waves they crave?

---

[38] See Fucecchi 2015.　[39] See Micozzi 2004; also Briguglio 2017: 25–32.
[40] On witchcraft and repetition in Latin poetry, see Pillinger 2012.

She is but the infant Opheltes' nurse, not a goddess. The woman is about to introduce herself, when she suddenly holds back from recounting her gruesome story. As the reader shall see, Hypsipyle's speech has only been postponed: in Books 5 and 6 it is precisely this speech that will be the longest delay in the poem, the *mora Nemea*, in a complex relationship between Callimachean principles and epic norms, as McNelis pointed out.[41] Georgia Nugent correctly notes that Hypsipyle again suppresses the embarrassing topic of her father's death at 5.34–6, showing reluctance to talk about the past:[42] *illa ego nam, pudeat ne forte benignae / hospitis, illa, duces, raptum quae sola parentem / occului. Quid longa malis exordia necto?*[43] This is surely correct, but what is more tantalizing, here, is the different role of the *aposiopesis*: despite her embarrassment, Hypsipyle is not going to conceal her past. Her perseverance in telling and retelling the story of the Lemnian women is one of her most noticeable traits: as Bruce Gibson and Laura Micozzi put it,[44] in this sense she is a *figura* of the epic narrator, always ready to start his account from the very beginning. Hypsipyle's *reticentia* cannot remain a really voiceless trope for long. Her story is a problematic epic[45] within the major epic, full of nuances that scholars have tried to explain in a number of different ways.[46]

In this case, *aposiopesis* is not a figure of silence or a way of silencing some parts of a literary tradition, but rather a figure of the craving for storytelling: the trope thus becomes a kind of generative force in a narrative context, and it does not close but rather opens the narrative. Arguably, a thirsty audience is not well disposed towards a long tale: thus *demoror* and the *reticentia* mark not only the *mora* (a distinguished feature of epic, as we know[47]), but also the troubles of an epic narrator as to where, when and to whom the story shall be told. The hesitation at 5.36 (*quid longa malis exordia necto?*) suggests the difficulty of finding a starting point for a tale, and connects to the same hesitation of the poet at 1.3–4: *unde iubetis / ire, deae?*[48]

---

[41] McNelis 2007; see also Parkes 2012 ad loc.   [42] Nugent 1996: 53–4.
[43] 'For I am she, captains, lest perchance you be ashamed of your kindly hostess, she who alone snatched her parent away and hid him. Why do I weave a long preamble to a tale of woe?'
[44] See Gibson 2004: 156–71; Micozzi 2008.   [45] Or a problematic *epyllion*, as Heslin 2016 argues.
[46] See e.g. Nugent 1996; Casali 2003; Ganiban 2007, ch. 4; Soerink 2014; Heslin 2016; Briguglio 2019.
[47] See e.g. Parkes 2012: XVII–XX.
[48] 'Where do you command me to begin, goddesses?'; see Briguglio 2017 ad loc.

Conclusion

In conclusion, in Licinia Ricottilli's words, *aposiopesis* intervenes to mark the violation of a code.[49] This is, perhaps, its most insightful definition, but we should meditate on two issues related to such a violation: what kind of code is being violated, and why are the rules of this code being enacted? The second question pertains not only to the sphere of literary criticism, but also to that of psychoanalysis, and this is not the place to refer to the Freudian *Verneinung* in literature.[50]

I think it is worth investigating the first point further. What code is being violated? Clearly, the one concerning moral, religion and good manners, as we saw at the very beginning of this paper. However, several examples in Statius' *Thebaid* broaden the range, and I have made the case that a generic code must be added to the list. The wide use of *aposiopesis* enables Statius and his readers to focus on the relationships between different genres in his epics. He also draws attention to his own poetic status, by using the explosive, post-Ovidian, innovations of imperial poetry, as well as to his role within a long epic tradition.

---

[49] 'In un certo senso, è come se l'aposiopesi scattasse quando, in uno stato di forte emotività, ci rendiamo conto all'improvviso che stiamo violando il codice. L'unica possibilità allora di rispettare la censura (eludendola insieme) è quella di troncare il discorso al punto giusto', 'in a sense, it is as if aposiopesis happened when, due to a strongly emotional state, we suddenly realized that we are in fact violating the code. In that case, the only possibility to respect, and at the same elude, censorship is to break off the speech at the right time' (Ricottilli 1984: 39, n. 47).

[50] For *aposiopesis* and psychoanalysis, see again Ricottilli 1984: 20–1; 27–9. On psychoanalysis and literature, the canonical treatment is probably Orlando 1973; for a recent survey, see Oliensis 2009, with detailed bibliography (discussed at 1–13). Heslin 2005: 277–300 devotes a chapter to Statius' *Achilleid* and Lacanian theories.

CHAPTER 3

Allegorical Absences
Virgil, Ovid, Prudentius and Claudian

Philip Hardie

Allegory 'speaks the other', that which was previously unspoken, and sometimes that which is unspeakable. Allegory also makes present what was absent; allegories are often absent presences. Allegory offers a fullness of meaning, but often succeeds only in delivering linguistic emptiness.

The 'allo' of 'allegory' refers to something that is 'other', elsewhere, not present in the surface or literal reference of an utterance or a text. Allegory enters into a range of relationships to what is spoken and what is not spoken, to absence and presence. Viewed at its simplest, and in accordance with the etymology of the word *allegoria*, allegory has a bipartite structure, operating on two levels, the first, let us call it literal, sense of what is 'spoken' (*agoreuo*), and the second, the 'other', over there. The relationship between the two levels could be one of co-presence. But this egalitarian model is rarely that simple. The 'reality', or importance, of one level is usually of a different order to the other, one being given ontological or semantic priority over the other. The surface image or narrative is a veil, an integument, concealing but also revealing, and so allowing to be spoken, a mystery or higher reality that claims our attention. This is the case both with Platonizing or Neoplatonizing allegorizations of myth and poetry, and with Christian sacramental symbolism, which views the things of this world as shadows of the realities of a higher world. Both Neoplatonism and Christianity deal in visible symbols of the invisible, or effable symbols of the ineffable, that which is unspeaking or unspeakable because it transcends the limits of human understanding and human speech.

In the case of biblical typology, the allegory of events, or concrete prophecy, the type, the prior event or person in the Old Testament is possessed of full historical reality, but it has a meaning that is only fully realized, or fulfilled, in the antitypes of the New Testament and the age of grace that supersedes the age of law. As foreshadowings, 'shadows' cast retrospectively by the later events, the types of the Old Testament lack the full illumination of their Christian fulfilments, and to that extent have a lesser reality. An extreme 'supersessionist' view of the relationship between the Jewish history of the Old Testament and the Christian history of the New would see the former as rendered redundant and superfluous by the latter.[1] Another way of conceptualizing the relationship between type and antitype is transformation: central to the Christian message is the idea of making new the old, a re-formation that may also be a trans-formation, but one in which something of the old survives in recognizable form.

This last formulation could also be applied to the typical narrative of transformation in Ovid's *Metamorphoses*, and there is indeed an allegorical quality to many of Ovid's stories of changes, in which the product of metamorphosis, the thing or creature that is 'other', *aliud*,[2] than the person or other object that undergoes metamorphosis, can often be read as an expression of something inherent, essential, but as yet not visible, in the original form.[3] The metamorphosed body can be read as an allegory of that original form. There is also in Ovid a deep connection between metamorphosis and a kind of allegory that I have not yet mentioned, personification, a trope that gives visible presence to something invisible or absent. Paradoxically, that which is most evident to the senses in a personification, the visible body of a concept, a city, etc., or the apparently living body of somebody who is dead, is that which has less reality than that of which it is an embodiment. Personification, or *prosopopoeia*, gives a mask, *prosopon*, *persona*, a face, a mouthpiece, to someone or something who is not present as an embodied individual, either because that someone is dead (as when in the *Pro Caelio* (33–4) Cicero summons up the long-dead person of Appius Claudius Caecus to rebuke his decadent descendant Clodia), or because that something never had a living body (such as the personification of the *patria* in Cicero's first Catilinarian, 27–9). The personification of some thing gives the potential of voice to a thing which cannot speak, although as a word or concept it can be spoken. Personification also exploits the

---

[1] On the debate over whether Christian constructions of history are supersessionist with regard to Jewish history, see Dawson 2002.
[2] For the 'otherness' of products of metamorphosis, see Ov. *Met.* 15.252–7: *nec species sua cuique manet, rerumque nouatrix / ex **aliis alias** reparat natura figuras, / nec perit in toto quicquam, mihi credite, mundo, / sed uariat faciemque nouat, nascique uocatur / incipere esse **aliud**, quam quod fuit ante, morique / desinere illud idem*, 'Nothing retains its own form; but Nature, the great renewer, ever makes up **forms from other forms**. Be sure there's nothing perishes in the whole universe; it does but vary and renew its form. What we call birth is but a beginning to be **other** than what one was before; and death is but cessation of a former state.' (Loeb transl.).
[3] Solodow 1988: 197–8 on metamorphosis as a making visible of essences. On the connections between metamorphosis and metaphor, simile, allegory, see Hardie 2002: ch. 7 'Absent presences of language'.

ever-present tension between the verbal and the visual, between text and image: what is seen in a personification is more vivid than that which is personified, but it is only a phantom of presence.

Allegory Absented

Before I turn to examine in more detail the complications of absence and presence, spoken words and seen images, in allegories that flaunt their status as allegories, in texts by Ovid, and by two late-antique poets who are profound readers of Ovid – Prudentius and Claudian – I will look at the curious case of the allegory whose voice has been suppressed in Virgil, the poet who speaks strongly through the works of Ovid, Prudentius and Claudian, not least in those writers' practice of allegory and personification. I return to typology, and to the analogy that has often been discerned between biblical typology and historical foreshadowing in Roman epic, in particular the *Aeneid*.[4] There is still a prejudice in some quarters against allegorical readings of ancient texts, a prejudice which results in the suppression of a voice, a gagging of speech. C. J. Fordyce's refusal to accept any symbolic meanings in the Hercules and Cacus narrative in *Aeneid* 8 is notorious. 'Political allusion need not be looked for here any more than in the Aristaeus episode of *Geo*. iv. In both places artistic purpose is justification enough. Virgil's introduction of this aetiological epyllion, appropriate to the scene, is a piece of literary technique, diversifying his narrative with an artful digression in which colourful realism and antiquarian appeal combine to hold his interest and the Cacus story is given life by the device of putting it into the mouth of an eyewitness.'[5] Forty years later, it might seem a waste of time to mention Fordyce's obstinate and wilful application of his blind eye to the exegetical telescope, were it not that his name has been taken, not in vain, by a recent interpretation of the *Aeneid*, Hans-Peter Stahl's *Poetry Underpinning Power. Vergil's Aeneid: The Epic for Emperor Augustus* (2015). On the story of Hercules and Cacus in *Aeneid* 8, Stahl comments: 'In spite of its artistically autonomous character, it has been connected to all sorts of (mostly political) references: Cacus ‑ Cleopatra; Hercules ‑ Augustus; Cacus ‑ Turnus; Hercules ‑ Aeneas, etc. Such interpretations are hardly based on the sequence of thought the text offers. Showing the flaws of some arbitrary readings,' says Stahl, 'Fordyce is right to ask the rhetorical question; "Would a tale of Hercules be expected by itself to make the reader think of Augustus?"'.[6]

[4] See Knauer 1964: 355–6; Horsfall 1995: 162–7. [5] Fordyce 1977: 226. [6] Stahl 2015: 322–3.

Stahl's endnote (n. 130) exposes the particular kind of fundamentalism by which Stahl steers his reading of the *Aeneid*, one that proceeds by a purely sequential reading of the text, in accordance with what is claimed to be 'the strict logical (and rhetorical) organization of ancient literary works'. This narrowly syntagmatic approach is contrasted with a paradigmatic approach which Stahl exemplifies, and criticizes, in Karl Galinsky's 1966 article on the Hercules and Cacus episode, relying, in Stahl's words, 'heavily on "parallels of imagery, language, symbolism and, partly, theme"'.

Stahl, following Fordyce, attempts to suppress voices in the name of a strict policing of the boundaries of sense and interpretability that lays down the law as to what is plausible and implausible, reasonable and far-fetched. We are all familiar with this when it comes to allusion and intertextuality, and Stephen Hinds has written eloquently on the dangers of both philological fundamentalism (very little goes) and intertextual fundamentalism (almost anything goes).[7] Allusion itself can be thought of as a form of allegory (of course, a case can be made that any act of interpretation, intertextual or otherwise, is allegory): al-lusion plays with the other of all-egory.[8] Allusion, like allegory, imports other, or further, voices into a text, voices which may either be given a hearing or be suppressed. Intertextuality and intratextuality often work together with allegory as it jostles for our attention, or as we readers play with the possibility of allegorical meanings. Some readers will see in Aeneas' killing of Turnus an allegory, prefiguration, of Romulus' killing of Remus, some will resist. The former will be encouraged by the echo in Aeneas' words to Turnus *poenam scelerato ex sanguine sumit* ('[Pallas] exacts this punishment from your criminal blood', *Aen.* 12.949) of Romulus' words to Remus in Ennius' *Annals*, on the point of killing him *nam mi calido dabis sanguine poenas* (*Ann.* 95 Sk.).[9] Those who resist may point out that those words are echoed elsewhere in the *Aeneid* in contexts where allusion to the death of Remus would seem to be out of place, and conclude that that allusion should not be heard here either.

Whether the voice of allegory is heard or not is related to the distinction, often made, between allegory and allegoresis, a distinction that is made by appeal to the intention of the author or text.[10] Allegory is used of a text which is intended to point to a level of meaning beyond the literal or

---

[7] Hinds 1998: ch. 2.
[8] For an important statement of the relationship between allusion and rhetorical figures, specifically metaphor, see Conte 1986: 52–7. A standard ancient definition of the trope of allegory is a 'succession of metaphors', *continuae tralationes* (Cic. *Or.* 94).
[9] See Tarrant 2012 ad loc.   [10] On the distinction, see, for example, Copeland and Melville 1991.

surface meaning, and allegoresis is used of a reading process that looks for another meaning or meanings in a text, whether or not these were intended by the author. Scepticism as to the possibility of the allegorical reading of Roman epic needs to be tempered by recollection of the fact that allegoresis was well embedded in ancient reading practices, as we know from the Homeric scholia, from works such as Heraclitus' *Homeric Questions*, and, with reference to a different kind of poetic production, from the Derveni Papyrus.

The ancients were already aware that allegories could be denied when it suits. The deniability of allegory, in the case of a text (or image) that does not overtly provide its own allegorical exegesis, can be a political convenience or safety net, as in the use by ancient orators and poets of figured speech, *emphasis*, the figure *quo aliud simulatur dici quam dicitur*, 'where the speaker pretends to be saying something other than what he is saying' (Quint. *Inst.* 9.1.14); *est emphasis . . . inter figuras, cum ex aliquo dicto latens aliquid eruitur*, 'Emphasis is a figure too [as well as a trope], when a hidden meaning is extracted from a phrase', 9.2.64; *quamlibet enim apertum, quod modo et aliter intelligi possit, in illos tyrannos bene dixeris, quia periculum tantum, non etiam offensa uitatur; quod si ambiguitate sententiae possit eludi, nemo non illi furto fauet*. 'For you can speak with success against those declamation tyrants as openly as you please, so long as what you say can be given a different interpretation, because it is only the risk of conviction, not also offence that has to be avoided. If this danger can be eluded by an ambiguous remark, everybody is in favour of the trick.' 9.2.67.[11] This *schema* is all-egorical (*aliud dici, aliter intelligi*). The difference from other brands of allegory is that the avoidance of danger lies in the fact that what has been said can be claimed not to have been said.

The Emptiness of Personification Allegory

I move on now from Virgil to Ovid, and to personification allegory. Those authors who develop lengthy or recurrent personification allegories are often highly self-conscious about the tensions and paradoxes involved in the device: think of Spenser's *The Faerie Queene*, or the striking figures of Sin and Death encountered by Satan at the gates of Hell in *Paradise Lost* (2.648–883), a passage that has been both a stumbling block and a stimulus to interpretation for generations of Milton's readers. For an example of the self-consciousness of these early modern authors, both thoroughly steeped

---

[11] On *emphasis*, see Ahl 1984.

in the Virgilian and Ovidian tradition, take Spenser's personification of Death, last to appear in the pageant of *Mutabilitie*:

> And after all came *Life*, and lastly *Death*;
> *Death* with most grim and griesly visage seene,
> Yet is he nought but parting of the breath;
> Ne ought to see, but like a shade to weene,
> Vnbodied, vnsoul'd, vnheard, vnseene.
>
> *Mutabilitie Cantos* VII.vii.46

This is aptly described by James Paxson as an 'absent-but-present personification',[12] no sooner offered to our mental vision than withdrawn, deprived of both inner essence and external manifestations of personhood.

Here, I shall look at the major personifications in Ovid's *Metamorphoses*,[13] a foundational text in the history of personification in western literature, and then at the late-antique text which is often taken to mark the beginning of medieval personification allegory, Prudentius' *Psychomachia*. My brief survey of Ovid's personifications will look at two aspects in particular: first the emergence from image into speech (a reversal of the process whereby visible personifications are conjured up out of words), and second Ovid's thematization of the essential emptiness, non-existence, of personifications, characterized by absent presence.

Of the four major personifications in the *Metamorphoses*, the first two, *Inuidia* (Envy) and *Fames* (Hunger), are embodiments of, respectively, an emotion, envy, and a physiological condition of the body, hunger. Neither is given an opportunity to be the mouthpiece for articulate speech. The personification of Envy is mandated by Minerva to infect the Athenian princess Aglauros with envy at her sister Herse's attracting the erotic attention of Mercury. Envy's self-consumption, associated with an atrabilarian humour (*pectora felle uirent*, 'her breast is green with bile', *Met.* 2.777), is felt as an effect on the body, and her operation on her human victim is also bodily.[14] The sense through which she operates is primarily sight, not hearing. Envy is a vice of vision, the sense that is contained within the word that is her name, *In-uid-ia*. Her utterances are confined to groans and sighs (*ingemuit uultumque una ac suspiria duxit*, 'she groaned, pulling a face and drawing sighs', 2.774). We are told that the bile that discolours her body is made vocal in the poison of her tongue, *pectora felle uirent, lingua est suffusa ueneno*, 'her breast is green with bile, her tongue is

---
[12] Paxson 1994: 160, cited by Hardie 2002: 236.
[13] In the following paragraphs I revisit and develop material discussed in Hardie 2002: 231–8, 272–82.
[14] See the fine discussion of Ovid's *Inuidia* in Feeney 1991: 243–7.

stained with poison', 777, but her poisonous words are not heard in Ovid's text. Instead we are shown the images of the object of her envy that *Inuidia* places before Aglauros' eyes, *germanam ante oculos fortunatumque sororis / coniugium pulchraque deum sub imagine ponit*, 'before her eyes she puts her sibling, her sister's happy marriage, and the image of the god [Mercury] in his beauty', 803–4. The conversion of speech into image, a speaking picture, coincides with the poet Ovid's use of words to conjure up vivid images, through *enargeia*, turning a speaking (or writing) volume into a picture gallery.

The second Ovidian personification, *Fames*, utters no sound at all, not even the groans of a starving person. Hunger is mandated by Ceres to inflict an insatiable hunger on Erysichthon, the *contemptor diuum* who has cut down an oak sacred to the goddess. We are not given a transcript of the actual words in which a mountain nymph conveys the orders of Ceres to Hunger, and are told only that the nymph conveys the goddess's commands (*refert mandata deae, Met.* 8.810), and that Hunger carries out Ceres' words (*dicta ... Cereris ... peragit*, 814–15). Nor does Hunger address any words to her victim; she works purely on the interior of the body of the sleeping Erysichthon. Hunger fills Erysichthon with a great emptiness; she is an empty personification of emptiness. *uentris erat pro uentre locus*, 'instead of a stomach there was the place for a stomach', 805, 'not a description of the stomach but of its absence', as Garth Tissol notes,[15] with perhaps a hint at the rhetorical sense of *locus*, a place-holder for a body. Ovid draws on the emptinesses and insubstantialities of Lucretian atomism to describe the para-physiology of hunger and the experience of dreaming. With *in uacuis spargit ieiunia uenis*, 'she spreads hunger in his empty veins', 820, E. J. Kenney ad loc. compares Lucretius on the distribution of food through veins, *facile in uenas cibus omnis induitur* 'all the food is easily distributed into the veins'[16], *De rerum natura* 2.1125. Kenney notes '*uacuis* is paradoxical: filling his veins with herself, Hunger empties them and creates a raging appetite'. In Lucretian terms, Hunger is void, not atomic substance. But the body of any personification, not just that of a deficiency like Hunger, is without substance. We are told that *seque uiro inspirat*, 'she breathes herself into the man', 8.819: but her 'self' has no reality, unlike the flesh and blood of the real human being she attacks.

To the emptiness, nothingness, of hunger/Hunger corresponds the emptiness and nothingness of the dream-food with which Erysichthon

---

[15] Tissol 1997: 69.
[16] Cf. also *De rerum natura* 2.1136; 4.955 (on the effect of food filling the veins in driving out soul particles and so causing sleep, analogously to the effects of invasive air in the body causing sleep).

tries in vain to fill himself in his sleep, insubstantial Lucretian *simulacra*, *petit ille dapes sub imagine somni / oraque uana mouet dentemque in dente fatigat*,[17] */ exercetque cibo delusum guttur inani / proque epulis tenues nequiquam deuorat auras*, 'In his dreams he craved for a meal, as he munched away on a void and ground his teeth to no purpose, gulping down imaginary food in his cheated oesophagus, vainly devouring a banquet of air without any substance',[18] *Met.* 8.824–7. Ovid swerves from Lucretius when Erysichthon's delusional dream of eating, feeding only on *simulacra*, turns into a waking insatiable hunger, however much real, solid food is ingested. Erysichthon turns into a black hole which insatiably and imperialistically swallows up the produce of the three world-divisions, sea, land and air, *nec mora, quod pontus, quod terra, quod educat aër, / poscit*, 8.831–2.

The poetic *imago*, i.e. the personification, of *Fames* is as *inanis* as the dream, the *imago somni*, in which Erysichthon imagines that he is eating. The emptiness of *Fames qua* personification is realised in, or transformed into, the emptiness which is the physiological cause and sensation of physiological *fames*. The unreality of *Fames* (with a capital *F*) is then reflected in the unreality of a narrative in which the emptiness of a limited flesh-and-blood body is incapable of being filled by endless amounts of solid food. Ovid is faithful to his model, Callimachus' *Hymn to Demeter*, where Erysichthon is similarly afflicted with a fairy-tale insatiable appetite, but there the goddess is the immediate agent, 'Straightway she sent on him a cruel and evil hunger – a burning hunger and a strong – and he was tormented by a grievous disease', 66–7. It is by inserting the intermediary of a personification that Ovid engineers the play on the emptiness of hunger and the emptiness of Hunger.

Erysichthon is assaulted by Hunger *sub imagine somni* 'a vision seen in sleep'. The third major Ovidian personification conjures up the *imago Somni*, an image of Sleep, i.e. a personification. Juno, tired of Alcyone's repeated prayers at her temple for the safe return of her husband Ceyx, who has been drowned at sea, commissions Iris to go to the House of Sleep and

---

[17] Cf. also *De rerum natura* 4.1108–9: *adfigunt auide corpus iunguntque saliuas / oris et inspirant pressantes dentibus ora*, 'they greedily attach themselves to each other's body and mingle the saliva in their mouths and breathe in each other, pressing on each other's mouth with their teeth', lovers in the vain pursuit of total bodily possession of each other.

[18] Lucretius describes the experience of dreaming of drinking water, rather than eating, *ut bibere in somnis sitiens cum quaerit et umor / non datur, ardorem qui membris stinguere possit, / sed laticum simulacra petit frustraque laborat / in medioque sitit torrenti flumine potans*, 'as when in sleep a thirsty man seeks to drink, and water is not given that might quench the heat in his limbs, but he pursues the images of water and toils in vain, and thirsts as he drinks in the middle of the raging river', 4.1097–1100.

order that a dream-vision of Ceyx should be sent to inform Alcyone of the truth. Here the words of the *mandata* (11.625: cf. 8.810) of the intermediary between divinity and personification, Iris, *are* relayed at length by the narrator. *Somnus* cannot be a waking anthropomorphic agent, able to interact with another individual for more than a short time, and then only after he has detached himself from the essence of what sleep is, *excussit tandem sibi se*, 'he shook himself off himself', 11.621. In the further chain of command, it is necessary that the dream to be sent to Alcyone should also be sufficiently anthropomorphic to respond to an order. We are not given the direct speech in which *Somnus* gives that order, but told instead that he performs an action that paradoxically denies his own essence, *excitat* 634, he 'rouses, wakes up' the vehicle for the dream itself. *Somnus*' choice from *populus natorum suorum* 'the race of his children' (cf. *Od.* 24.12 δῆμον Ὀνείρων 'land of Dreams') is Morpheus, who might be called a personification of dreaming, proficient in expressing both the visual and the verbal markers of a human being, *exprimit incessus uultumque sonumque loquendi*, 636, gait, appearance and sound of speaking, together making up the recognizable identity of an individual, a person. As personification of the *Meta-morphoses*, Morpheus is also adequate to the power of the poet Ovid both to use words effectively and to conjure up visual images of things that have no substantial existence. As a verbal-visual fiction, this personification is a fully adequate equivalent to that which he personifies, the verbal artefact that is the *Metamorphoses*. In that sense, he is *ipse ego* 'I myself' (668) (as he deceptively presents himself to the sleeping Alcyone in his impersonation of Ceyx): that is what the successful text is. The particular shape that he takes for this mission is the image of Ceyx, (Iris to *Somnus*) *somnia ... iube sub imagine regis / Alcyonen adeant*, 'tell dreams to approach Alcyone in the image of the king', 626–8: in rhetorical terms a *prosopopoeia* or personification of the dead Ceyx, a standard rhetorical use of the device. Quintilian uses the same verb, *excito*, of the use of *prosopopoeiai* to summon up the dead, that Ovid uses of Somnus rousing Morpheus, *quin deducere deos in hoc genere dicendi et inferos excitare concessum est*, 'We are even allowed in this form of speech to bring down the gods from heaven or raise the dead', Quint. *Inst.* 9.2.31. *excito* is also frequently used in other contexts of 'rousing', 'calling up' one of the dead.[19] The *imago Ceycis* is doubly absent, both as the likeness of an absent body, and the likeness of an absent

---

[19] Making the dead speak was sometimes called *eidolopoiia*, Hermog. *Prog.* 9; Aphth. *Prog.* 11; *eidolon* is the Epicurean term for films of atoms translated by Lucretius as *simulacrum*: cf. *Met.* 11.628: *simulacraque naufraga fingant* 'they feign the images of shipwrecks' (the operation of dreams).

body of one who is absent through death. Although Morpheus is not (the absent) Ceyx, *ipse ego* is true in the further sense that as a personification (of dreaming, of the *Metamorphoses*) Morpheus converges with the status of the *imago Ceycis* as personification of a dead person.

Morpheus is a powerful and affecting actor/orator in his address to the sleeping Alcyone.[20] This power of words is inherited by the fourth and last of the major Ovidian personifications, *Fama*, who, like Morpheus, is also a personification of the *Metamorphoses*, viewed within its place in the Greco-Roman literary tradition, in which Ovid locates himself as just one of a series of *auctores*: of the echo-chamber that is the House of *Fama* we read *auditis aliquid nouus adicit auctor*, 'Each new authority/author adds something to what he has heard',[21] 12.58. Like Morpheus, *Fama* is equally at home in the visual and the verbal: she sees everything that happens in the world, and the sounds of her house proliferate without check. Although she can see everything, however, we cannot see her: her chaotic body exceeds the visualizing powers even of that master of *enargeia*, Ovid. Nor, in fact, do we hear her speak, at least not in direct speech: the effect of her power is conveyed in a verb of doing, rather than speaking, as had been the case with *Somnus*: *fecerat haec notum* ... 'she had made it known', 64 ... (with a cross-lingual pun in *fecerat* on *poeta*, Greek ποιητής, from ποιέω = *facio*), followed by a report in indirect speech (in the footsteps of the Virgilian *Fama* in *Aeneid* 4, whose tendentious words are given in indirect speech), *Graias cum milite forti / aduentare rates*, '...that the Greek ships were approaching with a strong army', 64–5. As the final personification, *Fama* in the end does not point to any reality outside the text that we are reading: allegory collapses into tautology.

Prudentius' Christian Personifications

In my *Ovid's Poetics of Illusion* (Hardie 2002), I discussed the close links between personification and metamorphosis, following Joseph Solodow and Garth Tissol: so far from using words to relate to an extra-linguistic reality, personification allegory pulls off the trick of converting words into the vivid appearance, but appearance only, of a worldly presence. I turn now from Ovid to Prudentius. One of the marks of Prudentius' profound Ovidianism is the self-consciousness of his dealings with personification in the *Psychomachia*. In a sophisticated account of that poem, Georgia

---

[20] On the emptiness and absent presences of Morpheus, see Hardie 2002: 276–9.
[21] On Ovid's *Fama*, see Hardie 2012: ch. 5.

Nugent comments on the shiftiness involved in personification allegory, which 'performs yet another substitution, in fact, an inversion: allegory attempts to *turn* the word back into an object, to reify it. This is a fraudulent turn, or *trope*, which is inherent in the making of allegories' (my emphases).[22] This is a deception, Nugent says, that can only be resolved through the intervention of the divine *Verbum*, in the incarnation in solid flesh of the second person of the Trinity, a personification in the sense of the lending of a human body to a word which is absolute being and true presence, as a divine Person, who realizes that union of the verbal and the bodily, which, in the case of a poetic and rhetorical personification is no more than a feigning.

The relationship between personification allegory and the theology of the Incarnation is explored in the second of the encounters between Virtues and Vices in the *Psychomachia*, in which *Pudicitia* 'Chastity' defeats *Libido* 'Lust'. The manner of *Libido*'s death is in keeping with this Vice's enmiredness in the body, as her spirit/soul fails to detach itself from corporeal filth, *calidos uomit illa uapores / sanguine concretos caenoso;*[23] *spiritus inde / sordidus exhalans uicinas polluit auras* 'She spews forth hot fumes clotted with filthy blood; then the unclean breath pouring out defiles the air nearby', 50–2. If the concept of lust is the 'soul' of the personification of *Libido*, it is a soul that is unusually bound up with the fictional body of the personification; she is an embodiment of bodiliness. In her victory speech over the dead *Libido*, the chatty *Pudicitia* reaches out from her own existence within the fiction of personification allegory to the reality of Old Testament history, and asks how it is that *Libido* was not killed once and for all when Judith cut off the head of Holofernes, himself an *exemplum*, one might say embodiment or personification, of lust. *Pudicitia* then proceeds to give an answer to her question, 66–88:

> at fortasse parum fortis matrona sub umbra
> legis adhuc pugnans, dum tempora nostra figurat,
> uera quibus uirtus terrena in corpora fluxit
> grande per infirmos caput excisura ministros.
> numquid et intactae post partum uirginis ullum   70
> fas tibi iam superest? post partum uirginis, ex quo
> corporis humani naturam pristina origo
> deseruit carnemque nouam uis ardua seuit,
> atque innupta Deum concepit femina Christum,
> mortali de matre hominem, sed cum Patre numen.   75

---

[22] Nugent 1985: 30, cited by Hardie 2002: 232.
[23] *caenum* is often used of the mire of fleshly sinfulness in the Fathers.

inde omnis iam diua caro est quae concipit illum
naturamque Dei consortis foedere sumit.
Verbum quippe caro factum non destitit esse
quod fuerat, Verbum, dum carnis glutinat usum,
maiestate quidem non degenerante per usum   80
carnis, sed miseros ad nobiliora trahente.
ille manet quod semper erat, quod non erat esse
incipiens: nos quod fuimus iam non sumus, aucti
nascendo in melius: mihi contulit et sibi mansit.
nec Deus ex nostris minuit sua, sed sua nostris   85
dum tribuit nosmet dona ad caelestia uexit.
dona haec sunt, quod uicta iaces, lutulenta Libido,
nec mea post Mariam potis es perfringere iura.

But perhaps a woman still fighting under the shade of the law had not force enough, though in so doing she prefigured our times, in which the real power has passed into earthly bodies to sever the great head by the hands of feeble agents? Well, since a virgin immaculate has borne a child, have you any claim remaining—since a virgin bore a child, since the day when man's body lost its primeval nature, and power from on high created a new flesh, and a woman unwedded conceived the God Christ, who is man in virtue of his mortal mother but God along with the Father? From that day all flesh is divine, since it conceives Him and takes on the nature of God by a covenant of partnership. For the Word made flesh has not ceased to be what it was before, that is, the Word, by attaching to itself the experience of the flesh; its majesty is not lowered by the experience of the flesh, but raises wretched men to nobler things. He remains what He ever was, though beginning to be what He was not; but we are no longer what we were, now that we are raised at our birth into a better condition. He has given to me, yet still remained for Himself; neither has God lessened what is his by taking on what is ours, but by giving his nature to ours He has lifted us to the height of his heavenly gifts. It is his gift that you lie conquered, filthy Lust, and cannot, since Mary, violate my authority. (trans. H. J. Thomson, adapted (Loeb))

Pudicitia refers to the fundamental division in Christian history between the age of the law, and the age of grace, the two linked by the relationships of typology (lines 66–7). The recurrent embodiment of lust in human flesh, resulting in the ability of *Libido* to rise from the dead after being killed (*tene, o uexatrix hominum, potuisse resumptis / uiribus extincti capitis recalescere flatu*, 'Will you, o troubler of mankind, have been able to resume your strength and grow warm again with the breath of your extinguished life?', 58–9), derives from the fact that Judith was fighting in the shadow of the Old Testament law, a shadow contrasted with the strength of the truth of the age of grace, following the Incarnation of Christ. This is also the power (*fortis*, 66) of typology, lending the force of a providential Christian history to the shows of personification allegory. In her account of the Incarnation, Prudentius' personified *Pudicitia* plays with the mechanics of personification. *uera quibus uirtus terrena in corpora fluxit* (68) could be a description of the mechanism whereby an abstraction (*uirtus*) is embodied in a personification (*Virtus*) (absence), as well as an account of the incarnation of God the Father's *uirtus* in the body of the Virgin Mary (presence).[24] Should a modern text capitalize *Virtus*? The Virgin Mary has a real, historical, body, unlike that of the *uirgo* (47) *Pudicitia*, the personification of the virtue of which Mary is the greatest *exemplum*. The jingling *uera uirtus* poses further questions about the truth and reality of this *uirtus*: *uirtus* as a true substance, not just a concept or a word, or 'true man-hood', with reference to the orthodox doctrine that Christ truly became man at the Incarnation.

That play on the two senses of *uirtus*, 'virtue, or courage', and 'manhood' is found in Virgil's Numanus and Ascanius episode in *Aeneid* 9, both in Apollo's encouragement of Ascanius, *macte noua uirtute, puer*, 'congratulations on your newfound manhood, boy', 641, and, a few lines earlier, in Ascanius' own taunting of Numanus as he shoots him dead, '*i, uerbis uirtutem illude superbis*', 'now go and taunt courage with your proud words', 634. In that line the jingle *uerbis ... superbis* calls attention to the fact that the magniloquent Numanus comes close to being a personification of *Superbia*; Prudentius registers this in modelling the speech of his *Superbia* substantially on that of the Virgilian Numanus.[25] Numanus is also closely related to the personification of *Fama* in *Aeneid* 4, like her puffed up with words that have an imperfect relationship to the truth.[26] In reply, Ascanius makes an assonant contrast between *uerbis* and *uirtutem*, empty words and solid *uirtus*. Ascanius' arrow is launched with the backing of the supreme god Jupiter, whose presence is marked by the thunder which rings out in answer to Ascanius' vow and which accompanies the sound of the bow (*intonuit laeuum, sonat una fatifer arcus*, *Aen.* 9.631). This instrument of a divinely sanctioned *uirtus* passes through the *cava tempora*, 'hollow temples' (633) of Numanus, a phrase suggesting that Numanus is a hollow

---

[24] Christ as *uirtus* of the Father: Augustine *Catholic and Manichean Practices* 1.15.25 expounding 1 Cor. 1:23–4 *nos autem praedicamus Christum crucifixum, Iudaeis quidem scandalum gentibus autem stultitiam; ipsis autem uocatis, Iudaeis atque Graecis, Christum Dei uirtutem et Dei sapientiam* 'But we preach Christ crucified, unto the Jews a stumbling block, and unto the Greeks foolishness; but unto them which are called, both Jews and Greeks, Christ the power of God, and the wisdom of God.'

[25] Numanus is (*Aen.* 9.596) *tumidusque nouo praecordia regno* 'swollen in his heart with his new royalty'; at her first appearance *Superbia* has the epithet *inflata* (*Psychom.* 178); a few lines later (182) she is *tumido despectans agmina fastu* 'looking down on the ranks with swollen pride'. *Superbia*'s speech is modelled primarily on the speech of the puffed-up Numanus, as she claims to rule the whole man from the hour of his birth, ever since the expulsion from Eden.

[26] See Hardie 1994 on *Aen.* 9.595.

man, a boaster of no substance, all words and no action.[27] In *Pudicitia*'s **uera quibus uirtus** may be heard already a sonic foreshadowing of the word, *Verbum*, in Prudentius' elaboration (78–9) of the *et Verbum caro factum est* of John 1:14. Lust, we saw, is the enslavement of the spirit to the body. Flesh is equally inseparable from spirit in the doctrine of the Incarnation, but in this case, the co-existence of spirit and flesh does not sully the former or introduce any change: *Verbum quippe caro factum non destitit esse / quod fuerat, Verbum, dum carnis glutinat usum.* 'For the Word made flesh did not cease to be what it had been, that is, the Word, by gluing itself to the experience of the body.', 78–9. *glutino*, literally 'glue, glue together', is a remarkably concrete expression for the union of the Word and flesh, as vivid as the use of *concretus* of the inseparability of *Libido*'s spirit from the mire of her flesh, *uapores / sanguine concretos caenoso*,[28] 50–1. *Glutino* is elsewhere used of closing up or joining a wound (e.g. Prud. *Perist.* 10.874), and here there is perhaps the suggestion that the Incarnation heals the wound inflicted on mankind by original sin, so restoring the primal harmony of body and soul.

Dreaming Allegory in Claudian

Finally, I look at the knowing play with allegorical absences in another late-antique poet who writes in polemical dialogue with Prudentius,[29] and who, like Prudentius, is a subtle connoisseur of Lucretius, Virgil and Ovid: Claudian. My text is the elegiac *Praefatio* to Claudian's last panegyrical epic, his *Panegyric on the Sixth Consulship of Honorius*:[30]

> Omnia, quae sensu uoluuntur uota diurno,
>   pectore sopito reddit amica quies.
> uenator defessa toro cum membra reponit,
>   mens tamen ad siluas et sua lustra redit.

---

[27] Cf. Hor. *Carm.* 1.18.15 *tollens uacuum plus nimio Gloria uerticem* 'Glory raising her empty head far too much'.

[28] Cf. *TLL* s.v. *concresco* 4.0.96.28 f. 2 conglobari: **a** gloss. conglutinatum, conglobatum; conglobatos uel consolidatos; συνηθροισμένος. Prudentius also uses *glutino* at *Cath.* 11.49–52: *Hic ille natalis dies / quo te creator arduus / spirauit et limo indidit / sermone carnem glutinans*, 'This is the natal day on which the creator on high breathed you forth and set you in a frame of clay, uniting flesh with the Word'; *Perist.* 10.871–5: *'fortasse ceruix si secandam iussero / flecti sub ensem non patebit uulneri, / vel amputatum plaga collum diuidens / rursus coibit ac reglutinabitur / umerisque uertex eminebit additus'*, 'Perhaps his neck, if I order that it bend to receive the sword-stroke, will prove impervious to the blow, or the wound that cuts it in two will heal and join again, and his head be set on his shoulders and stand erect.'

[29] See Dorfbauer 2012.   [30] I owe much to the excellent commentary by Dewar 1996.

```
        iudicibus lites, aurigae somnia currus                           5
          uanaque nocturnis meta cauetur equis.
        furto gaudet amans, permutat nauita merces
          et uigil elapsas quaerit auarus opes
        blandaque largitur frustra sitientibus aegris
          inriguus gelido pocula fonte sopor.                           10
        me quoque Musarum studium sub nocte silenti
          artibus adsuetis sollicitare solet.
        namque poli media stellantis in arce uidebar
          ante pedes summi carmina ferre Iouis;
        utque fauet somnus, plaudebant numina dictis                    15
          et circumfusi sacra corona chori.
        Enceladus mihi carmen erat uictusque Typhoeus:
          hic subit Inarimen, hunc grauis Aetna domat.
        quam laetum post bella Iouem susceperat aether
          Phlegraeae referens praemia militiae!                         20
        additur ecce fides nec me mea lusit imago,
          inrita nec falsum somnia misit ebur.
        en princeps, en orbis apex aequatus Olympo!
          en quales memini, turba uerenda, deos
        fingere nil maius potuit sopor, altaque uati                    25
          conuentum caelo praebuit aula parem.
```

All the desires that our waking minds ponder by day, these does friendly sleep bring back to us when once our spirits are lulled in slumber. When the huntsman lays down his weary limbs upon his bed, all the same his mind returns to his familiar coverts and the woods. Judges dream of lawsuits, and the charioteer of his chariot as with his horses of the night he steers safely past a phantom turning-post. In stolen delights the lover finds his joy, the merchant barters his goods, and, on waking, the miser seeks in vain the riches that have slipped from his grasp, while to poor mortals stricken by thirst sleep streaming in lavishes – but all in vain – pleasing draughts from cool springs. Me too in the silence of the night devotion to the Muses commonly troubles with my accustomed craft. For I seemed to find myself in the very heart of the citadel of the starry heavens, bringing my songs before the feet of Jupiter the Most High. And, such is the flattery of dreams, the gods applauded what I sang, and so also all the sacred throng that stood around. Enceladus was my theme, and Typhoeus conquered (one lies beneath Inarime, the other weighty Etna holds in subjection); and how joyful was Heaven when, the war concluded, it welcomed Jupiter, receiving the spoils of battle on the fields of Phlegra! See how confirmation is now granted me, and my vision has not played me false, nor has the deceitful Gate of Ivory sent dreams that come to nothing. Behold our Prince, behold the world's pinnacle made level with Olympus! Behold the gods as I remember them, a venerable host! Sleep could imagine nothing greater, and this lofty hall has shown the bard a gathering that is the peer of heaven. (trans. Michael Dewar)

Claudian recounts a dream which proves to be true in waking reality, as had Erysichthon's nightmare.[31] The content of the dream, Claudian tells us, was pre-determined by his waking activities, according to a standard ancient view on the nature of dreams, but instead of a literal vision of what Claudian does when awake, i.e. produce poetry and perform it at the imperial court, the dream is an allegorical vision. The *Praefatio* offers a sophisticated commentary on figuration and fiction, on the relationship of allegory to reality and truth, on the gap between allegory and that of which it speaks.

Waking desires (*uota*) are the subject of dreams, Claudian tells us (*Praef.* 1–2). To the hunter, judge, charioteer, lover, sailor, the greedy man and the thirsty man dreams offer empty phantoms of waking reality (***uanaque** nocturnis meta cauetur equis*, 6, *et uigil **elapsas quaerit** auarus opes*, 8, *blandaque largitur **frustra** sitientibus aegris / inriguus gelido pocula fonte sopor*, 9–10). These are the delusive *simulacra* of the Lucretian dreamer (*De rerum natura* 4.962–1036), absent presences which Ovid had also built in to his narratives of *Fames*, and *Somnus* and Morpheus. 'Me too in the silence of the night zeal for the Muses usually stirs me with my accustomed craft' (11–12). But in Claudian's dream his craft is not practised in an illusory replica of his customary waking environment. He sees himself in the starry heavens, presenting his song at the feet of Jupiter, a song of Gigantomachy, Jupiter's victory over Enceladus and Typhoeus. The last three couplets offer an interpretation of the dream, beginning with a couplet which asserts the truth-value of the sleeping vision, in the language of Virgil,[32] Horace[33] and Ovid: *additur ecce fides nec me mea lusit imago, / irrita nec falsum somnia misit ebur*, 21–2. This is not a delusive image or a false dream, but something with 'credibility', *fides*. *Nec me mea lusit imago*: the poet is like Ovid's Narcissus, who recognizes the reality of what he sees, *nec me mea fallit imago*, 'my image does not deceive me', *Met.* 3.463. But the poet is unlike Narcissus in that the realization of the truth also brings him his heart's desire.[34] Narcissus is disillusioned of his belief that his reflection is another person, but continues to be cheated of, disappointed in, what he desires.

---

[31] For full discussion of the *Praefatio* and the traditions on which it draws, see Dewar 1996 ad loc. On Claudian's *Praefationes*, see Felgentreu 1999; Ware 2004.

[32] Cf. *Aen.* 6.895–6 the ivory gate of Sleep which sends *falsa insomnia* to the world above.

[33] Dewar on v. 21 cites Hor. *Carm.* 3.27.37–41: *uigilansne ploro turpe commissum, an uitiis carentem / ludit imago / uana, quae porta fugiens eburna / somnium ducit?*, 'Am I awake, deploring a crime I have committed? Or am I innocent, mocked by an empty vision escaping from the Gate of Ivory?'

[34] In context, following allusion to Lucretius on dreams, through window allusion Claudian also signals the Lucretian intertext for Ovid's Narcissus: see Hardie 2002: 150–63.

Michael Dewar takes *imago* here as 'dream', with a possible second sense of Epicurean *eidolon*, atomic 'image', the technical term which Lucretius translates by *simulacrum*. We could also take it of an artistic *imago*, either a visual or a verbal image. If we take it as a visual image, the point would be not that Claudian has not been taken in by a delusively lifelike representation, like the viewers of the likeness represented by Arachne on her marvellously verisimilar tapestry at Ovid *Met.* 6.103–4: *Maeonis elusam designat imagine tauri / Europen: uerum taurum, freta uera putares*, 'The Maeonian girl portrays Europa deceived by the likeness of a bull; you would think that it was a real bull, a real sea.' Viewers plural, rather than viewer, since Europa is taken in by the likeness of a bull which in truth is no bull but Jupiter in metamorphic disguise, and the deception practised on Europa by the supreme god Jupiter is mirrored in the deception practised by the supreme artist Arachne on the beholder of her tapestry, who is deceived into taking for a real bull, travelling over a real sea, what is only the artistic image of a bull travelling over the sea. Claudian's point, rather, is that this is *not* a representation of a reality other than the one to which the poet awakes, with the repeated *en* of *enargeia, en princeps, en orbis apex aequatus Olympo! / en quales memini, turba uerenda, deos!*, 23–4. The likeness of Jupiter (in his anthropomorphic appearance) does not deceive, since the god is manifested in waking reality in the person of the emperor.

As a verbal image, *imago* could be taken in the rhetorical-grammatical sense of 'comparison': 'my simile, comparison (of Olympus with the Palatine) has not deceived me'. But taking *imago* as literary comparison would be to step away from strict equivalence, to likeness. The *Praefatio* concludes, *fingere nil maius potuit sopor, altaque uati / conuentum caelo praebuit aula parem*, 25–6. The comparative *nil maius* suggests the hyperbolical synkrisis ('comparison'): when compared to Olympus, Honorius' court is found to be just as great, the equal (*parem*) of Olympus. What is really at issue, however, is not equality in the sense of sameness, but a com-parison, simile, or allegory: this is clear both from the synkrisis implied in *nil maius*, and from another Ovidian passage, the poet's comparison of Jupiter's palace to the Palatine House of Augustus, *Met.* 1.168–76, which anticipates the first formal simile in the *Metamorphoses*, which again establishes a correspondence, of a kind that could be called allegorical, between divine ruler and Roman ruler, in a comparison of the uproar in the palace of Jupiter to the uproar on earth at an assassination attempt on Caesar

(*Met.* 1.199–206).³⁵ The *Praefatio* to *On the sixth consulship of Honorius* anticipates the extended assimilation of Rome to, or allegorization of Rome as, a celestial city in the main panegyric that follows.

If the dream comes true, it is allegorically, connecting on the vertical axis the levels of heaven and earth, which are also connected by the fiction of imperial apotheosis, of which Claudian gives a dazzling account in the ascension of Theodosius' soul in *On the third consulship of Honorius* 162–88.³⁶ The notion of the allegorical dream is an addition to the Lucretian substrate of the passage, and it anticipates by some years Macrobius' pairing of discussion of the meaning of dreams and of allegoresis in his commentary on the *Somnium Scipionis*.

The poet realizes his self-regarding and narcissistic desire (*uotum*) to be received on 'Olympus' and to have the performance of his poetry applauded. He also realizes his ambition of producing a poetry that creates a persuasive illusion of the (allegorical) equation of the mythological gods and their starry *arx* with the court of Honorius. In other words, the poet turns dream into reality, the work of Ovid's Morpheus, whose operation is that of *fingere*, like that of Claudian's poetic dreaming (*fingere nil maius potuit sopor*).³⁷ As a Morpheus, Claudian is also a master of metamorphosis, changing Jupiter and his Olympian entourage into the likeness of Honorius and his court. What a poet dreams of might indeed have as much or as little reality as his waking compositions, images and words seen or spoken in dreams having as much substance and meaning as those seen and spoken while awake. This marks a difference from the activities of the other dreamers, which can only be empty *simulacra* of the waking equivalents.³⁸

---

³⁵ See Feeney 2014: 221–2.
³⁶ See Dewar 1996 on v. 13, referring to MacCormack 1981 on the connection between these lines and the language of pagan *consecratio*: MacCormack 1981: 138–40, 332 n. 214, 334 n. 223 on the connection between *6 Cons. Hon. Praef.* 13 ff., *namque poli media stellantis in arce uidebar* . . . and the language of *consecratio*; Septimius' dream of ascent to Heaven, SHA *Sept. Sev.* 22.1–2.
³⁷ See the language of Juno's address to Somnus at *Met.* 11.626–8: *somnia, quae ueras aequant imitantia formas . . . iube . . . Alcyonen adeant simulacraque naufraga fingant*, 'command the dreams that through imitation equal true shapes to approach Alcyone, and feign the likeness of a shipwreck'.
³⁸ With the possible exception of *furto gaudet amans*, 7: cf. the final examples in Lucretius' list at 4.1026–36, wetting the bed while dreaming of urinating, and erotic wet dreams, *ut quasi transactis saepe omnibus rebus profundant / fluminis ingentis fluctus uestemque cruentent*, 'with the result that often, as if they had completed the whole business, they pour forth huge floods of liquid, and stain their clothes', 1035–6, unlike the frustration of dreaming of imbibing water to satisfy a thirst. There is something doubly 'stolen', 'furtive' about sexual satisfaction in one's sleep. *sub nocte silenti*, 11 perhaps hints that it makes little difference whether he is in fact awake or asleep, this being the time for the *agrupnia* of the *uigil* poet, *noctes uigilare serenas*, Lucr. 1.142 (although 15 *utque fauet somnus is*

This extensive allusion to the Ovidian thematization of poetic illusion and the suspension of disbelief registers an awareness on Claudian's part that his panegyric operates in a sphere of poetic *ludus*, and all-egorical al-lusion. Panegyrical poetry such as that of Claudian, even in its 'waking' form, is a tissue of comparisons and equations which operate with a gap between poetic representation and reality, which is also the gap between the two levels of all-egory. Fritz Felgentreu in his book on Claudian's *Praefationes* refers to their 'gleichnishaft-allegorischer Stil'.[39] That is a characterization that could be applied to the panegyrics themselves. This is one of the ways in which the *Praefatio* to *On the sixth consulship of Honorius* is programmatic for the hexameter poem.[40]

Additur ecce fides[41] are the words with which Claudian announces that his dream has come true. The deictic *ecce* anticipates the threefold *en* two lines later, which announce the real presence of the emperor, of the emperor's seat brought level with Olympus, and the man-gods of the Palatine: 'real presence' which dissolves into panegyrical allegory (*princeps*, yes, 'the world's pinnacle made level with Olympus', well . . ., the 'gods as I remember them', well, not really – or did the fault lie in the poet's memory?). Reading backwards, one might ask whether *ecce* suggests the equally real, equally unreal, epiphany of *Fides* with a capital *F*, a divinity or virtue who appears in person elsewhere in Claudian's panegyrics.[42] But that is perhaps to introduce an allegory that my readers will not wish to allow to make itself heard.

---

unambiguous). This might help explain the ambiguity at *et uigil elapsas quaerit auarus opes*, 8: see Dewar 1996 ad loc.

[39] Felgentreu 1999: 212.

[40] See Dewar's commentary for some of the connections between *Praefatio* and poem.

[41] Cf. Ov. *Met.* 15.361: *siqua fides rebus tamen est addenda probatis*, 'if credence is to be given to things that have actually been tested'.

[42] *Fides* personified in Claudian: *huic diuae* [sc. *Clementiae*] *germana Fides eademque sorori / corde tuo delubra tenens sese omnibus actis / inserit*, 'Good Faith too Love's sister, has made her shrine in your heart, and joins herself to all your actions', *Cons. Stil.* 2.30–2; (return of Golden Age) *Concordia, Virtus / cumque Fide Pietas alta ceruice uagantur* (cf. *Aen.* 1.291–3), 'Concord and Virtue, Good Faith and Piety, wander abroad with heads held high', *In Ruf.* 1 52–3; *uirtutes uariae fructus sensere receptos; / depositum seruasse, Fides; Constantia, paruum / praefecisse orbi; Pietas, fouisse propinquum*, 'your many virtues have found their proper reward: loyalty that has kept safe that which was entrusted to it; firmness of purpose, in having set in dominion over the world one so small; family duty, in having cherished a kinsman', *6 Cons. Hon.* 584–6; *exultat cum Pace Fides*, 'Peace and Loyalty are exultant', *Pan. Manl. Theod.* 171. At *Epithal. Hon. Aug.* 240–1 a non-personified *fides* vouches for the reality of another epiphany, that of Venus, *mox uera fides numenque refulsit*, 'Soon came the proof; in all her beauty the goddess bursts upon them.'

The various senses of *fides* with a small *f*, 'trustworthiness, honesty', and 'plausibility, credibility', are the subject of frequent play by Ovid, and form a central part of the Ovidian poetics of illusion on which Claudian draws repeatedly in this *Praefatio*.[43] In Claudian's day *fides* was also a foundation stone and central virtue of Christianity, the Christian faith, a faith buttressed by what was, by the late fourth century AD, a highly developed exegetical tradition in which allegory played a major part. In Prudentius' *Psychomachia* the personification of Fides kills the first and last of the Vices who challenge the Christian faith, respectively from outside and within: first, *Veterum Cultura Deorum*, or pagan religion, a descendant, via the Virgilian Cacus, of that unreal monster defeated by Lucretius' Epicurus, the personification of *Religio*; and, second, *Discordia*, the divisions within the faith caused by heresy. I do not think that one could exclude the possibility that Claudian's audience, at the very Christian court of Theodosius and his son Honorius, would overhear a playful, but not necessarily disrespectful, hint of the Christian sense in Claudian's self-interpreting allegorical *Praefatio*, exploiting a theology of imperial power that implicitly acknowledges its status as founded on nothing more substantial than a poetics of illusion, and in which poetic words may equate human with divine, but in a manner very different from the (real) co-presence of man and god in the incarnated Word. There we are not dealing with the otherness of allegory, nor with the subordination of one level to another, but with the hypostatic union of Christ's humanity and divinity in one individual existence (*hypostasis*).

[43] Hardie 2002: index s.v. *fides*.

CHAPTER 4

Tamen apsentes prosunt pro praesentibus
Proxied Absences and Roman Comedy

Giuseppe Pezzini[*]

Casina, Prologue

In the opening of Plautus' *Casina* the (interpolated)[1] prologue warns the audience:

> hinc adulescentem peregre ablegauit pater;
> sciens ei mater dat operam apsenti tamen.
> Is, ne exspectetis, hodie in hac comoedia
> in urbem non redibit: Plautus noluit,
> pontem interrupit, qui erat ei in itinere.
>
> (Pl. *Cas.* 62–6)

The father sent off his lad abroad. Even so, his mother knowingly supports him in his absence. In case you're waiting for him, he isn't returning to the city in this comedy today. Plautus didn't want him to, he demolished a bridge on his way.[2]

The *adulescens* in question is Euthynicus, the young lover of the play, who is competing with his father Lysidamus for the love of an enchanting slave-girl, the eponymous Casina.[3] As emphatically announced, Euthynicus will never become present onstage; and yet he will not be completely absent either: as the prologue also declares, his mother 'knowingly supports him in his absence' (63), by fighting against her lascivious husband Lysidamus and ultimately devising the central ruse of the play, with the help of the maid Pardalisca[4] (cf. in particular, 685–8). The mother Cleostrata is not the

---

[*] I'm extremely grateful to the editors of this volume, and to Victoria Rimell, Peter Brown and William Fitzgerald for their invaluable comments and encouragement.
[1] On the interpolated nature of (parts of) *Casina*'s prologue, derived from a revision for a later revival, Paratore 1959: 5–12 is still useful. For a select bibliography, see Arnott 2003: 25 n. 4.
[2] All texts and translations of Plautus are from De Melo's Loeb Edition, unless otherwise specified.
[3] As suggested by line 32 (see next note), the original title of the play was *Sortientes*, while the name *Casina* was added at a later stage (cf. MacCary and Willcock 1976: 102).
[4] On Pardalisca's role in *Casina*, see Questa 2003.

only 'proxy'[5] character in Casina. In fact, both Lysidamus and Euthynicus have at their disposal two 'legions', prepared against each other (*sibi uterque contra legiones parat*, 50), that is, their slaves Olympio (the *uilicus*) and Chalinus (the *armiger*), who act as 'proxies' of their masters, the latter throughout the whole play. In particular, both slaves have been instructed to act as 'proxy-husbands' to secure Casina's possession; the 'proxy-marriage' will facilitate and conceal the sexual exploits of the masters.

In the passage above, the phrase *Plautus noluit* is revealing: a few lines before, the prologue-speaker has posited a clear authorial distinction between the Greek author Diphilus and the Latin Plautus.[6] In such a context, a unilateral reference to Plautus (65 *Plautus noluit*) and the deictic markers (64 *hodie in hac comoedia*) suggest that it was the Roman playwright who 'demolished the bridge', and thereby prevented the young lover from reuniting with Casina within the play's action, as presumably happened in the denouement of the Greek original.[7]

Accepting this plausible, and yet unverifiable reconstruction, in this chapter, I will speculate on the motivations that might lie behind Plautus' apparent decision to 'demolish the bridge'. More precisely, I will investigate the dramatic function of Euthynicus' (and many other characters') 'proxied absence' and argue for its central significance in Plautus and Terence's *palliata*, a Roman comic genre, performed and composed by 'proxies'. After a brief overview of Euthynicus' typology ('the proxied absentee') in Roman comedy, I will explore the potentially comic nature of 'proxy' characters, as vehicles for deception and misapprehension. I will then connect the prominence of 'proxiness' in Roman comedy with the iconic pre-eminence of slaves, 'proxies' *par excellence*, and as such sources of comic anxiety for their masters (on- and offstage), owing to the danger of their contradictory status, as instrumental and yet enterprising entities. Finally, I will relate the thematisation of 'proxiness' to comedy's treatment of theatricality more broadly, and to the plays' self-conscious status as

---

[5] The English term 'proxy' ultimately derives from Latin 'pro-curare', also attested in comedy, cf. *Men.* 966–9: *spectamen bono seruo id est, qui rem erilem | procurat (...) | ut absente ero rem eri diligenter | tutetur* (for the translation, see p. 75).

[6] Pl. *Cas.* 31–4: *Clerumenoe uocatur haec comoedia | Graece, latine Sortientes. Deiphilus | hanc graece scripsit, postid rursum denuo | Latine Plautus cum latranti nomine.* 'This comedy is called *Kleroumenoi* in Greek, in Latin "Men Casting Lots". Diphilus wrote it in Greek, and after that Plautus with the barking name wrote it again in Latin.'

[7] Cf. O'Bryhim 1989, esp. 82–3, and see also Paratore 2003: 60–70, Arnott 2003: 39–44, Umbrico 2009: esp. 39. For a select bibliography on the *uexata quaestio* of the relation between Plautus' and Diphilus' plays, see Arnott 2003: 23 n. 1, to which one can add Lowe 2003, Umbrico 2009 and Konstan 2014.

'proxies' of absent or concealed figures, texts and traditions. Whether in a theatrical, social or cultural-political dimension, 'proxied absences' always have a disruptive (and thus comic) potential in Roman comedy.

The 'Proxied' Absentees in Roman Comedy

The situation in Plautus' *Casina*, with a key character remaining absent for the whole play while proxies work on his behalf,[8] is by no means eccentric in Roman comedy. Indeed, Plautus' and Terence's plays are populated by a crowd of absent characters, who participate in the comic action through the intermediation of more or less reliable 'proxies'.[9] Most Roman comedies feature at least one absentee who is 'proxied' by another character on stage, in one or several scenes, or indeed for the whole duration of the play. For instance, in *Cistellaria* Selenium asks Gymnasium to act on her behalf while she is absent (Pl. *Cist.* 104–9). Epidicus, in his eponymous comedy, plots on the orders of his absent master Stratippocles, who communicates to him by letter (cf. e.g. *Epid.* 508–9). In *Amphitruo* the absent Jupiter and Amphitruo are respectively represented on stage by the slaves Mercurius and Sosia.[10] In this comedy, and many others, the 'proxied absentees' will eventually make their appearance on stage, and the role of their proxies will not necessarily cease because of that (i.e. Sosia will continue to act on Amphitruo's behalf even when the latter is present; cf. *Amph.* 630); here, however, my focus will mainly be on the 'proxying' of absent characters, that is, on the combination of 'proxiness' and 'absence'.

The function of proxy characters in Roman comedy is variable: some are sent as emissaries or message-carriers (such as Sosia; cf. e.g. *Amph.* 291); others act as intermediaries, deputies, or agents, or more often a combination of these; in many cases 'proxies' perform as masterminds or pawns in the elaborate ruses which are at the core of most comic plots (as Cleostrata, Chalinus and Pardalisca in *Casina*). I could go on, as the lists of both proxy characters and their functions are extensive, and could be further expanded by non-human proxies, such as letters and tokens.[11]

---

[8] On the act of 'proxying' *per se*, cf. Fitzgerald (this volume).
[9] Not all comic absentees are 'proxied' on stage, and the (prototypical) comic potential of absence extends well beyond its relation with 'proxiness'; I offer a full investigation of all types and functions of comic absenteeism in Pezzini 2019.
[10] Cf. Pl. *Amph.* 19–20, and the whole prologue, in general.
[11] Letters in particular, can be construed as involving two proxies, the message-carrier and the letter itself. Cf. e.g. Phoenicium's love letter in *Pseudolus* (Pl. *Pseud.* 51–74), Mnesicholus' letters in *Bacchides* (cf. Pl. *Bacc.* 728–48, 789–91, 995–1035), Curculio's counterfeited tables in his eponymous play (cf. Pl. *Curc.* 419–36), the several letters (fake or not) in *Persa* (196, 247–50, 497–527). Cf. also

To take a closer look, a good example of a proxy-character is the slave Harpax in Plautus' *Pseudolus*, who has been sent by the soldier Polymachaeroplagides to collect the girl Phoenicium from the pimp Ballio (cf. Pl. *Pseud.* 616–18). Harpax is introduced to the audience in a famous confrontation with the eponymous Pseudolus (595–666), who is himself a proxy, working on behalf of his master Calidorus. Harpax is the epitome of the well-intentioned proxy; he sees through his master's eyes:

> Hi loci sunt atque hae regiones quae mi ab ero sunt demonstratae,
> ut ego oculis rationem capio quam mi ita dixit erus meus miles.
> (Pl. *Pseud.* 594–6)

> These are the places and these the regions that I was shown by my master, that's how I draw the conclusion with my eyes from what my master told me.

and considers the master present, even when he is absent:

> Ego, ut mi imperatum est, etsi abest, hic adesse erum arbitror.
> (Pl. *Pseud.* 1113)

> When I'm given an order, I consider my master to be present, even if he's away.

Not all comic proxies are real or veracious, that is to say, not all of them have been rightfully appointed as such by their 'proxied' character: in *Asinaria*, for instance, the slave Leonidas postures as the trusted steward of the absent old man Demenaetus (Pl. *Asin.* 499–501); in *Pseudolus* the eponymous slave deceivingly pretends to be a proxy of the pimp Ballio (cf. Pl. *Pseud.* 607: HARPAX: *Tune es Ballio?* PSEUDOLUS: *Immo uero ego eius sum Subballio* 'HARPAX: Are you Ballio? PSEUDOLUS: No, rather I am his Under-Ballio').

The Comic Functionality of 'Proxiness': Deception and Misapprehension

Even when they are real and veracious, however, comic proxies are only rarely performing their duty in a frictionless manner; whether because of inability, ill-luck or (more often) bad intentions, 'proxiness' is never trouble-free in Roman comedy. In fact, the troubles originating from

---

Diabolus' contract in *Asinaria* (746–809). On the comic and meta-theatrical potential of Plautine letters, see Jenkins 2005, Barbiero 2014.

the frustration of 'proxiness' are of momentous importance both in the dramatic fabric of Roman comedy, and in its social and cultural-political framework. One of the first factors explaining the frequency of 'proxiness' in Roman comedy is indeed related to its inherent 'cognitive' dangers. 'Proxied', mediated relationships are less straightforward than direct, immediate ones: that is to say, 'proxiness' introduces a gap between the 'proxied' absent character and the intended receiver of the communication, a gap that can be intentionally exploited for deception, or (accidentally) result in misapprehension (the personified *Agnoia* of Menander's *Perikeiromene*).

Deception is accounted for in many of the examples quoted in the previous section, where 'proxiness' is capitalised on by a trickster to the detriment of the 'proxied' absentee. A good example of this is again Harpax's (and his master's) deception by Pseudolus, which involves two layers of 'proxiness', namely Harpax acting as an agent of his master Polymachaeroplagides, and Pseudolus pretending to deputise Ballio. This double 'proxiness' is exploited by the iconic Pseudolus ('the liar'), who disrupts the communication between Ballio and the soldier, i.e. the completion of the transaction of Phoenicium. The 'bug' which allows Pseudolus' 'hacking' is generated by the inherent danger of 'proxiness', of which characters are well aware.

In fact, Harpax is instructed to mistrust 'proxiness', and claims that he will give his money only to Ballio in person:

> HARPAX: Reddere hoc, non perdere erus me misit. (...)
> ego nisi ipsi Ballioni nummum credam nemini.
> (Pl. *Pseud.* 642, 644)

> My master sent me to pay this, not to lose it. (...)
> I won't entrust a single coin to anyone other than Ballio himself.

Despite his intentions and precautions, however, Harpax eventually falls into the cognitive trap of 'proxiness', and hands over to Pseudolus (the fake proxy) something even more important than the money; this is the soldier's letter, which Harpax has been ordered to hand over to Ballio together with the money and the seal (*symbolus*) imprinted on it, the token of the transaction:

> HARPAX: Tu epistulam hanc a me accipe atque illi dato.
> Nam istic symbolust inter erum meum et tuom de muliere.
> (Pl. *Pseud.* 647–8)

> You, take this letter from me and give it to him:
> the token between my master and yours about the woman is there.

Letters and tokens *per se* are common types of non-human proxies in Roman comedy, as already pointed out. The 'proxy' function of this particular letter is, however, further highlighted by the fact that the token consists in an effigy of the soldier:

> PSEUDOLUS: Scio equidem: ut qui argentum afferret atque **expressam imaginem**
> huc suam ad nos, cum eo aiebat uelle mitti mulierem.
> (Pl. *Pseud.* 649–50)
>
> I know: he said he wanted the woman to be sent with the man who brought the money and his **stamped image** here to us.

This effigy, a copy of which is in the hands of Ballio, is meant to be a further precaution against the dangers of 'proxiness'. It thus serves as a seal to secure the 'proxied' communication between the pimp and the soldier, but is also an icon of it; the absent soldier connects with Ballio through a faithful effigy of himself, carried over by a (supposedly) duteous proxy. The phrasing used by Pseudolus may even include a meta-theatrical allusion to theatrical 'proxiness' (on which, see further, p. 81), since the expression *expressam imaginem* is normally used in the context of artistic representation, including indeed comic mimesis.[12] By handing over the soldier's effigy to Pseudolus, Harpax is compromising the whole enterprise, exposing the vulnerability of 'proxiness' and paving the way to the play's deception, as Pseudolus immediately acknowledges:

> PSEUDOLUS: Nam haec allata cornu copiae est, ubi inest quicquid uolo: hic doli, hic fallaciae omnes, hic sunt sycophantiae, (...)
> (Pl. *Pseud.* 671–2)
>
> Yes, it was brought to me as a cornucopia which has everything I want inside. Here there are tricks, here there are all devices, here there are deceptions. (...)

Crucially, the key to dismantle the 'firewall' put up by the soldier and pimp to secure their 'proxied' communication is itself an instance of (fake) 'proxiness', that is Pseudolus' sudden decision to pretend to be Ballio's proxy, a '*Subballio*' (607). Again, Pseudolus is well aware of the momentousness of this decision:

> aurichalco contra non carum fuit
> meum mendacium, hic modo quod subito commentus fui,

---

[12] Cf. Cic. *Sext. Rosc.* 47 [in comedy] *expressam (...) imaginem uitae cotidianae uideremus*; Quint. 10.1.69 *Menander (...) omnem uitae imaginem expressit*.

> **quia lenonis me esse dixi**. Nunc ego hac epistula
> tris deludam, erum et lenonem et qui hanc dedit mi epistulam.
> (Pl. *Pseud.* 688–91)

> It wasn't dear at its weight in mountain copper, my lie which I came up with here so suddenly, **when I said I belong to the pimp.** With this letter I'll now deceive three people, my master and the pimp and the man who gave me this letter.

The deception in *Pseudolus* is a good illustration of the inherent vulnerability and deceiving potential of 'proxiness' in Roman comedy: despite all possible precautions and 'firewalls', proxies (human or mimetic) do not fully 'presentify' their masters' absence – that is, they do not provide flawless channels of frictionless communication, as expected by their masters. For this reason, proxies can be exploited as vehicles of deception, as cognitive interstices where the comic lie can be implanted and develop; this can happen either passively, as in the case of Harpax or the soldier's effigy, or actively, as with Pseudolus' fake *Subballio*, and many other equivalents in both Plautine and Terentian comedy.

In some cases, the deceiving potential of 'proxiness' may be stretched to a further degree, and proxies may act as (deceitful) impersonators, taking up (intentionally or not) the identity of the absentee who is 'proxied' by them: an example of this is the already-mentioned Gymnasium in *Cistellaria*, who, later in the play will be mistaken as, and pretend to be, the very woman she has been asked to deputise for (Pl. *Cist.* 306–71), to the derision of the old man.

The misapprehension engendered by proxy characters does not always result in humorous deception: in a more 'serious' (but no less comic) variant, especially common in Terence and probably inherited from Menander, the misapprehension caused by proxiness is used to introduce a separation or alienation between characters. For instance, in Terence's *Heauton Timorumenos* the young man Clitipho is estranged from his father Chremes and is living a debauched life behind his father's back. The main cause of this alienation is Chremes' characteristic tendency to communicate indirectly, by 'proxies' (*per alium*), as Clitipho himself declares:

> Mihi si umquam filius erit, ne ille facili me utetur patre.
> Nam et cognoscendi et ignoscendi dabitur peccati locus.
> Non ut meus, qui mihi per alium ostendit suam sententiam.
> (Ter. *HT* 217–19)

> If I ever have a son, he'll find me an easygoing father, believe me. There'll be times when misdeeds are looked into and times when they're overlooked.

I won't be like my own father, who reveals what he thinks through somebody else.[13]

In fact, later in the play, Chremes will offer a good specimen of his policy of 'proxiness', by instructing his fellow *senex* Menedemus to give money to his son *per alium*:

> MENEDEMUS: Quid faciam? CHREMES: Quiduis potius quam quod cogitas.
> Per alium quemuis ut des, falli te sinas
> techinis per seruolum.
>
> (Ter. *HT* 468–71)
>
> MENEDEMUS: What shall I do? CHREMES: Anything rather than what you are proposing. Contrive to give it through somebody else; let yourself be deceived by your slave's wiles.

The result of Chremes' policy will be the protraction of the alienation between Menedemus and his son Clinia (a key plot-catalyst in the play), and ultimately Chremes' own deception (see p. 79).

In sum, 'proxiness' in Roman comedy is above all a channel for deception, misapprehension and alienation. Since these are all prototypical ingredients of the comic recipe, as well known to both ancient and modern critics,[14] one might conclude that the first reason explaining the prominence of 'proxiness' in Roman comedy is its comic functionality.

Proxiness and Slavery

Yet, deception and misapprehension are not the only factors at play as far as comic 'proxiness' is concerned. Another important element to consider is the close connection between 'proxiness' and 'slavery', and in turn between 'slavery' and Roman comedy *per se*. Most of the proxy-characters analysed in the previous sections are slaves acting as agents for their (absent) masters (Sosia, Harpax, Pseudolus, Epidicus, Chalinus, etc.). This is not surprising: the slave is by nature the 'proxy' *par excellence*, since, to quote Aristotle's words (*Politics* 1255b), s/he is 'a part of the body of the master, alive yet separated from it'.[15] By virtue of this 'separation' slaves can be present when and where their masters are absent, but by virtue of their 'belonging' to

---

[13] All texts and translations of Terence are from Barsby's Loeb Edition, unless otherwise specified.
[14] See e.g. Petrone 1983, Nelson 1990 (esp. 138), Duckworth 1994: 305–30, Lowe 2008: 1–17, Halliwell 2008, esp. chapters 5 and 8, and p. 398 (on Theophrastus), Sharrock 2009, esp. 2–7; see also Muecke 1986 (on disguise in Plautus).
[15] See Fitzgerald (this volume).

them the slaves' presence is supposed to be a mere proxy for that of their masters. That is to say, the main function of slaves is to obviate absence for the sake of their masters. Slaves in Roman comedy are very well aware that this is what they are expected to be. Besides the aforementioned declaration of Harpax (Pl. *Pseud.* 1113), one can refer to two monologues by the slaves Messenio in *Menaechmi* and Sagaristio in *Persa*:[16]

> Spectamen bono seruo id est, qui rem erilem
> procurat, uidet, collocat cogitatque,
> ut apsente ero tam rem eri diligenter
> tutetur quam si ipse assit aut rectius.
> (Pl. *Men.* 966–9)

This is the touchstone for a good servant: that one is good who secures, watches, arranges, and has in mind his master's business, so that when his master is away he guards his master's business as diligently as if he were present in person or even better.

> Qui ero suo seruire uolt bene seruos seruitutem,
> ne illum edepol multa in pectore suo collocare oportet
> quae ero placere censeat praesenti atque absenti suo.
> (Pl. *Pers.* 7–9)

A slave who wants to serve his master well should place many things in his breast which he thinks will please his master when he's present as well as when he's absent.

In the case of Messenio, words match deeds: Messenio is one of the best embodiments of the 'ideal' slave, acting as a sort of active extension of his master. Despite (or perhaps because of) his mistreatment at his hands, Messenio is always compliant to his master Sosicles, consistently acts on his behalf in his absence and eventually confirms his contested identity (and thereby fully assures his presence). Messenio's initiative in the finale confirms that he is an extension of his master, but, crucially, not a passive, lifeless one: he knows that the good slave is the slave who acts even better (*rectius*, 969) when his master is not present. That is, he knows that his master expects him to be manageable and instrumental, and yet intelligent and enterprising; to be a good proxy is to have a double, contradictory nature, both submissive and independent, and this contradiction is at the origin of the masters' anxiety, as well as of comic disruptions (see p. 80 and cf. Fitzgerald 2000: 6–8). There are many other slaves

---

[16] For an analysis of these monologues, and of the 'good slave' motif in general, see McCarthy 2000: 35–76 (esp. 59–60, 71–2), 122–66 (esp. 130–3), Richlin 2017: 342–50 (esp. 347–9).

in Roman comedy who act as compliant, and yet enterprising proxies of their masters: an extreme example is the loyal Tyndarus in *Captiui*, whose proxy role will go as far as impersonating his master in the play (Pl. *Capt.* 35–9). Not surprisingly, both Messenio and Tyndarus will be rewarded with a happy ending.

That Messenio's and Tyndarus' behaviour corresponds to the masters' standard expectations is also suggested by the masters' attitude to their slaves, in *Persa* and *Captiui*, as well as in other plays. In the finale of *Rudens*, for instance, the old man Daemones has a harsh confrontation with his slave Gripus, which focuses on the re-assertion of the slave's contested 'proxiness'. Daemones is returning his trunk, lost during a shipwreck, to the pimp Labrax. In fact, it was Gripus, who found the trunk in the opening of the play, and stubbornly claimed possession of it, as a token for his freedom. Daemones has therefore no direct claim over the trunk and its finding, as his slave blatantly reminds him in protest:

> DAEMONES: Quando ergo erga te benignus ego fui atque opera mea
> haec tibi sunt seruata. GRIPUS: Immo hercle mea, ne tu dicas tua.
> DAEMONES. Si sapies, tacebis. (...)
> DAEMONES: Vidulum istunc ille inuenit, illud mancupium meum est;
> ego tibi hunc porro seruaui cum magna pecunia.
>
> (Pl. *Rud.* 1389–90, 1395–6)

> DAEMONES: Since I was kind towards you and by my attention your possessions have been saved...
> GRIPUS: No way, by god. By my effort; don't say by your effort.
> DAEMONES: If you are wise, you will hush up. (...)
> DAEMONES: (*to Labrax*) That man found that trunk; he's my slave; I have preserved it for you further, with a great sum of money.

And yet Gripus is silenced, and Daemones deals directly with the pimp, forcefully appropriating his slave's actions and behaving as the legitimate finder and keeper of the trunk; despite his protest, Gripus the 'trunk-finder' is thus treated by Daemones as a kind of prosthetic detector, an extension of his own authority. It does not matter that Daemones is looking after Gripus' interests, and will eventually concede to the slave the craved object of his desire, his freedom. What is important is that Gripus' active role in his *manumissio* is non-existent, since while he is a slave he and all his actions function as proxies for his master.

This kind of 'proxy' relation between master and slave is prototypical in Roman comedy, and is epitomised in the iconic scene of the slave hurrying about on behalf of his young master (*seruos currens*; cf. e.g. Ter. *HT* 37, *Eun.* 36,

Marshall 2006: 193–4), as well as its related conventional plot, featuring a cunning slave tricking out the money to fund his (young) master's revelries. Ideal proxies such as Messenio, or slapped-down rebels such as Gripo, could be construed as reflecting the anxieties of the Roman ruling class, worried about the assertion of their authority and the slaves' resistance to their expected 'proxy' nature (see McCarthy 2000, esp. 59–61, 71–6), and more generally about the inherent independence of intelligent instruments ('proxies'), an independence which is both expected and yet feared. Alternatively, following Parker 1989, comic slaves may well be interpreted as stand-ins for the Roman *adulescentes*, as alibis to vent the repressed aspirations of the Roman youth, under Saturnalian licence. Iconic in this respect is the behaviour of the free and young man Chaerea in Terence's *Eunuchus*, who impersonates a slave in order to rape the girl with whom he is infatuated.[17]

The repressions of the (comic) youth include revelry and debauchery, but also rebellion against their *patresfamilias*, and the authoritative system of Roman society, in general. In fact, Roman comedies are rich in rebellious slaves, who resist the ideals embodied in Messenio or Tyndarus, and make their expected 'proxiness' much more frictional and problematic. A good example is the already mentioned Sagaristio in *Persa*, who, after sketching the ideal of the good slave (Pl. *Pers.* 7–9, quoted on p. 75), immediately specifies that he himself does not adhere to it:

> Ego nec lubenter seruio nec satis sum ero ex sententia,
> sed quasi lippo oculo me erus meus manum apstinere hau quit tamen
> quin mi imperet, quin me suis negotiis praefulciat.
>
> (Pl. *Pers.* 10–12)

> As for me, I don't enjoy being a slave and I'm not sufficiently the way my master would want me to be, but nevertheless my master can't keep his hand away from me, as from a sore eye: so he gives me orders and uses me as support for his activities.

Sagaristio does not consider his 'proxy' role as being fully relieved (he still supports his master's activities), but as being imperfect (*nec satis ... ero ex sententia*, 10) and frictional, and this generates a 'sore' for his master: this 'sore' is archetypically comic and is often thematised in Roman comedy, which abounds in slaves showing disobedience, rebellion, disrespect against their (old) masters.[18] A good example is the slave Tranio, who fails to fulfil the primary role of the good proxy, i.e. to perform his master's orders in his absence, as his fellow-slave Grumio accuses him in the opening of *Mostellaria*:

---

[17] I owe this point to Victoria Rimell.   [18] On this, see Richlin 2017, esp. 203–51.

> Haecin mandauit tibi, quom peregre hinc it, senex?
> Hocin modo hic rem curatam offendet suam?
> Hoccin boni esse officium serui existumas
> ut eri sui corrumpat et rem et filium?
>
> (Pl. *Most.* 25–8)

> Is this what the old man told you to do when he went abroad? Is this how he'll find his business looked? Is this what you consider the duty of a good servant, to ruin his master's wealth and son?

And at the end of the play, in a meta-theatrical exchange with the master Theopropides himself, Tranio will explicitly describe his misbehaviour as the subject matter of the play, and of the comic activity as such (*ludificare*):[19]

> Si amicus Diphilo aut Philemoni es,
> dicito is quo pacto tuos te seruos ludificauerit:
> optumas frustrationes dederis in comoediis.[20]
>
> (Pl. *Most.* 1149–51)

> If you're a friend of Diphilus or Philemon, tell them how your slave made fun of you: you'll give them first-rate stories of imposture for their comedies.

In *Mostellaria*, as in many other trickster plays, the slave's subverted 'proxiness' is complemented by his loyalty to the *adulescens*, and often by the loyal 'proxiness' of another fellow slave (e.g. Grumio). In *Captiui*, for instance, the quintessentially bad slave Stalagmus, whose betrayal is at the origin of the play's complications, is contrasted with the embodiment of the good slave, the proxy-impersonator Tyndarus. At the end of the play Stalagmus is punished and Tyndarus is revealed as a free citizen; this kind of retributive framework could be (and has been) used to argue that Roman comedy mainly reflects the masters' point of view, but the situation is more nuanced than it may appear.

There are some plays in which loyal slaves do not feature at all. In *Persa*, for instance, a comedy where masters are never on stage, the only servile duty felt by the subversive Sagaristio is towards his fellow slave Toxilus. A problematic set of cases in particular, is that of the 'imperious proxies', i.e. slaves who, in their dutifulness towards their masters, transcend their servile status, and become authoritative and independent.[21] This is the case

---

[19] See Chiarini 1983: 215, Petrone 1983: 202–9.
[20] I here accept Kassel's (1991: 376) emendation of the manuscripts' *comoediis*.
[21] Cf. also Pl. *Cist.* 233–5 (Alcesimarchus insulted by his slave), *Curc.* 9 (Phaedromus teased for doing a slave's job), 298–9 (Phaedromus commenting on the freedom and overbearingness of (comic) slaves, with ref. to the iconic scene of the *seruos currens*). On this prototypical situation, see Richlin 2017, esp. 203–51 with bibliography.

of Pseudolus, who formally acts on behalf of his young master Calidorus, but does not hesitate to disrespect and command him (cf. Pl. *Pseud.* 1327: *fac quod te iubeo*). In Terence's *Heauton Timorumenos* the slave Syrus takes full control over his master Clitipho: he overzealously brings home his master's prostitute Bacchis, to his displeasure (cf. Ter. *HT* 311–3: *o hominis inpudentem audaciam*), blackmails him to secure his own mastery (338–52), and later sends him away from the comic action (585–9). Most authoritative slaves are purportedly acting on their master's behalf, and yet this does not necessarily result in the master's success, as Clitipho's eventual downfall in *HT* exemplifies.

An extreme example of an authoritative slave comes from Plautus' *Asinaria*, which features a particularly commanding proxy, Libanus. Together with his fellow Leonida, Libanus continuously crosses over his status, as epitomised in a famous scene in which he rides his master Argyrippus (Pl. *Asin.* 698–710). And yet, despite his subversive behaviour, Libanus is working throughout the play on behalf of Argyrippus himself, hunting for the money to fund the youth's revelries; moreover, in a key passage in the opening of the play, we find out that Libanus' tricks have been masochistically ordered by the *senex* Demaenetus himself (*me defraudato*, *Asin.* 91). This contradictory situation, featuring slaves ordered to act 'freely' against their masters, is paralleled in several plays. In *Heauton Timorumenos*, the slave Syrus is ordered by his master Chremes, albeit unconsciously, to perform a ruse against himself (543–58). There is one stock scene in particular, which epitomises this situation, which is that of the master handing over his authority to the slave and asking (and at times begging) him to act on his behalf.[22] An embodiment of this stock scene of inversion is also found in *Casina*, and features the old man Lysidamus and his proxy-husband Olympio:

> LYSIDAMUS: Seruos sum tuos. OLYMPIO: Optume est. LYSIDAMUS: Opsecro te,
> Olympisce mi, mi pater, mi patrone. OLYMPIO: Em, sapis sane. LYSIDAMUS: Tuos sum equidem.
> (Pl. *Cas.* 738–40)

---

[22] Cf. also Pl. *Capt.* 442–5: *haec per dexteram tuam te dextera retinens manu / opsecro, infidelior mi ne fuas quam ego sum tibi. / tu hoc age. tu mihi erus nunc es, tu patronus, tu pater, / tibi commendo spes opesque meas*, 'I entreat you by your right hand, holding you back with my right hand: don't be less faithful to me than I am towards you. Pay attention. Now *you* are my master, *you* are my patron, *you* are my father. I commend my hopes and my fortunes to you.' (Tyndarus/Philocrates to his slave Philocrates/Tyndarus); *Epid.* 381 (Stratippocles praising his slave Epidicus as his military leader); *Merc.* 171.

LYSIDAMUS: I'm your slave.
OLYMPIO: That's perfect.
LYSIDAMUS: I entreat you, my dear little Olympio, my father, my patron.
OLYMPIO: There you go, you really show sense.
LYSIDAMUS: I'm yours.

Social inversion, however one interprets it, is certainly an important feature of the Roman comic world: such inversion involving a master handing over his authority to his 'proxy' could be interpreted within a Saturnalian framework, as analogical to the withdrawal of the elite from the comic world and their temporary handing over of power (or at least prominence) in favour of the underclass.[23] And yet, as pointed out above, Olympio does remain a 'proxy' at the service of Lysidamus, and his independence is partial and restricted to the duration of the play.

In a less subversive variant of this situation, slaves are (temporarily) allowed by their masters a suspension of their proxy role, and this becomes the precondition and subject matter of the comedy. I am here thinking in particular about *Stichus*, a famously plot-less comedy, which is essentially an eponymous celebration of Stichus' 'holiday' from his servile duties, yet explicitly requested from and granted by his master Epignomus.

EPIGNOMUS: Age abduce hasce intro quas mecum adduxi, Stiche.
STICHUS: Ere, si ego taceam seu loquar, scio scire te
quam multas tecum miserias mulcauerim.
Nunc hunc diem unum ex illis multis miseriis
uolo me eleutheria capere aduenientem domum.
EPIGNOMUS: Et ius et aequom postulas: sumas, Stiche.
In hunc diem te nil moror; abi quo lubet.
Cadum tibi ueteris uini propino.

(Pl. *Stich.* 418–25)

EPIGNOMUS: Go on, take these girls inside whom I brought along with me, Stichus.
STICHUS: Master, whether I'm silent or whether I speak, I know that you know how many hardships I've given a hard time to with you. Now for this one day in recompense for those many afflictions I want to celebrate the Festival of Liberty on my arrival home.
EPIGNOMUS: What you say is just and fair; have it, Stichus. For this day I dismiss you: go where you like. I contribute a jar of old wine as a toast to you.

The paradox of 'proxies' ordered, begged, or allowed to cross over their 'proxiness' (with its comic implications) seems to be at the core of Roman

---

[23] See the classic Segal 1987; also Moore 1998: 181–96.

comedy, and is probably related to the general contradictory nature of slaves in Roman society, wavering between their double nature as tools and human beings, between their expected 'proxiness' and independence (on this, see Fitzgerald 2000: 6–8, McCarthy 2000). It also opens up the *uexata quaestio* about whether Roman comedy conveyed the slave's point of view (Richlin 2017), that of the citizen slave-owner (Parker 1989, McCarthy 2000) or a combination of both (Stewart 2012). This is a complex issue, which cannot be fully addressed here: I will only point out that the variety of approaches to 'proxiness', as outlined above, does not seem to allow for any unilateral interpretation.

In any case, the 'proxy' relation between slave and master, and the comic problems associated with that (self-inflicted or not), are iconic of the Roman *palliata*: internal evidence suggests that Roman comedies were performed by slaves (see Marshall 2006: 83–125) and that already in Plautus' time they were characterised by the prominent role slaves play in them (see e.g. Pl. *Most.* 1149–51, p. 78). If we add the fact that ancient traditions report that Roman playwrights were or had been slaves (Livius Andronicus, Plautus, Caecilius Statius, Terence),[24] and in at least one case (Terence) that they (allegedly) were mere proxy pennames for the Roman elite (see below pp. 85–6), we can conclude that the link between 'proxiness' and Roman comedy is very tight indeed. This also explains the (meta-)theatrical potential of 'proxiness', which we will explore in more detail in the next section.

Theatrical 'Proxiness'

There is indeed something inherently theatrical (and literary) about 'proxied absence': actors, playwrights and the plays themselves can all be considered as 'proxies' for someone else, and this is at times openly acknowledged in Roman comedy.

To focus on an illustrative example only, in the prologue of *Heauton Timorumenos* an unnamed veteran actor and troupe-leader (later identified with the 'star' Ambivius Turpio), enters on stage and introduces himself as the spokesman (*orator*) of the absent playwright, whose name he ostentatiously withholds:

> Nunc qui scripserit
> et quoia Graeca sit, ni partem maxumam
> existumarem scire uostrum, id dicerem.
> Nunc quam ob rem has partis didicerim paucis dabo.

[24] Cf. Richlin 2014: 211–12.

> Oratorem esse uoluit me, non prologum.
> Vostrum iudicium fecit, me actorem dedit.
>
> (Ter. *HT* 7–12)
>
> I would tell you who wrote it and the author of the Greek original, but I judge that most of you know this already. Now I will explain briefly why I have taken on this role. The playwright wanted me as an advocate, not as a prologue speaker. He has turned this into a court, with me to act on his behalf.

Ambivius is an *orator* and *actor* in both senses of the words (spokesman/advocate, actor/pleader): he has been sent by Terence, with the same authorial assertiveness (*uoluit*, 11) shown by Plautus in a similar context (*noluit, Cas.* 65), to deliver a memorised speech on his behalf, in a metaphorical trial in front of the audience/jury, in which the poet has been accused of having 'contaminated' Greek plays (*multas contaminasse Graecas*, 17) and of being a mere stand-in for powerful friends (*amicum ingenio fretum*, 24).

There are parallels in Roman comedies where actors present themselves as the performers of someone else's will (normally the leader of the company), and especially in prologues: cf. e.g. Pl. *Poen.* 4: *audire iubet uos imperator histricus* and especially *Amph.* 19–20: *Iovis iussu uenio . . . pater huc me misit ad uos oratum meus*, a passage that has several similarities with the prologue of *HT*. However, in *HT* there is an important hierarchical shift, from a secondary actor carrying the will of the leading actor in *Amph.* (cf. Oniga 1992: n. 26), to the leading actor carrying that of the poet in *HT*. Ambivius in *HT* presents himself as a mere 'proxy' for the absent poet, and this is further highlighted by his anxiety about the ability to perform his proxy role accurately:

> Sed hic actor tantum poterit a facundia
> quantum ille potuit cogitare commode
> qui orationem hanc scripsit quam dicturus sum?
>
> (Ter. *HT* 13–15)
>
> I only hope that the eloquence of the actor can do justice to the aptness of the arguments which the writer of this speech has contrived to put together.

As we have seen in the previous sections, 'proxiness' always carries with itself the anxiety about its unfulfillment, on the part of the master and/or the slave. Since Ambivius is not just an actor, but the leader of the troupe performing Terence's play, his anxiety encompasses the whole performance of the play, by the whole comic troupe. A similar concern, from a different perspective, is found in

Plautus' *Bacchides*, in a famous passage complaining about the bad performance of *Epidicus*:

> CHRYSALUS: Non res sed actor mihi cor odio sauciat.
> etiam Epidicum, quam ego fabulam aeque ac me ipsum amo,
> numquam aeque inuitus specto si agit Pellio.
>
> (Pl. *Bacc.* 213–15)
>
> It's not the success, but the actor that's wounding my heart with tedium. Even the Epidicus, a play I love as much as myself – well, there's no play I enjoy watching less if Pellio is acting in it.

Since, as argued by Brown (2002), it is likely that Pellio is also the leading actor of the comic *grex*,[25] Chrysalus' words voice the author's disappointment (real or fictional)[26] about the general performance of the play by a troupe of unreliable 'proxies', a disappointment which is similar in many respects to that of the master frustrated by the behaviour of his unsatisfactory or rebellious slave.

The 'demotion' of the actor to a mere proxy of the poet implies a confirmation of Terence's authorial authority, which is constantly highlighted in the prologue of *HT*.[27] The unnamed poet has assigned to the actor his part (*poeta dederit*, 2, *me actorem dedit*, 12), and crucially he has written (*scripserit*, 7, *scripsit*, 15) the script. The repeated use of the verb *scribere* is noteworthy, and is useful to introduce another important dimension of (meta)theatrical proxiness, which is related to the controversial relation between the Roman playwrights and their Greek models. The idea that Roman comedies are just an imperfect reflection of the splendour of their Greek originals does not belong only to German Romanticism: there is internal evidence in Roman comedy for the notion that Roman playwrights were supposed to be mere 'proxies' for their Greek models. The charge of *contaminatio* in particular, which Ambivius is refuting in the prologue of *HT*, implies a call for a strict adherence to the 'purity' of the originals. This is indeed what Terence explicitly attributes in disparaging terms to his detractor (cf. *obscuram diligentiam*, Ter. *An.* 21; *bene uortendo et easdem scribendo male*, *Eun.* 7), although he himself apparently claims

---

[25] On Pellio, see further Garton 1972: 172–4, Marshall 2006: 89–90, Fraenkel 2007: 417, speculating that Pellio may actually have been playing the part of Chrysalus.
[26] Mattingly (1960), followed by Zwierlein (1990–2: 4.202–12), considers these lines as a later addition; this is of course unverifiable, but even if the passage were interpolated, it would still introduce a (fictional) authorial concern about the reliability of the play's performers.
[27] On Terence's prologues, see in particular, Gilula 1989.

to have pursued literal or at least close translation in one scene (cf. Ter. *Ad.* 11: *uerbum de uerbo expressum extulit*).²⁸

In the prologue of *HT*, however, Terence clearly claims a degree of freedom in the adaptation of his Greek originals, following the *neglegentia* of his real models, Naevius, Plautus and Ennius, who accordingly would have been exposed to the same charge of *contaminatio* (cf. *An.* 18–21: *Naeuium Plautum Ennium / accusant quos hic noster auctores habet / quorum aemulari exoptat neglegentiam / potius quam istorum obscuram diligentiam*).²⁹ This apparent 'rebellion' of the Roman playwrights against a reduction of their literary activity as a 'proxying' translation is also suggested by the insistence on the act of writing (*scribere*): the reference to the play and its composition as the 'writing' of the Latin poet is a characteristic trait of Terence.³⁰ By contrast, in Plautus (and other earlier dramatists) the verb *scribere* is hardly ever associated with the composition of a theatrical piece. In the few Plautine cases in which the verb *scribere* does refer to the composition of a play, the subject is a Greek author (cf. *Demophilus scripsit*, *As.* 11, *Philemo scripsit*, *Trin.* 19, *antiquom poëtam* [i.e. Euripides?] *audiui scripsisse in tragoedia*, *Cur.* 591), whereas the act of the Latin poet is *uertere* 'translate' (cf. *Maccus uortit barbare*, *As.* 11, *Plautus uortit barbare*, *Trin.* 19). A possible exception is found in the prologue of *Casina* (*Diphilus / hanc graece scripsit, postid rursum denuo / latine Plautus cum latranti nomine*, 32–4),³¹ where, however, the Greek poet is still in a position of prominence. Conversely, in Terence the only occurrence of the verb *uertere* is found in a derogatory context (*qui bene uortendo et easdem scribendo male*, *Eun.* 7), probably with a negative connotation (cf. Don. *Eun.* 7: *uertendo, corrumpendo*), in which it is distinguished from *scribere* and associated with Terence's literary enemy. That is, if Plautus and above all Terence's enemy seem to consider themselves as (more or less complying) proxies subbing in for their Greek masters, Terence's emphasis on *scribere* betrays an urge for literary *manumissio*, although not yet complete independence (Menander, although unnamed, is still a looming shadow in the prologue of *HT*, cf. 7–9).

---

²⁸ See, however, Bettini 2012: 71–2 for a different interpretation of the passage.
²⁹ '(...) they are actually criticising Naevius, Plautus, and Ennius, whom he takes as his models, preferring to imitate their carelessness in this respect rather than the critics' own dreary pedantry'.
³⁰ Cf. *Poeta quom primum animum ad scribendum adpulit*, *An.* 1; *ne cum poeta scriptura euanesceret*, *Hec.* 13; *Postquam poeta sensit scripturam suam*, *Ad.* 1; *poetae ad scribendum augeat industriam*, *Ad.* 25.
³¹ 'Diphilus wrote it in Greek, and after that Plautus with the barking name wrote it again in Latin.'

The authority of the Greek models is not the only factor of anxiety for the Roman playwrights. The second charge addressed by the *actor* in the prologue of *HT* concerns another intricate dimension of 'proxiness', involving the relation between the playwright and the 'powerful friends' who patronise him:

> Tum quod maleuolus uetus poeta dictitat
> repente ad studium hunc se adplicasse musicum,
> amicum ingenio fretum, haud natura sua,
> arbitrium uostrum, uostra existumatio
> ualebit.
>
> (Ter. *HT* 22–6)

The malicious old playwright further asserts that our author has taken up the dramatic art rather suddenly, relying on the talent of his friends and not on his natural ability. This is a matter for your judgement; you shall decide the issue. (Trans. Barsby, with adjustments).

The accusation against Terence of being a mere 'proxy' of powerful friends becomes more explicit in the prologue of *Adelphoe*:

> Nam quod isti dicunt maleuoli, homines nobilis
> hunc adiutare **assidueque una scribere,**
> quod illi maledictum uehemens esse existumant,
> eam laudem hic ducit maxumam quom illis placet
> qui uobis uniuorsis et populo placent,
> quorum opera in bello, in otio, in negotio
> suo quisque tempore usust sine superbia.
>
> (Ter. *Ad.* 15–21)

As for the malicious accusation that members of the nobility assist our author and **collaborate with him in his writing all the time**, which his enemies consider a serious reproach, he regards it as a great compliment, if he finds favour with men who find favour with all of you and the people at large, men whose services have been freely available to everyone in time of need in war, in peace, and in their daily affairs.

The rumour that Terence was a mere proxy-name for the literary ambitions of the Roman elite is also confirmed by a passage of Suetonius' *Vita Terentii* 3; it opens up the crucial issue of the role of the Roman aristocracy in the integration of Greek culture in the Rome of the Middle Republic, and their (not always frictionless) patronage of the first 'culture brokers'[32] of Latin literature.

---

[32] See Feeney 2016: 67, and *passim* for the general issue (esp 65–91); the classic Gruen 1990 and 1992 are still useful.

As already noted by Suetonius, in both *HT* and *Adelphoe* Terence fails to refute the charge of being assisted by *homines nobiles*. Claiming a degree of independence from his Greek literary masters is one thing (and fits in with the widespread nationalistic discourse of the Rome of the time), quite another is to deny the patronage of powerful aristocrats. In particular, Terence's riposte in *HT* is apparently a mere appeal to the verdict (*arbitrium*, 25) and judgement (*existumatio*, 25) of the audience/jury, who are called to assess Terence's poetic talent and thereby the merit of his (forthcoming) play. These have been pre-emptively challenged by the charge of his detractor, who accused Terence of undeserved favouritism in his quick career; the refutation of this charge will require the examination of the whole play, and, in fact, the passage above is followed by a traditional request for an impartial hearing (*aequi sitis*, 28) of the forthcoming play. Terence's riposte to the charge of 'proxiness' marks therefore a key step of the prologue speech, by which Terence extends the forensic metaphor and reshapes it into a more traditional format, recasting its scope (the duration of the prologue > the duration of the whole play) and some of its structural elements, including the *orator* (Ambivius as an *actor* in the prologue > Ambivius as *actor* in the *Heauton Timorumenos*) and the *oratio* (the prologue speech > the play as a whole). This metaphorical extension also paves the way for the traditional request for fairness and attention (28–30, 35–6), and eventually the display of the evidence, i.e. the beginning of the play.

The prologue of *HT* thus introduces a final, important layer of literary 'proxiness': the *oratio* that the 'proxy' actor has been assigned to deliver is not just the prologue speech, but is extended to the whole comedy. A few lines later, this will be defined as a 'static' comedy (*stataria*), in which there will be only speech (*in hac est pura oratio*, 46):[33] against the accusation of having been undeservedly favoured in his career by the protection of powerful friends, Terence, through his 'proxy actor', cites his forthcoming comedy as a sort of 'evidence', proving the author's poetic talent. This situation can thus be construed as an embodiment of that prototypical

---

[33] Despite a popular and long-standing interpretation, *pura oratio* does not refer to Terence's pure language and/or style. *Oratio* is what is said, not the way it is said or written (which would rather be '*stilus*' or '*scriptura*'; cf. Ter. *An.* 12: *dissimili oratione sunt factae ac stilo*; *Ph.* 5: *tenui esse oratione et scriptura leui*). In a theatrical context the term refers to the content of the play in so far as it contributes to the entertainment of the audience, e.g. by means of verbal jokes, plot developments, characterisation, etc. (see *TLL* 9.2.884.65–77). Moreover, in early Latin *pura* does not mean 'elegant' or 'refined' but rather 'free from extraneous materials, physically undefiled', i.e., in this context, uninterrupted by stage activity. The inaccurate linguistic or stylistic interpretation is biased by Caesar's praise of Terence as a *puri sermonis amator* (*Carm.* fr. 1 Klotz), where, however, the word used is *sermo* and not *oratio*.

model of 'proxied absentee' which I have discussed in this chapter, with the performative comic text acting as a proxy for the author/playwright.

There are several remarks in Roman comedy presenting the comic plays as 'proxy' artefacts for the absent author, anticipating more elaborate variants on the theme in later Latin literature.[34] For reasons of space, I will only touch upon the most explicit of all, which describes the inherent (meta)theatricality of proxiness, and is again found in *Casina*'s prologue. In a passage that closely echoes the reference to Cleostrata's proxy role in the play (*sciens ei mater dat operam* **apsenti tamen**, 63), the prologue states that Plautus, by now a forever-absent character, can still be beneficial after his death, indeed by means of his plays:

> Ea tempestate flos poetarum fuit,
> qui nunc abierunt hinc in communem locum.
> Sed **tamen apsentes** prosunt pro praesentibus.
>
> (Pl. *Cas.* 18–20)

In that era the cream of poets lived, who've now gone away to the place to which all men go. But **even so** they benefit us **in their absence** as if they were present.

In conclusion, the prologues of *HT* and *Casina* reveal what is perhaps the most important dimension of absence and 'proxiness' in Roman comedy: the absent character *par excellence* is the author-playwright, who is 'proxied' by the actors and by the comedy they perform, and who is himself a 'proxy' for both the 'absent' Greek originals and the powerful Roman elite patronising Roman comedy. Just as all the other types of 'proxiness' discussed in this chapter, which pave the way for comic deception and misapprehension, or mirror the problematic relation between slaves and masters, this kind of literary 'proxiness' is never frictionless; rather, the complications related to the proxy-relations between Greek models, comic texts, Latin playwrights, the cultured elite and the social realities of the Middle Republic have engendered the most vexed problems that have tormented scholars and readers of Roman comedy for centuries: these include the relation with the absent Greek originals;[35] the identification of later interpolations and the unreliability of the canonical transmitted texts;[36] the authorial personality of the Roman playwrights

---

[34] Cf. e.g. Hor. *Epod.* 1.20, where the proxy-book is compared to a slave-boy leaving his master in search of pleasures in the city.
[35] Besides the classic Fraenkel 2007, see, for an overview, Halporn 1993 (esp. 191–3) and Petrides 2014.
[36] See e.g. the work of Zwierlein 1990–2, Goldberg 2005: 62–75, and for an overview Gratwick 1993: 3–4, Tarrant 1986: 302–3.

and the proportion of improvisation and script-adherence;[37] the supposed 'realism' of Roman comedy (are comedies reliable 'proxies' of contemporary social realities?[38]); and the interaction with the political background of the Middle Republic and its cultural discourses.[39] 'Proxiness' is a complex and elusive presence in Plautus and Terence, and yet pervasive and consistent: in one sense, it is at the origin of Roman comedy as we know it.

---

[37] See e.g. Lefèvre, Stärk and Vogt-Spira 1991, Benz, Stärk and Vogt-Spira 1995, and Stärk and Vogt-Spira 2000, Marshall 2006.
[38] See Pezzini 2021 with bibliography.
[39] See e.g. Gruen 1990: 124–57, Umbrico 2010, Feeney 2016, esp. 122–51.

CHAPTER 5

Absence Left Wanting
The Groove in Ovid's Remedia

Victoria Rimell

> Why doesn't art stop, why do people continue to create? Because in art as in sexual *jouissance*, we never say we've had "enough" of it. This idea makes no sense. If people continue to create and *jouir*, it's because desire doesn't stop when it takes one particular form. Because there is a constantly renewed desire, the desire to make new forms arise, that is, to make a new sensibility perceptible [*sensible*]. And this new sensibility is desired and created not because we lack something, or out of a compulsion for repetition, but because what is desired is the renewing of meaning *as such*. What art testifies to, then, is our desire to make sense infinitely.
>
> Jean-Luc Nancy with Adèle Van Reeth, *Coming* (2017)[1]

Getting Into the ...

By now, perhaps, everything has been spoken on Ovidian absence. This poet takes elegy – the poetry of loss, lack and mourning – and imagines its libidinal system taking root, object-less, in an empty heart (*in uacuo pectore, Am.* 1.1.26).[2] We have just begun reading and hearing a work whose chopped down, lighter form (from five to three books: *leuior demptis ... duobus, Am. Ep.* 4) announces itself as an epitaph to the first edition – a partial consolation for readers whose pain (*poena, Am. Ep.* 4) will, paradoxically or not, be lessened by this *petite mort*. In short, Ovidian elegy takes shape as a process of removal and mutilation: love's *uulnus,* inflicted on the masculine frame of epic, produces limping, excitable, unbalanced, attenuated, sometimes impotent bodies that rise and fall in music that is all about the drop and space – each pentameter's caesura –

---

[1] This chapter converses throughout with Nancy in dialogue with Van Reeth (Nancy 2017), which is recommended reading.
[2] Text of *Amores, Ars amatoria* and *Remedia amoris* throughout this paper is taken from Kenney 1995. All translations are my own.

before the beat (*surripuisse pedem, Am.* 1.1.4). When the poet-lover finally conjures up a girl, at first name-less, she is a cipher, a montage of limb and breast only half-seen, unattainable yet open to every man, *ante oculos* (*Am.* 1.5.17). His *ars* is the artistry of deception and concealment that entices with the promise of revelation, a peep into minds and behind closed doors. In the *Ars amatoria*, passion itself, like the elegiac couplet, waxes and wanes, waxes and wanes, a flame rekindled by the sulphur of longing, and the waning is expressed as a kind of hiding (*ignis / ipse latet, Ars* 2.439–40). Ovid's poet-lover is an arch-rhetorician fascinated by the violence of concealment and silencing (in human-animal transformation, in the butchering and slicing of bodies, in the drama of mute slavery), and by the texture and sound of silence. His career will end, or come full circle, in more poetry of loss – the *Tristia* and *Epistulae Ex Ponto* – brought into being (in the poet's world, at least) by the censorship of *carmina* now unspeakable, and sustained by the novelty of undoing and forgetting, the fantasy of un-learning Latin amidst barbarian noise.[3]

It is no coincidence that the title for the conference from which this volume evolved, *Unspeaking Volumes*, alluded to a well-known collection of essays centred on Ovid, a poet whose role here is glaring.[4] In the wake of Derridean deconstruction and Lacanian psychoanalysis, it has become commonplace to observe and track Ovid's tireless accumulation of stories and themes of absent-presence, launched in the first book of the *Amores*, as they wrestle playfully with Greco-Roman philosophy from Plato to Lucretius. As much as he toys with narrativizing the Lucretian doctrine of *simulacra* (in the story of Narcissus and of his many doubles), Ovid is an illusionist reliant on the striptease and the fetish, on a taking elsewhere, a trace, indentation, erotic memory or experience of ecstasis. Before she fades away, his Echo has a body that desires, and her (failed) coupling with Narcissus reverberates with difference, the miraculous, unlikely uniqueness of her voice.[5] As Philip Hardie points out in his landmark book, those who have fixated on Ovid's 'urbane vacuity' are missing the magic of the very process and possibility of conjuring.[6] Yet, what concerns me here is that critics still insist so often on parsing the obsessive, rhythmical oscillation between present-absence and absent-presence in Ovidian poetry in Freudian-Lacanian terms as a tragic or tragicomic performance of desire as frustration, futility, absence, rather than understanding the lull, space, or

---

[3] Cf. *Tr.* 3.14.45–6, 5.5.6–7, 5.7.21, 5.12.57–8, cf. *Rem.* 211, 297, 503.   [4] Barchiesi 2001.
[5] Cf. Rimell 2006: 79–83, with Cavarero 2005: 165–9, who strangely does not recognize the wit of Echo's 'replies' to Narcissus, and Butler 2015: 59–87.
[6] Hardie 2002: 13, where *Rem. am.* 717–34 are evoked as paradigmatic, 'a catalogue of stories and themes of absent-presence developed by Ovid at greater length elsewhere'.

'hiding of the flame' as an integral part or stage in the undular *propulsion* of desire.⁷ Ovid's critique of a metaphysics of presence could not be clearer: in his career-long experiment with elegy and the elegiac, his lover's desire flows as *uoluptas-poena*⁸ in the energetic matrix opened up by deferral as the renewal and return of pleasure. Yet we are still bound to that metaphysics in mourning a 'loss' that is itself predicated on a desire for true being and presence, and on an understanding of jouissance as consummation.⁹

This essay turns to Ovid's *Remedia amoris*, a poem which sets out to 'heal' where the poet has previously 'harmed', and considers it as an endgame exploration of the erotic experience of being 'stuck in a groove',¹⁰ a locus that is not a 'hole in the middle',¹¹ a fixed atemporality,¹² a feeling of failure or futility, or even a thing, but rather a force or relation, an invitation to (inter-)relate.¹³ And because in the *Remedia* reversability, contagion, the doubleness of *cura* as *pharmakon* are undeniable, unmistakable, even superficial, the poem's meaning-making is an affront to the professional reader as filler, unconcealer, knowing articulator of the unspoken, analytic dispenser of critical therapy as a (Freudian) archaeology of the repressed. Final fulfilment, in this mature, 'late' work¹⁴ which dwells on *tempora* (as a concern of medicine and of poetry, as the lover's unique, racing heartbeat), is rather beside the point, as we are swept up in the compulsive weave of erotic elegy as it regenerates itself. What follows is an attempt to surrender to the (im)possibility of giving an account of this phenomenon. That is, I am attempting to write down what I think is meaningful, productive and pleasurable about the rhythmic process of Ovidian *amor* in and of itself. The *Remedia* is an especially fascinating site for the reproduction of Ovidian desire, I will argue, as despite its latticework of (over-)familiar scenes and tropes, it is an uncanny work whose 'secret' is not its comic 'failure' (see section 2) but its provocative jolting of the desiring subject, its staging of departures from the (present, male, ideally invulnerable) self that channels the experience of jouissance as a going out or 'overflowing' (see section 5). It is in this sense that the *Remedia* performs absence as an 'undoing' (though not of the *Ars amatoria*, cf. *Rem. am.* 12) or, more precisely, an unmaking-remaking that leads lovers away from death. I discuss the basic structures of this process in

---

⁷ I.e. I am not seeking to privilege delay over gratification, circularity over drive, but rather to tune into the pleasure and fulfilment of desire as a productive process, that cannot be fixed in time but only performed, in Ovidian elegy. Cf. Rimell 2019.
⁸ *Am. Ep.* 3–4. ⁹ Cf. Nancy 2017: 70–87. ¹⁰ Gardner 2013: 80; cf. Gardner 2008.
¹¹ Lanham 1976: 50, explored by Hardie 2002: 27. ¹² Gardner 2013: 179.
¹³ Cf. Rimell 2006, 2019. ¹⁴ *Rem. am.* 109–10: *serior aegro / aduocor*.

sections 3 and 4 of this chapter, as a prelude to section 5, which explores – as paradigmatic of Ovid's method – the productive displacements involved in comparing male lover to mother in the *Remedia*.

Suspicion, Diagnosis and the Critic's Cure

Much recent scholarship on the *Remedia* has sought to preserve the critic's prerogative to unveil this text's quiet, buried secrets by suspending just the right amount of disbelief in the face of the poem's professed aim to cure (dangerous) passion, and occasionally, to that end, giving an oddly tendentious account of that aim. As Thorsen puts it, 'one of the most central lessons in the *Remedia amoris* is to unlearn how to love women',[15] but this is a misleading description, as Rosati notes.[16] Loving women in general is entirely unproblematic for Ovid here as long as its pleasure-pain does not tip over into death-drive (*ne pereat*, 16). The text itself can then be held to account for its failure and disingenuousness ('Is the *Remedia* a didactic failure? It is not a reliable self-help book . . . '[17]), when it is revealed that the poet 'repeatedly proves his own incapacity to bring help to the unhappy lover',[18] where 'help' is conceived as extricating that suicidal lover from the world of Ovidian *amor* rather than returning him to it. The critic, in this reading, dissects the deceptive, covert poem and diagnoses an unobvious pathology.[19] As Brunelle puts it, 'Ovid's conundrum' – that is, the ironic disjunction between the same, seductive poetic form and the work's ostensible didactic goal – 'does not display itself prominently and immediately on the surface of the text',[20] a variation on Conte's approach, which must, to some extent, accept at face value the poem's movement away from the enclosed elegiac world (making it not a cure for love, but 'a remedy against a form of literature')[21] while at the same time discovering the trick that *remedia amoris* are oxymoronic (it is impossible to be cured of love and to continue to write love elegy). Likewise, Gardner's recent mapping of the *Remedia,* in terms of an 'opening up' of the 'closed circuit of elegy', and

---

[15] Thorsen 2014: 190. Cf. Martelli 2013: 74 on the 'death of desire that the *Remedia* is designed to effect'.
[16] Rosati 2006: 151: 'Even a superficial analysis of the poem shows continuity with the *Ars* rather than a simple reversal, a continuity that is not camouflaged and is, at times, boldly exhibited.'
[17] Davvison 1996: 258. In their introduction to Gibson, Green and Sharrock 2006, the volume editors claim that the view of the poem represented in Davvison 1996 'has produced some of the most interesting scholarship of the present decade' (15).
[18] Fulkerson 2004 ('Why the *Remedia* fail').
[19] See Felski 2015: *passim* on the metaphor of critique as diagnosis and revelation.
[20] Brunelle 2000–1: 132.   [21] Conte 1989: 467.

therefore in terms of an exposure of 'women's time' and female desire (understood as limited, futile, torturous, circular in the Ovidian imagination) to the 'salutary' possibilities of history, linear time, or the adult, male world, must to some extent take Ovid's 'rehabilitation of subjects' literally.[22]

Yet by the time we get to the *Remedia,* Ovid is an 'unrepentant recidivist'[23] addressing not a novice-pupil but a worse-for-wear expert whom he himself has instructed, and the notion that *amor* as pathological impetus can be cured is not just a corny new paradox. We cannot fail to recognize that the duplicity of *cura* as both troubling anxiety and dispassionate (self-)care (*quaelibet huic curae cedere cura potest,* 'whatever care you have can yield to this care', 170) is a variation on all that has come before, and will come after, in Ovid. Taken literally, the surface premise that the poem will help suffering lovers to 'heal' rather than to love (*discite sanari per quem didicistis amare,* 'Learn to be healed by the poet from whom you learnt to love', 43) is always already unstable, and reversibility itself is invested with the momentum of unstoppable desire. As soon as you admit contagion, in a domino effect from the *Ars amatoria* onwards, there is nowhere desire cannot seep: its *imperium* is *sine fine.* Ovidian erotic elegy is not so much threatened in 'opening itself out' spatially and temporally to a series of outsides (as Conte argued), but the other way around. Every self-distancing, exiting and exile must replay the torture and pleasure of the *exclusus amator*; and every landscape 'opposed' to elegiac bedrooms and the languor of *otium* – Rome's fora and theatres, the battlefield and army barracks, fertile farmland and pastoral countryside, the scene of the hunt, seas and oceans – is designed to tease with barely suppressed metaphors and evocations.[24] Those healing and poisonous herbs – Ovid's examples are the rose and nettle – grow literally and symbolically close to one another (*urticae proxima saepe rosa est,* 46), sharing pleasant and unpleasant, medicinal and harmful properties (nettles sting, roses prick, and both plants have therapeutic uses).[25] Directionality, in space and time, is itself infected with duplicity in the poem, whose programmatic opposition between *ante* and *nunc* (8, 10), present and perfect tense (*discite . . . didicistis,* 43) is disturbed by *semper* (*ego semper amaui . . . nunc quoque . . . amo,* 'I have always loved . . . and now, also . . . I love', 7–8).[26] In line 41 (*ad mea, decepti iuuenes, praecepta uenite,*

---

[22] Gardner 2013: 167–80. [23] Rosati 2006: 152.
[24] For further exploration and examples, see e.g. Beasom 2013, Brunelle 2000–1, Davvison 1996, Fish 2004, Fulkerson 2004, Hardie 2006b, Houghton 2009, Rosati 2006, Shulman 1981.
[25] Cf. *Rem. am.* 323 *et mala sunt uicina bonis,* with Arist. *Rhet.* 1367a28–32, Quint. 3.7.25, and Pinotti 1988: 102–3.
[26] I read *nunc quoque* with *amo* rather than with *quid faciam* For discussion, see Pinotti ad loc., Goold 1967.

'Come, tricked youths, to my instructions') the homophony of *decepti* and *praecepta,* as Rosati observes, hints that current precepts might themselves be deceptive, that the contrast between past and present/future might collapse into an unchallenged contiguity or continuity.[27] Similarly, it is not quite the case that delay, or *mora*-as-*amor,* in opposition to speeding forward, always fosters desire (e.g. *nam mora dat uires,* 'For delay gives strength', 83), because hurrying (*sed propera,* 'but hurry', 93) is also laced with erotic urgency, the reminder that Ovidian eros is as much about getting off as frustration (compare *Ars am.* 2.727, after *Ars am.* 2.717: 'Venus' pleasure is not to be hurried'). Sex, like medicine, is all about context and timing; sometimes it is sexy to delay, other times to forge ahead.

It is indicative that the twice-mentioned historical model for the healing lover in this Janus-like text is the *fugax Parthus,* the fleeing Parthian (at 155–7, the suffering lover is told to conquer 'Parthian arrows', while at 224, he should act like the Parthian, who is 'safe' because he flees). This confusing shift from enmity to identification, Parthian as object to Parthian as model subject, is underpinned by the paradox of the *Parthus* himself, who as he 'flees', turns back on his horse and attacks, an image also employed in *Ars* 3 in advice on which sexual positions girls should experiment with to show off their best bits and hide their flaws (*ut celer auersis utere Parthus equis,* 'like the swift Parthian, use a backward-turned horse', *Ars.* 3.786).[28] When Ovid states in his proem *nec te, blande puer, nec nostras prodimus artes, / nec noua praeteritum Musa retexit opus* (*Rem. am.* 11–12), the couplet is usually translated as 'I betray neither you, seductive boy, nor my own arts, and a new Muse does not undo/cancel out the previous work (understood as the *Ars amatoria*)'. Yet *re-texit,* one of many verbs with this prefix in the poem, can mean both to unweave or unravel and to reweave or retrace ('to go back over a story, argument etc.').[29] The verb *retexo* is mostly used in

---

[27] Rosati 2006: 147. (Self-)deception, moreover, will retain its importance throughout the *Remedia* (see e.g. 212, 317–20, 325–6, 513–16), while *praecepta* (from *prae-cipio*) also emphasize *previously taken* advice. Thanks to E. Giusti for this point.

[28] Cf. *Ars am.* 1.211 (*fugis ut uincas*), and *Ars am.* 1.179–228 in general, which Sharrock (2006: 32) calls 'an orgy of Eastern conquest and projected triumph', not a digression from but a vehicle for the 'romanticisation of force' which is the story of this book.

[29] *OLD retexo* 3 (cf. Apul. *Met.* 9.17, Stat. *Theb.* 3.338). The verb means to 'redo' or 'retrace' a path at Verg. *Aen.* 12.763 (*quinque orbis explent cursu totidemque retexunt*), and 'to remake' or reform at Ov. *Met.* 15.249 (*idemque retexitur ordo*). Note that *retexo* is used in the context of a waning (and waxing) moon at *Met.* 7.530–1 (*expleuit ... / ... retexuit*), i.e. it is one movement in an oscillation. Cf. Martelli 2013: 76–7.

classical Latin literature in reference to Penelope's trick.³⁰ Ovid will not 'undo' the *Ars amatoria*, therefore, but he will perhaps not 'retrace' or 'remake' it either. These two movements are potentially in mutual conflict, while the hint at Penelope's cunning unravelling and reweaving of her tapestry as a *remedium* against the unwanted attention of the suitors is presented, paradoxically, as a rejected strategy. This Penelopean poet will not unweave-reweave, will not resist adultery. A Penelope who did not artfully unweave-reweave makes for a very different and novel *Odyssey* indeed, at the hands of a love poet who has made a career out of rewriting epic narratives from an expansionist elegiac perspective.³¹

At the same time, of course, while the double movement of *retexo* is ostensibly denied, it is also reactivated by the shuttle of the elegiac distich itself, conceived in *Amores* 1.1.1–4 as a composition and partial undoing that creates its distinctive shape and rhythm. As Adriana Cavarero writes, arguing against Plato's use of Penelope as an anti-model at *Phaedo* 84a, Penelope's work is *not* in vain: 'it has a rhythmic cadence and is thoroughly sustained by a precise intention that gives it a certain inexorability', whereas in the 'philosophers' tying and untying, there is neither design nor *metis*'.³² Cavarero's point is that Penelope tangles and holds together what philosophy (with its patriarchal underpinnings) wants to separate – body and soul. In denying her body to the suitors, she reaffirms her physical self and her sexuality as her own, invisible realm. Meanwhile the *Remedia*'s Penelopean Ovid, or his *nova Musa*, denies both unweaving and retracing, hinting both at his channelling of Penelope's creative world-making and at her yielding to temptation, after the *Ars amatoria*.

While the *praeceptor-amator* skips in this poem from one not quite convincing precept to the next (leave her, no stay with her, avoid sex, no lap it up, ditch all women, no embrace promiscuity, read me, don't re-read me), contradictions pile up and are underwritten by countless unlegislatable figurations and provocations of desire. The critic's expert unconcealment of the basic doubleness of the *Remedia*, as I have briefly outlined it, is hardly a revelation at all, and the problem with retaining this account of our experience of the poem is that it mimics Freud's account of the pleasure

---

[30] *quasi Penelope telam retexens*, Cic. *Acad.* 2.95; *nocturno tela retexta dolo*, Ov. *Am.* 3.9.30; cf. Stat. *Silu.* 3.5.9.
[31] Examples of this phenomenon are too many to list, from the inaugural transformation of Virgil's *Aeneid* in *Amores* 1.1.1–4, to the refashioning of epic heroes and heroines as lovers in the *Ars* (e.g. Ulysses at *Ars am.* 2.123–4), and throughout the *Heroides*, to further experiments in rerouting epic narratives in *Remedia*, e.g. 57–8, 65–6.
[32] Cavarero 1995: 28.

principle, offering a final diagnosis of unsatisfiability while at the same time marking its conclusion as a release from the tension of desire.³³ In this reading, the poem either fails because it does not succeed in its (tendentiously represented) aim of teaching lovers how to fall out of love, or it fails because it becomes the ultimate instantiation of desire as lack, an absence of something, a yearning for plenitude destined to fall short. In other words, the poem confirms that there is no escape from Ovidian *amor*, and from elegiac desire as – in Gardner's terms – futile, imprisoning, disempowering, static and tragic.³⁴ There is a fleeting hope of exiting this tomb and making it to the outside of poetic and historical 'flow' (Gardner 2013: 174), but alas, we are doomed to entrapment. Thus hysteric Phyllis, an example of the suicidal lover at *Remedia* 55–6 and 591–608,³⁵ treads the paradigmatic path of erotic elegy itself when she paces to and from the beach wishing for Demophoon's return, the same old Ovidian rut of desire.

Yet this opposition between Kristeva's 'monumental temporality' and the 'historical flow of time', which Gardner, after Conte, uses to stage the depressing and stagnant 'enclosure' of desire in the *Remedia*, is a false one. In Ovidian elegy, as this text hammers home, delay and drive are not antithetical modalities corresponding to (feminine) elegy/the semiotic and (masculine) epic/the Symbolic order respectively. Instead they overlap, swap position, and are connoted differently for individual lovers and lovemaking interactions, at different times.³⁶ Ovidian desire is not quite the movement from exciting absence to (failed) presence, but from differing permutations of absence-presence to absence-presence, a productive process that is pleasurable in itself, and that enlists the retracings and undoings of the critical reader in the renewal of elegiac desire and elegiac poetry as ebb and flow. This is not a question of denying lack, but of tuning into the *uoluptas* of lack as absence-presence and as an element that propels an interrelation – not a broken record, or a rut, but a groove.³⁷ The *Remedia* wants to make it a joy to keep on dancing – a joy that connects the sense-making process of interpretation with the life-affirming pleasure-pain of

---

³³ Freud 1961.   ³⁴ Gardner 2013 esp. 173–80.
³⁵ After *Her.* 2, *Ars am.* 3.37–8, and *Culex* 131–3. On Phyllis as 'female pupil', see Kennedy 2006: 62–74.
³⁶ For Kristeva herself, the semiotic is not strictly opposed to the symbolic order, which is composed of both semiotic and symbolic elements, but is rather part of it (although not confined to it). This is especially important for Kristeva 1984, as Oliver 1993 (esp. 101–3) observes.
³⁷ Cf. Gardner 2013: 175: 'The example of Phyllis (*Rem. am.* 591–608) illustrates these restricted impulses, for it demonstrates that women who attempt to leave their well-defined spaces do not get very far, but instead remain stuck, like a skipping record needle, in a groove they are bound to repeat'.

amor – and makes a joke of the very principle of reading as quasi-medical diagnosis. Who would want to cure this disease? Or if we understand disease in this context as an excess of suffering that transforms itself into suicidal impulse, is this not precisely the *remedium* required? We might say that the poem's false/failed exit from elegiac circuitry encodes and facilitates the 'going elsewhere' of jouissance. 'What we desire most strongly' as Nancy puts it, 'is to depart, to go out', in the sense that 'in jouissance, I stray from myself in such a way that I am sent back to a self beyond any possible identity'.[38] The *Remedia* stages a move to depart (*i procul*, 'go far away!', *Rem. am.* 214) as an *impetus* to return to the *uoluptas-poena* of the *exclusus amator*, a lover not just tortured and teased by being 'shut out', but by the thought of reliving that 'elsewhere' of erotic pleasure. I will explore how far that elsewhere might reach in the *Remedia* below (101–8). But first we must get with the beat.

Among the Conspiracy Theorists, Again

To say that the *Remedia* debunks or even mocks a hermeneutics of suspicion and diagnosis is not to impute that revelation of the unspoken becomes a flattened or irrelevant movement in the poem. On the contrary, it is a continual spur and provocation, despite the fact that broadly speaking we are always 'discovering' the same thing. The point is rather that the path or drive to get there, even in the same music, is always different, always differently pleasurable, and also that the process of (re-)discovery is by definition unclosed and productive: *augent secreta furores* ('secrecy fuels passions', 581). As Macherey wrote, 'the silence of the book is not a lack to be remedied, an inadequacy to be made up for.... We must distinguish the necessity of this silence' which 'gives it life'.[39] The problem with a hermeneutics of suspicion is that it rides tandem with the critic's pose as detective in pursuit of that 'smoking gun', or proof of the text's inadequacies, that will close the case.[40] Yet as Stephen Hinds argues in his reading of a 'poetics of conspiracy' in the exile poetry, attempts to distance ourselves from the fever of intense engagement with the (open) secrets of Ovidian *carmina-crimina*, to become dispassionate philologists rather than passionate conspiracy theorists, are futile, because the investigations set in motion by these texts will always tend to expose and taunt the abnormal, excited obsessiveness of the literary critic poring over their every tone, pitch and nuance. What Hinds communicates, but leaves unspoken, is that the

---

[38] Nancy 2017: 41–2.   [39] Macherey 1978: 84.   [40] Cf. Felski 2015: 14–51.

ultimate – the original – conspiracy theorist is the lover, crazed with desire and paranoia, reliving the not-quite-decipherable pleasure-pain of every encounter.[41] A key facet of Ovidian imperialism is that we are all lovers now.

We are and are not Phyllis, then. Or rather, the poem allows its participants a 'way out' of her tortuous zigzagging, to be performed again and again (if in Ovid's parallel universe she survives: 55–6), even as they follow in her (elegiac) footsteps. When Phyllis at *Remedia* 601–4 paces back and forth to the beach, and looks at her *zona* ('belt'), and then the tree, before raising her fingers to her neck, we grasp the implication that she is thinking about hanging herself from a branch. That is, she is not quite saying here what she wrote (silently) with her own hand in *Heroides* 2.141 (*colla quoque, infidis quia se nectenda lacertis / praebuerunt, laqueis inplicuisse iuuat*, 'my neck, too, because it was once offered to the bondage of your faithless arms, I could gladly have ensnared in a noose'), a couplet that already connects the pressure on her neck in Demophoon's tight embrace with the (erotic?) desire to experience the pleasure-pain of self-inflicted asphyxiation.[42]

Yet in this passage of the *Remedia*, desire is the memory not so much of a story but of a touch, a frisson, a flash or sensation, and it pervades this future intention which already in *Heroides* 2 was staged as a future potential in the past, *inplicuisse*.[43] Phyllis' wavering (*dubitat*, 603) now captures this temporal instability, deferring the suicide that is not described here (instead Ovid hints at her metamorphosis into an almond tree) and plunging us back into desire. In *Heroides* 2.115–16, Ovid's Phyllis recalls how Demophoon untied her *zona* and took her virginity (*cui mea uirginitas auibus libata sinistris / castaque fallaci zona recincta manu*, 'to you amid sinister omens my virginity was first bestowed, and my chaste belt undone by your lying hand', 115–16) and earlier in line 93, she remembered how he put his arms around her neck (*ausus es amplecti colloque infusus amantis / oscula per longas iungere pressa moras*, 'you dared to embrace me, and pouring yourself around/on/into the neck of your lover, to join close-pressed kisses in drawn-out delay', 93–4). Now in the *Remedia*, that

---

[41] Hinds 2007.

[42] Phyllis' suicide by hanging is also told or alluded to in Pliny *HN* 16.108, Serv. *ad Ecl.* 5.10. The verb *nectare* in *Her.* 2.141 suggests (an alternative to) *necare*, as does *laqueis*, used in the *Ars* and *Remedia* to indicate the 'snares' of passion lovers fall into, both literal and metaphorical (cf. *Ars am.*1.646, 2.580, 2.595, 3.591, *Rem. am.* 502), as opposed to the noose used in hanging (*Rem. am.* 17).

[43] Cf. Nancy 2017: 17–18, on 'why there is no solitary jouissance'. See Barchiesi 2001a: 105–28 on the 'future reflexive' in the *Heroides*.

lingering touching belongs to both past and future, and what remains is a scene of mourning that reignites the erotics of *flebilis elegia* and rustles throughout with non-verbalized sounds (from *nisi secretae laeserunt Phyllida siluae* in 591, and *ruptaque singultu uerba loquentis erant* in 598, to *non flesset positis Phyllida silua comis*, 606).[44]

Such is the sonic animation of *sola loca* ('lonely places') in this sensuous, post-Virgilian pastoral landscape, that we wonder whether what Ovid is suggesting in *aspicit et ramos* ('and she looks at the branches', 603) is not (only) future death by hanging from a branch, but also Phyllis' ecstatic Bacchic hallucination of the beginning of her own Myrrha-like transformation into a tree in the accelerating, overflowing present of jouissance. Is her 'flowing hair' (*fusis . . . comis*) in line 594 already now transformed into the *positis . . . comis* ('shed leaves/laid-aside human hair/neatly styled hair') of line 606, which may now belong not just to the *silua* but also to the girl-tree they echo, whose name derives from φύλλα, foliage?[45] Undone hair, *the* feature of the Bacchant, threatens to transform Phyllis from Ovidian lover into tragic suicide, yet *positis comis*, applied to Phyllis, and opposed in *Fasti* 1.405–6 to the *effusis comis* or 'loose hair' of Naiads, holds the tantalizing promise of restoration to Ovid's programmatically elegiac muse, the *compta puella comas* ('girl with a neat hair do', *Am.* 1.1.20).[46] We return/progress to Myrrha, who in *Metamorphoses* 10 attempts to hang herself from a branch with her belt (*zona*) but is 'saved' by her nurse. Like the doctor-poet in the *Remedia*, the nurse promises to bring her help (*opemque / me sine ferre tibi*, *Met.* 10.395–6; *nostrae sentiat artis opem*, *Rem. am.* 16, cf. 44, and 55, *si me foret usa magistro*) and is an expert in healing song and herbs (*habeo quae carmine sanet et herbis*, *Met.* 10.397, cf. *discite sanari*, *Rem. am.* 43; *salutares herbas*, *Rem. am.* 45). Yet of course, the nurse's intervention paves the way for Myrrha's death-drive to reassert itself as lust, and she becomes her mistress' accomplice, silencing the truth (*nec sentiet umquam / hoc pater*, 'Your father will never know of this', 10.409–10; *'potiere tuo' et*

---

[44] Phyllis appears several times as an icon of bucolic beauty and an inspiration for love song in the *Eclogues*, at 3.76, 5.10 and 7.59 as well as at 10.37, 41. Callimachus also wrote about Phyllis (see Pfeiffer 1949 on fr. 556, with Procop. *Epist.* 86 pp. 565–6). Ironically, unlike Gallus in *Ecl.* 10, who inhabits a responsive, animated woodland in which he is alone but never alone (*non canimus surdis, respondent omnia siluae*, 10.8), this Phyllis is truly abandoned, and her cries for help are ignored by a 'deaf' landscape (*surdas clamabat ad undas*, 597), despite the 'echoes' of Virgilian pastoral sibilance everywhere in this scene.
[45] Cf. also *Ars am.* 3.37–8 (*et audi / depositis siluas Phyllida flesse comis*).
[46] *Fasti* 1.405–6: *Naïdes effusis aliae sine pectinis usu, / pars aderant positis arte manuque comis*. The world of the *Ars amatoria* and the possibility of being a different kind of Phyllis also underwrites this scene: see again *Ars am.* 3.37–8.

non ausa 'parente' / dicere, '"Have your … "', and she did not dare say "father"', 429–30) while permitting the unspeakable. Myrrha, whose tale insinuates itself in the gaps revealed by Phyllis' wavering (*dubitat* 603, cf. *Met.* 10.374–5), daring (603, cf. *Met.* 10.429, 460–1) and erotic memories, takes us to other, less solitary *loca* – the places where desire is endlessly, differently, excessively replayed and made sense of in writing.

We might return again to Nancy's formulation: 'it is precisely this elsewhere that jouissance opens up'.[47] Phyllis is the paradigm case of the wretched lover whose way out is death by hanging (*Rem. am.* 17, 55–6). Yet in the other-world of this poem, the place we can access only *through* the particular meaning-making of Ovidian poetics, she can be saved/condemned again by the beat of desire that will not die, and that licenses her and her readers to remain in a space whose distinctive rhythms make time pass differently. Such rhythms move us away from Lacanian desire as continually projected into an eternal, tragically ungraspable future in which a void might be permanently fulfilled, and into the pleasure of jouissance in the vibrating, elegiac *now*. What we discover, in that space, is that the future becoming-other of metamorphosis can momentarily overwrite her suicide, returning her to the identity crisis/ecstasis of sexual bonding – or in Phyllis' own words 'in-pouring' – that of all art forms only poetry can capture in language (*Her.* 2.93–4: *colloque infusus amantis*, 'He poured himself around/onto/into the neck of his lover'). The memory of that liquidity and permeability between lovers, almost untranslatable and therefore concealed in English versions of the *Heroides*, returns here as the horrific-consolatory escape of physical transformation, the possibility that sobbing Phyllis might merge with a woodland that weeps in empathy: *non flesset positis Phyllida silua comis*, 'the wood would not have shed its leaves and wept for Phyllis' (*Rem. am.* 607), or 'the wood would not have wept for Phyllis after she had shed her leaves/redone her hair', after *Rem. am.* 594 (*ire solet fusis barbara turba comis*, 'she was going, as the barbarian throng is wont to go, with hair streaming out behind her'). As in *Heroides* 2.93–4, this is a transcendence – figured in the ever-changing tree – that comes to be about not (a tragic failure to achieve) spatio-temporal fixity and separation, but instead about new forms of intersubjective relation, a different kind of ecstasis.

---

[47] Nancy 2017: 87.

Going All the Way, and Back

Phyllis, had Ovid saved her, would not have been released from her repetitive pacing, but instead would have continued to tread the same circular route *saepius*, 'more often' (56). Yet some paths in *Remedia* do take us on a different trip. The most overt and outrageous instance of this phenomenon delights in revealing how sick the doctor-critic really is, how much embarrassing excitement can rev itself up in a familiar furrow (*et gyro curre, poeta, tuo,* 'run, poet, in your proper track' 398). The section of the *Remedia* that (re-)begins at line 397 offers a practical exercise to follow up on the rhetorical reconstructions recommended at lines 317–22 and 327–30, and supplements manipulations of the girl's behaviour suggested at 333–40. The poet instructs male lovers to exhaust their *uoluptas* with another woman first, which will render it *segnis* (slow, lingering – better for her? 403) when he visits the mistress. This almost commonsense precept is blurred by the next line (which is bracketed by Kenney): *sustentata Venus gratissima* ('deferred pleasure is enjoyed the most', 405), after *non est Veneris properanda uoluptas,* 'the pleasure of sex is not to be rushed', *Ars am.* 2.717. He then advises men to undermine the teachings of *Ars am.* 3 (and to go against the half-lit sexiness of *Amores* 1.5) by encouraging their girls to adopt the most unflattering positions during sex, with the windows open to let in as much natural light as possible (compare *Ars am.* 3.771–86, where women are advised to think about which parts of their body are more or less pleasing to the eye, and to position themselves accordingly for lovemaking).[48] At the same time, readers might intuit that this strategy is destined to fail precisely because of the successful dissemination of *Ars am.* 3. There is perhaps already something for the often excluded female audience of the *Remedia* at line 412, where the observation of *turpia . . . membra* might well evoke male body parts (you'll be on show too, *iuuenes*!) rather than generic 'ugly limbs'.[49] *Voluptas* lingers, and ends in simultaneous orgasm at *Rem.* 413–4 (*at simul ad metas uenit finita uoluptas / lassaque cum tota corpora mente iacent,* 'but as soon as pleasure has reached its goal, and both bodies and mind lie exhausted . . . '), reformulating *Ars am.* 2.727–8 (*ad metam properate simul: tum plena uoluptas, / cum pariter uicti femina uirque iacent,* 'Hurry to the post together: pleasure is full, when both woman and man lie conquered together') and reminding voyeuristic readers – before they even think of diagnosing Ovidian *cura*

---

[48] In particular, *figura* (407) and the verb *decere*, 408 (cf. *dedecuisse* 410) echo *Ars am.* 3.772 (*non omnes una figura decet*).
[49] See Adams 1982: 55–6 on *turpia* (with or without *membra*) as *pudenda*.

as failure – that the Circus's *meta* functions as both turning-post and end-post.⁵⁰ The climactic, 'fourth book' role of the *Remedia* in Ovidian erotodidaxis, which is itself an engine for jouissance not as plenitude but as acervation to the point of overflowing, is felt suggestively in the poet's interlude before the next scene, at 423–4 (*praeceptaque in unum / contrahe: de multis grandis acervus erit*, 'Draw my precepts together as one: from many you'll make a hefty pile').

And then comes *Amores* 1.5, again, with the lights on. Some (not all!) will be repulsed by their girlfriend, Ovid counsels, if they catch sight of **obscenas in aperto corpore partes** (literally, 'obscene parts in an open body', 429), a line which maps a photographic negative of hole between open legs, making instead the 'obscene parts' frame the opened body.⁵¹ He continues, '*ille quod a Veneris rebus surgente puella / uidit in immundo signa pudenda toro*', 'that man [checks his passion] because when his girlfriend gets up after sex, he sees the shameful traces on the dirty bed' (431–2). Yet unlike in the previous couplet (where in any case, *haesit amor* suggests physical clinging as well as putting the brakes on desire), Ovid does not spell out *ille*'s reaction: he just 'sees' those *signa pudenda* – 'signs to be ashamed of' – which suggest or put before our eyes the *pudenda*, genitals, that we see in and through their absence.⁵² Note that those revealed-concealed parts are now centrally placed in this verse and in this bed or body, where they belong (we are also almost exactly in the *middle* of the poem). *Signa* themselves are both present traces and the marks left by them (a *signum* is among other things the impression of a signet ring on wax), that obscene flash persisting from the previous couplet. As his readers are transfixed, Ovid digs them in the ribs: you're just feeble jokers (*luditis*, 433), if these things disturb you (*mouere*), although 'disturb' is not the only possible translation of *mouere* here. He is going to have to try harder. As a last resort, the male lover should hide, and secretly watch his girlfriend while she 'gives back obscene things (*reddente obscena*)', thus seeing what *mos* – the moral norm – forbids him from seeing (437–8). The neuter plural *obscena*, like *pudenda* (and like *talia*, in line 439, or like *ista* in 433, or *loca* at *Ars am.* 2.719) leaves those things unsaid, an absence or tease within a peepshow that draws on the perverse advice to a 'female' audience (while men watch) at *Ars am.* 3.225–30, when the *puella* is counselled to

---

⁵⁰ Cf. Sharrock 1994: 18–20.
⁵¹ *aperto* (*pace* Pinotti 1993: 216) does not simply mean 'uncovered'.
⁵² Holzberg 2006: 52: 'always an eyesore for the delicate ancient male' [sic]. Also see Martelli 2013: 90.

never let her boyfriend see her cosmetic preparations behind closed doors, after Lucretius 4.1175–92.

It is perhaps in part the redolence of stinking toilette scenes (despite the emphasis on the visual here, concealing unspeakable smells) that lead most commentators and translators to assume that *reddente obscena puella* (*Rem. am.* 437) is meant to evoke defecation.[53] The verb *reddo* (cf. *OLD* s.v. 4) can mean 'to expel from the body', yet the *re-* prefix (which itself comes to define the returns and reversals of *Remedia*) suggests more specifically the 'ejection of the waste products of substances previously taken'. Indeed, the *saucia turba* ('wounded crowd', 436), made up now not just of suffering lovers but of spectators vulnerable to desire, might surely infer that what is being expelled, or rather 'returned', is not digested food but the secretions suggested at 432 (*uidit in immundo signa pudenda toro*). Ovid may be hinting at a contraceptive technique mentioned by Hippocrates in *On the seed* ch. 5 ('When a woman has intercourse, if she is not going to conceive, then it is her practice to expel the sperm produced by both partners whenever she wishes to do so',[54] cf. ch. 13 of *The nature of the child*, where Hippocrates tells the story of a prostitute advised to jump up and down to make the male seed 'fall out', and who ended up expelling a small embryo). Ovid's Muse, identified with the prostitute Thais (385–6), is licentious in the face of (your) censorship ('there are those whose censorship dictates my muse is depraved', 362, cf. *Tr.* 2.354):[55] nothing shall remain unspoken. Indeed the ablative phrase *reddente obscena puella* fills in far too much, capturing the seductive horror of Kristeva's abjection from the point of view of both girl and male viewer: 'she expels', 'discharges', but literally 'gives back', 'returns'. Her *obscena* are and are not her *pudenda*, or are and are not part of her, as the synaloepha blurring the acting agent and the object in *reddente-obscena* also gestures towards.[56] Now that the lover hides in the space where he should not be, what is revealed is not just a different *puella*, but a different perspective on the

---

[53] Cf. Mela, *Chor.* 1.58.1 (*cibos palam et extra tecta / sua capiunt obscena intimis aedium reddunt*). See Pinotti 1993 and Lazzarini 1986 ad loc.; Holzberg 2006: 52. Strangely, Martelli 2013: 91 assumes without discussion or reference to other readings that the phrase suggests female masturbation: I find this unconvincing (in what ways could she be said to 'give back' *obscena* in masturbating?) although the interpretation is indicative of how much imaginative leeway the line allows, or fosters.
[54] Trans. I. M. Ionie in Lloyd 1978.   [55] On this passage, see also Holzberg 2006: 45–52.
[56] Cf. Kristeva 1981: 1: 'There looms, within abjection, one of those violent, dark revolts of being, directed against a threat that seems to emanate from an exorbitant outside or inside, ejected beyond the scope of the possible, the tolerable, the thinkable. It lies there, quite close, but it cannot be assimilated. It beseeches, worries, and fascinates desire, which, nevertheless, does not let itself be seduced'.

intersubjective connections that *uoluptas* fosters. This is what prevents Ovidian erotic poetry turning into what for us, alas, has become a mainstream norm of banal, violent porn that turns woman into thing and hole to stuff. There is always something that overflows, erupts, unbalances or tarries, even in Ovid's crassest, most brightly lit appeal to domination and the cliché of the male gaze: *obscena,* almost out of sight, are both *her* absent-present shit/genitalia, and *his* ejaculations, now 'given back' as if in reply (to vv. 429–32). We might add, excessively, that *reddo* is one of Ovid's favourite words for 'to echo': the girl giving back/uttering in reply 'obscene things' distils mischievous Echo's interaction with Narcissus in *Metamorphoses* 3, where she turns his 'innocent' words into suggestive phrases pregnant with the agency of her longing (*reddere de multis ut uerba nouissima posset,* 'so that she could only return the latest/most original words from many', *Met.* 3.361).[57] The readerly question 'What does the voyeur see?' in *Remedia* 429–40 is followed closely by 'what does he smell?' and 'what does he hear?' As the sick poet puts it, *talia ... / ... non sunt expedienda tamen* ('Such things ... are not to be tried out/ explained/ released', 439–40).

Mother-lover: the Subject in Jouissance

Can we go there? Do we want to? Should I go back and delete? Throughout the *Remedia,* although critics have tended to overlook (repress?) the agitation, Ovid uses exemplarity to jolt his readers into unexpected subject positions: specifically, he employs the analogy of (male) lover as a mother whose children render her especially vulnerable to loss. Indeed, this is the most overt manifestation of the phenomenon I have been discussing throughout this chapter, beginning with the lover both opposing himself to and then identifying himself/herself with the exemplary other who is not what he seems, the Parthian on horseback (*Rem. am.* 155–7, 224: see p. 94). Here, the ambiguity or inconsistency of the poet's address to male or male/ female readers is not incidental, and amounts to more than another instance of male didactic deceit, after the surprise of *Ars am.* 3. Having directed his *praecepta* towards *decepti iuuenes* in line 41, Ovid adds at lines 49–52 that everything he says to men is suitable advice for *puellae,* too; both sides will be given arms (*arma,* 50), and (gender is not specified, although the implication is that he is still referring to girls), if something (*siquid*) is not appropriate to 'your needs' (*uestros ... usus,* 51), then 'still, by example

---

[57] See also Rimell 2006: 79–80 on *Ars am.* 3.449–50 (*'redde meum' ... 'redde meum'*).

it can teach you much' (*at tamen exemplo multa docere potest*, 52). The double audience is alerted again at 608 ('O lover pained by his mistress, o girl pained by her man') and finally at 814 ('woman and man, healed by my song'). Yet, although many exemplified tragic cases are female, in the body of the poem (rather aptly, under the aegis of the *Remedia*'s supporting deity, *Lethaeus Amor*), the female audience tends to be forgotten, and it is men who are explicitly and implicitly addressed. At the same time, the text is punctuated by lessons which compare the suffering male lover to a mother who misses or mourns her lost or absent son.[58] As Davvison notes, the only critic to my knowledge to explore the uncanniness of this phenomenon at any length, 'maternal love appears surprisingly often in a poem professing to teach the calculated abandonment of love'.[59]

The poem as a whole is framed by tragic mother-daughter pair Pasiphae and Phaedra, at lines 63–4 and 743–5, women who in Ovid's counterfactual myth might (have) put aside their perverse zoophilic and incestuous desires. Thus the poet's attempt to reassure Cupid, who can stick to those 'maternal arts' (*maternas artes*) that were never (!) responsible for depriving a mother of a child (29–30), is tinged with risk from the start.[60] The countryside 'escape' from the elegiac cosmos already reverberates with Pasiphae's urges: the instruction to tame bulls (*tauros*) at line 171 brims with the urgency of Phaedra's inherited lust at *Heroides* 4.165–6 (*flecte ferox animos! potuit corrumpere taurum / mater; eris tauro saeuior ipse truci*? 'Bend your spirit, cruel one! Your mother could pervert the bull; will you yourself be fiercer than the savage bull?', cf. 4.21–3), and the landscape of healing *negotium* is haunted by animal maternal loss (*et queritur uitulum mater abesse suum*, 'and the mother bewails the absence of her calf', 184). In lines 127–8, the male lover, who, contrary to previous advice on never delaying treatment should not receive intervention immediately, is aligned with a mother mourning the death of a son: *quis matrem, nisi mentis inops, in*

---

[58] As if to emphasize the difference between Ovidian *praeceptor* and *Lethaeus Amor*, the latter evokes the male lover not as mother but as father (he is to distract himself by worrying over his daughter's marriage prospects: *te filia nubilis angat*, 571), which needless to say does not suggest itself as an escape from the world of *amor*. Comparing the male lover to a grieving mother has an important precedent in Verg. *Georg*. 4.511–15.

[59] Davvison 1996: 242. Henderson 1979: 108 states only that 'the image of the sorrowing or anxious mother seems to have had a powerful, and not very readily understandable, appeal for Ovid in this poem'.

[60] Pasiphae, Circe's sister, is the link between this maternal line and the other (aunt-niece) pair in the *Remedia*, Circe and Medea. On Circe, a herbalist and magician to rival (or not) this *Praeceptor*, see *Rem. am.* 261–88.

funere nati / flere uetet? ('Who, other than a fool, would forbid a mother to weep at the funeral of her son?'). The analogy reverses the scene in Ovid's proem, so that now instead of son (Cupid) supporting and doing the work of mother (*Venus*), the (male) mother who is being taunted by *uenus* has been abandoned by her own son/love-interest.[61] Then at lines 463–4, the explicitly male addressee, encouraged to take another lover to distract him from the first, is again compared to a grieving mother: *fortius e multis mater desiderat unum / quam quem flens clamat "tu mihi solus eras"*, 'A mother feels the loss of one son out of many more bravely than the woman who wails in tears, "you were my one and only!"'. Here the possible erotic register of *desiderat*, together with *fortius* (more heroically, or more strongly?), which places the emphasis not on the watering down of passion but the opposite, is filtered through Propertius 2.22a.41–2, a poem about why one girl is not enough (a ship is better protected by two cables, just as an anxious mother has less to fear in raising twins).[62] Again at 547–8, the male lover, who must let go of the anxiety that his *puella* will no longer be his, should heed the example of the mother who is more anxious about the son who is away at war (in this couplet, the hexameter echoes 463, with *mater* in the same metrical position, and *two* replacing *one* at the end of the verse). Yet the analogy reframes the initial precept (just stop caring) as ridiculous, and seems to corroborate the lover's anxiety – how can the mother, that *icon of caring*, just stop fearing for the son who is absent in battle? – especially as this advice follows recommendations that the lover over-indulge in his girl's presence. She is not absent at all, and still he 'loves more' (*plus amat*, 547).

Yet the mother herself is split: she is sometimes devoted, sometimes malicious, and her lack of separation from her children (or step-child, in Phaedra's case) can both heal and harm. She appears once more at lines 716–24, again as a model for the male lover, who should not be fearful of burning old love letters from his *puella*. After all, Althaea, mother of Meleager, had the courage to burn the log that represented the fate of her absent son, thus killing him in revenge for the murder of her brother. As Ovid tells the story in *Metamorphoses* 8, this scene is itself a drama of

---

[61] Lingering in the background here and throughout is Venus' other son, Aeneas, who is the implicit model in the *Remedia* for successful healing from passionate love when he leaves Dido (57–8). See also *Rem. am.* 5–6, where the poet announces he is *not* Diomedes, who wounded Venus after she rescued Aeneas from Diomedes' assault (cf. *Iliad* 5.333–80).

[62] *Rem. am.* 447 (*non satis una tenet ceratas ancora puppes*) announces the engagement to come with Prop. 2.22a.41–2; cf. Fedeli 2005: 648–9. *"tu mihi solus eras"* calques Prop. 2.7.19–20 (*tu mihi sola places: placeam tibi, Cynthia, solus: / hic erit et patrio nomine pluris amor*) and 1.11.23 (*tu mihi sola domus, tu, Cynthia, sola parentes*), through *Ars am.* 1.42 (*elige cui dicas "tu mihi sola places"*).

overlapping and conflicting familial roles: before she acts, the two names of 'mother' and 'sister' wrestle within her (8.462). It almost goes without saying that this *exemplum* as it appears in the *Remedia* is less than consoling, giving definition to the lover's treatment of a letter as fetish – a token of her absent-present body (her hand, her tears) that via the analogy of Althaea's log exceeds its status as fetish to become an *actual substitute* – and recalling both Meleager's fate (the cruel death *maternae artes* supposedly avoid) and Althaea's suicide. Althaea kills herself, like Dido, by stabbing her own *uiscera* or womb (*Met.* 8.532), the site of gestation. Just as Medea in *Remedia* 59 takes up arms against her own *uiscera* (innards/offspring), so too when Althaea murders her son, she murders herself, figuratively reversing time to re-perform the abortion by proxy that she un-did when she snatched the log from the fire (8.504–5).[63] The fleshy letter kills, and it feeds desire's flames.

Thus Ovidian *maternae artes*, which frame and punctuate the *Remedia*, are poised to excite, to elicit new joinings. The dislocations embedded in these *exempla* have to do not just with gender (exploiting the almost-buried competition and interaction between male and female addressees in a – now pressured? – heterosexual economy, after the *Ars*) but with time. The male lover, always a *iuuenis* in Ovid (although that youthfulness is perhaps stretched in the fiction of this 'late' work and cure: cf. *Rem. am.* 91, 109–10) becomes in flashes an older mother, missing not a daughter but a son, while female addressees striving to find something useful that applies to them discover in these comparisons and their revealing internal substitutions not so much a tradition of consolation that will culminate in Latin in Seneca's *Ad Helviam*, but the contagion of Phaedra's maternal line, the poison hidden in *remedia* all along (63–4).

The jolting analogy between erotic and maternal love suggests not just that escape from the former is not easy ('and perhaps not *honestum*', as Davvison censures),[64] but that in the re-volution or *lasciuia libera* of jouissance, which moves lovers out of separation and into the vitality of unfolding inter-connection, the one can contaminate the other. It is that latent threat of contamination, almost suppressed by the difference opened up in analogy, which lures us towards the tragic as that Oedipal zone in which connection and oscillating play becomes the horrifying collapse of kinship ties, and the joining of human and animal: as Myrrha, crazy with

---

[63] Cf. McAuley 2016: 139: 'the gesture repeats and reverses the double birth Meleager has already experienced'.
[64] Davvison 1996: 255.

longing, asks herself, *et quot confundas et iura et nomina, sentis?* ('Do you realize how many ties and names you are confusing?', *Met.* 10.346, after Sophocles *OT* 1403–8). Yet at the same time maternity, as it calls into question the border between subject and other, also exemplifies the overflowing of self that will rejuvenate Ovid's elegiac project in the same groove. That the maternal body 'encloses an other'[65] is the revelation that both propels elegiac duality and threatens to rupture its mechanisms. *Mater* is (almost) concealed in the *puella* as *materia* from the start (look at *Amores* 2.13–14). She is the fertility elegy must appropriate and erase, or in *Remedia* 437, 'give back' behind closed doors. That she cannot be absented from the project of *Remedia* comes to stand for the intensity and flow of Ovidian desire, as it continually shifts shape, making meaning on the page. There is nothing left but to stay with the groove.

Not the End: Desire and the Didactic Imperative

> ad mea, decepti iuuenes, praecepta uenite
> Ovid, *Rem. am.* 41

Come, tricked youths, to my instructions

> hic stupet, utque aciem partes dimittit in omnis,
> uoce "ueni!" magna clamat: uocat illa uocantem.
> Ovid, *Met.* 3.381–2

Amazed, he looks around in all directions, and in a loud voice yells "Come!"; and "Come!" she calls him calling.

Pleasure escapes, but it is in this escaping that there is pleasure. And that is where we find the other: escaping outside of oneself sends us to the other, the one to whom I say "Come!" and who answers me.
Jean-Luc Nancy with Adèle Van Reeth 2017: 20

---

[65] Oliver 1993: 100, on the trope of maternity in Kristeva's work.

CHAPTER 6

The Gaze on the Void
Hermeneutic Responses to Dido's First Appearance

Viola Starnone

In a text such as Virgil's *Aeneid*, equipped with such a long and rich hermeneutic tradition, every time that something is absent, and its absence is relevant, we are able to track down, through the centuries, a constant attempt to fill the void.[1]

In *Aeneid* 1, when Dido makes her first appearance in the poem, she is defined as most beautiful (*forma pulcherrima*, 496), she is escorted by a large company of youths (*magna iuuenum stipante caterua*, 497) and she is compared to Diana standing out from her nymphs (*deas supereminet omnis*, 501).[2] It is generally agreed that this is the moment when Aeneas sees her for the first time. But if we carefully follow what Virgil decides to narrate, when Dido comes on stage, making her way to the temple, we may have the impression that Aeneas is still involved in the contemplation of the frieze (*haec dum Dardanio Aeneae miranda uidentur, / dum stupet obtutuque haeret defixus in uno / regina ad templum … / incessit*, 'While Trojan Aeneas stood gazing, rooted to the spot and lost in amazement at what he saw, queen Dido … arrived at the temple', 494–7).[3] No passage in the narrative informs the reader that the hero has turned his gaze from the *pictura* to the *regina*. Actually, it is only the arrival of his companions, thought to be lost, that explicitly draws his attention (509–16). Thus we could say that the first look and impressions of the hero towards the heroine are absent from the text.[4]

---

[1] This chapter is partly based on a section of Starnone 2020.
[2] Virgil's text is from R. A. B. Mynors 1969 *OCT* edition.
[3] Translations from the *Aeneid* are by D. A. West with minor changes, unless otherwise specified.
[4] Few scholars seem to acknowledge this absence. See Farron 1980: 34–5: 'When Dido enters, Vergil describes her as extremely beautiful … and then compares her in a simile to Diana and portrays her as a great queen ruling her people …. But Aeneas' emotions are only for his newly found comrades'; Mackie 1988: 38: 'We could reasonably have expected a clear response from Aeneas to … the sight of Dido but this reaction is in fact more difficult to discern'; Fernandelli 1998: 170: 'non una parola descrive esplicitamente la reazione psicologica dell'eroe all'apparire della regina', 'Not a single word explicitly describes the hero's psychological reaction at the queen's appearance.'

Let us now temporarily put aside the reasons that may have led Virgil to leave this narrative void, in order to focus on the ways in which readers of all times have dealt with it. Right away, in fact, this absence ends up clashing with the expectations of the readers, both poets and commentators, who will often consider Aeneas' behaviour as inadequate.[5]

The readers' dissatisfaction may depend on different factors. Aeneas' condition of invisibility, due to the maternal cloud that makes him able to see without being seen, leads to a narrative focus on the character's point of view and subjectivity. This focus, while fully operating for the city under construction, for the contemplation of the *pictura*, and subsequently for the companions, seems to disappear when Dido makes her entrance. We have also learned that Venus (*Aen.* 1.314–417) has prepared Aeneas for this encounter, shaping in his mind the image of a woman of kindred spirit and similar destiny. Furthermore, Virgil tells us that Aeneas, once at the temple, is waiting for the queen, *reginam opperiens* (1.454). Last but not least, the poet emphasizes Dido's first reaction to the sight of Aeneas (613–4).[6] All these elements make the absence of any reactions to Dido all the more evident, when she finally appears in the flesh.

In addition, the readers may feel the necessity of Aeneas' gaze because the narrative situation recalls the moment when, in the ancient novel, the hero falls in love with the heroine at first sight.[7] After all, it was Virgil himself who had coined, on the basis of Theocritus, the famous *ut uidi, ut perii* (*Ecl.* 8.41), contributing to shape, in the Latin imagination, the idea of the man subject to a sudden erotic passion.[8] But while such behaviour on behalf of the gazing man is normally expected in comedy, pastoral poetry and elegy,[9] Virgil's solution is not uncommon in the epic genre, where the first appearance of the heroine does not provoke violent reactions in the hero, who usually does not fall in love at first sight. In the *Odyssey*, for example, when Nausicaa is compared to Artemis (6.102–9), Odysseus is still asleep; only when Athena wakes him up in order to let him *see* the girl (113) does he flatter the princess with 'words of honey' (146), in order to gain her help. Although impressed by Nausicaa's beauty, Odysseus obviously does not fall in love at first sight.

---

[5] The readers' dissatisfaction is not confined to this scene, but it is part of a bigger problem regarding the feelings of Aeneas in Book 4. See e.g. De Witt 1907: 27–37; Heinze 1908²: 122–3, n. 1.
[6] It is interesting that when Aeneas suddenly becomes visible Virgil defines him as *improuisus* (*Aen.* 1.595). On vision in the *Aeneid*, see Smith 2005 and Mac Gøráin 2018.
[7] See Hardie 1998: 78–9.
[8] See Heinze 1908²: 121 and n. 2. On the Virgilian expression and its literary models, see Timpanaro 1978: 219–87. On love at first sight in Greek and Latin literature, see e.g. Bellandi 2011.
[9] See De Witt 1907: 27 and Heinze 1908²: 123, n. 1.

Damien Nelis has convincingly argued that Virgil, for the first encounter between Dido and Aeneas, has mainly drawn inspiration from the third book of Apollonius' *Argonautica*, where Jason and Medea cross each other for the first time at Aeetes' palace.[10] I would add that the connection to Apollonius' passage is interesting in that, right where we would expect a verb describing Jason's first glance at the princess, there is presumably a textual lacuna preventing us from reading about that glance: 3.248–9 τῇ μὲν ἄρ' οἵ γε / < ... > / ἐκ θαλάμου θαλαμόνδε κασιγνήτην μετιοῦσαν ('Medea then they < ... > while she was going from chamber to chamber in search of her sister', trans. Seaton).[11]

Therefore, it is Virgil's quite traditional adaptation of the epic models[12] that tends to disappoint the readers. Why does the hero devote himself much more to a work of art (or to the city under construction or, later, to his companions) than to the woman he is about to love? Many readers have tried, more or less consciously, to fill up what they perceived as an unbearable void, looking for a trace of the missing gaze and emotions, just as though, concealed in the Virgilian text, there were another text, a sort of phantasmic *Aeneid*, containing Aeneas' absent reactions. As I will show in the next pages, this work of correction and integration is mainly conducted on what immediately precedes the arrival of the queen (i.e. the ekphrasis of the *pictura*: *Aen.* 1.453–95) and on the Diana simile following Dido's appearance (*Aen.* 1.498–504).

The Gaze and the Simile

The criticism that Marcus Valerius Probus directs at the Dido-Diana simile (Gell. 9.9.12–7) is well known.[13] In short, for the grammarian, the Virgilian parallel is less effective than its Homeric model, because, unlike Nausicaa and Artemis in *Odyssey* 6.102–9, Dido and Diana have almost nothing in common, and Virgil's simile cannot work properly. My

---

[10] Nelis 2001: 81.
[11] The ancient scholia, by noting that μετιοῦσαν is a predicative participle lacking a verb of sight (<μετιοῦσαν: λείπει> εἶδον, ed. Wender), seem to acknowledge the problem. The first among the moderns to postulate the existence of a textual lacuna is Madvig 1871: 287, n. 1. Fraenkel 1950: 126 suggests by way of example the following integration: Τῇ μὲν ἄρ' οἵγε <Μηδείῃ ξύμβληντο, τάφον δέ μιν εἰσορόωντες> ἐκ θαλάμου κτλ. 'Then they stumbled onto Medea, and they were looking at her in awe as she was going from chamber to chamber...' (cf. also Vian 1961 ad loc.: 'la rencontrèrent; ... ils la virent'); Hunter 1989 ad loc. proposes a more generic 'met'.
[12] Cf. also e.g. Cat. 64.86–93, where Ariadne's love at first sight does not correspond to any reactions on Theseus' part.
[13] See e.g. Austin 1971 *ad Aen.* 1.498.

suggestion, however, is that Probus' objections are only superficially concerned with the simile's functioning, and that they may depend instead on the absence of Aeneas' gaze. For Probus, the main flaw of the simile was that Virgil had neglected the Homeric *tertium comparationis*, that is, the prominence and visibility of the most beautiful woman over her female retinue.[14] But since Diana's visibility in the simile should correspond to Dido's visibility in the narrative, Probus here ends up suggesting that Dido too is scarcely visible. Therefore, the insistence of the grammarian on prominence may also conceal his disappointment, as a reader, over the absence of any clear signals of the queen's visibility.

It may be no coincidence that the Virgilian passage about Diana's prominence (*deas supereminet omnis, Aen.* 1.501 'she is the tallest of all the goddesses') is echoed by Ovid, in the episode of Diana and Actaeon narrated in the *Metamorphoses*.[15] In addition to being fully focused on the goddess' visibility, this Ovidian version of the myth is, in fact, based on an involuntary gaze. When the nymphs become aware of the intruder, they try to shield their mistress' nudity with their bodies. But Diana, famous for her height, remains visible (*supereminet omnis, Met.* 3.182). I believe that this passage may be a first critical response to the Virgilian scene.[16] Ovid seems to get to the heart of Probus' criticism: he makes explicit what Virgil has omitted, that is, the inescapable visibility of Diana, which Ovid describes by a deliberate allusion to the *Aeneid* – a visibility that is fundamental in order to render Actaeon's look unintentional as much as unavoidable. If, on the one hand, Ovid makes this correction to the *Aeneid*, on the other hand, he avoids mentioning explicitly Actaeon's profane gaze at the goddess, and he prefers to use a series of circumlocutions: he describes Diana's blush 'at *having been seen* without her robes' (*uisae sine ueste Dianae, Met.* 3.185), and the goddess sarcastically challenges Actaeon to tell the people, literally, 'of me *seen by you* without clothing' (*tibi me posito uisam uelamine, Met.* 3.192). Actaeon returns actively to use the sight only when he sees his brand-new beastly

---

[14] Gell. 9.9.17 *praeter ista omnia florem ipsius totius loci Vergilium uideri omisisse, quod hunc Homeri uersum exigue secutus sit:* ῥεῖά τ' ἀριγνώτη πέλεται, καλαὶ δέ τε πᾶσαι, *quando nulla maior cumulatiorque pulcritudinis laus dici potuerit, quam quod una inter omnis pulcras excelleret, una facile ex omnibus nosceretur.* ('Besides all this, Virgil seemed to have left out the flower of the whole passage, by giving only a faint shadow of this verse of Homer's: *And shone transcendent o'er the beauteous train*, for no greater or more complete praise of beauty can be expressed than that she alone excelled where all were beautiful, that she alone was easily distinguished from all the rest.' Trans. Rolfe).
[15] See e.g. Barchiesi and Rosati 2007 ad Ov. Met. 3, 182.
[16] On Ovid's criticism of the Dido-Diana simile, see Hardie 2004b: 7.

shape reflected in the water (*Met.* 3.200).¹⁷ We could say therefore that Ovid never mentions the direct gaze of Actaeon on the goddess, even though he is constructing a scene in which it is impossible for him not to see. This narrative choice is certainly dictated by the version of the myth that Ovid has selected, where Actaeon is simply an unlucky man, in the wrong place at the wrong time.¹⁸ But this solution seems also to be coherent with the lack of Aeneas' gaze, evoked by the allusion *supereminet omnis*. It is as if Ovid were saying that a gaze may be present even if not mentioned; and that indeed *that* gaze cannot be absent. He is the first to state that the absence in Virgil's passage is actually a stylistic void that can't be left empty, because, even when the hero is not intentionally seeing, he *is* seeing all the same, albeit involuntarily.¹⁹

Similarly to Ovid, Statius, in the *Achilleid*, offers to us his version of the scene, attributing to the Diana simile a narrative purpose that is explicitly erotic (*Achil.* 1.293–303). Statius' parallel is entirely focused on visibility: by comparing Deidamia to Venus, Diana, and Pallas, it praises the seducing sight of the princess leading the dances during Pallas' festival and standing out from her sisters, even though they are all beautiful and dressed the same. The comparison insists on the opposition of brightness and shadowing, as if the princess was the brightest star (*effulget*, 295; *flammatur*, 297; *lux*, 298), capable of outshining all the others (*obruit*, 294; *obstat*, 296).²⁰ Deidamia is so beautiful that Achilles, though observing the scene from afar, immediately casts his eyes on her and falls in love at first sight (*hanc ubi ducentem longe socia agmina uidit, / ... / deriguit totisque nouum bibit ossibus ignem*: 'When [he] ... saw her leading her attendant column from far ahead, he stiffened and drank novel flame in all his bones', 301–3, trans. Shackleton Bailey). Here the gaze that Virgil has omitted becomes a gaze that is explicitly narrated and erotically charged.²¹

---

¹⁷ On the contrary, in the exile poetry, where Actaeon's guilt becomes a paradigm for the poet's *error*, the gaze is described at length, but without the allusion to Virgil's passage. Cf. e.g. Ov. *Tr.* 2.103–5.

¹⁸ In any case, we should bear in mind that *Metamorphoses* 3 is focused on sight and blindness, and that Actaeon here is also superimposed on Callimachus' Tiresias. See e.g. Barchiesi and Rosati 2007 *ad Met.* 3.138–52.

¹⁹ That Ovid is aware of the absence of gaze in *Aeneid* 1 can be inferred from at least another episode of the *Metamorphoses*. When in Book 6 Philomela appears for the first time in front of Tereus (451–4), the poet attributes to the tyrant a sort of 'lust at first sight' (Hardie 2002: 260), filling up the Virgilian void with an overtly erotic gaze (Hardie 2014: 70).

²⁰ See Uccellini 2012 ad loc.

²¹ On this simile and its connections to Virgil's model, see e.g. Heslin 2005: 97–9.

These poets therefore, when leaving a trace of the scene in their texts, either seem to emphasize the visibility of the heroine, implying that the hero cannot but see her (Ovid), or they end up correcting Virgil, attributing to their character an erotic gaze (Statius). The absence of any reactions towards the woman seems intolerable to them.

The Gaze and the *Pictura*

But there is one, Valerius Flaccus, who pushes himself further in the investigation of the Virgilian absence. His Jason, just like Statius' Achilles, catches sight of Medea, perceives her prominence over the handmaids, and feels that she is their *dux* and *domina* (Val. Flacc. *Arg.* 5.377). But Valerius does not confine himself to attributing a look of love to his hero. When reusing the scene, he seems to single out the moment when – in his opinion – Aeneas must have necessarily turned to see the queen. The Virgilian expression *obtutuque haeret defixus in uno* (*Aen.* 1.495), describing Aeneas contemplating the *pictura*, is modified by Valerius into *haeret defixus in una* (*Arg.* 5.376–7),[22] describing Jason falling in love with Medea. In other words, Valerius feels the need to transform the Virgilian expression about the enjoyment of a work of art into a formula recounting the love at first sight of an epic hero. While Aeneas is formally left by Virgil as clinging to the *pictura*, his gaze absorbed by the artistic representation, Jason is fixated on the woman standing out alone from the women around her. The Flavian poet, therefore, as far as I am aware,[23] is the first to show that, when Dido appears, the fact that Aeneas is concentrated on the frieze complicates the scene, interfering also with the effectiveness of the Dido–Diana simile, which may seem purposeless. For this reason, Valerius, in his version of the episode, extracts from Virgil's text the words about the contemplation of the *pictura* and inserts them in a new context, one which is explicitly erotic. In doing so, Valerius seems to be aware that those words, especially the verbs *figo* and *haereo*, are often employed (even by Virgil himself) for the wound and arrow of love.[24] The problem is that, while it is certain that Aeneas is looking at the frieze, regardless of whether

---

[22] The allusion to Virgil is acknowledged by Wijsman 1996 ad loc.; see also Stover 2003: 126 and n. 12.
[23] But see also Ovid's Perseus, who reacts to the sight of Andromeda with a *stupor* (*Met.* 4.676) that has been connected to Aeneas' *stupor* for the *pictura* (Hardie 2002: 185). Furthermore, also the verb *deriguit* that Statius attributes to Achilles before Deidamia (*Achil.* 1.303) could derive from the description of Aeneas *defixus* in front of the *pictura*.
[24] Cf. e.g. Verg. *Aen.* 4.4; 68–73.

Dido is visible or not, nothing in the text states clearly that Aeneas is actually looking at her.

On the poetic level, Valerius works directly on Virgil's text, tracking down the eroticism, which is seemingly absent from the scene, into the gaze addressed by Aeneas to the *pictura,* and thus channelling into a woman the feelings originally addressed to a work of art.[25] The same tendency resurfaces in the late-antique commentary by Tiberius Claudius Donatus, although from a different point of view. As usual, Donatus is at pains to defend Aeneas' behaviour. At least for some readers, the hero, by being nurtured by the *pictura,* which is defined by Virgil as *inanis* (*Aen.* 1.464), could take the risk of becoming *inanis* himself, as if the adjective could taint his moral stature.[26] Aeneas could seem, in Donatus' words, *inanibus captus,*[27] fascinated by inane things, and not worried enough about the fate of his people: both the contemplation of the city and the immersion into the work of art may be considered as a waste of time, as occupations that are unworthy of a man of rank. But the truth, according to Donatus, is that Aeneas is performing his political duties: Virgil, in fact, says that he is there because he is waiting for the queen. Furthermore, his interest in the city and in the artistic representation is not frivolous at all, but has a practical purpose: by finding himself in front of these works in progress, Aeneas is learning how much *labor* is necessary in order to build a new *urbs.*[28] This assumption allows Donatus to focus on Dido's arrival, without resorting to the *ut uidi, ut perii* motif – which would be inconsistent with his moralistic interpretation. The commentator attributes to Virgil a narrative strategy based on what, in a subsequent note, he calls *repentinus euentus rerum*: the occurrence of a sudden event interrupts the main action, catching the attention.[29] For Donatus, Aeneas' *intentio,* while concentrated on the *pictura,* is interrupted by Dido: her entrance 'switches' (the Latin verbs are *commutare* and *conuertere*) Aeneas' *animus et studium* from the frieze to the queen.[30] Donatus, in other words, seems to imply the automatic transference to Dido of all the feelings previously felt for the *pictura*. For him, ultimately, the gaze on Dido ends up almost corresponding to the passionately political gaze with which Aeneas has been looking at the city and at the artistic representation. Donatus' comment upon this passage anticipates many modern and contemporary interpretations. It

---

[25] On the elegiac equivalence between the *puella* and a work of art, see Sharrock 1991.
[26] Cf. Serv. and *Serv. Dan. ad Aen.* 1.454.
[27] While Virgil attributes *inanis* to the *pictura,* Donatus seems to use it for all the things on which Aeneas is focused.
[28] Tib. Don. *ad Aen.* 1.453–6. [29] Ibid. 1.505–8. [30] Ibid. 1.494–7.

underlies in particular, the widespread assumption that Virgil narrates implicitly the transference to Dido of Aeneas' gaze, previously concentrated on the *pictura*.[31]

The seventeenth-century Jesuit La Cerda, while inheriting the interpretative work of the earlier centuries, reveals an extraordinary sensitivity for matters of sight. When commenting on the Aeneas–Apollo simile in Book 4 (141–50), he lists similarities and differences from the specular Dido–Diana simile, noticing the change of point of view on the two heroes. The comment is triggered by a Servian note about the anomalous definition of Aeneas as *pulcherrimus* right before the Apollo simile (4.141). Servius had made the suggestion that here the adjective may conceal the point of view of Dido: it is to her that Aeneas looks most handsome.[32] La Cerda associates this interpretation of *pulcherrimus* with the definition of Dido as *pulcherrima* in Book 1, right before the Diana simile, applying to the feminine superlative what Servius had conceived for the male one. In this way, for La Cerda, Dido seems *pulcherrima* to Aeneas, who is defined by the commentator as *spectator reginae*, thus becoming the internal focalizer of the scene.

La Cerda's note is also indebted to the complex hermeneutic tradition of *Aen.* 1.502, *Latonae tacitum pertemptant gaudia pectus* ('joy thrills Latona's silent breast'), the last line of the Diana simile. Through the centuries, this line, although being part of the simile and not of the narrative, will seem to encompass a secret point of view on the whole passage. This line too had been sharply criticized by Probus: for him the verb *pertemptant*, recounting Latona's maternal *gaudia* for Diana, was too mild to convey such a deep

---

[31] Some scholars theorize the equivalence between ekphrasis and simile, namely between Penthesilea (the last figure depicted on the murals before the arrival of the queen) and Dido as Diana: see e.g. Pöschl 1950: 104, n. 2, and 242, the first to see the Amazon queen as a sort of symbolic anticipation of Dido (see also Conte 1984: 107; Hardie 1998: 78–9; Putnam 1998: 34–6). Other interpreters connect the scene to other Virgilian *repentini euentus rerum*, e.g. the arrival of the Sibyl at the beginning of Book 6, interrupting the ekphrasis of the Cumaean frieze (Norden 1903 *ad Aen.* 6.34; Heinze 1908[2]: 317) or Aeneas catching sight of the *pictura* earlier in Book 1 (Pöschl 1950: 107–8, n. 1). But not everything feels right. There are huge differences between the two ekphraseis: in Book 1 Virgil describes at length Aeneas' gaze and emotions towards the *pictura*, while in Book 6 his point of view on the frieze is implied but almost left unspoken. Furthermore, while in Carthage, Aeneas' distraction from the *pictura* is never mentioned, whereas in Cumae the interruption is not only narrated, but also emphasized by the Sibyl's famous reproach to the hero (*Aen.* 6.37). Similarly, Aeneas' discovery of the *pictura* in Book 1 is marked by *uidet* (*Aen.* 1.456). On the contrary, as we have said, there is no hint at all of the fact that Dido has entered Aeneas' visual field. Even assuming that the shift of gaze occurs when the hero is looking at Penthesilea, one must consider that his emotive reaction to Dido is difficult to discern, while his reaction towards the companions is immediate and passionate.

[32] *Serv. Dan.* ad loc.

feeling (Gell. 9.9.15). But Servius felt differently: he opposed (and thus associated) the strength of *pertemptant gaudia*, concerning Latona at *Aen.* 1.502, to *gaudia pertemptant*, concerning Aeneas at *Aen.* 5.828, an almost identical expression that Servius however regarded as milder. It is precisely the 2,000-year discussion on the effectiveness of Latona's *pertemptant* (combined with both the Servian juxtaposition between Latona and Aeneas and with the humanists' notion that Latona's feelings towards Diana in the simile do not find any correspondences in the narrative) that – also through a long series of alterations, substitutions, misquotations – will end up producing a progressive 'eroticisation' of *Aen.* 1.502.[33] At the end of this tradition, Pöschl will state that *Aen.* 1.502 contains the effect that Dido has on the hero.[34] Virgil, in other words, would channel Aeneas' unexpressed reaction to the queen into Latona's silent reaction to her daughter. Latona's pleasure would symbolically represent Aeneas' excitement, his first erotic frisson for the heroine. Surprisingly, the reaction of a prospective lover ends up corresponding to the reaction of a mother.[35]

Conclusion – the Gaze and the Shade

I wish to suggest in conclusion that Virgil may have left the void in Book 1 on purpose, in order to fill it himself in the last encounter between Aeneas and Dido (*Aen.* 6.450–76).[36]

At least since the humanists, the Underworld scene has been studied mainly in connection to the dynamics of *Aeneid* 4: whereas, in Carthage, Dido had implored Aeneas, but he had remained impassive, in the *lugentes campi* it is Aeneas who asks for Dido's attention, while she completely ignores him.[37] As far as I am aware, only few scholars have associated the encounter in Book 6 with the encounter in Book 1: Michael von Albrecht has shown that while in Carthage Aeneas, who until then had been 'obscured' by Venus' cloud, finally appears to Dido *in clara luce*, while in the Underworld Dido, who is compared to a clouded moon, is seen by Aeneas as *obscura* (*Aen.* 6.450–5).[38] In the wake of von Albrecht, Antonio

---

[33] In Starnone 2020: 185–204 I explore in detail the genesis of this interpretation.
[34] Pöschl 1950: 111.
[35] This interpretation is adopted by many contemporary scholars: see e.g. Williams 1983: 61–2; Paschalis 1997: 48; Hardie 2006a: 26.
[36] In this sense, it appears that the author himself is the first reader, and rewriter, of his own work, setting the stage for further readers/rewriters to come.
[37] See e.g. Scaliger, *PLS* 3.XXV.114b; La Cerda *ad Aen.* 6.450–66 (*Explicatio*); Norden 1903 *ad Aen.* 6.456; von Albrecht 1999: 1–6.
[38] Von Albrecht 1999: 3.

Mauriz Martínez has argued that the description of Dido's ghost is meant to recall by contrast the queen's lively appearance at Juno's temple.[39] What seems to be missing here, and thus requiring investigation, is precisely the specularity existing between the absence of Aeneas' gaze and emotions towards Dido in Book 1 and the strong presence of his gaze and feelings for her in Book 6.

In the Underworld Aeneas is described, for the first time explicitly, as being entirely absorbed in the image of the queen.[40] Let us first concentrate on how Virgil has structured the scene (*Aen.* 6. 450–5):

> inter quas Phoenissa recens a uulnere Dido
> errabat silua in magna; quam Troius heros
> ut primum iuxta stetit agnouitque per umbras
> obscuram, qualem primo qui surgere mense
> aut uidet aut uidisse putat per nubila lunam,
> demisit lacrimas dulcique adfatus amore est.

Wandering among them in that great wood was Phoenician Dido with her wound still fresh. When the Trojan hero stopped beside her, recognizing her dim form in the darkness, like a man who sees or thinks he has seen the new moon rising through the clouds at the beginning of the month, in that instant he wept and spoke sweet words of love to her.

Dido's shadow is located in the midst of other heroines who have died for love (*inter quas*). This group of women may recall the throng of youths among which Dido had made her first appearance.[41] But usually the group is employed to introduce figures of rank,[42] a variation on this theme being the topos of the beautiful princess surrounded by her

---

[39] Martínez 2003: 283–91, focused on the ineffectiveness of language in the Underworld, on the impossibility of communication between the living hero and the dead queen.

[40] In *Aeneid* 4 Dido laments that Aeneas' gaze is not moved by her pleas (369): his eyes are concentrated on Jupiter's admonitions (331–2). However, we may infer that, at Carthage, Aeneas' gaze has actually been distracted by Dido: when Jupiter claims that the hero, rather than *inuidere* (i.e. literally 'looking at askance') Ascanius and the Roman citadel (234), rather than *exspectare* (225, literally 'looking at' Carthage), must 'look back' (225; *respicit* 235) on his promised land, he seems to imply that, while in Libya, Aeneas has been looking at something else (on this vocabulary, see Smith 2005: 40). It is interesting also that Dido's last words (*hauriat hunc oculis ignem crudelis ab alto / Dardanus*, 'may the cruel Trojan drink this fire with his eyes from the open sea', 4.661–2, my trans.) have to do with Aeneas' gaze on her. When she condemns him to 'drink with the eyes' the image of herself burning, it is as though she were condemning Aeneas to drink a sort of magic potion, whose effects he would display in the Underworld. Aeneas' visual return to Dido is already marked by the participle *respiciens*, 'looking back', at *Aen.* 5.3. This backward glance on Dido seems to anticipate his almost spellbound gaze on her ghost in the Underworld.

[41] Hornsby 1970: 98.

[42] Cf. e.g. Laocoon (*Aen.* 2.40); Dido herself (*Aen.* 4.136); Musaeus (*Aen.* 6.667–8); Amata (*Aen.* 11.478).

handmaids.⁴³ Virgil instead resorts to it in order to describe Dido as a shade among other shades, as *obscura*, scarcely visible, not immediately recognizable. Furthermore, members of the group escorting the leading figure are normally left anonymous, and the poet does not pay great attention to them; but Dido's companions in the Underworld are neither pale handmaids nor simple attendants. They have the power of outshining Dido, in that they are some of the most famous female figures of ancient mythology.

Virgil's untraditional use of the moon imagery is also relevant. As Norden has noticed, the moon is usually employed to highlight female beauty.⁴⁴ Furthermore, in comparison to other heavenly bodies, it may indicate extreme visibility.⁴⁵ In other words, the moon, just like the image of the group, is often used to underscore the prominence of one given character. But Virgil chooses another solution: in Book 1 Dido, at her first appearance in the poem, had been compared to Diana standing out from her nymphs; in the Underworld the queen, at her last appearance in the *Aeneid*, is compared to the moon – Diana's astronomic equivalent⁴⁶ – but as it appears when the clouds reduce her brightness. The inversion is all the more evident if we consider another glaring reversal. As I have tried to show, in Book 1 the prominence of Diana was often judged as purposeless, since Aeneas' point of view and erotic reactions towards Dido were absent from the narrative; in Book 6, although Dido is described as an overshadowed moon, Aeneas' point of view is strongly highlighted.

Virgil derives this focus on sight in a condition of low visibility from an Apollonian simile (4.1477–80). Heracles is lost; only Lynceus is able to spot him, far across the boundless earth, concluding that he is gone forever. The Apollonian passage is on the one hand totally focused on the miraculous eyesight of Lynceus; on the other hand the moon simile seems to undermine the power of his talent: Lynceus catching sight of Heracles is compared to someone who sees the moon at the beginning of the month, when it is small, almost indistinguishable, and, in addition, so overshadowed that it is difficult to say whether one is actually seeing it or is just *getting the impression* of seeing it.⁴⁷

Virgil, adapting the Apollonian simile, enhances the difficulty of sight. The participle ἐπαχλύουσαν, 'obscured' (4.1480), referring to the moon, and in ideal correspondence to the distance and boundlessness of the

---

⁴³ Cf. e.g. Nausicaa in *Odyssey* 6.102–9 or Sapph. fr. 16 L.–P. (on Helen).
⁴⁴ Norden 1903 *ad Aen.* 6.453 refers to *Hymn. Ven.* 89.
⁴⁵ Cf. e.g. Hor. *Carm.* 1.12.46–8 (for further examples, see Nisbet and Hubbard 1970 ad loc.).
⁴⁶ See e.g. Pöschl 1950: 249. See also Duclos 1969; Lee 1988; De Grummond 1997.
⁴⁷ On the unreliability of Lynceus, see Hunter 1989 ad loc. and Feldherr 1999: 102.

Libyan desert above which Lynceus' visual inquiry is conducted, is expanded: both the adjective *obscura* (6.453), assigned to Dido in the narrative, and the expression *per nubila* (6.454), 'among the clouds', associated with the moon in the simile, derive from it. While Lynceus' sighting is conducted from afar (4.1478 τηλοῦ), Aeneas must get close to Dido in order to identify her (*iuxta*, 6.452).[48] The latter's vision must face a wider range of obstacles: while Apollonius' scene is located in the desert, the Virgilian scene is set in a place where light does not exist, the Underworld; as we have seen, the other shadows (*per umbras*) outshine Dido, just as the moon is obscured by clouds (*inter nubila*); finally, Dido is herself a shadow, so she is inherently *obscura* (perfectly corresponding to the moon of the simile, in the first stages of its circle, and thus scarcely visible in itself). Precisely this emphasis on obscurity and on the impediments to vision makes it all the more evident that Aeneas is willing to see and recognize Dido. While Lynceus gives up his undertaking and goes back to the Argonauts (4.1481–2), Aeneas, after having seen or thought he had seen Dido, starts talking to her.

The epic successors of Virgil made up scenes where women were so beautiful that they were visible despite all sort of obstacles: Ovid's Diana was seen by Actaeon despite the efforts made by the nymphs to cover her; Statius' Achilles caught sight of Deidamia, although from afar and although she was amidst other similar girls; Valerius' Jason saw only Medea, although she stood among girls of the same age. Virgil's focus in *Aeneid* 6 is not on Dido's visibility, but on the efforts that Aeneas has to make in order to spot and recognize her now that she is just a mere shadow of herself. In short, when she was visible, he did not look at her; now that she is no longer visible, he desperately strives to see her. Surprisingly enough, Aeneas, as if epic were suddenly blurring into elegy, starts crying (*demisit lacrimas*, 455),[49] and Virgil, for the first time in the poem,[50] explicitly attributes to him *dulcis amor* towards the queen.[51] It is as though love at first sight on Aeneas' part were expressible only at the end of the story, only in the house of the dead, where, in order to see, one's eyesight must be more powerful than Lynceus': love at first sight becomes 'love at last sight'. In other words, we may retrospectively consider the absence of

---

[48] Feldherr 1999: 102. [49] On these tears, see e.g. Ricottilli 2000: 111–2.
[50] For another, more debated, example, see *Aen.* 4.395 *magnoque animum labefactus amore* ('with the heart shaken by great love'), where Servius makes the hypothesis that *amor*, rather than expressing the feelings of Aeneas, is to be referred to Dido.
[51] For the use of *amor* here, see e.g. Mackie 1988: 130. On the intimate tone of *adfari*, see Ricottilli 2000: 112.

gaze in Book 1 as a sort of missed elegiac strand,[52] which finds expression in Book 6, when we would least expect it.[53]

The emphasis on viewing here is even more evident if we consider that, in the Homeric encounter between Ajax and Odysseus (*Od.* 11.543–64), which is the main model for the Virgilian scene, the gaze of Odysseus on the dead hero is never explicitly registered. On the contrary, Virgil refers more than once to Aeneas' urge to look at Dido. Actually, the hero feels such a strong need not to lose sight of her, that his eyes follow the queen even when she refuses any contact with him (*teque aspectu ne subtrahe nostro*, 'do not leave my sight', *Aen.* 6.465),[54] even when she flees from him and joins Sychaeus (*prosequitur lacrimis longe*, 'long did he gaze after her with tears', 476). The insistence on Aeneas' gaze here may recall another Virgilian hero, Orpheus.[55] Aeneas' elegiac desire to look at Dido is in a way reminiscent of Orpheus' backward glance to Eurydice.[56] This proximity, acknowledged by Servius,[57] probably induced Ovid to draw upon this scene when writing his version of Orpheus' katabasis.[58]

Things in Book 1 were different. While Dido switched from *uultum demissa* (1.561, 'looking down') – the visual attitude with which she answered to the Trojans[59] – to *obstipuit primo aspectu* ('first [she] was amazed at the sight of him', 613) – her first reaction to the sight of Aeneas – Virgil decided not to attribute to Aeneas a similarly stupefied gaze on her. Now, at their last encounter, in a way that is significantly, and perhaps deliberately, antithetic, the poet opposes to the explicit presence of

---

[52] We could say that the absence in Book 1 has something 'aposiopesic', in the sense explored by Stefano Briguglio in this volume.

[53] On the elegiac undertones of the scene, see e.g. La Cerda, who associates Aeneas' words at 6.461 with the unreliability of lovers, quoting, among other things. Tibullus, 1.4.21–4 and Lygd. 3.7.47–50; Norden 1903 *ad Aen.* 6.430–40; Feldherr 1999: 112–5; Graverini 2016: 347. We should also bear in mind that the famous Catullan reference at *Aen.* 6.460 may contribute to cast a 'non-epic' tone on the scene. On the principle of something being repressed somewhere returning in another form later on, see Fitzgerald in this volume.

[54] It is noteworthy that at *Aen.* 6.698 Virgil assigns to Aeneas an almost identical exclamation, this time addressed to Anchises, but with *amplexu* instead of *aspectu*, which demonstrates once more the importance of gaze in the last encounter with Dido.

[55] We may also be reminded of Achilles, who fell in love with Penthesilea when she had just died (cf. e.g. Prop. 3.11.13–6).

[56] For Bernardus Silvestris the episode as a whole is a sort of symbolic backward glance on Aeneas' part: his contemplation of Dido is a meditation on his past *libido*, from which he has finally freed himself. For the commentator, Dido is dim because she represents the past: Aeneas no longer finds her so beautiful (*non enim tam pulchra sibi uidetur*). On the backward glance in Virgil, see Gale 2003.

[57] Serv. *ad Aen.* 6.459. See also Norden 1903 *ad Aen.* 6.475 and Bocciolini Palagi 1990: 143–4.

[58] See e.g. Bömer 1969 ad loc. and Reed 2013 ad loc.; Segal 1989: 64–5.

[59] On the opposition between this gesture and Dido's final description as *auersa*, see Ricottilli 1992: 215–8.

Aeneas' gaze on Dido the absence of Dido's gaze on him. Virgil indeed not only attributes to the dead queen the sublime silence of Ajax,[60] he also represents her with her eyes downcast, hostile (*illa solo fixos oculos auersa tenebat*, 469 'she kept her eyes upon the ground and did not look at him'),[61] and with her internal sight grimly focused on the memory of the great wrong that Aeneas has done to her (467–8).

In conclusion, it is as if, in this scene, Virgil were completing the game of visibility that he had started in Book 1, and, by doing so, explaining why he decided not to play it properly at that stage, thereby causing trouble and dissatisfaction to his readers. That poetic game could only be pursued in the Underworld. When the woman who was once *forma pulcherrima* no longer shines but fades instead into other women like the new moon into the clouds, the epic hero – the pious man, who is characterized by choices that are exclusively political and religious, and who must always act as a cold guide to his people, as a cruel executor of the gods' will – can finally reveal one of the most surprising fissures that his author has allowed him: a touch of elegy.

---

[60] On Dido's silence, see e.g. Ricottilli 2000: 106–16 and Graverini 2016.
[61] It is noteworthy that, while at first Dido may have seemed a flesh-and-blood realization of Penthesilea, and thus like a potential political ally for the Trojans (see Heerink 2014: 77, whose interpretation fits well Donatus' reading of Aeneas' gaze), she is now *inimica* (*Aen.* 6.472) and is matched by Virgil himself with the image of Athena, the old enemy who, in the Carthaginian *pictura*, refused to turn her gaze to the Trojan women in supplication (*Aen.* 1.482).

PART II
Absence in Context

CHAPTER 7

Speaking Silence in Cicero's Brutus *and Tacitus'* Dialogus de Oratoribus

Kathrin Winter

The silence of eloquence is usually viewed in connection with the political situation and its changes in the first century BCE. When *eloquentia* is taken as synonymous with *res publica* and free speech,[1] silence (all the more the silence of *eloquentia*) is, by analogy, to be understood as a signpost of restriction in democratic freedoms and the emergence of the Principate. In accordance with this, Cicero's *Brutus* is frequently read as an answer to the question: how do you speak when speech is banished? Cicero's answer is apparent: you write about the history of Roman eloquence. That way, the *Brutus* is aligned with a reading of Cicero's dialogues as attempts to continue political efforts by alternative means. Such readings look into Cicero's strategies in formulating and exerting less direct political influence in other realms (e.g. aristocratic erudition).[2] Naturally, Cicero intensifies these strategies in view of the changes brought about in the aftermath of civil war and Caesar's seizure of power.

A hundred and twenty years later, the form of government and the function of *eloquentia* as a means of political participation had changed drastically (or perhaps only developed consequentially). The question to be asked becomes instead: how do you speak if all speech is *per se* under suspicion and hence potentially dangerous for the speaker?[3] Tacitus' answer is difficult to describe – and this very fact already gives an answer to the question: you write a 'classical' dialogue on eloquence in (seemingly) Ciceronian language,[4] without being too clear in what you say. Ambiguity,

---

[1] Stroup 2010: 251–2; cf. also Lowrie 2008: 131–3.
[2] Cf. for example, Baraz 2012; Hanchey 2014: 73–5; Stroup 2010: 251–65.
[3] For various assessments of Tacitus' strategy, cf. Bartsch 1994 (probably the most consequential account of taking Tacitus' ambiguity seriously by interpreting it as the deliberate strategy of 'doublespeak'); Dressler 2013; Luce 1993: 18–38; Penwill 2003: 138–9; Schirren 2000: 243–4; Strunk 2010. A similar but much more aggravated situation is found in the *Epistles* of Seneca, who must not mention Nero while he cannot *not* refer to him either: cf. Edwards in this volume.
[4] Cf. Luce 1993: 26; Mayer 2001: 27–31.

which permeates the *Dialogus*,⁵ appears to state only one thing: when speech is suspicious, indeterminacy is the only possible form of expression.

However, this blueprint for the meaning of silence in the two dialogues neglects a crucial aspect: silence is only perceptible as silence and can only be understood as meaningful on the fringes of speech. In other words, silence comes from speech. The silence of eloquence which is treated in one form or the other in the *Brutus* and the *Dialogus* is inevitably part of their literary technique. That is to say, silence is not only a topic to be considered in the texts but is also exploited as a means of commenting about silence and its relationship to speech. In this way, the dialogues contribute to a discourse that reassesses and negotiates the position of eloquence (a notable symptom of the Republic).

This chapter looks into the means and techniques of silence employed in the dialogues in order to determine their dynamics. A fruitful tension between speech and silence plays a vital role here and is used effectively to create and channel a sense of desire for speech and eloquence. Yet, as will be shown, the form of silence and the use of desire differ significantly in the two dialogues. The means of silence influences the meanings of silence; it is part of the eloquent speech in these dialogues that, in fact, stages silence to highlight speech itself and to keep the discourse on the position of eloquence going.

Meaningful Silence: Cicero's *Brutus*

From the outset, silence is a crucial issue in the *Brutus*. Not only does the prologue open with the ultimate form of silence, death, when it laments that Hortensius has passed away, but the subsequent introductory scene, in which the characters Cicero, Atticus and Brutus gather together, is also punctuated by deliberate and meaningful silence. Both passages mark the loss of speech and connect it implicitly with the impossibility of delivering speeches and taking part in political decisions – a telling reticence that points to the causes of this loss: Caesar's seizure of power and the concomitant change in the political situation.⁶

---

⁵ The disagreement in research on even basic aspects of the text, such as the topic or the assessment of the characters, testifies to the difficulties that arise from Tacitus' masterly ambiguity: cf. e.g. Dressler 2013: 2–4; Goldberg 2009: 74, 81–4; Köves-Zulauf 1992: 332; Van den Berg 2014: 98–164.
⁶ Cf. Lowrie 2008 on the relationship between Caesar and Cicero in the *Brutus*.

It is the emotional reaction of Cicero as narrator and character that interlocks the two scenes:[7] at the end of the prologue, the narrator points out what a tremendous loss Hortensius' death is to the forum (*Brut.* 6) and then connects the death to his own sorrows and anxiety about the state and the current political situation (*Brut.* 9). These sorrows serve as a transition to the entrance scene of the conversation, where the figure of Cicero, deeply worried about the state, wanders around in his garden (*Brut.* 10), when Atticus and Brutus pay him an unexpected visit. Their first exchange of greetings, without mentioning the particulars, already points to the difficult circumstances, and the friends immediately agree 'not to talk about politics': *ut de re publica esset silentium* (*Brut.* 11).[8]

Thus, a massive central silence is established – one that is tightly connected with the desire for speech, and this interplay of silence and desire then determines the dynamics of the subsequent conversation. On the one hand, the silence is repeatedly pointed out;[9] on the other, it stimulates the production of more eloquent speech. The loss not only of Hortensius' voice but also of all eloquence in the forum and courtrooms sparks the burning desire to fill this void and thereby make present what is painfully missing. In accordance with this emotional response, the *Brutus* has been interpreted as Hortensius' *laudatio funebris* as well as the swansong of Roman eloquence.[10]

The desire created between speech and silence manifests itself in two forms: as figural and as narrative desire. The first is discernible when the interlocutors directly express their wish to speak into the silence. When they approach their chosen topic (*Brut.* 21–3), Atticus at first asks Cicero to start writing again, since he has been silent for a long time after the publication of his last book, *De Re Publica* (*Brut.* 19). But then, he urges Cicero not only to end the silence of his literary production,[11] but also to interrupt the present silence by resuming a talk he had begun previously, on the beginnings and history of Roman *eloquentia*. It was for this reason, Atticus adds, that Brutus, whom he had told about it, decided to accompany him on this visit: *magnopere hic audire uelle dixit*

---

[7] Making this distinction is reasonable for laying open the mechanism employed in the dialogue; it is, however, part of the rhetorical strategy of the text to confuse the two speakers. For the emotional reaction serving as a framework in the *Brutus*, cf. Schwindt 2000: 113–14.
[8] The text is H. Malcovati's Teubner; translations are adapted from L. G. Hendrickson and H. M. Hubbell (Loeb).
[9] For an overview of the passages that repeat this sort of 'interdictum', cf. Jacotot 2014: 194–7.
[10] For the *Brutus* as a funeral oration, see Stroup 2010: 253–6 and Dugan 2005: 173, 195.
[11] Writing is, of course, not the same as talking. On the substitution and its contexts in the *Brutus*, see p. 133; cf. also Schwindt 2000: 98–9; Stroup 2010: 251–65.

('he said he very much wanted to hear you', *Brut.* 20). Both have come to hear Cicero speak and Cicero grants their wish: *ego uobis . . . si potuero, satis faciam* ('I will satisfy your curiosity if I can', *Brut.* 21).

Cicero's answer in the subsequent passage displays a very similar desire to terminate silence with eloquent speech. Before discussing the beginnings of Roman eloquence, Cicero reminds Atticus of the beginnings of the *sermo* itself: they mentioned the topic, he says, because of Brutus' speech for king Deiotarus – although he was not present himself, he had heard about its elaborateness and eloquence.[12] Atticus agrees with Cicero and adds:

> scio . . . ab isto initio tractum esse sermonem teque [sc. Ciceronem] Bruti dolentem uicem quasi defleuisse iudiciorum uastitatem et fori. (*Brut.* 21)

> I recall that our talk started from that point, and that you, grieving for the lot of Brutus, fairly shed tears over the desolation of the courts and the forum.

Two things are conspicuous here. First, Brutus' lauded eloquence is immediately associated with the disruption of *eloquentia* itself, a connection that is to be repeated in the *Brutus*.[13] Second, the memory of that speech prompts an emotional outburst from Cicero, who explains his reaction by referring to Brutus' subsequent fate: despite being a gifted orator, Brutus did not have many possibilities left to engage in public speech and pursue a career suited to his talents. After all, Cicero concludes, 'there came a sudden collapse in other fields of public life, and eloquence, the theme of our present discussion, became mute' (*subito in ciuitate cum alia ceciderunt tum etiam ea ipsa, de qua disputare ordimur, eloquentia obmutuit*, *Brut.* 22). It is striking how the greater political changes and hence the causes of the deplorable situation are merely summarised as *alia ceciderunt*, whereas the silencing of eloquence (*tum etiam ea ipsa eloquentia obmutuit*) is foregrounded through the correlative conjunction *cum . . . tum*, which emphasises the second element.

The passage succinctly illustrates the intertwining of silence, desire and eloquent speech. Atticus and Cicero are careful to reconstruct how, at the moment eloquence became mute, their conversation began (*Brut.* 21–2), and why the forced termination of Brutus' eloquence initiated the conversation about eloquence itself. That way, the void that originated from the termination of eloquence is filled with speech again, and Cicero's

---

[12] Cf. Douglas 1966: 14.   [13] Especially in *Brut.* 328–30; see pp. 131–2.

emotional reaction implies that this is due to a burning desire for eloquence. When beginning and ending collapse into one, speech arises from muteness, since the characters crave to speak into the silence. The desire that the figures display is easily adopted and shared by the reader and thus can be used as an effective means of guiding him or her through the argumentation of the dialogue.[14]

This leads to the second drive used in the *Brutus* to fill the void of silence. That is, figural desire also feeds into narrative desire,[15] the structural and narrative means that govern the course of the dialogue. Cicero's talk on the history of Roman eloquence offers large numbers of earlier orators and plenty of eloquent speech. The plenitude of former speakers, however, paradoxically expresses the dearth and paucity[16] of eloquence, because none of the Roman speakers mentioned is adjudged a true orator. Rather, the eloquence of former centuries lacks qualities that are only available after considerable development; *eloquentia* slowly progresses from its origins to the height of its power. Consequently, as Schwindt and Dugan have shown,[17] a *telos* is formed towards which the whole narrative is geared. Atticus and Brutus continually express the drive towards this climax and do not leave any doubt as to where to find it: in Cicero himself.[18] Although he refuses several times to talk about himself, Cicero finally gives in and fills this gap, which then also fulfils the narrative desire that had been aiming at this *telos* throughout.[19] It is Cicero himself, who by means of *praeteritio* and *recusatio* – i.e. by voicing his intention to remain silent about himself – repeatedly reminds us of his ultimate position within the development and narrative.

As a result, Cicero, the *telos* of the narrative, is present all the time while the historical development is sketched out. Dugan pointedly calls this phenomenon 'simultaneously a history of ineloquence and eloquence':[20] Cicero, the apex of Roman eloquence, is, by his very absence, present throughout, overshadowing each and every orator mentioned while he assigns to them their place within the historical development – which, in comparison to its *telos*, must always remain a history of imperfection. The plenitude of orators thus also becomes an expression of the lack of perfect

---

[14] Dugan 2005: 210–11. Dugan also explains how Brutus' and Atticus' impatient desire to reach the end of Cicero's narrative is built up and projected onto the reader.
[15] Cf. for the concept of a narrative desire that drives towards the end of a story Brooks 1984.
[16] On paucity as a topos in Cicero's oratorical writings, cf. Van den Berg 2014: 208–12.
[17] Schwindt 2000: 97, 101–12, 116–21; Dugan 2005: 196–8, 204, 212–14.
[18] E.g. *Brut*. 150–1, 190, 232, 249–51, 253–4; cf. also Dugan 2005: 210–11.
[19] Cf. Schwindt 2000: 116–17; Dugan 2005: 248.   [20] Dugan 2005: 206–7.

eloquentia, which in turn requires the narrative of the pursuit of its perfection to continue.

Within the context of the conversation's setting, coming to the climax of the narrative means leading to inevitable disruption as the dialogue markedly joins eloquence with silence again. Just at the moment when, after long enumerations of minor orators, the height of eloquence is finally reached,[21] Roman eloquence abruptly falls silent (*Brut.* 328–30). This time the connection is more dramatic than before because the *telos* of the narrative fulfils the reader's desire but simultaneously flings him or her back into the silence of the beginning. The orator Cicero transforms from being absently (omni)present in his account of the development of eloquence to being, as the embodiment of perfect eloquence, presently absent, as it were – a living vessel of eloquence that is nevertheless no longer permitted to speak (*Brut.* 328).

Here, the second major point of silence in the *Brutus* comes to the fore again: Caesar.[22] When the end of the dialogue refers again to its beginning, the text reminds us of the fact that the conversation was motivated by the silence of eloquence, a silence that is caused by the political changes Caesar brought about. Although he is not markedly omitted in the way Cicero is, and although the agreement *ut de re publica sit silentium* is still in effect, Caesar is placed at the centre of this silence. Just as Cicero's shadow looms over the history of eloquence and the withheld *telos* of the narrative is kept present by means of *praeteritio*, Caesar is silently present throughout the dialogue. The interlocutors agree to be silent on politics yet continually fail to be so – without, however, mentioning Caesar's name. The technique could perhaps be termed a subsidiary *praeteritio*: only the result of Caesar's political doings is brought up several times and *then* glossed over by the initial agreement. Just as Cicero stands at the end of eloquence's history, Caesar stands at the beginning of the oppressive silence.

The setting of the conversation in the *Brutus* is carefully designed for this purpose. In the silence that falls after Caesar's unmentioned seizure of power, Cicero the orator talks with his friends about the rise of *eloquentia*. It is evident that the author Cicero is well aware of how to set an entrance scene effectively – he could have used a historical situation to create a distancing effect as he does in other dialogues. In the *Brutus*, however, he chooses a crucial moment of the contemporary

---

[21] The figure Cicero never calls himself *orator perfectus*, but nevertheless suggests it; for a neat illustration, see *Brut.* 321–2. Cf. also Lowrie 2008: 147.

[22] Caesar is only discussed as a historiographer, not as an orator or politician (Lowrie 2008: 139); cf. also Dugan 2005: 208–9.

present in which the crisis of the Republic and the unforeseeable future provide a dramatic backdrop for an eloquent, steady voice that speaks into the silence.[23]

Thus, it is the dialogue *Brutus* itself that creates the silence in the first place. It evokes the situation of outspoken silence, the 'unspeakability of the political situation'[24] and the burning desire for eloquence. That way, talking itself is foregrounded: despite external circumstances, the dialogue shows performatively that there is still eloquent speech even outside the forum. This is certainly a form of 'politics by other means', as found in Cicero's philosophical writings.[25] Eloquence is thus embedded in the dynamics of desire only to be exploited on a figural level (since the interlocutors are orators themselves) and a self-referential level (since the *Brutus* consists of eloquent speech, too).

Both the beginning (*Brut.* 21–3) and the epilogue (*Brut.* 328–33) of the dialogue highlight the intrinsic value of eloquent speech by means of the figure Brutus. When Cicero laments the muteness of eloquence and the missing possibilities for Brutus' oratorical talents (*Brut.* 23), Brutus answers that he studies and will continue to study *eloquentia* for its own sake even if there is no public use for it: *ceterarum rerum causa ... istuc et doleo et dolendum puto; dicendi autem me non tam fructus et gloria quam studium ipsum exercitatioque delectat*, 'For other reasons ... I share your grief and I recognize that it is a thing to be deplored; but so far as eloquence is concerned, my pleasure is not so much in its rewards and the renown that it confers, as in the study and training which it involves', *Brut.* 23. A parallel opinion is voiced in the epilogue. After concluding the history of the development of eloquence and its connection to the Republic's fate (*Brut.* 328–9), Cicero advises Brutus to preserve eloquence in private study and not to falter in his efforts.[26] The final scene corresponds precisely to the beginning. Both passages mention the disruption of eloquence and Brutus' career but at the same time express continuity[27] by stating – and showing performatively – that eloquence, if transferred to other realms, continues to exist even in the silence of the forum.

In both cases, it is the figure of Brutus who guarantees this persistence. He appears as a beacon of hope, the one who could and should have

---

[23] On Cicero's abilities in using fictional settings to make readers 'complicit in his reconstruction of the past', cf. Hanchey 2014 (quote on p. 74).
[24] Lowrie 2008: 139.   [25] Stroup 2010: 260–5; Baraz 2012: 149, 187–223.
[26] *Brut.* 330, 332. Cf. Stroup 2010: 260–5; Dugan 2005: 233–4, 243–8.
[27] Schwindt 2000: 97 on continuity and discontinuity in the *Brutus*.

succeeded Cicero when he was about to resign from his public duties: *cum tibi aetas nostra iam cederet fascisque submitteret*, 'when I, because of advancing age, was giving way to you and laying down my sceptre', *Brut.* 22.[28] In this notional period of transition, both Cicero's and Brutus' careers signify the disruption of eloquence, for the former was not yet finished and the latter had not yet begun.[29] The framing thus conveys the impression that, as Schwindt puts it, the teleology of eloquence is as much a process of perfection as the history of anticipated failure:[30]

> tuum enim forum, tuum erat illud curriculum, tu illuc ueneras unus, qui non linguam modo acuisses exercitatione dicendi, sed et ipsam eloquentiam locupletauisses grauiorum artium instrumento et isdem artibus decus omne uirtutis cum summa eloquentiae laude iunxisses. ex te duplex nos afficit sollicitudo, quod et ipse re publica careas et illa te. (*Brut.* 331)

> Yours was the forum, yours was that arena, you were conspicuous in bringing thither, not only a tongue sharpened by training to eloquence, but eloquence itself, enriched and equipped with arts of graver import, and through such studies you had joined to your renown for eloquence all that grace which belongs to the study of virtue. On your account a two-fold concern touches us, that you are bereft of the republic, and the republic of you.

The gaze into the past silently establishes continuity, evoking something like a counterfactual account of history. We can sense here what Brutus' eloquence would have done and meant to the forum. Cicero thus affirms the idea that Brutus would have been a worthy successor to him in great eloquence and projects his desire for *eloquentia* (to continue) onto Brutus.

The continuity refers to the silent equation of *eloquentia* with *res publica*, which is hinted at in the phrase *et ipse re publica careas et illa te*. Projecting the possibility of eloquence onto Brutus offers the possibility of keeping these values present and alive – even when eloquence is forced to be silent. It also implies the possibility of a return, i.e. if Brutus preserves eloquence and Republican values, he would be ready and present should the political

---

[28] Schwindt 2000: 100–1.
[29] Cf. *Brut.* 330: *doleo me in uitam paulo serius tamquam in uiam ingressum, priusquam confectum iter sit, in hanc rei publicae noctem incidisse*, 'I have indeed reason to grieve that I entered on the road of life so late that the night, which has fallen upon the commonwealth, has overtaken me before my journey was ended'. Cf. Dugan 2005: 243, 249–50.
[30] Schwindt 2000: 101.

situation change again.³¹ Brutus appears to be an implicit promise Cicero makes.

Besides referring to Brutus, the idea that 'there is still eloquent speech' is, of course, also self-referential. The dialogue *Brutus* does (or has already done) what Cicero admonished Brutus to do: preserve *eloquentia* in another, private field. In this case, the chosen form is writing, which in itself is just another form of speaking silently.³²

Writing is vital to staging the crucial moment of silence and eloquence in the dialogue. There is no other form in which fictive orality and the appearance of extemporisation are displayed so naturally and effectively; only here can several voices be heard at once and express so succinctly the intimidating circumstances. Silence could not be voiced without these written speeches. Moreover, writing is the foundation of the narrative desire employed here; without writing, it would be impossible to orient the narrative towards its *telos*. As before, desire is used as the major driving force: since the urgent desire to fill the void with speech drives the dialogue on, the reader can hardly encounter the disruption of eloquence without regret, a reaction likewise reflected by the interlocutors.

The literary technique of silence in the *Brutus* channels desire so that its vector points to a potential future beyond the dialogue. When the figure of Cicero projects his desire for *eloquentia* onto the figure of Brutus, the reader's desire is transferred to Brutus as well. For this purpose, the whole situation is carefully arranged: Cicero hints at the possibility of continuity when he reminds us of the effects Brutus' eloquence used to have (and still could have). Figural as well as narrative desire is thereby expressed: figural desire because it is Cicero's own hope, narrative desire because the narrative stages the disruption of *eloquentia* and its immediate consequences – the oppressive silence and uncertainty of facing a frightening and unforeseeable future – without offering a sense of closure. Almost. What Brutus could do implies a possibility onto which all desire for continuity and eloquence can be projected. It emerges as the only alternative to the repulsive silence. The fact that eloquent speech still exists seems to keep this possibility alive (and concomitantly contributes to the discourse on eloquence). And since the dialogue itself displays that the end of eloquent speech at times coincides with the beginning of other eloquent speech, any indicated ending should not be taken as final. Brutus and the *Brutus* guarantee that.

---

³¹ Cf. Stroup 2010: 262.
³² Dugan 2005: 230–1, 289–303; Lowrie 2008: 148, 152; Stroup 2010: 261–5. Cicero also stages silence in some of his (written and published) speeches, e.g. *Pro Marcello*; cf. Dugan 2013 and Marchese 2014.

Eloquent Silence: Tacitus' *Dialogus de Oratoribus*

Compared to the *Brutus*, the *Dialogus de Oratoribus* appears to be much more direct and outspoken. This is surprising, considering the political circumstances and the ways in which Tacitus must have experienced oppression and the limits of free speech.[33] But since Tacitus explains the changes in *eloquentia* by their historical contexts and connects them with political changes, the *Dialogus* appears to articulate openly what is withheld in Cicero's *Brutus*. However, as we will see, this outspokenness is deceptive and the *Dialogus* is, in fact, charged with silence. In this respect the work differs significantly from the *Brutus*: first, the form that silence assumes here is qualitatively different, because it is not the significant omission of something that creates the impression of silence, but rather silence is made perceptible because something unnoticeable is not made explicit. This kind of silence is more difficult to pinpoint since it occurs unobtrusively, albeit effectively. Second, silence in the *Dialogus* is not oriented towards an overarching aim but is dispersed and ubiquitous. Third, without a central aim, desire must be evoked and used in a very different way. All these factors contribute to the *Dialogus*' ambiguity of meaning and its overall effect of destabilisation.

The difference in the form and quality of silence is apparent from the *Dialogus*' beginning:[34]

> Saepe ex me requiris, Iuste Fabi, cur, cum priora saecula tot eminentium oratorum ingeniis gloriaque floruerint, nostra potissimum aetas deserta atque laude eloquentiae orbata uix nomen ipsum oratoris retineat; neque enim ita appellamus nisi antiquos, horum autem temporum diserti causidici et aduocati et patroni et quiduis potius quam oratores uocantur. (*Dial.* 1.1)

> You often put to me the question, Justus Fabius, how it is that, whereas former ages flourished in the genius and renown of many great orators, on our generation a signal blight has fallen: it lacks distinction in eloquence, and scarce retains so much as the name of 'orator', which we apply exclusively to the men of old times, calling good speakers of the present day 'pleaders', 'advocates', 'counsel' – anything rather than 'orators'.

Usually, the topic deduced from this passage is the difference between the flourishing eloquence of earlier times and the demise of oratory in

---

[33] On the differences and development in treating criticism (which is raised in anonymous defamatory verses) from Caesar to Tiberius, cf. Del Giovane in this volume.
[34] The text is taken from M. Winterbottom's and R. M. Ogilvie's *OCT* 1975; translations are adapted from E. Warmington et al. (Loeb).

contemporary times. But, it has been shown that this topic is less straight-forward than it seems.³⁵ Although the argumentation of the first sentence establishes a palpable contrast between present (*aetas nostra*) and earlier times (*priora saecula*), the comparison is not executed very precisely. When former times are characterised by *tot eminentium oratorum ingeniis gloriaque* ('an abundance of oratorical talents and renown'), it is to be expected that this earlier wealth would be met by a dearth of talents or eloquence nowadays. But instead, as Van den Berg points out, the present age is said to lack not *ingenia* or *eloquentia* but *laus eloquentiae*, 'distinction in eloquence'; it is merely the expectation of antithesis that may prompt readers to interpret 'a lack of talent' here.³⁶ Thus, the text creates a 'careful – yet significant – slippage in focus', because the loss of *laus eloquentiae* is not the same as the loss of *eloquentia* and hence does not 'unambiguously herald an unqualified decline'.³⁷ This small deviation from straightforward comparison has considerable impact on what one views as the topic of the dialogue and on whether one considers the argumentation to be positive or negative.³⁸

The passage serves as an instructive example of the kind of silence used in the *Dialogus*. Although earlier ages are characterised by abundance (*tot*) and the present by dearth (*deserta atque orbata*), it is not explicitly stated that the loss is connected with eloquence; rather, this information must be inferred from *ingenia oratorum* and *laus eloquentia*. Likewise, it is never stated explicitly that the object of loss is desirable – although this is crucial to establish the contrast just mentioned; if it were otherwise, raising the issue would be pointless. Moreover, the dearth found in the present age is paradoxically expressed by the abundance of other terms denoting eloquent men: *causidici, aduocati, patroni*. It is not clear to what these terms exactly refer, but from the implied context we can assume that they are somehow deficient if compared with *orator*. On the other hand, it is not clear either what *orator* means – to rank it indisputably above the other terms, it is usually understood as *orator perfectus*;³⁹ and though this reading is plausible, the text does not make it explicit. As before, a small omission has far-reaching consequences.

From the above we may draw two conclusions about silence in the *Dialogus*: first, presuppositions remain unspoken, though what is kept silent is small and not very specific. As a result, the *Dialogus* is permeated

---

³⁵ Dressler 2013: 3; Goldberg 2009: 74–5; Mayer 2001: 31–2; Van den Berg 2014: 101–8.
³⁶ Van den Berg 2014: 102.   ³⁷ Van den Berg 2014: 103.   ³⁸ Cf. Dressler 2013: 4–8.
³⁹ Cf. Van den Berg 2014: 103.

by little, unobtrusive gaps that the reader must – and does – fill continually in order to make sense of the text; depending on how the gaps are filled, the text's meaning is constituted differently.[40] Second, silence is dispersed and cannot be located precisely, which is why the many small fissures and rifts are not geared towards a specific aim as in the *Brutus*.

Although the *Dialogus* looks like a gauze of silence, the text is not incomprehensible; it even has the appearance of being perfectly intelligible. Yet this initial and superficially persuasive impression is accompanied by a second impression: the vague feeling that something else is being expressed along the way, something that has been overlooked or perhaps has not been explicitly stated; in short, that the text *may* not have just one meaning.[41] Paradoxically again, the suspicion that there is more meaning is created by saying less. It is crucial for the dialogue and also paradigmatic for the kind of silence exploited here that both impressions are created at the same time. It contributes to a subliminal destabilising effect beneath the coherent appearance of clarity.

One means to intensify this effect is to insert another level of distance and to put talk about talking on display.[42] This technique is frequently employed in the course of the dialogue; the introductory scene contains an instructive example. When Secundus, Aper and the narrator come to visit Maternus, it is explained that Maternus had offended the powerful with a recitation of his tragedy *Cato* the day before, which was the talk of the town:

> Nam postero die quam Curiatius Maternus Catonem recitauerat, cum offendisse potentium animos diceretur ... eaque de re per urbem frequens sermo haberetur... (*Dial.* 2.1)
>
> It was the day following that on which Curiatius Maternus had given a reading of his *Cato*, when court circles were said to have taken umbrage ... The thing was the talk of the town.

Although a great deal is said here *about* talking, there is no hint of what Maternus' *Cato* actually said or how people commented on it afterwards. The passive voice is also conspicuous: *diceretur* and *sermo haberetur* present speech without speaker as if it did not belong to anybody. Maternus,

---

[40] Gardini 2014: 83–5 aptly names this phenomenon in Tacitus' *Annals* 'lo stile lacunoso'. An illuminating example is also found in O'Gorman's reading of Tac. *Ann.* 1.3.7 (cf. her chapter in this volume).

[41] Cf. Goldberg 2009: 84; Van den Berg 2014: 1–14. On the *Dialogus* and doublespeak, see Bartsch 1994; on ambiguity as 'hermeneutics of suspicion', see Dressler 2013.

[42] Tellingly, the introductory question is presented as belonging to Fabius, not to the narrator. Cf. Mayer 2001: 31 n. 88; Müller 2013: 329–30; Van den Berg 2014: 102.

however, is even able to surpass this unspecific rumour himself: when Secundus cautions him to make his *Cato* a bit safer, he replies that his next play, *Thyestes*, will fill in what his *Cato* left out (*Dial.* 3.2–3). Here, too, the talk about talking does not inform us about specific content but creates a diffuse silence. This is also due to the fact that more than one subtext or cross-reference is possible, but there are no clear hints and no obvious suppressions.[43] By leaving things unsaid, the text continually creates the impression that more is being said.

On closer consideration, it must seem surprising that although this form of vague silence permeates the whole dialogue, its eloquent speech about eloquence never falters. As we have seen, Fabius' question, and accordingly also the topic of the dialogue, remains ambiguous. Nevertheless, the narrator and the interlocutors address the question as if its content were perfectly clear. In the *interludia*, the short transitional passages between the speeches, this behaviour is apparent: the interlocutors keep referring to the *quaestio* or use the term *requirere* to establish a connection with the initial question; Mayer in his commentary even talks about a 'key term'.[44] But naming the speech act does not tell us what the question is.[45] All interlocutors behave as if its precise content were obvious, and thus produce much eloquent speech about *eloquentia*, which, again, is not at all incomprehensible but also not unambiguous. The reader is carried along in this continuous flow of eloquent speech and adapts to the silently imposed rules.[46] The argumentation, as intelligible as it is, enforces the impression of a diffuse, silent subtext, which in turn intensifies the ambiguity because the reader can never be certain to have fully understood what the text is about. In the *Brutus*, it is clearly marked that silence is unusual; in the *Dialogus*, silence draws no commentary and thus gives the impression that it is perfectly normal – and yet, the absence of commentary leaves behind a vaguely uncomfortable feeling.[47]

---

[43] Examples are the striking similarity between Maternus and Crassus in the *De Oratore* (cf. Haß-von Reitzenstein 1970; Levene 2004: 188–95; Luce 1993: 12–13; Schirren 2000: 227–8; Van den Berg 2014: 212–40) or Messala's possible status as *delator* (cf. Goldberg 2009: 77–9; Mayer 2001: 37; Penwill 2003: 128–33; Schirren 2000: 232–4; Strunk 2010: 249–58).

[44] Mayer 2001: 137. [45] Cf. Goldberg 2012: 158.

[46] A similar manifestation of distorted speech that relies on misrecognition and withholds information is found in speech directed at the powerful in the imperial court: Winterling 2009: 111–13.

[47] As in the *Brutus*, this effect is achieved only in writing, especially in dialogue because its fictive orality allows for interaction as well as longer, coherent speeches. In the case of the *Dialogus*, the form is even more poignant since it fulfils exactly Cicero's demands on how to preserve *eloquentia*: privately.

Although the narrative dynamics of the *Dialogus* do not rely on a central and focused silence, they are – as in the *Brutus* – dependent on the principle of desire (it is characteristically left to the reader to infer that the desire is for eloquent speech). In contrast to the *Brutus*, the homodiegetic narrator of the *Dialogus* vanishes quickly after the prologue and introductory scene and is not mentioned again until the very last word: *cum adrisissent, discessimus* ('they laughed and we went our ways', *Dial.* 42 – he does not even take part in the laughter of the company).[48] Whereas Cicero the narrator and Cicero the character create coherence between prologue and setting, especially through their lament and wish to fill the silence with speech, the narrator in the *Dialogus* is certainly neither a central nor an authorial speaker;[49] and since the reader cannot sympathise with him in the way he or she does with the sorrows of Cicero, desire must be evoked in a different manner – it can hardly be the narrator's desire, personal grief or the acutely felt oppressive situation that drives the dialogue on.

Instead, the *Dialogus* works by means of the dynamics of a promise, which is set off by the narrator in the prologue and kept in effect even when the narrator's presence is no longer felt. It starts with a question, *saepe ex me requiris*, to which the phrase *percontationi tuae respondere ... uix ... auderem* responds only a little later (*Dial.* 1.2). Even though this corresponding sentence then proceeds in a different direction ('I would not dare to answer your question if not ...'), the simple and basic mechanism that a question requires an answer nonetheless exists. Again, this is talk about talking, for the answer is as reticent as the question is unclear; yet, a promise is given that the topic will be discussed, which indicates that there will be an answer. The underlying dynamics are based on the dynamics of silence, speech and desire: the question simultaneously signals the presence of something unknown, an absence and an aim, combined with the desire to know or obtain that object.[50] The promise raises the expectation that the desired object will be at one's disposal in due time. The desire behind the repeated question is to be satisfied by means of speech.

This mechanism lays the foundation for exploiting the desire for eloquence in Tacitus' *Dialogus*: the *Dialogus* never provides an answer but

---

[48] Luce 1993: 37.
[49] Cf. Levene 2004: 192–3. On a comparison of the interlocutors' behaviour in Tacitus' *Dialogus* and Cicero's *De Oratore*, cf. Köves-Zulauf 1992: 331–2.
[50] For a very similar technique, i.e. Tacitus' use of the rhetorical question in the *Annals*, cf. O'Gorman in this volume.

only the promise that there will be one.[51] The task is passed on from the narrator to the interlocutors (*respondere ... uix ... auderem si mihi mea sententia proferenda ac non disertissimorum ... hominum sermo repetendus esset*, 'I would hardly dare to answer ... if it were my own views that I had to put forward, instead of reproducing a conversation between very good speakers', *Dial.* 1.2), who, in turn, do not give an answer either, but merely promise to discuss the *quaestio*, whose exact content remains unspecified. In chapter 16.2, for example, Messala undertakes to give his views on the *quaestio* (*aperiam ... cogitationes meas*, 'I will let you know what I think', *Dial.* 16.2) and Maternus responds by promising that he and Secundus will answer Messala's speech and fill in the gaps that he will have left open: *pro duobus ... promitto; nam et ego et Secundus exsequemur eas partes quas intellexerimus te non tam omisisse quam nobis reliquisse*, 'I undertake for two of us; both Secundus and I will take up the points, which, as I see, you do not so much overlook as deliberately leave to us', *Dial.* 16.3.[52] It is striking how *promittere* and *omittere* are related to each other in this passage,[53] pointing out exactly the dynamic mechanism of speaking and silence that produces eloquent speech; but as this speech is permeated by eloquent silence, it can never come to any conclusion. Maternus' promise that his next play, *Thyestes*, will fill the gaps left in the *Cato*, works along the same lines. One promise leads to the next in a chain of deferral, using the desire for an answer (i.e. for speech) to persist endlessly. The promise is sustained right to the end of the dialogue, when Maternus promises at last to discuss the questions that were not answered at a later point in time (*et si qua tibi obscura in hoc meo sermone uisa sunt, de iis rursus conferemus*, 'And if anything in my argument may have struck you as needing further elucidation, we can then discuss it again', *Dial.* 42). The whole *Dialogus* appears to be nothing but an unending deferral: abundance of speech seemingly discussing the change in eloquence does not produce anything else but penury, thereby always fuelling the desire to reach an aim while permanently deferring it.[54] There is ample talk about talking that silently presupposes that the talk does have a content – which can neither be verified nor falsified.

---

[51] That way, the *Dialogus* is very much comparable to Felman's reading of Austin's *How to Do Things with Words* and Molière's *Don Juan*; see esp. Felman 2002: 15, 46–7.
[52] On Secundus' disappearance in the *Dialogus*, see Köves-Zulauf 1992; on the problem and extent of the lacuna, ibid. 318–22.
[53] I owe this observation to Ellen O'Gorman.
[54] Cf. Felman 2002: 15. This is why, as Dressler 2013: 25–6 has pointed out, there is no sense of closure in the *Dialogus*.

The situation is aggravated by an issue raised in the *interludia*. There, the interlocutors keep pointing out the fact that orators give opinions that are not their own; Dressler calls this phenomenon 'strategic speech', as distinguished from 'sincere speech'.[55] The most notorious instance of this phenomenon is the controversial question of whether Aper is an *aduocatus diaboli* or not:[56] does he really believe in what he says? Or does he display an essential ability possessed by every orator, namely to argue in favour of a position that is not his own?[57] The question inevitably remains unresolved because Aper himself stays silent on it. It is only the others who insist that Aper does not believe in what he says.[58] As a result, it is impossible to tell whether Messala and Maternus want to expose Aper's strategic speech or if they are trying to ease interpersonal tensions by pretending that everybody has the same opinion and all divergences are part of the rhetorical game.[59] All we can ascertain is the fact that the matter of strategic and sincere speech returns in all transitional passages. This is important for the whole *Dialogus* since, as Dressler shows, the interlocutors are presented in the introduction as the best speakers of their time. Accordingly, every one of them must be able to use strategic speech – not least the narrator.[60]

As it is in the nature of strategic speech to be silent on its true nature, it is impossible to distinguish it from sincere speech. This ambiguity is yet another example of the means by which one can keep presuppositions uncertain. Yet the impact on the whole *Dialogus* is enormous. After all, a promise, the driving force of this narrative, is a speech act – for it is not about propositional content but about action – and can hence be neither true nor false. It is only possible to consider whether its felicity conditions are fulfilled or not,[61] that is, whether the promise was given sincerely or not: a promise is only valid if the person making it really means it. In the *Dialogus*, this question must remain open because the issue of strategic or sincere speech cannot be resolved.

To sum up, the gauze of silence in the *Dialogus* renders all speech ambiguous: whenever something is said, other possibilities of meaning are offered subliminally and simultaneously. Indeed, the *Dialogus* takes ambiguity a step further, transferring it from content to the very act of speaking. All that remains in the end is a sense of desire, perhaps the least ambiguous constituent in the dialogue. Generated by the tension between

---

[55] Dressler 2013: 21.
[56] Goldberg 2012; Haß-von Reitzenstein 1970: 27; cf. also Luce 1993: 18–20; Mayer 2001: 45–6; Strunk 2010: 249–50.
[57] Dressler 2013: 20–4. [58] *Dial.* 16.3, 24.2, 27.1, 28.1. [59] Müller 2013: 337–46.
[60] Dressler 2013: 20–4. [61] See Austin 1975: 6–7, 40–7; Felman 2002: 17.

speech and silence, desire perpetually produces speech that is also laden with silence. What the reader is left with in the end is Maternus' promise to answer all open questions. We can take the *Dialogus* as a guarantee of that.

Conclusion: Speaking Silence

The forms and uses of silence differ considerably in the *Brutus* and the *Dialogus*. In the *Brutus*, two main and focused points of silence, Cicero and Caesar, determine the dynamics of the dialogue. Within the work's overall context and the structure, this kind of silence is not ambiguous and could be expressed well with words. In the *Dialogus*, however, silence cannot be pinpointed precisely or be identified with any specific event or person. It is dispersed throughout the dialogue and has a destabilising quality, both features that inhibit any attempt to assign to it any particular meaning. What the use of silence in the dialogue does do, however, is create the enduring impression of meaning. That is to say, the reader is continually given the impression that the speakers' words have some additional meaning, but precisely what that meaning is nevertheless remains elusive and polysemic. What is kept silent here cannot be easily transferred into an explicit formulation.

In both dialogues, the use of silence is tightly connected to desire, perhaps the most effective use of this literary technique. The *Brutus* evokes the desire for eloquence and continuity; in short, it evokes republican values that point beyond the dialogue to the potential of Brutus' eloquence and to the unspoken idea of an eloquent voice resounding in the courtrooms and the forum again. That way, the text not only claims but also shows that the discourse of negotiating eloquence and its place in Roman politics, history and society is still ongoing.[62] In the *Dialogus*, silence and desire affect the reader less directly. Eloquent speech that is permeated by silence renders all speech ambiguous because there is always the possibility that something else is being expressed too. This potential is, of course, ambiguous itself – because it is uncertain whether the silently perceptible sub-speech is really there, whether it is understood or not. But this ambiguity creates the vague feeling that there is more, and fuels the desire for an answer to the *quaestio* (whatever that *quaestio* is). That way, not having an answer points simultaneously beyond and back into the dialogue because it sustains the desire to keep looking – even though the *Dialogus* explicitly shows us that the continuation of the *sermo* is nothing but another (inevitably undelivered) promise. As in the *Brutus*, speaking silence is a means to continue not only eloquence but also the discourse on its position.

---

[62] Cf. Lowrie 2008: 151.

CHAPTER 8

Et sine auctore notissimi uersus
Unauthored Poetry and Rome's Authoritarian Turn

Barbara Del Giovane

This chapter engages with anonymous texts – texts whose anonymity revolves around the fundamental assumption that the authors *wanted to be* anonymous, that is, that they wanted to hide their name for a specific reason. These are the anonymous verses composed against powerful men – Julius Caesar and the emperors – quoted by Suetonius in his *Lives of the Caesars*.[1] In these cases, anonymity appears as a political necessity rather than a poetic choice, and it is my purpose to investigate the motives behind this necessity. In particular, this chapter focuses on the pivotal moment when changes in the political and social dimension of the late Republic and early Empire led some authors to self-censor their dissenting voice: authorial anonymity, I shall argue, is here to be interpreted as one of the first symptoms of Rome's authoritarian turn. It is no coincidence that the beginning of a consistent production of anonymous verses coincides with the time of Julius Caesar and his move towards autocracy. After investigating Caesar's reaction to these verses, I shall survey unauthored poetry under Augustus and Tiberius. In the early imperial era there is evidence of an initial awareness of the dangerousness of anonymous writing, followed by censorial measures together with other surprising attempts to keep the situation under control.

Republican verse invective was far from anonymous. Lucilius, for example, was famous not only for carrying on the old comic tradition of *onomastì komodèin*[2] ('to ridicule by name'), which enabled comic poets to pick on politicians using their real names; he was also directly present in the first person, that is, emphatically *not* anonymous. In Horace's portrait of Lucilius at *Serm.* 2.1.30–4, the Republican satirist is depicted as entrusting

---

[1] On the verses quoted by Suetonius, cf. Müller 1972; Cugusi 1979: 879–87; Gascou 1984: 563–5; Cupaiuolo 1993; Morelli 2000: 288–90; Morelli 2001: 61–3; Corbier 2006: 71–3; Zadorojnyi 2011: 120–30; Slater 2014; Del Giovane 2018.

[2] On the *onomastì komodèin*, see Degani 1993.

his secrets to his books, here defined as his 'loyal friends'. Both Lucilius' thoughts and deeds are so entirely transferred to his poems that his life turns into a votive tablet, its episodes clearly visible by everyone (*omnis ... pateat ... uita senis*). The use of the first person that we find in several fragments of Lucilius seems to be proof of such strong authorial presence.[3] Lucilius can thus be considered the paradigm of free speech, a freedom to speak about both himself and others.

It might sound like a foregone conclusion to say that it was in the imperial age that it became impossible to criticize by name the personalities who most embodied the exercise of power – the emperors – unless the emperor in question was a dead one. What comes immediately to mind is Seneca's *Apocolocyntosis*, presumably written after Claudius' death, or Juvenal's verses dedicated to Nero or Domitian, nicknamed the *caluus Nero*.[4] We may equally say that it was the necessity of reacting to power that led people to find different ways of making their voice heard. Through anonymous poetry, political messages can spread across the city, and thanks to their metrical form they can easily be memorized by people from different social levels. These verses circulated in Rome at different periods and under different political leaders.[5] They could spread in both written and oral form,[6] as poetic slogans or songs, but they could also be written in epigraphs, on walls or under the statues of the characters that they mocked.

Caesar and the Safe 'Delight' in Anonymous Free-speaking

In the Republican age, we have no evidence of slander or libel lacking an authorial name. Cicero (*Rep.* 4.12) mentions all authorial names when referring to Plautus and Naevius abusing the Scipios and Caecilius vilifying Cato, and his reference to the Twelve Tables, which prescribed the death penalty for singing or composing a song containing slander or insult to anyone (*si quis occentauisset siue carmen condidisset, quod infamiam faceret flagitiumue alteri*), does not imply anonymity either.[7] In fact, it seems to

---

[3] Cf. e.g. Lucil. fr. 712 M. [4] Juv. 4.38.
[5] In addition to the verses quoted by Suetonius (59 verses covering the lives of Caesar, Augustus, Tiberius, Caligula, Nero, Galba, Otho and Domitian), more have been handed down to us by Gellius, Macrobius and the *Historia Augusta*.
[6] See Suet. *Ner.* 39.2 *multa Graece Latineque proscripta aut uulgata sunt*.
[7] Fr. 8b of the Twelve Tables. Horace *Ep.* 2.1.152–4 *quin etiam lex / poenaque lata, malo quae nollet carmine quemquam / describi* is an allusion to the Twelve Tables and their legislation against slander and libel. Pliny *HN* 28.18 *qui malum carmen incantassit* (fr. 8a) refers to another offence: that of magical incantation (cf. Brink 1982: 196–8; Smith 1951: 169).

have been the personality of Julius Caesar, and his break with the Republican tradition, that first inspired the production of anonymous defamatory verses.

Suetonius actually gives us the names of some of the people who slandered Caesar through a defamatory book and highly abusive poems. These are Aulus Caecina[8] and Pitholaus, the former from the senatorial class, the latter a freedman of Pompey (Suet. *Iul.* 75.5):

> Aulique Caecinae criminosissimo libro et Pitholai carminibus maledicentissimis laceratam existimationem suam ciuili animo tulit.
>
> He bore with good grace the harm to his reputation caused by the most defamatory book written by Aulus Caecina and the highly abusive poems of Pitholaus.[9]

According to Suetonius, Caesar showed a permissive attitude towards these men, as well as on other occasions.[10] In particular, it is worth remembering Caesar's behaviour towards the famous epigram written by Licinius Calvus on Caesar's presumed homosexuality.[11] After Licinius' attempt at reconciliation through the mediation of common friends, it was the dictator who wrote to Calvus first, on his own initiative.[12] Similarly, in the case of Catullus, whose poems impressed *perpetua stigmata* on Caesar and Mamurra, Caesar does not appear to have held any grudges.[13] It is possible that knowledge of the authorial source made it tolerable for Caesar to have his reputation harmed by these works. As we shall see below, political hostility may not seem too dangerous to deal with when it comes under a specific name, while anonymous poetic propaganda is more threatening, since verses without a defined author could come from any possible socio-political background, and hold a kind of intimidating power that is potentially universal.

An extremely fascinating piece of evidence provided by Suetonius concerns the famous *carmina triumphalia*, 'triumphal songs' that soldiers addressed to a commander during a triumphal procession.[14] The playful feature of these verses was supposed to be a demonstration of relief at the moment of celebration for victory, but also a way to remove from the triumphal commander's head the possible envy of the gods.[15] Such verses walso have

---

[8] Caecina's book, mentioned by Cicero *Fam.* 6.6.8, was entitled *Querelae*.
[9] All translations of Suetonius are by Edwards (Oxford).
[10] Yavetz 1983: 205–6 recalls Dante's words *Segui il tuo corso e lascia dir le genti*.
[11] Suet. *Iul.* 49.1, cf. p. 148.   [12] Suet. *Iul.* 73.1.   [13] Ibid.
[14] See Cupaiuolo 1993: 12 n. 10; O'Neill 2003; Richlin 1992: 275; Beard 2007: 247–9.
[15] On the apotropaic character of the triumphal songs, cf. Versnel 1970: 70; Dupont 1976; Richlin 1992: 10; 94; O'Neill 2003: 3–4; Beard 2007: 248.

a 'sociological function', with the purpose of reintegrating the victorious general into his senatorial peer group.[16] With the end of the Republic and Caesar's ascent to power, we can see in the triumphal verses topics that reflect the influence of the political factions hostile to Caesar.[17] As will become clear,[18] these verses were not only sung by soldiers but began to spread everywhere through anonymous voices. It is not easy to explain how these verses were created and then disseminated. What we can do is consider the forces on the ground – the optimates, the soldiers, the plebs – as being aware of the importance of a mutual influence made possible by anonymity. The political impact of Caesar's conservative opponents is evident in the themes presented by the verses, as we shall see, but the plebs could be an ally in this political protest, and could function within an 'osmotic' process involving the creation and the distribution of these verses.[19]

As a first example of what I mean when I talk about the political impact of Caesar's opponents in anonymous verses, I shall discuss some triumphal verses that refer to a political move by Caesar, described by Suetonius as unprecedented, concerning the possibility that some 'half-barbarian Gauls' could receive the citizenship and then enter the Senate-house.[20] This decision is mentioned by Suetonius as one of those showing 'equal disregard for law and traditional practice' (*Iul.* 76.3 *eadem licentia spreto patrio more*). In the following verses sung by the soldiers, the Gauls, brought by Caesar into the Curia, are described as 'putting aside their barbarian trousers' in order to wear the broad stripe, typical of the senators (Suet. *Iul.* 80.2; *uers. triumph.* 2 Courtney 1993):[21]

---

[16] O'Neill 2003: 4; cf. Beard 2007: 248–9 n. 86.
[17] Cf. Morelli 2001: 61 as regards to the verses quoted by Suetonius on Caesar's homosexual relations with Nicomedes (see p. 148): 'io credo che sia chiaro che si tratta di un tema che doveva essere corrente nei Circoli politici avversi a Cesare, che lo diffusero largamente tra la popolazione di Roma'; see also Cèbe 1966: 164; Cupaiuolo 1993, 38–9; 44 and *passim*.
[18] See p. 150.
[19] See Horsfall 2012, an excellent study on the culture of the plebs (on the plebs in relation to anonymous verses, see pp. 38–9; 65; 111–2). I agree in interpreting the relation between elitarian and popular poetry in terms of a 'continua osmosi' (Cupaiuolo 1993: 23), of 'contaminazioni dallo spettro molto ampio' (Morelli 2000: 287). For evidence of the plebs being literate, see the poems from the fort of Bu Njem (in Tripolitania), written by centurions (with Adams 1999).
[20] Suet. *Iul.* 76.3 *eadem licentia spreto patrio more* [...] *ciuitate donatos et quosdam e semibarbaris Gallorum recepit in curiam*; see also *Iul.* 24.2, which mentions a legion recruited by Caesar from Gallia Transalpina, later rewarded with citizenship: *qua fiducia ad legiones, quas a re publica acceperat, alias priuato sumptu addidit, unam etiam ex Transalpinis conscriptam, uocabulo quoque Gallico—Alauda enim appellabatur—, quam disciplina cultuque Romano institutam et ornatam postea universam ciuitate donauit.*
[21] On these verses, see Cupaiuolo 1993: 44–6; Hickson Hahn 2015: 164–5; Corbeill 1996: 202 observes the similarity between this joke and a joke by Cicero against a man called Asinius, who was self-elected senator: *Phil.* 13.28 *mutauit calceos: pater conscriptus repente factus est*; see Del Giovane 2018 for a discussion on how Cicero could have inspired these jokes.

> Et illa uulgo canebantur:
>> Gallos Caesar in triumphum ducit, idem in curiam:
>> Galli bracas deposuerunt, latum clauum sumpserunt

> And the following verses were heard everywhere:
>> Caesar led Gauls in his triumph—and into the senate house;
>> The Gauls put aside their trousers and put on the broad stripe.

Cassius Dio, while mentioning the new kind of people who were awarded the senatorial rank by Caesar,[22] does not discuss the possibility of picking senators from the provinces, nor from the lands beyond the Alps, the only geographic origin that could warrant both Suetonius' expression *quidam e semibarbaris Gallorum* and the mention of Caesar's triumph in the verses cited above.[23] Even if it is possible that we may have lost further information about these Gallic senators, Syme sharply observes how unlikely it is that Caesar would have bestowed the senatorial rank on people who had just received the citizenship.[24] One hypothesis is that the mention of the 'half-barbarian Gauls' with senatorial rank, and the subsequent verses, actually reflects distorted propaganda against senators who originated from Latin colonies in Gallia Cisalpina. Cicero, for example, attacks Lucius Calpurnius Piso's maternal grandfather Calventius in an anti-Gallic vein, even though Calventius was a businessman from Placentia, a Latin colony in Gallia Cisalpina. Nevertheless, he is described by Cicero as if he were a merchant and an auctioneer – which is a more degrading job – from Mediolanum, the former capital of the Insubres,[25] while elsewhere he is even deemed to be from Gaul beyond the Alps.[26] The trouser joke of the verses resounds in the definition of Piso as 'the disgrace of his trouser-wearing kinsmen'[27] and, in Cicero's speech to thank the Senate, Piso's good qualities are damaged by Transalpine blood on his mother's side.[28] Syme concludes that 'the libel about Piso's ancestry will authorize the conjecture that some at least of the trousered Gauls were respectable citizens from Gallia Cisalpina'.[29] The citizenship was also bestowed upon several people close to Caesar originating from the Romanized

---

[22] Cf. Dio 42.51.5; 43.47.3; 52.25.6.
[23] See n. 22, for the mention of the legion from Gallia Transalpina receiving the citizenship.
[24] Syme 1979: 34.
[25] Cic. *Pis.* fr. 11a Clark *Insuber quidam fuit, idem mercator et praeco*; cf. also fr. 12 Clark; *Pis.* 26; 62.
[26] Cic. *Pis.* fr. 10 Clark *Prius enim Gallus, dein Gallica<nus>, extremo placentinus haberi <coeptus> est.*
[27] Cic. *Pis.* 53 *bracatae cognationis dedecus!*   [28] Cic. *Red. Sen.* 15.
[29] Syme 1979: 34–5; see also Wiseman 1985: 158.

province of Gallia Narbonensis,[30] and it would not be surprising if some of these received senatorial rank, becoming the focus of the verses' distorted perspective.[31] The lampoons seem to reflect a background in which the 'Romanized' Gallic origins of some people close to Caesar offered the chance for falsely propagating the rumour that Transalpine Gauls would become senators. Just before quoting these verses, Suetonius mentions an anonymous writing on a *libellus* (Suet. *Iul.* 80.2):

> peregrinis in senatum allectis libellus propositus est: 'Bonum factum: ne quis senatori nouo curiam monstrare uelit!'

> When foreigners were admitted to the senate, the following placard was set up: 'Well done, those who refuse to show a new senator where the senate house is!'

The expression *bonum factum* is a formula of well-wishing introducing the edicts by the magistrates; the construction *ne quis ... uelit* also recalls the language of the edicts.[32] The parody of the chancery style, while suggesting a familiarity with the language of administration and politics, creates a paradoxical edict against helping the new senators, who are deemed incapable of orientation in a different world with a different language.

Further condemnation of Caesar by anonymous verses involves anecdotes that would show him as disintegrating the Republican *mos*, through illicit love or sexual inversion, all the more so since these continue to feature his predilection for non-Roman people. Cassius Dio (43.20.3) gives us an interesting account of the triumphal songs on Caesar that mock his affair with Cleopatra and his relationship with Nicomedes IV, king of Bithynia. A poem on Caesar's 'passive' relationship with Nicomedes is mentioned by Dio; remarkably, we find the original version of this song, in trochaic septenarii, in Suetonius' text.[33] The irony is provided by the double meaning of the verb *subigo* ('to defeat, to submit'), which implies Caesar's military submission of Gaul but also his sexual submission to Nicomedes (Suet. *Iul.* 49.4; *uers. triumph.* 1 Courtney 1993):

---

[30] See Syme 1979: 35 for a survey of these people.
[31] Cf. Mela 2.74 for the 'other' name of the Narbonensis: *fuit aliquando Bracata, nunc Narbonensis*; cf. also Plin. *HN* 3.31.1.
[32] Cf. Suet. *Vit.* 14.4 for another parody of an edict by Vitellius; Plaut. *Poen.* 16; see Benner 1975: 33–4 for a discussion of this formula in Republican edicts.
[33] Cupaiuolo 1993: 39–42; Richlin 1992: 96; Hickson Hahn 2015: 160–2.

> Gallico denique triumpho milites eius inter cetera carmina, qualia currum prosequentes ioculariter canunt, etiam illud uulgatissimum pronuntiauerunt:
>
>> Gallias Caesar subegit, Nicomedes Caesarem.
>> Ecce Caesar nunc triumphat, qui subegit Gallias,
>> Nicomedes non triumphat, qui subegit Caesarem.
>
> Finally, in his triumph over Gaul, his men chanted, among the other songs soldiers usually come out with as they march behind the chariot, the following most notorious lines:
>
>> Caesar had his way with Gaul; Nicomedes had his way with Caesar:
>> Behold now Caesar, conqueror of Gaul, in triumph,
>> Not so, Nicomedes, conqueror of Caesar.

These verses reflect a poetic composition that is comparable, in tone and attitude, to the sceptic epigram as well as to some epigrams of Catullus. To dismiss the virile sexuality of a prominent man is an example of the 'politics of immorality' as a homo-social game played by the senatorial elite.[34] Not by chance, Caesar's homosexuality and the relation with the king of Bithynia are also the target of the only non-anonymous poem present in the *Lives of the Caesars*. These are the already mentioned 'notorious lines' by Licinius Calvus (Suet. *Iul.* 49.1; fr. 17 Courtney 1993):

> Pudicitiae eius famam nihil quidem praeter Nicomedis contubernium laesit, graui tamen et perenni obprobrio et ad omnium conuicia exposito. Omitto Calui Licini notissimos uersus:
>
>> Bithynia quicquid
>> et pedicator Caesaris umquam habuit.
>
> There were no stains on his reputation for manliness, apart from his stay with King Nicomedes, which was a constant source of criticism and was mentioned in taunts from every quarter. I shall not discuss the notorious lines of Licinius Calvus:
>
>> Whatever Bithynia ever owned
>> and Caesar's buggerer.

It is interesting to note that the verb *omitto* introduces a *praeteritio*, used by Suetonius to declare that he will not discuss the verses, but which has the

---

[34] Langlands 2006: 348–9 assumes that sexual slanders against Caesar and Augustus 'have a Republican flavour', comparable to charges moved by Cicero against a number of opponents.

opposite effect of giving them greater emphasis instead.³⁵ Calvus' verses are notorious (*notissimi*) and this could be a reason for quoting just a snippet of the poem. According to Suetonius, Caesar's friendship with Nicomedes was the worst injury to his reputation, causing him a *perenne opbrobrium* and taunts from every quarter. Thus, Calvus' verses on the same topic are not the only authorial products 'omitted' and at the same time quoted through the *praeteritio*: Suetonius 'won't mention' two more literary products by the elite, namely the speeches of Dolabella and Curio and the edicts of Bibulus.³⁶ Outside the *praeteritio*, he mentions the invectives of a certain Octavius and of Gaius Memmius, then a short extract from a letter by Cicero.³⁷ At the end of this list of (not only) omitted 'authorial' invectives on the homosexuality and effeminacy of Caesar, Suetonius quotes the above-mentioned anonymous verses, as to indicate an exegetical path to their interpretation, in a direction that would suggest the authors' belonging to the aristocratic milieu. Owing to their position, these verses seem to assume a special status, which endows them with a certain kind of finality and authority, and value as evidence.

Earlier in the *Life of Caesar* (*Iul.* 22.2), Suetonius reports Caesar's response to a similar insult about his effeminacy by an unmentioned individual. After acquiring Gallia Cisalpina, Illyricum and then Gallia Comata as his proconsular provinces, Caesar cannot stop boasting about his happiness in spite of his unwilling and complaining opponents. He is described as 'prepared to jump upon the heads of all his opponents' (*insultaturum omnium capitibus*), a gesture that according to some could also be taken in an obscene sense (referring to *fellatio*), as Caesar's response seems to suggest.³⁸ When someone replied that this would be a difficult thing for a woman to do, he answered: 'in Syria too Semiramis was queen and the Amazons once held sway over a great part of Asia'. While he does not reject the accusation of being a woman, Caesar deals with the invectives somewhat unexpectedly. As Corbeill points out,³⁹ Caesar deliberately created a public persona perfectly fitting to the insults by his opponents and consequently breaking with the morals pursued by the conservative factions. From this perspective, one can see how further signs of the senatorial voice against Caesar's 'transgressing' behaviours are those offered by the anonymous verses, which, as in the case of the passion for Nicomedes, expose moral or political behaviours that break with the

---

³⁵ On the use of *omitto* in Tacitus' *Dialogus de Oratoribus*, cf. Winter (in this volume).
³⁶ Suet. *Iul.* 49.1 *Praetereo actiones Dolabellae et Curionis patris [. . .]*. 2 *missa etiam facio edicta Bibuli*.
³⁷ Suet. *Iul.* 49.2–3.   ³⁸ Corbeill 1996: 196; Hallett 2015: 417.   ³⁹ Corbeill 2004: 137.

senatorial tradition.⁴⁰ Dio's passage on the triumphal song on Nicomedes confirms the political arguments for the triumphal songs against Caesar. In Dio's narrative the soldiers, after jesting about Caesar's affairs with Cleopatra and Nicomedes, appear to sing a 're-interpretation' of a nursery song in which Caesar's authoritarian turn into a genuine monarchy is affirmed.⁴¹

As I said, the reaction to the anonymous verses can also be useful for understanding the political value and the potential harmfulness attributed to these poems. As Morelli has pointed out, the context of the triumph, which activates the deviation from the norm, renders these verses harmless in terms of political damage.⁴² This idea could be confirmed by Dio's passage, which highlights Caesar's peaceful reaction to the triumphal songs: he is said to be delighted by the *parrhesia* of his soldiers (Dio 43.20.4 πάνυ ἔχαιρεν ὅτι τοσαύτῃ πρὸς αὐτὸν παρρησίᾳ), probably because he was aware that a degree of transgression was allowed in the triumphal ceremonies. However, Dio also singles out the poem on his intercourse with Nicomedes as the one exception to Caesar's otherwise tolerant behaviour to the triumphal songs: 'at this he was greatly vexed and manifestly pained; he attempted to defend himself, denying the affair upon oath, whereupon he incurred all the more ridicule'.⁴³ It may be telling that Suetonius refers to this poem as 'most notorious' or 'most widespread' (*illud uulgatissimum*), implying a circulation that would transcend the specific performance as well as the triumph's original performers and audience. It seems to me that as soon as the insults exit the socio-cultural frame of the triumphs it becomes more difficult to tolerate them. A rumour becomes more intimidating when it is disseminated by innumerable anonymous voices that stop coinciding with the original voices of the soldiers.⁴⁴ Accordingly, if libels by the authorial voices of the elite were tolerated and deliberately provoked by Caesar, when they are anonymously disseminated through all the people, the device of recognition of the enemy is turned into something much less controllable. Going beyond the specific

---

⁴⁰ I am close to the view expressed in Zadorojnyi 2011: 113 as regards graffiti: 'the polyphonous literary transcript of elite identity mobilises graffiti for their communicative and socio-political alterity—which it itself fastidiously creates'.

⁴¹ Dio 43.20.3: 'Finally, on top of all this, they all shouted out together that if you do right, you will be punished, but if wrong, you will be king' (all translations of Dio are taken from Cary's Loeb). Cf. Hor. *Ep.* 1.1.59–61 and Porphyrio's comment; O'Neill 2003: 5.

⁴² Morelli 2000: 290, 2001: 61–2; differently Cupaiuolo 1993: 42–3 does not consider the deviation from the norm affecting the *carmina triumphalia*: according to him, these verses, of senatorial origin, are considered vituperative actions *tout court* against Caesar, becoming a tool of 'political awareness'.

⁴³ Dio 43.20.4. See Corbeill 2004: 136 n. 153. ⁴⁴ Yavetz 1983: 220.

military moment, the anonymous background allows the poems to become adaptable to different situations. Everyone could appropriate a political message which, due to measured rhythms, alliterations, repetitions and wordplays, was purposefully conceived to be easily memorized and consequently, as both Dio and Suetonius confirm, to be repeated and spread everywhere.[45]

The history of Julius Caesar, in particular, the narrative of Brutus' and Cassius' conspiracy against him,[46] also offers a case of declared appropriation of anonymous writings by the elite. The sources describe an anonymous written campaign instigating Brutus' reaction against Caesar's dictatorship.[47] Graffiti were left in places linked to the political life of Brutus – e.g. the tribunal seat – but also under the statue of Brutus' ancestor, Brutus the Elder, to push the urgency of saving the Republic. In a true *peroratio*, Cassius aims at persuading Brutus to listen to these unnamed messages: his main argument is that the writings are by those with a high social profile rather than of the lower classes. Even if it was probably the senatorial elite who disseminated the written propaganda, this episode makes it clear how the anonymous feature allowed people to appropriate the possible context behind the nameless words, claiming them for any author, any source, any cause. Suetonius too mentions a sentence under the statue of Brutus the Elder, as well as two septenarii written under that of Caesar.[48] These verses propose the opposing couple of Brutus the Elder, who eliminated the monarchy, and Caesar, who instead reactivated it: thus, the anonymous written campaign and its poetic response can be considered a remarkable socio-political signal to understand the climate which led to Caesar's murder.

Sub diuo Augusto nondum hominibus uerba sua periculosa erant, iam molesta [49]

After Caesar, Augustus is central to our understanding of how powerful individuals at Rome perceived and reacted to anonymous invectives. It was during the Principate that slander and libel started to represent a problem and, consequently, we can witness a shift from authorial self-censorship to

---

[45] Horsfall 2012 gives illuminating hints on the matter of memorized song (by the plebs) as an instrument of politics. In particular, see pp. 38–9, 65, 111–2.
[46] Zadorojnyi 2011: 124–5.
[47] Plut. *Iul.* 62.7; Cic. *Brut.* 9.5–7; App. *B. Civ.* 2.16.112–3; Dio 44.12.3.
[48] Suet. *Iul.* 80.3 (*uers. pop.* 5 Courtney 1993) *subscripsere quidam Luci Bruti statuae: 'utinam uiueres!' item ipsius Caesaris: Brutus, quia reges eiecit, consul primus factus est: / hic, quia consules eiecit, rex postremo factus est.*
[49] Sen. *Ben.* 3.27.1 'under the deified Augustus, it was not yet true that a man's utterances endangered his life, but they did cause him trouble', translation by Basore (Loeb).

legislative censorship. Yet we can also detect a double stance. On the one hand, Augustus seems to show the same patient behaviour as Caesar. On the other, we will observe how the evidence of some legal actions belies this apparent tolerance.

Tacitus *Annals* 4.34.4 gives us Cremutius Cordus' ideal speech in defence of his praise of Brutus and Cassius, reported by clients of Sejanus.[50] This represents a crucial passage, since it reasserts again how Caesar and Augustus were indulgent towards defamatory writings. The doubt as to whether their actions are to be ascribed to forbearance or to wisdom (*moderatione magis an sapientia*) is a rhetorical device[51] and it suggests that Tacitus considers the behaviour of the Caesars to be dictated by a certain political strategy. Through Cremutius' words, Tacitus explains how persecution is a form of recognition. It is a concept which has been defined as 'la più lapidaria critica al meccanismo della censura'.[52] Tacitus' passage provides us with the names of well-known people who 'signed' vituperative actions against Augustus and Caesar: Antony through letters, Brutus through speeches, Bibaculus and Catullus through their poems. Despite the nonchalance exhibited by Augustus, the sources make it clear how the situation against compositions without a clear authorial source started to be taken more seriously, showing a consciousness and increasing worry on the part of the powerful. I would say that the absence of authors made a new problem present.[53] First, we know from Tacitus himself that Augustus was the first to have employed the *lex maiestatis*[54] in a trial against defamatory pamphlets (*cognitio de famosis libellis*).[55] In this case, the decision was taken in consequence of Cassius Severus' licentious writings (*procacia scripta*) against distinguished people (Tac. *Ann.* 1.72.1):

> Nam legem maiestatis reduxerat, cui nomen apud ueteres idem, sed alia in iudicium ueniebant, si quis proditione exercitum aut plebem seditionibus, denique male gesta re publica maiestatem populi Romani minuisset: facta arguebantur, dicta inpune erant. Primus Augustus cognitionem de famosis

---

[50] On this passage, cf. O'Gorman 2000: 97–105.   [51] Canfora 1993: 255.   [52] Ibid.: 256.
[53] I disagree with Cupaiuolo 1993: 55–60 when he maintains that in Augustus' age slandering verses are not to be interpreted as a protest against the established order. The verses on Augustus that survive are not numerous, but the juristic literature that we have provides us with enough evidence on how Augustus considered anonymous verses as a threat.
[54] On the *lex Iulia Maiestatis*, a law working during the Principate and probably created by Caesar rather than by Augustus, see Peachin 2015: 516 n. 54 with a bibliographical survey on the two positions.
[55] Levick 19992: 151–2; Pettinger 2012: 88 and n. 62; Peachin 2015: 529–30 and n. 102 with a delineation on the issue of dating.

> libellis specie legis eius tractauit, commotus Cassii Seueri libidine, qua uiros feminasque inlustris procacibus scriptis diffamauerat;

> He had brought back the law of treason. This had the same name in the time of the ancients, but different matters came to court, such as the impairment of an army by betrayal or of the plebs by sedition or, in fine, of the sovereignty of the Roman people by maladministration of the government. Actions were prosecuted, talk had impunity. Augustus was the first to handle a trial of defamatory documents under the category of that law, being roused by the passion with which Cassius Severus had defamed illustrious men and ladies in provocative writings.[56]

Second, turning to Suetonius, Augustus is depicted as not being frightened by 'pamphlets or poems defaming him circulating in the senate' (Suet. *Aug.* 55.1):

> Etiam sparsos de se in curia famosos libellos nec expauit et magna cura redarguit ac ne requisitis quidem auctoribus id modo censuit, cognoscendum posthac de iis, qui libellos aut carmina ad infamiam cuiuspiam sub alieno nomine edant.

> Even when pamphlets insulting him were circulating in the senate, he was not alarmed but took great care to refute them. Without enquiring about the authors, he merely prescribed that in future anyone who under a false name produced pamphlets or poems defaming someone should be brought to trial.

The mention of the *curia* provides us with the spatial and socio-political dimension of these messages, which are confuted by Augustus without any search for the authors. But the emotional response, perfectly controlled by the *princeps*, is one thing; quite another is the perception of a threat in the hostile political propaganda, indicated by the authoritarian legal reaction. In fact, Augustus prescribed trials (*id modo censuit, cognoscendum* ...) for everyone who would in the future produce pamphlets or defamatory poems under a false name (*sub alieno nomine*).

Remarkably, after the anonymous verses, we find here the introduction of a new kind of literary production elusive of authorship: *pseudonymous* writing.[57] Possibly, from Augustus' point of view, defamatory writings potentially bringing 'anyone' into play as their author could represent a threat even worse than anonymity. We might ask whether the 'other' name could be an invented one – a genuine pseudonym – or the name of a recognizable individual. It is possible, as we will observe below,[58] that

---

[56] All translations of Tacitus are by Woodman (Hackett).   [57] Peirano 2012: 47.   [58] p. 156.

invectives circulated under another living person's name, as in the case of Publius Rufus, in order to make someone else guilty in Augustus' eyes.[59] Immediately after the above-mentioned passage, Suetonius refers to an edict against spiteful or malicious jokes (56.1 *iocis . . . inuidiosis aut petulantibus*), but we do not find further evidence for these.

A later juridical text (but dealing with measures taken in the Augustan period, see p. 155), the commentary *Ad edictum* by Ulpian (quoted in the *Digest*) tells us more about these repressive measures against literary products without clear authorship, and it includes anonymous and pseudonymous writings.[60] The passage in question comes from a wider context regarding the books *ad infamiam alicuius pertinentes*, 'concerning someone's bad reputation'. Apparently, Ulpian quotes first the *lex Cornelia de iniuriis*,[61] a law from the period of Sulla contrasting, among other things, defamatory books (*D.* 47.10.5.9 *Si quis librum <u>ad infamiam alicuius</u> pertinentem scripserit composuerit ediderit doloue malo fecerit, quo quid eorum fieret*) even if edited under a different name or without a name (*etiamsi alterius nomine ediderit uel sine nomine*). Together with a pecuniary penalty, the condition of being *intestabilis* was prescribed. Ulpian then mentions a subsequent *Senatus Consultum* (*SC*) including anonymous authors of epigrams or of different unwritten forms of defamation (*D.* 47.10.5.10 *Eadem poena ex ex senatus consulto tenetur etiam is, qui* ἐπιγράμματα *aliudue quid sine scriptura in notam aliquorum produxerit*).[62] A penalty was prescribed also for those who took part in disseminating these compositions, purchasing or selling them (*item qui emendum uendendumue curauerit*).[63] Particularly interesting is the final passage of the *Digest*'s quotation, which specifies that the *SC* is necessary when the name of the

---

[59] Slater 2014: 296.   [60] D. 47.10.5.8–11, Ulp. 56 *ad ed.*
[61] D. 47.10.5 *pr.*, Ulp. 56 *ad ed. lex Cornelia de iniuriis competit ei . . .*
[62] It has been maintained that these could be drawings, graffiti, sculptures (Cerami 2015: 34), as well as oral songs or jokes (Smith 1951: 175).
[63] Bauman 1974: 37–9 following others assumes that the indication of the books which are anonymous or written under a different name is not part of the text of the *lex Cornelia*, but already an extract of the subsequent *SC*. Nevertheless, the other references by juridical texts to this *SC* talk about the persecution of *carmina famosa*, *psalteria* and *cantica* (D. 28.1.18.1, Ulp. 1 *ad Sab.*; Paul. *Sent.* 5.4.15; 5.4.16), expressions fitting *epigrammata* and non-written forms quoted in D. 47.10.5.10. Consequently, even if the issue is extremely complex to define (as demonstrated by the extensive scholarly controversy on this point), what we read in the juridical texts is about an *SC* extending the *lex Cornelia*, already devoted to 'books defaming someone' (*libri ad infamiam alicuius pertinentes*), whether anonymous or pseudonymous, to non-written forms of slander. It follows that the prohibition from buying or selling them explains how non-written compositions such as songs, jokes or performed poems constituted a risk in so far as they could later be published (Smith 1951: 175); see Manfredini 1979: 205–45 for a critique of Bauman's interpretation and a lucid analysis on the legal texts linked to the *SC*.

person who suffered the injury is missing (*D*. 47.10.6 *quod senatus consultum necessarium est cum nomen adiectum non est eius, in quem factum est*). This specification proves the presence of invectives where the labelling target is absent, probably due to an attempt to avoid any possible punishment: the political message is then left open to different interpretations but in its context it is arguably working as an in-joke. It follows that the paranoia of the people brought into play is further increased by an invective which 'could' be addressed to them only hypothetically, arousing suspicion and a sense of persecution. The difficulty in managing invectives that potentially do not attack anyone is that anyone is permitted to seek redress for the offence. Consequently, the *Senatus Consultum* got around this difficulty by establishing that these invectives were to be put down with a *publica quaestio*. It was not only the offended person who had the right to sue the offender for libel – anyone and everyone could do it.

As has been argued, Ulpian is referring to repressive measures taken by Augustus, in particular, to the *SC* issued to extend the *lex Cornelia*.[64] The *SC* would have been mentioned by Suetonius too with the juridical expression *id modo censuit* [. . .], even if Suetonius reports trials only against pseudonymous books and poems.[65] Curiously, after the verses on Caesar, which name him in almost all instances, all the anonymous poems on Augustus quoted by Suetonius lack the emperor's name, fitting perfectly with the circumstance sketched out by the *SC*.

A further piece of evidence to capture Augustus' attitude and the sociohistorical frame stimulating this literary production is offered by Cassius Dio.[66] He maintains that Augustus did not confine himself merely to ordering a search for anonymous authors who wrote vituperative pamphlets (βιβλία ἄττα ἐφ' ὕβρει), a measure in line with those attested by Suetonius and the juridical texts. According to Dio, Augustus' disquieting request to the aediles was to burn the pamphlets found in the city,

---

[64] Smith 1951: 173; Bauman 1970: 254 and n. 30; Bauman 1974: 37–51; Cerami 2015: 33; Levick 19992: 151 and n. 84 talks about the necessity of Augustus finding rulings that the defamatory writings were to be construed as constituting a diminution of *maiestas*; she does not mention the *SC*; already Mommsen 1899: 565; 800 assumes that the *SC* would have punished written and non-written forms of slander (anonymous and pseudonymous) under the ambit of the *maiestas*; see Giltaij 2018: 26–33 for a recent discussion on these legal measures.

[65] Scholars disagree on the interpretation. Bauman 1970: 251–7; Bauman 1974: 38–9 and *passim*; Smith 1951: 179 n. 6 connect the *SC* mentioned by juridical texts to Suetonius' *Aug*. 55; *censeo* is actually the technical verb referring to decrees issued by the Senate: see *TLL* s.v. *censeo*: 794–6; Muciaccia 1984 interprets Suetonius as evidence of a *cognitio extra ordinem* by Augustus against pseudonymous defamatory writing, while, according to him, the *SC* would deal with a *publica quaestio* only against slanders *in ignotam personam*.

[66] Dio 56.27.1; see Swan 2004: 286–7; Howley 2017: 229 and n. 90.

a repressive measure which reminds us of well-known literary dystopian scenarios.⁶⁷ Dio offers another valuable account of a situation which, in this case connects malcontent and pseudonymous writings (Dio 55.27.1–3):⁶⁸

> Now the masses, distressed by the famine and the tax and the losses sustained in the fire, were ill at ease, and they not only openly discussed numerous plans for a revolution, but also posted at night even more numerous pamphlets. Word was given out that all this had been planned and managed by one Publius Rufus, but suspicion was directed to others; for as Rufus could neither have devised nor accomplished any of these things, it was believed that others, making use of his name, were planning a revolution.

Dio focuses on a famine, dateable to 6 CE and associated with other calamities such as a fire in the city. The crowd is portrayed as discussing plans for revolution, but also as posting numerous pamphlets at night. According to Dio, rumours had it that at the heart of this event was an aristocrat called Publius Rufus, who has been plausibly identified with the Plautius Rufus quoted by Suetonius as one of the conspirators of the Augustan age, together with Aemilius Paullus.⁶⁹ Nevertheless, since Rufus was considered incapable of planning such deeds, suspicion was redirected to others, who were believed to be making use of Rufus' name to plan a revolution. Suetonius' connection with L. Aemilius Paullus is key to interpreting Dio's evidence. Aemilius Paullus was the husband of Augustus' granddaughter Julia the younger. Both were central to the conspiratorial *factio* against Augustus: a *scholium* to Juvenal 6.158 explains how Julia was relegated by Augustus after her husband Paullus was condemned to death due to a crime of high treason (*maiestatis crimine*).⁷⁰ Furthermore, Suetonius' *Life of Claudius* assumes that Aemilia Lepida, the daughter of Paullus and Julia, was repudiated by Claudius since 'her parents had offended Augustus'.⁷¹ Thus, Rufus' role has been interpreted as that of an intermediary with the plebs, who must have had an executive part in Julia's *factio*. Let me emphasize how this mediation between an

---

⁶⁷ Even if it is not a case of censorship against anonymous literary products, it is worth mentioning the burning of Titus Labienus' historical books by an *SC* under Augustus (Sen. *contr.* 10 *praef.* 4–8), on which see Howley 2017: 217 and n. 25, 223. Pettinger 2012: 89 argues that Labienus suffered the penalty of the *lex maiestatis*.
⁶⁸ See Swan 2004: 183–5.
⁶⁹ Suet. *Aug.* 19.1; those who support the identification: Levick 1976: 304–5; Levick 19992: 40; Pani 1979: 36; Rohr Vio 2000: 271; Pettinger 2012: 85; *contra* Swan 2004: 184.
⁷⁰ *Schol. in Iuu.* 6.158.1–2; *damnatio memoriae* followed: cf. *CIL* VI 4499 for the erasure of Paullus' name from public inscriptions; on these events connected to Julia and Paullus, cf. Levick 1976.
⁷¹ Suet. *Claud.* 26.1 *Parentes eius Augustum offenderant.*

absent plaintiff and the plebs, here depicted as openly discussing plans for a revolution, has been specially fulfilled through the use of an 'other name' which had been exposed by an investigation promoted by Augustus.[72] Dio does not mention how the story ended; he only writes that there were several accusations among much turmoil, which lasted until the end of the famine. Nevertheless, this narrative's reconstruction allows us to understand the sensitivity of an 'other name' and how Augustus was capable of fighting whatever or whoever was behind that name. It is *sub iudice* whether the passage of Dio is to be linked with the *SC* we have discussed (and eventually with Suetonius' *Aug.* 55).[73] If we take Pettinger's view that the events of 6 CE are unrelated to the *SC*, we would face a progression in censorial measures concerning pseudonymous 'enemies' over different periods and different kinds of crimes, from defamation to high treason.[74]

Tracking back to the triumviral period, we find a famous anonymous epigram on Octavian quoted by Suetonius, composed in a similar context of malcontent as that described by Dio: a famine resulted from the closure of Pompey's granary in 39–38 BCE. These are the 'very famous verses' on the so called 'dinner of the twelve gods' (δωδεκάθεος), a banquet organized by Octavian in which guests were requested to dress as gods.[75] Octavian himself dressed in the costume of Apollo, already prefiguring the

---

[72] Levick 1999²: 40–1; Pani 1979: 35–8; Rohr Vio 2000: 270–80; Pettinger 2012: 93–6; another case worth mentioning is the *asperrima epistula* against Augustus circulated by the plebeian Junius Novatus under the name of Agrippa Postumus (Suet. *Aug.* 51.1 *Cum ille* [sc. *Iunius Nouatus*] *Agrippae iuuenis nomine asperrimam de se epistulam in uulgus edidisset*, 'when Novatus had publicly circulated the most bitter letter concerning Augustus under the name of the young Agrippa'): the name of Agrippa could have been used by people from the anti-Tiberian faction, who made him a 'mouthpiece' of the opposition (Pettinger 2012: 117–22); Novatus, who was no more than a disseminator of the letter, was simply fined, while Agrippa, already *abdicatus*, was relegated (6 CE according to Levick 1999²: 237 n. 84).

[73] Mommsen 1899: 800 considers Suet. *Aug.* 55, Tac. *Ann.* 1.72 and Dio 55.27.1–3 all refer to the same events which led to an *SC* applying the *maiestas* to defamatory writings; according to Bauman 1974: 27–51, the events of 6 CE led to the *lex Cornelia* being extended through an *SC* (the one quoted by the *Digest* and perhaps mentioned by Suetonius) to anonymous and pseudonymous defamatory writings. Then in 8 CE, defamatory writings were punished in relation to the *lex maiestatis* (this is the context described by Tacitus as regards Cassius Severus); Pettinger 2012: 87–93 disagrees with this reconstruction, considering the revolts of 6 CE 'unrelated to the question of defamatory writing': since Rufus' issue concerns seditious writings, he relates it to the *lex maiestatis*. Muciaccia 1984 considers the events presented by Dio to be subsequent to the decisions mentioned by Suetonius; Levick 1999²: 237 n. 84 does not reject the possibility that Suet. *Aug.* 55.1 may be related to the events presented by Dio; Slater 2014: 296 has no doubts in considering Dio's passage to be connected with that of Suetonius.

[74] The *SC* has no certain dating; it is generally dated to the earlier years of Augustus' Principate (or more precisely in 6 CE, if connected to the events related by Dio). The first case of *maiestas* applied to Severus' defamation writings has been dated mostly to 8 or 12 CE. Smith 1951: 179 argues that the *maiestas* could represent the acme of Augustus' repression.

[75] Cupaiuolo 1993: 58–60; Scott 1933; Cresci Marrone 2002; Slater 2014: 297–8.

assimilation with the god that would gradually become more explicit (*Aug.* 70.1; *vers. pop.* 8 Courtney 1993):[76]

> Cena quoque eius secretior in fabulis fuit, quae uulgo δωδεκάθεος uocabatur; in qua deorum dearumque habitu discubuisse conuiuas et ipsum pro Apolline ornatum non **Antoni modo epistulae** singulorum nomina amarissime enumerantis exprobrant, sed et sine auctore notissimi uersus:
>
>> cum primum istorum conduxit mensa choragum,
>>   sexque deos uidit Mallia sexque deas,
>> impia dum Phoebi Caesar mendacia ludit,
>>   dum noua diuorum cenat adulteria:
>> omnia se a terris tunc numina declinarunt,
>>   fugit et auratos Iuppiter ipse thronos.
>
> auxit cenae rumorem summa tunc in ciuitate penuria ac fames, adclamatumque est postridie: omne frumentum deos comedisse et Caesarem esse plane Apollinem, sed Tortorem, quo cognomine is deus quadam in parte urbis colebatur.

> There were also stories about a rather secret dinner he arranged, which was commonly referred to as the dinner of the Twelve Gods. For this, the guests reclined in the dress of one or other of the gods or goddesses, with Augustus himself attired as Apollo. Not **only do Antony's letters** take him to task for this most acerbically, naming each of the guests, but there are also some notorious verses whose author is unknown:
>
>> As soon as that company of villains had hired their costumes,
>> Mallia saw six gods and six goddesses,
>> While Caesar impiously dared to play at being Apollo
>> And represented new adulteries of the gods at his banquet.
>> At this time all deities removed themselves from earth
>> And Jupiter himself abandoned his golden throne.
>
> Stories about the banquet were fuelled by the fact that the city was at that time suffering from hunger and food shortages and on the following day there was a protest that all the food had been eaten by the gods and that Caesar was indeed Apollo but Apollo the Tormenter (the god is worshipped under this title in one part of the city).

As already acknowledged, the passage fits perfectly with the political climate of the triumvirate marked by polemical toing and froing.[77] In

---

[76] Suffice to refer to Miller 2009, particularly ch. 1.   [77] Cresci Marrone 2002: 27 and n. 21.

Suetonius' introduction to the verses we find an interesting combination of different kinds of political vituperation. The first criticism of the dinner comes from Antony's letters, which acerbically name the participants, still embodying that Republican spirit of 'ridiculing someone by name' we mentioned above apropos of Lucilius' *Satires*. These letters appear also in Tacitus,[78] and Dio,[79] who explains how they were conceived as a public message to the people. More precisely, according to Dio, Octavian and Antony argued against each other through private messages, while Octavian talked to people through speeches, and Antony through public letters.

In Suetonius' passage, together with Antony's voice, there are some notorious unauthored verses, which recall the safer and most widespread habit of criticizing political figures in the early Empire. Not surprisingly, the verses also do not reveal the name of any table-companions present at the dinner. This is a case of anonymity with a double reference (which affects both addresser and addressees), the kind that Augustus will later make sure to punish with a specific sentence. Presumably, at the beginning of Octavian's political career, we still find this mixture of free speaking, as per the Republican way, and of the later, 'doubly-redacted' way of slandering.

The context of these verses is the same as the one mentioned by Dio, with the rumour of the dinner increased by hunger and food shortages. It seems to me that, although not in verse, Suetonius mentions two more lampoons on the event which presumably circulated orally (*adclamatumque est postridie*). The lampoons say that all the corn has been eaten by the gods, then make a pun insisting on the nature of Apollo's name which contrasts with the absence of Augustus's name: Caesar was indeed Apollo, but the Tormenter version.[80] A curious aetiological detail explains the use of the epithet, which was common in the god's worship in the *Vicus Sandalarius*, the part of the town between the *Carinae* and the Esquiline where the dinner happened.[81] Another crucial term playing with the name of Augustus in this passage may be *auxit* (< *augeo*), which refers to the

---

[78] Tacitus highlights the biting nature of Antony's letters, quoted together with the speeches by Brutus: *Ann*. 4.34.4 *Antonii epistulae Bruti contiones falsa quidem in Augustum probra set multa cum acerbitate habent*. After all, *asperrima* is also the letter 'by' Agrippa Postumus, see n. 72.

[79] Dio 50.2.1 'These were the charges they made against each other and were in a way their justification of their conduct, and they communicated them to each other partly by private letters and partly by public speeches on the part of Caesar and public messages on the part of Antony'.

[80] Scott 1933: 32 sharply offers the parallel of Antony's epithets χαριδότης, 'joy-giver' and μειλίχιος, 'gentle', which to the many become Ὠμηστής, 'savage' and Ἀγριώνιος, 'of wild nature' (Plut. *Ant*. 24.3–4).

[81] Coarelli 1993: 57–8 argued that the epithet could be related to a statue of Apollo skinning Marsyas erected in the *Vicus Sandalarius*. It is interesting to notice how Pompey the Great's *Domus rostrata* was in the *Carinae*, close to the *Vicus*: this suggests a strong presence of the clientele of Pompey's son,

increasing rumours. At the time of the dinner Octavian had not become 'Augustus' yet, but it is possible that Suetonius is playing on a pun that became common later: Augustus as the *auctor*, 'the increaser', who is capable of increasing only negative things, in this case the rumours rather than the food. As regards the composition of the verses, it seems plausible to suppose in this case too a reaction by Augustus' opponents, and plenty of names have been offered by scholars,[82] although nothing can be said with certainty. What is certain is the 'poetic' reaction: an anonymous poem aroused by the circles of influential people who thought that the absence of their name, as well as the absence of the addressee's name, was the best way to turn discontent into a plausible, successful popular protest.

We are now aware of the fact that from the age of Augustus the creation of political publications (or of texts that were potentially 'written' and publishable), whether anonymous (in terms of either addresser or addressee) or pseudonymous, started to be defined more clearly (*ioci inuidiosi aut petulantes* (*Aug.* 56.1); *libelli sub alieno nomine* (55.1); *libri ad infamiam alicuius pertinentes* ... *alterius nomine uel sine nomine* (*D.* 47.10.5.9); *carmina incertis auctoribus* (Tac. *Ann.* 1.72.4); *sine auctore* ... *uersus* (*Aug.* 70.1)). This production increased gradually, alongside Augustus' repressive measures. Suetonius claims an ambiguity in Augustus' attitude: the emperor shows a serene detachment from the matter (the propagandistic, programmatic and strategic *sapientia* mentioned by Tacitus) while implementing specific legal actions to counteract the political movements that opposed him.

Tiberius and His Revised Version of Atreus

After Augustus, Tiberius too had to deal with a political protest expressed in anonymous poetic form. Particularly interesting is a letter quoted by Suetonius from Augustus to his stepson, which, on the one hand reasserts Augustus' 'strategic tolerance'[83] against defamation, while on the other enlightens us with respect to a less programmatic impulse to anger starting from Tiberius (Suet. *Aug.* 51.3):

> Tiberio quoque de eadem re, sed uiolentius apud se per epistulam conquerenti ita rescripsit: "Aetati tuae, mi Tiberi, noli in hac re indulgere et nimium

---

Sextus Pompeius, and then a possible responsibility in the creation of the epigram (cf. Cresci Marroni 2002: 30 and n. 36 with bibliography).
[82] The main assumptions are Cassius of Parma, Asinius Pollio and Mark Antony.
[83] Roman 2014: 168.

indignari quemquam esse, qui de me male loquatur; satis est enim, si hoc habemus ne quis nobis male facere possit."

Moreover, when Tiberius complained rather forcefully about the same thing in a letter, Augustus replied: 'My Tiberius, do not give way to your youthful impulses or get too angry at anyone who speaks ill of me. We should be satisfied if we have the means to prevent anyone from doing us ill.'

Augustus' concern about Tiberius seems more than justified. According to Suetonius, when Tiberius takes over, his ambivalent behaviour will reveal much less self-control (*Tib.* 28.1):

Sed et aduersus conuicia malosque rumores et famosa de se ac suis carmina firmus ac patiens subinde iactabat in ciuitate libera linguam mentemque liberas esse debere; et quondam senatu cognitionem de eius modi criminibus ac reis flagitante: 'Non tantum,' inquit, 'otii habemus, ut implicare nos pluribus negotiis debeamus; si hanc fenestram aperueritis, nihil aliud agi sinetis: omnium inimicitiae hoc praetexto ad uos deferentur.'

More than that, he was self-contained and patient in the face of abuse and slander, and of lampoons on himself and his family, often asserting that in a free country there should be free speech and free thought. When the senate on one occasion demanded that cognizance be taken of such offences and those guilty of them, he said: 'We have not enough spare time to warrant involving ourselves in more affairs; if you open this loophole you will find no time for any other business; it will be an excuse for laying everybody's quarrels before you.'

First, Tiberius shows self-containment and patience in facing a hostile anonymous campaign made of abuses, slander and defamatory verses against himself and his family. Apparently pursuing the censorial policy towards freedom of speech which marks Tiberius' principate and which culminates in the trial of Cremutius Cordus, the Senate proposes to Tiberius a *cognitio*, a 'process' against these forms of defamation.[84] Nevertheless, in ensuring a fierce advocacy of both free-speaking and free-thinking, the emperor sticks to the policy of not prosecuting such offences (*Tib.* 66.1):[85]

---

[84] Pettinger 2012: 91–3 suggests that the Senate is here proposing to charge these crimes with *maiestas*. Since libel and slander were never treated as *maiestas* but rather under the heading of *iniuria* (cf. the SC), Tiberius would have come back with the impossibility for the Senate of 'opening such a window'. Nevertheless, in Tac. *Ann.* 1.73.4, the anonymous defamatory verses against Tiberius and his mother seem to provoke the question by the praetor Pompeius Macer whether to admit cases of treason for trial by assigning jurors to them (see Goodyear 1981: 152). Tiberius replied that the laws should be enforced (cf. Suet. *Tib.* 58).

[85] Rutledge 2007: 116.

> Urebant insuper anxiam mentem uaria undique conuicia, nullo non damnatorum omne probri genus coram uel per libellos in orchestra positos ingerente. Quibus quidem diuersissime adficiebatur, modo ut prae pudore ignota et celata cuncta cuperet, nonnumquam eadem contemneret et proferret ultro atque uulgaret.

> His troubled mind was further tormented by varied taunts from all quarters, for every single one of the condemned heaped all kinds of abuse on him either in his presence or through placards set up in the front row of the theatre. He reacted to these in very different ways, sometimes, through shame, wanting to keep them all unknown and hidden, sometimes making light of the same accusations and himself repeating and publicizing them.

In this second passage, Tiberius' tolerance is described as tested by the incessant reproaches, provoking a reaction close to a genuine anxiety disorder. In this case too the *princeps* is portrayed as dealing with a double kind of defamation: the first represents the straightest and freest form of communicating an offence – directly by the addresser to the addressed target, evidently possible since the addressers are people already condemned to death. The second brings into play the anonymity of the author, as Suetonius mentions pamphlets placed in the *orchestra* (*per libellos in orchestra positos*). Like the *curia*, the *orchestra* too is a socio-political space which serves as a stage for elite action. Tacitus confirms the poetic nature and the anonymity of these compositions when he talks about *carmina incertis auctoribus*, satirizing Tiberius' cruelty, arrogance and bad relationship with his mother Livia.[86] As in the case of the poems on Augustus, the verses on Tiberius in Suetonius' *Lives of the Caesars* never mention Tiberius' name.

In describing Tiberius' 'schizoid' reaction, Suetonius adds one more detail worth discussing. The *princeps* is on the one hand ashamed of the insults, and desires to keep them secret. On the other, he is portrayed not only as showing contempt towards libel and slander, but as allowing them circulation and – a point that I would like to stress –*publishing* them in the process. The use of the verb *uulgo* conveys the action of 'publishing a literary work':[87] the picture of the emperor becoming the publisher of the anonymous verses against himself sounds paradoxical, but possibly marks a further step in the reaction of powerful men faced with this sort of phenomenon. Compared with the conventional censorship exercised earlier by Augustus, Tiberius seems to explore a new approach to control the

---

[86] Tac. *Ann.* 1.72.4 *Hunc quoque asperauere carmina incertis auctoribus uulgata in saeuitiam superbiamque eius et discordem cum matre animum*. Suetonius quotes two elegiac couplets on Tiberius which involve Livia (Suet. *Tib.* 59.1 = *uers. pop.* 11a Courtney 1993).

[87] Cf. e.g. Mart. 10.93.3.

discontent of his opponents expressed in an anonymous form. The actions of circulating and publishing the anonymous pamphlets could reveal a more strategic political move. As 'the editor' of those writings, Tiberius makes it look like he is not only in full awareness of what is happening with the 'anonymous' adverse propaganda; he also appears in complete control, so sure of his political choices that he even becomes the mouthpiece of his own critics. Yet more than this: he stamps his 'editorial' name on the verses, authorizing and reclaiming them in the process. It seems to me that the production of anonymous verses provided Tiberius with the opportunity of exercising a programmatic tolerance, probably less easy to bear when facing cases of declared oppositions like that of Cremutius.

The conspicuous number of verses on Tiberius quoted by Suetonius[88] leads us to believe that Tiberius was truly besieged by anonymous slander and libel. However, it seems that he chose not to prosecute them, instead showing a strategic politics of tolerance while keeping the situation under control. After quoting them, Suetonius comments on the verses with an anecdote that perfectly sketches Tiberius' ambiguous behaviour (Suet. *Tib.* 59.2):

> quae primo, quasi ab impatientibus remedi<or>um ac non tam ex animi sententia quam bile et stomacho fingerentur, uolebat accipi dicebatque identidem: 'oderint, dum probent.' Dein uera plane certaque esse ipse fecit fidem.

> At first, he insisted that such things should be seen as made up by people who could not tolerate the treatment they deserved and were prompted by malice and ill-temper rather than expressing true feelings. He used to say repeatedly: 'Let them hate me provided they respect me.' Later he himself gave clear proof of their accuracy and firm foundation.

For the *princeps*, the malcontent expressed by the poems does not concern his reforms but expresses a sentiment of anger on behalf of his enemies. In response to the cruelty of the poems,[89] he offers a self-representation of a 'corrected' Atreus who is not interested in disseminating blood and terror but rather in finding approbation. The revised version of the famous senarius *oderint dum metuant* ('let them hate as long as they fear'), modified to *oderint dum probent*,[90] conveys the contradiction between granting the chance of being critical (as long as the critics are in anonymous form) and claiming total adherence to the established order.

---

[88] Seven elegiac couples, fourteen verses in total: Suet *Tib.* 59.1 = *uers. pop.* 11a-e Courtney 1993.
[89] E.g. Suet. *Tib.* 59.1 = *uers. pop.* 11d Courtney 1993. *Fastidit uinum, quia iam sitit iste cruorem: / tam bibit hunc auide, quam bibit ante merum.*
[90] Caligula will repeat Accius' verse in its original form (Suet. *Calig.* 30.1); on this passage, see Champlin 2003b: 307–8.

Conclusion

The choice of self-censoring one's own name when composing and disseminating poems dealing with a political topic is a signal of danger, true or potential, for free speech. By exploring the path from Caesar to Tiberius, we have observed how these powerful men had to deal with an anonymous anti-propaganda which involves different social backgrounds cooperating together from the stage of composition to that of circulation. The elite, accomplice in inventing political slogans and possibly taking mutual part in the composition of the verses, could not do without the plebs, which also provided the potent tool of dissemination and propagation of the verses. What allowed such different social levels to work together was anonymity, a democratizing feature, offering literary products suitable to everyone and potentially claimable by everyone.

The presence of anonymous or pseudonymous voices furnishes a means of testing the authoritarian climate and the different reactions between the three figures of power considered above. Caesar shows a calmness supported by the (anti-)institutional strength of the triumphal context. Nevertheless, outside this frame, the circulation of the verses appears more alarming. Augustus tries to censor anonymous propaganda by any means, from misleading strategies of tolerance to the possibilities offered by the law, even including book-burning procedures. Tiberius' behaviour is more complex. Despite his censorial politics against free speech, Tiberius claims not to censor anonymous slander and libel, to give a veneer of superficial tolerance. Such behaviour is moreover reinforced by the choice of becoming editor of the verses composed against him.

I have sketched how these verses play an important role for our understanding of both the socio-cultural and the political mechanisms starting from the end of the Roman Republic. It is thanks to anonymity that the protest against authority could express its voice. Is the situation so different nowadays? If we think of the name of the most important online form of activism against the established order – *Anonymous* – it would seem that this voice has not had the chance to speak openly yet.

CHAPTER 9

Looking for the Emperor in Seneca's Letters
Catharine Edwards*

Seneca's *Epistulae Morales* present themselves as a collection of apparently private letters from an elderly philosopher to his administrator friend, offering advice on how to become a better Stoic. Ostensibly – and self-consciously – these letters have almost nothing to say about politics – other than advising their addressee that he would be better able to focus on philosophical progress, if he were to withdraw from public office. Why should we be drawn to searching for the figure of the emperor in these letters? Gowers, in her contribution to *Reflections of Nero* (1994), articulates an underlying assumption of that collection: 'Neronian literature demands to be read in the shadow, or rather, glare of its ruler'.[1] But might not the *Epistulae Morales* be a notable exception to this claim?

Seneca had been one of Nero's closest associates since 49 CE, when he was recalled from exile, on the initiative, it seems, of Nero's mother Agrippina, and appointed to serve as tutor to the 11-year-old Nero (Suet. *Ner.* 7.1). After Nero's accession (aged 16), Seneca continued for many years as one of his most influential advisers. Nero is the addressee of Seneca's treatise *De clementia*, composed shortly after Nero came to power in 54 CE. Credited with many of the more positive features of Nero's early years as emperor, Seneca was also implicated in more questionable developments, allegedly composing Nero's self-exculpatory letter to the Senate, for instance, after the murder of his mother in 59 CE.[2] Seneca himself asked for permission to step down in 62 CE, citing the analogy of

---

* I am immensely grateful to the editors of this volume, to the other participants in the *Unspeaking Volumes* conference at St Andrews (July 2017) and to seminar participants in Stockholm (November 2017) and Munich (February 2018).
[1] Gowers 1994: 131.
[2] Tac. *Ann.* 14.11: *sed non iam Nero, cuius immanitas omnium questus anteibat, sed Seneca aduerso rumore erat quod oratione tali confessionem scripsisset*, 'But it was no longer Nero (whose appalling behaviour exceeded the criticism of all) but Seneca who was the subject of hostile rumour: with such language he had written his own confession.' Translations are my own.

Augustus' advisers Maecenas and Agrippa (if we believe Tacitus, *Ann.* 14.53). Nero refused, according to Tacitus (*Ann.* 14.53–6),[3] though Seneca contrived to keep a very low profile, in 64 CE, petitioning the emperor a second time for official permission to withdraw (*Ann.* 15.45). The *Epistulae Morales* were composed in these last years (before Seneca received the order from Nero in 65 to kill himself).

To Hold Back or to Speak Frankly?

Despite their profusion of apparently personal anecdote, Seneca's letters are in notable respects curiously reticent.[4] Much of his life was spent in Rome, but the empire's capital itself is barely mentioned in the *Letters*.[5] *Letter* 91 explores what consolation may be offered to a friend whose home town, Lyons, has been devastated by fire. This fire apparently struck in the late summer of 64 CE (according to Tac. *Ann.* 16.13.3), thus postdating the terrible fire of Rome (whose ravages are described at *Ann.* 15.38–41). Yet, though it was reported by Tacitus to have reduced a large part of the city to smouldering ruin (thereby offering Nero a splendid opportunity for palace building – to which we shall return), Seneca makes no mention of the Rome fire. Despite his key role in government over many years – the Elder Pliny (*HN* 14.51) describes him as *princeps potentia* – Seneca makes almost no explicit reference to his own political career.[6] And Nero himself, with whom Seneca had been so closely associated for so many years, features as a resounding absence, not mentioned once in 124, often very lengthy, letters. If writing about the emperor is necessarily political, not writing about the emperor, under some circumstances, may itself be a significant political choice. Ovid's poem on the Roman calendar, the *Fasti*, covers only the first six months of the year, thus failing to include those months named after Julius and Augustus – and Augustus' birth month, September. As Feeney comments: 'The silent second half of the poem has as much to say about the principate as the vocal first half.'[7]

Several of Seneca's other, earlier works, by contrast, make repeated reference to emperors and their relatives. The *Apocolocyntosis* pulls no

---

[3] As Wilson 2015: 144 underlines, the response Tacitus puts in Nero's mouth stresses the political interpretation that might be placed on Seneca's withdrawal (*Ann.* 14.56). For further discussion of this passage, see Ker 2009: 47–9.
[4] Wilson 2015 notes the silence of the letters in relation to current or recent political figures and events. Cf. Veyne 2003: 162.
[5] See Henderson 2004: 96–7; Edwards 2018.
[6] On Seneca's ambivalent treatment of public distinction in the *Letters*, see Edwards 2017.
[7] Feeney 1992: 12.

punches in its mocking critique of Nero's predecessor Claudius.[8] The *De clementia* (1.9–11) discusses at length Augustus' virtues – and indeed his earlier failings.[9] Augustus' wife Livia features as a fount of good advice in the same passage and, in Seneca's consolation to Marcia (2.3–3.2), as an exemplary instance of female fortitude in the face of bereavement. In *De ira*, Caligula's rages offer graphic illustration of the damaging effects of anger (1.20.8–9, 3.18.3–3.19.5), while that emperor's equally untrammelled grief (at the loss of his sister) serves to illustrate the inefficacy of attempts to seek relief in gambling and restless travel (*Cons. ad Polyb.* 17.3–6).[10]

The *Letters'* relative lack of explicit historical reference paradoxically serves to reinforce their philosophical appeal; their message remains readily applicable to future generations (Seneca makes clear early on his wish to offer advice to posterity, *Ep.* 8.2). But a case could also be made for seeing these silences as a dramatic act of self-censorship.[11] Explicit comment on Nero, when not complimentary, might certainly have been dangerous; Seneca's vast wealth made him especially vulnerable to accusations of *maiestas*, treason.[12] The protreptic strategy of Seneca's *De clementia*, addressed to Nero early on in his reign and praising the emperor for the qualities a ruler ought to have, had proved of limited efficacy.[13] In what terms could a retired adviser refer to the volatile autocrat, who had for years been ignoring his wise advice? Not referring at all to the emperor itself ran the risk of causing Nero significant annoyance, of course.[14] Indeed perhaps the most offensive aspect of the *Epistulae Morales* for the emperor – though he most likely did not go to the trouble of reading them himself – was their failure to mention him.[15]

Yet if Nero is not present explicitly, there are a number of respects in which Nero's domination of others, as well as his failure to exercise control over himself are, I shall argue, constructed as implicit and potent anti-models in the letters. Despite his virtually untrammelled power in the

---

[8] Most scholars agree in attributing this work to Seneca. For the debate around authorship, see Freudenburg 2015: 93–5. Claudius is presented more positively in the *Cons. ad Polyb.* composed during his reign.

[9] Augustus, reproving the anger of Vedius Pollio, also features in *De ira* 3.40.

[10] Part of a speech put in the mouth of the emperor Claudius Caligula also appears at *Brev. Vit.* 18.5–6, *Constant.* 18.

[11] Persius' comment (1.119–21) about entrusting the truth to a hole in the ground has been read as a reference to powerful inhibitions against speaking out under Nero. See Reckford 2009: 151.

[12] As Wilson rightly underlines (2015). [13] On the *De clementia*, see Braund 2009.

[14] The silence of Seneca's Stoic contemporary Thrasea Paetus was itself used against him, a little later in Nero's reign, by his political opponents (Tac. *Ann.* 16.22; Edwards 2007: 134–6).

[15] Soldo 2018 notes the conspicuous omission of reference to Nero in Seneca's insistence in *Ep.* 21 on the power of his letters to make their addressee's name live on in future generations.

political sphere, Nero, the *Epistulae Morales* insinuate, has no shred of control over his own desires and impulses. It is ultimately both much harder and much more important, Seneca asserts, to exercise *imperium* over oneself than over vast tracts of territory (113.30): *imperare sibi maximum imperium est.*

Nero himself is, we must assume, regarded as beyond redemption by this point in Seneca's career. Nero, it is reported, had no patience with philosophy.[16] The *Letters* have no ambition to cure the tyrant or indeed the hard-bitten voluptuary; they are addressed rather to the reader who is already committed to Stoic self-improvement. Yet in a world where Neronian standards hold sway, the work of the would-be philosopher is the more heroic, as he withstands the tide of luxury and vice engulfing his contemporaries.

Some comments can, of course, be read as oblique reflections on Seneca's relations with Nero.[17] 'The wise man will never provoke the anger of the powerful', *sapiens numquam potentium iras prouocabit*, he advises at 14.7 (an ironically ambiguous pronouncement). Yet the *potentes* might flare up on the slenderest provocation, he goes on to underline. In the concluding sections of *Letter* 47 (largely focused on the issue of slavery, literal and metaphorical), the topic of relations between rulers and their subjects is touched on, as an analogy for relations between masters and slaves; when masters are provoked to violence by trivial annoyances, they are like rulers who lash out, too ready to forget their own strength and the weakness of others: 'we [as masters] take on the spirit of kings', Seneca observes (47.20).[18]

The tendency of some rulers to react violently when their subjects offer unwelcome advice could all too easily induce subjects to behave like slaves. 'In the matter of vices, anger and flattery go

---

[16] Philostratus *Life of Apollonius* 4.35–6. Indeed, Agrippina had apparently stipulated that philosophy should not form part of young Nero's education (Suet. *Ner.* 52).

[17] Rimell observes (2015: 131–2) 'elsewhere in the *EM* Seneca comes closer to spelling out and satirizing the symbolic role of Nero himself in revived attempts to light up the night and in rebellious reactions to the disciplinary force of normative, official time in empire'. See also Habinek (2014: 14–15): 'Seneca displays his retirement and explains why he is doing so in the same collection of letters' (similarly Veyne 2003: 157–67).

[18] *regum nobis induimus animos* (using the first person plural Seneca assimilates himself and his addressee to the rulers/masters); cf. *regis quisque intra se animum habet ut licentiam sibi dare uelit*, 'every individual has the spirit of a king, so that he wants to use licence but not be the victim of it', *De ira* 2.31.3. The term *rex* often had negative overtones (cf. e.g. referring to Julius Caesar: *interfecto rege liberi non sumus*, 'though the king is dead, we are not free', Cic. *Att.* 14.11.1 = SB 365), but note that Seneca uses this term to refer to monarchs generally in the *Clem.* addressed to Nero. A parallel between household and state, *res publica*, is drawn at 47.14.

together', Foucault comments in his 1982 lecture on *parrhesia*, 'free speech'.[19] In Tacitus' *Annals* this dynamic frequently informs relations between emperors and senators.[20] Seneca (in Tacitus' version) presents himself as resisting the pressure to offer flattery; Tacitus reports his comment, when Nero's messenger, following the allegation that Seneca had been involved in the Pisonian conspiracy, brings the order to commit suicide. Nero, Seneca is made to assert, had more often experienced his outspokenness than his servility, *saepius libertatem Senecae quam seruitium expertus est* (*Ann.* 15.61.1), though as Ash notes, 'claiming outspokenness could paradoxically serve to flatter Nero as a *princeps* tolerant of straight-talking subordinates'.[21]

In Seneca's own writing, the term *libertas* rarely has an overtly political sense.[22] It is sometimes, however, used to express the kind of frank advice (characterised in Greek texts as *parrhesia*), which the teacher gives the student for the latter's own good. At *De ira* 3.13.4, for instance, Seneca advises:

> Rogemus amicissimum quemque, ut tunc maxime libertate adversus nos utatur, cum minime illam pati poterimus, nec adsentiatur irae nostrae.
>
> Let us beg all our best friends to use to the utmost such liberty towards us, particularly when we are least able to tolerate it, and let there be no approval of our anger.

Foucault, discussing Seneca's *Ep.* 75 which he describes as 'a veritable theory of speaking freely',[23] characterises *parrhesia* as 'the frankness, freedom, and openness that leads one to say what one has to say, as one wishes to say it, when one wishes to say it and in the form one thinks necessary for saying it'.[24] Its aim is to act on others 'so that they come to build up a relationship of sovereignty to themselves'.[25] The challenge for the philosophical adviser seeking to offer *parrhesia* to a ruler or even to a social superior was

---

[19] 2005: 374. On the political dimension of *parrhesia*, see Baltussen and Davis 2015. As their introduction notes, *libertas* has a broader significance. See also Ahl 1984, Sluiter and Rosen 2004. For *libertas* as free speech, see e.g. Hor. *Sat.* 2.7.4.
[20] See Lavan 2011. [21] Ash 2018 ad loc.
[22] Inwood 2005: 302–21. Inwood does not, however, discuss *libertas* in the sense of free speech. As Freudenburg observes (in a discussion of satiric *libertas*), one's *libertas* in the sense of freedom to speak, was only ever as good as one's *libertas*, in the sense of performatively free status (2001: 49).
[23] Foucault 2005: 383. Seneca contends (75.18), dismissing his addressee's concern for higher rank, that philosophy, banishing all fear of men and gods, brings true *libertas*, so that one possesses supreme *potestas* over oneself.
[24] Ibid.: 372. [25] Ibid.: 385.

a concern of numerous imperial writers (Galen, Plutarch).[26] 'How can one speak truthfully to the prince?'[27]

Seneca recognises that there is no point talking to someone who is unwilling to listen: *nulli enim nisi audituro dicendum est*, *Ep.* 29.1. He regards the indiscriminate *libertas* of the Cynics who offer advice to everyone they meet as ill-advised; such a strategy dilutes one's moral *auctoritas* (29.3). The *Epistulae Morales*, as we have noted, do not aim to achieve the impossible goal of leading their author's erstwhile pupil to a state of self-sovereignty. Yet there are moments when structures of political power, the nature of the state in which the would-be philosopher lives, impinge on Seneca's reflections. What kind of truth, what kind of *libertas*, might be on offer here?

Letter 73 muses on relations between rulers and philosophers; Seneca argues at some length that the philosopher above all is grateful to the ruler (*rex*, 'king', is used here as a positive term, as in Seneca's earlier *De clementia*), who, by ensuring the state is secure and peaceful (*securitas publica*), makes possible a life of philosophical leisure.[28] It is quite wrong, he asserts, to think of philosophers as stubborn and rebellious (*contumaces . . . ac refractarios*, 73.1). Here Seneca seems to be distancing himself from any association between Stoic philosophy and opposition to the emperor.[29] Might a contrast be implied between Seneca and others who had been openly critical of Nero? The term *libertas* seems to have been invoked as a watchword by the notoriously recalcitrant Thrasea Paetus (e.g. *Ann.* 14.49).[30] At the same time, Seneca's comments would scarcely qualify as unmitigated – servile – praise. 'Just as a man respects and reveres his teachers,' he observes, 'through whose help he has moved on from earlier wanderings, so too he regards those under whose protection he is able to live a philosophical life'

---

[26] Ibid. The interaction between Callisthenes and Alexander the Great (Diogenes Laertius 5.4–5) served as a paradigm (Baltussen and Davis 2015: 6).

[27] Foucault 2005: 381. See also Quint. *Inst.* 9.2.27: free speech, *oratio libera*, does not come under the heading of 'figurae orationis' unless it is feigned. 'Free speech which Cornificius calls *licentia* and the Greeks παρρησία. For what has less of a figure about it than true freedom (*uera libertas*). On the other hand, freedom of speech may frequently be made a cloak for flattery (*adulatio*)'.

[28] On this letter, see Veyne 2003: 159–62; Habinek 2014. For the resonance with Seneca's *De beneficiis*, see Griffin 2013: ch. 8. Rudich (1993: 109) sees this as a specific response to the slander campaign orchestrated by Tigellinus (Tac. *Ann.* 14.52).

[29] Seneca's nuanced exploration of this is discussed by Bartsch 2017. Wilson 2015 reads the earlier *Letters* as articulating a self-consciously Epicurean position (that withdrawal is the precondition for philosophy) as a strategy to distance Seneca from a more specifically Stoic doctrine that one should withdraw from politics only when the regime is corrupt.

[30] Cf. Tac. *Ann.* 14.12. On receiving the order to take his own life, he made a sacrifice to Jupiter liberator (Tac. *Ann.* 16.35), as did Seneca (15.64).

(73.4).³¹ Given his own pupil's increasingly errant behaviour – not to mention Nero's treatment of his teacher – it is hard to resist seeing a considerable irony in this analogy.³²

The letters repeatedly advocate withdrawal from the political sphere. Seneca's addressee Lucilius is urged to give up his post as procurator the better to devote himself to philosophy.³³ In Letter 68, Seneca warns Lucilius that it may be prudent to cloak philosophical withdrawal under the pretext of ill-health (*ualetudo, imbecillitas* 68.3–6). He himself is said by Tacitus to have feigned illness or used the excuse of his illness (*quasi ualetudine infensa*) to request withdrawal in 62 CE (*Ann.* 14.56).³⁴ Seneca comments earlier in the *Letters* (56.9):

> Although the impression is often given that we have withdrawn (*secessisse*) because of being fed up with the business of the state and regretful at our unfortunate and thankless position (*infelicis atque ingratae stationis*), still in the corner to which fear (*timor*) and exhaustion (*lassitudo*) have thrust us, ambition (*ambitio*) sometimes springs anew.

It would be unwise, however, to read any of Seneca's first-person comments as a straightforward reflection of his own experiences; this example, for instance, serves to illustrate the general claim that even in seclusion the would-be philosopher is still prey to mental disturbances such as anxiety – and ambition. Miriam Griffin and others have rightly highlighted the challenge of pinning down traces of the autobiographical in a text whose author, despite the apparently confessional tone he often adopts, frequently proves slippery and evasive.³⁵

This caution is in many ways well advised. And yet for all their aspirations to a transcendent, cosmopolitan perspective, the letters remain

---

³¹ *Quemadmodum praeceptores suos ueneratur et suspicit quorum beneficio illis inuiis exit et hos sub quorum tutela positus exercet artes bonas.*

³² At 73.8, Seneca refers particularly to *pax* and *libertas* as public goods, for the guarantee of which by the ruler the philosopher is especially grateful. In developing an analogy between the philosopher and Virgil's Tityrus (with quotations from *Eclogue* 1), Seneca, insofar as he is to be identified as the philosopher, is far from posing any threat to his ruler (Wilson 2015: 147–8). At the same time, Seneca opens up the possibility of assimilating Nero to Octavian/Augustus, the patron probably celebrated in Virgil's poem.

³³ See Bartsch 2015 and the detailed account in Griffin 1992: 315–66. Wilson 2015 reads this advice as a defensively Epicurean move, though it is notable that even in the first three books, Seneca makes clear that, while he approves of some aspects of Epicurean practice, he does not consider himself a follower of Epicurus. For a nuanced discussion of Seneca's engagement with Epicureanism in the *EM*, see Graver 2016.

³⁴ Tacitus reports rumours in 64 that Seneca, to avert opprobrium for Nero's increasingly shocking behaviour, had withdrawn to his bedchamber, *ficta ualetudine quasi aeger neruis*, 'having feigned illness from a muscular ailment', 15.45.

³⁵ Griffin 1992: 348–50; Edwards 1997; Jones 2014.

closely rooted in the political, cultural – and aesthetic – specificity of Neronian Rome. Seneca veers between intimate, confessional, hectoring and expository modes. He offers personalised advice to his addressee Lucilius, he chastises himself for his own failings, while later letters discourse at length on technical philosophical questions, such as the nature of the good. Yet even in these later letters, lengthy passages are devoted to excoriating in indignant detail the moral failings of Seneca's contemporaries. These passages are often dismissed as vapid moralising. We should not, however, underestimate their function as entertainment (their connections with earlier satiric traditions are notable). More importantly perhaps, as we shall see in due course, highly refined vices could even play a particular role in Seneca's model of philosophy's development.

First, however, I would like to explore the particular pertinence of the vices to which Seneca gives special attention. By this point, Seneca could hardly have expected his advice to exert any positive effect on his former pupil. That kind of *parrhesia* is, in the letters, directed at Lucilius – or at Seneca himself, or at other readers who chose to embrace the project of Stoic self-improvement. Yet, in relation to Nero, an inescapable presence in Seneca's world, Seneca also makes clear his refusal to stoop to flattery. Rather, I shall suggest (discussing particularly *Letters* 90 and 114), when Seneca reflects on the dynamics of vice in its more florid and imaginative forms, his terms frequently resonate quite specifically with ancient accounts of Neronian Rome (notably those of Tacitus and Suetonius) and other works of Neronian literature (particularly Petronius and Persius). Nero serves, if in a rather oblique manner, as an exemplar of the lack of self-command, of the surrender to vice, of the extreme rejection of nature, an arrestingly potent manifestation of the pathology of an individual utterly lacking sovereignty over himself.

Constructing Luxury

Luxurious building looms large among the vices of his age castigated by Seneca, who condemns at length the coloured marbles and elaborate water features adorning the homes of his contemporaries (notably in *Letters* 86, 90, 122). Seneca frequently contrasts such complex and lavish constructions with the simple structures of earlier times (e.g. *Ep.* 86, 90, *Helv.* 9.2–3). The author of the pseudo-Senecan tragedy *Octavia* (which seems to date from shortly after Seneca's death),[36] set in Nero's court, evidently

---

[36] On the dating, see Boyle 2008: lxvi.

regarded such sentiments as distinctively Senecan; the character 'Seneca' is made to give a similar speech ([Sen.] *Oct.* 397–406).[37] The evils of luxurious architecture are, of course, a theme prominent in attacks on luxury more generally. Elaborate ceilings (*laqueata tecta*) are criticised by Cicero, for instance (*Leg.* 2.2).[38] But such criticism had, it seems, particular purchase in Nero's Rome.

Suetonius comments on Nero: 'There was nothing in which he was more prodigal than in construction', *non in alia re tamen damnosior quam aedificando, Ner.* 31.1. In the wake of the fire of 64 CE, Nero constructed for himself a new palace, the Golden House, *domus aurea*, the most conspicuous symptom of a new (and more material) golden age.[39] Having noted the opulent decoration of the house (*cuncta auro lita, distincta gemmis unionumque conchis erant*, 'all covered in gold and picked out with gems and mother-of-pearl'), Suetonius attests (31.2–3) the emperor's taste for ingenious and lavish ceilings in particular: **cenationes laqueatae** *tabulis eburneis* **uersatilibus**, *ut flores* **fistulatis**, *ut unguenta desuper spargerentur; praecipua cenationum rotunda, quae perpetua diebus ac noctibus uice mundi circumageretur*, '**The banqueting halls had coffered ceilings** fitted with panels of ivory, **which would revolve**, scattering flowers, **and pipes**, which would spray perfume on those beneath. The principal banqueting chamber had a dome which revolved continuously both day and night like the world itself.'

Ceilings with moving panels are an architectural feature singled out for marked criticism in Seneca's *Letter* 90.15:

> Hodie utrum tandem sapientiorem putas, qui inuenit quemadmodum in immensam altitudinem **crocum latentibus fistulis exprimat**, qui euripos subito aquarum impetus implet aut siccat et **uersatilia cenationum laquearia** ita coagmentat, ut subinde alia facies atque alia succedat et totiens tecta quotiens fericula mutentur, an eum qui et aliis et sibi hoc monstrat, quam nihil nobis natura durum ac difficile imperauerit, posse nos habitare sine marmorario ac fabro, posse nos uestitos esse sine commercio sericorum,

---

[37] Ferri (2003 *ad* 433–4) sees the indictment of *auaritia* as strongly reminiscent of the critique offered by *Ep.* 90.38 of one who, 'through desiring much, has lost everything', *multa concupiscendo omnia amisit*.

[38] Degl'Innocenti Pierini 2008: 118–9. The Augustan moralist Papirius Fabianus is quoted at length in the *Controversiae* of Seneca's father (2.1.11–12), in a passage closely echoed by *Ep.* 90 (Degl'Innocenti Pierini, 2008: 109–114); at 100.12, Seneca recalls Fabianus' lectures with approval.

[39] On the display politics of the Golden House, see Champlin 2003a and most recently La Rocca 2017: 203–12. On the preoccupation with vice in the accounts of Nero's reign given by Suetonius, Tacitus and Dio, see Grau, who notes (2017: 269) the influence of the aesthetics of Senecan drama on the construction of Nero as a tyrant, particularly in Tacitus.

posse nos habere usibus nostris necessaria, si contenti fuerimus iis quae terra posuit in summo?

In our own times, which person do you consider the wiser – the one who invents a process **for spraying saffron perfumes** to a great height **from concealed pipes**, who fills or empties canals by a sudden flood of water, who so cleverly constructs **a banqueting hall with a ceiling of movable panels**, that it presents one pattern after another, the roof changing as often as the dishes, – or the one who proves both to others and to himself, that nature has imposed on us nothing harsh or difficult when she tells us that we can live without the marble cutter and the engineer, that we can clothe ourselves without trade in silk fabrics, that we have everything that is essential to our use, if only we can be content with what the earth has placed on its surface?

At 90.42–3 he returns to the topic:[40]

> Non impendebant **caelata laquearia**, sed in aperto iacentes sidera superlabebantur et insigne spectaculum noctium mundus in praeceps agebatur silentio tantum opus ducens. tam interdiu illis quam nocte patebant prospectus huius pulcherrimae domus. libebat intueri signa ex media caeli parte uergentia, rursus ex occulto alia surgentia. quidni iuuaret uagari inter tam late sparsa miracula? at uos ad omnem tectorum pauetis sonum et inter picturas uestras, si quid increpuit, fugitis attoniti. non habebant **domos instar urbium**.

> No **coffered ceilings** hung over them, but as they lay in the open air the stars glided quietly above them, and the firmament, the splendid nightly display, was being driven round at great speed, conducting its mighty work in silence. For them by day as well as by night, the visions of this most beautiful heaven were free and open. It was their delight to watch the constellations as they sank from the zenith, and others, again, as they rose from their hiding place. What else but delight could it be to wander among the marvels which stud the heavens, far and wide? But you of the present day shudder at every sound your houses make, and as you sit among your frescoes the slightest creak makes you retreat in terror. They had no **houses as big as cities**.

Suetonius reports jokes about the Domus Aurea: 'Rome is becoming one house', *Roma domus fiet* (*Ner.* 39).[41] Jaś Elsner has rightly emphasised the extent to which accounts of the Golden House are a product of Flavian propaganda.[42] Yet the close similarities between descriptions of Nero's palace and Seneca's denunciations of luxurious architecture also require scrutiny.

---

[40] Noted by Bradley 1978: 179–80 *ad* Suet. *Ner.* 31.
[41] Cf. Martial, *Spect.* 2, though the house as big as a city line was not altogether new.
[42] Elsner 1994. See now Varner 2017.

Nero's mechanism, with multiple moving parts to enable shifting celestial displays, was evidently complex; the cosmic motion in Suetonius' description elides the elaborate ceiling and the night sky; in Seneca's scheme these elements are prominent though strongly contrasted.[43] Parallels between the passages in Suetonius and Seneca have been widely noted (e.g. by Bradley in his commentary on Suet. *Ner.*).[44] Degl'Innocenti Pierini (2008: 127–8) also observes a suggestive resonance with the false ceiling (*lacunaria ... laxata machina*) of the boat through which Nero plotted to kill his mother, according to Suetonius (Suet. *Ner.* 34.2); in Nero's Rome a fear of collapsing ceilings might be amply justified. The manifestation of luxury in architecture – so closely associated with Nero himself – is treated in *Ep.* 90 as emblematic of both the moral failings of Seneca's contemporaries and the existential dangers these failings entail.[45]

In his attacks on luxurious building, Seneca repeatedly highlights the deliberate defiance of nature (cf. e.g. *a natura luxuria desciuit*, 'luxury has turned her back on nature', 90.19). According to Tacitus, Nero's architects Severus and Celer were celebrated for their ability to achieve through art what nature refused: *Seuero et Celere, quibus ingenium et audacia erat etiam **quae natura denegauisset** per artem temptare et uiribus principis illudere*, 'Severus and Celer, whose ingenuity and brazenness were such as to attempt by artifice **what nature had forbidden**, and to amuse themselves with an emperor's resources', *Ann.* 15.42. While the palace no doubt took some time to complete, we may well surmise that the plans were familiar to Seneca. Indeed Jacqueline Fabre-Serris (1999: 193) beguilingly suggests that aspects of Nero's ideology (including his building programme) took their form precisely in reaction against the views of his teacher, Seneca. Should we then see Nero's ingenuity as inspired precisely by that of Seneca?

Certainly Seneca's denunciations have played their own part, we may suspect, in fleshing out the image of Neronian Rome, with its prodigious palaces, overblown feasts, theatrical display and transgressive eroticism, so

---

[43] As to whether the comments in Suetonius relate to extant remains of the Golden House, see Champlin 2003a: 203–6; remains more recently discovered on the Palatine have also been identified with Nero's *cenatio*, Villedieu 2011: 282–7.

[44] Another Neronian text features a strikingly similar device; at one point in Trimalchio's banquet (Petron. *Sat.* 60.1–3), *repente lacunaria sonare coeperunt totumque triclinium intremuit* and panels shift to reveal a hoop hung with golden crowns and perfume vessels; the mechanisms are described in terms evoking those used in the theatre, as Panayotakis notes (1995: 90–1); cf. Plin. *HN* 36.117. Indeed, Seneca himself associates ingenious contrivances of this kind with the stage (88.22). On the resonances between the world of the *Satyricon* and Nero's Rome more generally, see Vout 2009 and Freudenburg 2017.

[45] Degl'Innocenti Pierini 2008: 109.

colourfully articulated by Tacitus and Suetonius, writing a few decades later.[46] It is perhaps ultimately Seneca's vision of Neronian Rome which has prevailed over that which the emperor, for all his claims to be a great *artifex*, sought to realise.[47]

The Morality of Style

A similar dynamic may be traced in Letter 114, the second of my two principal examples. Letter 114 offers an extended exploration of the moral implications of faults in literary style. Starting from the question of why a corrupt literary style flourishes at certain times, 114 alludes to some of the different faults which style may exhibit (§1). While the maxim that a man's literary style corresponds to the way he lives is extended to apply to societies (§2), Seneca focuses initially on the ways in which an individual's moral flaws are revealed in every detail of his bearing, dress and comportment (§3), his prime example being Maecenas, whose weaknesses of character (§4) are particularly reflected in his extraordinary literary style (§§5–8). Reprehensible style sometimes results from vices characteristic of society in general, which may reflect widespread moral laxity (§§9–11), Seneca argues, but he returns to the literary faults of specific individuals.[48]

Where literary faults are due to imitation (rather than originating with the writer) they do not necessarily indicate flawed character (§20); deliberate literary faults, like excesses in personal grooming, are the result of reprehensible attention-seeking (§21) and indicate significant disturbance of the mind (§22). Developing a political analogy for the relationship between the mind and the body, the concluding section of the letter (§§23–7) describes the dreadful consequences, when the mind rules not as a king but as a tyrant.

It is no surprise that Seneca associates a fashion for perverse literary style with periods when morals more generally are corrupt but he is more preoccupied in Letter 114 with literary faults whose genesis is to be found in the moral character of the specific individual. The prime example is Maecenas, confidante of the emperor Augustus. Seneca is unremitting in his critique of Maecenas' character more generally, as well as his writing (114.4):

[46] Some allusions to the *Epistulae Morales* in Tacitus' *Annals* are documented by Woodman 2010.
[47] Suet. *Ner.* 49: '*qualis artifex pereo!*' On the struggle for authorial control between author and emperor, see further, p. 183–4.
[48] Conceding that even the most admired have their failings, which may be an inextricable part of their greatness (§12).

> Quomodo Maecenas uixerit notius est, quam ut narrari nunc debeat, quomodo ambulauerit, quam delicatus fuerit, quam cupierit uideri, quam uitia sua latere noluerit. quid ergo? non oratio eius aeque soluta est quam ipse discinctus? ... uidebis itaque eloquentiam ebrii hominis inuolutam et errantem et licentiae plenam.

> How Maecenas lived is too well known to need present comment. We know how he walked, how over-refined he was, and how he desired to make a spectacle of himself and how unwilling he was that his vices should be overlooked. What then? Does not the looseness of his speech match his over-relaxed dress? ... His eloquence was that of an intoxicated man – twisting, wandering, full of self-indulgence.

There follows (114.5) a succession of brief quotations from Maecenas' prose, a jumble of bizarre phrases, which scholars have struggled to make sense of.

In criticising Maecenas' literary style, Seneca was not alone; Suetonius observes (*Aug.* 86.2) that the emperor Augustus: 'despised affected [*cacozelos*] writers ... and sometimes reproved them, particularly his friend Maecenas whose "scented curls" [*myrobrechis ... cincinnos*] as he called them, he attacked relentlessly, mocking him through parody'. Along similar lines are comments from Quintilian (*Inst.* 9.4.28)[49] and Tacitus's Messalla (*Dial.* 26.1),[50] while Macrobius (*Sat.* 2.4.12) quotes a letter of Augustus to Maecenas, itself perhaps a parody of Maecenas' style, which Macrobius interprets as a teasing comment on his wealth and sexual behaviour, as well as his recherché prose.[51]

Maecenas is also the object of criticism at *Letters* 19.9, 92.35,[52] 101.10–15 (where Seneca denounces *carminis effeminati turpitudo*, 'such womanish and shameless verse'), 120.19.[53] A leitmotif of these attacks is Maecenas' compromised masculinity; at *Prou.* 3.11 Seneca observes, commenting on those who envy Maecenas, that one who wishes to have been born Maecenas, such was his effeminacy, might just as well wish to have been his wife Terentia. At *Ep.* 19.9, for instance, Seneca comments that good fortune *eneruasset ..., immo castrasset*, 'had made him effeminate, if it had not castrated him'. Among Maecenas' compositions was a poem,

---

[49] Criticising Maecenas' perverse ordering of words.
[50] Like Augustus taking a metaphor from hairdressing, he derides his *calamistros* 'crimping'.
[51] Influenced by Seneca, suggests Graver 1998: 629–31.
[52] Though here Seneca contrasts a nice turn of phrase with the author's depraved character.
[53] Cf. *Prou.* 3.10–11: invoked as the antithesis of the noble Regulus, he serves as an emphatically negative exemplum, a figure for base self-indulgence; we should deem Regulus in his extreme sufferings for a virtuous cause more truly fortunate, Seneca insists, than Maecenas amid his luxurious pleasures.

composed in the distinctive galliambic metre, entitled *Cybele*.[54] Cybele's priests notoriously practised self-castration; Catullus' poem 63, also composed in galliambic metre, and in the voice of a priest of Cybele, famously explores such a transformation in graphic detail. Seneca's comment here that good fortune had castrated Maecenas is thus particularly telling.

Seneca's hostility to Maecenas' literary style has been diagnosed as a response to literary fashion at Nero's court, where, it is suggested, in the latter years of his reign, Maecenas' work was in circulation and inspiring imitators.[55] Certainly the literary politics of Nero's court were intense; Sullivan traces complex rivalries played out through parody, persuasively suggesting, for instance, that Petronius takes Seneca's writing as his target in passages in the *Satyricon*.[56] In Seneca's demonisation of Maecenas, Sharon Byrne detects a covert attack on Petronius, resented because he had recently come to exert a potent influence over Nero.[57] Yet, while Seneca is entertainingly critical in describing Maecenas' mode of life (going about accompanied by eunuchs,[58] wrapped up in a cloak like a runaway slave),[59] the chief concern of his attack is Maecenas' literary style; parallels between Petronius' style and that of Maecenas are far from obvious.[60] We should consider an alternative target.

The final three paragraphs of Letter 114 appear to take us in a quite new direction from the rest of the letter. Seneca now explores the proper relationship between mind and body in terms of analogies with different styles of autocracy, contrasting kingship (to which corresponds the rule of the healthy *animus*) and tyranny (the domain of an *animus* which is disordered). Nero himself, of course, is never explicitly mentioned. Yet the analogy, developed more fully here than in Letter 47, and underlining the dreadful consequences of disordered autocratic rule, recalls Seneca's earlier treatise on clemency, whose addressee was the young emperor. In

---

[54] Courtney 1993 frr. 5–6, Hollis frr. 188 + 189; Hollis (2007: 318) observes 'the influence of Catullus is almost overwhelming' (cf. Avallone 1962: 305–7).
[55] Lunderstedt (1911: 8, followed by Mayer 1982: 315). Morford 1972–3 argues that Lucan and Persius, along with Seneca, were reacting against this.
[56] Sullivan 1985: 172–6.
[57] Byrne 2006: 95–111. Certainly there are some parallels between the character of Maecenas in Seneca's 114 and Tacitus' (*Ann.* 16.18) portrait of Petronius. Byrne (2006: 92–3), noting that in Seneca's earlier *Ben.* (4.36.2, 6.32.2–4), Maecenas is mentioned in neutral or positive terms, argues that Seneca's critical remarks follow his withdrawal from Nero's inner circle in 62 (though on the difficulty of dating *Ben.*, see now Griffin 2013: 91–6).
[58] *spadones duo, magis tamen uiri quam ipse*, 114.6.
[59] *ut . . . in mimo fugitiui diuitis*, 'the rich man's runaway slave in the mime', 114.6.
[60] As Byrne concedes (2006: 104).

the *De clementia*, Seneca contrasted at length the rule of the *rex* and the rule of the *tyrannus* (see 1.3.4–5[61] and particularly 1.11.4,[62] with Braund ad loc.).

Literary style was a hot topic at the court of Nero. The emperor's own passion for literature was notorious; Tacitus (*carminum quoque studium affectauit*, 'Nero also adopted the pursuit of poetry', *Annals* 14.16.1) highlights the emperor's enthusiasm for composing poetry – though he suspects him of plagiarism;[63] Suetonius, by contrast, considers the blotchy crossings-out he has himself witnessed as authentic Neronian scribblings (*Ner.* 52). Some fragments of Nero's poetry survive;[64] Seneca himself elsewhere (*QNat.* 1.5.6) quotes and praises a line.[65] A scholiast on Persius' *Satire* 1.99–102 (a poem which Gowers 1994: 141 describes as itself 'a simulacrum of Nero's lost works') goes so far as to suggest these lines are from Nero's *Attis*:[66]

> Torva Mimalloneis inplerunt cornua bombis,
> et raptum uitulo caput ablatura superbo
> Bassaris et lyncem Maenas flexura corymbis
> Euhion ingeminat, reparabilis adsonat echo.

Their fierce horns they filled with Mimallonian booming and Bassaris, about to carry off the head ripped from the proud calf, and the Maenad, about to steer the lynx with ivy clusters, shouts again Euhoe and reverberating Echo chimes in.

Dio also reports (61.20.2) that Nero delivered an *Attis* or *Bacchae* at the Juvenalia of 59 CE (though does not make clear whether this was his own composition).[67] It seems hardly coincidental that the examples of 'groinless' (*delumbe*) compositions Persius chooses to attack are entitled *Maenas* and *Attis* (*Sat.* 1.104).[68] His term of disapproval is, we might note, another instance of marking a condemned literary style in terms of an effeminised body, a tendency which later finds its most graphic expression in

---

[61] Where he also draws an analogy between the power exercised by a ruler over his subjects (who are prepared to sacrifice themselves for him) and that properly exercised by the mind over the appetites of the body.
[62] *Quid interest inter tyrannum ac regem ... nisi quod tyranni in uoluptatem saeuiunt, reges non nisi ex causa ac necessitate*, 'what is the difference between a tyrant and a king ... unless it is that tyrants rage in pursuit of appetite, while kings only when there is necessary cause'.
[63] See also 13.3.3: *et aliquando carminibus pangendis inesse sibi elementa doctrinae ostendebat*, 'sometimes, too, in his verse composition he demonstrated that he had the rudiments of literary skill'.
[64] On which, see Bardon 1936: 337–49; Courtney 1993: 357–9; Baldwin 2005. Nero's poems are praised by Martial for their *doctrina* (8.70).
[65] *ut ait Nero Caesar disertissime*.
[66] *hi versus Neronis sunt*. Griffin 1984: 275 and Courtney 1993: 357–8 doubt their authenticity. As Baldwin notes, the *Vita* of Persius reports that a comment at 1.121 was toned down by Cornutus so that the posthumously published poems did not offend Nero (2005: 313).
[67] Griffin 1984: 150.   [68] Sullivan 1985: 102–4.

Quintilian's extended comparison of faulty writing to a castrated youth (*Inst.* 5.12.18).

Attis, the self-castrated priest of the Magna Mater, Cybele, might seem a quintessentially Alexandrian theme,[69] quite in keeping with what is otherwise known of Nero's literary tastes (the theatrical roles he chose to declaim, for instance, allegedly included Canace in labour with her incestuous offspring).[70] Features of the Attis story – gender subversion and self-castration in an exotic Trojan setting – resonate closely with themes prominent more generally in the accounts of Neronian Rome offered by Tacitus, Suetonius and Dio. Many anecdotes about Nero's own crossdressing, his 'marriage' to the castrated youth Sporus, his playing the part of the bride in another marriage to Doryphorus 'going so far as to imitate the cries and lamentations of a maiden being deflowered',[71] and his celebration of his family's Trojan ancestry relate to the later years of Nero's reign.[72] Yet we may readily imagine these predilections were foreshadowed even in the time of Seneca's ascendancy.

As for Nero's prose, while Seneca himself ghost-wrote Nero's speeches in the earlier part of his reign (Tac. *Ann.* 13.3, 11, 14.11), a lengthy inscription (*IG* 7. 2713) records a showy Neronian speech in Greek from 67 CE, in which experimental, Asianist features have been diagnosed by Jones; indeed, Jones (2000: 58–62) argues his Greek teacher may have been Niketes, whose florid, 'bacchic' style and daring phraseology are noted by Philostratus (*VS* 1.19.1). The emperor as author seems to have relished writing in a manner which deliberately scorned his old tutor's wise advice (Tac. *Ann.* 14.52).

Seneca's attention-seeking, pleasure-loving, gender-subverting Maecenas, who revels in producing inventive and obscure compositions, may be read, I would suggest, as resonating in important ways with representations of Nero himself.[73] Several parallels have been noted between Nero's own work and that of Maecenas.[74] Maecenas, we might

---

[69] See Harder 2004.
[70] Suet. *Ner.* 21.3. Griffin 1984: 150; cf. Sullivan 1985: 89–92. On Nero's *doctrina* (a feature of 'Alexandrian' style), see Martial 8.70.
[71] Suet. *Ner.* 28–9.
[72] Though see also Suet. *Ner.* 7.1–2 where young Nero pleads the case of the Trojans.
[73] Degl' Innocenti Pierini (2013: 61–2) briefly explores this possibility.
[74] Byrne 2006: 104–5. In terms of literary style, Seneca's Maecenas may not be an entirely plausible Petronius (despite Byrne 2006, 2007). Yet the parallels between Petronius' Trimalchio and Seneca's Maecenas are perhaps suggestive, given that a case has been made for interpreting Petronius' portrait of Trimalchio as refracting features of Nero as he was viewed by his court circle (Walsh 1970: 137–9; Rose 1971: 77–9, 82–6; Edwards 2007: 167–71; cf. Vout 2009, Freudenburg 2017).

also note, is compared in Letter 114 to a character from a mime, another respect in which he foreshadows the actor-emperor.[75] Indeed, recent scholarship has underlined Maecenas' leading role in the development of performance culture in Rome.[76] And while Rome burned, or so Suetonius reports (*Ner.* 38.2), it was from the tower of Maecenas (*e turre Maecenatiana*) that Nero watched the fire 'delighted with what he termed "the beauty of the flames" and, dressed in his stage attire, he sang "the fall of Troy"' (*laetusque flammae, ut aiebat, pulchritudine, Halosin Ilii in illo suo scaenico habitu decantauit*). The ferocity of Seneca's critique of Maecenas (which many critics have found surprising)[77] thus becomes far more understandable.[78] The coda to the letter, introducing an extended political analogy, which recalls the *De clementia* (itself addressed to Nero), surely lends further weight to this suggestion.

At the same time, the details of Seneca's criticism of Maecenas' writing suggestively recall the critical comments made by Augustus himself, an emperor whose authority was legitimated through his claim to be a restorer of Roman morals (specifically as the *auctor* of moral legislation, as he describes himself at *RG* 8.5).[79] In criticising Maecenas' literary style, Seneca thus assimilated himself to Augustus, Nero's ancestor and the emperor on whom Nero claimed, in a speech at the start of his reign written by Seneca, he would model himself (Suet. *Ner.* 10).[80] Pliny, as was noted earlier, described Seneca (*HN* 14.51) as *princeps potentia*; at the time of the Pisonian conspiracy, some expressed the view that Seneca himself might become emperor in Nero's place (Tac. *Ann.* 15.65). It is hard to imagine the elderly philosopher wishing to take up such a burden. He may, however, have relished the piquancy of assuming an *auctoritas* redolent of the first emperor's in offering an implicit critique of his descendant's literary excesses.

---

[75] Stories also circulated about Maecenas' passion for the actor Bathyllus (Tac. *Ann.* 1.54.2).
[76] Wiseman 2016.
[77] Degl'Innocenti Pierini (2013: 59): 'meno facile è ipotizzare i motivi per cui voglia individuare solo nella persona di Mecenate le cause del declino della letteratura contemporanea', 'It's less easy to conjecture the motives for his desire to individuate the causes of the decline of contemporary literature solely in the character of Maecenas.'
[78] Though curiously Tacitus (*Ann.* 14.53) has Seneca compare himself with Maecenas, inasmuch as the latter successfully sought permission from his emperor to retire as adviser (with Burrus implicitly cast in the role of Agrippa).
[79] On *auctoritas* as a central plank of Augustus' rule, see Galinsky 1996: 10–44; Lowrie 2009: 279–308. For the struggle for authorial control between emperor and writer, see also Ziogas 2015.
[80] Augustus is a more problematic model in the *De clementia* (1.11.1–2). On Augustus as an *exemplum* for Nero, see Champlin 2003a: 138–44.

For Yun Lee Too, the letters constitute a reassertion of Seneca's tutorial role in relation to Nero as emperor: 'Seneca rehearses and revises his prior relationship with the boy-emperor with ... Lucilius, under the ironic guise of urging his addressee to stand back from participation in the state' (Too 1994: 213). Arguing that the *Epistulae Morales* is a self-deconstructing project, Too contends that the paraded 'failure of the didactic project he undertakes with Lucilius in the early 60s' serves to pre-empt those who would credit the teacher Seneca with responsibility for the acts of his pupil Nero. I would not subscribe to Too's view of the letters as self-deconstructing; the progress made by his addressee is a crucial feature of their trajectory. But certainly they cannot altogether escape the subject of Nero.

Nero's presence in the *Epistulae Morales* may be shadowy but the dynamics of his pathology echo those of the tyrants of Senecan tragedy. These tyrants take particular pleasure in self-consciously embracing the extreme opposite of virtue. Indeed the author of the pseudo-Senecan *Octavia* (a work composed not long after Seneca's death) evidently perceived close affinities between the anti-heroes of Seneca's dramatic works and Nero himself, even if the *Octavia*'s Nero is rather less self-conscious in his transgressions than, for instance, Atreus in the *Thyestes*.[81] As Ferri notes, Nero's entrance at l. 438, at the climax of the character Seneca's tirade against the vices of *libido*, *auaritia* and *luxuria*, figures him as their embodiment.[82] Seneca himself, meanwhile, plays the role of unsuccessful *satelles*, whose advice is brusquely rejected.[83]

Echoes of the dialogue between Seneca's advice and Nero's practice resonate throughout the letters. Seneca offers florid anatomisations of moral and aesthetic defects implicitly exemplified by Nero in domains where the emperor claimed particular distinction. Nero's occluded presence in the letters can be construed as an attempt to recuperate his spectacular excesses for Seneca's Stoic project. These elaborate accounts of moral failings have a role to play in Seneca's overall enterprise in the *Epistulae Morales*. As Philostratus has Apollonius of Tyana comment in relation to Nero, 'If an emperor becomes a subject of people's

---

[81] Buckley comments on the character of Nero in *Octavia* (2013: 135) 'electing ... to actualize in his own person the stage tyrants of Seneca's ... tragedy ... his key model is Atreus of *Thyestes*'; Ferri (2003: 248) also sees strong parallels, though he regards *Octavia*'s Nero as 'more human'. He also notes (Ferri 2003 ad [Sen.] *Oct*. 430–1) a pointed allusion to Sen. *Phaedr*. 987. On specific Neronian allusions in the *Thyestes* itself, see Torre 2017: 141.
[82] Ferri 2003 ad loc.
[83] On the representation of Seneca as a character in *Octavia*, see Ginsberg 2017: ch. 3.

entertainment, making the crowd rejoice at his degradation, what thoughts may he not prompt in those who love wisdom?' (*VA* 4.36.2).

Philosophy's Fight against Corruption

In conclusion, let us return briefly to Letter 90. While Seneca is drawn to the idealisation of early human society which characterises so many Roman texts and also features at length in this letter, his nostalgia for primitive living is significantly tempered by his stress on the pre-eminent role of philosophy as something that must be deliberately striven for, that requires discipline – and without which a true life of virtue is not possible (cf. 90.1). Thus, as Seneca makes clear, however salubrious the simple life led in primitive times, the conditions then were not conducive to the mature development of philosophy.

Paradoxically, it is precisely the proliferation of vice which makes necessary, and indeed renders possible, the full flowering of philosophy, no longer just a matter of wise advice on how to live (*praecepta*), of the kind that early kings may have dispensed, but a body of thought underpinned by theoretical doctrine (*decreta*) (cf. 95.32–4). 'But however excellent and free of guile was the life of the men of that age, they were not wise men ... Through their ignorance of things the men of those days were innocent'. 'To become good is an art', *ars est bonum fieri* (90.44). Only when it is challenged by human corruption can philosophy develop to acquire its mature form as fully *contemplatiua*.[84] Nostalgia for the so-called golden age can serve as a valuable prompt, encouraging us to emulate the material simplicity of a life in accordance with nature, but the knowledge and the range of choices humanity has painfully acquired in making the transition to a more advanced existence are essential prerequisites for the practice of philosophy. A case could be made then for seeing the elaborate and ingenious vices of Neronian Rome generally – and the emperor himself in particular – as essential material for philosophical reflection. Only in an age of flagrant vice, perhaps, can a truly militant virtue come into its own.

At the same time, if the greatest *imperium* is *imperare sibi*, this is exactly what the *imperator* conspicuously fails to do, or so the *Epistulae Morales* slyly suggest. Even if the historical Nero was never quite the caricature of luxury and vice the letters implicitly constitute him to be, Nero, as he is imagined by his critics, lurks just out of sight at multiple points in the letters. Seneca keys in to tropes of the discourse of denigration, reinforcing

[84] Zago 2012: 130.

their association with Nero without mentioning him, as a consequence of the position from which Seneca speaks, in a final (possibly fatal) assertion of his own authorial power. Seneca's denunciation of the vices of Neronian Rome has left an indelible mark on later portraits of Nero himself, even if we may not be able to distinguish between the activities of the historical emperor, rebelling against his tutor's advice, and later portraits of Nero, themselves drawing inspiration from the same tutor's florid accounts of the vices of his age.

CHAPTER 10

Marcus Aurelius: Medi()ations Not Medi(c)ations
John Henderson

Let us leave, if possible, *myself*. – But 'tis impossible,
– I must go along with you to the end of the work.
(Sterne 1759–67: 6 Chapter 20)

Watch out for the paratext!
(Genette 1997: 410)[1]

Plenty of evidence shows that Roman emperors felt challenged to press their bid to command their own exemplarity by producing written versions of their name/fame of choice. A telling fictive instance sketches an acute version of the dynamics: *famae celebris Hadrianus tam cupidus fuit ut libros uitae suae scriptos a se libertis suis litteratis dederit, iubens ut eos suis nominibus publicarent* ('So desirous of a wide-spread reputation was Hadrian that he even wrote his own biography; this he gave to his educated freedmen, with instructions to publish it under their own names.' SHA *Hadrian* 16.1, perhaps the inaugural *Life* in the serialization).[2] A reign might strive mightily to centre on achievements in administration and foreign policy (conquest), on the here and now of bossing the empire, on processing that for worldwide consumption, but the story of each ruler's coming to power cast a long shadow forward over their significance in their role in the continuing saga of their management of succession: what no Caesar's autography could control would be the matching of their own induction to the success or otherwise of their oversight of replacement: paradigmatically, Augustus' *Res Gestae* is proclaimed a Tiberian document by their attribution as by *Diuus Augustus*, and textual blanketing of the *après moi* is turned on its head by Tacitus' (inaugural) account of the souring of the first

---

[1] Sterne here nails the insistence of the writing of 'I' within the written, including no matter how bleached ('un=spoken') a written 'I': the topic of this chapter. For stealthy permeation by paratext, see p. 191.
[2] See Westall and Brenk 2011 for political autobiographies/memoirs from Trajan through Caracalla.

emperor's last years through to the funeral/ascension with indignation at the prospect of Agrippa Postumus or Tiberius to come (*Annals* 1.4–10).

In Marcus Aurelius' case, his narrativization was always going to be dominated by the insistence of his elaborate co-optation into the line of imperial succession; and his last years portended commensurate anxiety over his provision for scheduling the future. While his track record in government was secure, and he battled on to the end to rack up a generalissimo's *res gestae* in the field around the Danube, neither consideration would count for much set beside the trajectory between acclamation for the schooling that brought him to power and the shifts he tried for handing the empire on, the trepidation he could not dispel, and the ruination he left at his demise/ascension, as first anticipated and then actualized. The SHA *Marcus* maps the reckoning in justly stark (and targeted) terms: the opening string of chapters devoted to Marcus' Succeeding as Emperor (A) first segues the ins and outs of the complex stages in his morphing into emperor with his matching scheme for the future (1–8):

A1   Succeeding as Emperor

1. Stemmatics. Birth – sibling – wife. Marcus morphed from 'Catilius' at the outset to 'Annius Ver(issim)us' as adult.
2. Childhood – a penchant for Philosophy. Tutors. At twelve turned to the Philosophical life. His Philosophy tutors. **3.** Attended lectures through to after his adoption by Antoninus Pius.
4. Under Hadrian, at six . . ., at eight . . . ; an omen of his rule. At fifteen betrothed. Attended games, races, fowling etc., but Philosophy distinguished his adolescence. **5.** At eighteen Pius, his uncle-in-law, was adopted by Hadrian, and Marcus was marked out for adoption by Pius (and, we're wrongly told, part of the plan was to adopt L. Verus!); the portentous 'ivory shoulders' dream.
6. Under Pius he was raised to 'Caesar'; then as consul married Faustina, daughter of Pius. And produced a daughter. A prediction of his rule. **7.** Over twenty-three years Marcus stuck by and with Pius, formally becoming his deathbed heir. On accession he made himself Rome's first ever co-emperor, with his 'brother' L. Verus, betrothing his daughter to Verus. **8.** The co-rule went well – Marcus continued his devotion to Philosophy.

Marcus, that is, travelled a multi-phase journey to the top, sucked into the orbit, then positioned as a cog in Hadrian's machined wheel, evincing preplanning way beyond the Nerva-through-Hadrian precedents. In modern times a system of 'adoptive emperors' has been starred, from Trajan through Marcus, for the very good reason of Marcus' own eventual legacy. But here special notice *is* taken of the invention of a shared throne, assigned by the *Life* to a 'philosophically' oriented reluctance.[3] Next, in stark concision, tumble out *Events, dear boy* (8–14):

A2 Success as Emperor

8. The régime faces war, in Parthia ... etc., etc.
9–12. Governance and admin – the business of courts, senate, finance, the people. The family celebrates a togetherness triumph.
13. War resumes, against the Marcomanni etc.
    Plague breaks out.
14. L. Verus dies. ||

In a flash, just when things were going so well, best-laid plans capsize. Narrative marks the disjuncture as the *Life* at once double-takes in twin recaps, turned/turning sour in underscored and motivated consternation:

B ~~Succession~~

15. Marcus suffers ridicule. As he presides over the ascension of *diuus Verus*, poisonous gossip disseminates poison gossip. A revolt breaks out.
16. Marcus' son – 'cursed and foul' – is promoted to Caesar.
    Marcus may make a good sole emperor, but Philosophy ... (reprise of 5).
17. That war goes on, against the Marcomanni (from 13.). After that plague. Good rule persists.
18. Marcus is loved, through a reign of eighteen years to his death/ascension. Yes he is blessed – except for that son.
19. Or was he no son of Marcus, considering Faustina's sluttery? No, no stain attaches to Marcus for that son – that gladiator, of that wife of a slut. He is still a god for you, Diocletian – and unmatchable, as emperor Philosopher. ||

For Marcus SHA is *the* dyarchic precedent, for Diocletianic tetrarchy; his reluctance to rule will be outdone by Diocletian's attempt to retire in one

---

[3] Material relating to formulaic polarity between philosophy getting into a Roman student and development into a properly wired Roman is collected in Woodman and Kraus 2014: 100 on Tac. *Agr.* 4.3.

piece from the throne, which was no philosophical cop-out but an attempt to 'adopt on' an empire with a prospect at least of ruling, and fighting, and leading, on more than one front, with a best shot at finessing revolt and coup d'état. Marcus' ('philosophically'?) pallid shot at realizing the Hadrian-Pius plan for a royal family with Verus would collapse at once into father-son succession by all accounts already cursed at the time (as acted out by the *Life*). *Commodus!*[4]

C1 Success *Downside* as Emperor

20. Marcus' *acta* after 14: his new start – as if glad. He re-married off his daughter, inaptly. His son Verus had died aged seven.
    There was that plague and that war, Marcomanni.
    He was a success, but Philosophically harsh – and resented by the people; gossip said he meant to substitute 'Philosophy for games'.
24. There was that revolt (reprise of **15**).
    Marcus brought peace out East, impressed Philosophy there.
27. Talk of 'Philosopher kings'.
    He meant to finish the Marcomanni war.

C2 ~~Succession~~

28. On his deathbed, lamented Commodus. His death (reprise of **17–18**). On that deathbed – 'think of plague, scorn death'. He wanted son dead.
29. He'd favoured wife's lovers. He was mocked on stage, by the people. Gossip said he was not as *uerus* as Pius or Verus etc. His parents were *diui*. After that wife Faustina died, Marcus took a concubine – there would be no stepmothers. ||

This is the sort of 'Good Emperor – except he couldn't fashion a repeat for Afterwards' profile that Marcus knew[5] he had coming through the final years spent on campaign over the Danube when he was writing what has become known as his album of *Meditations* (apparently) in twelve books ('*M*' hereafter).[6] The manuscript tradition is opaque, but that the first

---

[4] Thus, too, spake *Tristrapedia*: Sterne 1759–67: 6 ch. 5, recalling that 5/14 bad teachers were very soon cashiered by Marcus Aurelius but not before they'd done for Commodus.

[5] *M*10.36 has Marcus imagining what they'll say when he's gone (Brunt 1974: 12).

[6] The none too authoritative title for *M* of ΤΩΝ ΕΙΣ ΕΑΥΤΟΝ is too often twisted into validating dialogue with/address to self, but speaking 'to' is πρός in anyone's Greek, and Marcus' rubric would fit *M*4.3, εἰς ἑαυτὸν ἀναχωρεῖν, and the programmatically accented 8.61, εἰσιέναι εἰς τὸ ἡγεμονικὸν ἑκάστου· παρέχειν δὲ καὶ ἑτέρῳ παντὶ εἰσιέναι εἰς τὸ ἑαυτοῦ ἡγεμονικόν.

volume serves as a paratextual threshold to what follows is uncontroversial (though very often sidelined – dampened to the point of occlusion), and that it represents a narrative along the lines of the *SHA Life* displaced into a very different register and discourse becomes clear upon examination. *M*1 provides a starter-kit signature, a chronologically arranged composition with the built-in autobiographic dynamic of coherence through teleology, drawing ever closer to capturing the moment of narration in the 'I' of the 'Here' and 'Now'. We shall get to know a Marcus, the one who writes *M* by reading that Marcus. So much is *not* hard to make out, in this 'history of oneself through the mediation of others':[7]

[NB Rest assured that processing styles and annotations in this schematic anatomy of *M*1 will be explained in the reading that follows.]

A The Making of Marcus

1–4. Stemmatics. Grandfather (Annius) Verus. Father, Mother. Great-grandfather (Catilius). Home tutoring:

5–15. Tutors: **5.** at odds with races, games etc. **6.** no nonsense, e.g. quail-keeping etc. (ἐπτοῆσθαι pun) – but Philosophy. **Writing dialogues as a boy**. 'Greek' lifestyle. **7.** Rusticus **vs. logick, vs. writing theory or protreptic, vs. parading as ethical. vs. rhetoric, poetry, wit. Letters plain as his were to *MY* mama at 'S'** {= circumstantial detail}. **Close reading. Read Epictetus.** Apollonius, remaining the same e.g. on loss of child. Friends.

9. Friends. **11.** Training against tyrant habits. Aristos *AMONGST US* are cold. **12. Against writing '*I'M* busy'.**

13. Friends. 14 *MY* 'brother' Severus on Stoic politics. Friends.

15. Maximus.||

16. Father [Pius]: opposing pederasty. Councils. Friends. Measures *in his reign*. Good governance and admin. Using Fortune's gifts. Honouring true Philosophers. Managing without medication. Good governance and admin, lifestyle {NB **16.8.** a tricolon of nominatives + circumstantial details clothes from X, estates at Y, incident at Z}. Fortitude as e.g. in Maximus' illness. ||

B Being *Me*, Marcus

17.1–2. The Gods: grandfathers, parents, sister, tutors, family, friends (recap of **1–15**) and '...that *I* tripped over none of 'em, though

---

[7] Dickson 2009: 120.

but for Gods' blessing that would've failed *ME*'. No more time being reared with father's concubine (μὴ ἐπὶ πλέον refrain). Keeping youth safe, not manning up before adulthood – yes, and then some (ἔτι καὶ ἐπιλαβεῖν τοῦ χρόνου).

17.3. Subject to ruler and father that *would* remove *MY* pride (reprise of 16).

17.4. Fortunate to have a brother [= L. Verus], focusing *ME* on care of *MY*self and gladdening *ME*. *MY* children fine.

My not pressing on further in rhetoric and poetry etc., when *I* maybe would have got caught if *I*'d felt *I* was going places (μὴ ἐπὶ πλέον).

Getting those tutors hiked to the status they seemed *TO ME* to want, not deferring in hopes of *MY* doing it later, as they were still young. Getting to know Apollonius (~ **1.8**), Rusticus (~ **1.7**), Maximus (~ **1.15**).

17.5. Ideas on the Gods, reminders and (almost) 'tutoring from the Gods'.

17.6. *MY* body holding out so long in a life like this.

Not touching B or T {NB details left aside} but getting healthy in sexual bouts later too (ὑγιᾶναι). Getting cross often with Rusticus but doing nothing more *I*'d regret (μηδὲν πλέον).

My mother – though heading for a young death – living her last years *WITH ME*.

17.7. 'Every time *I* wanted to help someone out, *I* never heard there's no cash, and similar need never befell *ME*.' Having [had] such a nice wife. Having plenty of fine tutors for the children.

17.8. Getting help through dreams esp. for not spitting blood and dizziness, and that [!weird thing ?at Caieta?! = *locus desperatus*]. 'When *I* was smitten with Philosophy, **not falling into the hands of some pedant, not settling down ?over books?, not solving logical puzzles, or living cosmology**' ('reprise' of 7.). All these 'require Gods for helpers, and Fortune - x |.' ||

Through the idiom of a roll-call of exemplary presences in the Marcufacture of this emperor which runs along from origins through reigning, *M*1 sets up a priamel-cap rhetorical structure in which the adoptive father Pius arrives, as Grand Mediator, to comprise and outdo all the rest of the influences that have preceded, before both columns (**1–15** + **16**) are cashed out in **17**, the climactic finale where we meet Marcus in (first) person, as he is, praise the gods for the training he has highlighted in

1–16, another Pius, with no more call for medication than he. This familial Marcus, ready kitted out with wife and kids, in the business of providing training for the succession, gets no further, beyond contriving to intone in a rush 'and no more':

<s>C. Me writing 'and no more': mê epi pleon</s>

*M*1 shares the challenges of governance and admin as reflected in his Pius but entirely eschews *res gestae* and admits no reference to dyarchy,[8] to adoptive succession,[9] to pre-planning of his own. What had he to say, given that at the time of writing these beatitudes everyone mentioned has pre-deceased him? Beyond those tutorial friendships, in fact, this Marcus finds a format that skeletalizes narrativity almost to the point of disqualification (the only 'detail' that could count as fleshing out, let alone animating, proceedings was noticed at 7, 16, 17.6). *M*2–12 *will* contain mentions of court and the front, of children and an emperor's functions, and Marcus will never in the course of his *souci de soi* on paper quite bury reminders that this is the Antonine Roman emperor fashioning a self, a weird self perhaps, but one that requires no other form of medication than this practice of writing,[10] towards which he was steered in the course of his elaborated training (references to his preferred forms of writing appeared above **in bold**, chiefly through negation). Our paratext has advertised itself self-referentially as the approved scheme of writing in question – besides managing to smuggle in a generic self-classification as *bios* at the death (17.6):

τὸ ἀντισχεῖν μοι τὸ <u>σῶμα</u> ἐπὶ τοσοῦτον <u>ἐν τοιούτῳ βίῳ</u>

My body holding out so long IN A *LIFE* LIKE THIS

and indicating to us for envoi how to appreciate t/his self-medication, in what he hasn't written, in the rhetoric, scholarship, logic, and physics that he hasn't done, isn't doing, and won't do (17.8) – which must leave what we might call ethics, writing ethics as his *bios*?

But in squeezing out space or indeed function for negotiating the conduct of imperial rule as Marcus' Romans knew it from narratives such as Hadrianic Suetonius' *Lives,* this 'I' has contrived to self-erase so

---

[8] On this, see now Priwitzer 2017.
[9] Was there ever a principle? (Stanton 1969: 583–4). Hekster 2015: 55–6, 62–4 argues hard that father-son succession always conferred an extra layer of legitimacy on an emperor.
[10] See *M*3.13, where Dr Marcus is armed with *dógmata*-doct rin' for instruments and scalpels.

thoroughly as to evoke un-onymity precisely while marking out his formation as subject. In the 'précis' offered above, every first person verbalized in the course of *M*1 was marked *IN ITALIC CAPS*. Instead of the linguistic egocentricity expected of any project in imperatorial autodiegesis, *this* Caesar forgoes even the famous third person pioneered by Julius, and trusts his egos to a basket that eliminates his self altogether from his training.[11] (The redundant, so emphatic, '*MY* mama' and '*MY* brother' at 7 and 14 plus the incipiently anecdotal sentence for Pius nipped in the bud at 16.8 buck the ensemble/s of 1–16.) What allows this is the presentation of this moulding for life through a catena of items with παρά + the genitive, where the topic appears as τοῦ + the infinitive. This is understood to indicate the origination in experience of conceptualizations of particular phenomena or characteristics, so that the list cumulates to form a bundle of notions available to the thinking of the person checking out the items. Marcus got to know what 'good morals and/in combination with absenting of temper' amount to 'from granddad Verus'; he starts up, not claiming he's acquired the qualities (and so bragging), nor even attributing possession of the qualities to the mediary (and so hero-worshipping, and thereby self-heroizing by reflection), but claiming that he's made the acquaintance with, and internalized into his repartee, the existence of the stated entity (or, as I hinted in keeping open the play between two components represented by 'and/in combination with', what its slogan points to as a problematic, an issue). This philosophically inflected syntax often, as already here at the outset, features the jargonesque repertoire of second-century CE Greek moral-philosophical vocabulary/theorization,[12] so that the decision of this Roman emperor to commit to the Greek language for *his* encounter with self represents an extreme form of unLatinity, way beyond the reach of bureaucratese (of chancellery translatability à la *RGDA*, for example), and as such invents a specific Graeco-Roman Caesar-Writing Caesar. The type of this least Latin text that it can get away with showing us its being comes most appropriately from this opening salvo (*M*1.1–5):[13]

1. Παρὰ τοῦ πάππου Οὐήρου τὸ καλό-ηθες καὶ ἀ-όργητον.
2. Παρὰ τῆς δόξης καὶ μνήμης τῆς περὶ τοῦ γεννήσαντος τὸ αἰδῆμον καὶ ἀρρενικόν.

---

[11] Power 2014: 6–7 gives stats for the massive first person ego trips doled out to emperors in Suetonius' *Caesars*.
[12] Well-marshalled and interimplicated as associative swarms by Giavatto 2008 esp. Parte 1.
[13] The first persons introduced by the Loeb translator are struck through; in 1.1 and 1.5 the claim to virtue posited in 'I learned' is only the first such vicious misrepresentation.

3. Παρὰ τῆς μητρὸς τὸ θεο-σεβὲς καὶ μετα-δοτικὸν καὶ <u>ἀφ-εκτικὸν</u> οὐ μόνον τοῦ κακοποιεῖν, ἀλλὰ καὶ τοῦ ἐπὶ ἐννοίας γίνεσθαι τοιαύτης· ἔτι δὲ τὸ <u>λιτὸν</u> κατὰ τὴν δίαιταν καὶ <u>πόρρω</u> τῆς πλουσιακῆς διαγωγῆς.
4. Παρὰ τοῦ προπάππου τὸ <u>μὴ</u> εἰς δημοσίας διατριβὰς φοιτῆσαι καὶ τὸ ἀγαθοῖς διδασκάλοις <u>κατ'οἶκον</u> χρήσασθαι καὶ τὸ γνῶναι ὅτι εἰς τὰ τοιαῦτα δεῖ ἐκτενῶς ἀναλίσκειν.
5. Παρὰ τοῦ τροφέως τὸ <u>μήτε</u> Πρασιανὸς <u>μήτε</u> Βενετιανὸς <u>μήτε</u> Παλμουλάριος ἢ Σκουτάριος γενέσθαι· καὶ τὸ φερέ-πονον καὶ <u>ὀλιγο-δεές</u>· καὶ τὸ αὐτο-υργικὸν καὶ <u>ἀ-πολύπραγμον</u>· καὶ τὸ <u>δυσ-πρόσ-δεκτον</u> διαβολῆς.

1. From ~~my~~ grandfather Verus ~~I learned~~ <u>good morals</u> and <u>the government of</u> ~~my~~ <u>temper</u>.
2. From the reputation and remembrance of ~~my~~ father, <u>modesty</u> and a manly character.
3. From ~~my~~ mother, piety and beneficence, and <u>abstinence</u>, not only from evil deeds, but even from evil thoughts; and further, <u>simplicity</u> in ~~my~~ way of living, <u>far removed from</u> the habits of the rich.
4. From ~~my~~ great-grandfather, <u>not to</u> have frequented public schools, and to have had good teachers <u>at home</u>, and to know that on such things a man should spend liberally.
5. From ~~my~~ governor, to be <u>neither</u> of the green <u>nor</u> of the blue party at the games in the Circus, <u>nor</u> a partisan either of the Parmularius or the Scutarius at the gladiators' fights; from him too ~~I learned~~ endurance of labour, and <u>to want little</u>, and to work with ~~my~~ own hands, and <u>not to meddle with other people's affairs</u>, and <u>not to be ready to listen</u> to slander.

In *M1* 'I' arrives precisely at the point where the tome comes to me, at **1.17**, with the self-portrait of our emperor as a wizened dog, blessed by Fortune/ the gods with the intellectual repertoire he has sketched, and cognizant of the endowment that it all adds up to, a self-portrait founded in experience of others. Very little indeed of what he has written in the approach-work to this miniature *Life* is writable in Latin – all those multi-compounds, privative negations, and terms/*loci* from academic philosophy ... It must lodge with the reader, more pointedly, that so much of the thrust of this mental furniture consists in recommendation of the ~~prohibitive~~, of ~~negation/abstention/distantiation~~ (as underlined above). No, the joys of reading Marcus do not and cannot, *Quirites*, replicate in Romespeak: thus, an exquisite favourite turn of his style consists precisely in rhetorical figures in and around 'l'axiôma sterêtikon', where:

> ≪l'enunciato privativo≫] ... aiuta a confermare l'importante sfumatura che distingue il termine negativo dal termine privativo (eventualmente, a sua volta negato): quest'ultimo è più specifico, perché contiene già in sé l'elemento di cui costituisce l'opposto.[14]

> [the privative statement] ... helps confirm the important nuance that distinguishes the negative term from the privative term (which is eventually, in turn, negated): this last is extra specific as already containing within itself the core of what it sets up as its opposite.

With this starkly graphematic livery goes the displacement of accountability by/for this self for rulings made and missed, and deeds done or undone – and for his vindication of the training that has made him in the training programme that will leave the empire to its outcome. Instead, Marcus determines to define Marcus strictly as practising – as event-proof *writing* – product, and suppress the duty of anticipation. Stuck at *SHA Marcus* 14 and not about to budge! In return, we recognize (variously) how in the diplomatics of first-person self-promotion, concentrated absenting delivers strongly motivated presencing:

> We must not conclude that Marcus is absent from his *Meditations*. Rather, he is present in them in many ways, and the work has an autobiographical value which is limited, but very real.[15]
>
> This rigorous asceticism, which amounts practically to cutting out whole areas of experience, helps explain the intensity, the claustrophobic concentration, of his writing.[16]

So much for *M*1, as conditioning entrée to the enter-prise, prejudicing but not fixing what lies ahead, what truths. For:

> The ultimate destiny of the paratext is sooner or later to catch up with its text in order to *make a book.*[17]

For a preponderance of scholarship, *M* is, and has been, important-through-crucial not as text, but as practice, as thoughts, as access to *thinking*.[18] On the one hand, Marcus wrestles up front with the undeniable

---

[14] Giavatto 2008: 131.   [15] Hadot 1998: 257.   [16] Rutherford 1989: 120–1.
[17] Genette 1997: 403.
[18] The classic account was Misch 1950: 443–85: 'The *M* of Marcus Aurelius', where 'this mature beauty and goodness of soul shine out ... in self-communion ... (which) only produced a literary publication because it *happened* to have been recorded in writing.' Still, a book: 'Marcus collected into a book the notes that had then accumulated' (443–4). On Misch's mythology, see Güthenke

givenness of his identity as Roman, Antonine, Emperor, interset with his prerogative of eluding any dampeners on his capacity to self-define that stereotyping expectations might nevertheless apply: what does Marcus spell? Not (any old) Caesar, is what counts:

Ἐάν τίς σοι προβάλῃ <u>πῶς γράφεται τὸ Ἀντωνίνου ὄνομα</u>, μήτι κατεντεινόμενος προοίσῃ ἕκαστον τῶν στοιχείων; τί οὖν ἐὰν ὀργίζωνται, μήτι ἀντοργιῇ; μήτι οὐκ ἐξαριθμήσῃ πρᾴως προιὼν ἕκαστον τῶν γραμμάτων; (M6.26)

If any man should propose to thee the question, <u>how the name Antoninus is written</u>, wouldst thou with a straining of the voice utter each letter? What then if they grow angry, wilt thou be angry too? Wilt thou not go on with composure and number every letter?

But on the other:

Ὅρα μὴ <u>ἀποκαισαρωθῇς, μὴ βαφῇς</u>: γίνεται γάρ. τήρησον οὖν σεαυτὸν ἁπλοῦν, ἀγαθόν, ἀκέραιον, σεμνόν, ἄκομψον, τοῦ δικαίου φίλον, θεοσεβῆ, εὐμενῆ, φιλόστοργον, ἐρρωμένον πρὸς τὰ πρέποντα ἔργα. ἀγώνισαι, ἵνα τοιοῦτος συμμείνῃς, οἷόν σε ἠθέλησε ποιῆσαι φιλοσοφία. αἰδοῦ θεούς, σῷζε ἀνθρώπους. βραχὺς ὁ βίος: εἷς καρπὸς τῆς ἐπιγείου ζωῆς, διάθεσις ὁσία καὶ πράξεις κοινωνικαί. 2 <u>πάντα ὡς Ἀντωνίνου μαθητής</u> ... (M6.30.1–2)

<u>Take care that thou art not made into a Caesar, that thou art not dyed with this dye</u>; for such things happen. Keep thyself then simple, good, pure, serious, free from affectation, a friend of justice, a worshipper of the gods, kind, affectionate, strenuous in all proper acts. Strive to continue to be such as Philosophy wished to make thee. Reverence the gods, and help men. Short is life. There is only one fruit of this terrene life, a pious disposition and social acts. 2 <u>Do everything as a disciple of Antoninus</u> ...

What matters to this writing is indeed energetic drive, serious application of applied seriousness – to the exclusion of anecdote, specifics, events (i.e. 'detail'), and, for the most part, linkage into the frames of educated culture. The barrage of non-sequitur topics alluding to mainstream Stoic self-regulatory discourse 'after Epictetus' blocks out a programme of gnomic pro-imperatives delivered in a stop-start ferment of imaginative sound bites, parading anti-compositional traits that connote in-the-moment urgency, complete with the hustle of self-flagellating authenticity and anti-book-learning of the mortal in a hurry. The stylistic contortions and antics constitute a diary in denial, as historicality

---

2016: 35–9. Giavatto 2008 brightly highlights the image-fecundity and expressive brio of *M* (esp. Parte 2).

remains a rejected blank, and the entries pound their aleatory workout from the repertoire for the intellect.[19] This has made of Marcus, beyond hagiography for an intelligent pagan asceticism, a precious survival of the Hellenistic-imperial elite 'Greek' lifestyle. Not, insist the philosophers, a Philosopher caught at it, churning away at churning away in readiness for revisionary impact while exemplifying and inducing ever-renewed dedication to the ethical self; but, say cultural historians, in the process of re-locating Philosophy from creed and dogma to scrupulous practice, to vigilance through self-goading; precisely, that is to say, to a vocal-verbal-rhetorical 'meditation', now preserved in the aspic of Marcus' writing frenzy. Against the various sides of this disputation over the academic, and indeed 'spiritual', status of such philosophizing comes the recent iconoclasm of the re-location of *M* to the status of a well-documented style of regular professional class workout through rhetorical limbering which elite officials and rulers used to set themselves up across the period begun with the late Republic's plunge into Greek schooling and in full swing under the Antonines:

> Jamais Marc Aurèle ne se présente comme un philosophe stoicien, et c'est la raison pour laquelle les humanistes, qui savaient faire la différence entre un empéreur et un philosophe, se sont bien gardés de le traiter comme tel.[20]
>
> Not once does Marcus Aurelius present himself as a Stoic philosopher, and that's why the Humanists – who knew how to tell the difference between an emperor and a philosopher – took care not to treat him as such.

Here we catch the Roman emperor setting himself up to perform his public/official roles ('droiture'). Yet this restitution of *M* to the hand of the Roman emperor still treats him as a generalizable member of the Graeco-Roman elite, distinguished mainly by the fact that his routine of private antics/agilities has, no doubt because he *is* the apotheosed emperor of blessed memory, beaten their constitutive ephemerality and made it on through. While recognizing the power of paratextuality to mis-presage its text, I regard the entrapment as the contrast between the taut control of *M*1's para-*bios* formatting and the veritable κυκεών[21] of scrambled paragraphs to follow, whereas the upheld cueing lies in the due presentation of *M* as indeed one contained and shaped *composition* framing this special/weird emperor's autographic mode of choice.

For a start, *M*2–12 is encased in a frame that heralds a book-text programme 'from start to exit-line':

---

[19] 'Spiritual diary' ... 'his own private devotions' was the position sponsored by Brunt 1974: 1, 5.
[20] Vesperini 2016: 17.   [21] *M*6.10, 9.39, with ramifying amplifications elsewhere.

Dawn's up (2.1–5)[22]

2.1. ‖ Ἕωθεν προλέγειν ἑαυτῷ: συντεύξομαι περιέργῳ, ἀχαρίστῳ, ὑβριστῇ, δολερῷ, βασκάνῳ, ἀκοινωνήτῳ: πάντα ταῦτα συμβέβηκεν ἐκείνοις παρὰ τὴν ἄγνοιαν τῶν ἀγαθῶν καὶ κακῶν. ἐγὼ δὲ ...

Begin the morning by saying to thyself, I shall meet with the busybody, the ungrateful, arrogant, deceitful, envious, unsocial. All these things happen to them by reason of their ignorance of what is good and evil. But I ...

2.2. Ὅ τί ποτε τοῦτό εἰμι, σαρκία ἐστὶ καὶ πνευμάτιον καὶ τὸ ἡγεμονικόν. ἄφες τὰ βιβλία: μηκέτι σπῶ. οὐ δέδοται, ἀλλ' ὡς ἤδη ἀποθνῄσκων τῶν μὲν σαρκίων καταφρόνησον: λύθρος καὶ ὀστάρια καὶ κροκύφαντος, ἐκ νεύρων, φλεβίων, ἀρτηριῶν πλεγμάτιον. θέασαι δὲ καὶ τὸ πνεῦμα ὁποῖόν τι ἐστιν: ἄνεμος, οὐδὲ ἀεὶ τὸ αὐτό, ἀλλὰ πάσης ὥρας ἐξεμούμενον καὶ πάλιν ῥοφούμενον. τρίτον οὖν ἐστι τὸ ἡγεμονικόν. ὧδε ἐπινοήθητι: γέρων εἶ: μηκέτι ...

Whatever this is that I am, it is a little flesh and breath, and the ruling part. Throw away thy books; no longer distract thyself: it is not allowed; but as if thou wast now dying, despise the flesh; it is blood and bones and a network, a contexture of nerves, veins, and arteries. See the breath also, what kind of a thing it is, air, and not always the same, but every moment sent out and again sucked in. The third then is the ruling part: consider thus: Thou art an old man. No longer ...

2.3. τὴν δὲ τῶν βιβλίων δίψαν ῥῖψον, ἵνα μὴ γογγύζων ἀποθάνῃς

But cast away the thirst after books, that thou mayest not die murmuring ...

2.4. Μέμνησο ἐκ πόσου ταῦτα ἀναβάλλῃ καὶ ὁποσάκις προθεσμίας λαβὼν παρὰ τῶν θεῶν οὐ χρᾷ αὐταῖς. δεῖ δὲ ἤδη ποτὲ αἰσθέσθαι ... αὖθις οὐκ ἐξέσται.

---

[22] Cf. 5.1: Ὄρθρου, ὅταν δυσόκνως ἐξεγείρῃ, πρόχειρον ἔστω ὅτι ἐπὶ ἀνθρώπου ἔργον ἐγείρομαι: τί οὖν δυσκολαίνω, εἰ πορεύομαι ἐπὶ τὸ ποιεῖν ὧν ἕνεκεν γέγονα καὶ ὧν χάριν προῆγμαι εἰς τὸν κόσμον; ἢ ἐπὶ τοῦτο κατεσκεύασμαι, ἵνα κατακείμενος ἐν στρωματίοις ἐμαυτὸν θάλπω; 'In the morning when thou risest unwillingly, let this thought be present – I am rising to the work of a human being. Why then am I dissatisfied if I am going to do the things for which I exist and for which I was brought into the world? Or have I been made for this, to lie in the bed-clothes and keep myself warm?'

> Remember how long thou hast been putting off these things, and how often thou hast received an opportunity from the gods, and yet dost not use it. Thou must now at last perceive ... it will never return.

2.5. Πάσης ὥρας φρόντιζε στιβαρῶς ὡς Ῥωμαῖος καὶ ἄρρην τὸ ἐν χερσὶ μετὰ τῆς ἀκριβοῦς καὶ ἀπλάστου σεμνότητος καὶ φιλοστοργίας καὶ ἐλευθερίας καὶ δικαιότητος πράσσειν καὶ σχολὴν σαυτῷ ἀπὸ πασῶν τῶν ἄλλων φαντασιῶν πορίζειν.

> Every moment think steadily as a Roman and a man to do what thou hast in hand with perfect and simple dignity, and feeling of affection, and freedom, and justice; and to give thyself relief from all other thoughts.

And in the End...

12.36. Ἄνθρωπε, ἐπολιτεύσω ἐν τῇ μεγάλῃ ταύτῃ πόλει: τί σοι διαφέρει, εἰ πέντε ἔτεσιν ἢ τρισί; τὸ γὰρ κατὰ τοὺς νόμους ἴσον ἑκάστῳ. τί οὖν δεινόν, εἰ τῆς πόλεως ἀποπέμπει σε οὐ τύραννος οὐδὲ δικαστὴς ἄδικος, ἀλλ' ἡ φύσις ἡ εἰσαγαγοῦσα, οἷον εἰ κωμῳδὸν ἀπολύοι τῆς σκηνῆς ὁ παραλαβὼν στρατηγός; —ἀλλ' οὐκ εἶπον τὰ πέντε μέρη, ἀλλὰ τὰ τρία. —καλῶς εἶπας: ἐν μέντοι τῷ βίῳ τὰ τρία ὅλον τὸ δρᾶμά ἐστι. τὸ γὰρ τέλειον ἐκεῖνος ὁρίζει ὁ τότε μὲν τῆς συγκρίσεως, νῦν δὲ τῆς διαλύσεως αἴτιος: σὺ δὲ ἀναίτιος ἀμφοτέρων. ἄπιθι οὖν ἵλεως: καὶ γὰρ ὁ ἀπολύων ἵλεως. ||

> Hey, you, member of the human race, you've lived as a citizen in a great city. Five years or a hundred – what's the difference? The laws make no distinction. And to be sent away from it, not by a tyrant or a dishonest judge, but by Nature, who first invited you in – why is that so terrible? Like the impresario ringing down the curtain on an actor: 'But I've only gotten through three acts ... !' Yes. This will be a drama in three acts, the length fixed by the power that directed your creation, and now directs your dissolution. Neither was yours to determine. So make your exit with grace – the same grace shown to you. ||

Within these bookends, the third tranche encases its own self within strongly marked borders:

3.1. || Οὐχὶ τοῦτο μόνον δεῖ λογίζεσθαι, ὅτι καθ' ἑκάστην ἡμέραν ἀπαναλίσκεται ὁ βίος καὶ μέρος ἔλαττον αὐτοῦ καταλείπεται, ἀλλὰ κἀκεῖνο λογιστέον, ὅτι, εἰ ἐπὶ πλέον βιώῃ τις, ἐκεῖνό γε ἄδηλον, εἰ ἐξαρκέσει ὁμοία αὖθις ἡ διάνοια πρὸς τὴν σύνεσιν τῶν πραγμάτων καὶ τῆς θεωρίας τῆς συντεινούσης εἰς τὴν ἐμπειρίαν τῶν τε θείων καὶ τῶν ἀνθρωπείων. ἐὰν γὰρ παραληρεῖν ἄρξηται ... χρὴ οὖν ἐπείγεσθαι οὐ μόνον τῷ ἐγγυτέρω τοῦ θανάτου ἑκάστοτε γίνεσθαι, ἀλλὰ καὶ διὰ τὸ τὴν ἐννόησιν τῶν πραγμάτων καὶ τὴν παρακολούθησιν προαπολήγειν. ||

We ought to consider not only that our life is daily wasting away and a smaller part of it is left, but another thing also must be taken into the account, that if a man should live longer, it is quite uncertain whether the understanding will still continue sufficient for the comprehension of things, and retain the power of contemplation which strives to acquire the knowledge of the divine and the human. For if he shall begin to fall into dotage ... We must make haste then, not only because we are daily nearer to death, but also because the conception of things and the understanding of them cease first. ||

3.14–16. Μηκέτι πλανῶ· οὔτε γὰρ τὰ ὑπομνημάτιά σου μέλλεις ἀναγινώσκειν οὔτε τὰς τῶν ἀρχαίων Ῥωμαίων καὶ Ἑλλήνων πράξεις καὶ τὰς ἐκ τῶν συγγραμμάτων ἐκλογάς, ἃς εἰς τὸ γῆρας σαυτῷ ἀπετίθεσο. σπεῦδε οὖν εἰς τέλος καὶ τὰς κενὰς ἐλπίδας ἀφεὶς σαυτῷ βοήθει, εἴ τί σοι μέλει σαυτοῦ, ἕως ἔξεστιν.

No longer wander at hazard; for neither wilt thou read thy own memoirs, nor the acts of the ancient Romans and Hellenes, and the selections from books which thou wast reserving for thy old age. Hasten then to the end which thou hast before thee, and throwing away idle hopes, come to thy own aid, if thou carest at all for thyself, while it is in thy power.

3.16. εἰ δὲ ἀπιστοῦσιν αὐτῷ πάντες ἄνθρωποι, ὅτι ἁπλῶς καὶ αἰδημόνως καὶ εὐθύμως βιοῖ, οὔτε χαλεπαίνει τινὶ τούτων οὔτε παρατρέπεται τῆς ὁδοῦ τῆς ἀγούσης ἐπὶ τὸ τέλος τοῦ βίου, ἐφ' ὃ δεῖ ἐλθεῖν καθαρόν, ἡσύχιον, εὔλυτον, ἀβιάστως τῇ ἑαυτοῦ μοίρᾳ συνηρμοσμένον. ||

And if all men refuse to believe that he lives a simple, modest, and contented life, he is neither angry with any of them, nor does he deviate from the way which leads to the end of life, to which a man

> ought to come pure, tranquil, ready to depart, and without any compulsion perfectly reconciled to his lot. ||

For sure, the anti-compositional mêlées mushroom helter-skelter (!), but within the show*case*. The *non-dit* of the *M* is that their status as dummy autobiography serving the emperor's self by dressing in new 'Rhetorical Philosophy' clothes represents an abjuration of the mundane but prime responsibility to regulate the succession in Rome that couldn't possibly cut it – for all the blanket of formal limitation to self-address, eschewal of 'publication', and erasure of temporality beyond the moment of inscription. As has been written, 'neither an emperor's life nor an emperor's thoughts can ever be private'. The furthest he could bury the job in self-erasure, he wrought *and wrote* autocratography into the representation of an imperial Roman Life marooned on the head of a painful pin.

...absence on the whole being preferable...[23]

---

[23] Brookner 2009: 152.

CHAPTER 11

Lost in Germania
The Absence of History in Tacitus' Ethnography
James McNamara

Introduction

Absences in both context and content loom large in any reading of Tacitus' *Germania*. This little book comes down to us bereft of peers, as no other ethnographic monograph has survived from antiquity. The form of the text shows some notable absences: no prefatory remarks, for instance, and few recent historical reference points.[1] Readers of *Germania*, used to encountering ethnography in the context of historiography, have frequently supplied a contextualising historical narrative in order to 'explain' the description, making *Germania* a warning about the dangers beyond the empire's frontier or an exhortation to further conquest.[2] If, however, the work is taken on its own terms, its absences may speak loudly. Tacitus' emphasis on the Germanic *gens* as 'similar only to itself' (*tantum sui similem gentem*, *Germ*. 4.1) may in turn reflect

---

[1] For centuries, readers of *Germania* have filled its perceived gaps with information from the present or from more recent history, often conflating *Germania* and *Deutschland*. For its reception in the Renaissance, cf. Krapf 1979; Krebs 2005. That is not my focus in this chapter, though it is worth noting that the modern reception history of *Germania* is amongst the most intensive and controversial of any ancient text, cf. Krebs 2011 for its appropriation by National Socialism. Momigliano 1954=1960: 13–14, speaking of books that have inspired wars, famously suggested that the *Germania* might be numbered among 'the one hundred most dangerous books ever written'. Krebs 2011 employs the metaphor of the virus, living from its hosts. The reception of *Germania* is often a story of attempts to fill gaps; this chapter is an attempt to allow absence to speak for itself.

[2] Recently, for instance, Krebs 2005 reads the work as a kind of preparatory treatise for a Roman invasion. Lund 1991a: 1954–6 allows *Germania* a more descriptive function, explaining Rome's inability to conquer the territory through a portrayal of Germanic *libertas*. The Celtic and Germanic ethnography that has come down to us from ancient Rome is inextricably bound up with conquest, mostly appearing in excursuses in historical works; Tacitus refers to the interest and colour such passages lend to a history (*Ann*. 4.33.3). The legacy of Said (1978) offers a model for understanding literary description of the Germani as a justification of empire and the imposition of a system of knowledge and understanding that acts as symbolic control over the territory, perhaps a preliminary to conquest. The modern concern with supplying a contextualising narrative may also have its roots in a more general tendency among literary critics to put description in the service of narrative, as discussed by Fowler 1991.

on *Germania*.³ Where history does make an appearance in the text, it is subject to disintegration, and Tacitus' treatment of chronology can be as disorientating as his handling of space. In Germania, systems of organising knowledge risk becoming lost, bogged down and defeated.

The present paper focuses in particular on the absence of key features of historiography and historiographical ethnography in the *Germania*, in particular the absence of historiographical narrative, and the absence of reliable information worthy of historical trustworthiness (*fides*). Rather than attempting to fill gaps and 'explain' the content of the text, as has often been done, I wish to concentrate on the ways in which Tacitus' unconventional composition highlights the strangeness and inaccessibility of his subject matter. Tacitus does not, I argue, merely leave gaps; rather, he shows the intractable nature of the information available to a Roman attempt to subject Germania to Latin literary prose.⁴ In the first part of this chapter, I introduce the absence of conventional features of ethnography by comparing *Germania* with *De Bello Gallico*. I shall then discuss the role of digressions in the *Germania* that briefly touch on historical events, in order to show how Tacitus banishes the subject matter and the narrative structure of historiography from his text. Next, I shall consider how Tacitus represents his source traditions; I argue that Tacitus puts on show the lack of *fides* (trustworthiness) in many of his sources, and in the process renders his subject matter something other than the stuff of history. Finally, I shall reflect on the possibilities opened by a reading that takes the absence of history in *Germania* as a positive quality and not as a gap that needs to be filled.

A Non-history of Not-Gaul

A useful first step in recognising historiographical absences in *Germania* can be made through comparison with Caesar's *De Bello Gallico*. The *Germania* may be read as a distorted inversion of ethnography in the Caesarian mould. Caesar's *commentarii* enter into geographic description without any prefatory remarks; rather, the geographic and ethnographic information serves as a preface to the narrative of the wars. Ethnography later appears in excursuses, notably regarding the Suebi in book 4 and more generally the Gauls and Germani in book 6. Tacitus' work is more

---

³ For productive readings that employ this conflation, cf. Tan 2014, discussed on p. 204, and O'Gorman 1993 on Germania/*Germania* as a territory 'created' by Tacitus; my reading explores the room for doubt in the omniscient authorial attitude that O'Gorman posits.
⁴ For Tacitus' representation of conflicting ethnographic theories and *topoi*, cf. Woolf 2011: 101.

mysterious; the subject traditionally assigned to prolegomena or excursus has itself become the main text, and historical events and chronological narrative appear in excursuses of the barest kind.

Historical and geographical absences are made strikingly apparent from the outset of Tacitus' text, where resemblances to Caesar's *De Bello Gallico* make it clear what *Germania* is not. At the start of the second half, where Tacitus turns from general description of the Germani to a periegetic guide to individual tribes, Caesar stands as the only named source in the whole work, lauded as 'the highest authority' (*summus auctor*, *Germ.* 28.1). The presence of Caesar, the conqueror of Gaul and author of *De Bello Gallico*, at two important structural points of the text, and his absence at the end, are significant for the negative definition of Germania, text and territory, rendered in opposition to Caesar's representation of Gaul.

The abrupt opening of the work recalls, as is widely recognised, the first words of Caesar's *De Bello Gallico*:[5]

> Germania omnis a Gallis Raetisque et Pannoniis Rheno et Danuvio fluminibus, a Sarmatis Dacisque mutuo metu aut montibus separatur. (*Germ.* 1.1 – Winterbottom in Winterbottom and Ogilvie 1975)
>
> All of Germany is separated from the Gauls, Raetians and Pannonians by the rivers Rhine and Danube, from the Sarmatians and Dacians by mutual fear or mountains.

> Gallia est omnis diuisa in partes tres, quarum unam incolunt Belgae, aliam Aquitani, tertiam qui ipsorum lingua Celtae, nostra Galli appellantur. hi omnes lingua, institutis, legibus inter se differunt. Gallos ab Aquitanis Garunna flumen, a Belgis Matrona et Sequana diuidit. (Caes. *BGall.* 1.1)
>
> All of Gaul is divided into three parts, one of which is inhabited by the Belgae, another by the Aquitani, and the third by those who in their own language are called Celts, and in our language, Gauls. These all differ from each other in language, institutions and laws. The river Garonne separates the Gauls from the Aquitani; the Marne and Seine separate them from the Belgae.

Like Caesar, Tacitus makes the subject of his work the first word, and begins with an overview (*Germania omnis*) that simultaneously defines the subject as a unity.[6] The verbal echo *Germania omnis* ~ *Gallia . . . omnis* is accompanied by a verb of division in each text; Tacitus varies Caesar's *diuisa est* with *separatur*.

---

[5] Tan 2014: 182–8 with references: Melin 1960, Thielscher 1962.
[6] For the political value of Caesar's claim to comprehend and completely subdue Gaul, cf. Riggsby 2006: 30.

Caesar immediately enlarges upon divisions within Gaul, while Tacitus delays that approach until the second half of the work, first presenting a barely filled outline. Caesar's boundaries are rivers, while Tacitus' boundaries are both physical and affective: rivers, mountains, but also fear. Caesar's boundaries are natural and the prevailing impression is of fixity, while the human and emotional element in Tacitus' opening immediately makes the furthest boundary a less certain one, whether for the Germani and their neighbours, or for Tacitus attempting to describe the further reaches of the territory. The abstract *metus* suggests a boundary that has no physical location but is dependent on the psychology of peoples: an early sign of the elevated register (whether 'oratorical', 'rhetorical' or 'poetic') that pervades *Germania*.[7] Tan makes a strong case for the unconventional character of *Germania* in comparison with broader traditions of Greco-Roman geographical description. She notes, 'many standard features of ancient geographical writing are absent from the text, with the effect that our understanding – our ability to mentally "acquire" Germania – is consistently restricted'.[8] Both descriptive detail and aids to orientation are notably absent.[9] Tacitus delineates his subject as a territory beyond the bounds of the empire.

Tacitus opens *Germania* by establishing boundaries, but there is room for fluctuation where Caesar had once delineated fixed points of reference. At the outset of the periegetic second half, Tacitus again refers to Caesar, but in order to establish that the Rhine is not a defining line between Gauls and Germani. Tacitus seems specifically to be drawing on the following passage in Caesar's ethnographic excursus in book 6:

> ac fuit antea tempus, cum Germanos Galli uirtute superarent, ultro bella inferrent, propter hominum multitudinem agrique inopiam trans Rhenum colonias mitterent. (Caes. *BGall.* 6.24.1)
>
> There was an earlier time when the Gauls surpassed the Germani in prowess, waged war of their own accord and used to set up colonies east of the Rhine owing to the burgeoning population and the lack of farmland.

Caesar mentions a time (*fuit antea tempus*) when the Gaulish Volcae Tectosages crossed into the area around the Hercynian forest. He gives

---

[7] The words 'mysterious', 'enigmatic', 'strange' are frequently to be found in commentary and criticism on the *Germania*, cf. Tan 2014. For poetic language in *Germania*, cf. Thomas 2009.
[8] Tan 2014: 181. Cf. Timpe 1992: 271, 276.
[9] An exception to the absence of fixed points of reference to situate the tribes discussed in the work's second half (28.2) is instructive, since it occurs when Tacitus is locating Gaulish tribes on the edge of Germania in an area described by Caesar – such reference points are not provided in the case of Germania libera.

their reasons, too: a growing population and a shortage of cultivated land. He then employs the authorial first person (signalling his activity as a scholar, rather than as the commander of the military narrative) to remark upon his knowledge of Greek geographical tradition: Eratosthenes and 'certain Greeks' are aware of the Hercynian forest by repute (*fama*).[10] Caesar thus establishes himself as a pioneering Roman in two respects at once, surpassing Greek geographical knowledge with Roman knowledge through exploration and conquest.[11] Zeitler remarks, further, on Caesar's competition with Greeks, in this instance as an indirect suggestion that he is a Roman Alexander, opening new fields of geographical knowledge in the course of distant conquests.[12] Tacitus draws a different, more nebulous picture than Caesar; he does not name the Volcae Tectosages, but imagines a time of loose political allegiances, predating kingship, during which the Rhine fades into insignificance as a barrier to the ebb and flow of surrounding tribes:

> quantulum enim amnis obstabat quo minus, ut quaeque gens eualuerat, occuparet permutaretque sedes promiscas adhuc et nulla regnorum potentia diuisas! (*Germ.* 28.1)[13]
>
> How little effect the river had in preventing the tribes, according to their relative strength, from occupying and changing their territories which were yet held indiscriminately without being divided by the dominion of kings!

Once again, Caesar's imposition of *ratio*, the willingness to impose clear distinctions, contrasts with Tacitus' emphasis on fluctuation, uncertainty and contestation.[14] Caesar, himself a great breaker of political and geographical boundaries, enters Tacitus' text at those moments when the uncertain borders of Germania are under discussion.

Tacitus' engagement with Caesar offers, I suggest, a guide on how to read his unconventional handling of ethnography. Rather than trying to fill in perceived gaps in what Tacitus could have provided in the way of information about the Germani, it is more rewarding to accept the text as a radical departure from *De Bello Gallico*. Fluctuation and inexactitude

---

[10] Caesar corrects the form of the name given by Eratosthenes.   [11] Zeitler 1986: 47–8.
[12] Pelling 2006 explores Caesar's reputation as a boundary-breaker, both in his exploits which included bridging the Rhine and crossing the Ocean to Britain, and in his political role as the liminal figure between republic and principate.
[13] On the notion of a time predating regal power, cf. Lund 1991a: 1921.
[14] Devillers 2014: 22 notes that by offering Caesar the most prominent place amongst his predecessors, and naming only Caesar among his sources, Tacitus downplays the importance of more recent authors, implying that little progress has been made in understanding Germania since Caesar's time.

take the place of Caesar's imposition of order and boundaries, and spatial vagueness provides a setting in which a teleological narrative of conquest and subjugation loses its way. Tacitus' frequent references to defeating the *Germani* remain partial or wishful. Caesar, the *summus auctor*, bears that authority through his combination of literary and military mastery. The Gaul that he defines and describes is the territory he conquered. Germania, by contrast, is located outside the empire. It is well recognised that the *Germania* makes a mockery of Domitian's claims to have conquered Germany.[15] The attempt to describe Germania requires different kinds of absence to be confronted, including both that which was never in Rome's grasp, the most distant lands where *fabulae* abound, and also territory once conquered, grasped and known but since lost.[16] Ignorance and loss prove immensely productive of stories, and it is this mass of tradition that Tacitus puts on display in the *Germania*.[17]

Digressions into Non-history

The most controversial of the historical passages, and one of the most discussed statements in the *Germania*, is the reflection on a recent event on the eastern side of the Rhine:

> iuxta Tencteros Bructeri olim occurrebant: nunc Chamauos et Angriuarios immigrasse narratur, pulsis Bructeris ac penitus excisis uicinarum consensu nationum, seu superbiae odio seu praedae dulcedine seu fauore quodam erga nos deorum. nam ne spectaculo quidem proelii inuidere: super sexaginta milia non armis telisque Romanis, sed, quod magnificentius est, oblectationi oculisque ceciderunt. [2] maneat, quaeso, duretque gentibus, si non amor nostri, at certe odium sui, quando urgentibus imperii fatis nihil iam praestare fortuna maius potest quam hostium discordiam. (*Germ.* 33.1–2)
>
> Next to the Tencteri the Bructeri were once to be found: now it is reported that the Chamavi and Angrivarii have moved in, expelling the Bructeri and eradicating them with the approval of the neighbouring tribes, either

---

[15] Rives 1999: 51–3; Ash 2014: 186–7.
[16] The Elbe (Albis) is mentioned once as a river that used to be well known but is now no more than a name: *nunc tantum auditur* (41.2). The implied move from vision to hearing represents a shift from visual *enargeia* based on past knowledge to the rumours that make up the contemporary understanding of Germania. Cf. O'Gorman in this volume. As Tan 2014: 194 notes, rivers conventionally aid orientation in geographical description. Tacitus instead locates the river in terms of the tribe, and shows the decay of knowledge since the time when Rome had that territory in its grasp.
[17] Cf. Paul in this volume for lost spaces as a productive source of historical mythologising; her discussion offers a perspective both on the relationship of *Germania* to the lost and desired territory of Germania and the eagerness of readers to fill in perceived absences in the text.

because of hatred of their arrogance or the enticement of plunder or some favour of the gods towards us; for they did not even begrudge us the spectacle of battle. More than sixty thousand fell not by Roman arms and weapons but, even more splendidly, for the delight of our eyes. May there remain, I pray, and persist among the nations, if not love for us, then at least hatred for each other, since with the fate of the empire driving us on, fortune can provide nothing greater than the discord of our enemies.

It is notable how the battles of the Bructeri and their neighbours, which represent a minimal historical excursus, are presented as a gladiatorial spectacle: a major historical event is reduced to the object of Rome's gaze. Just as the *mores* of the Germani are put on display by the ethnography, and it becomes clear what they lack by comparison with the empire, their history, too, enters the text at this moment, not as a series of events worth the name of history, but as an entertainment for the Romans, presumably the Roman army, watching and interpreting it in Roman terms. The downfall of the tribe occurs beyond the bounds of history. The Roman policy of seeking to destabilise the Germanic tribes might even bring to mind the notion of a spectacle controlled and overseen by the Romans. While the destruction of the Bructeri might be reassuring to a Roman, and it is celebrated with a kind of bitter exultation, it is not the stuff of history, and *Germania* displays to its readers no Roman victories, only a decontextualised spectacle.[18]

The longest passage of historical material in *Germania* is at 37.2–6. When the periegesis of the second half of the work comes to the Cimbri, Tacitus is reminded of their fateful entry into Roman history and the unresolved conflicts that have stretched down to his own time:

> sescentesimum et quadragesimum annum urbs nostra agebat cum primum Cimbrorum audita sunt arma Caecilio Metello ac Papirio Carbone consulibus. ex quo si ad alterum imperatoris Traiani consulatum computemus, ducenti ferme et decem anni colliguntur: tam diu Germania uincitur. medio tam longi aeui spatio multa in uicem damna. non Samnis, non Poeni, non Hispaniae Galliaeue, ne Parthi quidem saepius admonuere: quippe regno Arsacis acrior est Germanorum libertas. quid enim aliud nobis quam caedem Crassi, amisso et ipse Pacoro, infra Ventidium deiectus Oriens obiecerit? at Germani Carbone et Cassio et Scauro Aurelio et Seruilio Caepione Maximoque Mallio fusis uel captis quinque simul consularis

---

[18] The similarity to a staged fight may be enhanced if the battle is related to Vestricius Spurinna's installing of a new king among the Bructeri, recorded by Pliny *Ep.* 2.7.2. It is possible that the battle, known only from *Germ.* 33, resulted from Roman efforts to stoke discord among the Germani (Rives 1999: 257–8).

> exercitus populo Romano, Varum trisque cum eo legiones etiam Caesari abstulerunt; nec inpune C. Marius in Italia, diuus Iulius in Gallia, Drusus ac Nero et Germanicus in suis eos sedibus perculerunt: mox ingentes C. Caesaris minae in ludibrium uersae. inde otium, donec occasione discordiae nostrae et ciuilium armorum expugnatis legionum hibernis etiam Gallias adfectauere ac rursus pulsi. nam proximis temporibus triumphati magis quam uicti sunt. (*Germ.* 37.2–6)
>
> It was the six hundred and fortieth year of our city, when the arms of the Cimbri were first heard in the consulship of Caecilius Metellus and Papirius Carbo. Counting up to the second consulship of the emperor Trajan would make nearly two hundred and ten years: this is how long the conquest of Germania is taking. Many mutual losses have been suffered in the course of such a long extent of time. The Samnite, the Carthaginians, the Spanish and Gaulish lands, even the Parthians have not cautioned us more often, for the freedom of the Germani is fiercer than the rule of Arsaces. What else can the East cast in our teeth but the slaughter of Crassus, when the East, losing Pacorus, was itself cast down under Ventidius? The Germani, defeating or capturing Carbo, Cassius, Aurelius Scaurus, Servilius Caepio and Mallius Maximus, robbed the Roman people of five consular armies at once, and even robbed Caesar of Varus and three legions with him. Not without loss did Gaius Marius strike them down in Italy, the Divine Julius in Gaul, Drusus and Nero and Germanicus in their own territory; soon the mighty threats of Gaius Caesar became a laughing stock. Then came inactivity, until, taking advantage of our discord and civil war, they sacked the legions' winter quarters, began even to move on Gaul, and were beaten back; for in recent times they have been the subjects of triumphs rather than conquest.

The passage recalls the first time the Romans met a Germanic army in battle during the migration of the Cimbri and Teutones. Ash remarks on the momentary 'frame breaking' of this diachronic account, and the reflection on the present day against the 'timeless ethnographical present (where things are *always* true)'.[19] Where the emphasis in the excursus on the Bructeri had been on vision, it is hearing that brought the Cimbri to the Romans' attention.[20] The phrase *Cimbrorum audita sunt arma* collapses the distinction between those present and those who hear tell of the events, since the words may have the sense 'Cimbrian arms were heard (clattering in battle)' or 'reports were heard of Cimbrian arms'. The effect

---

[19] Ash 2014: 187. More specifically – since the excursus occurs in the second half of the work where Tacitus frequently invokes a dichotomy between the more and less distant past, or then and now – the unusual feature of the cited passage is the hint of chronological narrative.

[20] Here, as elsewhere, that which is heard, or heard of, is less securely known than things seen. Cf. the remarks on *enargeia* on p. 206 n. 16 and O'Gorman in this volume, who embeds 'seeing' in a rich sensory experience of presence.

of Germanic battle chants is one of the first features of Germanic culture mentioned at *Germ.* 3.1, and there is an ominous effect in the progression from Roman viewing of a gladiatorial spectacle at 33.2 to the onset of a Germanic invasion at 37.2; the sense of hearing, experienced internally in the body, has an invasive effect different from the external experience of vision.[21] The Teutones themselves are absent from this historical summary, and it has long been noted that although Tacitus includes a Roman commander defeated by the Helvetian Tigurini in 107 BC, L. Cassius Longinus, he omits M. Iunius Silanus, who was routed by the Cimbri themselves in 109 BC.[22] The overriding principle is not narrative but the force of the argument that Germania remains unconquered.

As in the excursus on the Bructeri, Tacitus moves from a report of an event to an authorial judgment introduced by a first-person verb, this time in the plural (*computemus*). Subsequent encounters, the cause of great losses on both sides, are then listed. In a text overwhelmingly concerned with collectives rather than individuals, this passage stands out for the many personal names, nearly all Roman, though the absence of Germanic names is accentuated by the presence of two Parthians, Arsaces and Pacorus.[23] Names are a crucial feature in the structure and content of *Annales*, providing consular dates (as here) and being central to the record of those events (including victories, defeats, triumphs) deemed worthy of history.[24] The Cimbrian excursus is a defective historical overview *ab urbe condita*, in which Rome's imperial expansion gives way to *otium* and *ludibrium*. The sequence of Romans is related without a clear distinction between republic and empire, otherwise a central organising principle of Roman history in Tacitus, including summary.[25] Absent from the passage is any sense of progress, as Roman history falls into disarray, those central annalistic *realia*, victories and triumphs, revealed as a lie, hollow and absurd.[26]

---

[21] Rosenbloom 2006: 68–9.
[22] Furneaux 1894: ad loc. Perl 2005: 171–3 remarks on the greater prominence of the Longinus case in rhetorical tradition and attributes the selection of *exempla* to this consideration.
[23] 'Arsaces' need not refer to an individual; the name of the Arsacid dynasty's founder stands as a Parthian counterpart to 'Caesar', which itself appears twice in the summary, for Augustus and Gaius (Anderson 1938: 175).
[24] As has been widely noted, Tacitus omits the name of Domitian from the summary, enacting a kind of *damnatio memoriae*.
[25] On this break as an underlying structure in Tacitean historical summary, cf. McNamara 2014: 143–6. Ellen O'Gorman has suggested reading the passage as a reflection of the chronology-defying impression created in Germania by the Roman military personnel serving there, who would appear as a constantly renewing stream of men of military age, cf. Said 1978: 42.
[26] There is a portentous ring to the concluding *sententia*, which ends in nine consecutive heavy syllables.

The Stuff of Non-history

The denial of history in foreign cultures is a well-recognised means of subordinating the Other.[27] It has widely been noted, and it is unnecessary for me to rehearse at length, that Tacitus' portrait of Germanic *mores* has a timeless and ahistorical quality. I should like, however, to turn from tacit absences to those that are marked by the fleeting suggestion of presence or knowledge. Tacitus does not deny that historical change occurs in Germania; what is absent is chronological narrative. As Lund notes, the Germanic past is most often mentioned as an earlier state of affairs with which the present is compared.[28] Description is patterned through a series of antitheses: contemporary Germani are measured against contemporary Romans, but also against their own past, and a Roman past; frequently the comparison between present-day Germani and Romans serves to point out a contrast between the Rome of today and a simpler, less corrupt stage of Roman society.[29] The work opens with origins, and the second half frequently compares the more distant past with the present or more recent past.[30] Chronology is reduced to dichotomy, and narrative, which might explain the connection between 'then' and 'now', is absent.[31]

In a literal sense, Tacitus' Germani do not have history, which is to say, they do not have historiography. In Germania, stories of the past belong to the realm of myth and song:

> celebrant carminibus antiquis, quod unum apud illos memoriae et annalium genus est, Tuistonem deum terra editum. ei filium Mannum, originem gentis conditoremque, Manno tris filios adsignant, e quorum nominibus proximi Oceano Ingaeuones, medii Hermiones, ceteri Istaeuones uocentur. quidam, ut in licentia uetustatis, pluris deo ortos pluresque gentis appellationes, Marsos Gambriuios Suebos Vandilios, adfirmant, eaque uera et antiqua nomina. (*Germ.* 2.2)

> In their ancient songs, which are their only kind of history, they sing the renown of Tuisto, a god born from the earth. They assign him a son, Mannus, the origin and founder of the race, and to Mannus three sons, the founders, from whom those closest to the Ocean take the name Ingaevones, those in the middle the Hermiones, and the rest the Istaevones. With the licence accorded to antiquity, they claim there were more born from the god, giving their name to tribes: the Marsi, Gambrivii, Suebi, Vandilii, and those names are real and ancient.

---

[27] For this approach to *Germania*, cf. for instance O'Gorman 1993. [28] Lund 1988: 46–7
[29] O'Gorman 1993: 148–9, 153 n. 28.
[30] For the difficulty in establishing whether Tacitus' information is current, cf. Lund 1991a: 1939–40; Rives 1999: 231–2; Tan 2014: 193.
[31] E.g. 28.2; 33.1; 36.1–2; 37.1.

The songs are 'ancient' and tell tales of the divine, so have more in common with epic than with prose *annales*. They are compared with Roman historiography, as the combination of the nouns *memoria* and *annales* suggests a hendiadys: written history.[32] The hendiadys allows further reflection on the nature of recorded memory in Germania. Romans had numerous kinds of written record, which included epic *annales* and historical *origines*.[33] The Germani, by contrast, have only one system of recording the past, and history and myth blur together in it. The account of Germanic origins brings Tacitus' source traditions dimly into view and Tacitus remarks on the dubious quality of the available traditions. The Germanic songs, which have reached Tacitus' text by a route that is impossible to trace, are hardly the stuff of Tacitean historiography, yet Tacitus follows them with a sceptical attitude towards the available Roman and/or Greek authors, left unnamed (*quidam*).[34] As Lund notes, the reference to *licentia uetustatis* is a commonplace of historiographical critique.[35] While the tales of Tuisto, Mannus and Mannus' sons may be taken on their own terms as origin myths, Tacitus voices scepticism when Greco-Roman authors attempt to claim trustworthiness in their narratives based on such myths.

When Tacitus proceeds to recount the story of Ulysses' travels to Germany, he again expresses a dismissive attitude when he judges that his sources have taken liberties, spinning unreliable narratives around a mixture of real and dubious evidence. The name of Asciburgium stands out as the only named Germanic settlement outside the empire, but like the names of Mannus and his sons, it becomes a source of unreliable historical information. Monuments laid down by Ulysses are said to be still standing, but Tacitus offers no check on the veracity of the story. Like the northern Pillars of Hercules mentioned at 34.2 ('rumour has spread the story (*fama uulgauit*) that Pillars of Hercules still remain'), it is unclear whether a real monument has been surrounded with unreliable myth, or whether the existence of the monument is itself a fiction. Drusus' attempt to establish its existence might have brought this monument/landscape feature into the realm of history, but his efforts were inconclusive, and only

---

[32] Lund 1988 ad loc.
[33] The passing suggestion of Ennius and Cato has an appropriately archaic ring.
[34] Tacitus is less forthcoming than Caesar (*BGall.* 6.24.2) who cites 'certain (other) Greeks' alongside Eratosthenes. The high degree of authority attributed to indigenous *logoi* is a *topos* reaching back to Herodotus (Lund 1991a: 1872). It is notable here that Tacitus twice in quick succession reports a Germanic *logos* without judgment before criticising a literary *logos*.
[35] Lund 1988: ad loc.

rumour remains, and spreads. When Tacitus forbears to go further into such material, the effect is twofold. By laying out the content of tradition, even if he does not lend credence to it, he provides a sense of the *Germania* that is accessible to a Roman, the product of doubtful narratives. At the same time, Tacitus suggests that these doubtful subjects have been wrongly handled if they are accorded the status of a historical reality:

> quae neque confirmare argumentis neque refellere in animo est: ex ingenio suo quisque demat uel addat fidem. (*Germ.* 3.3)
>
> It is not my intention to make arguments to confirm or deny these things: let each lend or deny trustworthiness to them from his own intellect.

Here, his attitude to the Ulysses stories in his sources is reminiscent of Livy, who shows no interest in confirming or denying traditions more suited to adorning the works of poets.[36] These are something other than the stuff of history, and the same applies to what passes for historiography in Germania, leaving a great gulf between mythical origin stories and the uncertain present. Rives interprets the phrase *ex ingenio suo ... fidem* as a comment on the credence of readers, translating 'Each reader may withhold or bestow credence according to his own inclination'. It seems to me, however, that Tacitus may be commenting on the practice of authors who might choose to be in favour of such traditions or against; his practice, by contrast, is to show the content of traditions about Germania, rather than to waste effort on promoting or refuting what is fanciful. When the available information about Germania is so unreliable, what matters is not recourse to a universal epistemology to find an underlying truth, but to represent the state of Roman understanding: small bright spots of knowledge amidst a vast expanse of thicket.

Doubtful Traditions

In the *Germania*, absence of history is partly, but not comprehensively, explicable in terms of imperialistic denial of history to the Other. It is striking that the landscape of Tacitus' Germania is in fact marked by traces of earlier times, but they are no 'uncorrupted monuments' (to borrow

---

[36] Lund 1988: 121, noting the deployment of a historiographical *topos*. Livy states: *quae ante conditam condendamue urbem poeticis magis decora fabulis quam incorruptis rerum gestarum monumentis traduntur, ea nec adfirmare nec refellere in animo est* (Livy 1.pr.6). 'It is not my intention to confirm or deny those traditions regarding the time before the city's foundation, or before it was to be founded, which appropriately adorn poetic tales rather than uncorrupted historical monuments.'

Livy's phrase cited above). Tacitus instead emphasises their decay or the dubious traditions that they have inspired. The Cimbrian excursus, discussed on p. 209, is prompted by ruins:

> ueteris ... famae lata uestigia manent, utraque ripa castra ac spatia, quorum ambitu nunc quoque metiaris molem manusque gentis et tam magni exitus fidem. (*Germ.* 37.1)
>
> Extensive marks of their ancient renown remain: sprawling forts on both sides of the river, the scale of which allows you to gauge the might and main of the people, and stands as evidence of their mighty migration (downfall?).

Tacitus uses the second person singular subjunctive to encourage the reader to imagine pacing out the scale of these remnants. All that their great bulk can explain, however, is the scale of destruction, and *ueteris ... famae* suggests not only the renown that the Cimbri once commanded, but the state of current knowledge of the Cimbri as an ancient rumour. The ensuing historical summary, discussed on p. 209, picks up on the sense of fragmentary historical *fides* offered by the ruins of the Cimbri.[37] Roman loss and Germanic loss are mirrored.

Unlike the nearer bounds of Germania, the furthest places described by Tacitus were never under Roman control, and information can only have reached him indirectly. While Caesar provides a point of reference for what nearer Germania could have been (but is not), there is no authoritative Roman agent amongst the Fenni, the Hellusii and the Oxionae. Geographical writers, particularly those who are willing to include tales of half-humans in distant climes, do not offer the same authoritative grasp of foreign places as a conqueror, whose knowledge Tacitus privileges.[38] In the absence of Caesar, we are left in the hands of Pliny the Elder and Mela. Roman writers are divided on the question of whether half-bestial humans inhabit the ends of the earth. Tacitus is neither one of those authors who

---

[37] In the grove of the Nahanarvali, Tacitus manages to draw evidence from the very absence of *uestigia*; judging the cult of the Alci to be ancient since it involves 'no effigies, and no trace (*uestigium*) of foreign superstition' (43.3).

[38] In the *Agricola*, Tacitus asserts his claim to outdo previous writers on Britain because he is writing of a territory that has now been conquered: *ita quae priores nondum comperta eloquentia percoluere rerum fide tradentur*, 'Thus those things that earlier writers elaborated with their eloquence, though they were not yet ascertained, will be handed down with the trustworthiness of history.' (*Agr.* 10.2) His criterion is the historian's virtue of *fides*; cf. Mela 3.49 for *rerum fides* as a consequence of Claudius' conquest of Britain; *incorrupta rerum fides* describes the work of Cremutius Cordus at Sen. *Cons. ad Marc.* 1.3. Tacitus claims that others employ *eloquentia*, but it is not yet well established (*comperta*) since, as Sailor 2008: 82 puts it: 'Conquest makes the difference ... what is "subjugated completely" ... is also "known" ... and what is not yet subjugated does not count as fully known.' Cf. Hardie 2012: 277–8.

states their existence outright like Pliny and Mela, nor one of those who banishes them from the work: once again Tacitus brings the content of tradition to the fore, showing his readers what is said.[39] There is no Roman historical agent to act as guide to the furthest reaches of Germania:

> cetera iam fabulosa, Hellusios et Oxionas ora hominum uultusque, corpora atque artus ferarum gerere: quod ego ut incompertum in medium relinquam. (*Germ.* 46.6)
>
> After this the rest is the stuff of stories: that the Hellusii and Oxionae have the faces and expressions of men but the bodies and limbs of beasts – since this is uncertain, I shall leave it open.

By this point, Tacitus has reached the truly unverifiable and fantastical, but he has not reached the end. Germania may continue indefinitely as far as we know. While the world might be bounded by Ocean to the west and north, the Germanic territories offer no boundary, only an endless series of fluctuating peoples and borders. Germania itself is *sine fine*. Tacitus offers, in *oratio obliqua*, a summary of the content of *fabulae* that extend beyond where he leaves off his work. The stuff of these tales is *incompertum* – it has not been established – but there is more of it than Tacitus chooses to relate; there is more of Germania to describe, but the text leaves off where knowledge breaks down. As knowledge becomes ever harder to gain, Tacitus is forced to end on a kind of *aposiopesis*.[40] Returning to the question of the text's descriptive character, its lack of historical-narrative framing and its susceptibility to gap-filling interpretations, the final clause (*quod . . . relinquam*) might be seen as a peculiarly brusque statement of publication. Instead of a text dedicated to an individual or 'published' in the familiar sense, with a verb such as *edo*, Tacitus 'leaves' the *fabulosa*, and indeed the whole text, *in medium*, that is 'before the eyes' of the readership or 'in public' (with the suggestive force of 'submitted without comment' or 'I'll just leave this here'). The descriptive text might even be taken as a series of images, ecphrastic in nature, placed verblessly before its readers.[41] Tacitus acknowledges the indeterminacy of his portrait and its openness

---

[39] Cf. *Ann.* 2.24.6 where the returning members of Germanicus' scattered fleet tell of *miracula*, including half-bestial people. Thanks to Sarah Lawrence for throwing light on Tacitus' position relative to Pliny and Mela.

[40] Cf. Briguglio in this volume, especially with reference to 'generic aposiopesis', when the text threatens to go beyond the bounds of its genre.

[41] Although *quod* at 46.4 refers, in the immediate context, to the *cetera . . . fabulosa*, the passage follows a description of the Fenni notable for its strangeness, and it is not clear where the boundary can be drawn between *fabulae* and more secure information. On ethnographic *thaumata* in the portrayal of the Fenni, cf. Thomas 2009: 69–70.

to interpretation by its readers, to whom it is 'left'. Furthermore, it is open to future writers to develop their own works on the basis of Tacitus' text, in a gesture that recalls the rhetorical posture of Caesar's *commentarii*, avowedly the material on which historiography may be based.[42]

The end of the text returns in ring composition to the sense of fluctuating borders that marks the opening chapters and the transition to the periegesis at *Germ.* 28. Tacitus' ethnography may be read as an inversion of Caesar's, emphasising indeterminacy in its spatial descriptions, and breaking down the narrative of Roman expansion when it reaches Germania. Tacitus seems to be sceptical about the capability of a totalising epistemology to comprehend Germania. The *Agricola* provides an illustrative contrast. By 82 Agricola has control as far as 'the boundary of Britain' (*Britannia terminus, Agr.* 23.2; 27.1). Beyond that is Caledonia, whose inhabitants, according to the chieftain Calgacus, are 'the furthest people in land and liberty' *terrarum ac libertatis extremos, Agr.* 30.3); beyond the Caledonians there lies Thule (called *ultima*, sighted but not conquered), and there remains the unanswered question of how easily Agricola might have taken Hibernia.[43] Agricola emphasises the connection between conquest and understanding when he tells his troops:

> ergo egressi, ego ueterum legatorum, uos priorum exercituum terminos, finem Britanniae non fama nec rumore, sed castris et armis tenemus: inuenta Britannia et subacta. (*Agr.* 33.3)
>
> I have gone beyond the bounds of the old generals, and you of earlier armies and we have the end of Britain in our grasp, not through boasting and rumour but with arms and camps: Britain has been discovered and subjugated.

The ends of the earth in the *Agricola* are where glory can be won; but besides the traditional martial understanding of the distant battlefield, Agricola's words have philosophical connotations.[44] Agricola assures his

---

[42] *Praeteritio* of this kind is traceable in other literary contexts, as Tom Geue has pointed out: at Verg. G. 4.148, Virgil leaves subject matter (gardening) or, rather, a garden landscape, the subject of an excursus, to future readers and writers with the verb *relinquo*.

[43] It may be significant that Calgacus is unaware of Thule beyond Caledonia, which Agricola's exploration reveals. Calgacus cites the Caledonians' remoteness, the Romans' ignorance and the rumours it produces, as a kind of protection – again, productive absence (*Agr.* 30.3). Cf. Hardie 2012: 277–8.

[44] For the ability to extend one's understanding to the bounds of nature through philosophical education, cf. Quintilian's report that Cicero said he would never have had such oratorical resources to draw on 'if he had bounded his intellect with the enclosure of the forum and not the very limits of

troops, 'it would be no disgrace to fall at the very end of land and nature' (*nec inglorium fuerit in ipso terrarum ac naturae fine cecidisse*, *Agr.* 33.6). It makes sense to read Agricola's speech in a philosophical framework, since Agricola himself has already been introduced as a sophisticated and highly practical, distinctively Roman, philosopher in the account of his education (*Agr.* 4.5). Agricola combines a traditional Roman view of conquest as a source of glory with a practical understanding of the moral implications of reaching the ends of the earth.[45] He is able to make sense of his place in Caledonia because he has the power to impose Roman imperial frameworks of understanding. In *Germania*, by contrast, there is no authoritative Roman present to make history, much less to practise philosophy.

In the absence of conquest, epistemology can make no headway. In part this reflects the Roman understanding of ethnography as a product of imperial expansion which, in Germania, has been rebuffed. Nevertheless, there is also a sense in which Tacitus suggests the existence of a world greater than was sometimes acknowledged by Roman authors. Tacitus shows his own enquiring mind being denied the kind of victory that Seneca imagines for the philosopher's elevated spirit. Seneca portrays the educated soul approaching the viewpoint of the gods; here, geography appears clearly laid out in a manner quite foreign to Tacitus' depiction:[46]

> o quam ridiculi sunt mortalium termini! ultra Istrum Dacos <nostrum> <arc>eat imperium, Haemo Thraces includat; Parthis obstet Euphrates; Danuuius Sarmatica ac Romana disterminet; Rhenus Germaniae modum faciat ... si quis formicis det intellectum hominis, nonne et illae unam aream in multas prouincias diuident? cum te in illa uere magna sustuleris, quotiens uidebis exercitus subrectis ire uexillis ... libebit dicere: "it nigrum campis agmen". (Sen. *QNat.* 1. pr.9–10)

> O how laughable are the boundaries of mortals! It may be that the empire keeps the Dacians at bay beyond the Ister, encloses the Thracians with the Haemus, that the Euphrates blocks the Parthians, the Danube separates Sarmatian from Roman territory, the Rhine establishes a limit for Germany ... [but] if one should give human understanding to ants, they

---

nature' – *si ingenium suum consaepto fori, non ipsius rerum naturae finibus terminasset* (Quint. *Inst.* 12.23.1).

[45] For Agricola's ethical understanding of conquest to the ends of the earth, cf. McNamara 2014: 80–4.
[46] The sole reference to *sapientia* in the *Germania* is in a *sententia* that unmasks it as good fortune, and reveals that in the Germanic context it is not possible to live a life reminiscent of Roman *otium*, or of the *moderatio* that merits such praise in *Agricola*. Through a long period of enervating peace, the Cherusci have become the victims of the Chatti, who can lay claim to *sapientia* as well as *modestia* and *probitas* because they are militarily stronger (*Germ.* 36.1). The guiding power is *manus*, rather than *mens*.

will surely divide one yard into many provinces. When you raise yourself up to true magnanimity, you will be pleased to say, whenever you see the armies going back and forth with their standards, "the black column trails across the fields".[47]

Seneca's philosopher sees borders clearly, as Agricola did, and in contrast to Germania where boundaries are fluid and unclear. The sublimity of philosophical understanding allows borders to be viewed from a perspective where they do not serve as significant barriers.[48] Like the borders of Tacitus' *Germania*, they are imposed by human psychology, but while Seneca's exalted philosopher is able to stand above those boundaries, for Tacitus the border between Rome and Germania is a true barrier to understanding, and in the more distant places lie the enemies of philosophy: superstition, rumour and baseless stories. While Seneca is dismissive of borders imposed by conquest and military power, Tacitus' insistence on Rome's limits leaves room to critique claims to the universal power of Roman epistemologies. His 'flight of the mind' results not in the sense that the Roman subject transcends all the world's boundaries, but that there remains much beyond Rome's grasp, intellectually as well as politically.

Conclusion

There is a fascinating quality to Tacitus' ethnography that arises from its representation of the struggle to understand Germania and represent it in literary form. Rather than regarding the work as an orphan excursus in need of supplementation and explanation, I suggest that taking the work's absences on their own terms leads to a richer understanding of this unique piece.[49] While Roman ethnography frequently attempts symbolic control over the Other through Roman epistemology and its codification in literary form, what seems to me particularly striking about Tacitus' *Germania* is the air of uncertainty and mystery surrounding much of what Tacitus has to say about Germania and the Germani. The

---

[47] Seneca cites Verg. *Aen.* 4.404; cf. Tamás in this volume for emphasis on distant viewing in this line as a poignant experience of separation, rather than the imperious oversight in Seneca's reading, which has more in common with the distanced perception of Lucr. 2.7–13.
[48] On Seneca's reception of the Lucretian sublime, cf. Williams 2015: 173–9. For the flight of the mind as a philosophical tradition operative in didactic poetry, cf. Volk 2001. The didactic elements of Tacitus' *Germania* have been suggestively noted by Thomas 2009: 62 and Pagán 2017: 85–7, but deserve to be the subject of a separate investigation.
[49] Cf. Tamás in this volume on the tension between a desire to supplement and an acceptance of perceived absences as a part of the text.

imperialistic perspective of the text must always be kept in view, but forbearing to read *Germania* in terms of an absent narrative of Roman triumph or doom allows the qualities of Tacitus' description to come to the fore. Indeed, Tacitus' reluctance to subject his material either to historical narrative or to a 'higher' viewpoint such as that of Seneca's natural philosophy can be seen as an absence that makes his world greater. While Rome's limits are acutely apparent in *Germania*, Tacitus creates the impression of another world that cannot easily be grasped in Roman terms. This quality, emerging from the absence of secure knowledge, can easily cause readers to become lost in *Germania*. Unlike many of his readers, however, Tacitus does not attempt to claim an empty triumph of *ratio* over a territory that is resistant to it.

CHAPTER 12

Conspicuous Absence
Tacitus' De Re Publica

Ellen O'Gorman[*]

quotus quisque reliquus, qui rem publicam uidisset?

'how many were left, who had seen the Republic?' (Tac. *Annals* 1.3)

The climactic phrase in the preface to Tacitus' *Annals* around which this chapter is organised expresses the condition of Augustan senators in AD 9 as an absence of political experience. But what does it mean to see – or no longer to see – the Republic? As I hope to show, the visual terms of this phrase enable Tacitus to explore concepts of bodily presence, representation as a supplement for absence, and the implication of both presence and absence in the transmission of political practice over time.[1] In these respects, Tacitus' exploration of the *res publica* as something that can be experienced – or missed – through visuality also constitutes an extended meditation on Cicero's expression of loss in book 5 of *De Re Publica* where he likens the state to a faded masterpiece:

> Nostra uero aetas cum rem publicam sicut picturam accepisset egregiam, sed iam euanescentem uetustate, non modo eam coloribus isdem quibus fuerat renouare neglexit, sed ne id quidem curauit ut formam saltem eius et extrema tamquam liniamenta seruaret. Quid enim manet...? (Cic. *Rep*. 5.1)

> But our generation has inherited the Republic as if it were a painting, an exceptional work of art, but already fading with age, and we have not only failed to renew its colours as they were but have even failed to preserve its overall image and its outlines, so to speak. So what remains...?[2]

---

[*] My thanks above all to Tom Geue and Elena Giusti, for their inspiration and editorial advice. Various drafts of this paper have benefitted from discussion with Rhiannon Ash, Hannah-Marie Chidwick, Esther Eidinow, William Fitzgerald, Emily Gowers, Will Guast, Philip Hardie, John Henderson, Kurt Lampe, Aske Damtoft Poulsen, Bella Sandwell, Lydia Spielberg, and especially Edwin Shaw.

[1] My discussion of these issues draws (tangentially) on Panagia 2009.

[2] All translations, unless otherwise indicated, are my own.

This striking metaphor – distinctively Cicero's own[3] – presents a paradoxically vivid image of an image fading from view. It's also notable that the *res publica* as painting does not evoke any intense language of visuality: Cicero and his generation are imagined not as spectators, but as curators.[4] Hence the concept of viewing the Republic remains suspended; by the end of the passage, Cicero laments the loss of *res publica* in terms of representational words, not images. *rem publicam uerbo retinemus, re ipsa uero iam pridem amisimus*: 'we still have the Republic in name, but we have long since lost the thing itself.'

When Tacitus asks how many men were left who had seen the Republic, he inverts the metaphorical–visual balance of Cicero's image. Abstracting the metaphor which would 'make sense' of his question, he leaves us to supply elements which will mediate between 'seeing' and 'the Republic'.[5] That omission requires us to work with a certain absence in the phrase itself, an absence perhaps signalled by the form of the rhetorical question, which both demands and denies a response. In the following sections of the chapter, I will supplement the absence of metaphor in Tacitus' phrase with various cultural practices which enable us to 'make sense' of the concept of seeing the Republic – and to challenge the senses that are made. Visuality, explored through these cultural practices, emerges as an exceptionally rich medium of experience, combining intellectual, sensory, and affective modes.[6] It gives flavour and dimension, in turn, to the experience of the Principate as an experience of absence.

'So what remains...?' Cicero, like Tacitus, turns to the form of the rhetorical question to express his sense of loss. But, as I've already suggested, rhetorical questions are delivered as a demand to respond, even as they enjoin silence. They conjoin speaker and listener in a shared sense of something missing: a response, a remainder, or possibly even knowledge of how much remains.[7] Tacitus, I believe, responds to this sense by speaking of political loss in terms which elide the differences between senatorial experience of 51 BC (the time of Cicero's *Republic*), of AD 9 (the time of the

---

[3] Büchner 1984: 392.
[4] On the political significance of 'care for the things of the world' in *De Re Publica* and *Tusculanae Disputationes*, see Hammer 2008: 42–61.
[5] Similarly, Kathrin Winter in this volume observes of Tacitus' *Dialogus* that it is 'permeated by little, unobtrusive gaps that the reader must... fill continually in order to make sense of the text'.
[6] An excellent recent overview of the connotations of sight is Squire 2016. See also Grethlein 2017. For visuality and historiography, Feldherr 1998.
[7] As Tom Geue has pointed out to me, Tacitus' question may well be predicated on the impossibility of *knowing* how many were left who had seen the Republic. See also James McNamara in this volume, for an exploration of how Tacitus resists easy claims to command of knowledge.

Annals preface), and of AD 98 (the time of Tacitus' emergence as a historian). Thus Tacitus' own experience of Domitian's reign and its immediate aftermath, of which he speaks in *Agricola*, draws on the same sensory palette of loss and alienation with which he expresses the situation of the Augustan senate. Absence as an experience transcends historical and political particularity, creating a different kind of knowledge of the past.

quotus quisque reliquus. . .?

The context of Tacitus' phrase draws our attention to the primary sense of loss here: embodied presence:

> Domi res tranquillae, eadem magistratuum uocabula: iuniores post Actiacam uictoriam, etiam senes plerique inter bella ciuium nati: quotus quisque reliquus, qui rem publicam uidisset? (Tac. *Ann.* 1.3.7)

> Domestic politics were peaceful, the titles of magistrats remained the same: the younger men had been born after the victory at Actium, even many old men had been born into the midst of civil war: how many were left who had seen the Republic?

The absence of men who had been physically present in the Republican era is not just an effect of Augustus' longevity; the intervening years of civil war have mortally disrupted physical presence, and engendered a self-consciousness about the fragility of embodied connections to the past. In the same vein Cicero asks *Nam de uiris quid dicam? Mores enim ipsi interierunt uirorum penuria* (Cic. *Rep.* 5.1), 'and what should I say about the men? For our practices themselves are lost because of the deficit of men.' The emphatic gender of *quotus quisque reliquus* keeps our attention on the loss of those Romans involved in the formal political sphere, and also those more vulnerable to the predations of civil war. But a few books later in the *Annals*, Tacitus presents us with a figure whose embodied experience of the Republic would make her name an appropriate response to this rhetorical question: Junia Tertulla, relative of the two most prominent killers of Julius Caesar, and 'a relic of a distant age'.[8]

Junia's funeral in AD 22,[9] at the end of the third book of the *Annals*, concludes with one of Tacitus' most distinctive and famous *sententiae* –

---

[8] Pelling 2006: 148; Woodman and Martin 1996: 490 explicitly link Junia to the *quotus quisque reliquus?* question.
[9] Of the four funerals in the Tiberian hexad of the *Annals*, Junia's is the only non-imperial ceremony. Germanicus (*Ann.* 3.4) and Drusus (*Ann.* 4.9) represent the *iuniores*, both born after Actium (respectively 16/15 and 13 BC). Augustus (*Ann.* 1.8–10), like Junia ten years his senior, represents the *senes*. There may be some residual wordplay between Junia's name and her old age.

appropriately enough, about the envisaging of absence. In addition to this, the funeral as a whole dramatises the situation which Tacitus has already summed up in the preface. The traditional spectacular displays of Roman funerals, which perform the continuity of the past through the procession of ancestral masks, make this cultural practice an obvious site for making sense of 'seeing the Republic'.[10] Polybius remarks, in his well-known description of the Roman funeral, on 'the sight of all the images (εἰκόνας) gathered together of men with a reputation for excellence, as if living and breathing.' (Polyb. 6.53.10) But the 'as if' in his final phrase points to the way in which the absent bodies of these men have been replaced by representations (masks, *eikones* or *imagines*).[11] Tacitus' account of Junia's funeral shows us both the vulnerability and the resilience of these and other representations of the Republic:

> Et Iunia sexagesimo quarto post Philippensem aciem anno supremum diem expleuit, Catone auunculo genita, C. Cassii uxor, M. Bruti soror. Testamentum eius multo apud uulgum rumore fuit, quia in magnis opibus, cum ferme cunctos proceres cum honore nominauisset, Caesarem omisit. Quod ciuiliter acceptum, neque prohibuit, quominus laudatione pro rostris ceterisque sollemnibus funus cohonestaretur. Viginti clarissimarum familiarum imagines antelatae sunt, Manlii, Quinctii aliaque eiusdem nobilitatis nomina, sed praefulgebant Cassius atque Brutus eo ipso, quod effigies eorum non uisebantur. (Tac. *Ann.* 3.76)

> And Junia passed away, in the sixty-fourth year after the battle of Philippi, born with Cato for an uncle, the wife of C. Cassius, the sister of M. Brutus. Her will occasioned much gossip among the common people because, endowed with great wealth, when she had made honourable mention of almost all the notable men in the state, she left out Tiberius Caesar. He accepted this in a civic spirit and did not obstruct the honours of her funeral: the oration from the rostra and the other rituals. Twenty funeral masks preceded her, from the most splendid families – the Manlii and Quinctii and other names of equal nobility – but Cassius and Brutus shone forth above all because of this very thing, that their images were not to be seen.

The conclusion is generally understood to celebrate the triumph of social memory over autocratic control. But it does so by working against the move from embodied presence to representation. The practices and achievements of Brutus and Cassius are transmitted despite the absence

---

[10] Holliday 2002: 122–8; Turner 2016: 147–9. [11] Potter 2014: 40–3.

of their representations. As A. J. Woodman puts it, they are 'somehow "really" present...'.[12] We note how the language of visuality underscores this presence without capitulating to the idea of representation. Brutus and Cassius outshone the twenty *imagines* which were present, from the most splendid families: *clarissimi* is so idiomatic that its association with brightness and clarity can be taken for granted. *Praefulgebant*, however, asserts a visuality which is non-literal, not only because the *imagines* of Brutus and Cassius are not present but because they would not in any case shine, being wax masks. Indeed, since these masks would be over 60 years old, they would be well on their way to becoming the *fumosae imagines* alluded to by Cicero and Juvenal.[13] *Imagines*, incidentally, as a visual form of commemoration which supplies both tangible and representational links to the past, are quite unlike Cicero's painting. The more they are revered and cultivated, the dirtier they will become. They are thus ideal vehicles for a visual, non-mimetic representation of the illustrious ancestor.

The illogicality of Brutus and Cassius' splendid visibility presents us with the same gap between 'seeing' and 'the Republic' which we have already confronted in Tacitus' prefatory statement. This illogicality has been enshrined in the English coinage 'conspicuous by its absence': the Tacitean origins of this phrase constitute a popular anecdote in current scholarship.[14] But Lord Russell's coinage merits a closer look for a moment, because it points to the role of expectation in making an absence conspicuous. Russell, as a prominent member of the Liberal Party in opposition, commented on the Conservative Reform Bill that:

> Among the defects of the bill, which were numerous, one provision was conspicuous by its presence, and one by its absence; a non-resident right of voting boroughs was introduced ... By the same clause freeholders whose property was in boroughs were deprived of their votes for the county ... The absence of any provision to reduce the franchise in boroughs and the hard line of separation thus left between the middle orders and those who earn their livelihood by manual labour would have tended to foster discontent and make a war of classes...[15]

---

[12] Woodman and Martin 1996: 498. [13] Flower 1996: 186; Henderson 1997: 46.
[14] 'When Lord John Russell in a speech to the electors of London in 1859 used the phrase "conspicuous by its absence", he went on to say "It is not an original expression of mine, but is taken from one of the greatest historians of antiquity." Tacitus' political quip [sic] created an image so striking, so universally comprehensible, that it continues to enrich our language two millennia later.' Mellor 1993: 133. 'It was this passage ... which gave rise to the modern phrase "conspicuous by its absence", first used by Lord John Russell on 15 April 1859.' Woodman and Martin 1996: 498 n. 1. '... so here we find the origin of the modern expression, "conspicuous by its absence"'. Pagán 2017: 91.
[15] Lord John Russell 'Address to the Electors of the City of London' [6 April 1859], *The Examiner*, 9 April 1859, 232 col. 2.

The fact that a newspaper critic of Disraeli echoed the phrase only a few days later suggests that Russell's coinage attracted attention – perhaps as much as the term 'fancy franchises' formulated around the same time.[16] Hence Russell defended his expression in a subsequent speech, and this is what most Tacitus scholars cite.[17] A century and a half later, the modern reader who is not expert in the franchise debates of the mid-nineteenth century has to read the address very carefully to understand which feature of electoral reform was conspicuous by its absence from this bill. But this was clear enough to the electors, since Russell's address was praised in the *London Daily News* as 'plain, dignified, and to the purpose', 'qualities which every Englishman will appreciate':[18] the electors notice the same absence as Russell does because they are looking for provision to redistribute the borough franchises.[19] In the same way, Tacitus shows us public expectation at Junia's funeral and suggests that Brutus and Cassius are present, not because their images are present, nor because people expect their images to be present, but because people expect their images to be *absent*.[20]

This public expectation derives from the sense of what Junia means in the political history of the Late Republic; the same charged awareness makes the Roman public hypersensitive to the rhetoric of her will and to the conspicuous absence of the emperor's name from her list of bequests.[21] Tacitus thus shows us how a visual sense of the *res publica* is achieved, in the absence of embodiment or representation, through a commonly held social memory expressed in non-formal speech.[22] Hence the usual reading of this passage is optimistic, seeing it as attesting 'an independent system of value under the Principate';[23] 'bear[ing] witness to the power of memory'[24] in keeping the Republic visible (as if living). But the dazzling presence of Brutus and Cassius outshines other, competing Republican presences in

---

[16] 'The Political Examiner', *The Examiner*, 9 April 1859, 1 col. 3.
[17] Russell's address to the Liberal Electors Committee [15 April 1859], *The Morning Chronicle*, 16 April 1859, 6 col. 1.
[18] *London Daily News*, 7 April 1859, 1 col. 2.
[19] For further context and discussion, Taylor 1995: 309–21.
[20] There may not have been a formal embargo on the public exhibition of these *imagines* – Junia's family may have independently chosen to omit them (Woodman and Martin 1996: 497; Sailor 2008: 25). This funeral takes place only two years after the senate had formally banned the appearance of a senator's *imago* in future processions (*SCPP* 81–2), so the public would have been hypersensitive to potential absences. On the legacy of Cassius and Brutus in imperial literature, Rawson: 1986.
[21] Champlin 1991: 5–6 comments on the Roman will as public document; 13–14 on pointed omissions, of which Junia's is 'the most dramatic'.
[22] Bruce Gibson has pointed out to me the associations between the brightness of eloquent speech (e.g. *Dial.* 20) and the splendour of Brutus and Cassius.
[23] Sailor 2008: 26–7.   [24] Pagán 2017: 91.

Junia's funeral and its narration. Each of these has its own 'blind spot', showing us that even Junia and her relatives fall within Tacitus' criterion of 'people born into the midst of civil war' – for their experience of the Republic seems to overlay and blot out older senses of the past.

First, Junia's birth date is omitted in favour of the more politically charged date at which she became a widow. As Thomas Strunk has observed, it is 'a moment recognised as a dramatic break between historical periods';[25] it also suggests that Junia's life before that period is somehow extraneous to her political significance and the significance of her funeral. Similarly, her genealogy is mobilised in order to prioritise the status of Brutus and Cassius[26] and thereby create in the reader that same expectation of conspicuous absence which the public entertain at the end of the episode. Junia's father, for instance, D. Iunius Silanus, is upstaged as progenitor by uncle Cato – who had tutelary guidance of Brutus certainly, but probably not of his half-sisters. We would also expect the father in the procession of *imagines* – as consul-elect in 63 BC no less, Iunius Silanus would certainly be more prominent than Brutus or Cassius, both praetors in 44. Indeed, the account of the procession lacks any mention of representatives from the family of Iunii, Silani or Servilii. These are replaced by the more ancient – and much more tenuously related – Manlii and Quinctii: a detail which considerably exercised the ingenuity of Sir Ronald Syme.[27] As a result, Junia's funeral erases various significant Republican components in order to present us with two very specific and limited images of the Republic: one a remote antiquity without a clear connection to the present scene; the other a recent past in which all other political issues are swallowed up in the single-minded drive to wipe out Caesar the dictator. And Junia herself lends her will to that drive when she leaves out Tiberius' name from her list of bequests: *Caesarem omisit*. The experience of the Republic, whether Junia's or that of the spectators at her funeral, is confined to a Republic caught up in trying and failing to effect the absence of Caesar.

This limited Republican past, and the way it is bound up in the significant absence of Caesar, is illuminated by the first funeral in the *Annals*, that of Augustus. This is also where we see in more detail the representational work that lies behind the presence of Brutus and Cassius at Junia's funeral. First, in order to get a sense of how sparsely Tacitus

---

[25] Strunk 2016: 177–8; see also Gingras 1992: 248–9.
[26] For comparable manipulation of genealogy at another *matrona*'s funeral, see now Osgood 2019: 138–42.
[27] Syme 1980: 158–9.

describes this ceremony, we need to turn to Dio's lovingly detailed account of the same event:

> Then came his funeral. There was a couch made of ivory and gold and adorned with coverings of purple and gold. In it his body was hidden (συνεκέκρυπτο), in a coffin down below; but a wax image of him in triumphal garb was visible (ἐξεφαίνετο). This image was borne from the palace by the officials elected for the following year, and another of gold from the senate-house, and still another upon a triumphal chariot. Behind these came the images of his ancestors and of his deceased relatives (except that of Caesar, because he had been numbered among the demigods) and those of other Romans who had been prominent in any way, beginning with Romulus himself. An image of Pompey the Great was also seen, and all the nations he had acquired, each represented by a likeness which bore some local characteristic, appeared in the procession. After these followed all the other objects mentioned above.' (Dio Cassius 56.34.11–4, trans. Carey)

There are many innovations in this ceremony – the opulence of the funeral couch, the inclusion of prominent Romans who were not part of the family, the order of procession – but the traditional continuities are also maintained.[28] What I want to focus on is the proliferation of images and other objects of display, which Dio intensifies by describing them and then mentioning their presence in the procession: 'after these followed all the other objects mentioned above'. In the middle of all this paraphernalia, not least of which are the three images of the dead man himself, we find – the absence of Caesar. This is an honorific absence; as a *heros* he is afforded a different kind of presence.[29] But it is striking because Tacitus' account of the same ceremony reverses the order of display; no images are shown, but only soldiers:

> Die funeris milites uelut praesidio stetere, multum inridentibus qui ipsi uiderant quique a parentibus acceperant diem illum crudi adhuc seruitii et libertatis improspere repetitae, cum occisus dictator Caesar aliis pessimum, aliis pulcherrimum facinus uideretur: nunc senem principem, longa potentia, prouisis etiam heredum in rem publicam opibus, auxilio scilicet militari tuendum, ut sepultura eius quieta foret. (Tac. *Ann.* 1.8.6)

> On the day of his funeral soldiers stood there as if for defence and were mocked thoroughly by onlookers who had themselves seen, or had heard from their parents, about that day when servitude was still fresh and the attempt to gain liberty had gone badly, when the killing of Caesar the dictator seemed to some the worst and to others the finest of deeds: now

---

[28] Sumi 2005: 256–61; on Dio's account, Swan 2004: 319–25.   [29] Bodel 1999: 260–1.

they said an old emperor, of long-lived power, after seeing to the supply of heirs for the state, needed military support for his protection, indeed, so that his burial would be peaceful.

'This brevity invites further comment.'[30] Instead of gazing at the impressive display of masks, the onlookers focus on the soldiers, a gaze which exposes the military force underpinning the specious display of precedent – precisely the point which Tacitus has made about the Augustan constitution in his opening chapters. The presence of the military also allows the absent Caesar and his funeral to overshadow what is taking place – a situation already anticipated by Tiberius himself, who warned the people in an edict not to aim for a repeat performance of that disruptive scene.[31] But even Caesar is upstaged by the tyrannicides: although Brutus and Cassius are not mentioned, it is their act which draws the focus of public memory. The popular, verbal commentary on the funeral becomes the alternative site of representation:[32] here is where Caesar, Brutus, and Cassius are present at Augustus' funeral and, as I suggested on p. 225, at Junia's. This verbal commentary is also underpinned by autopsy. The people who recall Caesar's death are those who saw, or whose parents saw: *qui uidisset?* is answered by *qui uiderant* (respectively the first and third uses of this verb in the text so far). But these onlookers, too, have a viewpoint which falls short of the Republic and which affirms Tacitus' lament. They had seen a time 'when servitude was still fresh' – the same time which directs the attention of the participants at Junia's funeral eight years later. Who, then, was left, who had seen the *res publica*?

... *qui* ... *vidisset?*

Roman funerals are no different from any other, in that they perform rituals of loss and consolation, negotiating absence and the substitution which makes absence bearable.[33] In Dio's account of Augustus' funeral, the dead body of Augustus is hidden and images of Augustus converge from various significant locations in the city, illustrating – to excess – how the dead 'take on new forms of visibility'.[34] Tacitus' account of the same event

---

[30] Goodyear 1972: 151.   [31] Gowing 2005: 28–30.
[32] Compare Barbara Del Giovane, in this volume, on the political dimension of popular chants at the triumph of Caesar.
[33] Erik Fredricksen in this volume elaborates on the anxiety underlying this act of substitution in Catullus' and Carson's poetry of loss.
[34] Turner 2016: 143.

invites us instead to examine the spectators and the act of viewing and to recast his rhetorical question with the same shift of emphasis: who was left to see, or what was left of the act of seeing?

As I've already suggested, *uidere* denotes a range of sensory, affective, and intellectual experiences: Polybius' spectator at the Roman funeral is 'inspired' by the nobility of the assembled ancestor masks, so that seeing becomes bound up with desire to perform one's social role.[35] Conversely, the absence of the Republic in Tacitus can be denoted by a change in the valence of seeing: a lack of stimulus, a succession of negative emotions ranging from grief to hatred, and a diminishing of knowledge and expertise. Some of these effects are more evocatively expressed in Tacitus' other historical prefaces, to the *Agricola* and the *Histories*; the relative sparseness of the preface to the *Annals* is a point I will address at the end of this section.

Here I also want to bring in a parallel text by Tacitus' colleague Pliny, which, as Chris Whitton has ably shown, engages extensively with all three of the Tacitean prefaces.[36] As Pliny laments the decline of expertise in senatorial procedure after the disastrous reign of Domitian, he too asks the question *quotus quisque*, when he says *Quotus enim quisque tam patiens, ut uelit discere, quod in usu non sit habiturus?* (Pliny *Ep.* 8.14.3): 'Who indeed is there so patient, that he would want to learn a skill which he would never be able to put to use?'[37] The restrictions on political participation result in a loss of knowledge in senatorial *ius*, practised through speaking, listening, reading, and exercising judgement. Hence when Pliny speaks of senatorial practice in visual terms, he prioritises the intellectual aspect of seeing; but in his lament at the loss of an embodied transmission of knowledge he evokes the experiential diversity of the senatorial career past and present:

> Erat autem antiquitus institutum, ut a maioribus natu non auribus modo uerum etiam oculis disceremus, quae facienda mox ipsi ac per uices quasdam tradenda minoribus haberemus. Inde adulescentuli ... honores petituri adsistebant curiae foribus, et consilii publici spectatores ante quam consortes erant. ... At nos iuuenes ... prospeximus curiam, sed curiam trepidam et elinguem, cum dicere quod uelles periculosum, quod nolles miserum esset. ... Eadem mala iam senatores, iam participes malorum multos per annos uidimus tulimusque; quibus ingenia nostra in posterum quoque hebetata fracta contusa sunt. (Plin. *Ep.* 8.14.4, 5, 8, 9)

---

[35] O'Gorman 2011. [36] Whitton 2010.
[37] The answer to this (rhetorical) question, as Kathrin Winter's analysis shows, might be Cicero's Brutus, whose claim to rejoice in the study of *eloquentia* for its own sake makes him a guarantor of continuity (*Brut.* 23). Equally, Pliny's question could be an exasperated rejoinder to such naivety.

> It was the practice of antiquity for us to learn from our elders not only with our ears, but with our eyes also, what we needed to do ourselves, which in turn we needed to pass on to the younger generation. Hence young men ... who had ambition for office were accustomed to attend at the doorway of the senate house and to be spectators of political deliberation before they took part in it themselves. ... But when we were young ... we gazed upon a senate house trembling and robbed of speech, when it was perilous to say what you wished to say, and wretched to say what you did not wish. ... Now as senators we have witnessed, and endured, and been participants in these evils for so many years in which our abilities were dissipated, broken, and shattered, and remained so for some time thereafter.

Pliny evokes the tradition of young men learning from bodily co-presence with their elders, a tradition in which Tacitus situates his own education in his *Dialogus de Oratoribus*:

> Marcus Aper et Iulius Secundus, celeberrima tum ingenia fori nostri, quos ego utrosque non modo in iudiciis studiose audiebam, sed domi quoque et in publico assectabar ... ut fabulas quoque eorum et disputationes et arcana semotae dictionis penitus exciperem... (Tac. *Dial.* 2.1)

> Marcus Aper and Julius Secundus, the best-known public speakers of our time, both of whom I not only listened to most attentively when they spoke in the law courts but even followed to private and public gatherings ... so that I could catch even their anecdotes and conversations and intimate remarks ...

Tacitus' emphasis on co-presence remains at the auditory level; as a keen young student of rhetoric he strives to 'pick up' different modes of speaking from his role models. But in Pliny's account of the same process of education, the visual medium gains dominance over the act of hearing as the medium of instruction: his *adulescentuli* attend the senate as spectators rather than as audience. And spectating is the necessary prelude to participating: from this perspective Tacitus' rhetorical question in the *Annals* can be rendered 'who was left who had even seen the Republic (let alone participated in it)?' This might suggest that survivors of the Republic were too young to have reached the stage of political participation. Or Tacitus could be speaking of the years before Augustus in terms of political alienation. Either way, it draws attention to a rupture in the transmission of knowledge, referred to in the *Histories* as *inscitia rei publicae ut alienae* (*Hist.* 1.1.1), 'ignorance of state affairs as if they were the property of another'.[38] An equivalent rupture is dramatised in Pliny's account of his

---
[38] Damon 2003: 79 on the translations of *ut*.

own youth, where the spectacle of the senate becomes a scene where sensory apprehensions are fragmented. Unlike the *adulescentuli* of old, who look at *consilia publica* (which implicitly would have been heard as well as seen), Pliny's generation gaze upon a silent image: *curiam elinguem*. Tacitus observes a similar disaggregation of sight and sound in the *Agricola*, speaking of the same time:

> Sicut uetus aetas uidit quid ultimum in libertate esset, ita nos quid in seruitute, adempto per inquisitiones etiam loquendi audiendique commercio. (Tac. *Agr.* 2.3)

> Just as antiquity saw the extreme in liberty, so we saw the extreme in servitude, having lost, under hostile inquiry, even the interchange of speaking and hearing.

The act of seeing here has an affective as well as an intellectual dimension, as the senators look upon their own silence with grief; the political experience of loss here is also felt audibly, as the interchange of speech is replaced by a one-sided *inquisitio* which robs the subject of words. Witnessing here, and in Pliny, becomes a new form of participation: endurance. Tacitus returns to and intensifies the affective language of visuality at the end of the *Agricola*, when he details the miserable spectacle in the senate which Agricola did not live to see:[39]

> Non uidit Agricola obsessam curiam et clausum armis senatum et eadem strage tot consularium caedes... (Tac. *Agr.* 45.1)

> Agricola did not have to see the senate-house under siege, the senators constrained by armed guards, the slaughter of so many consular men in one act of carnage...[40]

The debilitation of senatorial excellence which is inflicted by such experiences combines the affective and cognitive dimensions, so that the Roman senator is faced with an awareness of his limitations and with the burden of grieving the loss of his own ability. As Tacitus puts it in the preface to *Agricola*, *nostri superstites sumus* (*Agr.* 3.3): 'we have become survivors of ourselves'. The senator becomes spectator and *imago* at the funeral of his own political potential. In this context, Tacitus' rhetorical question suggests not the absence of survivors – 'who was left who had seen the

---

[39] Again, Kathrin Winter's reading of *Brutus* shows us how Tacitus' and Pliny's vocabulary of loss draws them closer to Cicero, who speaks of Hortensius not living to see the forum bereft of *eloquentia* (*Brut.* 6).
[40] Keitel 2014: 63 on the *euidentia* of this episode.

Republic?' – but rather a survival which is bereft of anything more than bare life: 'who was left for whom seeing the Republic was a meaningful act?'

Reading Pliny alongside the prefaces to the *Agricola* and the *Histories* provides a wealth of intellectual, sensory, and affective dimensions to the act of seeing. Putting them alongside Tacitus' rhetorical question draws our attention to how this sentence stands out at the end of the first three chapters of *Annals*, which have created a political landscape almost bereft of sensory or affective terms. Tacitus' opening chapter, infamously, sketches the history of Rome under almost Oulipan constraints, using mostly abstract nouns for power and temporality.[41] Indeed, across the first three chapters which make up the preface, the language of affect is confined to about twelve terms – appropriately enough for a historian who professes to write without anger or excessive attachment.[42] Meanwhile the concept of perception is only gestured towards with the term *species* (1.3.2).[43] We might compare this with the denser experiential language of the *Histories*: even before we get to the dramatic table of contents in the second chapter of that work, we have encountered nearly twenty experiential terms within more sustained phrases of affect, considerably greater than the first chapter of *Annals*.[44] The preface to the *Annals*, then, seems to be doing something different from the *Histories*, even though it says more or less the same thing. Specifically, the peculiar semantic limitation of these chapters seems to create the effect of sensory deprivation in the reader, to recreate for us the lack of stimulus which is one aspect of the political experience of absence. It's notable in this context that the first affective word we encounter in *Annals* 1.1.1 is *fessa*: 'tired'. By the time we reach the words *quotus quisque reliquus, qui rem publicam uidisset*, we may be too tired to notice that so far there really has been nothing to see.

And this leads me to a more text-centred, literal-minded way of reading this rhetorical question, for if the opening chapters of the *Annals* omit the language of experience, they undoubtedly parade a plenitude of language for political structures, positions, and power. But the one term that does not appear in the preface, until the very end of chapter 3, is *res publica*. Who was left, who had even seen the <u>word</u> *res publica*?

---

[41] This analysis supplements the insights of Kraus 2009.   [42] A point made to me by Tom Geue.
[43] *fessa* (*Ann.* 1.1.1); *adulatione deterrerentur; ob metum falsae; recentibus odiis* (1.1.2); *sine ira et studio* (1.1.3); *contentum; dulcedine otii; ferocissimi* (1.2.1); *suspecto* (1.2.2); *flagrantissime cupiuerat* (1.3.2); *ferocem* (1.3.4); *cupidine* (1.3.6).
[44] *libertate; libidine adsentandi; odio* (*Hist.* 1.1.1); *cura posteritatis inter infensos vel obnoxios; ambitionem; obtrectatio et liuor; adulationi; malignitati falsa species libertatis* (1.1.2); *iniuria; neque amore quisquam et sine odio; felicitate ubi sentire quae uelis et quae sentias dicere licet* (1.1.3).

...*rem publicam*...?

Julius Caesar is supposed to have provided his own variation on Cicero's 'we still have the Republic in name, but we have long since lost the thing itself':

> Nihil esse rem publicam, appellationem modo sine corpore ac specie (Suet. *Iul.* 77)
>
> The *res publica* was nothing, a name only without substance or appearance.

His claim, perceptively analysed by Llewelyn Morgan as both a political reproach and a remark about semantics,[45] draws its power from the difficulty of conceptualising *res publica* in the abstract, without *species* or outward appearance.[46] We have seen how that difficulty is posed again by the peculiarity of Tacitus' phrase *rem publicam uidere* and is surmounted by the translation of that action into various cultural practices of spectating, most of which involve looking at senators and senatorial representations. Tacitus himself juxtaposes the abstract and the embodied immediately after he has posed the question:

> quotus quisque reliquus, qui rem publicam uidisset? igitur uerso ciuitatis statu nihil usquam prisci et integri moris: omnes exuta aequalitate iussa principis aspectare. (Tac. *Ann.* 1.3.7–1.4.1)
>
> How many were left, who had seen the Republic? Therefore, with the constitution of the state overturned, there was a complete absence of the old, uncorrupted modes of behaviour: everyone, stripped of their equality, turned their eyes to the commands of the Princeps.

This, too, mediates Cicero's lament in a new age, for Cicero ties the loss of the Republic to the impossibility of maintaining ancient *mores*, embodied practices, in the absence of virtuous men:

> Quid enim manet ex antiquis moribus, quibus ille dixit rem stare Romanam, quos ita obliuione obsoletos uidemus, ut non modo non colantur, sed iam ignorentur? Nam de uiris quid dicam? Mores enim ipsi interierunt uirorum penuria... (Cic. *Rep.* 5.1)
>
> For what remains of those ancient practices, on which Ennius said the Roman state was founded, which we now see blotted out by forgetfulness, so that not only are they not cultivated, but they are not even understood?

---

[45] Morgan 1997.   [46] Hodgson 2017.

Indeed, what should I say about the men? For our practices themselves are lost because of the deficit of men ...

Tacitus translates that deficit of men and *mores* into depersonalised absence – not *nemo* but *nihil prisci moris*. The Augustan senators turn their gaze away from the silent senate house towards the *iussa principis*. We might understand this as the senators viewing an imperious gesture of command, such as a master would give a slave,[47] or as another example of Tacitus presenting a gap between the act and the object of seeing. In either case, it evokes the absence of *prisci mores* in a new and impoverished experience of political community: silence, one-way communication, bodily submission,[48] even slavery.

Tacitus' transition from *nihil* to *omnes* demonstrates what Cicero has stated explicitly: the impossibility of conceiving of *mores* without their embodied practitioners. Related to this is the difficulty of seeing the Republic unless one envisages the Republic as a set of embodied practices. Cicero's reflection on men and *mores* takes as its starting point the line from Ennius: *moribus antiquis res stat Romana uirisque* (Ennius *Ann.* 156 Sk.), 'on ancient practices rests the Roman state, and on its men.' What Cicero and in turn Tacitus might elicit from Ennius is a relation between men, *mores*, and *res publica* which does not rely on representation or metaphor, but rather on embodiment as the sequence through which the Republic can be apprehended by the senses. It is not that men 'stand for' the Republic but that the Republic is substantiated by men and *mores*: without them, it becomes a mere word *sine corpore ac specie* 'without substance or outward appearance'.[49]

Envisaging the Republic as a set of actions or practices, often understood as the 'exemplary' as opposed to the 'constitutional' idea of *res publica*, underscores the way in which the Republic, about which so much is written, is also fundamentally unwritten.[50] While Cicero, Tacitus, and Pliny pinpoint the vulnerability of a *res publica* which depends on

---

[47] This suggestion was made to me by William Fitzgerald.
[48] The initial sense of *aspectare* suggests that the viewer turns bodily to look at a particular object (*OLD* 1); this provides the physical corollary to its sense of turning one's attention towards an object (*OLD* 2b, where this passage is cited).
[49] Morgan 1997: 23–4 juxtaposes Seneca's discussion of semantics, which similarly explores the substance of action, which can only be perceived through its embodied performance. For an analysis of how the concept of the 'body politic' is worked out through visual images of Augustus, see Squire 2015.
[50] The comments of Peachin 2007: 88 are especially useful here: '...we must remember several things about the Republican "constitution": a) it was unwritten, which left plenty of room for debate about its proper nature and rightful content, along with significant leeway for the invention and/or re-invention of many of its aspects...'.

embodied practice and its transmission through co-presence, they also might gesture towards the possibility of its recovery not through co-presence but through texts which evoke the sensory plenitude of past political experience. Tacitus' early work, the *Agricola*, is well known as giving an account of recovery which it also enacts as a piece of writing. It begins with Tacitus conceiving of political restoration in terms of bodily healing (*Agr.* 3.2) and concludes with the injunction to remember Agricola not through representation but through the shaping of one's own self:[51]

> praeceperim ... memoriam uenerari ut omnia facta dictaque eius secum reuoluant, formamque ac figuram animi magis quam corporis complectantur ... quam tenere et exprimere non per alienam materiam et artem sed tuis ipse moribus possis. (Tac. *Agr.* 46.3)
>
> I would advise them ... to revere his memory by recalling all his actions and words and to hold in their minds the image and outlines of his character rather than of his body ... which you can comprehend and express not through non-human material and representative art but through your own embodied practices.

Tacitus' repudiation of statuary here resonates provocatively with Cicero's figure of the Republic as a painting. The rejection of a strongly visual but silent medium directs us back to the primary sense involved in political *mores* – sound, and speech – and reminds us that Tacitus characterises his biography of Agricola as a recovery of voice. We can return to Pliny's letter to get a sense of what, by implication, the full presence and plenitude of political experience might be: mature senators visible and audible, in the company of young men spectating, desiring, and preparing to participate in politics. In the absence of this plenitude, Tacitus' writing aims to fill the gap, and achieve some future reactivation of integrated political senses.[52]

A glimpse of such a happy future is offered in the preface to Tacitus' *Histories*, after the historian has lamented the rupture in the transmission of senatorial knowledge effected by the Augustan regime. Tacitus himself writes:

> rara temporum felicitate, ubi sentire quae uelis et quae sentias dicere licet. (Tac. *Hist.* 1.1.4)
>
> In that rare happiness of times, when you can feel/think what you like, and say what you feel/think.

---

[51] Harrison 2007; O'Gorman 2020.
[52] In this respect, Tacitus' move from specific third person plural at the beginning of this exhortation to generalised second person singular (Woodman and Kraus 2014: 326) signals the transmission of Agricola's *figura animi* beyond the immediate present: O'Gorman 2020.

Intellectual and affective experience is here united, as is the seamless continuity between inner and outward life. *Sentire*, in particular, conveys the double meaning of sensory experience and political opinion. This compressed and repetitive phrase – a *sententia* about political sensation – picks up on the sort of multi-sensory engagement Pliny evokes when he speaks of a lost political plenitude. Under Domitian, Tacitus and Pliny have felt politics as absence and deficit, expressed in narratives of muted or fragmented senses. And the recurring imagery associating visuality with silence has become a potent expression of the disaggregration or fragmentation of the senses, and a metaphor for the absence of full political experience. When Tacitus reclaims full political experience under Nerva and Trajan, he does so by announcing a recovery of speech integrated with will, sensation, and opinion. And he does so, crucially, by expressing senses as internalised, not offered to others as externalised spectacle. If there is a message of hope in this declaration, it could provide one more way of reading Tacitus' rhetorical question in the *Annals*: for who can see the Republic, if it resides within them?

PART III
Going Beyond

CHAPTER 13

The Slave, Between Absence and Presence

William Fitzgerald

I was reading one of those annoying books which disdain footnotes while intriguing you with statements that you trust are true. Making the point that the slave's presence was not always registered by the Romans, the author related that one of Horace's poems begins by describing himself as alone, but reveals some lines later that he is accompanied by a slave. Naturally, I was curious. Which poem? The author wasn't telling, so there was no alternative but to rummage through my Horace *OCT* to find this fascinating poem that seemed to have slipped my attention. After about an hour, I came to the conclusion that the poem in question must be *Satires* 1.9, nicknamed in modern times The Bore, or more recently The Pest, which begins:

> Ibam forte Via Sacra, sicut meus est mos,
> nescioquid meditans nugarum, totus in illis . . .
>
> (Hor. *Sat.* 1.9.1–2)

> I happened to be walking on the Via Sacra, as I do,
> pondering some triviality, completely absorbed in that. . .

Of course, Horace does not say that he is alone in the opening of this poem. It just sounds, to a twentieth-century reader, as though Horace, absorbed in composing poetry, must be telling us that he is alone. So who is ignoring the slave here, Horace or his modern expositor? To whom does the scandal adhere?

In the modern scholar's remark, we experience the meeting of a modern prejudice (anyone absorbed in thought must be alone) with an ancient prejudice (the presence of the slave goes without saying). The modern prejudice has to do with notions of privacy and interiority. When Horace uses the word *meditans* of his activity on the Via Sacra, moderns tend to assume that the activity is happening in his head (meditation), whereas a glance at the *OLD* shows that the word covers a spectrum from the interior to the externalizing (with meanings from 'ponder', 'contemplate', 'rehearse', 'practise', 'say to oneself', 'practise public speaking', to 'work over in performance'). Horace's slave is likely to be taking dictation from a poet who is rehearsing a poem (*nugae*) out loud. And, of course, there's a slave there! The poet need not explicitly tell us. But the fact that he doesn't say 'I was walking down the Via Sacra with my slave the other day' makes the sudden materialization and immediate disappearance of the slave later on in the poem noteworthy to the modern mind.

Here, to refresh your memory, is what happens in this poem: Horace is strolling down the Via Sacra when someone known to him only by name joins him and insists on accompanying him. Horace tries to shake him off by various shifts; first he walks faster, then he walks slower, and then he whispers something in his slave's ear (*in aurem dicere nescio quid puero*, 9–10). But the Pest is persistent, and it quickly transpires that what he wants is an introduction to Maecenas, offering himself as a useful ally in the manoeuvrings within that circle. Horace insists that his interlocutor has got Maecenas wrong, but to no avail. Eventually, the pair encounter Horace's friend Aristius Fuscus, but in spite of Horace's hints Fuscus does not save him from his annoying companion, leaving him in the lurch. Finally the Pest's opponent in law meets them and makes a citizen's arrest, since the Pest has jumped bail, asking Horace to act as witness (*licet antestari*, 76). Horace assents in the ritual way, by offering his ear to be touched (*oppono auriculam*, 77), and he is saved.

In this poem, Horace's slave is introduced to serve a purpose in the narrative and then disappears from view. Or does he? Here we come to another case of modern blindness. It used to be the case that scholars discussing this poem took considerable relish in castigating the Pest as everything that Horace is not: ambitious, self-promoting, unscrupulous, importunate, and so on. The poem was a lesson in manners and taste by opposition. More recent readings of Horace's satire, against the grain, have been keen to point out that Horace seems blind to the fact that he and the 'Pest' (now in scare quotes) are not as different as we have wanted to believe. Schlegel (2005: 126) comments: 'Shrewd readers (Johnson, John Henderson, Oliensis) observe that Horace has portrayed himself as every bit as vulnerable to the scorn saved for the interlocutor as the interlocutor is.'[1] Furthermore, as Gowers (2012: 282) puts it, expounding Henderson 1993: 'When the conversation triangulates, H's frantic appeal to his mock-obtuse friend Fuscus is choreographed as a replica of the pest's frustrated

---

[1] In what follows re: *Satires* 1.9, I recapitulate material from Fitzgerald 2011: 179–80.

approach to him.' So, there are plenty of parallels between the three characters, but what about the slave? His introduction as an ear (*in aurem dicere nescio quid puero*, 9–10) should alert us to his significance. Ears are important in this poem, which describes the unpleasant experience of having one's ear bent, and which ends when deliverance comes from an ear.[2] So the fact that the slave materializes as an ear connects him with the imagery of the poem as a whole. Let us include the slave in the play of similarity and difference between the characters in this scenario and see what happens. To begin with, we can note that Horace's slave stands in a similar relation to his master as his master does to the Pest: Horace whispers any old thing (*nescioquid*, 10) into the slave's ear in a futile attempt to shake off the Pest, while the latter rattles on to Horace about anything that occurs to him (*cum quidlibet ille / garriret*, 12–13). Once Horace realizes that his attempt has been futile, he resigns himself with a bad will to his fate, and once again the focus is on ears:

> demitto auriculas, ut iniquae mentis asellus,
> cum grauius dorso subiit onus.
>
> (Hor. *Sat.* 1.9.20–1)
>
> I droop my ears, like a resentful ass
> when its back has taken on too heavy a load.

Here, the poem speaks back to itself by indicating to us precisely what it refuses to say: Horace buttonholed by the Pest may be like the burdened ass, but he is also like his own slave, whose ears are constantly at the disposal of his master. Strolling along the Via Sacra, Horace seems to be composing poetry (*nescioquid meditans nugarum*, 2)[3] which, presumably, the slave must remember or record. Horace's slave, for whom carrying burdens is *not* a metaphor, can also be expected to be as resentful (*iniquae mentis*, 20) as an ass, and for the same reason as Horace is resentful of the Pest – he is being forced to listen. In the expression *demitto auriculas* the act of listening, of resigning the ears (***dimitto***) to their fate is also an expression of resentment, as the ears are drooped (***demitto** auriculas*).[4] With reference

---

[2] Tom Geue suggests to me that Persius' image of the satirist (like Midas' barber) confiding his words to a hole in the ground before he asks 'Who does not have asses' ears?' (*auriculas asini quis non habet?*, 1.121) is in dialogue with this poem. He also points out that at Juvenal 11.56–9 whispering in the slave's ear is again a figure for the confiding of the master's true feelings. In Juvenal the hypocritical master who parades his ascetic diet whispers 'cake, cake' in the ear of his slave.
[3] Compare *Tityre tu ... silvestrem tenui Musam meditaris auena* (Verg. *Ecl.* 1.1–2).
[4] Gowers 2012: 288 notes that the phrase can also mean 'to deign to listen to', 'to bring oneself down to someone's level'.

to the ass, commentators have been quick to point out that Horace is probably punning on his name, Flaccus (flop-eared). But they are missing something more obvious here, if we consider the common association in Latin literature between asses and servitude (we will have another example of this later).[5] Horace may be like the burdened ass, but so, more appropriately, is his slave: no less than the put-upon Horace, he can never shake off the master who is dictating poetry to him. In another respect, though, the slave is like the Pest himself, who sticks to the poet through thick and thin, for that is the duty of a slave. Only, *he* can be ignored, unlike the Pest, and *his* presence can be taken for granted. The one thing the master will not do is to set free, or release (again, *dimitto* perhaps shadows *demitto*) the ear that is, for him, the slave. Emily Gowers (2012: 286), as far as I know the only one to make anything of the slave, introduces another figure to which the slave alludes when she points out that Horace's aside to his slave mimicks his shared joke with the reader.[6] As I have argued elsewhere (Fitzgerald 2000), the slave, present and yet not present, often serves as a figure for the reader in Latin poetry. So, if we make Horace's vestigial slave into a presence in this poem, not only does it begin to say things that can't be directly said about slavery, but it reorients the axis of blindness in and to this poem: we have failed to see how integral the figure of the slave is to this poem, and Horace has failed to see how ironic his complaints would sound to the ear of his slave, who might appropriate the resentment of the ass with droopy ears as a figure for *himself*. Insofar as slavery is a relation characterized by blindness to the subjectivity of another human being, this text has much to say about slavery, and it locates the master's blind spot, from which the slave might speak back, with some precision.

Is it anachronistic of us to be surprised, or outraged, at Horace's revelation of the slave's presence so casually and fleetingly, without him having been properly introduced? An ancient reader is unlikely to have been surprised at the sudden appearance of the slave because that reader would naturally have assumed that a member of the elite, strolling on the Via Sacra, would be accompanied by a slave. The text can remain unspeaking on this point because it can be taken for granted. But to take someone for granted might be to assume their presence without noticing it. If our hypothetical ancient reader wouldn't imagine Horace wandering down the Via Sacra, lost in thought and bumping into people in the solitary

---

[5] For more on slaves and domestic animals, particularly asses, see Fitzgerald 2000: 99–102 and Bradley 2000.

[6] Although, as Tom Geue points out to me, the slave is privy to information from which the reader is excluded, and the indefinites *nescioquid* (2) and *quidlibet* (12) leave us out of the loop.

absentmindedness of his composing, neither would that reader necessarily picture a slave at his side, witnessing the whole scene. We can tell this, I think, because Ovid makes that very distinction, between assuming and noticing, into a dramatic event in the paired poems *Amores* 2.7 and 8. In this well-known diptych Ovid first defends himself against his mistress' paranoid suspicions that he is having sex with her slave Cypassis and then, in the next poem, addressed to the slave herself, asks how her mistress could have found out about what they have done.[7] The important point, for my purposes, is that Ovid makes it clear that Cypassis was present in the altercation described in the previous poem ('didn't I play my part well?', he asks her, complaining that she almost gave the game away, *Amores* 2.8.7–16). Ovid draws our attention to the fact that though the slave was, as we might assume, present during Ovid's altercation with his mistress, we didn't notice her. The change that Horace's satire undergoes once we accommodate the slave to its scenario is made by Ovid into the focus of his diptych. We re-read *Amores* 2.7 in the light of Cypassis' presence, and we note how the axis Ovid–Corinna (with the slave as an excluded third person) is now replaced by the axis slave–Ovid (with Corinna the excluded third person). 'Ah, you hadn't thought of that', says Ovid (like the literary critic). 'Gotcha!'

The Master's Prosthesis

Is the slave in these unspeaking volumes, then, the 'taken for granted' or might there be other ways of thinking about this presence which is not declared? One of the most notorious slave-absences in Latin literature is in Vergil's *Georgics*. It is clear that the farms Vergil is describing in the *Georgics* must have been large estates that would have been worked by slaves for absentee masters. Yet, as Brendon Reay (2003) points out, neither slaves nor the term *dominus* appear in the poems, and instead Vergil addresses his advice to an *agricola*, *colonus* or *pastor*, usually in the second person singular, as though that *agricola* were himself doing the farming. The *Georgics*' erasure of the slaves allows the elite to imagine themselves as individual farmers and herdsmen, as the modern embodiment of culture heroes like Cincinnatus and Romulus, and for that the agency of the slaves needs to be absorbed by the master. Particularly striking are passages in which Vergil moves seamlessly between telling the singular addressee to do something and telling that addressee to *order* it to be done:

---

[7] More on this diptych in Fitzgerald 2000: 63–7.

> rara sit an supra morem si densa *requires*
> (altera frumentis quoniam fauet, altera Baccho,
> densa magis Cereri, rarissima quaeque Lyaeo),
> ante colum *capies* oculis, alteque *iubebis*
> in solido puteum *demitti*, omnemque *repones*
> rursus humum, et pedibus summas *aequabis* harenas.
> (Verg. *G.* 2.227–32)

> If you *ask* whether the soil is thin or unusually dense
> (since one favours corn, the other Bacchus,
> the dense is better for Ceres, the thinnest kind Lyaeus),
> you must first *look out* a place, and then *order* a deep pit
> *to be sunk* in the solid ground, and you will *replace*
> all the soil, and with your feet *even out* the earth on top.

How can these two very different kinds of action be equivalent? Reay argues that the Romans thought of their slaves as prostheses, so that what is done by the slave is, in effect, done by the master.[8] Before we leave the *Georgics* to follow the slave-as-prosthesis model in a different context, let me suggest where the unspoken of the *Georgics* might come to the fore. If we follow the principle that everything suppressed at one point of the text returns in another form elsewhere, it is not difficult to imagine where we might find the missing slave gang. The bees of *Georgics* 4 are a collectivity devoted to efficient work. Their individuality is subordinated to the group. Whatever else they are doing in the *Georgics* I would suggest that their eruption into the text is partially driven by the suppression of the agricultural slave gang.[9] *Examen* (swarm) is clearly a word that Roman writers considered appropriate for a gang of slaves.[10] This is not to say that Vergil's bees are a figure for the missing slaves, and nothing else; simply that the significant appearance of such a collectivity devoted to labour allows what has been so strenuously suppressed to find an expressive (and very reassuring) outlet.[11]

But, to return to the slave as prosthesis. First of all, we should acknowledge that the prosthesis phenomenon is not restricted to the ancient world; think of statements like 'We've just re-modelled our kitchen'.

---

[8] Reay 2003: 36–7.
[9] See now Geue 2018, a sharp analysis of the (occluded) distribution of work over the *Georgics*' trajectory. Geue's bees allow the oppressed provincials of Egypt, the new imperial province, (not) to come into sight.
[10] Cicero *Har. resp.* 25 *examina tanta seruorum*; Plautus, *Truc.* 534 (on a gift of slave girls): *paenitetne te quot ancillas alam, quin examen super inducas.*
[11] On the relation of the spoken to the unspoken in literary texts, see Macherey 1978: 84–9 (original French version published in 1966).

Let's not be smug.[12] In the context of Latin literature, Sarah Blake has applied Brendon Reay's suggestion to some other Latin texts, citing Bruno Latour's 'actor network theory' (Blake 2012). In a subsequent study (Blake 2016) she cites Pliny's famous statement, in the first of his epistles, that he has not bothered to put the letters in any particular order, but simply published them *ut quaeque in manus uenerat* ('as each one came to hand', *Ep.* 1.1). If we imagine Pliny with all his letters spread out on the floor, picking up one or the other at random, we would be wrong. 'As my slave handed them to me' would be a more accurate expression of what Pliny is describing in the phrase *ut quaeque in manus uenerat*.[13] And, as Blake points out, *manus* is a significant word when it comes to slaves, who are in the *manus* of their master. Following the prosthesis model, we can also say that the slave is the master's *manus*. Let us push the idea of the hybrid body, in which slave and master form a continuous whole, and ask whether the tail could wag the dog? Vergil's *Georgics* leave no doubt as to who is absorbing the agency of whom. But a more equal relationship in the hybrid body of master and slave is suggested by an epigram from Martial's *Apophoreta*, his book of gift-tags, in which each epigram is a couplet imagined as accompanying a Saturnalian gift:

> *Notarius*
> currant uerba licet, manus est uelocior illis:
> nondum lingua suum, dextra peregit opus.
>
> (Mart. *Ep.* 14.208)

> *Stenographer*
> However fast the words run, the hand is faster than them.
> The tongue has not yet finished its job when the right
> hand has finished its own.

As Blake points out (2012: 203), if we didn't have the lemma *Notarius* heading the poem we would assume that tongue and hand belong to the same body. But the lemma announces that the couplet accompanies the gift of a (slave) stenographer and so the tongue is the master's and the hand the slave's. The syntax of the couplet, however, enhances the sense of a continuum between bodies, with the main verb, *peregit* (accomplished),

---

[12] Bertolt Brecht mocks this way of describing historical events ('Caesar conquered Gaul') in his poem *Fragen eines lesenden Arbeiters*.
[13] For the use of this locution to allude to the work of a slave, see Persius, *Satire* 3.11, *inque manus chartaeque nodosaque uenit harundo*. The preceding '*ocius adsit / huc aliquis. nemon? turgescit uitrea bilis*' (7–8) indicate that a slave has been called, but the knotty texture (*nodosa*) of the pen is more vividly present than the slave who proffers it.

postponed and governed by both *lingua* (tongue) and *dextra* (right hand). The object of both *lingua* and *dextra*, *suum* ... *opus*, is distributed so that the postponement of the noun *opus* questions the possession emphasized by the possessive *suum*. Whose *opus* is this, hand's or tongue's? Does *dextra* 'steal' *opus* from the tongue's possessive (*suum*)? There's no slave in this poem, but there's no master either, just body parts, and both of them are instrumental, both are functions of a task. It is as though the instrumentalization of the slave has infected the master too.

The first line of Martial's couplet conjures up a different scenario. Words seem to be trying to escape the hand, which always catches them. We might think of a runaway slave. The slave is in the *manus* of the master, but here the *manus* is the slave's. So, again, the reduction of persons to instrumentalized body parts allows some play within the master-slave relation. The line focuses on a paradox, namely that the writing *dextra* is *faster* than the dictating tongue. How can that be? We can imagine such a thing more easily than a Roman could: we need only consider our own prosthesis, the iPhone, with its auto-correct function which finishes the *opus* before our hand has finished its job. Looking backwards rather than forwards in time, we might ask if there is a double entendre in Martial's second line, with *dextra peregit opus* alluding to Ovid's scenario of furtive mutual masturbation at a dinner party:

> saepe mihi dominaeque meae properata uoluptas
> ueste sub iniecta *dulce peregit opus*. (Ov. *Am*. 1.4.47–8)
>
> Often the pleasure sought by my mistress and me
> *finished the pleasurable job* beneath the cover of a robe.

What to make, then, of the fact that in Martial, *lingua* and *dextra* compete to complete the *opus*? Or is the subtext of Martial's second line metaliterary rather than pornographic? No sooner have we started reading the epigram than the poet wraps it up, an *opus* swiftly accomplished, over when it has scarcely begun. In fact, the elegiac couplet and its characteristic word patterning are so familiar that we might indeed have finished it before we reach an end which we had already anticipated. One part of us has got ahead of another.

The lemma saves us from the couplet's rampant imaginings by anchoring the body parts to separate agents; like the solution to a riddle, it explains that 'these words accompany the gift of a slave stenographer', closing down the free play of meanings by locating us firmly within the trade in persons that is slavery. And yet, the epigram's pragmatic purpose, indicated by the lemma, doesn't *only* work to close down the potential mushrooming of subversive relations. The gift has to be 'talked up', and it is the process of talking up the gift as something wondrous that gets us into the confusion of free-floating body parts and unruly meanings that I have elaborated. So, while the slave may be erased by being subsumed into the master's agency, as in the *Georgics*, the fact that the slave is something to be given as a gift allows the magic of prosthesis to eat away at the master's own agency, conjuring up a vision of ownerless body parts in a text that leaves the agents unspoken.

The Not-Spoken

Returning to Horace, I want to consider a text where the slave is very much present, but only as metaphor, and here I will examine the *not-*spoken rather than the *un*spoken. I want to ask how specifically a text might not say what it does not or cannot say. Can we identify the actual words that it is not saying?[14] I turn to the last epistle of Horace's first book (*Epistles* 1.20), in which Horace sends his book out into the world in an extended metaphor which casts the book as a slave looking forward to manumission. Here, a slave is present throughout, as a personification of the book. Horace's book-as-slave is eager to leave the family nest, and the author expresses his anxieties about publication through an argument with his 'slave' that describes the dangers and unpleasantness awaiting the slave who has detached himself from his master's presence. But I want to focus on a passage that is not usually remarked upon. Horace says that when the book/slave regrets that he has disregarded his master's advice to stay at home, he – Horace – will laugh

> ut ille
> qui male parentem in rupes protrusit asellum
> iratus: quis enim inuitum seruare laboret?   (Hor. *Epist.* 1.20.14–16)
>
> like one
> who thrusts the recalcitrant ass over a cliff
> angrily: for who would labour to save one unwilling (to be saved)?

---

[14] I recapitulate here Fitzgerald 2011: 178.

Here, Horace alludes to a fable of Aesop in which a recalcitrant ass wanders from the trodden path until it is in danger of falling over a cliff (Aesop 197 Hausrath). The driver tries to pull it back but, faced with the continued resistance of the ass, he finally lets go, saying 'it is a bad victory that you have won'. Let me confess that, as a student, I used to misread the last line of this passage and translate 'for who would labour to serve against his will?', as though Horace had written *quis enim inuitus serui*re *laboret?* The *enim* now applies not to the action of the owner ('for who would bother to save a subordinate who doesn't want to be saved?') but to the fact that the slave is *male parens* (disobedient)! Of course, the slave/ass is disobedient, 'for who would labour to serve against his will?' One might say that Horace very nearly *did* say that (he was only two letters off!) or that he never came *anywhere near* to saying it (if we consider explicit Roman attitudes, behaviour, environment, and indeed the logic of the passage). So near and yet so far! We are distinguishing two ways in which the poem speaks: through its words or through what it says, text or utterance. We might say that I misread the passage because it made more sense to my twenty-first century outlook to read it that way. We might, if we wanted to be bold, attribute these two very different meanings inhabiting virtually the same letters to two different voices in Horace's text. Roman etymology did, after all, connect *seruire* with *seruare*.[15] Furthermore, the sonic structure of Horace's line might encourage my misreading, for it is held together by the similar sounds of *iratus* and *inuitum*, each of which words is a molossus; ir*a*tus, we might say, takes us to *seruare*, and in*ui*tum to the forbidden *seruire*. At the very least I would say that these lines are playing with fire.

Can we say that our own misreadings are part of what a text doesn't say? When is it useful, or revealing, or true, to say that some things are said by a poem under erasure, so to speak? The opening of *Satires* 1.9, for instance, *doesn't* say that Horace is alone, and that fact speaks volumes. But it takes my scholar's misreading to make the text not-say specifically *that*. In this case, what the text does not say measures the distance between our taken-for-granted and the ancient world's taken-for-granted. But is it just a matter of the difference between ancient and modern attitudes and assumptions? In the case of slaves, perhaps the most obvious locus of the unspoken in Latin literature, we can articulate the situation more sharply if we say that, for the masters, the institution of slavery is a kind of blindness.[16] The critic's task, then, might be to locate the point where those blind spots can be found, or where the text might speak to, against, or from its own blind spots.

[15] Maltby 1991: 564.   [16] See Fitzgerald 2011: 176.

Presence as Diversion

I have said that slaves are perhaps the most *obvious* locus of the unspoken in Latin literature. And maybe this obviousness is itself a strategy, albeit not one that has been consciously concocted. I take my lead from one of the most brilliant and thought-provoking studies of the partially visible in literature, and that is Bruce Robbins' *The Servant's Hand* (1993), a study of servants in the nineteenth-century English novel. What concerns Robbins is not just the fact that servants appear only as 'expository prologues, oracular messengers, and authorial mouthpieces, rhetorical "doublings" of the protagonist, accessories used to complicate or resolve the action', but that these literary servants are substituted for 'full representations of the life of the people'.[17] It is convenient that the people – those who do not belong to the classes whose story the novel will tell – should be represented by servants, who are integrated into the paternalistic world of the middle-class family. In other words, these vestigial presences serve to cover more significant absences. Transferring this to our Roman context, can we say that the vestigial appearance of the slave in Latin literature covers, and distracts us from, a more significant absence, that of the free poor?

Robbins goes on to say something that concerns us as classicists and historians more closely. He is struck by the annoying sameness of the formal manifestations of literary service, from Homer to Virginia Woolf. The literary servant does not seem to change with the times. Robbins tells us that, like many a good historicist of the eighties (his book was originally published in 1986), he set out to reassert 'the principle that social being determines social consciousness by displaying the historical variables that this apparent consistency concealed'. But, he tells us, this project had to be abandoned, because he found that the *differences* between the devices that made up the literary servant from Terence to Thackeray were less illuminating than an 'analysis of the disturbing fact of *continuity*'. Perhaps the most scandalously unspeaking volume is the one that does not speak of its own time.

---

[17] Robbins 1993: x.

CHAPTER 14

In Search of the Lost City
The Enduring Absence of Pompeii

Joanna Paul*

For a place that looms so large in the cultural imagination, Pompeii's presence is surprisingly insubstantial, its anchor in both space and time only provisional. It might seem ludicrous to question, doubt, or even erase or conceal the very existence of an ancient site which at times suffers from an *excess* of materiality[1] – but in fact this has been a recurrent theme in responses to and receptions of Pompeii ever since the disaster that befell it in the year 79 CE. The repression of Pompeii begins with the near-contemporary poems of Martial and Statius, and becomes a trope that continues through to the present day – a trope in which Pompeii and its inhabitants can variously be conceived of as forgotten, lost, empty, or dislocated.[2] This chapter sets out to examine the ways in which Pompeii's absent presences, from antiquity to the present, might be noticed, and argues that these absences are an important part of understanding Pompeii's long afterlife. They also help us to understand our other encounters with the ancient world, for nearly all the wormholes that hollow out classical antiquity, from lost texts to disappeared frescoes, ruined buildings to nameless and voiceless people, can be tracked through this Campanian site.[3] By embracing the counterintuitive possibility that Pompeii is, in a sense, *never there*, we might therefore gain new

---

* I wish to thank the organisers and attendees of the conference at which the original version of this paper was delivered, and colleagues at the University of Leeds Classics research seminar, for their helpful comments and suggestions.
[1] The sheer number of exhibitions of Pompeian artefacts is just one marker of the site's material abundance; see Coates, Lapatin and Seydl 2012: 242–50 for a helpful catalogue, to which many new examples can already be added. Osanna 2017 emphasises the materiality of Pompeii as a key factor in promoting a sense of familiarity and proximity between past and present ('la possibilità di tendere un filo di Arianna attraverso il labirinto del tempo', 96). Objects, 'nella lora duratura materialità' (97), provide the biographies of people who have left no other trace in history.
[2] I regard this trope as distinct from the more common conception of antiquity as fragmented, or only partially absent, an aesthetic which is particularly strong in, though by no means limited to, modernist receptions of antiquity (explored by Nochlin 1994, for example.)
[3] Morley 2018: 51–9 summarises the effect of these 'absences' on our study of antiquity.

appreciations of its importance as a *locus* (or anti-*locus*) for understanding the widespread absences that permeate classical culture, and our modern receptions of it.

Pompeii's Poetic Absences

After the eruption that devastated the Campanian cities, it didn't take long for the poets of the age to ruminate on its demise. Martial's *Epigram* 4.44 was published a decade after the event and probably after the poet spent a summer on the Bay of Naples:

> Hic est pampineis uiridis modo Vesbius umbris,
>   presserat hic madidos nobilis uua lacus:
> haec iuga quam Nysae colles plus Bacchus amauit;
>   hoc nuper Satyri monte dedere choros;
> haec Veneris sedes, Lacedaemone gratior illi;
>   hic locus Herculeo nomine clarus erat.
> cuncta iacent flammis et tristi mersa fauilla:
>   nec superi uellent hoc licuisse sibi.

Here is Vesuvius, that till recently was green with shady vines. Here did the noble grape load the vats with juice; here was the ridge that Bacchus loved more than the hills of Nysa; on this peak, not long ago, Satyrs held their dances. Here was Venus' seat, that she favoured over Sparta; this spot was famous for its Herculean name. All lie sunk in flames and dismal ash. The gods themselves must have wished this was not in their power.[4]

A sense of what has been lost is clearly the driving force here, in keeping with the poem's literary influences, primarily the Hellenistic genre of epigrams lamenting a destroyed city,[5] and the epitaphic genre. After the solemn anaphora of *hic, haec* and *hoc*, and the funerary connotations of flames and ash (Newlands 2010: 110; Watson & Watson 2003: 333), the poem hinges on the strong contrast between what *was*, the vision of fecundity and life in the first six lines, and what *is* now, when everything lies submerged, *cuncta iacent mersa*. And submerged beneath this vivid imagery, are, first and foremost, the names of the Vesuvian towns, a notable omission given that the name of the deceased typically appears in Martial's other epitaphic poems (Henriksen 2006: 358). Pompeii and Herculaneum are instead referred to in mythological terms as *Veneris sedes*

---

[4] Translation by Nisbet 2015.
[5] These are often cities destroyed by war, such as Corinth (*Anth. Pal.* 9.151) and Troy (*Anth. Pal.* 9.62, 9.152–6).

and *locus Herculeo nomine*; and perhaps an echo of Pompeii's name is tantalisingly traced in the adjective *pampineis* in line 1. In fact, deceased people are emphatically not the subject of this epigram; as Carole Newlands points out, the neuter plural of *cuncta* elides the loss of human life (Newlands 2010: 111), and the third person address of the poem maintains a distancing effect. What is named is Vesuvius, not blamed as the aggressor, but named, unlike the towns, as part of the devastated landscape (Watson and Watson 2003: 333).

This repression of Pompeii's name, and a focus on Vesuvius, characterises the references to the disaster throughout the *Siluae* of the Neapolitan poet Statius, too. Although his poetic career was forged at Rome, he remains, to borrow Carole Newlands' phrase (2012), a poet 'between Rome and Naples', thus displaying a particularly acute sensitivity to the trauma suffered by his home region. *Siluae* 3.5, published in 93 or 94, is at the hinge of this bicultural identity. Writing to his wife, he attempts to persuade her to return with him to Naples. After appeals to her conjugal loyalty, he offers a *laudes Campaniae*, an encomium to the region which emphasises its security and resilience, in comparison with the turbulence of Rome (Newlands 2012: 142–5). The events of 79 frame this encomium, but this time serving as evidence of the region's regeneration, rather than conveying the funereal solemnity of Martial's verse:

> **non adeo Vesuuinus apex et flammea diri**
> **montis hiems trepidas exhausit ciuibus urbes:**
> **stant populisque uigent.** hinc auspice condita Phoebo
> tecta Dicaearchi portusque et litora mundi   75
> hospita, at hinc magnae tractus imitantia Romae
> quae Capys aduectis impleuit moenia Teucris,
> nostraque nec propriis tenuis nec rara colonis
> Parthenope, cui mite solum trans aequora uectae
> ipse Dionaea monstrauit Apollo columba.   80
> (Stat. *Silu.* 3.5.72–80)

Not so entirely has Vesuvius' summit and the flaming tempest of the fire mountain drained the terrified cities of their population; they stand and flourish with folk. On one side are the dwellings of Dicaearchus [Puteoli] founded under Phoebus' auspices and the harbour and world-welcoming strand, on the other the walls that Capys filled with Teucrian migrants [Capua], mimicking the expanses of great Rome. There is also our Parthenope [Naples], neither meagre in her own folk nor lacking in settlers; to her, a traveller from overseas, Apollo himself showed a gentle soil with Dione's dove.[6]

Here, then, we see a rather different take on the absence trope. Seeming to correct Martial's *cuncta iacent* (Newlands 2010: 112), Statius tells us that cities stand and their populations flourish, *stant populisque uigent* (74); but these cities are Puteoli, Capua, Naples itself, and, a little later in the poem, *Stabias renatas*, 'Stabiae reborn' (104). Pompeii remains conspicuous by its absence, the loss of its population thrown into sharper relief by the emphatic *stant populis* of the other urban centres.

It has been suggested that Statius' optimistic depiction of Vesuvius and its environs here is somewhat manipulative, deliberately skewed to reassure his wife (Newlands 2010: 112) – and it is certainly true that the poet's subsequent references to the Vesuvian disaster recapture the sense of loss and desolation seen in Martial. Books 4 and 5 of the *Siluae* were published in the mid-90s, Statius now back in Naples, and the destructive power of Vesuvius literally always on the horizon, even fifteen years after the eruption. *Siluae* 4.4 vividly evokes the ongoing shock occasioned by the loss of Pompeii and its surroundings:

> Haec ego Chalcidicis ad te, Marcelle, sonabam
> litoribus, fractas ubi Vesuius erigit iras
> aemula Trinacriis uoluens incendia flammis.   80
> mira fides! **credetne uirum uentura propago,**
> **cum segetes iterum, cum iam haec deserta uirebunt,**
> **infra urbes populosque premi proauitaque fato**
> **rura abiisse pari?** necdum letale minari
> cessat apex. procul ista tuo sint fata Teate   85
> nec Marrucinos agat haec insania montes.
>
> (Stat. *Silu.* 4.4.78–86)

This song I sing to you, Marcellus, on Chalcidian shores where Vesuvius rears his broken wrath, rolling out fires to rival Trinacrian flames. Wonderful but true! **Shall future progeny of men believe, when crops grow again and this desert shall once more be green, that cities and peoples are buried below and that an ancestral countryside vanished in a common doom?** Nor does the summit yet cease its deadly threat. Far be that fate from your Teate, nor let this madness drive Marrucinian mountains!

In this poem, Statius compares his home region (the *Chalcidicis . . . litoribus* referring to early Greek colonisation of the Bay of Naples) with that of his addressee, Vitorius Marcellus, hoping that it will not undergo the same

---

[6] All Statius' translations are by Shackleton Bailey (Loeb).

devastation; and in so doing, he rather contradicts the rosy picture of Campania reborn that he gave his wife in *Siluae* 3. The overwhelming impression is one of absence and desolation. This *deserta* has not yet been re-greened, and the again unnamed *urbes populosque* are buried out of sight; the fact that the lost land is ancestral, *proauita ... rura* (83–4), emphasises the shock of its disappearance.[7] Although there is optimism that the crops and greenery *will* return (Newlands 2010: 114), still Statius questions whether future generations will believe what was there before (Coleman 1988: 154). Pompeii's name and people are already lost to posterity, no match for the madness of Vesuvius, *insanus* both at line 86 here, and later on in *Siluae* 4.8, when Statius hopes that the recent birth of a son to Julius Menecrates will compensate for some of the losses inflicted by the volcano:[8]

> clari genus ecce Menecratis auget
> tertia iam suboles. procerum tibi nobile uulgus
> crescit et insani solatur damna Veseui.
>
> (Stat. *Silu.* 4.8.3–5)

A third scion now gives increase to renowned Menecrates' line. Your noble crowd of grandees grows, solacing the losses of mad Vesuvius.

Finally, two poems in book 5 of the *Siluae* connect Statius' father with the events of 79. In 5.3, Statius is lamenting his father's death, and summoning Parthenope to pay tribute to him:

> Exsere semirutos subito de puluere uultus,
> Parthenope, crinemque afflatu montis adustum
> pone super tumulos et magni funus alumni,
> quo non Munychiae quicquam praestantius arces
> doctaue Cyrene Sparteue animosa creauit.
>
> (Stat. *Silu.* 5.3.104–8)

Raise your half-buried countenance from the sudden shower of dust, Parthenope, and place your locks, singed by the mountain's breath, on the tomb and body of your great foster son, than whom Munychia's towers created nothing finer, nor learned Cyrene or valiant Sparta.

The siren, Parthenope, is 'a metonymic figure for the damaged city' (Newlands 2010: 120), Naples, covered in ash and half-ruined, *semirutos*

---

[7] The nature of the ancestral land's disappearance changes with the variant reading of *fato ... pari*; read as *toto ... mari*, it is rendered as 'and that our ancestors' fields have disappeared in such a great inundation' (Coleman 1988).

[8] Though it is not clear that these are losses felt specifically by Menecrates' family, as suggested by Cooley (2003: 51).

(104)⁹ – so while there is, again, hope in future regeneration, conveyed by the opening imperative *exsere* (104), 'rise' or 'come forth', the region is still characterised by damage and loss. These lines focus on Naples, but a little later, when Statius is describing the poem that his father had planned to write about the eruption, he reminds us of the wide extent (*late*, 208) of Vesuvius' impact, and the losses, *damnis* (206), over which he will weep:

> iamque et flere pio Vesuuina incendia cantu
> mens erat et gemitum patriis impendere damnis,
> cum Pater exemptum terris ad sidera montem
> sustulit et late miseras deiecit in urbes.
> (Stat. *Silu.* 5.3.205–8)

And now it was your purpose to weep Vesuvius' flames in pious melody and spend your tears on the losses of your native place, what time the Father took the mountain from earth and lifted it to the stars only to plunge it down upon the hapless cities far and wide.

So once again, no mention of Pompeii, no Herculaneum – just *urbes*. In all of these poems, the city's name has been erased.¹⁰ Should this strike us as odd? We must, of course, beware of looking too hard for something *we* expect to find, of deeming something conspicuous by its absence when contemporary audiences might not have noticed it; some have even argued that small-town Pompeii was simply not famous enough to warrant naming in this way.¹¹ Even a more prosaic near-contemporary account seems not to bother; in Tacitus' brief reference to the eruption, the destroyed cities are again simply *urbes*:

> Iam uero Italia nouis cladibus uel post longam saeculorum seriem repetitis adflicta. **haustae aut obrutae urbes, fecundissima Campaniae ora**; et urbs incendiis uastata, consumptis antiquissimis delubris, ipso Capitolio ciuium manibus incenso. (Tac *Hist.* 1.2)

Moreover, Italy was distressed by disasters unknown before or returning after the lapse of ages. **Cities on the rich fertile shores of Campania were swallowed up**

---

⁹ See Gibson 2006: 305 and Newlands 2010: 120 for variant readings of line 105.
¹⁰ Just one mention of Pompeii appears in the *Siluae*: Statius uses *Pompeiani* as an epithet for the river Sarnus when praising the newlywed (and fellow Neapolitan) Violentilla (1.2.265).
¹¹ Zissos 2016 distinguishes between the status of the Vesuvian settlements at the time of their destruction, and their later significance: 'Vesuvius' eruption destroyed three unimportant towns of decidedly modest size; the economic damage, its jolting impact notwithstanding, was of an essentially transient kind. But in the Western imaginary. Pompeii, the city suddenly destroyed by the forces of nature has attained the status of an archetype.' (523)

or overwhelmed; Rome was devastated by conflagrations, in which her most ancient shrines were consumed and the very Capitol fired by citizens' hands.[12]

But is Tacitus perhaps playing with the namelessness of a city? After all, hot on the heels of the *haustae aut obrutae urbes* comes the description of another city burned, *urbs incendiis uastata*, but we readily infer that this is the city – The City, Rome – which needs no name because it is so overwhelmingly famous and significant (though the translator yet sees fit to restore it).[13] And in fact, Pompeii is far from absent from pre-79 literature, and it does get named plenty of times.[14] Cicero refers to the area in various letters, naming the city (e.g. *QFr.* 2.6, 2.13; *Fam.* 7.4, 12.20), while Cato tells us that a mill can be bought for 384 sesterces there (*Agr.* 22). The younger Seneca opens book 6 of his *Quaestiones naturales* on earthquakes, with the words *Pompeios, celebrem Campaniae urbem* (6.1.1), before going on to describe the earthquake that strikes the city in 62. Not only is the city's name emphasised in his first word, it is qualified as 'famous', the phrasing reflected almost exactly by Tacitus' account of the earthquake, where the named Pompeii, though now an *oppidum*, is also *celebre* (*et motu terrae celebre Campaniae oppidum Pompei magna ex parte proruit, Ann.* 15.22). Tacitus also doesn't hesitate to name the city when reporting on the riot in 59 between the Pompeians and Nucerians (*inter colonos Nucerinos Pompeianosque, Ann.* 14.17), and we could probably assume that if the parts of the *Historiae* that dealt with the events of 79 were not themselves lost, that the city would have been named there too (Dewar 2016: 471). In later accounts of the destruction, Dio Cassius (66.23.4) names the 'two entire cities, Herculaneum and Pompeii' that were buried (τό τε Ἑρκουλάνεον καὶ τοὺς Πομπηίους), as does Tertullian in his description of how Pompeii was drenched in fire from 'its own mountain' (*Pompeios de suo monte perfudit ignis*, 40.8). Finally, it is notable that Marcus Aurelius invokes Pompeii and Herculaneum in his meditation on mortality and the impossibility of outrunning death, asking us to reflect on 'how many entire cities are, if I may use the expression, dead, Helice and Pompeii and

---

[12] Translation by Moore (Loeb).
[13] See Edwards 1996: 86–8 on Rome as *urbs aeterna*. Virgil also plays with the namelessness of towns and cities at *Aeneid* 6.776, when Anchises indicates the future heroes who will build the great Latin towns of Nomentum, Gabii, Fidenae and so on. Here, the anonymity is not the fate of the city, but its precondition: *haec tum nomina erunt, nunc sunt sine nomine terrae*. But as Denis Feeney 1986 and others have argued, the irony was that for Virgil's original audiences, the reference was to towns that had, in many cases, subsequently been destroyed or deserted once the region fell under Roman control.
[14] Cf. *OLD* s.v. 'Pompeianus[1]', 'Pompeii', 'Pompeius[2]'.

Herculaneum, and others without number' (πόσαι δὲ πόλεις ὅλαι, ἵν' οὕτως εἴπω, τεθνήκασιν, Ἑλίκη καὶ Πομπήϊοι καὶ Ἡρκλάνον καὶ ἄλλαι ἀναρίθμητοι, *Meditations* 4.48). Here, strikingly, it is the Vesuvian cities that are privileged with a name, along with the Peloponnesian city destroyed by an earthquake in 373 BCE, set against the countless others whose identity is suppressed.[15]

Given this backdrop of Pompeii being named and indeed celebrated in other texts, then its suppression in Statius and Martial is worthy of comment and requires some explanation. Perhaps the magnitude of the event and the totality of its disappearance have made the name unsayable (especially in the sense of the Latin *infandus*, which captures the ineffability of the shocking and abominable occurrence).[16] Carole Newlands, for example, argues that Pliny, Statius, and Martial attempt to alleviate the catastrophe, primarily by adopting literary forms – the epitaph and the letter – which lend 'authenticity and directness to the described experience' without the kind of 'sentimentality or sensationalism' that might come from, say, epic (Newlands 2010: 118). Like the poets, Pliny passes over the names of the Vesuvian towns in both *Ep.* 6.16 and 6.20: his description of the death of his uncle, Pliny the Elder, uses a similar formulation as the examples already seen, referring to the disaster which also befell 'whole cities and their people' (*ut populi ut urbes*, 6.16.2). Failing to name Pompeii could thus be seen as a way of maintaining distance and coping with the extent of the disaster. However, Newlands also proposes that what is really important here is not Pompeii, but Vesuvius (2010: 111–14). Mountains and volcanoes are seen as 'testing ground' for poets, and Statius in particular, on account of his close personal identification with the region, yokes himself and his poetic ambitions to Vesuvius and its power, providing a kind of heroic amplification for his own activities, and allowing him to connect Campania's regeneration with his own poetic renewal.[17]

---

[15] See Walter 2017 for discussion of Helice as an instance of divine retribution for human misbehaviour in ancient texts.
[16] The ineffability of catastrophic and traumatic events has been discussed particularly in the context of the Holocaust; see, e.g., Waxman 2008: 152–84.
[17] Cf. the two references to Vesuvius in Valerius Flaccus' *Argonautica* (seen by Stover 2012 as a *terminus ante quem* for the dating of the poem's composition): at 3.209, the volcano is the *mugitor*, 'bellower', in a simile that describes the raging of the battle between the Argonauts and the Doliones; the 'terror-stricken cities' (*attonitas ... urbes*) roused by the volcano remain anonymous. In the simile at 4.507–8, Vesuvius simply brings destruction to Hesperia, Italy as the western land.

Maintaining Absence and Anonymity

Even if we conclude that Pompeii and its people were not necessarily that important to the Flavian poets, still their erasure of the city's name is frequent enough to seem significant. Moreover, as the second half of this paper will explore, the poetic absence initiates an ongoing failure to recognise or remember the city or its inhabitants, even to wilfully deny its physical presence. To that end, it's worth pausing to reflect on the extent to which the literary absence of the city might have reflected the physical reality. Was, as *Siluae* 4.4 suggests, everything really vanished and buried below? What remained accessible or visible of Pompeii is not that easy to determine.[18] The consensus is that 'within another generation [of the eruption] the sites would seem to have passed out of memory' (Winsor Leach 2016: 328), in keeping with Plutarch's account of 'the destruction of so many great towns, so that their location is imperceptible (ἄγνοιαν) and uncertain (ἀσάφειαν) to anyone going there in broad daylight, now that the land has been turned topsy-turvy' (*Moralia: The Oracles at Delphi* 398E).[19] There was regeneration in the area: for example, repairs to roads and infrastructure were made by early in the second century, and there is evidence for resumption of viticulture (Cooley 2003: 60–1) – but certainly no attempts to build a New Pompeii. Instead, the forgetting of Pompeii – what Robert Boissier calls *un oubli* (2011: 42) – is emblematised in the new name that, by the Middle Ages, locals would give to the area: it is simply *Civita*.

Yet the idea that Pompeii descends into *total* oblivion is misleading (Rowland 2014: 30). The archaeological evidence for scavenging and/or salvaging, in the form of tunnels, finds of post-79 objects such as lamps, and even apparent disturbances to the otherwise distinct stratigraphy of the eruption, is well known. This suggests that returns to the site were made, in both houses and areas such as the forum, and not only in the immediate aftermath.[20] And as we move through the centuries, the faint but persistent presence of Pompeii's name can be tracked through a handful of texts,

---

[18] Cooley 2003: 50–64 provides an overview of the years between 79 and the official rediscovery of the Pompeiian sites in the eighteenth century.

[19] In this part of the Pythian dialogues, Plutarch is praising oracles' veracity and accuracy in predicting Vesuvius' eruption. See Brenk 1999: 211–25.

[20] Dio Cassius' claim (66.24) that Titus authorised the redistribution of property of victims also suggests the site remained at least partly accessible. Mau 1902 (cited in Descoeudres 1992: 167) declared that 'the first excavations at Pompeii were undertaken by the survivors shortly after the destruction of the city'. It has also been pointed out, though, that the evidence is not conclusive and that holes in the houses may represent escape attempts as much as post-eruption salvage or looting (Cooley 2003: 54–5; Allison 2004: 179–82). See also Ling 2005: 155–7.

from a ninth-century account of a battle between Prince Sicardo of Beneventum and the Saracens, in which he's described as camping *in Pompeio campo*, to Boccaccio in the fourteenth century, and Flavio Biondo in the fifteenth;[21] the town is also mapped on the thirteenth-century Peutinger Table (Cooley 2003: 51). In 1504, a particularly evocative example emerges in the *Arcadia* of Neapolitan poet and humanist Jacopo Sannazaro.[22] In the following passage, the narrator Sincero, who traverses Campania on a quest for a pastoral idyll before returning to Naples to find his lover, is taken on a journey under Vesuvius by a nymph:

> 'So also under great Vesuvius I would make you hear the terrifying groans of the giant Alcyon ... There certainly was a time when all the neighbours heard them, along with the damage they suffered when, with storms of flame and ashes, he covered the countryside round about, as even now the liquefied and burnt stones clearly testify ... under which who will ever believe that both people and villas and most noble cities are buried? (*Sotto ai quali chi sarà mai che creda che e populi e ville e città nobilissime siano sepolte*). As they really are there (*come veramente vi sono*), not only those which were covered by the burnt pumice stones and the wreckage of the mountain but this one which we see in front of us which, without any doubt, was a famous city once in your country called Pompeii (*la quale senza alcun dubbio celebre città un tempo nei tuoi paesi, chiamata Pompei*) ... and it was by a sudden earthquake swallowed up by the earth ... Certainly a strange and horrifying manner of death for living people.'
>
> I marvelled at our speedy progress, that in so brief a time we could have arrived this far from Arcadia. [...] And with these words we were almost at the city she described, and its towers, houses, theatres, and temples could be picked out nearly intact. (*Arcadia* 12.28–34)[23]

Sannazaro's engagement with classical literature pervades the *Arcadia*, and here, it is as if he is answering Statius' question in *Siluae* 4.4 over whether or not future generations of men will know that Pompeii lies beneath them. The nymph appears to confirm that on the surface, such uncertainty indeed persists, and she underlines the shock of the fate that befell the city – now not only destroyed, but also forgotten – by reminding Sincero that the city was once famous (*celebre*), the choice of words recalling Seneca and Tacitus. But having been granted a privileged glimpse of the buried city lying nearly intact beneath the earth, Sannazaro also invites his readers to regard and recognise, in some way, the city beneath their feet, restoring

---

[21] Garcia y Garcia 1998: 61–2 collects these citations; see also Moormann 2015: 9–10.
[22] Kidwell 1993: 65–6 provides a partial English translation; see also Cooley 2003: 62–3.
[23] Translation by Kidwell 1993.

its name and physical existence to their imaginations, if not yet fully in reality.

Although the *Arcadia* facilitates an imaginary encounter with Pompeii only through the magical capabilities of the nymph, Sannazaro's literary fantasy surely reflects the fact that the city must have continued to make its presence felt in the collective memory and perhaps even in physical traces too. Sannazaro was a knowledgeable antiquarian, often guiding visitors around the city of Naples and its environs (including subterranean areas; de Divitiis 2015: 202–5), alongside other antiquarians who were beginning to speculate on what really lay beneath the hill of Civita. In 1514, Ambrogio Leone, in his *De Nola*, proposed that it was Stabiae under Civita, and speculatively placed Pompeii north-west of Naples in the map engraved for his volume by Girolamo Mocetto (Darley 2011: 36–7);[24] a century later, in 1607, Giulio Cesare Capaccio's history of Naples suggested that Pompeii could be found under Torre Annunziata (Rowland 2014: 33–4). In fact, a few years previously, Pompeii had been 'excavated' for the first time in the modern era when, in the late 1590s, Domenico Fontana's construction of an aqueduct, leading from the River Sarno to Torre Annunziata, cut a 1600-metre channel through the Civita hill, uncovering a few inscriptions along its way (Cooley 2003: 62; Bowersock 2009: 68–9). Then, in 1637, Lucas Holstein proposed that it was indeed Pompeii that lay under Civita, but he was paid no heed, to the extent that even when an inscription reading POMPEI was recovered from Civita in 1689, it was assumed to refer to Pompey the Great (Bowersock 2009: 69–70). Furthermore, there is evidence to suggest that parts of Pompeii were actually visible above ground, or could very easily be uncovered. Writing in 1658, Holstein could not have been more clear in his assertion that 'it is as certain as can be that Pompeii must have been where the biggest ruins can be seen, in the place that people call Civita, which Ambrose of Nola once thought must be Stabiae' (cited in Rowland 2014: 39); later on, in 1776, François Latapie describes his tour of the site (where excavations had only recently begun), explaining how ruins could sometimes be seen above the surface of the ground, or were covered only lightly (Cooley 2003: 64; a few years earlier, in his letter on the discoveries at Herculaneum, Winckelmann had also described how easily Pompeii's amphitheatre could be seen above ground). It is therefore no great leap to imagine that Sannazaro could have seen parts of Pompeii above ground even in the early sixteenth century.

[24] See De Divitiis, Lenzo and Miletti 2018.

Yet despite all of this, when official excavations began at Pompeii in 1748 (having commenced at Herculaneum a decade earlier), the identity of the site was still subject to question until the 1760s.²⁵ Certainly from the Renaissance onwards, and perhaps even earlier, the whole issue of Pompeii's identity and whereabouts seems to have been held in a tension between reality and the collective imagination. Pompeii had not been entirely erased from the landscape, but its visible fragments were apparently misinterpreted, perhaps even wilfully ignored, as though confusion and concealment were preferable to recognising and identifying the city beneath their feet; and yet nor was it ever completely forgotten by the collective imagination. In these long centuries between death and resurrection, then, Pompeii maintained its anonymity and absence against the odds, while yet finding ways to insist upon its former fame, particularly through literary encounters such as Sannazaro's imaginary journey; it remained a city both there and not-there.

Pompeii's Modern Absences

Pompeii's 'lost centuries' might seem to be over, now that no one can doubt either its material presence or its identity. But in fact this is far from the case, for Pompeii's absence continues to preoccupy visitors, writers, artists, and scholars, in a myriad of ways. We can sample only a small selection here, but it should be sufficient to show how the rich reception history of the city is very often predicated on the idea that something fundamental is *missing* at Pompeii. Early literary responses to the city often drew attention to the obvious absence of the city's inhabitants, prompting Schiller to explore the 'silent halls' in his 1797 poem 'Pompeii and Herculaneum' ('how lone the clear streets glitter in the quiet day', in Bulwer-Lytton's translation); while Madame de Staël, in her 1807 novel *Corinne, or Italy*, meditates on the abandoned amphorae and the wheeltracks still visible on the paving, and laments the loss of the 'thoughts and feelings' of the men who left these traces (Book 11, Chapter 4). This absence of humanity would unsurprisingly provide suitable subject matter for the profoundly nihilistic Giacomo Leopardi, whose 1836 poem 'La Ginestra' ('The Broom', referring to a shrub that tenaciously grows on the slopes of Vesuvius) elaborates on

---

²⁵ Moormann 2015: 25 n. 76 sets out the appearances of the name of Pompeii in the early excavation reports, along with the claim made by Francesco La Vega, an early chief engineer/excavator, that Pompeii had been identified with certainty only in 1763.

the utter desolation of the once 'great cities' (*città famose* at line 29, again recalling the formulation in our Latin literary examples), and the Pompeians themselves who were destroyed 'so utterly that they scarce leave behind a memory' (*distrugge sì che avanza / a gran pena di lor la rimembranza*, 109–10).

Of course, within a few decades, Pompeii's inhabitants would begin to be returned to the city in the startling re-embodiments of Giuseppe Fiorelli's plaster casts.[26] But even though these figures would seem to answer the Romantic desire for access to the people who walked Pompeii's streets – resurrecting their feelings and emotions all too vividly by capturing their death throes – still they remain a haunting reminder of the absence, both literal and figurative, of the Pompeians. The casting process, after all, depends upon the discovery of a void in the volcanic material, the body made present again only by filling the void with plaster.[27] The sculptural quality of Fiorelli's casts has in turn inspired artists, and particularly in the twenty-first century, a number of works have used the casts as a spur to consider the sense of absence that characterises our encounter with the past at a place like Pompeii. In *The Presence of Absence* (2014; Figure 14.1), Tom Price used coal to cast a series of male and female figures in progressive states of decay, the increasing fragmentation of their bodily substance highlighting 'awareness that what we are observing is an almost tangible presence of a person who is now clearly absent', and prompting us to reflect on our own mortality by drawing attention to the fact that, 'when we go, we leave in our place an absence'.[28]

Price acknowledges the inspiration derived from the Pompeiian casts, as does fellow British sculptor Antony Gormley, whose *Untitled* (2002; Figure 14.2) is another piece that plays with the idea of an absent corporeality by fragmenting the bodily form, this time into small steel blocks.[29] Gormley explains how the 'lost bodies' of Pompeii are the starting point for exploring the gulf between human fragility and sculptural solidity that characterises much of his work (quoted in Coates, Lapatin, and Seydl 2012: 234):

> 'The "lost body" – as the most extreme form of translation from life to something close to art – is a radical replacement for the lost wax process, and is more direct, more shocking, more about human fragility and our desire for

---

[26] See Dwyer 2010 for an overview of the production of and responses to the casts, which began in the 1860s.
[27] See O'Gorman (this volume) for discussion of the substitution of the absent body at Augustus' funeral.
[28] www.tom-price.com/the-presence-of-absence, accessed June 2018.
[29] A similar work from the same series, *Spleen II*, is also titled *Suspend Pompeii*.

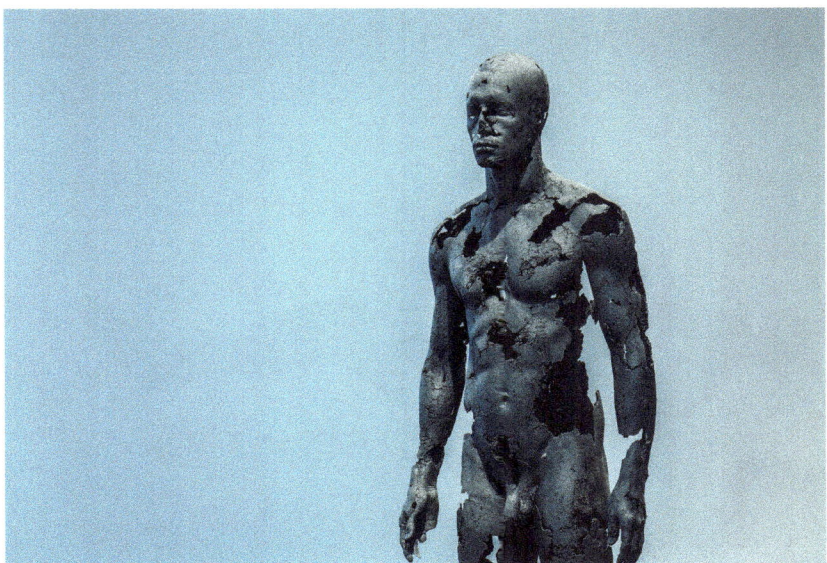

Figure 14.1 Tom Price, *The Presence of Absence*. Photo: Jaroslav Moravec

survival. They are shadows that have been made solid, holes that have been filled. I started my work making moulds which were left empty or filled with a darkness which I associated with our experience of body's darkness. The plaster forms cast from these Pompeian holes are very much masses that materialise a human space in space – a spatial displacement rather than a figural representation.'

By contrast, Allan McCollum's *The Dog From Pompei* (1993; Figure 14.3) maintains the bodily coherence of its subject, but draws attention to the 'enormous, monumentally sad absence of a whole world we'll never retrieve again' by displaying numerous casts of the famous Pompeian dog side by side (quoted in Coates, Lapatin and Seydl 2012: 232). Not only does the 'original' cast depend on the dog's absence in order to exist but each new iteration, in failing to return the creature itself to life, reminds us of the permanent absence and irremediable fragility of existence.

So the absence of Pompeii's people is certainly a recurrent motif – but what about the absence of the city entire? In some strands of Pompeian reception, the abundant materiality of the city takes centre stage, and as we glory in its perhaps unexpected resurrection – and as it seduces us with its tableaux of ancient domesticity – the presence of Pompeii, post-1748, is harder to doubt or

Figure 14.2 Antony Gormley, *Untitled*, 2002. Bright mild steel blocks 25 x 25 x 50 mm. 17 11/16 x 74 7/16 x 20 7/8 in. (45 x 189 x 53 cm). © Antony Gormley. Photo © Stephen White Courtesy White Cube

conceal than the presence of its people. As Goran Blix has shown, in the 'tug-of-war between memory and forgetting' that characterised nineteenth-century discourse, Pompeii could function as a 'reassuring myth of survival, the guarantee of a durable archive' (2009: 184). In texts such as Théophile Gautier's *Arria Marcella* (1903), a modern visitor's experience of the site is so powerful as to effect transportation, whether through reverie, hallucination, or time travel, to the past itself, even facilitating an erotic encounter with the eponymous Arria; in narratives of this kind, the leap between present and past effectively elides the intervening centuries of Pompeii's absence, as if the city has always already been there.[30] But as Genevieve Liveley has argued, 'the promise of presence, of immediacy and intimacy' in Gautier's novella is interwoven with 'the tease of ellipse, absence and mystery' (2011: 117),

---

[30] See also William Beckford's Pompeian reverie in *Dreams, Waking Thoughts and Incidents* (1783), discussed by Baum 2011.

Figure 14.3 Allan McCollum, *The Dog from Pompei*, 1991, Polymer modified hydrocal, 53 x 53 x 53 cm each. Courtesy of the artist and Petzel, New York

especially as Arria herself is summoned from the fragmentary and hollow imprint of her breast in the lava.[31]

In more recent texts, the time-travel conceit is exploited and expanded so that it is the city itself that slips its moorings in real-world geography and chronology, to become lost in time or space. Amelie Nothomb's short novel *Péplum* (1996) takes the form of a dialogue between a late-twentieth

---

[31] Alexandra Tranca explores how Gautier (and the contemporary photographer Eugene Atget) 'adopt the contemporary topos of the disappearing city and explore post-apocalyptic visions to articulate urban identity as essentially fragmented, fragile, and displaced' (2016: 261).

century woman, A.N., who wakes up in the twenty-sixth century, and the mysterious Celsius, who, the woman learns, triggered the eruption of Vesuvius in the year 2579.[32] He did so because in the twenty-second century, Earth's 'South' – including Pompeii – was obliterated; centuries later, gaining access to ancient texts, a time-travelling Celsius interprets Pompeii as the city which best represents antiquity's zenith, particularly in its art, and so he longs for its material presence to be preserved. And so, through various means, the eruption is caused from 2,500 years into the future, ensuring Pompeii's preservation, and allowing Celsius to bear witness to the city. In a more recent novel, Daniel Godfrey's *New Pompeii* (2016), new technology has allowed the transportation of the entire population of Pompeii to a replica of the city in central Asia, thus saving them from the eruption. Nor is this kind of interference with Pompeii's spatio-temporal location limited to the genre of science fiction. The 'New Chronological' school of pseudohistory, developed in the 1990s by Anatoly Fomenko, has homed in on Pompeii as one of the main pieces of evidence for its theory that history only begins circa 800 CE and that everything before that is a fabrication – Pompeii, claims Fomenko, is clearly a medieval or Renaissance town destroyed by a later eruption of Vesuvius (2007: 61–5).

These narratives rest on the conceit that Pompeii was not destroyed when we think it was, or that the city itself, and its people, are not where we think they are.[33] Pompeian sci-fi narratives may, in part, simply result from the broader appeal that antiquity holds for sci-fi and speculative fiction – hence the number of stories of how the Roman empire never fell, or the Greek gods still walk among us (Rogers and Stevens 2015). But Eric Moormann may be mistaken to suggest that the Pompeii setting is totally inconsequential (2015: 329), because both Nothomb and Godfrey arguably do use Pompeii for a specific reason, exploiting its capacity to address anxieties over human behaviour. Moralising responses to the eruption in the nineteenth century tended to frame these anxieties in terms of mankind's punishment by the Judeo-Christian God (taking a cue from ancient accounts of the disaster such as that of Dio Cassius, in which he describes how 'some thought the giants were rising in revolt', 66.23), but since the mid-twentieth century, this has been replaced by anxieties about mankind's

---

[32] See Moormann 2015: 328–9 for a summary.
[33] Cf. Pompeii's role in the *Doctor Who* episode 'The Fires of Pompeii' (2008); although the Doctor travels back in time to 'Volcano Day', the city and the moment of its destruction remain firmly rooted in time and space; in fact, the Doctor emphasises that the eruption is a fixed point in history which cannot be interfered with. See Hobden 2009.

relationship with the natural world. The eruption symbolises Nature's superior power, and even her revenge for man's mistakes and hubris with respect to natural resources. So, in *Péplum*, we learn that the destruction of 'the South' in the second millennium was a result of an energy crisis, and in *New Pompeii*, the masterminds behind Pompeii's dislocation are a villainous multinational energy corporation. Even beyond the sci-fi genre, we can find Robert Harris describing his 2003 novel, *Pompeii*, as explicitly concerned with man's misuse of natural resources (Hales and Paul 2011: 336), and in Tom Price's account of his sculptures, he explains the significance of his use of coal, not only because it recalls the carbonisation of objects and victims at Herculaneum, but also because we 'depend on coal for much of our energy, a reliance that simultaneously sustains and threatens our existence. This apparent dichotomy echoes the conflicting yet dependent bond between presence and absence and the duality of life.'

Pompeii is thus well placed to help us reflect on man's place in the world and our responsibility towards it. Whether the disaster is viewed as punishment by the gods or the planet, it is easily framed, in both ancient and modern narratives, as a punishment that the human race brings upon itself. Employing the trope of Pompeii's absent presence in these narratives only underlines the extent of humanity's hubris, and the severity of the punishment. By making Pompeii itself slip through cracks in time, or drawing attention to the absence of its people, we see how the destroyed city 'models the end of the human project and gives us a foretaste of our own demise', in Antony Gormley's words (quoted in Coates, Lapatin and Seydl 2012: 234). In another recent artwork, the end of the human project is effectively already completed at Pompeii. Laurent Grasso's video installation, *Soleil Noir* (2014), consists of footage shot by a drone as it flies over the site (along with another volcano, Stromboli). Over 11 minutes and 40 seconds, we witness this unmanned machine's aerial footage of an entirely unmanned site – the only visible living creature a dog – where, as the artist explains, 'humanity exists only in the negative, the absent mode'.[34] Pompeii is now a 'post-human landscape ... [an] ode to obsolescence'[35] – a simple but striking manifestation of one possible consequence of our disregard for the world. The ghost town of antiquity comes to represent the

---

[34] www.perrotin.com/artists/Laurent_Grasso/190/soleil-noir/29340. After its initial exhibition, *Soleil Noir* was shown at the 2015 Pompeii exhibition at Montreal's Museum of Fine Arts, and then as part of 'The Silent Echo' exhibition at the Museum of Baalbek in 2016. See Paul 2019 for more detailed discussion of the significance of aerial views of Pompeii.

[35] *The Silent Echo* exhibition catalogue: http://media.wix.com/ugd/8574eb_6f15e879c68642afadd03d37fe93ae51.pdf

ghost town of a global apocalypse, with the absence of the city's ancient inhabitants now foreshadowing the potential absence, or at least the vulnerability, of humankind entire.

In these final examples, then, Pompeii is used as a way of thinking about the implications of our Anthropocene world and the post-human reality that might await us: a scenario that gains power from its fixation on the idea of Pompeii as an absent presence. Ever since the poets of the first century initiated that absence by refusing or resisting its name, Pompeii has eluded our grasp even when we think it's right in front of us, or right beneath our feet, and it continues to challenge our received ideas about the security and longevity of humankind in an unstable environment. It is, as Serenella Iovino (2016: 17) has described, a site of profound 'epistemic rupture', a 'spatiotemporally porous' zone that is 'founded on hollows' such as the voids left by its dead inhabitants, 'bodies in which, as in Pompeii's plasters, an absence is often encapsulated: it is the absence of citizenship and of collective protection, the absence of a political ecology both of things and humans' (ibid., 38).[36]

At the same time, reflecting on the nature of Pompeii's absence allows us to better understand our desire for it. It is easy to play along with the idea that Pompeii is a time capsule, granting us direct and complete access to the moment of its destruction and making the Roman world newly present. Not only that, our need for Pompeii to keep on making meaning has turned it into a touchstone for practically all destroyed cities, whether ancient or modern, along with any newly discovered archaeological sites that offer the merest glimpse of a slice of ancient life; in these contexts, Pompeii's name is hardly absent, but entirely overused, such that anything from a ravaged New Orleans to a recovered Bronze Age village in Cambridgeshire becomes a 'new Pompeii'.[37] But as Mary Beard has argued (2008: 19–20), our certainty that Pompeii's apparent and seductive presence can transport us to the past is only ever an illusion, as is its relevance in many of the contexts into

---

[36] It is perhaps curious that Pompeii has not thus far played a bigger role in the growing literature on posthumanism and ecocriticism, save for Iovino 2016: 13–46. Schliephake 2017 (ed.) responds to the relative lack of attention paid to antiquity in ecocriticism thus far, but finds no place for sustained discussion of Pompeii.

[37] See Paul 2009 for an account of Pompeii's recurrence in contemporary discussions of natural and man-made disasters. A blog post by Peter Kruschwitz, 'Pompeiis Everywhere!' (https://thepetrified muse.blog/2014/07/25/pompeiis-everywhere/) helpfully catalogues the use of Pompeii in media discussions of other archaeological discoveries, up to 2014.

which its name spreads itself.³⁸ Instead, it is the complex interplay of Pompeii's presence and the absences that permeate it that shapes our repeated attempts to encounter the site. This is the dialectic that Joshua Billings identified as key to the 'erotics of reception', through which we should be 'sensitive to the ways in which the classical world is absent as well as present in modernity' (2010: 21).³⁹ Absence, he argues, is key to understanding the distinctiveness of our 'powerful and ambiguous' desire to regain, restore, and receive the classical past, such that 'it is only by recognizing the absence at the heart of classical reception that we can fully understand antiquity's presence' (ibid., 23). So, too, recognising the absence at the heart of Pompeii is crucial to our understanding the true complexity of the site and its meaning in the modern world.

---

³⁸ As Jennifer Wallace 2004: 100 argues, Pompeii is 'a place of hidden and forbidden desire, a place which inspires lurid fantasy because the hard facts are not readily available, a site of repression and half-acknowledged memory'.
³⁹ Levin 2005 explores the symbolism of Pompeian absence as a marker of desire in the works of Conrad, Freud, and Derrida.

CHAPTER 15

Omnibus umbra locis adero
Elena Ferrante and the Poetics of Absence

Francesca Bellei*

Strictly speaking, Elena Ferrante does not exist, but it was not so long ago that journalists and scholars of all persuasions raced one another to find out who she 'really' was – an aggressively literal-minded operation.[1] There has been endless speculation about Ferrante's absence from the public eye, but very little has been said about absence *in* Ferrante,[2] which is curious enough, given that her most popular work, the tetralogy collectively known in the English-speaking world as the Neapolitan Quartet, begins with, and is born out of, the disappearance of one of its two protagonists.

Covering much of Italy's modern history, from post-war to post-Berlusconi, the tetralogy follows the lives of Elena Greco and Lila Cerullo, born in one of the poorest neighbourhoods in Naples, known only as the *rione*. The relationship that quickly develops between them is so visceral and raw as to shatter any rose-tinted, hand-holding notion of female friendship™ into smithereens. Both have a ferocious desire to escape

---

* This chapter first came into being as a 2016 paper for Francesco Erspamer's seminar on contemporary Italian literature. I am grateful to him both for being its first reader and for believing in the importance of teaching, reading, and writing about Ferrante. I thank Emily Gowers for being the first to transmit her own Ferrante Fever to me, for teaching me the best parts of what I know about how to read Latin literature, and being an honest and encouraging reader of my drafts. I cannot imagine a better place to learn about intertextuality than the 2017 seminar on Virgil taught by Richard Thomas, whose comments knocked my drafts into fighting shape. I would never have figured out what I did not know I knew about Ferrante without the long conversations with Barbara Del Giovane and Ronit Matalon, whose absence is sorely felt. Most of all, I must thank the editors of this volume for giving me the opportunity to be a part of this project: Elena Giusti in particular for her transformative comments and labour on this chapter, and loving mentorship throughout the years; and Tom Geue, for being the most brilliant interlocutor I could have wished for on all things (Ferrante), and for seeing my voice long before I did. As for its *mancanze*, I alone am responsible.
[1] Or an aggressively political one: cf. Geue 2016a.
[2] As her famous soundbite goes: 'I didn't choose anonymity; the books are signed. Instead, I chose absence.' (2016: 255). For Ferrante's untying of her texts from her 'real' identity as a desire to partake in the condition of the Classics, see Geue 2016b. All translations of Ferrante's work are by Ann Goldstein (Ferrante 2012b, 2013b, 2014b, 2015), unless otherwise specified. The date and page numbers reported after quotations correspond to the Italian original, which, for reasons of space, have been included for the Neapolitan Novels only, but not for *Frantumaglia*.

poverty, which is to say the *rione*, which is – perhaps – themselves. But only one of them will make it out in the end, and we are left wondering which one. Elena and Lila are each other's one and only, and yet they are tied together by a third woman: Virgil's Dido.

What I argue in this chapter is that Ferrante, herself the archetypal absent author, uses Dido as a model for both Elena and Lila in order to interrogate Virgil's own silences and omissions, thus enabling a more general reflection on the absent presence of literary models, and what it does both for literary criticism and for literature. To explain what I mean by this, however, I first need to outline a definition of 'intertextuality' specific to this context.

In terms of reception, the childless Dido is one of Virgil's most progenitive characters, and also his most divisive, because she has a direct bearing on who gets to claim Virgil for their own.[3] The dominant understanding of intertextuality in Classics, as is still taught in most schools and universities, has long brought with it an assumption of 'serious' authorial intention,[4] which Stephen Hinds spotlighted by ventriloquizing it as a 'tidy contract between author and reader, where the author is *serious* about the references *he* puts in ... and the reader is guaranteed a reward for being equally *serious* about recognizing models and applying them to the text'.[5] Ironically, even though it was the feminist scholar Julia Kristeva who first coined the term 'intertextuality',[6] the 'seriousness' that often permeates this concept in Classics is clearly charged in terms of both gender and genre – two words for which the language of Ferrante only has one, *genere*.[7]

Complaints that the reception of Virgil's epic has now run its course,[8] or that Dido has found no postmodern interpreters[9] can be resolved by widening our definition of what literary texts are, and which ones are worthy of scholarly attention, as has already been suggested.[10] But while the poststructuralist call for an expanded notion of intertextuality has

---

[3] Thomas 2001: 154.
[4] For an example of how intertextuality can be productively used in playful ways, cf. Rimell in this volume.
[5] Hinds 1998: 22. Emphasis is my own. [6] Baraz and van den Berg 2013: 1.
[7] Feldherr highlights how the *Aeneid*'s multivocality is also expressed in terms of genres mapping onto genders: 'As Dido is distorted by being interpreted through the lens of epic, so Aeneas' words and actions acquire a contradictory meaning when read against the traditions of amatory poetry' (1999: 104–6). Thomas complicates Feldherr's neat polarity by pointing to Virgil's use of Catullus' elegiac treatment of Ariadne's abandonment as a blueprint for his Dido (2001: 157). See also Hardie's contribution to this volume.
[8] Hardie 1993: xii.   [9] Savage 1998: 34.   [10] Fowler 2000: 128.

largely been heeded,[11] and brought some significant gains to the field, from a theoretical standpoint we are still learning to come to terms with the hardcore pantextualist's wish to do without authorial control, which is freedom from political and moral responsibility. Simply shifting that weight from the writer to the reader won't cut it, all the more so since every writer is first and foremost a reader.

Ferrante's treatment of Virgil, as I will argue, can productively be read in light of Fowler's poststructuralist inversion of the directionality between source and target texts.[12] It is more than a simple case of modern constructions affecting our readings of antiquity.[13] Fowler's claim that no one familiar with Lacan can read the story of Narcissus without thinking of the mirror stage 'left in the text, patent or latent, over or under erasure'[14] must perforce imply that texts are built not just from what is present in their sources, but also from what is forgotten, erased, and omitted.

But while Elena (Ferrante)'s relationship with Virgil is built on an 'intertextuality of absence', Elena (Greco)'s relationship with Lila explicitly takes that poststructuralist vision to task, by voicing Elena's anxiety about the derivativeness of her work, which she unfailingly sees as having originated from the much more powerful raw material of her brilliant friend's own writing,[15] which is pointedly absent from the text, always jealously sheltered from her readers' eyes by Elena's own retelling of it. Elena is almost always the only reader of Lila's writing, making it impossible for anyone but herself to gauge the extent and honesty of her intertextual practices with Lila's Urtext. The open question of how much responsibility Elena's cannibalization of Lila's life in her books bears in Lila's disappearance is therefore a direct challenge to the 'absent' poststructuralist author, made all the more poignant by Ferrante's own choice to exist only in her texts.

Virgilian Presences: Hunting for Dido in Ferrante's Naples

Before I can begin teasing out how Virgil's absences make themselves felt in the Neapolitan Novels, I must first ascertain his presence. Dido is a spectre who haunts Lila and Elena from the very beginning of their relationship

---

[11] If anything, Classics might be failing to move on from it, as other disciplines have done. This is an issue which is confronted head-on in Baraz and van den Berg 2013:1–8, König and Whitton 2018, and in the introduction to this volume; but the next theoretical overhaul in Classics is yet to come.
[12] Fowler 2000: 130.   [13] Ibid.: 129.   [14] Ibid.
[15] The title is intentionally misleading. Readers are led to believe that Lila is Elena's brilliant friend, up until, at the very end of Book 1, we discover that it is Lila who says it to Elena: *Tu sei la mia amica geniale, devi diventare la più brava di tutti, maschi e femmine*, 'you're my brilliant friend, you have to be the best of all, boys and girls' (2011: 309).

with men, when both are 14 years old. When Elena tells Lila about Gino, her first teenage fling, Lila sarcastically comments: *brava, hai ceduto, ti sei innamorata come la fidanzata di Enea*, 'good for you, you've given in, you're in love like Aeneas' lover' (2011: 156). In her eyes, getting involved with a boy signals a failure to preserve oneself from the evils to come – an outcome that only readers who are already familiar with the fate of Virgil's Dido are able to glimpse. Though Dido's name here is pointedly absent, this is a reference to the *Aeneid* in its 'most basic form',[16] the degree zero of allusion.

But where Classical authors might have placed an 'Alexandrian footnote',[17] to show off their scholarly and literary knowledge,[18] Ferrante here alludes to Virgil as two teenagers reading the *Aeneid* for the first time would: Elena through the formal education she has been allowed, if begrudgingly, to pursue, and Lila completely on her own, since her parents would not let her go beyond primary school. And yet, it is from her that Elena, who presents herself as a slower and less perceptive reader, first learns about Dido:

> Mi chiese anche dell'*Eneide*, si era appassionata. L'aveva letta tutta in pochi giorni ... Mi parlò dettagliatamente di Didone, figura di cui io non sapevo nulla, quel nome lo sentii per la prima volta non dalla scuola, ma da lei. E un pomeriggio buttò lì un'osservazione che mi colpì molto. Disse: 'Se non c'è amore, non solo inaridisce la vita delle persone, ma anche quella delle città.'

> She also asked me about the *Aeneid*, she was crazy about it. She had read it all in a few days ... She talked in great detail about Dido, a figure I knew nothing about, I heard that name for the first time not at school but from her. And one afternoon she made an observation that impressed me deeply. She said, 'when there is no love, not only the life of the people becomes sterile, but the life of cities.' (2011: 156)

This passage foreshadows a pervasive thread linking Naples and Carthage throughout the novels.[19] But for Elena, Lila's idea that Carthage ultimately perishes for 'lack of love' immediately brings Naples to mind:

---

[16] Hinds 1998: 2. [17] Ross 1975: 78.
[18] This is not, of course, the only way or the only reason for authors to do this. Notably, Hinds (1998: 11) observes that, though 'scholarship' is commonly read as a metaphorical 'vehicle' for the underlying idea ('tenor', using I. A. Richards' terminology) of 'allusion', the paradigm can be upended by reading 'allusion' as a vehicle to talk about 'scholarship'.
[19] As was first pointed out me by Emily Gowers, the two colonies are both named 'new city', from the Greek Νεάπολις and the Phoenician *Qart-ḥadašt* respectively. For parallels between the fate of the city and that of its (re-)founding heroine as a crucial term of comparison between Dido and Lila, see Galippi 2016 and C. Barchiesi 2018: 9–53.

> Non mi ricordo come si espresse di preciso, ma il concetto era quello, e io lo associai alle nostre strade sporche, ai giardinetti polverosi, alla campagna scempiata dai palazzi nuovi, alla violenza in ogni casa, in ogni famiglia... (ibid.)
>
> I don't remember exactly how she expressed it, but that was the idea, and I associated it with our dirty streets, the dusty gardens, the country-side, disfigured by new buildings, the violence in every house, every family...

Carthage, in its state of post-Aeneas desolation, which in Virgil prefigures the outcome of the Punic Wars, in Ferrante comes to mirror the havoc of post-war Naples,[20] a landscape of violence and deprivation from which both protagonists want out. That is exactly what happens to Elena, but is denied to Lila, despite her independent and fiery intelligence – far superior, Elena suspects, to her own: *Mi dedicai allo studio e a molte altre cose difficili, solo per restare al passo con quella bambina terribile e sfolgorante*, 'I devoted myself to studying and to many things that were difficult, alien to me, just so I could keep pace with that terrible, dazzling girl.' (2011: 43).

From her degree in Classical literature at the Scuola Normale Superiore (where she wrote a thesis on *Aeneid* 4) to her career as a writer, Elena is perpetually haunted by how much she owes to Lila. The idea of the 'city without love', which wins her so much admiration and praise at school and beyond, is a textbook example of authorial anxiety:

> Certo, mi dicevo, sicuramente lo svolgimento su Didone è mio, la capacità di formulare belle frasi è roba che viene da me; certo, ciò che ho scritto su Didone mi appartiene; ma non l'ho elaborato insieme con lei, non ci siamo stimulate a vicenda, la mia passione non è cresciuta al calore della sua? E quell'idea della città senza amore, che era piaciuta tanto ai professori, non mi era venuta da Lila, anche se poi l'avevo sviluppata io, con la mia capacità? Cosa devo dedurne?
>
> Of course, I said to myself, the essay on Dido is mine, the capacity to formulate beautiful sentences comes from me; of course, what I wrote about Dido belongs to me; but didn't I work it out with her, didn't we excite each other in turn, didn't my passion grow in the warmth of hers? And that idea of the city without love, which teachers had liked so much, hadn't it come to

---

[20] As Elena explicitly reveals when asked what 'a city without love' meant: *Pensai alle discussioni che avevo fatto con Lila e Pasquale per tutto settembre e le sentii all'improvviso come una vera scuola più vera di quella che facevo tutti i giorni. 'L'Italia sotto il fascismo, la Germania sotto il nazismo, tutti quanti noi esseri umani nel mondo d'oggi'*, 'I thought of the discussions I'd had with Lila and Pasquale in September and I suddenly felt that they were a true school, truer than the one I went to everyday. "Italy under Fascism, Germany under Nazism, all of us human beings in the world today".' (2011: 184).

me from Lila, even if I had developed it, with my own ability? What should I deduce from this? (2011: 184)

While Elena gets bogged down in the books and chases after good grades, Lila takes Virgil's text as a model through which she can interpret life. She highlights Dido's affinity with Melina, a poor widow from the *rione* who was driven mad after having been abandoned by Donato Sarratore, a married neighbour (as well as amateur poet and father of Elena's future lover Nino) rumoured to be her lover.

Melina's predicament contains a dark foreboding of Lila's own future, mediated through Dido, who famously reacts to Aeneas' untimely apology in the Underworld by freezing on the spot like a statue.[21]

> illa solo fixos oculos auersa tenebat
> nec magis incepto uultum sermone mouetur
> quam si dura silex aut stet Marpesia cautes.
> (Verg. *Aen.* 6.469–71)

She turned away, eyes fixed to the ground, and when he begins to speak her features do not move any more than if she stood firm like hard flint or Marpesian rock.[22]

Surprisingly, the echo of that ghostly encounter, impossibly far in time but geographically adjacent to Ferrante's *rione*, lingers as much in Melina as it does in Lila:

> Ferma dentro ciò che la parente di sua madre stava facendo, *ferma per la pena, ferma di sale come le statue di sale*. Aderente. *Tutt'uno con Melina*, che aveva sul palmo lo scuro sapone tenero appena acquistato nello scantinato di don Carlo, e ne prendeva con l'altra mano e se lo mangiava.
>
> Firm in what her mother's relative was doing, *firm in the pain, firm in silence as a statue is firm*. A follower. *One with Melina*, who was holding in her palm the dark soft soap she had just bought in Don Carlo's cellar, and with the other hand she was taking some and eating it. (2011: 36)

---

[21] Virgil's text is from R. A. B. Mynors 1969 *OCT* edition, translations are my own unless otherwise specified. For an analysis of Dido and Aeneas' hellish rendezvous, cf. Starnone in this volume.

[22] As Feldherr points out (1999: 114), this line 'recalls precisely the description of another sculptural image that turns away from Trojan prayers, the figure of Athena on the temple of Juno at Carthage, *diua solo fixos oculos auersa tenebat* (1.482).' Like Sarratore's mediocre poetry, Aeneas' narrative about his abandonment (ambiguously positioned with respect to Virgil's own poetic fiction) turns Dido into a mute and immobile artistic object. Her return to Sychaeus means a return to an independent personhood, and, simultaneously, a banishment from the realm of epic: 'as the frozen Dido ... resumes her motion, exchanging the brightness of Parian marble for a shadowy grove, she also quite literally excises herself from the poem's narrative' (ibid.).

Lila sees and understands the way in which Donato only gained from his affair with Melina, while she lost both her reputation and her mind. This is a dynamic that keeps repeating itself since antiquity: Ariadne[23] helped Theseus out of the Cretan labyrinth; Medea[24] aided Jason in his quest for the Golden Fleece through her command of magic; Dido opened the doors of Carthage to Aeneas and his companions without reserve, and even provided him with a blueprint for founding a new city: not a single one of these women escaped madness, despair or death, while the men who seduced, used, and abandoned them went on to fulfil their mission and become heroes.[25]

As if aware of this long history, Lila swears to her friend that she will never fall in love. When Elena retorts that others might fall for her regardless, and suffer as Dido did, Lila prophetically replies: *No, si andranno a fidanzare con un'altra, proprio come ha fatto Enea, che alla fine si è messo con la figlia di un re*, 'No, they'll go and find someone else, just like Aeneas, who eventually settled down with the daughter of a king.' (2011: 157). In the years to come, Nino will in fact end up marrying Eleonora, a rich Neapolitan whose family connections will help Nino in his career, like Aeneas marries Lavinia to secure his political standing in Latium.

This is far from an isolated instance of dramatic irony in Ferrante, who explicitly traces the origins of her fascination with this device to Virgil's treatment of the Dido myth. In *Frantumaglia*, Ferrante singles out the moment when Aeneas, immediately before meeting Dido, stops to admire the images of the Trojan War that adorn the temple of Juno (*animum pictura pascit inani*, 'he feeds his soul with empty images', *Aen.* 1.464). Here, Ferrante zooms in on the raging Amazon Queen Penthesilea, stating that she had 'always been disturbed by stories that introduce an almost imperceptible sign of future imbalances into a happy scene, that take your breath away with the spectre of an abrupt reversal of fate' (2016: 146).

---

[23] Explicitly mentioned by Ferrante as the model of abandoned woman in *Frantumaglia*, 2016: 107. For a sustained analysis of the parallels between Elena and Lila and Ariadne, see C. Barchiesi 2018. Particularly striking is her observation that Elena and Lila's dolls mirror those of Ariadne and her sister Phaedra, as recounted in Robert Graves' *Greek Myths*, which Ferrante explicitly mentions in *Frantumaglia*.

[24] The comparison between Dido and Medea is not an unusual one; cf. Henry 1930, Collard 1975, Muecke 1983, Nelis 2001, Schiesaro 2008, and Giusti 2018: 115–27.

[25] This is not the only possible reading, and Thomas is right to caution against the idea of Virgil's Dido as a stable entity on which reception is based. Simultaneously, Thomas is not unaware of the suggested direction in which Dido's story could, and has, mainly been read: 'an Augustan reading will always attempt to subordinate Dido to Aeneas, but it will also just as surely fail to convince that the heroism of the latter is the only lesson of the episode' (2001: 155–6). For more 'generous' interpretations of Aeneas' behaviour and motivations, see D'Anna 1989: 30–1 or Zarker 1967. Schiesaro 2008 makes use of poststructuralist and psychoanalytic theory in order to resist the idea of Dido as a victimized and/or fully sympathetic character.

Her choice of words is a curious one. For Ferrante, the irony lies in the fact that Dido, who at that moment is still in the fullness of her strength as a monarch and as a woman, will soon become *furens* (*Aen.* 1.491) like Penthesilea, even though neither she nor Aeneas know it yet.[26] But the idea that Penthesilea might be a 'spectre' carries with it the echo of Virgil's *inani*, as Austin points out in his commentary to the passage: '*Inani* has much pathos: the "insubstantial" painting on which he [Aeneas] "feeds his thoughts" is full of ghosts for him' (1971: 157). And for *her*, is Ferrante's rejoinder.

The knowledge of Dido's fate haunts Elena and Nino's story from their first kiss. This comes at the end of an argument in which Nino disavows his father's treatment of Melina, and pompously swears he will become a different man. The dramatic irony (and childish naiveté) of Elena's final words at this time is hard to miss: *Lui e Melina sono stati travolti dalla passione, come Didone ed Enea. Sono cose che fanno male, ma anche molto commoventi*, 'He [Donato] and Melina were overcome by passion, like Dido and Aeneas. These are things that are hurtful, but they're also very moving' (2011: 217). She won't find them so moving anymore, after being made to walk in Melina's shoes decades later.

While Dido betrays the vow to remain celibate after the death of her first husband Sychaeus,[27] Lila and Elena both betray and abandon their first (still living) husbands to be with Nino, which, *mutatis mutandis*, attracts the same amount of moralizing reproaches in the respective societies within which these women operate. Stefano Carracci, Lila's first husband, bears some resemblance to King Iarbas, an old suitor of Dido's who could not overcome his bitterness at having been rejected by her, particularly in view of how 'generously' he welcomed her when she fled Tyre (*Aen.* 4.211–14). In truth, Iarbas only gave Dido the hide of one bull and told her that she could have as much land as the skin could cover, as a slight. But she proved herself far cleverer than Iarbas, and divided the hide into impossibly thin strips, which were sewn together so they could enclose an area big enough for a whole city, Carthage (*Aen.* 1.365–8).

Lila is also characterized by a sharp, creative intelligence, which enlarges the possibilities of everything she does: like Dido, for instance, she is skilled in the art of sewing leather.[28] What Ferrante writes in *Frantumaglia* fully corroborates this association:

---

[26] Ferrante 2016: 140.   [27] *Aen.* 4.15–27.

[28] The association between weaving (the female craft *par excellence*) and cunning intelligence (with a duplicitous edge) runs throughout Greek thought, particularly with reference to Athena, Penelope, and Helen. Cf. Detienne and Vernant 1978, Bergren 1983, and Scheid 1996. For a link

'And here I should tell you that my mother was a dressmaker ... With needle, thread, scissors, fabric, she could do anything. She altered old clothes, made new ones, sewed, unsewed, let out, took in, made tears invisible with skilful mending. Because I had grown up in the middle of all that sewing, the way Dido tricks the king of the Gaetuli immediately convinced me.' (2016: 147–8)

The idea of designing luxury shoes comes to Lila when her cobbler father Fernando forces her to quit school and work for him at the shoe shop. Against all odds – and her father's wishes – Lila eventually finds an investor: her future husband Stefano. He is the first man to truly notice Lila's talent (Elena has known for years), but his decision to invest in the Cerullo shoes is inextricably linked to his desire to make Lila his; to possess her.[29] For both Iarbas and Stefano, then, having been rejected by the women they had 'invested in', and therefore felt 'entitled to', is the biggest slight of all.

On the other hand, Iarbas' derogatory designation of Aeneas as *ille Paris* (*Aen.* 4.215) cannot but remind us of Helen of Troy, who is often assimilated to Dido, as Elena Giusti argues: '[in] recognition of their stories as aetiological *fabulae* for the outbreak of international conflicts which are envisaged in the form of a huge clash of continents, and represent these women as the pivot around which myth, history and politics rotate'.[30] Lila's beauty, like Helen's, is excessive, dangerous, and gradually drags the whole *rione* – which faithfully reproduces, on a micro-level, the flawed macro-structures of Naples, Italy, and the entire world[31] – into a state of open warfare. But if Nino is Aeneas who is in turn Paris, then Helen is also Elena, whose surname, Greco, simultaneously reinforces and eludes her identification with Menelaus' wife, since Helen's Greek identity is subsumed under her new Trojan one.[32]

---

between sewing and women's storytelling, cf. Rimell in this volume on un-sewing and re-sewing as a Penelopean archetype (after Cavarero).

[29] See especially Ferrante 2012a: 238. [30] Giusti 2016: 46.

[31] *Me l'ero battuta infatti. Ma solo per scoprire, nei decenni a venire, che mi ero sbagliata, che si trattava di una catena con anelli sempre più grandi: il rione rimandava alla città, la città all'Italia, l'Italia all'Europa, l'Europa a tutto il pianeta. E oggi la vedo così: non è il rione a essere malato, non è Napoli, è il globo terrestre, è l'universo, o gli universi,* 'I had fled, in fact, only to discover, in the decades to come, that I had been wrong, that it was a chain with larger and larger links: the neighbourhood was connected to the city, the city to Italy, Italy to Europe, Europe to the whole planet. And this is how I see it today: it's not the neighbourhood that's sick, it's not Naples: it's the entire earth, it's the universe or universes.' (Ferrante 2013a: 19).

[32] The importance of Elena's name, like Ferrante's, is deeply tied to her identity as a writer. After the publication of her first book and in view of her imminent wedding, Elena declares that, although she will take her husband's surname, Airota, she will always sign her books under the name Greco. (2012a: 467).

Virgilian Absences: What Virgil Never Said

So far, I have limited myself to surveying the more straightforward ways in which Ferrante signals to her readers the presence of a Virgilian intertext. But recognition of this explicit model also invites the readers to create further links between the Neapolitan novels and what is left unrevealed or unspoken in the *Aeneid*.

One obvious way in which Ferrante invites us to look inside and beyond Virgil's text is in the parallel between Lila and Elena and Dido and her sister Anna, whom Virgil strikingly describes as *unanima* (Aen. 4.8). But while the idea that Dido and Anna act as mirror images of one another[33] is waiting in the wings of the *Aeneid*, with Elena and Lila it takes centre stage. *Quello che fai tu, faccio io*, 'What you do, I do' (2011: 51), are Elena's first words to Lila, thus initiating a lifelong pattern of mimicry that is both moving and sinister. Their bond is one of friendship and sisterhood, but also of sexual rivalry and unspoken desire.

When Elena helps Lila get dressed for her wedding she sees her naked for the first time, and falls into a state of agitation, later recognized as *la vergogna di poggiare con piacere lo sguardo sul suo corpo, di essere la testimone coinvolta della sua bellezza di sedicenne poche ore prima che Stefano la toccasse, la penetrasse, la deformasse, forse, ingravidandola,* 'the intense embarrassment of gazing with pleasure at her body, of being the not impartial witness of her sixteen-year-old beauty a few hours before Stefano touched her, penetrated her, disfigured her, perhaps, by making her pregnant' (2011: 309). The homoerotic subtext of Elena's gaze finds no further outlet, except for the rushed, painful wish to be Lila, by virtually being in Lila's marital bed. All Elena wishes for is: *trovare un angolo abbastanza appartato perché Antonio facesse a me, nelle stesse ore, la stessa identica cosa,* 'to find a corner secluded enough so that Antonio could do to me, at the same time, the exact same thing.' (2011: 310).

Later on, like Virgil's Anna,[34] Elena finds herself implicated in the relationship between her quasi-sister Lila and Nino, acting as a go-between and trying to keep them both in check:

> Avvertii, quel giorno, che parlare di Lila con Nino poteva essere nelle settimane a venire una modalità nuova del rapporto tra noi tre. Né io né lei lo avremmo mai avuto. Ma potevamo ottenere entrambe, per tutta la

---

[33] See D'Anna 1989: 159–96; Schiesaro 2008: 96–9.
[34] *Aen.* 4.548–9 *tu lacrimis euicta meis, tu prima furentem / his, germana, malis oneras atque obicis hosti*, 'you, my sister, surrendered to my tears, and you were the first to oppress my folly with this torment, and drive me into the arms of my nemesis'.

durata della vacanza, la sua attenzione, lei in quanto oggetto di una passione senza sbocco, io in quanto savia consigliera che teneva sotto controllo la follia sia di lui che di lei.

I felt, that day, that to speak of Lila with Nino could in the weeks to come give a new character to the relationship between the three of us. Neither she nor I would ever have him. But both of us, for the entire time of the vacation, could gain his attention, she as the object of a passion with no future, I as the wise counsellor who kept under control both his folly and hers. (2012a: 241)

Many readers of Virgil, however, starting with Ovid,[35] have seen Anna's involvement as repressed desire for Aeneas. Though pointedly absent, this alternative plot line[36] is hinted at in Dido's characterization of her sister's closeness to the Trojan hero: *solam nam perfidus ille / te colere, arcanos etiam tibi credere sensus; / sola uiri mollis aditus et tempora noras*, 'since that traitor trusted you and you alone, since he shared with you even his deepest feelings, only you will know when to approach him persuadingly', (*Aen.* 4.421–3).

The sexual overtones of *mollis aditus* are fully brought out in Ferrante, by having both women fall in love with the same man. But Ferrante's text does more than create a story out of Virgil's erasures. Elena tacitly implies that Dido's myth, which had made such an impression on the two young girls, may have been actively implicated in her acceptance of Lila's disastrous romance with Nino:

Evocai versi e romanzi come tranquillanti. Forse, pensai, aver studiato serve solo a questo: a calmarmi. Lei gli aveva acceso la fiamma in petto, lui per anni l'aveva custodita senza accorgersene: ora che quella fiamma era divampata, cos'altro poteva fare se non amarla.

I called on poems and novels as tranquillizers. Maybe, I thought, studying has been useful to me just for this: to calm myself. She had kindled the flame

---

[35] As Schiesaro points out (2008: 97), in *Fasti* 3, Anna comes to Latium as an exile, and is welcomed by Aeneas, who has established his rule there, thanks in part to his marriage to Lavinia. This arouses the suspicion of his new bride, who begins to plot against Anna, as Dido once plotted against Aeneas: *furialiter odit, / et parat insidias et cupit ulta mori* (3.637–8). Dido's ghost appears to Anna and warns her to flee, as Mercury had Aeneas. Starnone's chapter in this volume explores more fully a range of creative responses to the notable absence of Aeneas' gaze on Dido in Book 1, including, but not limited to, Ovid's *Met.* 3.

[36] The Servian *corpus* makes mention of Varro's version of the myth, according to which it was Anna, and not Dido, who had killed herself after a failed love affair with Aeneas: 'Serv. auct. *ad. Aen.* IV, 682, *Varro ait non Didonem sed Annam amore Aeneae impulsam se supra rogum interemisse*; Serv. *ad. Aen.* V, 4, *Sane sciendum Varronem dicere Aeneam ab Annam amatum.*' as quoted in D'Anna 1989: 159.

in his breast, he had preserved it for years without realizing it. Now that the flame had flared up, what could he do but love her. (2012a: 237).

The mention of 'poems and novels', as well as 'studying' may seem generic enough, but the *topos* of love as fire, though hackneyed, acquires a distinctively Virgilian flavour in the context of the explicit invocation of Dido as a model everywhere else in the text. Virgil's famous and culturally ubiquitous *caeco carpitur igni*[37] and *agnosco ueteris uestigia flammae*[38] can only be repressed with some effort. Although Elena can say that Nino's love for Lila 'flared up' by locating its inception in the past, the idea of a resurgence could, on a metaliterary level, also refer to Aeneas and Dido's love affair in the *Aeneid*.

Ferrante employs here what Conte[39] called 'modelling by code', whereby Virgil is present in her text not so much in 'single word[s] to be precisely imitated', but 'as the representative of the epic institution that guarantees the ideological and literary functions of poetry itself',[40] but she does not do so uncritically. The 'poems and novels' to which Elena refers have become normative both on a literary and on an emotional level; they are the institutions within which girls are raised, the pill ('tranquillizer', or *pharmakon*) they have been made to swallow, to lace the pain of being played with the intoxicating knowledge of their belonging to a (fictional) line of suffering heroines.

Thus, Ferrante's relationship with Virgil addresses his *mancanze*, meaning both 'faults' and 'things which are lacking or absent', but it also simultaneously credits him with a higher sensitivity than other interpreters have attributed him. For instance, her consistent depiction of the passion between Lila and Nino (and Elena) as mutual[41] draws out the intensity of what might have been Aeneas' feelings for Dido, which remain largely unspoken in Book 4.[42] This is particularly evident in the dissolution of

---

[37] 'she is seized by a blind fire' (*Aen.* 4.2).
[38] 'now I remember the signs of the old flame' (*Aen.* 4.23).
[39] The chronology of Elena's life, moreover, has her studying Latin literature at the Scuola Normale in Pisa shortly after Conte, which, while it does not constitute hard evidence, is a suggestive hint at the theoretical *zeitgeist* of which Elena might have been a part.
[40] Conte 1986: 31.
[41] Cf. Virgil's *Aen.* 4.4–5 *haerent infixi pectore uultus / uerbaque, nec placidam membris dat cura quietem* ('but his features and words cleave stuck to her soul, and the thought of him forbids her body from finding a moment's rest') and Lila's *Ma è notte, non riesco più ad addormentarmi, ho in testa tutte le parole che lui ha detto, tutte quelle che non vedo l'ora di dirgli io*, 'But it's night, I can't sleep anymore, I have in my head all the words he said, all the ones I can't wait to tell him.' (2012a: 255). While Virgil focuses exclusively on Aeneas' *uerba*, Ferrante stresses Lila's eagerness not only to listen, but also to speak to her lover.
[42] Cf. Feeney 1983.

Elena's relationship with Nino. After discovering he cheated on her with almost every single woman she has ever met, Elena reacts with a fury so intense as to provoke a dissociative episode:

> Lo colpii a pugni chiusi sul petto e mentre lo facevo mi sentii come se ci fosse una me scollata da me che voleva fargli ancora più male, che voleva schiaffeggiarlo ... strappargli gli occhi. ... *Sono sempre io quest'altra così furiosa? Io qui, a Napoli, in questa casa lurida, io che se potessi uccidere quest'uomo, gli ficcherei con tutte le mie forze un coltello nel cuore? Devo trattare quest'ombra – mia madre, tutte le nostre antenate – o devo scatenarla?*
>
> I hit him in the chest with my fists and as I did I felt as if there were a me unglued from me who wished to hurt him even more, who wanted to beat him ... tear out his eyes. ... *Am I always this other furious I? I, here in Naples, in this filthy house, I, who if I could would kill this man, plunge a knife into his heart with all my strength? Should I restrain this shadow – my mother – all of our female ancestors – or should I let her go?* (2014a: 85)

Who are, in fact, Elena's ancestors? Dido, certainly, who, at the height of her madness, cries to Jupiter:

> non potui abreptum diuellere corpus et undis
> spargere? non socios, non ipsum absumere ferro
> Ascanium patriisque epulandum ponere mensis?
>
> (*Aen.* 4.600–2)

Couldn't I have torn his body limb for limb and scattered it at sea? Couldn't I have murdered his companions and even Ascanius himself with a sword, and served them to be eaten at his father's table?

Dido's ancestors, in turn, are Thyestes, who fed his brother Atreus the flesh of his children for dinner (*patriisque epulandum ponere mensis*); Medea, who, in Apollonius' *Argonautica*, murdered her brother Absyrtus and scattered his limbs in the sea (*abreptum diuellere corpus at undis / spargere*), and the bacchants, followers of Dionysus, whose rituals culminated in the *sparagmos*, the dismemberment of the god himself, followed by the consumption of his flesh.[43] As Dido's madness progresses, she is afflicted by hallucinatory dreams (*Aen.* 4.465–73) in which she is pursued by Aeneas just as Pentheus and Orestes were pursued by the Furies, the former for violating the secret of the Dionysian orgies,[44] the latter for killing his

---

[43] Dido is explicitly likened to a bacchant twice (*Aen.* 4. 300–3 and 346). For Dido's bacchic connections, see Krummen 2004.
[44] *Eumenidum ueluti demens uidet agmina Pentheus*, 'just like Pentheus, in his frenzy, saw an army of Furies', *Aen.* 4.469.

mother Clytemnestra.[45] But what are we to make of the fact that, later on, Dido will invoke those very same female avenging spirits[46] (*Aen.* 4.610 *Dirae ultrices*) to persecute Aeneas?

Schiesaro argued that Dido's 'seeing double'[47] is not only an allusion to Euripides' *Bacchae*,[48] but also an indication that, though psychoanalysis would have the 'diffraction of the dreamer's self' as a normal phenomenon that occurs in dreams,[49] there is more to Dido's hallucinations than that. By opening up the range of identities Dido assumes in her delirium, Virgil is working within the tradition of Classical tragedy by making her both innocent and guilty, active and passive, prey and predator: 'Just as Dido's immense suffering subverts the comfortable "Jovian" reading of Aeneas' departure as inevitably destined *ad maiorem gloriam*, Dido's covert aggressiveness, in turn, destabilises an over-romanticised reading of her character as a forlorn elegiac heroine, the entirely passive victim of an emotionally challenged cad.'[50]

Dido's potential to harm, which in the *Aeneid* is suggested through the absent presence of murderous literary ancestors, in Ferrante is simultaneously fulfilled and repressed through Elena and Lila's respective reactions to trauma. While Elena merely contemplates murder, Lila, we are led to believe, is the one who executes it, after her 4-year-old daughter Tina suddenly vanishes, never to be seen again. Many decades later, after Lila's own disappearance, Elena's friend Pasquale suggests that the Solara brothers, the camorristi whom Lila had repeatedly rejected, publicly denounced and therefore humiliated, were behind Tina's abduction.[51] He then added: '*Vuoi che ti dica anche chi ha ammazzato quei due pezzi di merda?*', 'Do you also want me to tell you who murdered those two pieces of shit?' Even though Elena is not always a reliable (or sympathetic) narrator, the insinuation is a heavy one: *gli ho letto all'improvviso nello sguardo qualcosa che mi*

---

[45] *aut Agamemnonius Poenis agitatus Orestes*, 'or as when Agamemnon's Orestes, was hounded by the Furies', *Aen.* 4. 471.
[46] Hardie sees the Furies' power to destabilise identity as a metapoetic device: 'The Fury is like a virus, that replicates herself in her victim, often in multiple copies (just as, one might add, Virgil's Allecto episode will reproduce itself in the works of the successors of Virgil).' (1993: 41).
[47] *et solem geminum et duplicis se ostendere Thebas*, 'a double sun and two Thebes appear', *Aen.* 4.470.
[48] Almost a direct quotation from one of Pentheus' hallucinations (Eur. *Bacch.* 918–22).
[49] Schiesaro 2008: 199.   [50] Schiesaro 2008: 227.
[51] Foreshadowed by a violent altercation between Lila and Michele Solara, at the conclusion of which he violently hits her in the face: *Tu invece sì che sei qualcuno, persino la tua ombra è meglio di qualsiasi persona in carne ed ossa. Però non l'hai mai volute capire, e allora peggio per te. Ti leverò tutto quello che hai ... Lila vomitava in dialetto parole e sangue (ti uccido, quant'è vero Dio, siete già morti tutt'e due)*, 'You are someone, even your shadow is better than any flesh-and-blood person. But you would never understand, so much the worse for you. I'll take away everything you have. ... Lila vomited in dialect words and blood (I'll kill you, by God, you are both dead already).' (2014a: 289).

ha fatto orrore – un rancore inestinguibile – e gli ho detto no. Ha scosso la testa tenendosi per un po' il sorriso in faccia. Ha mormorato: "Vedrai che quando Lila deciderà si farà viva." 'suddenly I read in his gaze something that horrified me, an inextinguishable rancour – and I said no. He shook his head and continued to smile. He said: "You'll see that when Lila decides to, she'll show up."' (2014a: 449).

Ferrante's bold claim consists in linking the dissociative potential of female trauma with the power of (literary) creation and destruction. As she states in *Frantumaglia*, the crowding of the female 'I' is explicitly linked to 'a long history of oppression and repression ... [it] tends to shatter as it's tossed around, and to reappear and shatter again, always in an unpredictable way' (2016: 322). *Frantumaglia*, or 'fabric scraps', a word Ferrante claims to have learned from her seamstress mother, is a metaphor for 'the large quantity of heterogeneous fragments' tossing up inside (ibid.) Ferrante's women, but also an allusion to their resourcefulness, to their ability to sew them back together into something beautiful and meaningful, be it a city, a humble pair of shoes, or a novel. The crowd of ghosts suffering can conjure from the dregs of time, Ferrante suggests, is what gives writing its edge.

This is exemplified by Elena Greco's career as a writer, which begins with a story based on her first sexual experience with Donato Sarratore, Nino's father, when Elena was just 15 years old, the same night Lila made love to Nino for the first time. Shrouded in the secrecy of a deserted beach, the predatory *paterfamilias* both excites and traumatizes a teenage Elena, who struggles to reconcile herself with the fact until she manages to write about it. This too is a pairing which activates and reverses Virgil's latent suggestion of incest, as Dido's desire for Aeneas is channelled through Cupid disguised as Ascanius.[52] It should come as no surprise that Elena writes her first novella at the same time as her dissertation on *Aeneid* 4.[53] Cast deep into the achrony of Dido's trauma, Elena finally comes to terms with her own.

The spectre of Dido in Ferrante's texts, however, is never exclusively summoned by men's violence or absence. *My Brilliant Friend* opens with

---

[52] Oliensis 1997: 305–7.
[53] *Da un certo punto in poi vidi Pietro sempre di meno con la scusa che ero indietro e rischiavo di non finire in tempo la tesi. Una mattina comprai un quaderno a quadretti e cominciai a scrivere in terza persona di ciò che mi era successo a Barano*, 'At a certain point I began to see Pietro less frequently, with the excuse that I was behind and was in danger of not finishing my thesis on time. One morning I bought a graph-paper notebook and began to write, in the third person, about what happened to me that night on the beach near Barano.' (2012a: 431–2).

an epitaph from Goethe's *Faust*: '...Man's active nature, flagging, seeks too soon the level; / Unqualified repose he learns to crave; Whence, willingly, the comrade him I gave, / Who works, excites, and must create, as Devil.'[54] On the one hand, the Devil is the force that never lets Man find satisfaction and repose, stirring desire, greed and ambition in him. On the other, that force is Eve, 'the comrade' God gave to man (without a capital M), the woman-devil who falls into and is herself temptation. In the Neapolitan Novels, Lila is Elena's Devil, and her Eve-Adam is completely eliminated from the picture.[55] Ultimately, the novels exist because of Lila, in more ways than one.

Omnibus umbra locis adero: the Return of the Muse

Like Elena, Lila begins to write after a traumatic event that has upended her life, namely, Tina's disappearance. Elena, though she never manages to find evidence that Lila is indeed writing, and the latter firmly denies it, is convinced that such a text exists almost until the end, and this is partly why she begins to write her own:

> Nei momenti di maggiore cupezza ero sempre più sicura che Lila avesse scritto la storia dettagliata di sua figlia, ero sempre più sicura che l'avesse mescolata a quella di Napoli ... Poi capivo che si trattava di una mia fantasia ... Io scrissi in pochi giorni una storia che per anni, auspicando e temendo che la stesse scrivendo Lila, avevo finito per immaginare in ogni dettaglio.
>
> In the moments of greatest darkness I was sure that Lila had written the detailed story of her daughter, sure that she had mixed it into the history of Naples. ... Then I understood it was a fantasy of mine. ... Within a few days I wrote a story that over the years, hoping and fearing that Lila was writing it, I had imagined in every detail. (2014a: 440–2)

Elena's first novel is based, by her own admission, not only on her own experience and Dido's, but on a brilliant short story Lila wrote when they were children, *The Blue Fairy*. Lila's brilliance, however, is blinding, excessive, destructive; it cannot be channelled into the ordained structure

---

[54] Translation by Bayard Taylor.
[55] The biblical reference assumes further significance through Elena's second book, a critique of several creation myths in which woman is presented as deriving from man: *Io sono Ish e lei è Isha'h ... porto dentro il suo Verbo. Lei è dunque un puro suffisso applicato alla mia radice verbale, può esprimersi solo dentro la mia parola*, 'I am Ish and she is Isha'h. ... I carry within me his Word. She is therefore a pure suffix applied to my verbal root, she can express herself only within *my* word.' (2013a: 332).

of a novel, the routine of a job, or the strictures of marriage: *essa si distingueva tra tante perché con naturalezza non si piegava a nessuna addestramento, a nessun uso e a nessun fine*, 'she stood out among so many because she, naturally, did not submit to any training, to any use, or to any purpose.' (2014a: 383).

Like Naples, Lila always has to contend with her inner Vesuvius;[56] her creativity is a volcanic force that shapes and fructifies the landscape around her, but is also the incandescent matter that threatens to destroy it, the fire that consumes her from within, the earthquake that shatters the outlines of the self and of reality, as is evident in her recurring episodes of *smarginatura*, or 'dissolving margins'.[57]

Her self-destructive tendencies are apparent throughout the tetralogy. When Elena brings her *The Blue Fairy* decades after she had written it, Lila simply throws it on the fire and watches it burn (2012a: 465). When a stunning life-sized photograph of Lila on her wedding day is hung (against her will) at the shoe shop in Piazza Dei Martiri, she enlists Elena's help to excise her own face from it – with the unexpected consequence of turning it into a much-appreciated work of postmodern art (2012a: 118–19). Towards the end of her life, the desire to cancel all traces of her presence becomes an all-consuming obsession,[58] which is finally brought to bear when Elena breaks her promise to Lila never to write about her daughter's disappearance.

It is impossible not to notice, however, that Elena is always extremely implicated in, if not directly responsible for, Lila's self-erasure. Elena creates from the raw material that Lila destroys: herself. And yet, through Elena's writing, Lila is also granted existence, *despite* herself. It is worth repeating that the Neapolitan Novels begin when Elena, outraged at her friend's final act of self-erasure, decides to write down the story of their friendship, in an attempt to thwart Lila's stubborn desire to cancel herself off the face of the earth. Lila, therefore, can never truly disappear. First,

---

[56] For classical instances of Mount Vesuvius being appropriated as a source of poetic energy, cf. Paul in this volume.

[57] As Lila tells Elena in detail after one such episode, which occurs during the earthquake of 1980: *lei aveva avuto l'impressione che qualcosa di assolutamente materiale, presente intorno a lei e intorno a tutti e a tutto da sempre, ma senza che si riuscisse a percepirlo, stesse spezzando i contorni di persone e cose rivelandosi*, 'she had the impression that something absolutely material which had been present around her and around everyone and everything forever, but imperceptible, was breaking down the outlines of persons and thing and revealing itself.' (2011: 85–6).

[58] Cf. 2014a: 433: *Quell'idea di cancellarsi l'aveva espressa spesso, ma a partire dalla fine degli anni Novanta, soprattutto dal 2000 in poi, diventò una sorta di ritornello sfottente*, 'She had often expressed the idea of eliminating herself, but, starting in the late nineties – and especially from 2000 on – it became a sort of teasing chorus.'

because she, like Dido, now exists in literature, and second because Elena's writing is repeatedly presented as feeding off Lila's own absent texts. That Elena's writing about Lila is precisely what occasioned the latter's disappearance[59] is a dramatic paradox of the most Virgilian kind, insofar as the metapoetic function of Dido's death, as Hardie points out, lies in her post-mortem survival as a Fury:

> ...sequar atris ignibus absens
> et, cum frigida mors anima seduxerit artus,
> omnibus umbra[60] locis adero. dabis, improbe, poenas
> audiam et haec Manis ueniet mihi fama sub imos.
>
> (*Aen.* 4.384–7)

...though absent, I will hound you with the black flames of my torches, and when cold death will have pried the soul from my bones, as a ghost I will haunt you everywhere. Bastard, you will pay, and I will hear of it, the tale will reach me down in the depths of Hell.

The coupling of *sequar absens* and *umbra adero*, though a contradiction in terms, is associated with the eternal *kleos* bestowed upon both Dido and Virgil by the *Aeneid*. As Hardie puts it, this points to a 'persistent association in Latin epic of the powers of the Fury and of *Fama*, as a mythological personification merely the negative aspect of the *fama* that is the *raison d'être* of epic' (1993: 41).

The poetic mechanism that Hardie unearthed in the *Aeneid* rings true in Ferrante's novels, and finds a confirmation in *Frantumaglia*, with one crucial deviation; namely, that it is inextricably entangled with the lived experience of womanhood:

> I've described women at moments when they are absolutely alone. But in their heads there is never silence or even focus. ... I can't even think without the voices of others, much less write. ... I'm talking about the past, what we generally call tradition; I'm talking about all those others who were once in the world and who have acted or now act through us. Our entire body, like it or not, enacts a stunning resurrection of the dead just as we advance towards our own death. We are, as you say, interconnected. And we should teach ourselves to look deeply at this interconnection – I call it a tangle, or, rather, *frantumaglia* – to give ourselves adequate tools to describe it. In the most absolute tranquillity or in the midst of tumultuous events, ... we are a crowd of others. And this crowd is certainly a blessing for literature. (2016: 356)

---

[59] In fact, it is only after the publication of Elena's latest book, *A Friendship*, in which she recounts Tina's disappearance, that the latter takes off, never to be seen again.
[60] For Lila as shadow, see n. 51.

The story of Elena and Lila is the story of Ferrante's own descent into the Avernus, her own epic journey through the bowels of Naples. While for Aeneas the encounter with Dido is, yet again, an incidental moment on his trajectory to lay the foundations of the Roman empire, for Ferrante that is the whole point; it is her *telos* and her *kleos*. Through a sustained and sophisticated engagement with Virgil, Ferrante fiercely reclaims the ghosts of her female ancestors and places them at the centre of her literary universe. She takes women's pain, she takes the trauma that splits them in two, or three, or more, and turns it into literature, but she does not shy away from showing the ugly side of what would otherwise seem like an emptily triumphalist narrative.

While Elena, like Ferrante, gains fame and notoriety, Lila, like whoever Ferrante may 'really' be, sinks further and further into obscurity, until there is nothing left of her, and yet, it is thanks to Elena (Ferrante) that she will be remembered even after Elena's life, though not her name, is long forgotten. Ferrante's work, then, is both a homage to muses past and present as absent authors of their own texts, and a meditation on the generative power of their absence. In writing Elena and Lila in the shadow of Dido, and simultaneously as Dido's (and her own) 'internal others,' Ferrante overcomes the pre- and post-structuralist dilemma of whether the point at which meaning is realized resides with the author or the reader, by finally giving it back to the Muse.

CHAPTER 16

The Philology of Grief
Catullus 101 and Anne Carson's Nox

Erik Fredericksen

It is a particular embarrassment to be good with words in the face of loss. As a number of critics and theorists have elaborated, mourning is a process that happens crucially through language, but literary and linguistic skill can do little, if anything, to make that mourning easier.[1] Indeed, while language and mourning are intimately related, grief is often what exceeds language, resists articulation, and reduces the mourner to non-linguistic cries and utterances. This problematic relationship is only complicated further when a mourner begins to write. Writing is for oneself, or for absent readers, or for posterity – but it is most certainly not for the deceased. Writing poems of mourning can risk becoming a self-centered betrayal of grief's demanding focus on what has been lost. Moreover, creating a successful poem out of loss can create the uncomfortable situation of a poet profiting or reaping reward from the loss of a loved one, what has been called the economic problem of elegy.[2] In a variety of ways, grief puts particular and contradictory pressures on a poet. In this article, I examine this fraught relationship between poetic creation and loss in two related texts of mourning: Catullus' poem 101 and Anne Carson's 2009 book *Nox*, which translates and transforms Catullus 101.

Both these works take the loss of a brother as their reason for existence, growing out of an absence and responding to that lack. Both Carson and Catullus react to the loss of a brother by writing poetry, and each poet, as we will see, questions this move from mourning to poetic creation. In what follows, I examine how Catullus can help us read Carson, how Carson can

---

[1] Oliensis 2009: 14 sums up this relationship between language and mourning: 'Mourning happens – not exclusively, but crucially – in and through language ... From Freud's account of his grandson's attempts to master loss via the paradigmatic repetitions of the fort/da game, to Lacan's seminar on mourning in Hamlet, to Abraham and Torok's studies of melancholic incorporation as anti-metaphor, to Peter Sacks' psychogeneric reading of English elegy: to write about the "work of mourning" is to write about the mournful and melancholy words that help accomplish that work.'
[2] See Ramazani 1994: 6–8.

help us read Catullus, and how both poets can help us think about the intersections of absence, intimacy, and poetic learning. What does the world of literary tradition or scholarly learning have to offer a mourner? What does literary skill avail in the face of loss? And how are the tasks of the poet, the mourner, and the scholar all related? In thinking through these broad questions with Catullus and Carson, I will first offer a reading of Catullus 101, tracing the movements the poem makes in response to loss and drawing out the problems that linger for Catullus as a poet and as a mourner. Next, I will turn to Carson's *Nox*, to explore how that book takes up Catullus 101 and its problems. *Nox* alternates from page to page between mourning and remembering Carson's brother, and breaking down and examining Catullus' poem. The book becomes a twin exercise in grieving and in an obsessive philology, and my aim will be to examine the relationship Carson creates between philology and mourning as two related responses to loss. I will conclude by reading Carson's reception back onto Catullus, suggesting that while loss and absence condition poetry and philology, the literary has its own answer to absence, and perhaps even a lesson for grief.

Catullus 101: Substitution and Its Discontents

Catullus' *Carmen* 101 is, by all accounts, a remarkably effective poem. In poems 65 and 68 (both 68a and 68b), the loss of Catullus' brother interrupts, forestalls, and threatens his poetic composition, but this short poem is conspicuously successful in merging what are elsewhere the drastically opposed obligations of mourner and poet, creating what has long been singled out as one of Catullus' miniature masterpieces. But the poem is also effective in another sense. As a speech act, the poem professes to effect something for its speaker.[3] In particular, Catullus 101 effects a process of mourning through substitution. In a study of the English elegy, Peter Sacks has argued that elegies do not simply describe or represent loss, but in fact perform the work of mourning.[4] A similar process is at

---

[3] Skinner 2003: 128 reads poem 101 as an unsuccessful performative utterance. Feldherr 2000: 211 sees the poem as engaging with funerary ritual in order to effect the same social transformations as such rites. See Selden 2007: 520–44 on Catullan poetry's performativity more generally.

[4] Sacks 1985. Such an approach resonates with the fact that ancients often traced elegiac form back to actual cries of lamentation, as the common etymologizing of the Greek ἔλεγος from ἐλέγειν attests. See, for example, Horace *Ars P.* 75 with Maltby 1991: 201–2. Sacks, of course, is using elegy in the modern sense of a poem of lament.

work in Catullus' poem, though, as we will see, there are also signs that Catullus has reservations about the work that this poem accomplishes.

Sacks' influential work borrows the idea of substitution from Freud, who claims that a healthy mourning process involves withdrawing affection from what has been lost and redirecting it to a substitute object of attachment.[5] In a reading of the story of Apollo and Daphne from Ovid's *Metamorphoses*, Sacks concisely explains what is for him a classic example of this process: 'Daphne's "turning" into a tree matches Apollo's "turning" from the object of his love to a sign of her. It is this substitutive turn or act of troping that any mourner must perform.'[6] Jahan Ramazani summarizes Sacks' approach with a description of the traditional elegiac consolation, something he suggests modern poets have rebelled against: '[The poet] finds recompense ... in making this very poem, redirecting his affection from the lost friend to the brilliant artifact that is in some measure a replacement for the man it mourns.'[7] It is not only modern poets, though, who have reacted against the neatness of this process.[8] While Catullus 101 effects a substitutive process of mourning akin to that described by Sacks, problems and anxieties surrounding the turn from lost brother to polished poem linger just beneath the textual surface.[9]

According to Catullus' poetry, his brother died in the Troad, in Asia Minor. Unable to be present for his death and burial, Catullus must travel belatedly to see his brother's tomb. This spatial and temporal displacement compounds Catullus' loss, as the time needed to travel is time no longer shared between his brother and him. The closer Catullus comes to his brother geographically, the farther away he becomes temporally. The opening lines of the poem take the reader through Catullus' long journey but then immediately situate the poem in a vivid present moment:

> Multas per gentes et multa per aequora uectus
>   aduenio has miseras, frater, ad inferias,
> ut te postremo donarem munere mortis
>   et mutam nequiquam alloquerer cinerem,

---

[5] On the uses and limits of Freud and psychoanalysis more generally in interpreting poems of mourning, the remarks of Ramazani 1994: 28–31 are useful.
[6] Sacks 1985: 5. While not engaging explicitly with Sacks, Hardie 2002: 63–5 offers a similar reading of Ovid's Daphne and Hyacinthus narratives, emphasizing the transformation of Apollo's beloveds into kinds of texts.
[7] Ramazani 1994: 3.
[8] Ibid.: 9 recognizes this: 'In rejecting the premodern elegy, the modern elegy may really elaborate one set of transhistorical tendencies long embedded in the form.'
[9] On the hermeneutic value of positing something like a textual unconscious, see Oliensis 2009: 3–13.

> quandoquidem fortuna mihi tete abstulit ipsum,
> heu miser indigne frater adempte mihi.
> nunc tamen interea haec, prisco quae more parentum
> tradita sunt tristi munere ad inferias,
> accipe fraterno multum manantia fletu,
> atque in perpetuum, frater, aue atque uale.

> Through many peoples and through many seas I was carried,
> to come to these wretched rites, brother, to present you
> with the final gift of death, and to speak in vain to mute ash,
> since fortune has snatched you yourself away from me –
> ah! Poor brother, taken undeservedly from me.
> But now, for now, take this – what has been handed over
> in the ancient custom of our fathers with grim duty to the dead,
> take it dripping with the many tears of a brother
> and for the rest of time, brother, be well and farewell.[10]

The immediacy of this moment – a fleeting pause between the long journey that preceded it (1–2) and the eternity it looks ahead to (10) – is achieved in part through the poem's two key uses of deixis: *has inferias*, 'these funeral rites' (2), and *haec*, 'these things, these offerings' (7). Both serve to render a 'here' for a reader to occupy imaginatively. And yet, both instances also point to 'this' poem of which they are a part, another offering from Catullus. For Catullus' address to mute ash is also a written utterance addressed in part to his readers. It is they, after all, who receive (*accipe*, 9) the mournful gift of this poem.[11] The very vagueness of *haec* ('these things') helps with this slippage of reference, which crucially redirects affective attachment away from Catullus' brother. *Has* and *haec* are the deictic hinges by which the poem pivots from 'this' funeral offering to 'this' poetic gift, from absent brother to present poem. The polished Neoteric creation substitutes for the lost brother, and in the process the failed dialogue between brothers becomes a felicitous poetic utterance shared between friends.[12]

---

[10] All translations are my own. For the text of Catullus I use Thomson 1997.
[11] Cederstrom 1981 reads the gift of poem 101 as the poem itself. Skinner 2003: 128 similarly notes that poem 101 is 'the munus of which it speaks.' A poem is a *munus* in the related poem 68, at 68(b).149. On *munus* as a term of reciprocal textual exchange in the late Republic, see Stroup 2010: 66–100, esp. 72–88 on Catullus.
[12] This is the sort of substitution that Janan 1994: 118 notes Catullus is unable to accomplish in poems 65 and 68. Feldherr 2000: 229 notes how Catullus' poems themselves forge and maintain ties of *amicitia* among the social circle they represent. On his reading of poem 101, Catullus moves from isolation from his social world to reintegration precisely through the poetry that binds his friendships together.

Now, this is a very neat and tied-up reading of the poem, one that would perhaps make Dr. Freud very happy, with Catullus well on his way to healthy mourning. But in fact this movement of substitution leaves Catullus and his poem with some problems. For one thing, it is not clear that the move from absent brother to present poem actually overcomes absence. And, perhaps more fundamentally, reading poem 101 alongside Catullus' other poems dealing with his brother's death raises the question of whether this process of substitution is not in fact a betrayal of his brother – not a successful completion of the process of mourning, but an abandonment of it.

Early in the poem, Catullus recognizes the futility of his own graveside utterance: he comes to his brother's burial site in order to address the mute ash of his brother in vain (*nequiquam*, 4).[13] The poem implicitly asks why Catullus even speaks these words that will not be heard, much less answered. Of course, the answer is that these words will be heard by Catullus' readers, who in classic lyric fashion 'overhear' the address to his brother.[14] As mentioned before, thinking of Catullus' utterance as a written poem seems to redeem the otherwise unsuccessful dialogue he attempts to have with his brother. However, writing does not so much solve the problem of absence as it does multiply it. Catullus himself will turn out to be as absent and unreachable to his readers as his brother is to him. As William Fitzgerald has observed, 'in the case of poem 101, there is a congruity between the frustrated communication between Catullus and his dead brother and the fact that the (written) poem is a communication from one who is absent, even dead.'[15] Far from remedying the problem of mutual absence between speakers, the written nature of the poem implies the mutual absence of poet and readers.[16]

Again, Catullus' slippery use of deixis is instructive. On the one hand, deictic self-reference creates a sense of immediacy around a shared textual object, but on the other hand it also defines our distance from Catullus' text, which we access only through the mediation of textual dissemination and transmission.[17] Catullus offers up a gift wet with tears, but we do not

---

[13] Skinner 2003: 128 suggests 'no poem of lament has ever brought home more powerfully, and more paradoxically, the uselessness of lamentation.'
[14] On this form of lyric address, see Culler 2015: 186–243.   [15] Fitzgerald 1995: 200–1.
[16] While poetic composition in Catullus can be part of a social world of interpersonal textual exchange (as in Catullus 50), the poem's intertextual engagement with Homer and Hellenistic epigram indicates that Catullus is well aware of written poetry as something that goes on being read in the absence of its author, even after the author's death. Catullus' wish in poem 1 – that his writings last for longer than one *saeculum* – suggests that he wants his poetry, too, to have this continued readership after his own death.
[17] Lowrie 2006: 125–6 makes a similar observation about deixis in poem 68b.

hold his tear-stained page.[18] The poem we read and hold is not exactly the one Catullus writes, because we do not hold the same book.[19] Since deictic reference is indexed to its speaker, our 'this' and his are not the same.[20] The shared poetic object that was to connect Catullus to his readers only discloses the distance between them.

Loss and absence are therefore not overcome by Catullus' act of poetic substitution, but merely deferred and reinstated in the relationship between Catullus and his future readers. As we will later see in greater depth, this absence does not cancel out the possibility of any meaningful relationship, but it does mean that Catullus' substitution merely recreates the graveside scenario it turns away from.[21]

Regardless of the success or failure of Catullus' turn from his brother to the creation of a poem, there is an even more fundamental problem with this movement, namely that writing the poem may have more to do with Catullus than his brother, who will of course never read it. As Fitzgerald asks, 'if the poet cannot communicate with his brother across the grave, then where does the poem go and who is it for?'[22] One discomfiting answer is that the poem is for Catullus himself. His brother's death has furnished him the opportunity to craft an accomplished poem. The potential that Catullus 101 is written not to grieve for Catullus' brother, but rather to display literary ingenuity, leads to a tension between learned poetic skill and mourning in the poem.

This tension confronts us in the poem's first line: the opening words establish the pathos of the poem's dramatic situation, and the repetition of *multa ... multas* begins what will be the poem's languorous obsession with the murmuring letter m.[23] But, as most Latinists today would not fail to point out, the line does something else: it points to the famous opening of the *Odyssey*, making Catullus a kind of Odysseus and his journey a sort of anti-*nostos* and failed *nekyia*, all in one.[24] This intertextual opening creates

---

[18] Propertius will later play with tear-stained pages at 4.3.2–3, simultaneously suggesting an intimacy with the materiality of Arethusa's letter and marking our distance from it. Ovid continually takes advantage of similar references in the *Heroides* and in his exile poetry. See Ovid, *Heroides* 3.3–4, 4.175–6, and 15.97 and *Tristia* 1.1.13–14, 3.1.15–16, and 4.1.95–6.

[19] This is true for most readers, but especially for us, with our sorry state of knowledge about Catullus' original poetry book or books.

[20] Cf. Lowrie 2006: 117–18.

[21] Kennedy (this volume) examines this kind of relationship built on mutual absence in greater depth.

[22] Fitzgerald 1995: 210.

[23] Fordyce 1990: 388 calls the repetition of m-sounds 'a piece of studied technique.' See further Biondi 2007: 185–6 (an English translation of his earlier Italian article).

[24] Conte 1986: 32–9 identifies the allusion. See Biondi 2007: 188–9 on the relevance of the *nekyia* scene of the *Odyssey*.

a rich set of implications for Catullus' poem.[25] What I would like to emphasize, though, is how odd it is that Catullus' outpouring of fraternal grief begins with a complexly clever allusion to Homeric epic. The poem begins with a gesture not toward Catullus' lost brother, but toward a Greek poetic model. We thus confront a perennial issue in Catullus, as summarized by Michele Lowrie: 'the Catullan question is how to resolve the relationship between the sense of lived experience the poetry conveys and the similarly strong impression created of literary artificiality.'[26] Of course, it is important not to construct an overly simplified binary opposing sincere individual emotion to tradition or literary artifice.[27] Nonetheless, the particularly learned play of Catullus' Homeric allusion – the way it plays with genre, injecting epic into a funerary epigram, and the way it takes advantage of the apparent coincidence of his brother's death near Troy – seems potentially out of place in poem 101. It brings to mind Samuel Johnson's famous verdict on Milton's *Lycidas*: for him, that poem 'is not to be considered as the effusion of real passion; for passion runs not after remote allusions and obscure opinions.'[28] He goes on to quip, 'where there is leisure for fiction, there is little grief.'[29] So, with reference to Catullus' poem, where there is leisure for Homer, is there much grief?[30]

It can be argued that in asking this question I am projecting modern criteria of sincerity onto Catullus, and that Dr. Johnson's reaction is ill suited to Catullus' very different understanding of poetic propriety. So David Wray notes that while the *Odyssey* allusion has troubled the sensibilities of some modern readers, 'performative verbal wit in the face of death and grief did not seem any more out of place to Catullus than it had to his Hellenistic predecessors.'[31] In fact, though, Catullus himself voices some of the very concerns that such an approach would historicize away, as we can see by reading poem 101 alongside his other poems on the death of his

---

[25] In addition to Conte 1986: 32–9 and Biondi 2007: 188–9, see Fitzgerald 1995: 187–9; Feldherr 2000: 227; and Stevens 2013: 173–4 and 185–7.
[26] Lowrie 2006: 115.
[27] In poem 101, for example, writing in the tradition of funerary epigram does not vitiate Catullus' personal feelings of grief, nor do the trappings of Roman funerary ritual. See Feldherr 2000: 209–10 against readings that see ritual and tradition in poem 101 as inadequate to Catullus' personal grief. On the relevance of Hellenistic funerary epigram to this poem, particularly *Anth. Pal.* 7.476 (by Meleager), see Gutzwiller 2012: 105–7 and Paratore 1963: 563–72.
[28] Johnson 2006: 278.   [29] Johnson 2006: 278.
[30] Cf. Fitzgerald 1995: 186, who asks more generally of the brother poems, 'If Catullus can, and must, write from other motives than grief for his brother, then has he not betrayed that grief?'
[31] Wray 2001: 52. Cf. Williams 1968: 185: 'It may be thought at least mistaken to look for literary ancestry in the case of a poem so obviously personal and immediate. But these criteria that come so readily to the sympathetic reader are often illusory and are certainly dangerous.'

brother.³² Poem 65 begins by stressing Catullus' inability to compose poetry while grieving: *etsi me assiduo confectum cura dolore / seuocat a doctis, Hortale, uirginibus...*, 'even though, as I'm exhausted by constant pain, grief calls me away, Ortalus, from the learned maidens...', 65.1–2. Here *doctis* is particularly marked, not just a conventional epithet for the Muses. To indulge in the learned play that defines much of Catullus' poetry is to belie or betray the constant, unremitting nature of the grief afflicting him. If *dolor* is really *assiduus*, there is no time for *doctrina*. We may compare this with lines from poem 68a, where Catullus explains that he used to indulge in happy, playful poetry, but can no longer do so after his brother's death:

> Tempore quo primum uestis mihi tradita pura est,
>   iucundum cum aetas florida uer ageret,
> multa satis lusi: non est dea nescia nostri,
>   quae dulcem curis miscet amaritiem.
> sed totum hoc studium luctu fraterna mihi mors
>   abstulit... (68a.15–20)

> At the time when the white garment was first given to me,
> when flowering youth was passing a pleasant spring,
> I played enough at many things: the goddess is not ignorant of me,
> she who mixes sweet bitterness with cares. But all this pursuit
> the death of my brother has carried off from me with grief...

These lines suggest that the grieving Catullus has no room in his mind for the pleasant trifling of literary play. He goes on to say, *tota de mente fugaui / haec studia*, 'I have banished these pursuits entirely from my mind,' 68a.25–6. It is worth emphasizing the recurrence of *studium* and *studia* here. It is the whole learned pursuit and laborious endeavor of the Neoteric poetry that Catullus crafts that is unthinkable in the context of grief. There is much more to say (and indeed much more has been said) about the pressures grief puts on Catullus as a poet and the complex ironies and indirections this gives rise to in poems 65 and 68 – not least of which that Catullus' inability to create poetry is expressed in poems, though of an odd sort.³³ But, for our present purposes, the important question is what happens to these issues in poem 101.

---

³² The near-verbatim repetition of 68.20 and 68.92 at 101.5–6 would seem to demand that we read these poems together.

³³ See in particular Janan 1994: 115–42, esp. 115–19; Fitzgerald 1995: 185–211; Oliensis 2009: 15–17 and 25–54; and Woodman 2012. Most recently, Stevens 2013: 123–72 examines poems 65 and 68 in the context of Catullus' interest in forms of silence.

The Philology of Grief 297

If turning to studious poetry and the learned Muses is a betrayal of Catullus' constant mourning, is this not precisely the kind of poetic *studium* with which poem 101 opens, with its *Odyssey* allusion? Or consider the brilliance of line five: *quandoquidem fortuna mihi tete abstulit ipsum*. With the elision in *tete abstulit*, the word for 'you' becomes absorbed into the verb of loss – it is literally snatched away by 'snatched away.' In fact, it is precisely because *te* would disappear into *abstulit* that we need the emphatic reduplicated form *tete*. Not ready to let go of his brother, Catullus adds a repetitive excess of the signifier *te* to form a buffer, to stave off loss from 'you.' The intensive *ipsum* at the end of the line even seems to point to this failed attempt: death has robbed Catullus of his actual brother himself (*te ipsum*), leaving him with nothing but substitutes, words for 'brother' and 'you.' Remembering how grief elsewhere forbids Catullus from engaging in learned poetic play, what are we to make of these flashes of ingenuity? Do they call attention to Catullus' pain or to his own literary skill? Just whom are these shows of poetic learning for?

It is possible to read the poetic craft of poem 101 as working in sync with mourning, rather than at odds with it.[34] And for some, the poem may exemplify a positive process of 'transforming lamentation into poetry, loss into art.'[35] However, the strong opposition in poems 65 and 68a between mourning and poetic *studium* means that anxieties about this move from loss to art persist just beneath the surface of poem 101. In order to write this very text, Catullus has had to turn away from his brother and toward the learned Muses. As Ellen Oliensis describes it, 'the performance is almost too efficient, the seal almost too tight, as if the poem meant to put an end to the brother once and for all.'[36] The poem's closural speech act, *aue atque uale*, exorcizes the brother so that Catullus can compose. Or perhaps, a reader of poems 65 and 68 might suggest, this closure has already happened before the poem's first word. Hasn't Catullus already had to put an end to real mourning, so that writing could begin?

This and other troubling questions linger for readers beneath the apparent neatness of poem 101, all clustering around the fraught relationship between creating learned poetry and being in mourning. Why turn at all

---

[34] Thus, for example, Howe 1974 and Syndikus 1987: 108–9. Quinn 1959: 83 claims poem 101 succeeds, as poems 65 and 68 do not, in making poetry out of Catullus' experience of loss. For Feldherr 2000, the skill of the poem makes it a more effective quasi-ritual performance.
[35] Martin 1992: 145.
[36] Oliensis 2009: 16. Quinn 1972: 181 already shows a hint of this reading: 'The reader who has read the collection feels Catullus is saying, as well, "I addressed you in Poem 65, I addressed you in Poem 68, now I address you for the last time".'

from brother to poem, if that poem will merely confront Catullus with further forms of absence, and if it necessitates turning his back on his deceased brother? In short, what does the literary have to offer the mourner? We can gain some traction on these issues by looking to a recent reception of Catullus' poem, Anne Carson's 2009 book *Nox*, which uses poem 101 in order to come to terms with the loss of Carson's own brother.

Anne Carson's Work of Mourning

In poem 65, Catullus writes that amid grief he can only produce a translation of another poet's work.[37] Out of the loss of her own estranged brother, Carson produces in *Nox* a book that is at once not even a translation and much more than one. The back cover of the book informs us: 'When my brother died I made an epitaph for him in the form of a book. This is a replica of it, as close as we could get.'[38] The accordion-like book unfurls scrapbook remembrances of her brother alongside meditations on historiography and her attempt to know him, the practice of translation, and other topics. Throughout the book, Carson's reflections and memories are interspersed with lexicographical entries for every single word of Catullus 101, a poem that forms the spine of this (spineless) book. The first page of *Nox* is a tear-stained copy of the Latin poem, while a ripped and smudged English translation appears about three quarters of the way through (there are no page numbers). This translation then reappears on a piece of paper ripped into strips that are superimposed on each other. The final page of *Nox* takes the same translation and blurs it beyond legibility with what looks like water damage, or perhaps tears.

Nox is built around a translation of Catullus 101 that is continually withheld; even after we glimpse what seems like a final version, Carson continues to transform and deform it. It is the relationship between this poem and Carson's own poetic lament that I want to examine here, although *Nox* is also interested in other questions, involving for example the materiality of the book, and the relation between history and memory. In taking up Catullus 101, Carson makes Catullus' poem of brothers into a sister's lament.[39] She also takes up crucial questions facing any author of

---

[37] Catullus 65.15–16, on which see Fitzgerald 1995: 191–2. [38] Carson 2009.
[39] On the importance of the symmetrical brother-to-brother relationship in Catullus 101, see Feldherr 2000: 217–18. On Carson's *Nox* as claiming Catullus' poem out of a long tradition of male receptions, see Theodorakopoulos 2012: 156–9. Carson perhaps gestures toward this issue with her entry for *frater*, which notes that in the plural the word can refer to 'brother and sister.'

an elegy, of the sort we saw in Catullus 101. Like Catullus, Carson's *Nox* enacts a turn from lost brother to created poetic artifact, but also questions and problematizes this move.

Nox explores and is marked by absences of varying kinds, spurred by the loss of an estranged brother who was never all that present to Carson to begin with. *Nox* or night, taken from Catullus 5 where it refers to the *nox perpetua* of death, comes to stand for death and absence in the book, but also for the opacity of the brother she will never fully know.[40] Carson experiments with different ways of representing absence, probing the possibilities of making present what is fundamentally a non-presence. For example, the book is fascinated by shadow, a motif that appears throughout *Nox*. In one particular photograph we see the shadow made by a body not in the image.[41] In other words, what we see is a particular shape created by the absence of light, caused by a body itself absent to us. Similarly, another image shows an empty swing, and what appears to be the shadow of a child we don't see in another swing – again, what is absent leaves a visual impression through a medium of lack (shadow). In both cases, Carson deploys photography – a medium of exact likeness well equipped to furnish the substitutive image of an absent person – to render only the absence of a body. Another page confronts one with the question 'WHO WERE YOU,' whose letters seem to be formed by erasure. What is normally the empty space surrounding signifying language (the white of the page) here becomes the material of language itself – the absence of letters becoming letterforms. Everywhere we look in *Nox*, absence seems to multiply itself – when we see a picture of an empty chair, for example, are we looking at the presence of a chair or the absence of someone who might have been sitting in it?[42] Meanwhile, fragments of postcards, letters, and photographs tease us with the absent wholes they imply.

For much of the book, Carson seems less interested in attempting to overcome absence than in dwelling in it, exploring its own contours and possibilities. Nonetheless, Carson's creation of *Nox* engages in a similar substitutive process as that we saw with Catullus 101. Out of the loss of her brother, she has constructed an object now shared with readers. Indeed,

---

[40] Marsden 2013 explores Carson's interest in what she calls the fundamental opacity of human being' through the figure of night in *Nox*.
[41] The photograph appears opposite the short text labeled 1.2.
[42] Marsden 2013: 194 further suggests, 'certain images [in *Nox*] have a spectral quality, not simply because they are devoid of human subjects – an empty swing or garden chair – but because they exhibit unusually long perspectives of domestic exteriors, with low lights and low contrast, as if announcing an absence in advance of itself: a loss that is destined to come.'

Carson counterbalances the numerous forms of absence in *Nox* with a remarkable degree of intimacy between herself and her readers. To read the book is to flip through her diary of mourning, to see personal correspondences and idiosyncratic handwriting. With all of the book's carefully scanned folds, wrinkles, and staples, Carson painstakingly seeks to create an intimate, tactile relationship between readers and her creation, as though we can touch the very object she made in grief.[43]

The crafted book as a site of care, attention, and attachment potentially substitutes for the absent brother, and gestures toward a shared, intimate relationship with the readers it is meant for. However, as with Catullus, this kind of substitution only overcomes absence to re-inscribe it elsewhere. In unfolding the pages of *Nox*, a reader cannot help but run her or his fingers over what appear to be creases, staples, and smudges. But to do so is to register instantly the distance between us and the original object of which the book is a copy.[44] The scrapbook quality of *Nox* invites a tactile engagement with it as an art object, but the smoothness of every page reminds us that this is a facsimile. The work simultaneously invites and refuses intimacy, gesturing toward presence only to return us to absence and distance.

More fundamentally, though, it is worth asking whether this substitutive turning, failed or not, is what Carson's *Nox* really attempts to accomplish. Does she turn from her brother to Catullus, and from mourning to poetic creation like Sacks' Apollo turns from Daphne to the laurel? The layout of *Nox*, in which pages devoted to Carson's brother tend to alternate with pages devoted to the words of Catullus 101, stages this movement again and again: every turn of the page replicates Carson's turning from sisterly loss to scholarly contemplation, and back again. Over the course of the book, Carson's scholarly-poetic activity collapses into the process of mourning it might seem to deflect from or keep at bay. The words *nox* and 'night' surface repeatedly in Carson's lexicographical entries for unrelated words: the entry for *multas* offers various examples of usage but culminates with the phrase '*multa nox*: late in the night, perhaps too late.' Similarly, for *gentes*, Carson runs through a variety of English meanings but also slips in '*noctis gentes*: nightpeople.' Even the entry for the conjunction *et* leads to an

---

[43] Readers often remark on the tactile quality of the book. For example, Sikelianos 2015: 148 notes, 'this is a touchable book about an untouchable brother.' Plate 2015 suggests that the material qualities of *Nox* entangle the reader in webs of social relations.

[44] Similarly, Marsden 2013: 190: 'The eye demands that the fingers should touch these troubled surfaces but the fingers return only a perfect numbness as if the power to feel has been flattened, the affects denied.'

evocative phrase: '(to mark a parenthesis) and by the way, (*et nocte*) (you know it was night).' These irruptions of night – evocative of her brother's death – into the dispassionate listing of dictionary meanings function like the exclamations that interrupt Catullus 68. Grief finds its way into the endeavor that was to distract from it. And if her brother's death infects the project of Carson's translation-cum-decomposition of Catullus, her scholarly endeavor also influences her treatment of her brother. Her searching after and curating of every trace of his life comes to resemble the obsessive scholarly focus she directs toward Catullus' poem. Catullus, as we have seen, is haunted by the idea that turning to learned poetry might be a betrayal of his brotherly grief. But for Carson her scholarly-poetic work becomes complementary to it. The two blend and enrich – or contaminate – each other.

It is worth examining why these two impulses, so opposed to each other for Catullus, are so intertwined for Carson. She herself elaborates a parallel between translation and mourning in *Nox*:

> I never arrived at the translation I would have liked to do of poem 101. But over the years of working at it, I came to think of translating as a room, not exactly an unknown room, where one gropes for the light switch. I guess it never ends. A brother never ends. I prowl him. He does not end.[45]

Carson's endeavors both to translate Catullus and to know her brother are likened to an endless process of approximation. Her translation work dovetails with her work of mourning, as both demand gaining familiarity with absence, never arriving at a solution or consolation, but rather coming to know a lack, gaining a feel for the contours and textures of a room we cannot see. As Neil Corcoran puts it, 'if a dead brother is like a dead language, he can be recovered only in traces, fragments, memorial ruins, hauntings, approximations, and vanishings.'[46] Carson has to piece together the life of her deceased brother like the well-trained philologist of fragments she is.

Indeed, Carson's translation project in *Nox* is marked by the trappings of classical philology, repurposed for her own poetic aims. Her lexicographical entries for Catullus recall philology's ambitions of scientific precision and encyclopedic exhaustiveness (think, for example, of the *Thesaurus Linguae Latinae*), while the way these entries anatomize the poem into a series of lemmata plays with and parodies classical

---

[45] Carson 2009. She repeats the parallel two pages later, with the line 'prowling the meanings of a word, prowling the history of a person, no use expecting a flood of light.'
[46] Corcoran 2012: 377. Cf. Fleming 2016: 66.

commentary. While Carson links translation to mourning, she never addresses in *Nox* these markers of philological work. What is the relationship between her mourning and this philology? In the following section, I will argue that Carson exploits constitutive tensions in classical philology as a discipline organized in response to a loss – to the perceived absence of a classical culture it attempts to reconstitute or revivify, even though it will never fully do so. The grieving Carson is interested in the methods of philology because philology itself is an endless work of reconstruction subtended by loss.

The Philology of Grief

Philology, whether conceived of as a discipline or a method, is a contested concept, even more so as it has come to enjoy a resurgence in popularity.[47] What Carson alludes to in *Nox* is a particular form of classical philology, one that directs painstakingly detailed attention and labor toward a valorized past. It is fundamentally a response to a perceived loss, as we can see from the beginnings of the discipline. To begin with the philhellenism underlying philology, Winckelmann offers the following instructive vignette in his *History of the Art of Antiquity*, originally published in 1764:

> Just as a beloved stands on the seashore and follows with tearful eyes her departing sweetheart, with no hope of seeing him again, and believes she can glimpse even in the distant sail the image of her lover – so we, like the lover, have as it were only a shadowy outline of the subject of our desires remaining. But this arouses so much the greater longing for what is lost, and we examine the copies we have with greater attention than we would if were in full possession of the originals.[48]

Winckelmann's echoes of Ariadne (and indeed of Catullus 64) position the abandoned female lover as the quintessential philhellene, desiring after what has been lost.[49] And if the distance between Theseus and Ariadne is the gap between ancient and modern, philology will be the activity that could – perhaps – close that distance. We can see this in the work of August

---

[47] On the recent resurgent interest in philology amid confusion and contestation as to what exactly the term refers to, see Gumbrecht 2003: 1–4; Pollock 2009: 933–4; Gurd 2010: 1–12; Pollock 2015: 2–6; and Lönnroth 2017: xviii–xix.
[48] Winckelmann 2006: 351.
[49] On this famous passage and its implications, see Davis 1994; Potts 1994: 48–50; Güthenke 2010: 123–6; Harloe 2013: 123–5; and Billings 2016: 54–6. Cf. also Bellei (this volume).

Boeckh, a crucial figure in the development of classical philology as a quasi-scientific academic discipline. In his *Encyclopedia and Methodology of the Philological Sciences* (edited and compiled from earlier lectures), he is at pains to distinguish philology from the mere gathering of historical details:

> In truth, philology has a higher aim, which is the historical reconstruction of the whole of knowledge as well as of its parts, and the study of the ideas which are stamped into it . . . To re-learn what has been known, to present it in a pure state, to remove the falsifications of time, the misconceptions, to make what does not appear whole into a whole – these are not superfluous activities, but something very essential, without which all knowledge would soon be finished.[50]

As 're-construction' and 're-learn' suggest, philology is a seeking after what used to be, a recovery of what is now absent. Boeckh's famous definition of philology as 'die Erkenntniss des Erkannten' (the knowledge of what has been known) makes it a recapturing of what has been lost, while his emphasis on remaking the whole or the unity of classical antiquity emphasizes a reparative response to a loss or injury.

Classicism posits a gulf between the present and the classical past, and philology offers the fantasy that scholarly activity can repair this rift. The philologist's urge to fill in gaps, discussed elsewhere in this volume by Ábel Tamás, may be symptomatic of a larger imperative to fill in *the* gap that separates a scholarly present from a classical past. Philology, in short, is underwritten by a desire for the presence of the absent past.[51] But more than this, it is the activity or practice that seeks to make good on this desire, to do the hard work of making present what would otherwise remain absent. For Wilamowitz, this work resembles Odysseus' *nekyia*, a raising of the dead: 'The tradition is dead; our task is to revivify life that has passed away. We know that ghosts cannot speak until they have drunk blood; and the spirits which we evoke demand the blood of our hearts.'[52] There is, to be sure, more to the story of how engagement with a literary past has often been entwined with ideas of commerce and contact with the dead.[53]

---

[50] Boeckh 1877: 14–15, trans. Pritchard in Boeckh 1968: 13, modified.
[51] Thus Gumbrecht 2003: 3 speaks of philology's 'emergence from a desire for the textual past.'
[52] Wilamowitz-Moellendorff 1908: 25. Cf. the axiom of Hamacher 2009: 37: 'philology is *nekyia*, descent to the dead, *ad plures ire*.'
[53] Such a story would include, among many others, Propertius' *Callimachi manes* (3.1.1), Horace's vision of Sappho and Alcaeus in the underworld (*Odes* 2.13), Petrarch's letters to dead authors, and Pound's version of the *nekyia* in *The Cantos*. See also Richardson 2016 on the intersections of Classics and spiritualism in nineteenth-century Britain, where classicists' desires for encounters and dialogues with the dead were often literalized in the performances of mediums and spiritualists.

Carson, though, gestures in *Nox* to the particular disciplinary history of Classics and its methods of philology. Philology, like mourning, is a response to loss, working scrupulously to regain the presence of what is gone.

Of course, philology never fully arrives at this goal of repairing the gap between then and now. As Boeckh describes it, 'like every science, philology is an endless pursuit of approximation.'[54] It is this infinite and asymptotic approximation that makes the philological method particularly useful to Carson. Akin to a process of mourning, philology becomes for Carson a way of not letting go. She refuses to complete her project that is part philology, part translation, and part poetic composition – *Nox* draws out poem 101, presenting us not with the product of translation but with translation as process.[55] Carson's philological activity never reaches full completion, and indeed it never could: no work could exhaust every possible meaning of every word of any poem. Ironically, in taking to an extreme the tools of a traditional philology often concerned with closing down meaning, Carson fashions a philology that produces and proliferates ever-extending meanings.

Never reaching its final destination, Carson's philological method constitutes an ongoing intimacy, a tarrying with details and traces. In this, Carson's literary endeavor offers a lesson for grief: while mourning exposes the affective structure of classical philology, philology shows a way of working with what has been lost. By never completing the perfect translation, Carson also never stops mourning, refusing to complete the process of substitution that gives Catullus such qualms. Keeping the project of Catullan translation alive means denying the tight closure and conclusion that Catullus puts on his poem and his brother alike.

Carson takes from Catullus the central problem of what it means for a poet to create something out of loss, to turn away from a lost loved one and toward the world of words and texts that would seem to have nothing to offer the mourner but more absence – and perhaps guilt. But Carson uses the tools of philology to show a different relationship between learned poiesis and grief. Her poetic *studium* is not opposed to mourning but offers a practice for working with loss. What emerges from *Nox* is a melancholic philology and a philological melancholy, which mutually reinforce each

---

[54] Boeckh 1877: 16, trans. Pritchard in Boeckh 1968: 14, modified.
[55] Plate 2015: 104 similarly notes that in *Nox* Carson 'emphasizes (never-ending) process over (finished) product.'

other. Carson's melancholic philology refuses to arrive at a final translation of Catullus 101 but continues to pull it apart, holding onto every word of it; and her philological melancholy examines every fragment left behind by her brother, seeking not to put an end to him and complete the mourning process, but to maintain an always ongoing engagement with the traces of his past presence.[56]

Conclusion

Both Catullus and Carson create poetic artifacts out of grief while simultaneously probing the problems and possibilities of such an undertaking. The poetic and scholarly activities that would represent a turning away from the object of loss – Catullus' turning from his brother to poetry and Carson's turning from her brother to Catullus – seem only to multiply absence rather than substitute for it, and lead to difficult questions about betraying or abandoning the obligations of mourning. In Catullus 101, these concerns linger just beneath the surface of a poem that appears to seal off grief most effectively and tidily. Carson, on the other hand, constructs a book object whose central project of translation resists completion, finding in the endlessness of her poetic task a way of never fully turning away from her brother. Her philological relationship with Catullus offers a model for an enduring intimacy with the traces and memories of her brother.

Catullus does not have a tradition of modern classicism and classical philology at his disposal. Nonetheless, Carson's use of Catullus can reveal something at work in his poem as well. Catullus' intertextual engagement with Homer arguably shows a similar intimacy with a classical text as Carson's with Catullus. Both these relationships show how intricate bonds can be constructed over and out of absence and loss. Catullus' relationship to Homer and Carson's to Catullus establish relationships over a gulf of absence that is already there. In other words, Carson never had a relationship with Catullus before he was lost to her. He became important to her after already being gone. And this is as true of Catullus'

---

[56] There is perhaps something disconcerting about this model of endless grief, as Carson herself recognizes. Opposite her entry for *nunc*, she writes of the room to which she compares her process of translation and mourning, 'in one sense it is a room I can never leave, perhaps dreadful for that.' Nevertheless, I am reluctant to import, for example, Freud's normative, pathologizing distinction between (healthy) mourning and (unhealthy) melancholy. *Nox* in part shows the creative fertility of a certain kind of melancholy.

working with Homer as it is of Carson's dissection of Catullus. Whether through Carson's philological scrutiny or Catullus' intertextual play, in both poets the world of literary tradition does in fact have something to offer the mourner. It does not overcome absence but teaches one how to work with it. Read together, Catullus and Carson demonstrate that absence need not be the end of closeness but can be the ground of new intimacies. This is not exactly substitution, or consolation – but it is not nothing.

CHAPTER 17

Absence, Metaphysically Speaking
From Reception to Instauration?
Duncan F. Kennedy[*]

A quarter of a century ago, in the collection of essays he co-edited on the reception of Horace, *Horace Made New*, Charles Martindale wrote: 'Many writers, including most of those discussed in this book, and a great many readers, have had a friend – in Quintus Horatius Flaccus. More, perhaps, than any other ancient poet his writings have encouraged, and continue to encourage, reading in terms of what is now sometimes called "the poetics of presence", the belief that literature makes present to us the consciousness and mind of the author behind or beyond the text.'[1] Deconstruction underpinned Martindale's defamiliarization of the poetics of presence with its reliance on the meeting of two conscious minds. This was the residue of a metaphysical tradition, an amalgam of Platonic and Christian ideas that envisaged soul communicating directly with soul or with God. In turn, Derridean notions of dissemination and différance destabilized ideas of originary meaning generated by a mind wholly present to itself.[2] '*Meaning*', Martindale suggested, '*is always realized at the point of reception.*'[3] This encouraged a scholarly turn towards contexts of reception, though sometimes without the equivalent metaphysical caution that deconstruction enjoined, particularly the endless deferral of final or definitive meaning suggested by dissemination and différance.[4] The sender, the receiver and the modes of communication are all constitutive and continuing issues of

---

[*] Responsible readers and interlocutors have played a significant role in the coming-into-being of this essay: the editors of this volume, Charles Martindale, Pantelis Michelakis, Ellen O'Gorman, Alexei Zadorojnyi.
[1] Martindale and Hopkins 1993: 1.
[2] Cf. Martindale 1993: 7: 'we cannot get back to any originary meaning wholly free of subsequent accretions'.
[3] Ibid.: 3; original emphasis.
[4] The debate set in train by Martindale 1993 continues apace. Dufallo 2018: 8–12 offers a shrewd and concise summary of the current arguments, which in the main fight shy of the metaphysical issues which will be addressed here.

concern in reception studies.[5] Questions of the interaction of human beings involve metaphysical assumptions about what is to *be* a human being and about ontological issues more generally. My aim in this essay is to refresh debates about presence and absence with the help of some recent metaphysical thinking, particularly the work of Samuel Scheffler and Bruno Latour, and John Durham Peters' reflections on communication. The texts that will provide points of reference in my discussion are those of Horace (particularly his *Epistles*) and the 'Letter to Horace' written by Joseph Brodsky (1940–1996) in what was to be the last year of his life.[6] To get this going, then, a study in reception that focuses these issues.

The Challenges of Communication: Dialogue and Dissemination

For Brodsky, the relationship he has to Horace's poetry is characterized not so much by presence as by absence. In his 'Letter to Horace', what is lacking in his relationship with Horace is a sense of reciprocity: he can read Horace's poems, but Horace can never read his. He mentions that he is writing this letter in a continent (North America) Horace didn't know existed while reading Horace's poems in a translation into a language (Russian) that didn't exist in Horace's time; 'We weren't even we', he says.[7] As he remarks in his essay, 'Homage to Marcus Aurelius': 'While antiquity exists for us, we, for antiquity, do not. We never did, and we never will. This rather peculiar state of affairs makes our take on antiquity somewhat invalid';[8] and a few pages later: 'The most definitive feature of antiquity is our absence.'[9] Brodsky gestures towards what we might call the 'metaphysics of absence' and the 'Letter to Horace' explores its associated poetics.

Brodsky's piece is explicitly framed as a *letter* to Horace, and we might recall (particularly through Janet Gurkin Altman's classic exploration of what she called the 'bridge/barrier function' of epistolary form) how the letter was one of the great sites of deconstructive debate about the interplay of presence and absence.[10] However, epistolarity was a particular instance

---

[5] Cf. Willis 2017: 5: 'At its simplest, the idea of "reception" suggests a sender (an author), a message (a text) and a receiver (a reader), but it also implies that there must be a communications system which facilitates the sending and receiving of the message ... Thinking about reception entails thinking about the system itself: about the people, processes and institutions involved in the production, transmission, distribution and circulation of messages and texts.'
[6] Brodsky 1995: 428–58.   [7] Cf. Brodsky 1995: 430.   [8] Ibid.: 267.   [9] Ibid.: 272.
[10] Altman 1982.

of the dualism of communication more generally, at once bridge and chasm, a dualism that could be differently addressed in different media of transmission (writing, the telephone, radio, internet and so on). In *Speaking into the Air: A History of the Idea of Communication*, John Durham Peters suggests that '[t]he deprivation of presence, in one way or another, has always been the starting point of reflection about communication'.[11] Peters historicizes two notions, first that of *media*, and suggests that new media change the dynamics of communication without resolving the dualism.[12] Second, the notion of *communication*: he contrasts the Platonic/Christian picture of a communion of souls, of direct presence, with the idea of communication as an insurmountable barrier, which he suggests was at the heart of literary and aesthetic modernism, and of modernist philosophy.[13] He cites Heidegger in *Being and Time*: 'Communication is never anything like a transportation of experiences such as opinions and wishes from the interior of one subject into the interior of another.'[14]

Brodsky's 'Letter' resonates with this. In seeking points of commonality with Horace, he recalls Horace's interest in sex (mentioning the anecdote from the Suetonian Life that his bedroom was lined with mirrors) and himself talks a lot about sex, recounting experiences he has had, from memory in the Suburra when he visited Rome, more recently in dreams he says were prompted by his reading of Horace. This reflects the metaphysical tradition which in Plato's *Phaedrus* and *Symposium* links dialogue and desire in the quest for oneness. The language of communication is troped around images of intercourse and relations (conversely the language of sexual intercourse can be expressed by co-presence, 'to be with', σύνειμι and *esse cum*). Brodsky's sexual reminiscences chime with his meditations on absence; the portrayal of his own sexual encounters seems to involve only a limited sense of mutuality. Even in his dreams, he says, 'two torsos can't shrink into one limb; no subconscious is that economical'.[15] The anecdote about Horace's mirrors, the spectating of the self in the course of prosecuting physical relations, resonates with his anxiety that he is in effect writing to himself: in the absence of communication, all one is left with is the contemplation of one's own reflection.[16] To paraphrase Brodsky, while

---

[11] Peters 1999: 36.   [12] Cf. Ibid.: 5.
[13] The idea of course informs *Speaking into the Air* itself. Cf. Krämer 2015: 68–74.
[14] Peters 1999: 16, citing Heidegger 1962a [1927]: 162 = Heidegger 1962b: 205.
[15] Brodsky 1995: 436. For many readers this will recall the speech of Aristophanes in *Symposium* 189d–191c, and his 'myth' that explains how people in love are looking for their other halves.
[16] Cf. Ibid.: 441: 'At the very least, I can sit down in front of my mirror and talk to it.' For Peters even this would not resolve the bridge and chasm of communication: Brodsky is not wholly present even to himself.

Horace exists for us, we, for Horace, do not. We never did, and we never will. Brodsky's bleak reflections suggest to him that poetry is not written for one's contemporaries or posterity, but for one's predecessors;[17] his own poetry is his homage to Horace.

Brodsky's text falls into a venerable genre of writing, letters addressed to great figures of the past. The figure of Petrarch comes to mind here especially, and we may also recall that amongst his letters is one addressed to posterity, which takes the form of an incomplete autobiography. With that in mind, I want to explore the poetics of absence where the perspective is towards the future as well as the past, partly to re-assess Brodsky's loneliness, but mainly to open out further some of the metaphysical questions his 'Letter' raises. Of course, Horace himself is the author of *Epistles*, and although he does not explicitly *address* posterity in the way that Petrarch does, the future is very much in play in his text. Peters suggests there are two great models of communication, dialogue and dissemination. He associates the former particularly with Socrates and Plato's *Phaedrus*, the latter with Christ in the synoptic gospels, who speaks of spreading his message in the imagery of broadcast seeds, some of which will fall on stony ground, some on fertile ground. Socrates privileges face-to-face dialogue and is famously suspicious of writing, which is associated with dissemination: it is addressed to nobody in particular (*Phaedrus* 275d–e). Socrates too uses the image of the seed, but speaks of sowing as husbandry, seeking out the right ground (an individual receptive to one's dialogue), planting the seed and nurturing it (*Phaedrus* 276b).

But these two models of communication need not be categorically differentiated as Socrates differentiates them, for his own metaphysical purposes.[18] For Peters, dialogue and dissemination share the challenges of communication across any distances. Whatever the mode of mediation (speech, writing, telephone, social media), communication involves distances (temporal as well as spatial), even (arguably acutely so) in the physical proximity of conversations. The issue cannot be reduced to a technical one associated with modes of transmission: 'The problem of communication becomes not only one of getting messages across the waste expanses traversed by telegraph wires or the interference-prone "ether" of radio transmission, but one of making contact with the person sitting next

---

[17] Ibid.: 439.
[18] The privileging of speech over writing and its specific role in underpinning the Platonic metaphysics of presence was the object of Derrida's deconstruction in his reading of the *Phaedrus* in 'Plato's Pharmacy': Derrida 2016 [1972].

to you.'[19] Sybille Krämer remarks that, for Peters, 'the problem of communication is rooted in the unbridgeable divide between the self and the other'.[20] One could take issue with this formulation (bridge/chasm is constitutive of communication for Peters as well as its 'problem'), but the metaphysical point is well made. Indeed, it could be pressed further than Krämer does: is the self ever wholly present to itself? Brodsky sitting down in front of a mirror and *talking* to it offers a poignant image of a distance even within the self that he is seeking to bridge. Peters is the philosopher who best probes the issue of the lack of reciprocity that Brodsky raises, and, even as Plato's Socrates exalts dialogue as reciprocal communication, so Peters finds much to celebrate in the lack of reciprocity of dissemination. His peroration is worth quoting in full:[21]

> There is, in sum, no indignity or paradox in one-way communication. The marriage of true minds via dialogue is not the only option; in fact, lofty expectations about communication may blind us to the more subtle splendors of dissemination or suspended dialogue. Dialogue still reigns supreme in the imagination of many as to what good communication might be, but dissemination presents a saner choice for our fundamental term. Dissemination is far friendlier to the weirdly diverse practices we signifying animals engage in and to our bumbling attempts to meet others with some fairness and kindness. Open scatter is more fundamental than coupled sharing; it is the stuff from which, on rare, splendid occasions, dialogue may arise. Dissemination is not wreckage: it is our lot.

The difficulties of communication lead Peters to see it as an ethical rather than a semantic problem, still less, to put it crudely, one of data transfer. The otherness of those we encounter must be respected and met 'with some fairness and kindness'.

An 'Earthly Afterlife'? Communication with the Unknown, Not-yet-existent

To open out these issues further, let us shift orientation in this communicative action to explore some perspectives offered by Brodsky's addressee, Horace. In the first book of his *Epistles*, nineteen poems are addressed to various (mostly named) contemporaries from whom their author is separated in one way or another. Broadly, these adopt the mode of dialogue, and Horace himself describes them in seed imagery as *sermones* ('conversations'; he never refers to them as epistles, though they display marks of that

[19] Peters 1999: 178.   [20] Krämer 2015: 69.   [21] Cf. Peters 1999: 62.

form).²² But the final poem (1.20) is addressed to the book which assembles them into a collection and which is about to be consigned to the booksellers: dialogue gives way to dissemination, framed — luridly so — in the sexual imagery associated with communication. The book (*liber*, 1), no longer Horace's slave, subject to his master's attentions only, but now, punningly, 'free' (*liber*), will come to the notice of 'lovers', readers who will get their fill of it (*et scis / in breve te cogi cum plenus languet amator*, 7–8), will be able to command a high price at Rome until youth has deserted it (*carus eris Romae donec te deserat aetas*, 10), when it will become grubby by being fingered by all and sundry (*contrectatus ubi manibus sordescere uulgi / coeperis*, 11–12). The poems have specific named addressees but will be broadcast to no addressees in particular, and their publication combines the facets of dialogue and dissemination. In particular, their dissemination, as Horace's image of his book as having a life cycle like that of a freed slave indicates, weaves into the text a further, and extended, *temporality*: its 'reception' over time by a promiscuous and anonymous readership.

Horace's collection has a prospective, and anxious, eye on its own future. But how is this future construed? I'll approach this with two perspectives on absence. First, thinking about a future in which *we* do not exist: what is our relationship to that world? Second, how do we model communication with a future populated by the *unknown not-yet-existent*? Horace's eclectic philosophizing in the *Epistles* embraces Epicureanism: he styles himself in letter 1.4 to Albius as 'a porker from Epicurus' herd', 16.²³ But Epicurus is invoked here in a specific context: Albius is invited to visit Horace and live for the moment: 'amidst hope and care, amidst fears and angers, believe that every day that has dawned is your last. Welcome will come the addition of the hour unhoped for', 12–14. The invitation to Albius to share the simple pleasures of friendship and conversation opportunistically invokes Epicurus to entice someone portrayed as involved in poetic activity or philosophical reflection (3–5) to seize the moment. Horace, who describes himself in *Epistles* 1.1.14 as *nullius addictus iurare in uerba magistri* ('not bound to swear as any one master dictates'), was no card-carrying Epicurean, but, as John Moles has shown, Epicureanism provided an important co-ordinate for his thinking.²⁴ What, then, of Epicurus' dictum that 'the most horrible of evils, death is nothing to us,

---

²² Cf. de Pretis 2002: 7. She reminds us that 'Aristotle [had] already defined the letter as "the half of a *dialogue* between friends"', and goes on to track 'how ancient stylistic theories stressed the spoken nature of epistolary utterance'.
²³ Text and translation in the Appendix at the end of this chapter.   ²⁴ Moles 2007.

since so long as we are, death is not with us; but when death is with us, then we are not' (*Epistle to Menoeceus* ap. Diog. Laert. 10.125)?

Fear of dying as a painful and drawn-out process is understandable; but Epicurus is suggesting that the state of being dead is nothing to be feared, since it is the end of consciousness and we are no longer experiencing subjects. However, the fear of death targeted in Lucretius' diatribe at the end of Book 3 of *De rerum natura* is the notion that there is an experience of being dead, whether pleasant or painful, such as we are presented with in some religious images of the afterlife. At the beginning of the diatribe, Lucretius ventures a dramatic thought experiment that culminates in the ultimate doomsday scenario (3.832–42):[25]

> et, uelut anteacto nil tempore sensimus aegri,
> ad confligendum uenientibus undique Poenis,
> omnia cum belli trepido concussa tumultu
> horrida contremuere sub altis aetheris oris ...   835
> sic, ubi non erimus, cum corporis atque animai
> discidium fuerit, quibus e sumus uniter apti,
> scilicet haud nobis quicquam, qui non erimus tum,   840
> accidere omnino poterit sensumque mouere,
> non si terra mari miscebitur et mare caelo.

And, as in time past we felt no discomfort, while from all directions the Carthaginians were advancing to the attack, when the whole world, shaken by the terrifying tumult of war, shivered and quaked under the lofty regions of the heavens ... (837) so, when we shall no longer be (*ubi non erimus*), when the separation shall have come about between body and soul from which we are fitted together into a single whole, then for sure nothing at all will be able to happen to us, who will then no longer be (*qui non erimus tum*), or to make us experience sensation, not when earth will be mingled with sea and sea with sky.

Is death, his future non-existence in the Epicurean sense, nothing to Horace? Not if a statement such as 'I shall not completely die, and a large part of me will escape Libitina [goddess of funerals]' (*non omnis moriar, multaque pars mei / utabit Libitinam*, *Odes* 3.30.6–7) are given any weight: what happens after he ceases to be an experiencing subject seems to matter quite a lot to him. Of course, what happens to people one cares about after one dies matters to one, but what of the nameless multitudes in the future one will never know of, let alone know?

---

[25] What follows is generally known as the 'Symmetry Argument' and *may* be new to Lucretius. For a full discussion, see Warren 2004: 57–108.

To get some purchase on this, let us turn to Samuel Scheffler's book *Death and the Afterlife*, which seeks to address the Epicurean conundrum. He proposes in turn a couple of related thought experiments which similarly picture doomsday scenarios. Taking his cue from P. D. James's novel *The Children of Men*, he asks you to imagine that the human species had become infertile and would cease to exist as its remaining members died off; or suppose you knew that, shortly after your own death, an asteroid would strike the earth and wipe out all human life. In James's novel, people are gradually overcome by what her protagonist calls an *ennui universel*, which he observes in others and senses in himself.[26] In the absence of a future for the human species, Scheffler suggests, people's lives and activities would become drained of meaning, and their projects, however visionary (curing cancer or saving the environment), become pointless if there is nobody in the future to benefit from them. These extreme scenarios lead Scheffler to a seemingly counterintuitive conclusion: 'the fact that we and everyone we love will cease to exist matters less than would the non-existence of future people whom we do not know and who, indeed, have no determinate identities';[27] and it is this earthly 'afterlife' (which we ourselves will not experience and will have no knowledge of) that sustains our projects here and now in ways that we can easily take for granted.

Scheffler's conclusion may seem counterintuitive and we may not be prepared to accept it in its strong form; but we should give some consideration to how such arguments work. By provoking a strong emotional reaction, his thought experiments bracket off what we take to be obvious (our concern for those we love) so as to focus upon something noteworthy that might otherwise escape our attention (our investment in the existence of humanity after our death). The premise of his thought experiments (the *imminent* destruction of humanity) pushes him towards 'clean abstraction' and the extreme formulation we have just seen.[28] If we entertain his argument in something less than its maximal form, it does help us not to take for granted our psychic dependence on an 'earthly' afterlife. Scheffler is keen to distinguish this earthly afterlife from its religious counterparts, though there are some similarities. Like the religious afterlife, it can act as a vehicle for deferred fulfilment: we imagine we would receive what we believe to be our just recognition. Contrariwise, the absence of an afterlife

---

[26] James 1992: 12. In Lars von Trier's 2011 film, the planet that is going to collide with the Earth, and gives the movie its title, is called *Melancholia*.
[27] Scheffler 2013: 45. [28] Cf. Srinivasan 2014: 13.

(earthly or religious) would tend to make us answerable only to the present, constricting our ability to think about our larger projects, and what we might do to bring them about. It may even lead us into a form of self-obsession. Recall Albius, wandering silently in the woods 'giving thought to whatever is worthy of one who is wise and good' (1.4.5). Pondering such things needs space, and not simply physical space. Within a restricted temporal reach, ethical or political challenges can feel oppressive, thinking about them tinged with futility. Perhaps Horace harbours concerns about Albius' well-being, perhaps not; whatever moves Horace to pen this epistle is never made wholly explicit. Nonetheless, it concludes with an invitation that precisely imagines on his friend's behalf a *very* brief temporal reach as a respite.

In practice, we order our lives as though what we are doing has meaning and purpose beyond the day or the moment. We all have our 'projects', those things we *cast in front* of us and which provide existential bearings for us beyond the day and the moment. These projects may be long-term or brief; Scheffler himself mentions play (where the meaning and purpose is in the activity itself): '[The] clearest examples of particular things that we value but do not want preserved are all *events*, like meals or performances. And in these cases ... the point may be less that we resist preservation of the valuable item than that the valuable item cannot be preserved as such by being prolonged. Temporal extension does not preserve it as a valuable item but rather transforms it into something less valuable.'[29] Horace's injunction to Albius is to live for the moment; but the references earlier in the poem to previous 'conversations' (1) and to Albius' attributes more generally (6–11) may point to a concern for his well-being in a broader temporal context, with this epistolary invitation thus being part of a project concerned with the longer-term well-being of his friend more than simply a proposed get-together.

Scheffler's concern is, of course, with projects whose temporal reach extends beyond our individual deaths, and he sees the importance of the earthly afterlife as lying in the logic of value. Valuing, he suggests 'has a temporal dimension', and is oriented towards the future: 'to value X is normally to see reasons for trying to preserve or extend X over time ... what matters to us now depends on what we think will happen later'.[30] But what about beyond the moment of our death, when we shall no longer be, when the capacity to preserve and sustain through our personal agency ostensibly ends? That a researcher may not live to see the cure for cancer

[29] Scheffler 2013: 191; original emphasis.   [30] Ibid.: 60.

towards which they are working is no barrier to committing themself to this work (though Scheffler's contention is that their commitment would wither in the absence of a future for humanity). Scheffler asks the same question of creative and scholarly projects that have no obvious practical aim, and responds that '[t]here is something approaching a conceptual connection between valuing something and wanting it to be sustained and preserved'.[31] His thought experiment leads him to suggest that '[r]ather than looming as a blank eternity of nonexistence, the future can be conceptualized with reference to an ongoing social world in which one retains a social identity'.[32] Recall how Horace sees the preservation of his work in terms of cultural continuity: he will ever grow fresh in the praise of posterity *so long as* the pontifex climbs the Capitol with the silent virgin (*usque ego postera / crescam laude recens, dum Capitolium / scandet cum tacita uirgine pontifex*, *Odes* 3.30.7–9). Scheffler views the function of tradition through this lens, and importantly gives it a temporal reach that stretches into the future as well as the past. 'Participation in a tradition is not only an expression of our natural conservatism about values but also a way of achieving a *value-based* relation to those who come after us', he says. 'We can think of our successors as people who will share our values, and ourselves having custodial responsibility for the values that will someday be theirs'.[33] By subsuming our lives, our projects and our individuality into a larger narrative of human history that embraces both past and future, we project our *selves* into the future, and personalize our relation to it.

Scheffler leaves aside the exercise in pure abstraction of his thought experiments to accept in practice that, while humanity will eventually become extinct, crucially it will be at a moment not defined and hopefully distant. He suggests that 'in valuing we lay claim to the future – we arrogate to ourselves the authority to make judgments about how the future *should* unfold. In a sense, valuing is a way of trying to control time'.[34] Scheffler speaks of the future as populated by beings that 'have no determinate identities'; however, values are attributed to them. It is worth thinking about what Virgil attempts in the *Aeneid*: value is sustained by tying us into not simply a larger narrative of human history, but Jupiter's narrative of *imperium sine fine* (1.279), power or empire not delimited by time or space, and constructed with the help of an elaborate scaffolding of a theological world view and a theological afterlife.[35] In his 'Letter to Horace', Brodsky compares

---

[31] Ibid.: 25.   [32] Ibid.: 29.   [33] Ibid.: 33; original emphasis.   [34] Ibid.: 61; original emphasis.
[35] For this distinctively 'metaphysical' take on empire and power, cf. Kennedy 2013: 43–83.

Virgil unfavourably with Horace: 'for all his expansive gestures, your friend, my dear Flaccus, was just craving metaphysical security'.[36] Brodsky describes 'metaphysical security' as 'a contradiction in terms' and feels a greater affinity with Horace's more relaxed attitude (cf. '*so long as* the pontifex climbs the Capitol. . . .'). Alongside values, I would invoke the notion of *interests*. Thus Horace imagines being *spoken of* in the future as 'the first to have brought Aeolian poetry to Italian measures' (*dicar . . . princeps Aeolium carmen ad Italos / deduxisse modos*, Odes 3.30.10–14). This act of dissemination on the part of Horace enables Brodsky to feel there *is* something *between* him with Horace that *mediates* a relationship of communication: a shared *inter-est* in metres – albeit different metres that are historically, linguistically and culturally specific.

In modelling communication with a future populated by the unknown not-yet-existent, the ontological question of what it is to be a human being must now be addressed. Epicureanism has its own very particular answer. It sees human beings as material compounds subject to an impending non-existence when nothing will matter to them. Scheffler's thought experiments have given us some purchase on the dissatisfaction that has often been felt about that Epicurean view of death, and one way it does so is by leading us to question the Epicurean way of thinking about what it means for a human being to exist. In seeking to reduce human beings to a single mode of existence, physics, it succumbs to an idealism of matter. However, to be human is to be something more than a temporary compound constituted by the buzz of atoms in motion. Perhaps this helps to make a point of interest for us with Horace. *Non tu corpus eras sine pectore*, he says to Albius ('you were never a body without soul', 1.4.6), as he then goes on to list at some length the specific attributes that make Albius the person he, distinctively, *is* (6–11), and to advise him to live with his concerns by periodically changing the temporal parameters within which he experiences them (*inter spem curamque, timores inter et iras, / omnem crede diem tibi diluxisse supremum*, 'amid hopes and cares, amid fears and angers, believe that every day that has dawned is your last', 12–13). A temporal thought experiment, might we say, to encourage him to re-assess and re-adjust who (he thinks) he is? As Scheffler suggests, human beings are characterized by concerns that reach towards a future – and a past – in

---

[36] Brodsky 1995: 444, where he also remarks: '[Virgil] had a terrific metaphysical instinct, a real nose for things' spiritual linings . . . Still, whatever his sources were – Pythagoras, Plato's *Phaedrus*, his own fancy – he blows it all for the sake of Caesar's lineage.'

which they themselves do not exist physically. Scheffler does not mention Heidegger, but his intervention, in arguing that questions of being are bound up with time, has been profoundly influential in recent discussions.[37]

Responsibility and Instauration

There has been a noteworthy turn over the past few years to ontological issues, especially from perspectives that emphasize time, in respect of entities coming-into-being and passing-out-of-being.[38] These approaches are noteworthy for the sheer plurality of entities whose existence they entertain. Thus for Markus Gabriel, lots of things exist *in some sense*: 'There are planets, my dreams, evolution, the toilet flush, hair loss, hopes, elementary particles, and even unicorns on the far side of the moon.'[39] As Patrice Maniglier remarks: '"To be" does not mean the same thing for a Higgs boson as it does for the Argentinian peso, but both equally *are*, and the task of the metaphysician is to exhibit that equality and diversity.'[40] Unicorns on the far side of the moon exist in the field of sense of Gabriel's argument, just as a pig with the features and Epicurean inclinations of Horace exists in the field of sense of *Epistles* 1.4. The task of metaphysics is seen not as the exploration of Being (capital B) in a monolithic Parmenidean sense, but as an attempt to account for the multiplicity of things that exist alongside others *in one field of sense or another*.[41] This recent turn resists reduction of being to one mode of existence (whether that be Parmenides, Plato, Epicurus or, for that matter, Heidegger). Thus Bruno Latour explores not existence *per se*, but *modes of existence*, not what exists, but how what exists exists – comes into existence and ceases to exist. He posits at least fifteen such modes, which variously intersect.[42] One of these he calls **FICTION**, which includes our capacity to generate the 'scripts', as Latour calls them, in which we organize our existence and are organized in turn (**ORGANIZATION** is another of

---

[37] For Heidegger, the human being (*Dasein*) is characterized by what he calls 'care' (*Sorge*).
[38] Hacking 2002 surveys some of these approaches and suggests the catch-all title 'historical ontology'. I discuss these issues in detail in Kennedy forthcoming.
[39] Gabriel 2015a: 1.   [40] Maniglier 2014: 42; original emphasis.   [41] Cf. Gabriel 2015b.
[42] Latour's fifteen 'modes of existence' (summarized 2013: 488–9): Reproduction, Metamorphosis, Habit, Technology, Fiction, Reference, Politics, Law, Religion, Attachment, Organization, Morality, Network, Preposition, Double Click. These fifteen modes are explicitly not meant to be definitive, rather prompts to argument. When referring explicitly to one of Latour's suggested modes, I shall distinguish it by bold font and capitalization.

Latour's modes).⁴³ *Epistles* 1.4, an invitation that may or may not be accepted, is just such a script, which may, in ways that cannot be known fully in advance, affect Albius' being. Since the effects on another cannot be fully calculated in advance, responsibility (the sense of being answerable) is involved in making such interventions, as Peters reminded us. Another mode is **ATTACHMENT**: 'We *are* what we are attached to', says Latour; these attachments – family, friends, rivals, localities, culture, values, scripts (recall Albius once more) – are tied up with our desires, needs and lack and are, as Latour likes to put it, anthropogenic, they *make* us what we *are*.⁴⁴

We are born ('thrown', as Heidegger would put it) into a **NETWORK** of attachments which we negotiate during our lives and leave our impress upon, even as our bodies pass out of being. **ATTACHMENT** is closely associated with the social or collective dimension of our existence of which Scheffler speaks when he talks of our 'participation in a tradition'.⁴⁵ Latour suggests we not think of human beings as if they existed in and of themselves – thus somewhat less than the indivisible individual of much social theory and some philosophical schools. Within these modes of existence, being human is a temporal process that extends into the past and the future; it is also a relational process, with being not inherent in any one person or thing, but distributed across its attachments. Latour suggests that '[t]here is no better definition of any existent whatsoever beyond th[e] list of the other beings through which it must, it can, it seeks to pass'.⁴⁶ This leads us to perhaps the crucial feature of Latour's metaphysics. He studies, he says, not being-as-being, but being-as-other. Being-as-being 'seeks support in a *substance* that will ensure its continuity' (one thinks, above all, of Aristotle's *ousia*), whereas beings-as-other 'depend not on a substance on which they can rely but on a *subsistence* that they have to seek out at their own risk'.⁴⁷ Being-as-other makes for a tremendously

---

⁴³ For 'scripts', which can be any form of communication (conversations, texts, pictures and so on), cf. Latour 2013: 390–6. The 'alteration' brought about by **FICTION** is to 'multiply worlds'.

⁴⁴ We *are* at any moment at the intersection of many scripts which play upon our needs and desires – far more than we are ever conscious of, and only some of which we ourselves initiate: think of advertisements, especially now in social media platforms like Facebook, which mines the attachments we wittingly and unwittingly register, the better to direct scripts at us personally, scripts in this case that are not directly traceable to any personalized agency, but serially generated through those quasi-autonomous, but deeply ideological, modes of **ORGANIZATION** called algorithms. It is sometimes said that entities like Facebook know who we are better than we know ourselves; rather Facebook seeks to make us who we are – with little of the sense of responsibility I shall go on to discuss.

⁴⁵ Scheffler 2013: 33.

⁴⁶ Latour 2013: 425. He suggests his metaphysics is constituted around the verb 'to have' rather than 'to be'; the being that *possesses* attachments and the being that is *possessed* by those attachments.

⁴⁷ Ibid.: 162; emphasis original.

fragile existence. Our selves, distributed across time and the attachments that make us up, are vulnerable things, prone to psychic disorders and malaises: 'If there is anything guaranteed to produce insanity, it is an autonomous self, without attachments and without an owner; it will be left without care, without defense against attacks.'[48] Might Albius, either absorbed in poetic composition or wandering in the woods and thinking about philosophy without talking to anybody (cf. *tacitus*, 1.4.4), be in danger of becoming, as we might put it, a bit *detached*? Or Brodsky, the long-term exile conscious that his failing health means that he is not long for this life, who is reduced to thinking about talking to himself in the mirror, an act that may only deepen his sense of alienation from himself?

The distributed self craves the (temporality of) presence of the other. This is associated by Latour with a different mode of existence, the one he calls **RELIGION**, the trajectory of which is 'the engendering of persons', and is associated by him with what he calls 'the passage of words that *make the subject exist* as a *unified person*',[49] words that 'gather us in and straighten us up by *addressing* us unmistakably: "It's you, it's me, it's us."'[50] He suggests you think of words expressing love:

> Words of love have the particular feature of endowing the person to whom they are addressed with the existence and unity that person has lacked ... to close one's ears to these words – or never pronounce them for others – is to disappear for good, or to make the others disappear for good. What could be more miserable than never being the intended recipient of a loving word: how could anyone who had never received such gifts feel like a person? Who could feel like *someone* without having been addressed in this way? What wretchedness, never to have aroused anything but indifference! For we don't draw the certainty of existing and being close, of being unified and complete, from our own resources, but from elsewhere: we receive it as an always unmerited gift that circulates through the narrow channel of these salutary words. Our experience as recipients of such gifts is what gives us the confidence to start over, again and again.[51]

From the perspective of Horace, as he issues his invitation, Albius' situation is unclear to him (it may be of serious concern, it may not), a response is awaited, and may even not come, but the crucial thing is that the words have been addressed – words that '*resuscitate* those to whom they are

---

[48] Ibid.: 302. [49] Ibid.: 310; original emphasis.
[50] Ibid.: 302; he continues: 'The nuance may be subtle, but it doesn't escape those who are involved in intimate interactions and who have to sort out this crossing in the tumult of crisis.'
[51] Ibid.: 302–3; original emphasis. Contrariwise, hate crimes are ontological: attacks on human beings and the attachments that make them who they are.

addressed'[52] and work to ensure continuity in being. For Brodsky too: Horace will never know 'Brodsky' exists, but through his texts Brodsky feels addressed nonetheless. It's me, it's you, it's us. He has a friend in Quintus Horatius Flaccus, and Brodsky's faltering reading of Horace's texts resuscitates him – and them.

'The confidence to start over and over again'; words that '*resuscitate* those to whom they are addressed': phrases like these mark the fragile subsistence of beings-as-other of which Latour speaks. He is referring to human beings here, but his remarks resonate strongly also for the entities we have been most concerned with in this essay. Values, traditions, texts can be viewed as beings-as-other too, never existing 'in themselves' and which rely for their subsistence on acts of resuscitation. If, with Latour, we see being as processual and relational, we should not think of human beings as atomized individuals, 'as if they were always points of emission and reception of scripts'.[53] This should give us pause when we speak, as we habitually do, of the 'point of reception' and even 'reception studies'. Latour prefers to speak of *instauration*, a term he has resuscitated from a largely forgotten philosopher of a previous generation, Étienne Souriau (1892–1979).[54] Souriau's concern is with 'the existential incompleteness of every thing':

> Nothing, not even our own selves, is given to us other than in a sort of half-light, a penumbra in which only incompleteness can be made out, where nothing possesses either full presence or evident patuity, where there is neither total accomplishment, nor plenary existence.[55]

Latour picks up with enthusiasm Souriau's reflections on instauration as the mode of existence of a work-to-be-made. An artist is 'never the creator,'[56] but always the instaurator of a work that comes to him but that, without him, would never proceed toward existence. If there is something that a sculptor never asks himself, it is this critical question: "Am I the author of the statue, or is the statue its own author?"'[57] When is a painting, sculpture, poem or essay 'finished'? Latour asks us to recall the

---

[52] Ibid.: 303; original emphasis. [53] Ibid.: 422.
[54] Latour, with his frequent collaborator Isabelle Stengers, oversaw the re-publication of Souriau's *Les différents modes d'existence* of 1943 and a lecture of 1956, 'L'oeuvre à faire' (translated as 'Of the Mode of Existence of the Work-to-be-made'), and equipped them with a sizeable introduction: Souriau 2015.
[55] Ibid.: 220.
[56] By which Latour means the sole point of emission, a God-like figure who can see the whole work in advance of its accomplishment.
[57] Latour 2013: 160.

painter of *La Belle Noiseuse* in Balzac's story 'The Unknown Masterpiece', who

> ruined everything in his painting by getting up in the dark and adding one last touch that, alas, the painting *didn't require*. You have to go back again and again, but each time you risk losing it all ... Everything depends on what you are going to do next, and you alone have the competence to do it, and *you don't know how* ... You're not in control, and yet there's no one else to take charge. It's enough to make anyone wake up at night in a cold sweat. Anyone who hasn't felt this terror hasn't measured the abyss of ignorance at whose edge creation totters.[58]

The emergent *being* of the work-to-be-made signals a lack of ultimate control and demands a responsibility that the term *instauration* gestures towards: 'the act of instauration has to provide *the opportunity to encounter beings capable of worrying you*',[59] the obligation to do your best by them. As the instaurator of *Epistle* 1.4, Horace may have pondered whether he had written a word too many or too little, responsible not only for the 'well-*being*' of the script but that of its recipient. This metaphysics of multiple, emergent ontologies feels very different from a world view that would oppose *one* objective reality to an autonomous and sovereign human subjectivity. What Latour says of the 'point' of emission in respect of instauration can be extended to the 'point' of reception as well, where the distributed self is no less responsible for beings that cannot be captured in their essence or entirety, and must exercise, and be exercised by, a similar concern. The being of a text, script or work of art is fragile, all too likely to collapse into disappearance and non-being, its subsistence never guaranteed. Where human beings were concerned, Latour looked to the mode of existence he called **RELIGION**, with its words of love, to engender a sense of personhood. That mode seems also in play in those acts of instauration we call reception, and likewise works to engender a sense of presence amidst the flux of experience. The process ontology Latour describes has affinities with certain approaches to theology, the subject of Latour's doctoral dissertation, in which he argued that God is not a transcendent absolute, but the very being that reveals its presence in a moment of revelation when one exegesis is resumed by another.[60] The subsistence and presence of a porker from Epicurus' herd emerge from such acts of instauration, the readings of Albius and unknown others yet-to-be; while the presence of Horace can be felt by a lonely emigré under the shadow of his own impending

---

[58] Ibid.: 160–1; original emphasis.   [59] Ibid.: 161; original emphasis.
[60] On this, see de Vries 2016: 17–20.

non-being, reading a Russian translation in a chilly house far from his roots as the twentieth century draws to a close.

Appendix: Horace *Epistle* 1.4

> Albi, nostrorum sermonum candide iudex,
> quid nunc te dicam facere in regione Pedana?
> scribere quod Cassi Parmensis opuscula uincat,
> an tacitum siluas inter reptare salubris,
> curantem quidquid dignum sapiente bonoque est?
> non tu corpus eras sine pectore. di tibi formam,
> di tibi diuitias dederunt artemque fruendi.
> quid uoueat dulci nutricula maius alumno,
> qui sapere et fari possit quae sentiat, et cui
> gratia, fama, ualetudo contingat abunde,
> et mundus uictus non deficiente crumina?
> inter spem curamque, timores inter et iras,
> omnem crede diem tibi diluxisse supremum.
> grata superueniet quae non sperabitur hora.
> me pinguem et nitidum bene curata cute uises
> cum ridere uoles Epicuri de grege porcum.

Albius, shining critic of my 'chats', what shall I say you now are doing in your country at Pedum? Writing something to surpass the pieces of Cassius of Parma? Or strolling quietly amid the healthful woods, and musing on all that is worthy of one wise and good? (5) Never were you a body without soul. The gods gave you beauty, the gods gave you wealth, and the art of enjoying it. For what more would a fond nurse pray for her sweet ward, who like you has the ability to think aright and utter his thoughts, and to whose lot there falls abundantly favour, fame, health (10), decent means, and a never failing purse? Amid hope and care, amid fears and angers, believe that every day that has dawned is your last. Welcome will come to you the addition of an hour unhoped for. As for me, when you want a laugh, you will find me in fine fettle, fat and sleek, (15), a porker from Epicurus' herd.

AFTERWORD

Lights Out

Emily Gowers

The party's over and the guests have gone. How to wrap up these meditations on loss, silence, longing, haunting and not being there, when they already have a thumping introduction and a near-perfect ending? First thoughts from a distance (though I *was* at the original conference, with its fizzing conversations): what a spur to creativity absence is. Without it, what need would there be for words to conjure presence or fill the page with descriptions, lists, variations and other gestures towards completeness? Erasmus understood this in *De Copia*: where would all those messenger speeches be, or accounts of yesterday's debauchery, or longing letters from one shore to another? Without absence, there is no stretch for the imagination to make. As Ábel Tamás puts it: 'Textual absence is one of the most effective "presence effects" that a literary work can generate.' In that paradoxical frame of mind, think how many figures of speech are compensations or circumlocutions for absence (some of them richly explored in these pages by Briguglio, Hardie and others): allegory, aposiopesis, *ecphrasis, enargeia,* euphemism, irony, litotes, metonymy, paraphrase, *praeteritio, prosopopoeia, recusatio,* simile, synecdoche . . . And how sometimes, sparingly used, the sheer loss of words can open up a drop onto the sublime: *quem iam tibi Troia. . .*[1]

Feeling absence lets us take the oblique view or the ironic view, see things two ways at once. Erik Fredericksen asks of a photograph in Anne Carson's *Nox*: 'When we see a picture of an empty chair, for example, are we looking at the presence of a chair or the absence of someone who might have been sitting in it?' The unspoken answer: the frame makes it both at the same time, like those photos of lonely shoes in city gutters, sole survivors of coupledom and reminders of their owners' once purposeful direction. 'Conspicuous by its absence' is a phrase Ellen O'Gorman traces to the letter of Victorian politics, but its spirit we know above all from the glaring textual 'appearance' of the busts of Brutus and Cassius missing

---

[1] 'whom already to you [at] Troy. . .', *Aen.* 3.340.

from Junia's funeral, where Tacitus makes havoc of the Roman cult of monuments and *imagines*: 'They shone out all the more for not being seen' (*Ann.* 3.76). O'Gorman pits this against Tacitus' ironic account of Augustus' funeral, where Julius Caesar's image is absent – but for a different reason altogether, because he is already a god.

In this volume about unspeaking, absence makes its presence felt in multiple ways: in the rush of eloquence that compensates for the loss of Republican free speech (Winter); in the explosive squibs of the anonymous (Del Giovane); not to mention the sullen hovering of slaves (Fitzgerald) – the corner of the eye that always needs scratching.[2] In imperial times, it is just as often the emperor who is the elephant in the room: in Seneca's *Letters* (as Catharine Edwards shows) or in Persius' *Satires*, where the legend goes that the inflammatory 'King Midas has ass's ears' was scrubbed out in favour of a bland 'Who doesn't have ass's ears?' by his posthumous editor (Suet. *Vita Persi*). In Marcus Aurelius' *Meditations*, a ruler even rules out autocracy to showcase Stoic self-rule (Henderson). The Romans had a system for still mattering *in absentia*: the *ratio absentis*, the right to canvass for election from outside Rome, which worked infamously to Julius Caesar's advantage.[3] Is that also how language works for Ovid in exile, which should be such living hell for a narcissist cut off from his supply, the literate populace of Rome? Against all odds, faintness and lack make Ovidian expression abundant and demanding, echoing as it does off the hard Pontine rocks.[4] In elegy, separation and frustration make the heart grow fonder – or, as Propertius doesn't put it (now that Heyworth has excised the couplet): 'Passion is always more ardent when lovers are absent; long supply blunts the appeal of persistent suitors.' (2.33b [43–4]). Even Ovid's cure for love, Victoria Rimell reveals, is just a back step in the ongoing dance of desire.

Much is said here about how reflections on absence in ancient Rome mimic our own relationship to antiquity, as if we were archaeologists clambering over the ruins, piecing fragments into meaningful mosaics and plugging textual lacunae, or hopeless romantics pining like Ariadne or Dido after unresponsive deserters.[5] Pompeii is the cenotaph that guidebooks and novellas can never resist repopulating, packing its hollow enclosures with imaginary bodies (Paul); post-modernists like Carson pay homage to antiquity by constructing purpose-built fragments of

---

[2] Plautus' phrase (*Persa* 11 *lippo oculo*). [3] Gruen 1974: 449–98.
[4] As if *ante emoriar quam sit copia nostri* ('I'd sooner die before you get your fill of me', *Met.* 3.391) had become *sit tibi copia nostri* ('May you get your fill of me', *Met.* 3.392).
[5] See Billings 2010: 21 on the 'erotics of reception'.

their own. There is much, too, about how the Romans conjure feelings of absence in relation to their own past: imperial writers imagining the sunlit uplands of a never-real Republic, for example. Less is said about the relationship with Greece, above all Roman nostalgia for the lost perfection of the symposium and for Homer as the author who said it all already, out loud, twanging his live wires at some ancient feast. Such visions of primitive plenitude are of course a mirage: with his capsule plots, arbitrary beginnings and endings, microcosmic Shield and appeals for a sturdier constitution, even Homer had gestured towards a more distant totality that could never be recovered.[6] But the feeling of not having been at yesterday's party may be a particularly Roman legacy. Catullus' fantasy of being there ('wanting to see the light, to speak with you and be with you', *cupiens uidere lucem, / ut tecum loquerer, simulque ut essem*, 50.12–13) is directed as much towards the swooning Sapphic stanzas about to be revived in the poem that follows as it is to last night's fun with Calvus. If erotic love needs a minimal gap in order to function healthily, so creative juices flow all the more freely the morning after.

With the Romans (and the later Greeks) stuck like this between 'them' and us, questions of perspective arise. Who exactly is absent, and from whom? Virgil, who had such 'a terrific metaphysical instinct, a real nose for things' spiritual linings', put his finger on this very pulse, and one need look no further for examples.[7] 'The magic of an inflected language', in Roland Austin's words, allows Dido to 'lock Aeneas in her thoughts', in an extraordinary collocation whose refusal to be translated brings home our own separation from the original:[8]

> illum <u>absens absentem</u> auditque uidetque   (*Aen.* 4.83)
>
> <u>Absent</u>, she sees and hears him <u>absent</u>

In a banal sense, this is a neat Latin way of saying 'when the two of them weren't together'. But if it's clear enough that she feels *his* absence, how is *she* absent? Because her subjectivity is being displaced by someone else's?[9] Because in revenge or nightmare she sees herself coming from somewhere else or already left behind, 'always being left alone by herself' (*semperque relinqui / sola sibi*, 4.466–7)? Dido's paradoxical threats, 'In my absence,

---

[6] Ford 1992: 57–89.   [7] Joseph Brodsky, quoted by Kennedy.
[8] Austin 1955: 47. This is Virgil's first use of *absens*. On his inversion of the idiom *praesens praesentem*, 'right before my eyes', see Serv. ad loc.; Wills 1996: 283; Hardie 2002: 12.
[9] Giusti 2017a: 5 discusses *Aen.* 4.83 in connection with Foucault's idea of the mirror as a heterotopia through which 'I discover my absence from the place where I am'.

I will follow you with dark fires' (*sequar atris ignibus absens*, 4.384) and 'I will be present as a ghost' (*umbra ... adero*, 4.386), speak for all women who feel they do not fully belong in men's stories (Bellei). Yet once Virgil slipped that invented African winter into a fold of historical time, his Dido came so close to hijacking the narrative – Tyrian and female, but more vital, more vocal than any faceless, taciturn hero.[10]

When the cat's away, the mice will play: absent Achilles, absent Aeneas, Odysseus absent but present in his own house – all make room for other players to flex their muscles.[11] Aeneas was huge at Troy, he tells us in his unreliable messenger speech (*pars magna fui*, 'I played a large role', *Aen.* 2.5), but later he can afford to depart from his own saga for an entire book, so clearing a space for unknown lovers to perish (in)gloriously and for his son to kill his first man.[12] Statius' *Achilleid* prepares its hero for Iliadic downtime by removing him from one epic to play prima donna in another: *omnis in absentem belli manus ardet Achillem* ('All the forces of war burn for absent Achilles', *Ach.* 1.473).[13] As for Odysseus, his semi-truancy from his epic is often signalled by the deictic pronoun (*e*)*keinos* ('that man'). Here is Anna Bonifazi on its many cognitive and pragmatic meanings, all of which conjure an absentee's latent presence:[14]

> that one whom you already know and who now is becoming a relevant piece of information; in particular:
> that one is now present to my eyes;
> that one whom all of us know about;
> that one I/we am/are venerating;
> that one I/we am/are venerating and lamenting over, since he is dead;
> that one I/we are detesting or that one I/we want to distance;
> that one that cannot be mentioned by name (but you all know whom I/we refer to);
> that one, that is, Odysseus.

In turn, Virgil's *ille Aeneas* (*Aen.* 1.617) acquires a further significance: not just 'that man Aeneas' but 'that Aeneas you already know from Homer'.[15]

Absence, as much as presence, then, is the key to recognition.[16] Virgil's Andromache, speaker of the ungraspable *quem iam tibi Troia...*, sees her

---

[10] See Giusti 2018: 170–6 on the extra winter; Feeney 1983 on the taciturn hero. NB Homer's Aeneas had already normalized masculine reticence by dismissing women who quarrel in the middle of the street (*Il.* 20.254).
[11] See Pezzini here on proxy characters in comedy.
[12] See Wiltshire 1999 on *Aeneid* 9 and 'the man who was not there'.
[13] For Michelakis 2002, Achilles' absence is a fertile 'problem' for Greek tragedy and satyr play.
[14] Bonifazi 2012: 67.   [15] Cf. *Aen.* 2.274–5 *illo / Hectore*.
[16] Cave 1988: 22: 'Recognition always reaches back analeptically to earlier narratives.'

dead son conveniently superimposed on nephew Ascanius: 'O, the living image of my Astyanax. That's just how his eyes were, his hands, his face', *Aen.* 3.489–90. At the same time, her words regress to an equivalent Homeric moment: Menelaus seeing Odysseus in Telemachus. Just so, Elena Greco, narrator of the novels of Elena Ferrante, describes encountering her lost lover Nino in the face of his child by another woman.[17] For all that he spots *himself* in pictures from his Trojan past, Aeneas looks through or away from Dido when she first comes into view (so Viola Starnone persuades us), thus galvanizing Virgil's cheated successors into supplying the lovers with that resounding 'love at first sight' which would cast them as Achilles and Penthesilea in the picture from which Aeneas' eyes never stray. Yet *absens absentem* pinpoints the blind spots that will always be there for two lovers who converge so briefly ('together', 'to the same cave') before looking past each other again.[18]

Not looking, and not recognizing, is just as much this hero's destiny. Juno throws back Venus' words with contempt: 'So what if "Aeneas is absent and in the dark": let him be absent and in the dark.'[19] He will, for instance, never cross paths or meet eyes with that other Amazon, Camilla. Sergio Casali (an important absent friend to textual absence) has detected in Daedalus' unfinished Theseid at Cumae the blatant unmentionable, that red flag to a bull – Ariadne – which makes the Sibyl sweep Aeneas so hastily on, only for him to run smack into abandoned Dido soon after.[20] Yet even Aeneas' vision of Dido's ghost is no more than a partial recovering: he half-sees her, receding from his consciousness, like a man who 'sees or thinks he sees' a crescent moon through clouds (6.451–4).[21] After all this build-up comes a supreme moment of ecphrastic *non*-recognition, which invites us to fill in or at least mind the teasing gap ourselves. Aeneas, a man wearing a flaming helmet, sees a man wearing a flaming helmet at the centre of the shield Venus gives him, and this time he doesn't say: Look, that's me.[22]

For infinitely receding absence-presence, it's hard to beat the Cyclops episode in *Aeneid* 3, where Virgil reaches towards epic origins by recalling a Homeric event that celebrates lack: Odysseus in and out of the Cyclops' cave; 'No-man' versus a monster with a missing eye (unmentioned in Homer), then

---

[17] Dido dreams of a little Aeneas, 'whose face will even so recall yours' (*qui te tamen ore referret*, *Aen.* 4.329).
[18] Aeneas <u>unaque</u> miserrima Dido, *Aen.* 4.117; <u>speluncam</u> Dido dux et Troianus <u>eandem</u> / deuenient, *Aen.* 4.124–5.
[19] "*Aeneas ignarus abest*': *ignarus et absit*', *Aen.* 10.85. [20] Casali 1995.
[21] Virgil might have agreed with Étienne Souriau: 'Nothing, not even ourselves, is given to us other than in a sort of half-light'; see Kennedy.
[22] *Aen.* 8.620 ~ *Aen.* 8.680–1.

no eye. The experience is conjured up through vivid *enargeia*, just as Odysseus recalled it to the Phaeacians, when Achaemenides, left behind by his ruthless leader (a nobody in Odysseus' story, even as 'Ulixes' is now absent from his), gives his Trojan rescuers a chilling eye-witness account of the Cyclops's brutality (*uidi egomet*, 'I saw with my own eyes', 3.623). But then, unexpectedly, blind Polyphemus heaves once more into view, as oppressively present as his belching one-eyed counterpart, Etna. First he plants his footsteps (*uestigia*, 659, 669) on the beach – like Virgil groping towards Homer's infinite ocean. Then he wades out to sea by 'feeling' it ('After he felt the waves get deep', *postquam altos <u>tetigit</u> fluctus*, 662).[23]

Just before these words sits one of Virgil's notorious half-lines, barely a half-line at that: *solamenque mali* ('consolation for his woes', 661). It describes the giant's flock of ewes, his only delight (*sola uoluptas*, 660), now that the rams are dead. Sparrow calls it 'an indication, and the only indication, that the passage in which it occurs is unfinished'. Horsfall notes 'paronomasia between *sola* and *solamen*', while Heyworth and Morwood supply the etymological point (consolation lightens isolation). All ignore the temptation to read something expressive into the textual void that follows, embedded though it is among phrases that fill the gap where the monster's eye used to be, describing either the hole – *luminis effossi* ('dug out eye') and *cui lumen ademptum* ('whose eye was gone') – or the props that inadequately replace it – *trunca pinus* (pine crutch) and *sola uoluptas* (the sheep).[24] Even if an echoed 'whose eye was gone' were supplied here from several lines above, that still leaves a gap of one *metrum*: one eye, already a lack, reduced to a gaping hole?[25]

Most immediately, the blank suggests hiatus: cognitive, temporal and spatial. A blind man leans on his sheep, faltering between sand and water – before he plunges in:

> solamenque mali.
> postquam altos tetigit fluctus et ad aequora uenit...   (*Aen.* 3.661–2)
>
> consolation for his woes.
> After he felt the waves get deep and reached the open sea...

---

[23] *pace* Horsfall, and Henry before him, *tetigit* doesn't just mean 'reached' if you are blind.
[24] Heyworth and Morwood 2017: 51 include it with half-lines where 'joins have not been resolved', rather than those that are 'strikingly effective' (such as 5.639–40 *funem / rumpite...*, 'break the cable...'). See Tamás in this volume on 4.400 *infabricata fugae studio* ('[logs] unhewn, in their eagerness for flight'). For the remaining eye as solitary, cf. 3.636 [*lumen*] *solum*.
[25] Modern editors reject the supplement *de collo fistula pendet*.

But out of this hole, this 'unbearable void' (Starnone's phrase), more meanings keep on erupting, the further we care to burrow into what Ellen Oliensis (sadly, a late withdrawal from the conference) calls the 'textual unconscious'.[26] After all, this isn't just a sequel to Achaemenides' tale of grief: it's also a section of Aeneas' memoir, warmed up for Dido. The encounter with the Cyclops is the prelude to a further trauma, a father's unpredicted death. All too soon, Aeneas will uncannily approximate his description of Polyphemus' sheep when he mourns Anchises as 'the lightener of all my anxiety and suffering' (*omnis curae casusque leuamen*, 3.709). With this later sorrow in mind, the repressed matter of the Cyclops episode, which describes, according to some, wreckage from the symbolic castration of a giant father figure,[27] floats to the surface: *lumen ademptum* swims into focus as a textual echo of an immortal moment of grief, Catullus' regret for the light of life taken from his beloved brother (Cat. 68b.93), while *sola ... uoluptas* will be exposed as the temporary balm that staves off a son's imminent loss (Evander to doomed Pallas: *care puer, mea sola et sera uoluptas*, 'Dear boy, my only, late delight', *Aen.* 8.581). This makes the textual gap after *solamenque mali* far more than just an icon of physical maiming. It opens up a meaningful hole in Aeneas' speech, a sublime loss of words as he recognizes his own grief in another's.

No surprise, then, that the looming absent-presence of the Cyclops left such a cavernous space for creative in-filling.[28] Ovid would conjure up another survivor, Macareus, and so prolong the chain of belatedness.[29] Horace's 'Journey to Brundisium' (*Satire* 1.5) took a different path in the shadow of the *Odyssey*, yielding a catalogue of mutilations and lost landmarks, among them Horace himself, pedestrian Cyclops and blinkered observer of contemporary politics, and Venusia, his Ithaca, occluded but erupting in a rash of v-words.[30] Notoriously, the 'castrated' monster would rear its head again as the one-eyed trouser-snake in Ausonius' naughty late-antique pastiche of Virgilian fragments: *monstrum horrendum informe ingens cui lumen ademptum*, 'a monster, terrible, ugly, vast, whose eye was gone' (*Aen.* 3.658 = *Cento Nuptialis* 108). In the twentieth century, something of the Cyclops informs John Banville's essay on the obstacle that is James Joyce, for him a towering figure, one of those unfathomable forebears ('*mysterious* at their core') among whom he also includes Virgil.

---

[26] Oliensis 2009: 6.   [27] Miller 2003; Glenn 1978.
[28] See e.g. Davis 2008: 188–207 on Dryden's cyclopean extravagances.   [29] Hinds 1998: 111–15.
[30] Gowers 2012: 207–8.

Joyce is the 'great looming Easter island effigy of the Father', 'that stone Nobodaddy at my shoulder'. Coming after is a mixed blessing:

> When I think of Joyce I am split in two. To one side there falls the reader, kneeling speechless in filial admiration, and love; to the other side, however, the writer stands, gnawing his knuckles, not a son, but a survivor. (Banville 1990: 73–4)

Such conflicted feelings about succession – reverence, nostalgia, revenge, competition, inadequacy, fear, grief, anger, survivor's guilt – are equally familiar from Roman writers' encounters with their absent sources. All ghosts are insubstantial, but the Romans seem peculiarly aware of their tendency to clutter the vacated spaces of Hellenic culture with all-too-material 'stuff'. Still, the gap between Greek soul and Roman body could be a productive one. If it hadn't been for the broken bridge that interrupted a lover's journey home in Plautus' *Casina*, so the prologue tells us, a grossly physical Roman farce would have been just another clichéd Hellenizing romance. As it is, the telltale vegetable bulge under a fake bride's dress makes its presence all too felt, while Casina herself, elusive object of desire, is never seen, only smelled, like the exotic whiff of cinnamon in her name. As Giuseppe Pezzini points out, this is a play that clings in re-performance to the optimism of its glory days (*flos poetarum*) and consoles itself with a fantasy of continuity with yesterday's winners: 'Still, even though they're gone, they're as useful as if they were present' (*sed tamen apsentes [poetae] prosunt pro praesentibus*, *Cas.* 20). Like the Cyclops, *Casina* incidentally attunes us to a hierarchy among the senses where effects of presence are concerned: sight, taste and touch coming above sound and smell.[31]

On the other hand, Roman writers are every bit as conscious that they will one day be literature's absentees.[32] Vitruvius, for example, imagines a future reading community that bridges time with 'face-to-face' conversations, more substantial in virtual form than they could ever be in reality. In so doing, he hints at his own hopes for communication with posterity, by analogy with those recently departed:

> Many also, born in time to come, will seem with Lucretius to investigate *The Nature of Things*, as it were face to face (*coram*), or with Cicero, *The Art of the Orator*; many of our future descendants will converse with Varro *On The Latin Language*; no less, either, will many scholars, deliberating with the thinkers of Greece, seem to hold private conversations with them (*secretos*

---

[31] See O'Gorman on the 'sensory deprivation' of imperial politics.
[32] See Kennedy on Horace; cf. Fowler 2000: 193–4 on Ausonius *Ep.* 37.

cum his uidebuntur habere sermones). In a word, the ideas of scientific writers who are absent in the body, old and yet ever new, are present at our counsels and investigations; and all have greater authority (*maiores auctoritates*) than if they were present with us. Vitr. 9 *praef.* 17

Thanks to the accidents of survival (perhaps even helped by his canonizations here), Vitruvius' predictions came true, except for Varro's 'Latin Tongue', cut short like Cicero's. But could we still dream of a far less fragmented community of texts, one that included not just the much-lamented losses of Latin literature – Republican tragedy, Varius' *Thyestes* and Ovid's *Medea*, most of Ennius, Livy and Petronius, the end of Tacitus' *Histories* and *Annals*, Agrippina's memoirs – not just the voices of the crushed and silent, but even a fantastical counterfactual library of never written works: Ovid's resumed gigantomachy or uninterrupted coitus with Corinna; Virgil's late cosmological work and completed gardening poem; months 7–12 of the *Fasti*; Tacitus' history of the present day; or Statius' Achilles led all the way through Troy and out the other side to meet his Penthesilea? All those *ecphrases* that point to paths not taken – re-runs of old material, propaganda, entire sagas or universes – would be blown into blockbusters in their own right. On second thoughts, would we really want Latin literature complete? Doesn't what's left have, for better or worse, 'greater authority' (*maiores auctoritates*), because we like to believe that the fittest have (mostly) survived the 'crises of selection' faced first by their (mostly male) authors, then by their transmitters?[33]

In his 'Letter to Horace', discussed here by Duncan Kennedy, Joseph Brodsky is eloquent about the loneliness of the long-distance reader who, as far as antiquity is concerned, has never existed and never will. When Kennedy responds with a brighter metaphysical conviction that we do attain presence as distributed selves through our attachments to other presences, past and future, he sounds remarkably like James McNamara on the scattering of 'x's on the Roman imperial map ('small bright spots of knowledge amidst a vast expanse of thicket') or Elena Ferrante on the literary community that binds lonely women ('We are ... interconnected ... we are a crowd of others'). Absent, we hear and see them absent: *apparent rari nantes in gurgite uasto* (*Aen.* 1.118). Don Fowler (a towering absent friend to Roman absence, whose voice is still so present in his writing) saw antiquity's ruins, both textual and monumental, not as an end point but as a starting point on our 'journey back', a stimulus for rebuilding.[34] At the time of writing, a small town in California with an

---

[33] The term is Ford's (1992: 71). [34] Fowler 2000: 199.

inauspicious name has been devastated by wildfires: Magalia, 'Cottages', is originally a Punic word, given by Virgil to the makeshift huts that Carthage will displace (1.421), then proleptically revert to (4.259), in the *Aeneid*. A new-world perspective extends the ancient ironies of city-building, but at the same time the old world tilts a little more on its axis. To adopt the less passive model of reception that Kennedy proposes, every time we meet those absent friends, we aren't just taking them in: we're also setting out with them all over again on another sea.

Bibliography

Adams, J. N. 1982. *The Latin Sexual Vocabulary*. London.
  1999. *The Poets of Bu Njem: Language, Culture and the Centurionate*, JRS 89: 109–34.
Adorno, T. 1990. *Negative Dialectics*, trans. by E. B. Ashton. London.
Ahl, F. 1984. 'The Art of Safe Criticism in Greece and Rome', *AJP* 105: 174–208.
Albrecht, M. von 1999. 'The Art of Mirroring in Virgil's *Aeneid*', in Hardie, P. (ed.) *Virgil. Critical Assessments of Classical Authors*. London and New York, 1–12.
Allison, P. 2004. *Pompeian Households. An Analysis of the Material Culture*. Los Angeles.
Altman, J. G. 1982. *Epistolarity. Approaches to a Form*. Columbus.
Anderson, J. G. C. 1938 *Cornelii Taciti de origine et situ Germanorum*. Oxford.
Ankersmit, F. R. 2005. *Sublime Historical Experience*. Stanford.
Aricò, G. 1987. 'Analecta scaenica', in *Filologia e forme letterarie. Studi offerti a Francesco Della Corte*, I, Urbino, 201–12.
Arnott, W. G. 2003. 'Diphilus' Κληρούμενοι and Plautus' *Casina*', in Raffaelli, R. and Tontini, A. (eds.) *Lecturae Plautinae Sarsinates VI, Casina*. Urbino, 23–44.
Ash, R. 2014. 'Act Like a German! Tacitus *Germania* and National Characterisation in the Historical Works', in Devillers, O. (ed.) *Les* opera minora *et le développement de l'historiographie tacitéenne*. Bordeaux, 185–200.
  2018. (ed.) *Tacitus Annals XV*. Cambridge.
Augoustakis, A. 2016. *Statius, Thebaid 8*. Oxford.
Austin, J. L. 1975. *How to Do Things with Words*. Cambridge, MA.
Austin, R. G. 1955. *P. Vergili Maronis Aeneidos Liber Quartus*. Oxford.
  1971. *P. Vergili Maronis Aeneidos Liber Primus*. Oxford.
Avallone, R. 1963. *Mecenate, con edizione dei frammenti*. Naples.
Baldwin, B. 2005. 'Nero the Poet' in Deroux, C. (ed.) *Studies in Latin Literature and Roman History* XII. Brussels, 307–18.
Baltussen, H. and Davis, P. J. 2015 (eds.) *The Art of Veiled Speech: from Aristotle to Hobbes*. Philadephia.
Baltussen, H and Davis, P. J. 2015. 'Parrhesia, Free Speech and Self-Censorship', in Baltussen and Davis (eds.), 1–17.

Banville, J. 1990. 'Survivors of Joyce', in Martin, A. (ed.) *The Artist and the Labyrinth*. London, 73–81.
Baraz, Y. 2012. *A Written Republic. Cicero's Philosophical Politics*. Princeton.
Baraz, Y. and Van den Berg, C. S. 2013. 'Introduction,' *AJP* 134.1: 1–8.
Barbiero, E. A. 2014. *Reading Between the Lines: Letters in Plautus*. PhD Diss. Toronto.
Barchiesi, A. 2001a. *Speaking Volumes: Narrative and Intertext in Ovid and Other Latin Poets*. London.
   2001b. 'Genealogie letterarie nell'epica imperiale. Fondamentalismo e ironia', in *L'histoire littéraire immanente dans la poésie latine*, Fondation Hardt («Entretiens sur l'antiquité classique» 47), Vandoeuvres-Geneva, 315–47.
   2005. *Ovidio Metamorfosi, libri i-ii*, vol. 1. Milan.
Barchiesi, A. and Rosati, G. 2007. *Ovidio Metamorfosi, libri iii-iv, vol. 3*. Milan.
Barchiesi, C. 2018. *Donna Ferrante's Library: Resonance of the Classics in the Neapolitan Novels*. MA Thesis. Georgetown. https://repository.library.georgetown.edu/handle/10822/1050795 [Accessed 7 July 2018]
Bardon, H. 1936. 'Les poésies de Néron', *Revue des Études Latines*: 337–49.
   1943. 'Le silence, moyen d'expression', *REL* 21:102–20.
Bartsch, S. 1994. *Actors in the Audience. Theatricality and Doublespeak from Nero to Hadrian*. Cambridge, MA and London.
   2015. 'Senecan Selves' in Bartsch, S. and Schiesaro, A. (eds.) *The Cambridge Companion to Seneca*, Cambridge, 187–98.
   2017. 'Philosophers and the State under Nero', in Bartsch, S., Freudenburg, K. and Littlewood, C. (eds.) *The Cambridge Companion to the Age of Nero*. Cambridge, 151–63.
Baum, C. 2011. 'Ruined Waking Thoughts: William Beckford as a Visitor to Pompeii', in Hales and Paul (eds.), 34–47.
Bauman, R. 1970. *The crimen maiestatis in the Roman Republic and Augustan Principate*. Johannesburg.
   1974. Impietas in Principem: *A Study of Treason Against the Roman Emperor with Special Reference to the First Century A.D.* Munich.
Beard, M. 2007. *The Roman Triumph*. Cambridge, MA and London.
   2008. *Pompeii: The Life of a Roman Town*. London.
Beasom, P. T. 2013. 'Forgetting the *Ars Memoriae*: Ovid, *Remedia Amoris* 579–84', *CQ* 63.2: 903–6.
Bellandi, F. 2011. 'Colpi di fulmine e patologie d'amore da Omero a Catullo: qualche considerazione', *BStudLat* 41.1: 1–30.
Benjamin, W. 1997. 'The Translator's Task', trans. by S. Rendall, *Traduction, Terminologie, Rédaction* 10.2: 151–65.
Benner, M. 1975. *The Emperor Says: Studies in the Rhetorical Style in Edicts of the Early Empire*. Göteborg.
Benz, L., Stärk, E. and Vogt-Spira, G. 1995 (eds.) *Plautus und die Tradition des Stegreifspiels*. Tübingen.
Bergren, A. 1983. 'Language and the Female in Early Greek Thought.' *Arethusa* 16.1: 69–95.

Berlincourt, V. 2013. *Commenter la* Thébaïde *(16ᵉ-19ᵉ s.). Caspar von Barth et la tradition exégétique de Stace*. Leiden-Boston
Bessone, F. 1997. *P. Ovidii Nasonis Heroidum Epistula XII. Medea Iasoni*. Florence.
    2011. *La Tebaide di Stazio. Epica e potere*. Pisa-Rome.
Bettini, M. 2012. *Vertere. Un'antropologia della traduzione nella cultura antica*. Turin.
Billings, J. 2010. 'Hyperion's Symposium: an Erotics of Reception', *CRJ* 2.1: 4–24.
    2016. 'The Sigh of Philhellenism', in Butler, S. (ed.) *Deep Classics: Rethinking Classical Reception*. London, 49–65.
Biondi, G. G. 2007. 'Poem 101', in Gaisser, J. H. (ed.) *Catullus*. Oxford, 177–97.
Bishop, J. 1985. *Seneca's Daggered Stylus: Political Code in the Tragedies*. Königstein.
Blake, S. 2012. 'Now You See Them: Slaves and Other Objects as Elements of the Roman Master', *Helios* 39.2: 193–211.
    2016. 'In Manus: Pliny's Letters and the Art of Mastery', in Keith, A. and Edmondson, J. (eds.) *Roman Literary Cultures: Domestic Politics, Revolutionary Poetics, Civic Spectacle*. Toronto, Buffalo and London, 89–107.
Blix, G. 2009. *From Paris to Pompeii: French Romanticism and the Cultural Politics of Archaeology*. Philadelphia.
Bocciolini Palagi, L. 1990. 'Enea come Orfeo', *Maia* 42: 133–50.
Bodel, J. 1999. 'Death on Display: Looking at Roman Funerals', in Bergmann, B. and Kondoleon, C. (eds.) *The Art of Ancient Spectacle*. New Haven, 259–81.
Boeckh, A. 1877. *Encyklopädie und Methodologie der philologischen Wissenschaften*, E. Bratuscheck (ed.) Leipzig.
    1968. *Interpretation and Criticism*, trans. by J. Pritchard. Norman, OK.
Boissier, R. 2011. *Pompéi. Les doubles vies de la cité du Vésuve*. Paris.
Bolonyai, G. 2007. 'Fenség és nézőpont', in Hajdu, P. and Odorics, F. (eds.) *Retorika és narráció*. Budapest, 205–27.
Bömer, F. 1969. *P. Ovidius Naso, Metamorphosen: Kommentar*. Heidelberg.
Bonifazi, A. 2012. *Homer's Versicolored Fabric: the Evocative Power of Ancient Greek Epic Word-making*. Washington, DC.
Bowersock, G. 2009. *From Gibbon to Auden: Essays on the Classical Tradition*. Oxford.
Boyle, A. J. (ed.) 2008. *The Octavia: Attributed to Seneca*. Oxford.
Bradley, K. 1978. *Suetonius' Life of Nero: An Historical Commentary*. Brussels.
    2000. 'Animalizing the Slave: the Truth of Fiction', *JRS* 90: 110–25.
Braund, S. M. 2009. *Seneca: De Clementia*. Oxford, New York.
Brenk, F. 1999. *Clothed in Purple Light: Studies in Vergil and in Latin Literature, Including Aspects of Philosophy, Religion, Magic, Judaism, and the New Testament Background*. Stuttgart.
Briguglio, S. 2017. *Fraternas acies. Saggio di commento a Stazio, Tebaide, 1, 1–389*. Alessandria.
    2019. 'Ritratti di signora. Ipsipile tra Ovidio e l'epica flavia', in Bessone, F., Stroppa, S. (eds.), *Lettori latini e italiani di Ovidio. Atti del convegno – Università di Torino, 9-10 novembre 2017*, Pisa-Rome, 41–9.

Brink, C. O. 1982. *Horace on Poetry. Epistles Book II: The Letters to Augustus and Florus*. Cambridge.
Brodsky, J. 1995. *On Grief and Reason: Essays*. London. ('Homage to Marcus Aurelius' pp. 267–98; 'Letter to Horace' pp. 428–58).
Brookner, A. 2009. *Strangers*, London.
Brooks, P. 1984. *Reading for the Plot. Design and Intention in Narrative*. Cambridge, MA and London.
Brown, P. G. M. 2002. 'Actors and Actor-managers at Rome', in Easterling, P. E. and Hall, E. (eds.) *Greek and Roman Actors: Aspects of an Ancient Profession*. Cambridge, 225–37.
Brunelle, C. 2000–1. 'Form vs. Function in Ovid's *Remedia Amoris*', *CJ* 96: 123–40.
Brunt, P. A. 1974. 'Marcus Aurelius in his *Meditations*', *JRS* 64: 1–20.
Büchner, K. 1984. *M. Tullius Cicero. De Re Publica*. Heidelberg.
Buckley, E. 2013. '*Nero Insitivus*: Constructing Neronian Identity in the Pseudo-Senecan *Octavia*', in Gibson, A. G. G. (ed.) *The Julio-Claudian Succession: Reality and Perception of the Augustan Model*. Leiden, 133–54.
Budick, S. and Iser, W. (eds.) 1989. *Languages of the Unsayable: The Play on Negativity in Literature and Literary Theory*. New York.
Butler, S. 2015. *The Ancient Phonograph*. Cambridge, MA and London.
Butler, S. (ed.) 2016. *Deep Classics: Rethinking Classical Reception*. London.
Byrne, S. N. 2006. 'Petronius and Maecenas. Seneca's Calculated Criticism', in Byrne, S. N., Cueva, E. P and Alvares, J. (eds.) *Authors, Authority, and Interpreters in the Ancient Novel*. Groningen, 83–111.
  2007. 'Maecenas and Petronius' Trimalchio Maecenatianus', *Ancient Narrative* 6: 31–49.
Calboli, G. 1969. *Cornifici rhetorica ad Herennium*. Bologna.
Canfora, L. 1993. *Studi di storia della storiografia romana*. Bari.
Carson, A. 2009. *Nox*. New York.
Casali, S. 1995. 'Aeneas and the Doors of the Temple of Apollo', *CJ* 91: 1–9.
  2003. 'Impius Aeneas, impia Hypsipyle: narrazioni menzognere dall'Eneide alla Tebaide di Stazio', *Scholia* 12: 60–8.
Cavarero, A. 1995. *In Spite of Plato. Feminist Rewriting of Ancient Philosophy*, trans. by S. Anderlini-D'Onofrio and A. O'Heely. London.
  2005. *For More than One Voice: Toward a Philosophy of Vocal Expression*, trans. P. A. Kottman. Palo Alto, CA.
Cave, T. 1988. *Recognitions: a Study in Poetics*. Oxford.
Cèbe, J. P. 1966. *La caricature et la parodie dans le monde romain antique des origines a Juvénal*. Paris.
Cederstrom, E. 1981. 'Catullus' Last Gift to his Brother (*c.* 101)', *CW* 75: 117–18.
Cerami, P. 2015. '*Tabernae librariae*. Profili terminologici, economici e giuridici del commercio librario e dell'attività editoriale nel mondo romano', *AUPA* 58: 9–36.
Champlin, E. 1991. *Final Judgements. Duty and Emotion in Roman Wills, 200 BC – AD 250*. Berkeley.

2003a. *Nero*. Cambridge, MA.
2003b. 'Agamemnon at Rome. Roman Dynasts and Greek Heroes', in Braund, D. and Gill, C. (eds.) *Myth, History and Culture in Republican Rome: Studies in Honour of T.P. Wiseman*. Exeter, 295–319.
Chiarini, G. 1983. *La recita: Plauto, la farsa, la festa*, 2nd ed. Bologna.
Coarelli, F. 1993. 's.v. Apollo Sandalarius and Apollo Tortor', in Steinby, E. M. (ed.) *Lexicon Topographicum Urbis Romae*, I. Roma, 57–8.
Coates, V., Lapatin, K. and Seydl, J. (eds.) 2012. *The Last Days of Pompeii: Decadence, Apocalypse, Resurrection*. Los Angeles.
Coleman, K. 1988. Statius *Silvae IV*. Oxford.
Collard, C. 1975. 'Medea and Dido', *Prometheus* 1: 131–51.
Conte, G. B. 1984. *Virgilio. Il genere e i suoi confini*. Milan.
 1986. *The Rhetoric of Imitation: Genre and Poetic Memory in Virgil and other Latin Poets*, trans. by C. Segal. Ithaca, NY and London.
 1989. 'Love Without Elegy: the *Remedia Amoris* and the Logic of a Genre', *Poetics Today* 10: 441–69 (= Conte, G. B. 1994. *Genres and Readers*. Baltimore, 35–65).
 2016. 'On the Text of the *Aeneid:* An Editor's Experience', in Hunter, R. and Oakley, S. P. (eds.) *Latin Literature and Its Transmission. Papers in Honour of Michael Reeve*. Cambridge, 54–67.
Cooley, A. 2003. *Pompeii*. London.
Copeland, R. and Melville, S. 1991. 'Allegory and Allegoresis, Rhetoric and Hermeneutics', *Exemplaria* 3.1: 159–87.
Corbeill, A. 1996. *Controlling Laughter. Political Humor in the Late Roman Republic*. Princeton.
 2004. *Nature Embodied. Gesture in Ancient Rome*. Princeton.
Corbier, M. 2006. *Donner à voir, donner à lire. Mémoire et communication dans la Rome ancienne*. Paris.
Corcoran, N. 2012. 'A Brother Never Ends.' Review of Carson 2009. *The Cambridge Quarterly* 41: 371–8.
Costa, S. (ed.) 2014. *Maecenas: Frammenti e Testimonianze Latine*. Milan.
Courtney, E. 1993. *The Fragmentary Latin Poets*. Oxford.
Cresci Marrone, G. 2002. 'La cena dei dodici dèi', *RCCM* 44.1: 25–33.
Cucchiarelli, A. 2012. *Publio Virgilio Marone. Le Bucoliche* (Intr. and Comm.; trans. by A. Traina). Rome.
Culler, J. 2015. *Theory of the Lyric*. Cambridge, MA.
Culpepper Stroup, S. 2010. *Catullus, Cicero, and a Society of Patrons. The Generation of the Text*. Cambridge.
Cupaiuolo, G. 1993. *Tra poesia e realtà. Le pasquinate nell'antica Roma*. Naples.
Damon, C. 2003. *Tacitus*. Histories Book 1. Cambridge.
Dangel, J. 1995. *Accius. Oeuvres (fragments)*. Paris.
D'Anna, G. 1989. *Virgilio, Saggi Critici*, Rome.
Darley, G. 2011. *Vesuvius: The Most Famous Volcano in the World*. London.
Davis, P. 2008. *Translation and the Poet's Life: the Ethics of Translating in English Culture, 1646–1726*. Oxford.

Davis, W. 1994. 'Winckelmann Divided: Mourning the Death of Art History', in Davis, W. (ed.) *Gay and Lesbian Studies in Art History*. New York, 141–59.

Davisson, M. H. T. 1996. 'The Search for an "*Alter Orbis*" in Ovid's "*Remedia Amoris*"', *Phoenix* 50: 246–61.

Dawson, J. D. 2002. *Christian Figural Reading and the Fashioning of Identity*. Berkeley, Los Angeles, London.

De Divitiis, B. 2015. 'Memories from the Subsoil: Discovering Antiquities in Fifteenth-Century Naples and Campania', in Hughes, J. and Buongiovanni, C. (eds.) *Remembering Parthenope: The Reception of Classical Naples from Antiquity to the Present*. Oxford, 189–216.

De Divitiis, B., Lenzo, F. and Miletti, L. (eds.) 2018. *Ambrogio Leone's De Nola, Venice 1514: Humanism and Antiquarian Culture in Renaissance Southern Italy*. Leiden and Boston.

Degani, E. 1993. 'Aristofane e la tradizione dell'invettiva personale in Grecia', in Bremer, I. M. and Handley, E. W. (eds.) *Aristophane: Fondation Hardt Entretiens 38*. Vandoeuvres–Geneva, 1–36.

Degl'Innocenti Pierini, R. 2008. *Il parto dell'orsa*. Florence.

2013. 'Seneca, Mecenate e il ritratto in movimento', in Gasti, F. (ed.) *Seneca e la letteratura greca e latina: per i settant' anni di Giancarlo Mazzoli*. Pavia, 45–66.

De Grummond, W. W. 1997. 'The «Diana Experience»: A Study of the Victims of Diana in Virgil's *Aeneid*', *Latomus* 239: 144–57.

De Lacy, P. 1964. 'Distant Views: the Imagery of Lucretius 2', *CJ* 60: 49–55.

Deleuze, G. and Guattari, F. 1983. *Anti-Oedipus: Capitalism and Schizophrenia*, trans. by R. Hurley, M. Seem and H. R. Lane, preface by M. Foucault. London.

1987. *A Thousand Plateaus*. London.

Del Giovane, B. 2018. 'Il consolato di Cesare e Bibulo e un epigramma anonimo tramandato da Svetonio: per un'analisi del retroterra ciceroniano', in Audano, S. and Cipriani, G. (eds.) *Aspetti della Fortuna dell'Antico nella Cultura Europea: Atti della Quattordicesima Giornata di Studi, Sestri Levante, 10 marzo 2017*. Foggia, 323–38.

De Melo, W. D. C. 2011–12. *Plautus*, 5 vols. Cambridge, MA and London.

De Pretis, A. 2002. *'Epistolarity' in the First Book of Horace's Epistles*. Piscataway, NJ.

Derrida, J. 1976. *Of Grammatology*, trans. by G. C. Spivak. Baltimore.

2016 [1972]. 'Plato's Pharmacy', in Derrida, J. (ed.) *Dissemination*, trans. by B. Johnson. London, 65–181.

Descoeudres, J. 1992. 'Did some Pompeians Return to Their City after the Eruption of Mt Vesuvius in AD 79? Observations in the House of the Coloured Capitals', in Franchi dell'Orto, L. (ed.) *Proceedings of the International Congress Ercolano 1738–1988: 250 anni di ricerca archeologica, held in Pompeii, Herculaneum, and Naples in October-November 1988*. Rome, 165–78.

Detienne, M. and Vernant, J. P. 1978. *Cunning Intelligence in Greek Culture and Society*. Atlantic Highlands, NJ.

Devillers, O. 2014 'Les Opera Minora "Laboratoire" des Opera Maiora', in Devillers, O. (ed.) *Les opera minora et le développement de l'historiographie tacitéenne*. Bordeaux, 13–30.
De Vries, G. 2016. *Bruno Latour*. Cambridge.
Dewar, M. 1996. *Claudian. Panegyricus de sexto consulatu Honorii Augusti*. Oxford.
  2016. 'Lost Literature', in Zissos, A. (ed.) *A Companion to the Flavian Age of Imperial Rome*. Malden, MA and Oxford, 469–83.
De Witt, N. W. 1907. *The Dido Episode in the Aeneid of Virgil*. Toronto.
Dickson, K. 2009. 'Oneself as Others: Aurelius and Autobiography', *Arethusa* 42: 99–125.
Dimock, W. C. 2006. *Through Other Continents: American Literature Across Deep Time*. Princeton.
Dolar, M. 2006. *A Voice and Nothing More*. Cambridge, MA and London.
Dorfbauer, L. J. 2012. 'Claudian und Prudentius: verbale Parallelen und Datierungsfragen', *Hermes* 140: 45–70.
Douglas, A. E. 1966. *M. Tullius Cicero, Brutus*. Oxford.
Dressler, A. 2013. 'Poetics of Conspiracy and Hermeneutics of Suspicion in Tacitus's *Dialogus de Oratoribus*', *ClAnt* 32: 1–34.
Duckworth, G. 1994. *The Nature of Roman Comedy: A Study in Popular Entertainment*, 2nd ed. Bristol [1st ed. Princeton 1952].
Duclos, G. S. 1969. 'Dido as *triformis* Diana', *Vergilius* 15: 33–41.
Dufallo, B. (ed.). 2018. *Roman Error: Classical Reception and the Problem of Rome's Flaws*. Oxford.
Dugan, J. 2005. *Making a New Man. Ciceronian Self-Fashioning in the Rhetorical Works*. Oxford.
  2013. 'Cicero and the Politics of Ambiguity. Interpreting the Pro Marcello', in Steele, C. and van der Blom, H. (eds.) *Community and Communication. Oratory and Politics in Republican Rome*. Oxford, 211–25.
Dupont, F. 1976. 'Signification théâtrale du double dans l'Amphitryon de Plaute', *REL* 54: 129–41.
Dwyer, E. 2010. *Pompeii's Living Statues: Ancient Roman Lives Stolen from Death*. Ann Arbor.
Edwards, C. 1994. 'Beware of Imitations: Theatre and the Subversion of Imperial Identity', in Elsner, J. and Masters, J. (eds.) *Reflections of Nero*. London, 83–97.
  1996. *Writing Rome: Textual Approaches to the City*. Cambridge.
  1997. 'Self-scrutiny and Self-transformation in Seneca's Letters', *G&R* 44.1: 23–8.
  2007. *Death in Ancient Rome*, New Haven and London.
  2008. *Suetonius Lives of the Caesars*. Oxford.
  2017. 'Seneca and the Quest for Glory in Nero's Golden Age' Bartsch, S., Freudenburg, K. and Littlewood, C. (eds.) *Cambridge Companion to the Age of Nero*. Cambridge, 164–76.
  2018. 'On not Being in Rome: Exile and Displacement in Seneca's Prose', in Fitzgerald, W. and Spentzou, E. (eds.) *The Production of Space in Latin Literature*. Oxford, 169–94.

Elsner, J. 1994. 'Constructing Decadence: the Representation of Nero as Imperial Builder' in Elsner, J. and Masters, J. (eds.) *Reflections of Nero*. London, 112–27.
Ernst, W. 2001. 'Absenz', in Barck, K. *et al.* (eds.), *Ästhetische Grundbegriffe*, vol. I. Stuttgart/Weimar,1–16.
Fabre-Serris, J. 1999. 'Néron et les traditions latines de l'âge d'or', in Croisille, J.-M., Martin, R. and Perrin, Y. (eds.) *Neronia V. Néron: histoire et legend*. Brussels, 187–200.
Fantuzzi, M. and Hunter, R. 2004. *Tradition and Innovation in Hellenistic Poetry*. Cambridge.
Farrell, J. 1998. 'Reading and Writing the *Heroides*', *HSCPh* 98: 307–38.
  2009. 'The Impermanent Text in Catullus and Other Roman Poets', in Johnson, W. A. and Parker, H. N. (eds.) *Ancient Literacies. The Culture of Reading in Greece and Rome*. Oxford,164–85.
Farron, S. 1980. 'The Aeneas-Dido Episode as an Attack on Aeneas' Mission and Rome', *G&R* 27: 34–47.
Fedeli, P. 2005. *Properzio Elegie Libro II. Introduzione, testo e commento*. Cambridge.
Feeney, D. 1983. 'The Taciturnity of Aeneas', *CQ* 33: 204–19.
  1986. 'History and Revelation in Vergil's Underworld'. PCPhS 32: 1–24.
  1991. *The Gods in Epic: Poets and Critics of the Classical Tradition*. Oxford.
  1992. '*Si licet et fas est:* Ovid's *Fasti* and the Problem of Free Speech under the Principate', in Powell, A. (ed.) *Roman Poetry and Propaganda in the Age of Augustus*. Bristol, 1–25.
  2014. 'First Similes in Epic', *TAPA* 144: 189–228.
  2016. *Beyond Greek: The Beginnings of Latin Literature*. Cambridge, MA.
Feldherr, A. 1998. *Spectacle and Society in Livy's History*. Berkeley.
  1999. 'Putting Dido on the Map: Genre and Geography in Vergil's Underworld', *Arethusa* 32: 85–122.
  2000. '*Non inter nota sepulcra*: Catullus 101 and Roman Funerary Ritual', *ClAnt* 19: 209–31.
Felgentreu, F. 1999. *Claudians Praefationes: Bedingungen, Beschreibungen und Wirkungen einer poetischen Kleinform*. Stuttgart.
Felman, S. 1982. 'Turning the Screw of Interpretation,' in Felman, S. (ed.), *Literature and Psychoanalysis: The Question of Reading: Otherwise*, Baltimore: 94–207.
  2002. *The Scandal of the Speaking Body. Don Juan with J. L. Austin, or Seduction in Two Languages*. Stanford.
Felski, R. 2011. 'Suspicious Minds', *Poetics Today* 32.2: 215–34.
  2015. *The Limits of Critique*. Chicago and London.
Fernandelli, M. 1998. 'Virgilio imitatore: quattro ipotesi a proposito di *Eneide* I', *Lexis* 16: 163–99.
Ferrante, E. 2011. *L'amica geniale*. Rome.
  2012a. *Storia del nuovo cognome*. Rome.
  2012b. *My Brilliant Friend*, trans. by A. Goldstein. New York.

2013a *Storia di chi fugge e di chi resta*. Rome.
2013b. *The Story of a New Name*, trans. by A. Goldstein. New York.
2014a. *Storia della bambina perduta*. Rome.
2014b. *Those Who Leave and Those Who Stay*, trans. by A. Goldstein. New York.
2015. *The Story of the Lost Child*, trans. by A. Goldstein. New York.
2016. *Frantumaglia: a Writer's Journey*, trans. by A. Goldstein. New York.
Ferri, R. 2003. *Octavia*. Cambridge.
Fetscher, J. 2001. 'Fragment', in Barck, K. et al. (eds.) *Ästhetische Grundbegriffe* vol. II. Stuttgart and Weimar, 551–88.
Finamore, J. F. 1984. 'Catullus 50 and 51: Friendship, Love, and otium', *CW* 78: 11–19.
Fish, J. 2004. 'Physician, Heal Thyself: the Intertextuality of Ovid's Exile Poetry and the "*Remedia Amoris*"', *Latomus* 63: 864–72.
Fitzgerald, W. 1995. *Catullan Provocations: Lyric Poetry and the Drama of Position*. Berkeley.
2000. *Slavery and the Roman Literary Imagination*. Cambridge.
2011. 'The Slave as Minimal Addition in Latin Literature', in Alston, R., Hall, E. and Profitt, L. (eds.) *Reading Ancient Slavery*. London and New York, 175–91.
Fleming, J. 2016. '"Talk (why?) with Mute Ash": Anne Carson's *Nox* as Therapeutic Biography', *Biography* 39.1: 64–78.
Flower, H. 1996. *Ancestor Masks and Aristocratic Power in Roman Culture*. Oxford.
Fomenko, A. 2007. *History: Fiction or Science? New Chronology: 1*. Bend, Oregon.
Ford, A. 1992. *Homer: the Poetry of the Past*. Ithaca, NY.
Fordyce, C. J. 1977. *Aeneidos libri VII-VIII*. Oxford.
1990. *Catullus: A Commentary*. Oxford.
Foucault, M. 1966. *The Order of Things: An Archaeology of the Human Sciences*. New York.
2005. *The Hermeneutics of the Subject: Lectures at the Collège de France 1981–2* (ed.) F. Gros, trans. by G. Burchell. London.
Foucault, M. and Miskowiec, J. 1986. 'Of Other Spaces,' *Diacritics* 16: 22–7.
Fowler, D. 1990. 'Deviant Focalisation in Virgil's *Aeneid*', *PCPhS* 36: 42–63.
1991. 'Narrate and Describe: the Problem of Ekphrasis', *JRS* 81: 25–35.
2000a. 'Postmodernism, Romantic Irony, and Classical Closure', in Fowler, D. *Roman Constructions. Readings in Postmodern Latin*. Oxford, 5–33.
2000b. 'The Ruin of Time: Monuments and Survival at Rome', in *Roman Constructions. Readings in Postmodern Latin*. Oxford, 193–217.
Fraenkel, E. 2007. *Plautine Elements in Plautus*, trans. by T. Drevikovsky and F. Muecke. Oxford [1st German ed. Berlin 1922; Italian ed. Florence 1960].
Fraenkel, H. 1950. 'Problems of Text and Interpretation in Apollonius' Argonautica', *AJPh* 71: 113–33.
Freud, S. 1961. *Beyond the Pleasure Principle*, trans. by J. Strachey. New York and London.
Freudenburg, K. 2001. *Satires of Rome: Threatening Poses from Lucilius to Juvenal*, Cambridge.

2015. 'Seneca's Apocolocyntosis', in Bartsch, A. and Schiesaro, A. (eds.) *The Cambridge Companion to Seneca*. Cambridge, 93–105.

2017. 'Petronius, Realism, Nero' in Bartsch, S., Freudenburg, K. and Littlewood, C. (eds.) *The Cambridge Companion to the Age of Nero*. Cambridge, 107–20.

Frings, I. 1991. *Gespräch und Handlung in der Thebais des Statius*. Stuttgart.

Fucecchi, M. 2015. 'Passato da rimuovere e passato da rivivere: l'incubo della guerra civile (e la sua 'metabolizzazione') nell'epica flavia', in Esposito, P. and Walde, C. (eds.) *Letture e lettori di Lucano. Atti del Convegno Internazionale di Studi, Fisciano 27–29 marzo 2012*. Pisa, 231–53.

Fulkerson, L. 2004. '*Omnia Vincit Amor*: Why the *Remedia* Fail', *CQ* 54: 211–23.

2005. *The Ovidian Heroine as Author: Reading, Writing, and Community in the Heroides*. Cambridge.

Furneaux, H. 1894. *De Germania Cornelii Taciti*. Oxford.

Gabriel, M. 2015a. *Why the World Does Not Exist*. Cambridge.

2015b. *Fields of Sense: A New Realist Ontology*. Edinburgh.

Gaisser, J. H. 2009. *Catullus*. Malden, MA, Oxford and Chichester.

Gale, M. 2003. 'Poetry and the Backward Glance in Virgil's *Georgics* and *Aeneid*', *TAPA* 133.2: 323–52.

Galinsky, G. K. 1966. 'The Hercules-Cacus Episode in *Aeneid* VIII', *AJP* 87: 18–51.

1996. *Augustan Culture: an Interpretive Introduction*. Princeton.

Galippi, F. 2016. 'In Search of Parthenope and the "Founding" of a New City', in Bullaro, G. and Love, S. V. (eds.) *The Works of Elena Ferrante: Reconfiguring the Margins*. New York, 101–27.

Ganiban, R. T. 2007. *Statius and Virgil. The* Thebaid *and the Reinterpretation of the Aeneid*. Cambridge.

Garcia y Garcia, L. 1998. *Nova bibliotheca Pompeiana. 250 anni di bibliografia archeologica*. Roma.

Gardini, N. 2014. *Lacuna. Saggio sul non detto*. Turin.

Gardner, H. H. 2008. 'Women's Time in the *Remedia Amoris*', in Liveley, G. and Salzman-Mitchell, P. (eds.) 2008. *Latin Elegy and Narratology*. Columbus, OH, 68–85.

2013. *Gendering Time in Augustan Love Elegy*. Oxford.

Garton, C. 1972. *Personal Aspects of the Roman Theatre*. Toronto.

Gascou, J. 1984. *Suétone Historien*, Rome.

Genette, G. 1997. *Paratexts: Thresholds of Interpretation*. Cambridge.

Geue, T. 2016a. 'Elena Ferrante has her Reasons for Anonymity – We Should Respect Them.' *The Conversation*. Available at: https://theconversation.com/elena-ferrante-has-her-reasons-for-anonymity-we-should-respect-them-66436 [Accessed 30 May 2018]

2016b. 'Elena Ferrante as the Classics.' *Melbourne Historical Journal; The Amphora* 44.2: 1–31.

2018. 'Soft Hands. Hard Power: Sponging Off the Empire of Leisure (Virgil, *Georgics* 4)', *JRS* 108: 115–40.

Giavatto, G. 2008. *Interlocutore di se stesso: la dialettica di Marco Aurelio.* Hildesheim.

Gibson, B. J. 2004. 'The Repetitions of Hypsipyle', in Gale, M. (ed.) *Latin Epic and Didactic Poetry: Genre, Tradition and Individuality.* Swansea, 149–80.

2006. *Statius Silvae 5.* Oxford.

Gibson, R. 2003. *Ovid Ars Amatoria Book 3.* Cambridge.

Gibson, R., Green, S. and Sharrock, A. (eds.) 2006. *The Art of Love. Bimillennial Essays on Ovid's* Ars Amatoria *and* Remedia Amoris. Oxford.

Giltaij, J. 2018. 'The *lex cornelia de iniuriis* and "Hyperlinks" in Roman Law', *Fundamina* (online) 24.2: 21–34.

Gilula, D. 1989. 'The First Realistic Roles in European Theatre: Terence's Prologues', *QUCC* 33: 95–106.

Gingras, M. T. 1992. 'Annalistic Format, Tacitean Themes, and the Obituaries of Annals 3', *CJ* 87: 241–56.

Ginsberg, L. 2017. *Staging Memory, Staging Strife: Empire and Civil War in the Octavia.* Oxford.

Giusti, E. 2016. 'My Enemy's Enemy Is My Enemy: Virgil's Illogical Use of *Metus Hostilis*' in Hardie, P. (ed.) *Augustan Poetry and the Irrational.* Oxford, 37–58.

2017a. 'Virgil's Carthage: a Heterotopic Space of Empire', in Asper, M. and Rimell, V. (eds.) *Imagining Empire: Political Space in Hellenistic and Roman Literature.* Heidelberg: 133–50.

2017b. 'Cronaca del Convegno: *Unspeaking Volumes: Absence in Latin Texts*, University of St Andrews, 29 June–1 July 2017', *BSL* 47.2: 808–13.

2018. *Carthage in Virgil's* Aeneid: *Staging the Enemy under Augustus.* Cambridge.

Glenn, J. 1978. 'The Polyphemus Myth: Its Origin and Interpretation'. *G&R* 25: 141–55.

Godfrey, D. 2016. *New Pompeii.* London.

Goldberg, S. M. 2005. *Constructing Literature in the Roman Republic.* Cambridge.

2009. 'The Faces of Eloquence: the *Dialogus de Oratoribus*', in Woodman, T. (ed.) *The Cambridge Companion to Tacitus.* Cambridge, 73–84.

2012. 'Appreciating Aper: The Defence of Modernity in Tacitus' *Dialogus de Oratoribus*', in Ash, R. (ed.) *Tacitus.* Oxford, 155–79.

Goldhill, S. 1991. *The Poet's Voice. Essays on Poetics and Greek Literature.* Cambridge.

Goldschmidt, N. 2018. 'Ovid's Tombs: Afterlives of a Poetic *Corpus*', in Goldschmidt, N. and Graziosi, B. (eds.) *Tombs of the Ancient Poets: Between Literary Reception and Material Culture.* Oxford, 101–20.

Goodyear, F. R. D. 1972. *The* Annals *of Tacitus. I. 1–54.* Cambridge.

1981. *The* Annals *of Tacitus. II. 1. 55–81 and Annals 2.* Cambridge.

Goold, G. P. and Mozley, J. H. 1969. *Ovid The Art of Love, and Other Poems.* Cambridge, MA.

Gowers, E. 1993. 'Horace, *Satires* 1.5: an Inconsequential Journey", *PCPS* 39: 48–66; reprinted in Freudenburg, K. (ed.) 2009. *Oxford Readings in Horace II: Sermones and Epistles.* Oxford, 156–80.

1994. 'Persius and the Decoction of Nero', in Elsner, J. and Masters, J. (eds.) *Reflections of Nero*. London, 131–50.
 2012. *Horace, Satires Book 1*. Cambridge.
Gowing, A. 2005. *Empire and Memory. The Representation of the Roman Republic in Imperial Culture*. Cambridge.
Gratwick, A. S. 1993. *Plautus Menaechmi*. Cambridge.
Grau, D. 2017. 'Nero: the Making of Historical Narrative', in Bartsch, S., Freudenburg, K. and Littlewood, C. (eds.) *The Cambridge Companion to the Age of Nero*. Cambridge, 261–75.
Graver, M. 1998. 'The Manhandling of Maecenas: Senecan Abstractions of Masculinity', *AJPh* 119: 607–32.
 2016. 'The Emotional Intelligence of Epicureans: Doctrinalism and Adaptation in Seneca's *Epistles*', in Williams, G. and Volk, K. (eds.) *Roman Reflections: Studies in Latin Philosophy*. Oxford, 192–210.
Graverini, L. 2016. 'Il silenzio di Didone, le parole di Cornelia. Due note su Virgilio e Properzio', in Setaioli, A. (ed.) *Apis Matina. Studi in onore di Carlo Santini*. Trieste, 343–5
Greene, E. 1995. 'The Catullan Ego: Fragmentation and the Erotic Self', *AJPh* 116: 77–93.
 1999. 'Re-figuring the Feminine Voice: Catullus Translating Sappho', *Arethusa* 32: 1–18.
 2007. 'Catullus and Sappho', in Skinner, M. B. (ed.) *A Companion to Catullus*. Malden, MA, Oxford and Carlton, 131–50.
Grethlein, J. 2017. *Aesthetic Experiences and Classical Antiquity*. Cambridge.
Griffin, M. 1984. *Nero: the End of a Dynasty*. London.
 1992. *Seneca: a Philosopher in Politics*. 2nd ed. Oxford.
 2013. *Seneca on Society: A Guide to De Beneficiis*. Oxford.
Gruen, E. S. 1974. *The Last Generation of the Roman Republic*. Berkeley.
 1990. *Studies in Greek Culture and Roman Policy*. Leiden [repr. Berkeley 1996].
 1992. *Culture and National Identity in Republican Rome*. Ithaca, NY.
Gumbrecht, H. U. 1997. 'Eat Your Fragment! About Imagination and the Restitution of Texts', in Most, G. W. (ed.) *Collecting Fragments – Fragmente Sammeln*. Göttingen, 315–27.
 2003. *The Powers of Philology. Dynamics of Textual Scholarship*. Urbana, IL.
 2004. *Production of Presence. What Meaning Cannot Convey*. Stanford.
 2012. *Atmosphere, Mood, Stimmung. On a Hidden Potential of Literature*, trans. by E. Butler. Stanford.
Gurd, S. 2010. 'Introduction', in S. Gurd (ed.) *Philology and Its Histories*. Columbus, OH, 1–19.
Güthenke, C. 2010. 'The Potter's Daughter's Sons: German Classical Scholarship and the Language of Love circa 1800', *Representations* 109: 122–47.
 2016. '"Lives" as Parameter: The Privileging of Ancient Lives as a Category of Research', in Fletcher, R. and Hanink, J. (eds.) *Creative Lives in Classical Antiquity: Poets, Artists, and Biography*. Cambridge, 29–48.

Gutzwiller, K. 2012. 'Catullus and the *Garland* of Meleager', in Du Quesnay, I. and Woodman, A. J. (eds.) 2012. *Catullus: Poems, Books, Readers.* Cambridge, 79–111.
Habinek, T. 2014. '*Imago vitae suae:* Seneca's Life and Career' in Damschen, G. and Heil, A. (eds.) *Brill's Companion to Seneca.* Leiden, 3–31.
Hacking, I. 2002. *Historical Ontology.* Cambridge, MA.
Hadot, P. 1998. *The Inner Citadel: The Meditations of Marcus Aurelius,* trans. by J. M. Chase. Cambridge, MA.
Hales, S. and Paul, J. (eds.) 2011. *Pompeii in the Public Imagination from its Rediscovery to Today.* Oxford.
Hallett, J. P. 2015. 'Making Manhood Hard: Tiberius and Latin Literary Representations of Erectile Dysfunction', in Masterson, M., Sorkin Rabinowitz, N. and Robson J. (eds.) *Sex in Antiquity. Exploring Gender and Sexuality in the Ancient World.* New York, 408–21.
Halliwell, S. 2008. *Greek Laughter.* Cambridge.
Halporn, J. 1993. 'Roman Comedy and Greek Models', in Scodel, R. (ed.) *Theatre and Society in the Classical World,* Ann Arbor, 191–213.
Hamacher, W. 2009. '95 Theses on Philology', *Diacritics* 39: 25–44.
Hammer, D. 2008. *Roman Political Thought and the Modern Theoretical Imagination.* Norman, OK.
Hanchey, D. 2014. 'Days of Future Passed: Fiction Forming Fact in Cicero's Dialogues', *CJ* 110: 61–75.
Harder, A. 2004. 'Catullus 63: A "Hellenistic Poem"?', *Mnemosyne* 57.5: 574–95.
  2012. *Callimachus. Aetia,* 2 vols. Oxford.
Hardie, P. 1993. *The Epic Successors of Virgil: A Study in the Dynamics of a Tradition.* Cambridge.
  1994. *Virgil. Aeneid Book IX.* Cambridge.
  1998. *Virgil.* Oxford.
  2002. *Ovid's Poetics of Illusion.* Cambridge.
  2004a. 'Don Fowler and Middles', in Kyriakidis, S. and De Martino, F. (eds.) *Middles in Latin Poetry.* Bari, 25–6.
  2004b. 'Approximative Similes in Ovid. Incest and Doubling', *Dictynna* 1: 1–16.
  2006a. 'Virgil's Ptolemaic Relations', *JRS* 96: 25–41.
  2006b. '*Lethaeus Amor:* the Art of Forgetting' in Gibson, Green and Sharrock (eds.) 6–90.
  2009. *Lucretian Receptions. History, the Sublime, Knowledge.* Cambridge.
  2012. *Rumour and Renown: Representations of Fama in Western Literature.* Cambridge.
  2014. 'Dido and Lucretia', *PVS* 28: 55–80.
Harloe, K. 2013. *Winckelmann and the Invention of Antiquity: History and Aesthetics in the Age of Altertumswissenschaft.* Oxford.
Harrison, S. J. 2007. 'From Man to Book: the Close of Tacitus' *Agricola*', in Harrison, S. J., Fowler, P. G. and Heyworth, S. J. (eds.) *Classical Constructions: Papers in Memory of Don Fowler, Classicist and Epicurean.* Oxford, 310–19.

Haß-von Reitzenstein, U. 1970. *Beiträge zur gattungsgeschichtlichen Interpretation des Dialogus 'de oratoribus'*. Cologne.
Heerink, M. 2014. 'Valerius Flaccus, Virgil and the Poetics of *Ekphrasis*', in Heerink, M. and Manuwald, G. (eds.) *Brill's Companion to Valerius Flaccus*. Leiden and Boston, 72–96.
Heidegger, M. 1962a [1927]. *Sein und Zeit*. Tübingen:Niemeyer = 1962b. *Being and Time*, trans. by J. Macquarrie and E. Robinson. Oxford.
Heinze, R. 1908². *Vergils Epische Technik*. Leipzig.
Hekster, O. 2015. *Emperors and Ancestors: Roman Rulers and the Constraints of Tradition*. Oxford.
Henderson, A. A. R. 1979. *P. Ovidi Nasonis Remedia Amoris*. Edinburgh.
Henderson, J. 1993. 'Be Alert, Your Country Needs Lerts', *PCPhS* 39: 67–93.
  1997. *Figuring out Roman Nobility. Juvenal's Eighth Satire*. Exeter.
  2004. *Morals and Villas in Seneca's Letters*. Cambridge.
Henriksen, C. 2006. 'Martial's Modes of Mourning. Sepulchral Epitaphs in the Epigrams', in Nauta, R., Van Dam, H. and Smolenaars, J. (eds.) *Flavian Poetry*. Leiden and Boston, 349–67.
Henry, J. 1878. *Aeneidea: or Critical, Exegetical, and Aesthetical Remarks on the Aeneis; vol. 2: Books II, III, and IV*. Repr. 2013.
Henry, R. M. 1930. *Medea and Dido*, CR 44: 97–108.
Hershkowitz, D. 1998. *The Madness of Epic: Reading Insanity from Homer to Statius*. Oxford.
Hertz, N. 1983. 'A Reading of Longinus', *Critical Inquiry* 9: 579–96.
Heslin, P. 2005. *The Transvestite Achilles. Gender and Genre in Statius' Achilleid*. Cambridge.
  2008. 'Statius and the Greek Tragedians on Athens, Thebes, and Rome', in Smolenaars, J. J. L., Van Dam, H.-J. and Nauta, R. R. (eds.) *The Poetry of Statius*. Leiden, 111–28.
  2016. 'A Perfect Murder: The Hypsipyle Epyllion', in Manioti, N. (ed.), *Family in Flavian Epic*. Leiden-Boston, 89–121.
Heyworth, S. J. 1992. '*Ars Moratoria* (Ovid, *A.A.* 1.681–704)', *LCM* 17: 59–61.
Heyworth, S. and Morwood, J. 2017. *A Commentary on Vergil* Aeneid 3. Oxford.
Hickson Hahn, F. 2015. 'Triumphal Ambivalence: The Obscene Songs', in Dutsch, D. and Suter, A. (eds.) *Ancient Obscenities: Their Nature and Use in the Ancient Greek and Roman Worlds*. Ann Arbor, 153–74.
Hinds, S. 1993. 'Medea in Ovid: Scenes from the Life of an Intertextual Heroine', *MD* 30: 9–47.
  1998. *Allusion and Intertext: Dynamics of Appropriation in Roman Poetry*. Cambridge.
  2007. 'Ovid Among the Conspiracy Theorists' in Heyworth, S. J. (ed.) *Classical Constructions. Papers in Memory of Don Fowler*. Oxford, 194–220.
Hobden, F. 2009. 'History Meets Fiction in Doctor Who, 'The Fires of Pompeii': A BBC Reception of Ancient Rome on Screen and Online', *G&R* 56.2: 147–63.

Hodgson, L. 2017. *Res Publica and the Roman Republic: 'Without Body or Form'*. Oxford.
Hofmann, J. B. 1965. *Lateinische Umgangssprache, 3* Auflage. Heidelberg.
Hofmann, J. B. and Szantyr, A. 1965. *Lateinische Syntax und Stilistik*. Munich.
Holliday, P. J. 2002. *The Origins of Roman Historical Commemoration in the Visual Arts*. Cambridge.
Hollis, A. S. 2007. *Fragments of Roman Poetry*. Oxford.
Holmes, B. 2017. *Liquid Antiquity*. Geneva.
Holzberg, N. 2006. 'Staging the Reader Response: Ovid and his "Contemporary Audience" in Ars and Remedia' in Gibson, Green and Sharrock (eds.) 40–53.
Hornsby, R. A. 1970. *Patterns of Action in the Aeneid. An Interpretation of Vergil's Epic Similes*. Iowa City.
Horsfall, N. M. 1995. *A Companion to the Study of Virgil*. Leiden.
  2006. *Virgil,* Aeneid *3: a Commentary*. Leiden.
  2012. *The Culture of the Roman Plebs*. Bristol.
Houghton, L. B. T. 2009. 'Sexual Puns in Ovid's "Ars" and "Remedia", *CQ* 59: 280–5.
Howe, N. P. 1974. 'The "Terce Muse" of Catullus 101', *CPh* 69: 274–6.
Howley, J. H. 2017. 'Book-Burning and the Uses of Writing in Ancient Rome: Destructive Practice Between Literature and Document', *JRS* 107: 213–36.
Hunter, R. 1985. *The New Comedy of Greece and Rome*. Cambridge.
  1989. *Argonautica Book III*. Cambridge.
  2019. 'Notes on the Ancient Reception of Sappho', in Thorsen, T. S. and Harrison, S. (eds.) *Roman Receptions of Sappho*. Oxford, 45–59.
Hutchinson, G. O. 2001. *Greek Lyric Poetry. A Commentary on Selected Larger Pieces*. Oxford.
Inwood, B. 2005. *Reading Seneca: Stoic Philosophy at Rome*. Oxford, New York.
Iovino, S. 2016. *Ecocriticism and Italy: Ecology, Resistance, and Liberation*. London.
Iser, W. 1978. *The Act of Reading; A Theory of Aesthetic Response*. Baltimore, MD and London.
  1989. 'The Play of the Text', in Budick and Iser (eds.) 325–39.
Jacotot, M. 2014. 'De re publica esset silentium. Pensée politique et histoire de l'éloquence dans le *Brutus*', in Aubert-Baillot, S. and Guérin, C. (eds.) *Le 'Brutus' de Cicéron: rhétorique, politique et histoire culturelle*. Leiden, 193–214.
James, P. D. 1992. *The Children of Men*. London.
Jameson, F. 1981. *The Political Unconscious: Narrative as a Socially Symbolic Act*. London and New York.
Janan, M. 1994. *'When the Lamp is Shattered': Desire and Narrative in Catullus*. Carbondale, IL.
Jenkins, T. E. 2005. 'At Play with Writing: Letters and Readers in Plautus', *TAPA* 135: 359–92.
Johnson, S. 2006. *The Lives of the Most Eminent English Poets; With Critical Observations on Their Works* (ed.) R. Lonsdale. Oxford.
Jones, C. P. 2000. 'Nero Speaking', *HSCP* 100: 453–62.

Jones, M. 2014. 'Seneca's Letters to Lucilius: Hypocrisy as a Way of Life' in Wildberger, J. and Colish, M. L. (eds) *Seneca Philosophus*. Berlin, Boston, MA, 393–429.
Kassel, R. 1991. *Kleine Schriften*. Berlin.
Keitel, E. 2014. 'No Vivid Writing Please: *Evidentia* in the *Agricola* and the *Annals*', in Devillers, O. (ed.) *Les opera minora et le développement de l'historiographie tacitéenne*. Bordeaux, 59–70.
Kennedy, D. F. 2002. 'Epistolarity: The *Heroides*' in Hardie, P. (ed.) *The Cambridge Companion to Ovid*, Cambridge: 217–32.
   2006. 'vixisset Phyllis, si me foret usa magistro: Erotodidaxis and Intertextuality' in Gibson, Green and Sharrock (eds.) 54–74.
   2013. *Antiquity and the Meanings of Time: A Philosophy of Ancient and Modern Literature*. London.
   2014. 'Crossing the Threshold: Genette, Catullus and the Psychodynamics of Paratextuality', in Jansen, L. (ed.) *The Roman Paratext. Frame, Texts, Readers*. Cambridge, 19–32.
   Forthcoming. 'Views from Here and There: Reflections on History and Metaphysics', in Lianeri, A. and Cambiano, G. (eds.) *The Edinburgh Critical History of Greek and Roman Philosophy*. Edinburgh.
Kenney, E. J. 2004. *Ovidio Metamorfosi, libri vii-i, vol. 4*. Milan.
Ker, J. 2009. *The Deaths of Seneca*. Oxford.
Kermode, F. 1979. *The Genesis of Secrecy: On the Interpretation of Narrative*. Cambridge, MA.
Kidwell, C. 1993. *Sannazaro and Arcadia*. London.
Kittler, F. A. 1986. *Grammophon – Film – Typewriter*. Berlin.
König, A. and Whitton, C. (eds.) 2018. *Roman Literature under Nerva, Trajan and Hadrian: Literary Interactions, AD 96–138*. Cambridge.
Konstan, D. 2014. 'Turns and Returns in Plautus' *Casina*', in Perysinakis, I. N. and Karakasis, E. (eds.) *Plautine Trends*, Berlin, Munich, Boston, 3–11.
Korenjak, M. 1996. *Die Erichtoszene in Lukans* Pharsalia, Einl. Text, Übersetz., Komm. Frankfurt am Main.
Kőrizs, I. 2004. 'Szerencsétlen-e Catullus, és ha igen, miért nem?', in Horváth, L., Laczkó, K., Mayer, Gy. and Takács, L. (eds.) *ΓΕΝΕΣΙΑ. Tanulmányok Bollók János emlékére*. Budapest, 701–7.
Köves-Zulauf, T. 1992. 'Reden und Schweigen im taciteischen *Dialogus de Oratoribus*', *RhM* 135: 316–41.
Knauer. G. N. 1964. *Die Aeneis und Homer. Studien zur poetischen Technik Vergils mit Listen der Homerzitate in der Aeneis*. Göttingen.
Krämer, S. 2015. *Medium, Messenger, Transmission. An Approach to Media Philosophy*, trans. by A. Enns. Amsterdam.
Krapf, L. 1979. *Germanenmythus und Reichsideologie: Frühhumanistische Rezeptionsweisen der taciteischen Germania*. Tübingen.
Kraus, C. S. 2009. 'The Tiberian Hexad', in Woodman, A. J. (ed.) *The Cambridge Companion to Tacitus*. Cambridge, 100–15.

Krebs, C. 2005. *Negotiatio Germaniae: Tacitus' Germania und Enea Silvio Piccolomini, Giannantonio Campano, Conrad Celtis und Heinrich Bebel*. Göttingen.
  2011. *A Most Dangerous Book: Tacitus's Germania from the Roman Empire to the Third Reich*. London.
Kristeva, J. 1981. *Powers of Horror. An Essay on Abjection*, trans. by L. S. Roudiez. New York.
  1984. *Revolution in Poetic Language*, trans. by M. Waller. New York.
Krummen, E. 2004. 'Dido als Mänade und tragische Heroine. Dionysische Thematik und Tragödientradition in Vergils Didoerzählung', *Poetica* 36: 25–69.
Lacan, J. 2013. *Le désir et son interprétation, 1958–1959* (ed.) Jacques-Alain Miller. Paris.
Langlands, R. 2006. *Sexual Morality in Ancient Rome*. Cambridge.
Lanham, R. A. 1976. *The Motives of Eloquence. Literary Rhetoric in the Renaissance*. New Haven and London.
La Rocca, E. 2017. 'Staging Nero: Public Imagery and the *Domus Aurea*', in Bartsch, S., Freudenburg, K. and Littlewood, C. (eds.) *The Cambridge Companion to the Age of Nero*. Cambridge, 195–212.
Latour, B. 2013. *An Inquiry into Modes of Existence: An Anthropology of the Moderns*, trans. by C. Porter. Cambridge, MA.
Lausberg, H. 1998. *Handbook of Literary Rhetoric: A Foundation for Literary Study* (eds.) D. E. Orton and R. D. Anderson, trans. by M. T. Bliss, A. Jansen and D. E. Orton. Leiden.
Lavan, M. 2011. 'Slavishness in Britain and Rome in Tacitus' *Agricola*', *CQ* 61: 294–305.
Lazzarini, C. 1986. *Ovidio. Rimedi contro l'amore*. Venice.
Lee, M. O. 1988. '*Per nubila lunam*: The Moon in Virgil's *Aeneid*', *Vergilius* 34: 9–14.
Lefèvre, E., Stärk, E. and Vogt-Spira, G. 1991. *Plautus barbarus*. Tübingen.
Lesueur, R. 1994. *Stace. Thébaïde, Tome III, Livres IX-XII*. Paris.
Levene, D. 2004. 'Tacitus' "Dialogus" as Literary History', *TAPA* 134: 157–200.
Levick, B. 1976. 'The Fall of Julia the Younger', *Latomus* 35.2: 301–39.
  1999². *Tiberius the Politician*. London.
Levin, Y. 2005. 'Conrad, Freud, and Derrida on Pompeii: A Paradigm of Disappearance', *Partial Answers: Journal of Literature and the History of Ideas* 3.1: 81–99.
Ling, R. 2005. *Pompeii: History, Life & Afterlife*. Stroud.
Liveley, G. 2011. 'Delusion and Dream in Theophile Gautier's Arria Marcella: Souvenir de Pompéi' in Hales and Paul (eds.) 105–17.
Lloyd, G. E. R. (ed.) 1978. *Hippocratic Writings*. London.
Lönnroth, H. 2017. 'Introduction: Why Philology Matters', in Lönnroth, H. (ed.) *Philology Matters! Essays on the Art of Reading Slowly*. Leiden, xiv–xxvi.
Lovatt, H. 1999. 'Competing Endings: Re-Reading the End of the Thebaid through Lucan', *Ramus* 28.2: 126–51.

Lowe, J. C. B. 2003. 'The Lot-Drawing Scene of Plautus' *Casina*', *CQ* 53: 175–183.
Lowe, N. J. 2008. *Comedy*. Cambridge.
Lowrie, M. 2006. '*Hic* and Absence in Catullus 68', *CPh* 101: 115–32.
  2008. 'Cicero on Caesar or Exemplum and Inability in the *Brutus*', in Arweiler, A. and Möller, M. (eds.) *Vom Selbstverständnis in Antike und Neuzeit / Notions of the Self in Antiquity and Beyond*. Berlin and New York, 131–50.
  2009. *Writing, Performance, and Authority in Augustan Rome*. Oxford.
Luce, T. J. 1993. 'Reading and Response in the *Dialogus*', in Luce, T. J. and Woodman, A. J. (eds.) *Tacitus and the Tacitean Tradition*. Princeton, 11–38.
Lund, A. A. 1988. *Germania. P. Cornelius Tacitus. Interpretiert, Hrsg., Übertragen, Kommentiert und mit einer Bibliographie versehen*. Heidelberg.
  1991a. 'Versuch einer Gesamtinterpretation der "Germania" des Tacitus, mit einem Anhang: Zu Entstehung und Geschichte des Namens und Begriffs "Germani"', *ANRW* II.33.3: 1858–988.
  1991b. 'Kritischer Forschungsbericht zur 'Germania des Tacitus', *ANRW* II.33.3: 1989–2222.
Lunderstedt, P. 1911. 'de C. Maecenatis fragmentis' *Commentationes philologae Ienenses* 9.1. Leipzig.
Lyne, R. O. A. M. 1987. *Further Voices in Vergil's Aeneid*. Oxford.
Lyotard, J.-F. 2012. 'The Sublime and the Avant-Garde', trans. by G. Bennington and R. Bowlby, in Tanke, J. and McQuillan, C. (eds.) *The Bloomsbury Anthology of Aesthetics*. New York, London, New Delhi and Sydney, 531–42.
MacCary, W. T. and Willcock, M. M. 1976. *Plautus: Casina*. Cambridge.
MacCormack, S. 1981. *Art and Ceremony in Late Antiquity*. Berkeley, Los Angeles and London.
Mac Góráin, F. 2018. 'The Poetics of Vision in Virgil's *Aeneid*', *HSCP* 109: 1–56.
Macherey, P. 1978. *A Theory of Literary Production*, trans. by G. Wall. London and Boston.
Mackie, C. J. 1988. *The Characterization of Aeneas*. Edinburgh.
Madvig, J. N. 1871. *Adversaria critica ad scriptores graecos et latinos*. Hauniae (Copenhagen).
Maltby, R. 1991. *A Lexicon of Ancient Etymologies*. Leeds.
Manfredini, A. 1979. *La diffamazione verbale nel diritto romano. I. Età Repubblicana*, Milan.
Maniglier, P. 2014. 'A Metaphysical Turn? Bruno Latour's *An Inquiry into Modes of Existence*', *Radical Philosophy* 187: 37–44.
Manioti, N. 2016. 'Becoming Sisters: Antigone and Argia in Statius' Thebaid', in Manioti, N. (ed.) *Family in Flavian Epic*. Leiden-Boston, 122–42.
Marchese, R. R. 2014. 'Speech and Silence in Cicero's Final Days', *CJ* 110: 77–98.
Marsden, J. 2013. 'In Search of Lost Sense: The Aesthetics of Opacity in Anne Carson's *Nox*', *Comparative and Continental Philosophy* 5: 189–98.
Marshall, C. W. 2006. *The Stagecraft and Performance of Roman Comedy*. Cambridge.

Martelli, F. 2013. *Ovid's Revisions. The Author as Editor.* Cambridge.
Martin, C. 1992. *Catullus.* New Haven.
Martindale, C. 1993. *Redeeming the Text: Latin Poetry and the Hermeneutics of Reception.* Cambridge.
Martínez, M. 2003. *La palabra y el silencio en el episodio amoroso de la Eneida.* Frankfurt am Main.
Martindale, C. and Hopkins, D. (eds.) 1993. *Horace Made New.* Cambridge.
Massimilla, G. 2010. *Callimaco.* Aitia. *Libro terzo e quarto*, intr., testo critico, trad. e comm. Pisa-Rome.
Mattingly, H. B. 1960. 'The First Period of Plautine Revival', *Latomus* 19: 231–5.
Mau, A. 1902. *Pompeii: Its Life and Art.* New York.
Mayer, R. 1982. 'Neronian Classicism', *AJPh* 104: 305–18.
  2001. *Tacitus. Dialogus de Oratoribus.* Cambridge.
McAuley, M. 2016. *Reproducing Rome. Motherhood in Virgil, Ovid, Seneca, and Statius.* Oxford.
McCarthy, K. 2000. *Slaves, Masters, and the Art of Authority in Plautine Comedy.* Princeton.
McKeown, N. 2007. *The Invention of Ancient Slavery.* London.
McNamara, J. 2014. *Magna Eloquentia in Tacitus: Finding a Role for Oratory in the Principate.* PhD Diss. Cambridge.
McNelis, C. 2007. *Statius' Thebaid and the Poetics of Civil War.* Cambridge.
Melin, B. 1960. 'Zum Eingangskapitel der Germania', *Eranos* 58: 112–31.
Mellor, R. 1993. *Tacitus.* London.
Mezei, G. 2017. 'The Text as Body: William Shakespeare and Lőrinc Szabó', in Bengi, L., Kulcsár Szabó, E., Molnár, G. T. and Kelemen, P. (eds.) *Hungarian Perspectives on the Western Canon. Post-Comparative Readings.* Newcastle upon Tyne, 61–75.
Michelakis, P. 2002. *Achilles in Greek Tragedy.* Cambridge.
Micozzi, L. 2004. 'Memoria diffusa di luoghi lucanei nella Tebaide di Stazio', in Esposito, P. and Ariemma, E. M. (eds.) *Lucano e la tradizione dell'epica latina. Atti del convegno internazionale di studi, Fisciano-Salerno, 19-20 ottobre 2001.* Naples, 137–51.
  2008. '*Ille referre aliter saepe solebat idem.* Ripetizione e sperimentalismo narrativo nella Tebaide di Stazio', *MD* 61: 211–27.
  2015. 'Statius' Epic Poetry: a Challenge to the Literary Past', in Dominik, W. J., Newlands, C. E. and Gervais, K. (eds.) *Brill's Companion to Statius.* Leiden-Boston, 325–42.
Miller D. L. 2003. *Dreams of the Burning Child: Sacrificial Sons and the Father's Witness.* Ithaca, NY.
Miller, J. F. 2009. *Apollo, Augustus and the Poets.* Cambridge.
Misch, G. 1950. *A History of Autobiography in Antiquity Part 2*, London.
Moles, J. 2007. 'Philosophy and Ethics' in Harrison, S. (ed.) *The Cambridge Companion to Horace.* Cambridge, 165–80.
Momigliano, A. D. 1960. *Secondo Contributo alla Storia degli Studi Classici.* Rome.
Mommsen, T. 1899. *Römisches Strafrecht.* Leipzig.

Moore, T. J. 1998. *The Theater of Plautus: Playing to the Audience*. Austin, TX.
Moormann, E. 2015. *Pompeii's Ashes: The Reception of the Cities Buried by Vesuvius in Literature, Music, and Drama*. Boston.
Morelli, A. M. 2000. *L'epigramma latino prima di Catullo*. Cassino.
  2001. 'L'eternità di un istante. Presupposti ellenistico-romani della poesia leggera di Catullo tra cultura letteraria, epigrafica e "mondana"', *A&R* 46: 59–79.
Morford, M. 1972–3. 'The Neronian Literary Revolution', *CJ* 68: 210–15.
Morgan, L. 1997. '*Levi quidem de re* ... Julius Caesar as Tyrant and Pedant', *JRS* 87: 23–40.
Morley, N. 2018. *Classics: Why it Matters*. Cambridge.
Muciaccia, G. 1984. 'In tema di repressione delle opere infamanti (Dio 55, 27)', in *Studi in onore di Arnaldo Biscardi*, vol. V, Milan, 61–78.
Muecke, F. 1983. 'Foreshadowing and Dramatic Irony in the Story of Dido', *AJPh* 104: 134–55.
  1986. 'Plautus and the Theater of Disguise', *ClAnt* 5.2, 216–29.
Müller, G. M. 2013. '*Si mihi mea sententia proferenda ac non disertissimorum, ut nostris temporibus, hominum sermo repetendus esset*. Zur Funktion der Gesprächshandlung in Tacitus' *Dialogus de oratoribus*', in Föllinger, S. and Müller, G. M. (eds.) *Der Dialog in der Antike. Formen und Funktion einer literarischen Gattung zwischen Philosophie, Wissensvermittlung und dramatischer Inszenierung*. Berlin and New York, 327–63.
Müller, W. 1972. 'Sueton und seine Zitierweise in "Divus Iulus"', *SO* 47: 96–9.
Mynors, R. A. B. (ed.) 1958. *C. Valerii Catulli Carmina*. Oxford.
  1969. *P. Vergili Maronis Opera recognovit brevique adnotatione critica instruxit R. A. B. Mynors*. Oxford.
Nancy, J.-L., with Van Reeth, A. 2017. *Coming*, trans. by C. Mandell. New York.
Nelis, D. 2001. *Vergil's* Aeneid *and the* Argonautica *of Apollonius Rhodius*. Leeds.
Nelson, T. G. A. 1990. *Comedy: An Introduction to Comedy in Literature, Drama, and Cinema*. Oxford.
Newlands, C. 2010. 'The Eruption of Vesuvius in the Epistles of Statius and Pliny', in Miller, J. and Woodman, A. (eds.) *Latin Historiography and Poetry in the Early Empire: Generic Interactions*. Leiden and Boston, 105–22.
  2012. *Statius, Poet Between Rome and Naples*. London.
Nisbet, G. 2015. *Martial Epigrams*. Oxford.
Nisbet, R. G. M. and Hubbard, M. 1970. *A Commentary on Horace: Odes Book I*. Oxford.
Nochlin, L. 1994. *The Body in Pieces: The Fragment as a Metaphor of Modernity*. London.
Norden, E. 1903. *P. Vergilius Maro Aeneis Buch VI*. Leipzig.
North, J. 2017. *Literary Criticism: A Concise Political History*. Cambridge, MA.
Nothomb, A. 1996. *Peplum*. Paris.
Nugent, G. 1985. *Allegory and Poetics. The Structure and Imagery of Prudentius'* Psychomachia. Frankfurt and New York.

1996. 'Statius' Hypsipyle: Following in the Footsteps of the Aeneid', *Scholia* 5: 46–71.
O'Bryhim, S. 1989. 'The Originality of Plautus' *Casina*', *AJPh* 110: 81–103.
O'Gorman, E. 1993. 'No Place like Rome: Identity and Difference in the *Germania* of Tacitus', *Ramus* 22.2: 135–54.
  2000. *Irony and Misreading in the Annals of Tacitus*. Cambridge.
  2011. 'Repetition and Exemplarity in Historical Thought: Ancient Rome and the Ghosts of Modernity', in Lianeri, A. (ed.) *The Western Time of Ancient History: Historiographical Encounters with the Greek and Roman Pasts*. Cambridge, 264–79.
  2020. *Tacitus' History of Politically Effective Speech. Truth to Power*. London.
O'Hara, J. J. 2010. 'The Unfinished *Aeneid*?', in Farrell, J. and Putnam, M. C. J. (eds.) *A Companion to Vergil's* Aeneid *and Its Tradition*. Malden, MA, Oxford and Chichester, 96–106.
O'Higgins, D. 1990. 'Sappho's Splintered Tongue: Silence in Sappho 31 and Catullus 51', *AJPh* 111: 156–67.
Oliensis, E. 1997. 'Sons and Lovers: Sexuality and Gender in Virgil's Poetry,' in Martindale, C. (ed.) *The Cambridge Companion to Virgil*. Cambridge, 294–311.
  2004. 'The Power of Image-Makers: Representation and Revenge in Ovid *Metamorphoses* 6 and *Tristia* 4', *ClAnt* 23: 285–321.
  2009. *Freud's Rome. Psychoanalysis and Latin Poetry*. Cambridge.
Oliver, K. 1993. 'Julia Kristeva's Feminist Revolutions', *Hypatia* 8.3: 94–114.
O'Neill, P. 2003. 'Triumph Songs, Reversal and Plautus' Amphitruo', *Ramus* 32: 1–38.
Oniga, R. 1992. *Anfitrione*. Venice.
Orlando, F. 1973. *Per una teoria freudiana della letteratura*. Turin.
Orrells, D. and Roynon, T. (eds.) 2019. 'Ovid and Theory', *IJCT* 26.
Osanna, M. 2017. 'Pompei: la prossimità del passato', in Osanna, M. and Villani, A. (eds.) *Pompei@Madre. Materia archeologica*. Milan, 91–101.
Osgood, J. 2019. 'Family History in Augustan Rome', in Gildenhard, I., Gotter, U., Havener, W. and Hodgson, L. (eds.) *Augustus and the Destruction of History. The Politics of the Past in Early Imperial Rome*. Oxford, 135–56.
Pagán, V. E. 2017. *Tacitus*. London.
Panagia, D. 2009. *The Political Life of Sensation*. Durham, NC.
Panayotakis, C. 1995. *Theatrum Arbitri: Theatrical Elements in the Satyrica of Petronius*. Leiden.
Pani, M. 1979. *Tendenze politiche della successione di Augusto*. Bari.
Paratore, E. 1959. *Casina*. Florence.
  1963. 'Osservazioni sui rapporti fra Catullo e gli Epigrammisti dell'*Antologia*', in *Miscellanea di studi alessandrini in memoria di Augusto Rostagni*. Turin, 562–87.
  2003. *Anatomie plautine*. Urbino.

Parker, H. 1989. 'Crucially Funny or Tranio on the Couch: The Servus Callidus and Jokes about Torture', *TAPA* 119: 233–46.
Parkes, R. 2012. *Statius. Thebaid 4*, ed. with an intr., trans. and comm. Oxford.
Paschalis, M. 1997. *Virgil's Aeneid: Semantic Relations and Proper Names*. Oxford.
Paul, J. 2009. '"I Fear It's Potentially like Pompeii": Disaster, Mass Media and the Ancient City', in Lowe, D. and Shahabudin, K. (eds.) *Classics for All: Reworking Antiquity in Mass Culture*. Cambridge, 91–108.
  2019. 'Drones Over Pompeii: Cinematic Perspectives on Antiquity in the Digital Era', *CRJ*: 274–95.
Paxson, J. J. 1994. *The Poetics of Personification*. Cambridge.
Peachin, M. 2007. 'Exemplary Government in the Early Roman Empire', in Hekster, O., de Kleijn, G. and Slootjes, D. (eds.) *Crises and the Roman Empire*. Leiden, 75–95.
  2015. 'Augustus' Emergent Judicial Powers, the "Crimen Maiestatis", and the Second Cyrene Edict', in Ferrary, J. L. and Scheid, J. (eds.), *Il princeps romano: autocrate o magistrato? Fattori giuridici e fattori sociali del potere imperiale da Augusto a Commodo*. Pavia, 497–553.
Peirano, I. 2012. *The Rhetoric of the Roman Fake: Latin Pseudepigrapha in Context*. Cambridge.
Pelling, C. B. R. 2006. 'Breaking the Bounds: Writing About Julius Caesar', in McGing, B. C., Mossman, J. M. and Bowie, E. L. (eds.) *The Limits of Ancient Biography*. Swansea, 255–80.
  2009. 'Tacitus' Personal Voice', in Woodman, A. J. (ed.) *The Cambridge Companion to Tacitus*. Cambridge, 147–67.
Penwill, J. L. 2003. 'What's Hecuba to Him . . .? Reflections on Poetry and Politics in Tacitus' Dialogue on Orators', *Ramus* 32: 122–47.
Perl, G. 2005. 'Tacitus, *Germania* 37, 2 und 4', *Philologus* 149.1: 170–4.
Perysinakis, I. N. and Karakasis, E. (eds.) *Plautine Trends*. Berlin, Munich, Boston.
Peters, J. D. 1999. *Speaking into the Air: A History of Communication*. Chicago.
Petrides, A. K. 2014. 'Plautus between Greek Comedy and Atellan Farce: Assessments and Reassessments', in Fontaine, M. and Scafuro, A. C. (eds.) *The Oxford Handbook of Greek and Roman Comedy*. Oxford and New York, 424–46.
Petrone, G. 1983. *Teatro antico e inganno*. Palermo.
Pettinger, A. 2012. *The Republic in Danger: Drusus Libo and the Succession of Tiberius*. Oxford.
Pezzini, G. 2019. 'Pontem interrumpere: Plautus' Casina and absence in Roman comedy', Pan 8: 185–208.
Pezzini, G. 2021. 'Terence and the Speculum Vitae: Realism and (Roman) Comedy', *HSCP* 111.
Pfeiffer, R. 1949. *Callimachus*, 2 vols. Oxford.
Pillinger, E. 2012. 'And the Gods Dread to Hear Another Poem: the Repetitive Poetics of Witchcraft from Virgil to Lucan', *MD* 68: 103–43.
Pinotti, P. 1988. *Remedia Amoris. Introduzione, testo e commento*. Bologna.

Plate, L. 2015. 'How to Do Things with Literature in the Digital Age: Anne Carson's *Nox*, Multimodality, and the Ethics of Bookishness', *Contemporary Women's Writing* 9: 93–111.
Pollock, S. 2009. 'Future Philology? The Fate of a Soft Science in a Hard World', *Critical Inquiry* 35: 931–61.
　2015. 'Introduction', in Pollock, S., Elman, B. A. and Chang, K. K. (eds.) *World Philology*. Cambridge, MA, 1–24.
Pollmann, K. 2004. *Statius. Thebaid 12*, intr., text and comm. Paderborn-Munich-Vienna-Zürich.
Porter, J. I. 2016. *The Sublime in Antiquity*. Cambridge.
Pöschl, V. 1950. *Die Dichtkunst Virgils, Bild und Symbol in der Äneis*. Innsbruck and Vienna.
Potter, D. 2014. 'The Social life of the Senses: Feasts and Funerals', in Toner, J. (ed.) *A Cultural History of the Senses in Antiquity, 500 BCE – 500 CE*. London, 23–44
Potts, A. 1994. *Flesh and the Ideal: Winckelmann and the Origins of Art History*. New Haven.
Powell, B. B. 2016. *The Aeneid. Vergil*. New York and Oxford.
Power, T. 2014. 'Introduction: The Originality of Suetonius', in Power, T. and Gibson, R. K. (eds.) *Suetonius the Biographer: Studies on Roman Lives*. Oxford, 1–18.
Prins, Y. 1999. *Victorian Sappho*. Princeton.
Priwitzer, S. 2017. 'Marc Aurel und der Doppelprinzipat', in Grieb, V. (ed.) *Marc Aurel: Wege zu seiner Herrschaft*. Gutenberg, 1–22.
Purcell, Henry. 1689. *Dido and Aeneas*, libretto by Nahum Tate. New York.
Putnam, M. C. J. 1998. *Virgil's Epic Designs. Ekphrasis in the* Aeneid. New Haven and London.
Questa, C. 2003. 'Pardalisca regista della Casina', in Raffaelli, R. and Tontini, A. (eds.) *Lecturae Plautinae Sarsinates VI, Casina*, Urbino, 45–60.
Quinn, K. 1959. *The Catullan Revolution*. Melbourne.
　1972. *Catullus: An Interpretation*. London.
Ramazani, J. 1994. *Poetry of Mourning: The Modern Elegy from Hardy to Heaney*. Chicago.
Rawson, E. 1986. 'Cassius and Brutus: the Memory of the Liberators', in Moxon, I. S., Smart, J. D. and Woodman, A. J. (eds.) *Past Perspectives. Studies in Greek and Roman Historical Writing*. Cambridge, 101–19.
Reay, B. 2003. 'Some Addressees of Vergil's *Georgics* and their Audience', *Vergilius* 49: 17–41.
Reckford, K. 2009. *Recognising Persius*. Princeton.
Reed, J. D. 2007. *Virgil's Gaze. Nation and Poetry in the* Aeneid. Princeton.
　2013. *Ovidio Metamorfosi, libri x–xii*, vol. 5. Milan.
Ribbeck, O. 1875. *Die römische Tragödie im Zeitalter der Republik*. Leipzig.
Richardson, E. 2016. 'Ghostwritten Classics', in Butler, S. (ed.) *Deep Classics: Rethinking Classical Reception*. London, 221–38.
Richlin, A. 1992. *The Garden of Priapus*. Oxford.
　2014. 'Talking to Slaves in the Plautine Audience', *ClAnt* 33: 174–226.

2017. *Slave Theatre in the Roman Republic*. Cambridge.
Ricoeur, P. 1970. *Freud and Philosophy: An Essay on Interpretation*. New Haven.
Ricottilli, L. 1984. *La scelta del silenzio. Menandro e l'aposiopesi*. Bologna.
   1992. '*Tum breviter Dido vultum demissa profatur* (*Aen.* 1, 561): individuazione di un '*cogitantis gestus*' e delle sue funzioni e modalità di rappresentazione nell'*Eneide*', *MD* 28: 179–222.
   2000. *Gesto e parola nell'Eneide*. Bologna.
Riggsby, A. 2006. *Caesar in Gaul and Rome: War in Words*. Austin, TX.
Rimell, V. 2006. *Ovid's Lovers. Desire, Difference and the Poetic Imagination*. Cambridge.
   2015. 'Seneca and Neronian Rome', in Bartsch, S. and Schiesaro, A. (eds.) *The Cambridge Companion to Seneca*. Cambridge, 122–34.
   2015. *The Closure of Space in Roman Poetics: Empire's Inward Turn*. Cambridge.
   2019. 'After Ovid, After Theory', in Orrells and Roynon (eds.) = *IJCT* 26: 446–69.
Rives, J. 1999. *Tacitus. Germania. Translated with Introduction and Commentary*. Oxford.
Robbins, B. 1993. *The Servant's Hand: English Fiction from Below*. Durham and London.
Rogers, B. and Stevens, B. (eds.) 2015. *Classical Traditions in Science Fiction*. Oxford.
Rohr Vio, F. 2000. *Le voci del dissenso. Ottaviano Augusto e i suoi oppositori*. Padua.
Roman, L. 2014. *Poetic Autonomy in Ancient Rome*, Oxford.
Rosati, G.-P. 2006. 'The Art of Remedia Amoris: Unlearning to Love?' in Gibson, Green and Sharrock (eds.), 143–65.
Rose, F. C. K. 1971. *The Date and Author of the Satyricon*. Leiden.
Rosenbloom, D. S. 2006. *Aeschylus: Persians*. London.
Ross, D. O. 1975. *Backgrounds to Augustan Poetry: Gallus, Elegy, and Rome*. Cambridge.
Rowe, G. 2002. *Princes and Political Cultures: The New Tiberian Senatorial Decrees*. Ann Arbor.
   2013. 'Reconsidering the *auctoritas* of Augustus', *JRS* 103: 1–15.
Rowland, I. 2014. *From Pompeii: The Afterlife of a Roman Town*. Cambridge, MA and London.
Rudich, V. 1993. *Political Dissidence under Nero: the Price of Dissimulation*. London.
Rutherford, R. B. 1989. *The Meditations of Marcus Aurelius: A Study*. Oxford.
Rutledge, S. H. 2007. 'Oratory and Politics in the Empire', in Dominik, W. and Hall, J. (eds.) *A Companion to Roman Rhetoric*. Malden, MA, 109–21.
Sacks, P. 1985. *The English Elegy: Studies in the Genre from Spenser to Yeats*. Baltimore.
Said, E. 1978. *Orientalism*. London.
Sailor, D. 2008. *Writing and Empire in Tacitus*. Cambridge.
Savage, R. 1998. 'Dido Dies Again' in Burden, M. (ed.) *A Woman Scorn'd: Responses to the Dido Myth*. London, 3–38.

Scharnowski, S. 2001. '"Es spricht nicht, es rauscht und toset nur!" Eine kurze Geschichte der Ästhetik des Erhabenen und des Rauschens', in Hiepko, A. and Stopka, K. (eds.) *Rauschen. Seine Phänomenologie und Semantik zwischen Sinn und Störung.* Würzburg, 43–55.

Scheffler, S. 2013. *Death and the Afterlife.* New York and Oxford.

Scheid, J. 1996. *The Craft of Zeus: Myths of Weaving and Fabric.* Cambridge, MA.

Schiesaro, A. 2008. 'Furthest Voices in Virgil's Dido', *SIFC* 100: 60–109 and 94–245.

Schirren, T. 2000. '*campus oratorum – vatum nemora.* Apers und Maternus' Kontroverse im *Dialogus de oratoribus* im Lichte einer Topographie der *eloquentia*', in Neumeister, C. and Raeck, W. (eds.) *Rede und Redner. Darstellung und Bewertung in den antiken Kulturen. Kolloquium Frankfurt a. M. 14.–16. Oktober 1998.* Möhnesee, 227–48.

Schlegel, C. 2005. *Satire and the Threat of Speech.* Madison, WI.

Schliephake, C. (ed.) 2017. *Ecocriticism, Ecology, and the Cultures of Antiquity.* Lanham.

Schönberger, O. 1965. 'Zum Weltbild der drei Epiker nach Lucan', *Helikon* 5: 123–45.

Schubert, C. 2014. *Studien zum Nerobild in der lateinischen Dichtung der Antike.* Leipzig.

Schwindt, J. P. 2000. *Prolegomena zu einer 'Phänomenologie' der römischen Literaturgeschichtsschreibung. Von den Anfängen bis Quintilian.* Göttingen.

Scott, J. C. 1990. *Domination and the Arts of Resistance: Hidden Transcripts.* New Haven.

Scott, K. 1933. 'The Political Propaganda of 44-30 B.C.', *MAAR* 11: 7–49.

Segal, E. 1987. *Roman Laughter: The Comedy of Plautus*, 2nd ed. Oxford.

1989. *Orpheus: The Myth of the Poet.* Baltimore and London.

Selden, D. L. 2007. '*Caveat Lector:* Catullus and the Rhetoric of Performance', in Gaisser, J. H. (ed.) *Catullus.* Oxford, 491–559.

Shackleton Bailey, D. R. 2003. *Statius. Thebaid, Books 8-12; Achilleid*, vol. III, ed. and trans. Cambridge, MA and London.

Sharrock, A. 1991. 'Womanufacture', *JRS* 81: 36–49.

1994. *Seduction and Repetition in Ovid's* Ars Amatoria II. Oxford.

2006 'Love in Parentheses: Digression and Narrative Hierarchy in Ovid's Erotodidactic Poems' in Gibson, Green, Sharrock (eds.), 23–39.

2009. *Reading Roman Comedy: Poetics and Playfulness in Plautus and Terence.* Cambridge.

Shulman, J. 1981. '*Te quoque falle tamen:* Ovid's Anti-Lucretian Didactics', *CJ* 76: 242–53.

Sikelianos, E. 2015. 'Sentences on Nox', in Wilkinson, J. M. (ed.), *Anne Carson: Ecstatic Lyre.* Ann Arbor, 148–51.

Skinner, M. 2003. *Catullus in Verona: A Reading of the Elegiac* Libellus, *Poems 65–116.* Columbus, OH.

Slater, N. W. 2000. *Plautus in Performance.* Princeton.

2014. 'Speaking Verse to Power: Circulation of Oral and Written Critique in the Lives of Caesar', in Scodel, R. (ed.) *Between Orality and Literacy: Communication and Adaptation in Antiquity.* Leiden, 289–308.
Sluiter, I. and Rosen, R. (eds.) 2004. *Free Speech in Classical Antiquity.* Leiden.
Smith, R. A. 2005. *The Primacy of Vision in Virgil's* Aeneid. Austin, TX.
Smith, R. E. 1951. 'The Law of Libel at Rome', *CQ* 1 3.4: 169–79.
Smolenaars, J. J. L. 1994. *Statius. Thebaid VII. A Commentary.* Leiden.
Soerink, J. 2014. 'Tragic / Epic: Statius's Thebaid and Eurpides' Hypsipyle', in Augoustakis, A. (ed.) *Flavian Literature and its Greek Past.* Leiden, 171–91.
Soldo, J. 2018. *Commentary on Seneca Letters Book 2.* PhD diss. LMU. Munich.
Solodow, J. B. 1988. *The World of Ovid's Metamorphoses.* Chapel Hill.
Souriau, É. 2015. *The Different Modes of Existence.* Introduction by I. Stengers and B. Latour, trans. by E. Beranek and T. Howles. Minneapolis.
Sparrow, J. 1931. *Half-lines and Repetitions in Virgil.* Oxford.
Spentzou, E. 2003. *Readers and Writers in Ovid's* Heroides: *Transgressions of Genre and Gender.* Oxford.
Squire, M. 2015. '*Corpus Imperii*: Verbal and Visual Figurations of the Roman "Body Politic"', *Word & Image* 31: 305–30.
  2016. 'Introductory Reflections: Making Sense of Ancient Sight', in Squire, M. (ed.) *Sight and the Ancient Senses.* London, 1–35.
Srinivasan, A. 2014. 'Review of Scheffler 2013', *London Review of Books.* 25 September.
Stahl, H.-P. 2015. *Poetry Underpinning Power. Vergil's* Aeneid: *The Epic for Emperor Augustus.* Swansea.
Stanton, G. R. 1969. 'Marcus Aurelius, Emperor and Philosopher', *Historia* 18: 570–87.
Stärk, E. and Vogt-Spira, G. 2000. *Dramatische Wäldchen.* Hildesheim.
Starnone, V. 2020. *Nessuno guarda Elissa: Due passi del primo libro dell'Eneide e il disagio degli interpreti*, Pisa-Roma.
Sterne, L. 1759–67. *The Life & Opinions of Tristram Shandy*, London.
Stevens, B. E. 2013. *Silence in Catullus.* Madison, WI.
Stewart, R. 2012. *Plautus and Roman Slavery.* Malden, MA and Oxford.
Stover T. 2003. 'Confronting Medea: Genre, Gender, and Allusion in the *Argonautica* of Valerius Flaccus', *CP* 98.2: 123–47.
  2012. *Epic and Empire in Vespasianic Rome: A New Reading of Valerius Flaccus' Argonautica.* Oxford.
Stroup, S. C. 2010. *Catullus, Cicero, and a Society of Patrons. The Generations of the Text.* Cambridge.
Strunk, T. E. 2010. 'Offending the Powerful. Tacitus' Dialogus and Safe Criticism', *Mnemosyne* 63: 241–67.
  2016. *History after Liberty. Tacitus on Tyrants, Sycophants, and Republicans.* Ann Arbor.
Sullivan, J. P. 1985. *Literature and Politics in the Age of Nero.* Ithaca, NY and London.

Sumi, G. 2005. *Ceremony and Power. Performing Politics in Rome between Republic and Empire*. Ann Arbor.
Svenbro, J. 1993. *Phrasikleia. An Anthropology of Reading in Ancient Greece*, trans. by J. Lloyd. Ithaca, NY.
Swan, P. M. 2004. *The Augustan Succession. An Historical Commentary on Cassius Dio's* Roman History. *Books 55–56 (9 BC–AD 14)*. Oxford.
Syme, Sir R. 1979. *Roman Papers*, Oxford =*JRS* 72 (1934): 127–37.
   1980. *The Augustan Aristocracy*. Oxford.
Syndikus, H. P. 1987. *Catull: Eine Interpretation. Dritter Teil, Die Epigramme (69–116)*. Darmstadt.
Tan, Z. 2014. 'Subversive Geography in Tacitus' *Germania*', *JRS* 104: 181–204.
Tarrant, R. 1986. 'Plautus', in Reynolds, L. D. (ed.) *Texts and Transmission: A Survey of the Latin Classics*, 2nd ed. Oxford, 302–7.
   2005. 'Roads Not Taken: Untold Stories in Ovid's *Metamorphoses*', *MD* 54: 65–89.
   2012. *Virgil. Aeneid Book XII*. Cambridge.
Taylor, M. 1995. *The Decline of British Radicalism, 1847–1860*. Oxford.
Theodorakopoulos, E. 2012. 'Women's Writing and the Classical Tradition', *CRJ* 4: 149–62.
Thibault, J. C. 1964. *The Mystery of Ovid's Exile*. Berkeley.
Thielscher, P. 1962. 'Das Herauswachsen der "Germania" des Tacitus aus Cäsars "Bellum Gallicum"', *Das Altertum* 8: 12–26.
Thomas, R. 2001. *Virgil and the Augustan Reception*. Cambridge and New York.
   2009. 'The Germania as Literary Text' in Woodman, A. J. (ed.) *The Cambridge Companion to Tacitus*. Cambridge, 59–72.
Thomson, D. F. S. (ed.) 1997. *Catullus*. Toronto.
Thorsen, T. S. 2014. *Ovid's Early Poetry: From His Single Heroides to His Remedia Amoris*. Cambridge.
Timpanaro, S. 1978. *Contributi di filologia e di storia della lingua latina*. Rome.
Timpe, D. 1992. 'Die Landesnatur der Germania nach Tacitus', in Neumann, G. and Seemann, H. (eds.) *Beiträge zum Verständnis der Germania des Tacitus, II*. Göttingen, 258–77.
Tissol, G. 1997. *The Face of Nature. Wit, Narrative, and Cosmic Origins in Ovid's Metamorphoses*. Princeton.
Too, Y. L. 1994. 'Educating Nero: a Reading of Seneca's EM', in Elsner, J. and Masters, J. (eds.) *Reflections of Nero*, 211–24.
Torre, C. 2017. 'Senecan Drama and the Age of Nero', in Bartsch, S., Freudenburg, K. and Littlewood, C. (eds.) *The Cambridge Companion to the Age of Nero*. Cambridge, 137–50.
Tranca, A. 2016. 'From Pompeii to Paris: Ghostly Cityscapes and the Ruins of Modernity in Théophile Gautier and Eugène Atget', *Word & Image* 32.3: 251–63.
Trapp, J. B. 1973. 'Ovid's Tomb: The Growth of a Legend from Eusebius to Laurence Sterne, Chateaubriand and George Richmond', *Journal of the Warburg and Courtauld Institutes* 36: 35–76.

Turner, S. 2016. 'Sight and Death: Seeing the Dead through Ancient Eyes', in Squire, M. (ed.) *Sight and the Ancient Senses*. London, 142–60.

Turpin, W. 2008. 'Tacitus, Stoic Exempla, and the *praecipuum munus annalium*', *CA* 27: 359–404.

Uccellini, R. 2012. *L'arrivo di Achille a Sciro: Saggio di commento a Stazio Achilleide 1,1-396*. Pisa.

Umbrico, A. 2009. '"Casinus" sotto il velo nuziale: ancora sul rapporto tra Casinaplautina e Κληρούμενοι difilei', *GIF* 61: 15–45.

2010. *Terenzio e i suoi nobiles: invenzione e realtà di un controverso legame*. Pisa.

Van den Berg, C. 2014. *The World of Tacitus' Dialogus de Oratoribus. Aesthetics and Empire in Ancient Rome*. Cambridge.

Varner, E. 2017. 'Nero's Memory in Flavian Rome', in Bartsch, S., Freudenburg, K. and Littlewood, C. (eds.) *The Cambridge Companion to the Age of Nero*. Cambridge, 237–57.

Vásári, M. 2012. 'Latency and Atmosphere: the Sensuous Dimension of Literary Texts', in Bárdosi, V. (ed.) *Tanulmányok. Irodalomtudományi Doktori Iskola*. Budapest, 225–38.

Versnel, H. S. 1970. *Triumphus: An Inquiry into the Origin, Development and Meaning of the Roman Triumph*. Leiden.

Vesperini, P. 2016. *Droiture et mélancholie. Sur les écrits de Marc Aurèle*. Paris.

Veyne, P. 2003. *Seneca: the Life of a Stoic*, trans. by D. Sullivan. London.

Vian, F. 1961. *Apollonios de Rhodes, Argonautiques chant III. Édition, introduction et commentaire*. Paris.

Villedieu, F. 2011. 'Une construction Néronienne mise au jour sur le site de la Vigna Barberini: la *cenatio rotunda* de la *Domus Aurea?*', *Neronia Electronica* 1: 37–52.

Volk, K. 2001. 'Pious and Impious Approaches to Cosmology in Manilius', *MD* 47: 85–117.

Von Trier, L. (dir.). 2011. *Melancholia*.

Vout, C. 2009. 'The Satyrica and Neronian Culture' in Prag, J. R. W. and Repath, I. D. *Petronius: A Handbook*, Chichester; Malden, MA, 103–13.

Wallace, J. 2004. *Digging the Dirt: The Archaeological Imagination*. London.

Walsh, P. G. 1970. *The Roman Novel: the Satyricon of Petronius and the Metamorphoses of Apuleius*. Cambridge.

Walter, J. 2017. 'Poseidon's Wrath and the End of Helike: Notions about the Anthropogenic Character of Disasters in Antiquity', in Schliephake (ed.), 31–43.

Ware, C. 2004. 'Claudian: The Epic Poet in the Prefaces', in M. Gale (ed.) *Latin Epic and Didactic Poetry*. Swansea, 181–201.

Warren, J. 2004. *Facing Death: Epicurus and his Critics*. Oxford.

Watson, L. and Watson, P. 2003. *Martial: Select Epigrams*. Cambridge.

Watson, P. A. 2002. '*Praecepta amoris*: Ovid's Didactic Elegy', in Boyd, B. W. (ed.) *Brill's Companion to Ovid*. Leiden, 141–65.

Waxman, Z. 2008. *Writing the Holocaust: Identity, Testimony, Representation*. Oxford.

Westall, R. and Brenk, F. 2011. 'The Second and Third Century', in Marasco, G. (ed.) *Political Autobiographies and Memoirs in Antiquity: A Brill Companion.* Leiden, 363–416.

Whittington, L. Forthcoming. *Supplementing the Classics: Ancient Texts and Renaissance Continuations.*

Whitton, C. L. 2010. 'Pliny, *Epistles* 8.14: Senate, Slavery and the *Agricola*', *JRS* 100: 118–39.

Wijsman, H. J. W. 1996. *Valerius Flaccus Argonautica, Book V. A Commentary.* Leiden.

Wilamowitz-Moellendorff, U. von. 1908. *Greek Historical Writing and Apollo: Two Lectures Delivered before the University of Oxford, June 8 and 4 1908,* trans. by G. Murray. Oxford.

Wiles, D. 1988. 'Greek Theater and the Legitimation of Slavery' in Archer, L. (ed.) *Slavery and Other Forms of Unfree Labor,* London and New York, 53–67.

Williams, G. D. 2015. 'Minding the Gap: Seneca, the Self and the Sublime', in Williams, G. D. and Volk, K. (eds.) *Roman Reflections: Studies in Latin Philosophy.* Oxford, 172–91.

Williams, G. W. 1968. *Tradition and Originality in Roman Poetry.* Oxford.

1983. *Techniques and Ideas in the* Aeneid. New Haven and London.

Willis, I. 2017. *Reception.* Abingdon.

Wills, J. 1996. *Repetition in Latin Poetry: Figures of Allusion.* Oxford.

Wilson, M. 2015. '*Quae quid fugit damnat*: Outspoken Silence in Seneca's Epistles', in Baltussen and Davis (eds.), 137–56.

Wiltshire, S. F. 1999. 'The Man Who Was Not There: Aeneas and Absence in *Aeneid 9*', in Perkell, C. (ed.) *Reading Vergil's Aeneid.* Norman, OK, 162–77.

Winckelmann, J. J. 2006. *History of the Art of Antiquity,* trans. by H. F. Mallgrave. Los Angeles.

Winsor Leach, E. 2016. 'Flavian Pompeii: Restoration and Renewal', in Zissos, A. (ed.) *A Companion to the Flavian Age of Imperial Rome.* Malden, MA and Oxford, 327–43.

Winterbottom, M. and Ogilvie, R. M. (eds.) 1975. *Cornelii Taciti opera minora.* Oxford.

Winterling, A. 2009. *Politics and Society in Imperial Rome.* London.

Wiseman, T. P. 1985. *Catullus and His World: A Reappraisal,* Cambridge.

2016. 'Maecenas and the Stage', *PBSR* 84: 131–55.

Woodman, A. J. 2010. '*Aliena facundia:* Seneca in Tacitus' in Berry, D. H. and Erskine, A. (eds.) *Form and Function in Roman Oratory.* Cambridge, 294–308.

2012. 'A Covering Letter: Poem 65' in Du Quesnay, I. and Woodman, A. J. (eds.) *Catullus: Poems, Books, Readers.* Cambridge, 130–52.

Woodman, A. J. and Martin, R. H. 1996. *The* Annals *of Tacitus. Book 3.* Cambridge.

Kraus, C. S. and Woodman, A. J. 2014. *Tacitus.* Agricola. Cambridge.

Woolf, G. 2011. *Tales of the Barbarians. Ethnography and Empire in the Roman West*. Oxford.
Wray, D. 2001. *Catullus and the Poetics of Roman Manhood*. Cambridge.
Yavetz, Z. 1983. *Caesar and his Public Image*. Ithaca, NY.
Young, E. M. 2015. *Translation as Muse. Poetic Translation in Catullus' Rome*. Chicago.
Zadorojnyi, A. V. 2011. 'Transcripts of Dissent? Political Graffiti and Elite Ideology Under the Principate', in Baird, J. A. and Taylor, C. (eds.) *Ancient Graffiti in Context*. New York, 110–33.
Zago, G. 2012. *Sapienza filosofica e cultura materiale: Posidonio e le altre fonti dell'Epistola 90 di Seneca*. Bologna.
Zarker, J. W. 1967. 'Aeneas and Theseus in *Aeneid* 6', *CJ* 62: 220–6.
Zeitler, W. 1986. 'Zum Germanenbegriff Caesars. Der Germanenexkurs im sechsten Buch von Caesars Bellum Gallicum', in Beck, H. (ed.) *Germanenprobleme in heutiger Sicht*. Berlin, 41–52.
Ziogas, I. 2015. 'The Poet as Prince: Author and Authority under Augustus', in Baltussen and Davis (eds.), 115–36.
Zissos, A. 2016. 'Vesuvius and Pompeii', in Zissos, A. (ed.) *A Companion to the Flavian Age of Imperial Rome*. Malden, MA and Oxford, 515–34.
Zwierlein, O. 1990–1992. *Zur Kritik und Exegese des Plautus*, 4 vols. Mainz.

General Index

abolitio. *See* damnatio memoriae
absence. *See also* presence
   absence as presence in Marcus Aurelius, 194
   absent author in Roman comedy, 87
   absent narrator in *Dialogus*, 138
   absent presence, 47, 52, 56
   as filling the void, 109
   as Roman legacy, 326
   as undoing, 91
   authorial absence in Ferrante, 271
   creating greater sense of authority, 332
   creating knowledge of past, 221
   expectation of absence, 225
   generative absence, 3, 5, 13, 14, 45, 288, 324
   of historiographical and ethnographic knowledge in *Germania*, 201–218
   of history in representation of marginalised, 249
   operational absence, 13
   origins of 'conspicuous by absence', 223
   phrase 'conspicuous by its absence', 324
   slavery between absence and presence, 239–249
   textual absence, 13
   writing and, 4
   writing multiplying problems of, 293
absence-presence
   in Ovid *Remedia*, 96
Absyrtus, 282
Accius, 40
Achaemenides, 329, 330
Achilles, 113, 120, 121, 327, 328, 332
Actaeon, 120
actor network theory, 245
address
   engendering subject in Latour, 320
Adrastus, 44
Aeetes, 111
Aemilia Lepida, 156
Aemilius Paullus, 156
aemulatio, 33
Aeneas, 106, 326, 327

Apollo simile in *Aeneid* 4, 116
   as elegiac lover, 122
   inadequate first glance at Dido, 110
   lack of Aeneas' gaze, 113, 115
   presence of Aeneas' gaze in *Aeneid* 6, 118
Aesop, 248
aesthetics, 20
afterlife
   as sustainer of current projects in Scheffler, 314
agency
   slave compromising agency of master, 247
Aglauros, 52
Agricola, 215
Agrippa, 166, 181
Agrippa Postumus, 157, 186
Agrippina, 165
Ajax, 121
Alcyone, 54, 55
Alexander the Great, 170
Allecto, 283
allegoresis, 50
allegory, 13, 24, 47–66, 324
   and tautology, 56
   and the *Aeneid*, 49–51
   and theology, 57
   deniability of, 51
   in Claudian, 60–66
allusion
   and allegory, 50, 65
Althaea, 106
ambiguity
   in *Dialogus*, 140
   of *Dialogus*, 134
   of speech in *Dialogus*, 126
ambivalence, 8
amicitia, 292
Amphiaraus, 37
Anchises, 121, 330
Andromache, 327
animal
   joining of human and animal, 107

General Index 365

Anna, 279
anonymity, 13
  and absence, 325
  and widespread circulation, 151
  as democratising feature, 164
  as protest, 164
  of both source and target, 159
  of target in invective, 155
  political motives behind, 142
  spread of anonymous verses, 143
Antigone, 38
Antoninus Pius, 186
Antony, 152, 159, 160
Aper, 136, 140
Apollo, 157, 291, 300
Apollonius of Tyana, 182
aposiopesis, 6, 13, 23, 324
  and colloquialism, 36
  and intertextuality, 40
  as violation of code, 46
  definition of, 36
  ending *Germania*, 214
  in Statius, 35–46
  metapoetics of, 37
Arachne, 63
archaeology, 1, 2, 325
Arethusa, 294
Argia, 38
Ariadne, 271, 276, 302, 325, 328
Aristius Fuscus, 240
Arsaces, 209
Artemis, 110, 111
Ascanius, 59, 118, 282, 284, 328
Asciburgium, 211
Asinius Pollio, 160
Astyanax, 328
Athena, 275, 277
Atreus, 163, 182, 282
attachment, 13
  as mode of existence in Latour, 319
  substitute object of attachment in mourning, 291
Atticus, 126
Attis, 180
auctoritas, 181
audience
  gender of in Ovid *Remedia*, 105
Augustus, 49, 142, 166, 171, 176, 185, 221
  ambivalence towards lampoons, 160
  and anonymous abuse, 151–160
  and *augeo*, 160
  Augustus' funeral in *Annals*, 225
  reaction to pseudonymous writing, 153
  Seneca as, 181
Aulus Caecina, 144

authorial intention, 22
autocracy, 178, 325
autodiegesis, 192
autography, 185, 196
auaritia, 173
Avernus, 288

Bacchus, 41
being
  as processual and relational, 321
belatedness, 39, 43
Bibaculus, 152
Bibulus, 149
blindness
  and slavery, 242
  to slavery, 240
Boeckh, August, 303
boundaries
  in *Germania* and *De Bello Gallico*, 204
  lack of boundaries for philosopher in *Natural Questions*, 217
  lack of in *Germania*, 214
Brodsky, Joseph, 332
  Letter to Horace, 308–310
Bructeri, 207
Brutus, 126, 151, 159, 222, 227, 324
Brutus the Elder, 151
Burrus, 181

C. Cassius, 222
Cacus, 66
Caecilius, 143
Caesar
  indulgent reaction to anonymous verses, 150
Caledonia, 215
Calgacus, 215
Callisthenes, 170
Calventius, 146
Calvus, 326
Camilla, 328
Canace, 180
carmina triumphalia, 144
Carson, Anne, 11
Carthage, 333
  link to Naples in Ferrante, 274
Casina, 331
Cassius, 151, 160, 222, 227, 323, 324
Cassius Dio, 155
Cassius Severus, 152
Cato, 143, 222
Catullus, 152
censorship, 90, 162
  and anonymity, 142
  of obscene in Ovid, 103
  self-censorship, 164

censorship (cont.)
    self-censorship in Seneca, 167
    shift from self-censorship to legislative censorship, 152
Ceres, 53
Ceyx, 54, 55
Christianity
    Christian symbolism, 47
chronology
    absence of in *Germania*, 210
Cimbri, 207, 208, 213
Cincinnatus, 243
Circe, 105
Claudius, 143
Cleopatra, 49, 147
Clytemnestra, 283
code model, 281
commentarii, 202, 215
Commodus, 188
communication, 308, 309, 317
    contrast between communion and barrier, 309
    frustrated communication in Catullus 101, 293
comparative literature, 16
concealment
    and revelation, 90, 95
consecratio, 64
consolation, 306
conspiracy
    lover as conspiracy theorist, 98
    poetics of, 97
contaminatio, 83
contamination, 107
context, 2
Corinna, 243, 332
correction
    of missing look of Aeneas, 111
counterfactual
    repertory of unwritten works, 332
Cremutius Cordus, 152, 161, 163
critic
    as detective, 97
critical race theory, 14
critique
    as diagnosis, 97, 101, 102
cultural memory, 14
Cumae, 328
Cupid, 105, 284
Curio, 149
Cyclops
    as episode of absent-presence in *Aeneid*, 328
Cynicism, 170
Cypassis, 243

D. Iunius Silanus, 225
Dacians, 216

damnatio memoriae, 14, 209
Danube, 216
Daphne, 291, 300
death
    as experience in Lucretius, 313
deception, 71
Deconstruction, 307, 308
defamation, 154, 157, 161
deferral
    as renewal of pleasure, 91
    Dialogus as deferral, 139
Deidamia, 113, 120
Deiotarus, 128
deixis, 293
    and absent Odysseus, 327
    in Catullus 101, 292, 293
delay
    in Ovid *Remedia.*, 94
Demophoon, 98
Derrida, Jacques, 4, 90, 307
Derveni Papyrus, 51
desire, 7, 89
    and promise, 138
    and silence, 141
    as ebb and flow, 96
    as frustration, 90
    as groove, 96, 108
    as lack, 96
    as rut, 96
    figural desire, 127, 133
    for eloquence, 129
    for eloquent speech in *Dialogus*, 138
    in Cicero *Brutus* and Tacitus *Dialogus*, 126
    in Ovid, 325
    infiniteness of, 93
    narrative desire, 127, 129, 133
    propulsion of desire, 91
    to fill void with speech, 133
destabilising
    effect of *Dialogus*, 136
deterritorialisation, 16
diagnosis
    critique as diagnosis, 92
dialogue, 310, 312
Diana, 109, 111, 113, 120
    and Actaeon, 112–113
dictation, 240
Dido, 106, 325, 326
    absence of Dido's gaze, 122
    and moon imagery, 119
    as narrative hijacker, 327
    as shade, 119, 120
    difficulty of seeing Dido in *Aeneid* 6, 120
    first appearance in *Aeneid*, 109
    in Ferrante, 272–278

invisibility of, 112
transference of gaze onto, 115
différance, 307
digression
  in *Germania*, 202
Diocletian, 187
Diomedes, 106
Dionysus, 282
Diphilus, 68
Discordia, 66
dissemination, 307, 310, 311, 312
  and extended temporality, 312
Dolabella, 149
Domitian, 143, 235
Donatus, Tiberius Claudius, 115
doomsday, 314
Doryphorus, 180
doublespeak, 8
dream
  and allegory, 62–66
Drusus, 211, 221
dyarchy, 191

ears
  in Horace Satire 1.9, 241
Echo, 90, 104
ecphrasis, 324, 328, 332
ecstasis, 100
edicts
  parody of edict style, 147
eidolopoiia, 55
ekphrasis
  and simile, 116
elegy
  economic problem of elegy, 289
  rhythm of the distich, 95
elision
  and loss in Catullus 101, 297
eloquence
  becoming mute, 128
  Cicero as telos of, 129
  continuity of, 132, 133
  disruption of eloquence, 132
  in writing, 133
  persistence of eloquence by other means, 131
  teleology of, 132
eloquentia
  loss of *eloquentia*, 135
emphasis, 51
emptiness
  and Hunger, 53
  of Hunger, 54
enargeia, 53, 56, 63, 324, 329
Enceladus, 62
Ennius, 232, 233

epic
  vs. tragedy, 39
Epictetus, 195
Epicureanism, 11, 171
  in Horace *Epistles*, 312
  inadequate view of death, 317
epistemology
  limits of Roman epistemology in
    Germania, 217
  of *Agricola*, 216
  scepticism towards totalising epistemology in
    Germania, 215
epistolarity, 5, 308
Erasmus, 324
erasure
  in *Nox*, 299
Eratosthenes, 211
Erichtho, 43, 44
erotodidaxis, 102
Erysichthon, 53, 62
ethnography, 201, 207, 215
Etna, 329
Eumenides, 38
euphemism, 324
Euphrates, 216
Europa, 63
Eurydice, 121
Evander, 330
Eve, 235
exchange, 292
exclusus amator, 93
excursus
  Germania as excursus, 203
existence
  being-as-other in Latour, 319
  modes of existence in Latour, 318

facsimile
  Nox as facsimile, 300
Faustina, 186
feminism, 14
Fenni, 213
fiction, 62
  as mode of existence in Latour, 318
figures
  of speech as compensations for
    absence, 324
fire
  love as fire in Ferrante and *Aeneid*, 281
Fowler, Don, 332
fragment, 305, 325
fragmentarity, 20, 23, 27, 28, 29, 33
fragments, 301
free speech
  loss of, 325

Freud, Sigmund, 2, 7, 12, 289, 305
  pleasure principle in, 96
Furies, 282, 283, 287
  Dido as Fury, 287
  Fury and *Fama* in *Aeneid*, 287
future
  in Horace *Epistles*, 312
  personal investment in future, 316

Gaius Memmius, 149
Gallus, 99
Gambrivii, 210
gap
  gaps in *Dialogus*, 136
  in scholarship, 2
Gauls
  Caesar and granting Gauls citizenship, 145
gender, 271
genre, 5, 271
  and law, 38
  generic comprehensiveness in *Thebaid*, 37
  generic conflict, 35, 37
Germania
  as negation of Gaul in Germania, 202–206
Germanicus, 221
ghosts
  of Greece in Rome, 331
  reclaimed ghosts in Ferrante, 288
Gigantomachy, 62
Goethe, 285
grace
  age of, 58
grief
  and language, 289
  and poetry-scholarship as complement, 301
  infecting lexicography in *Nox*, 301
groove, 2

Hadrian, 185, 186
  and fake biography, 185
Haemus, 216
Hamlet, 289
Heidegger, Martin, 309, 318, 319
Helen, 277, 278
Hellusii, 213
Heracles, 119
Hercules, 37
  and Cacus, 49
  Pillars of Hercules, 211
hermeneutics of suspicion, 8, 97
Herminones, 210
Herodotus, 211
heterotopia, 15

hiatus, 24, 26, 329
Hibernia, 215
historicism, 8–11, 16, 249
  new, 8, 14
historiography, 201
  absence of in *Germania*, 210
Honorius, 64, 66
Hortensius, 126
hypostasis, 66
Hypsipyle, 44

Iarbas, 277
ideology critique, 3, 10
imagines, 325
  at Junia Tertulla's funeral, 223, 224
incompleteness, 20
  existential incompleteness, 321
Ingaevones, 210
instauration
  artist as instaurator, 321
  in Latour, 321
interests, 317
interpolations
  in Roman comedy, 87
interruption
  in the *Aeneid*, 115
intertextuality, 6, 7, 12, 50, 271
  and authorial intention, 271
  and mourning, 306
  and silence, 6
  between Elena and Lila in Ferrante, 272
  between unspoken in *Aeneid* and Ferrante, 279–285
intratextuality, 5, 50
Iris, 54
irony, 324
  dramatic irony in Ferrante, 276
Istaevones, 210
Ister, 216
Ithaca, 330
Iulius Secundus, 229
Iunii, 225

Jason, 111, 114, 120, 276
jouissance, 89, 91, 97, 98, 102, 107
  as alternative to Lacanian desire, 100
Joyce, James, 330
Judith, 58
  and Holofernes, 57
Julia the younger, 156
Julius Caesar, 142, 168, 221, 325
  and anonymous abuse, 143–151
  as highest authority in *Germania*, 203, 206
  surpassing Greek geographical tradition, 205
Junia, 325

Junia Tertulla, 221
Junius Novatus, 157
Juno, 40, 54, 328
Jupiter, 41, 59, 62

katabasis, 42
kinship
  collapse of, 107
knowledge
  and conquest in *Germania*, 213, 216
  lack of in *Germania*, 212
  loss of embodied knowledge in Tacitus, 228
Kristeva, Julia, 271
  abjection, 103

Lacan, Jacques, 1, 90, 272, 289
lacuna, 1, 3, 325
  as generator of meanings, 330
  half-lines in Virgil, 329
  in Apollonius, 111
  in Catullus 51, 6, 22, 27, 29, 34
Latona, 116
  reaction of Latona expressing Aeneas' non-reaction, 117
Lavinia, 276
law
  age of, 58
learning
  function of poetic learning in Catullus 101, 297
letter
  as interplay of presence and absence, 308
lex Cornelia de iniuriis, 154
lex maiestatis, 152, 155, 157, 167
libertas, 169, 170
  in Seneca, 169
Licinius Calvus, 144, 149
listening
  in Horace Satire 1.9, 241
litotes, 324
Livia, 167
logocentrism, 26
Longinus, L. Cassius, 209
looking
  not looking in *Aeneid*, 328
loss
  philology and loss, 302
love
  at first sight motif, 110
  at last sight, 120
Lucilius, 142, 159
  in Horace, 142
Lucius Verus, 186
Lucretius, 90

luxury
  in Seneca, 172–176
Lynceus, 119

M. Brutus, 222
Macareus, 330
Macrobius
  attacks on Maecenas, 177
Maecenas, 9, 166, 240
  as example of style is the man, 176
  as figure for Nero, 180
  effeminacy of, 177
  in Seneca, 176–181
Mamurra, 144
Manlii, 225
Mannus, 210
Marcia, 167
Marcus Aper, 229
Marcus Aurelius, 9, 308, 325
  and autobiography, 189
  and first-person mode, 185–200
  and self-erasure, 200
  and succession, 186
  non-specificity in *Meditations*, 195
  relationship with father Pius, 190
  unspoken politics in, 200
  use of Greek as unLatinity, 192
  writing out the self in, 192
Marsi, 210
Marsyas, 159
materiality
  of the book, 298
Maternus, 136
meaning
  and purpose in life, 315
Medea, 105, 107, 111, 114, 120, 276, 282
mediation, 310, 317
melancholy
  philological melancholy, 304
Meleager, 106
melos, 29
memory
  and mourning, 290
  of the Republic in Tacitus, 224
  recorded memory in *Germania*, 211
  relationship with history, 298
Menelaus, 278, 328
metamorphosis
  and allegory, 48
metaphysics
  as account for multiplicity of being, 318
  metaphysical assumptions in reception, 308
  of absence, 308
metapoetics, 5
  of creative process in Ferrante, 288

meta-theatricality, 72, 78
metonymy, 324
Midas, 325
mimesis
    in comedy, 72
Minerva, 52
misreading
    of the not-spoken in Horace, 248
modernism, 309
mora, 45
Morpheus, 55–56, 64
    as poet of the *Met.*, 55
mother
    as lover in Ovid, 104–108
    as split figure in Ovid *Remedia*, 106
    maternity questioning border between self and other, 108
mourning, 289
    parallel to translation, 301
    relationship with philology in *Nox*, 298–302
    tension between poetry and mourning in Catullus 101, 290–298
Muse, 288, 296, 297
Myrrha, 99

Naevius, 143
Nahanarvali, 213
name
    importance of in Ferrante, 278
names
    in annalistic history, 209
Naples
    link to Carthage in Ferrante, 273
Narcissus, 62, 90, 104, 272
narrative
    absence of in *Germania*, 210
    unreliable narrative in *Germania*, 211
Nausicaa, 110, 111
negation, 12, 46
    in Marcus Aurelius' Greek, 193
    Marcus Aurelius' use of in *Meditations*, 191
negativity, 12–13, 16
nekyia, 294, 303
Neoteric poetry
    incompatible with grief, 296
Nero, 8, 9, 143
    and literature, 179
    and the Golden House, 173
    as exemplar of vice in Seneca, 172
    as oblique presence in Seneca, 183
    ideology of luxury as response to Seneca, 175
    Nero's *Attis*, 179
Nerva, 235
network
    as mode of existence in Latour, 319

neuter plural
    as absence in Ovid, 102
New Testament, 47
Nicomedes IV
    Caesar's submission to, 147
noise, 30
nostos, 294
Numanus, 59

Octavian
    and the banquet of the twelve gods, 157
Octavius, 149
Odysseus, 110, 121, 294, 327
Old Testament, 47, 57
omission, 14, 148
    and promise, 139
    of Tiberius in Junia's will, 225
ontology
    as multiple and emergent, 322
    historical ontology, 318
    ontological turn, 318
Opheltes, 45
optimates, 145
orator
    meaning in *Dialogus*, 135
Orestes, 282, 283
organisation
    as mode of existence in Latour, 318
orientalism
    as paradigm for *Germania*, 201
original sin, 60
Orpheus, 37, 121
otium, 33
outspokenness
    in Seneca, 169
Ovid
    exile, 5
    tomb, 5
Oxionae, 213

Pacorus, 209
Pallas, 113, 330
Papirius Fabianus, 173
paradigmatic reading, 50
paraphrase, 324
paratext, 185, 189, 191, 194, 196
paratextuality, 33
Paris, 278
paronomasia, 329
parrhesia, 169, 172
Parthians, 216
Pasiphae, 105
pathology
    critic as pathologist, 92

patronage
  of Terence, 86
Penelope, 95, 277
Penthesilea, 116, 121, 122, 276, 328, 332
Pentheus, 42, 282, 283
performativity, 290
persona, 5
personification, 48
  and allegory, 51–56
  and metamorphosis, 56
  Christian personification, 56–60
  of Chastity, 57
  of Death, 52
  of Envy, 53
  of Faith, 65
  of *Fama*, 56, 59
  of Hunger, 53–54
  of Lust, 57
  of Pride, 59
  of Sleep, 54–56
  of Virtue, 59
Petrarch, 310
Phaedra, 105, 106, 107
pharmakon, 281
philhellenism, 302
  erotics of, 302
Philippi, 222
philology, 11, 20
  and desire for the past, 303
  and intimacy, 304
  and mourning, 290
  and scientific precision, 301
  as endless work of mourning/grief, 302–305
  as *nekyia*, 303
  as reparation for loss, 303
  as work of reconstruction, 302
  melancholic philology, 304
  relationship with mourning in *Nox*, 298–302
philosophy
  and dependence on vice in Seneca, 183
  in Seneca as active goal, 183
  relation between rulers and philosophers, 170
Philostratus, 182
phonocentrism, 4, 26
phonograph, 28
Phyllis, 96, 98
  in Ovid *Remedia*, 98–100
Pirithous, 37
Piso, 146
Pitholaus, 144
Plato, 90
Plautius Rufus, 156
Plautus, 143
pleasure
  of Ovidian *amor*, 91

plebs, 245
plenitude
  lost primitive plenitude and Greece, 326
Pliny the Elder, 166, 213
Pluto, 38
politics of immorality, 148
Polyphemus, 329, 330
Pompeii, 1, 11
  as cenotaph, 325
Pompeius Macer, 161
Pompey, 144, 157, 159, 226
Pomponius Mela, 213
poor
  absence of free poor in Latin literature, 249
posterity
  in Horace *Epistles*, 310
  in Vitruvius, 331
poststructuralism, 271, 276, 288
potestas, 169
Pound, Ezra, 303
praeteritio, 6, 14, 148, 324
  in *Brutus*, 129
presence. *See also* absence
  Cicero's absent-presence in *Brutus*, 129
  metaphysics of presence, 91
  poetics of presence, 307
  presence effect, 20, 29
  self not fully present to itself, 311
presentism, 315
Principate
  experience of as experience of absence, 220
Probus, Marcus Valerius, 111
prosopopoeia, 48, 324
proxies
  actor as proxy for poet, 82
  and absence, 69
  and alienation, 74
  and deception, 73
  and metatheatricality, 81–88
  and slavery, 68, 74–81
  and theatricality, 69
  dangers of, 71
  disrupting communication, 71
  in Roman comedy, 67–88
  independent proxies, 78, 83
  non-human, 69, 72
  proxiness and translation, 84
  proxy-marriage, 68
  Roman comedies as proxies for Greek models, 83
  Terence as proxy for Roman elite, 85
  text as proxy for author, 87
pseudepigrapha, 6
pseudonymity, 153, 157

psychoanalysis, 7, 46, 90, 276, 283, 291
Publius Rufus, 154
pudenda
　as absences in Ovid, 102

queer theory, 14
Quinctii, 225

ratio
　emptiness of in *Germania*, 218
ratio absentis, 325
realism
　in Roman comedy, 88
reception, 9, 11, 13, 15
　as instauration, 333
　critique of 'point' of, 322
　erotics of, 325
　turn to contexts of reception, 307
reciprocity
　lack of reciprocity in communication, 311
recusatio, 324
religion
　as mode of existence in Latour, 320, 322
Remus, 50
repression, 7, 91
　repressed matter returning, 330
Republic
　as faded image in Cicero, 220
　as unwritten embodied practice, 233
　embodied experience of, 221
　loss of as sensory impoverishment, 228
　representations of at Junia Tertulla's funeral, 222
reticentia, 36, 40, 44
rhetorical question, 220, 228, 230, 231
Rhine, 216
Romulus, 50, 226, 243
rumour
　in *Germania*, 212–217

Sacks, Peter, 289
Sarmatian, 216
Saturnalia
　and inversion, 80
Scipio, 143
scripts
　in Latour, 318
Secundus, 136
Sejanus, 152
self
　distributed self in Latour, 320
self-destruction
　of Lila in Ferrante, 286
self-erasure
　resistance to in Ferrante, 286

semiotic order, 96
Seneca
　and attacks on luxury in building, 175
　and autobiographical, 171
　and Nero, 165–184
　and political withdrawal, 171
　and satire, 172
　and tyrants in Senecan tragedy, 182
　lack of historical reference in *Letters*, 167
　Maecenas, Nero and literary style in, 176–183
　moralising about literary style, 176
　oblique comments on Nero, 168
　responsibility for later reception of Nero, 184
　reticence of the *Letters*, 166
senses
　hierarchy of senses, 331
　sensory deprivation in opening of *Annals*, 231
　sensory disaggregation in Tacitus, 230, 235
　sensory experience in *Histories*, 235
sermones, 311
servants, 249
Servilii, 225
Sextus Pompeius, 160
shadow
　as motif of absence in *Nox*, 299
Sibyl, 116, 328
Silani, 225
Silanus, M. Iunius, 209
silence, 4, 13
　about Caesar in *Brutus*, 130
　about politics, 127
　and aposiopesis, 35
　and political constraint, 126
　and speech, 10
　and writing, 28
　as implicit argument in *Dialogus*, 135
　as political statement, 166
　as restricted speech, 125
　as sign of political loss in Tacitus, 233
　defined by speech, 126
　generative silence, 141
　giving impression of meaning, 141
　highlighting eloquence, 126
　in Catullus 51, 29, 296
　in Cicero *Brutus*, 125–133
　in Ovid, 90
　in Tacitus *Dialogus*, 134
　of language, 30
　silent subtext in *Dialogus*, 137
　unobtrusive silence in the *Dialogus*, 134
　unspeakability of politics, 131
simile, 324
sincerity
　in Catullus, 295

sisterhood
  between Elena and Lila in Ferrante, 279
slavery
  absence of slaves in *Georgics*, 243–244
  and absence, 325
  and proxiness, 10
  and repressed *adulescentes*, 77
  and Roman comedy, 74–81
  as blindness, 248
  as prosthesis, 76, 243–247
  as state between presence and absence, 239–249
  bees as slaves in *Georgics*, 244
  book as slave, 247
  disobedient slaves, 77
  Horace as slave in Satire 1.9, 242
  instrumentalising of slave, 246
  ruler-subject and slave-master analogy, 168
  running slave, 76
  slave as master's *manus*, 245
  slave as reader in Latin poetry, 242
  slave performers in Roman comedy, 81
  slaves as both instrumental and intelligent, 75, 81
smarginatura
  in Ferrante, 286
soldiers, 145
speech
  Dialogus as speech act, 140
  strategic vs. sincere speech in *Dialogus*, 140
speech act
  Catullus 101 as, 290
speechlessness, 30
spiritualism, 303
Sporus, 180
Statius
  and Lucan, 42–44
Stoicism
  Stoic opposition, 170
  Stoic self-improvement, 172
subjectivity
  autonomous subjectivity as hollow, 322
sublime, 24
substitution, 292, 306
  and grief in *Nox*, 299
  and loss/mourning, 290
Suburra, 309
succession, 331
  adoptive succession, 191
  imperial succession, 191
  of emperors, 185
Suebi, 210
Sulla, 154
supplement, 6, 22, 25
  and Catullus 51, 33
  in Catullus 51, 34

suprematism, 31
Sychaeus, 121, 275, 277
Symbolic order, 96
synaloepha, 103
synecdoche, 324
synkrisis, 63
syntagmatic reading, 50

tactility
  in *Nox*, 300
talk
  about talking in *Dialogus*, 137
Telemachus, 328
teleology
  absence of in *Germania*, 206
Terence, 249
Terentia, 177
Teutones, 208
Thackeray, 249
Thebes, 283
Theodosius, 64, 66
theology, 322
therapy
  critic as therapist, 91
Theseus, 37, 276, 302
Thracians, 216
Thrasea Paetus, 167, 170
Thule, 215
Thyestes, 282
Tiberius, 142, 186, 222
  ambivalent reaction to anonymity, 162
  and anonymous abuse, 160–163
  avoiding of Tiberius' name, 162
  dealing with slander by publicising, 162
  tolerance to slander, 163
  tolerance towards anonymous abuse, 162
Tigellinus, 170
Tigurini, 209
time
  deep time, 16
Tiresias, 42
Titus Labienus, 156
Tityrus, 171
tomb
  of Ovid, 15
touch
  in Ovid *Remedia*, 98
tradition, 319
Trajan, 235
transcript
  hidden, 8
  public, 8
translation
  Anne Carson's *Nox* as more than translation, 298

translation (cont.)
  in Catullus 51, 27–31, 32, 33
  incompleteness of translation in *Nox*, 305
  parallel to mourning, 301
trauma, 283, 284, 285, 288
  and dissociation, 284
Trinity, 57
Tucca, 21
Tuisto, 210
Twelve Tables, 143
Typhoeus, 62
tyranny, 178

Ulpian, 154
Ulysses
  in Germania, 211
uncertainty
  in *Germania*, 217
unconscious, 7
  textual unconscious, 291, 330
undoing
  in Ovid *Remedia*, 95
unspoken
  giving impression of depth, 137
  in the *Aeneid*, 279
  unspoken presuppositions in *Dialogus*, 135

unweaving
  in Ovid *Remedia*, 94

value
  and the afterlife, 315
  connection between value and need to preserve, 316
Vandili, 210
Varius, 21
Varro, 280
Venus, 106, 110, 113, 328
Venusia, 330
Vesuvius, 286
vision
  vs. hearing in *Germania*, 209
visuality
  as way of engaging with Republic in Tacitus, 219–231
voice, 26, 28
  recovery of voice in *Agricola*, 234

women
  mythical women as pivots for conflict, 278
wounding, 27
writing
  as substitute for lost political plenitude, 234

Index Locorum

Anthologia Palatina 7.476, 295
Achilles Tatius
   1.4.4, 110
Apollonius Rhodius
   Argonautica 3.248–9, 111; 4.1477–80, 119; 4.1481–2, 120
Appendix Vergiliana, 6
Appian
   Bellum Ciuile 2.16.112–3, 151
Apuleius
   Metamorphoses 9.17, 94
Aristotle
   De anima 420, 30
   Politics 1255b, 74
   Rhetoric 1367a, 28–32, 93
Augustus
   Res Gestae, 185; 8.5, 181
Aulus Gellius
   9.9.12–7, 111; 9.9.15, 117; 9.9.17, 112
Ausonius
   Cento Nuptialis 108, 330
   Epigrams 37, 331

Caesar
   Bellum Gallicum 1.1, 203; 6.24.1, 204; 6.24.2, 211
Callimachus
   Aitia 4, 40
   fr.556 Pf., 99
   Hymn to Demeter 66–7, 54
Catullus
   1, 293; 101, 34, 290–298; 14.17, 33; 42, 33; 50, 293; 50.12–13, 326; 50.2, 34; 50.16, 33; 50.7–17, 32; 51, 6, 13, 27–34; 51.6: 32; 51.6–8, 27; 51.7–8, 22; 51.8, 22, 34; 63, 178; 64, 302; 64.86–93, 111; 65, 355.1, 292; 65.1–2, 296; 65.15–16, 298; 68, 356.1, 292; 68.20, 296; 68.92, 296; 68a.15–20, 296; 68a.25–6, 296; 68b, 293; 68b.93, 330
Cicero
   Ad Atticum 14.11.1 = SB 365, 168

Ad familiares 6.6.8, 144; 7.4, 182, 256; 12.20, 182, 256
Ad Quintum fratrem: 2.6, 256; 2.13, 256
Brutus 11, 127; 6, 127; 9, 127; 10, 127; 19, 127; 20, 128; 21, 128; 21–2, 128–129; 21–3, 127, 131; 22, 132; 23, 131; 321–2, 130; 328–29, 131; 328–30, 128, 130; 328–33, 131; 330, 132; 330, 131; 331, 132; 332, 131
De haruspicum responso 25, 244
De republica 4.12, 143; 5.1, 219, 221, 232
De legibus 2.2, 173
In Catilinam 27–9, 48
In Pisonem 26, 146; 53, 146; 62, 146
   fr. 10 Clark, 146; fr. 11a1 Clark, 146
Philippics 13.28, 145
Post reditum in senatu 15, 146
Pro Caelio 33–4, 48
Pro Marcello, 133
Pro Sexto Roscio 47, 72
Claudian, 7
   De tertio consulatu Honorii 162–88, 64
   De sexto consulatu Honorii Pref 1–26, 57–59; 584–6, 65
   De consolatu Stilichonis 2.30–2, 65
   De raptu Proserpinae 1.68–9, 38; 2.307, 38
   Epithalamium de nuptiis Honorii 240–1, 65
   In Rufinum 1.52–3, 65
   De consulatu Manlii Theodori 171, 65
Culex
   131–3, 96

Digest
   28.1.18.1, 154; 47.10.5 pr., 154; 47.10.6, 155
Dio
   42.51.5, 146; 43.20.3: 1025.1, 150; 43.20.4, 150; 43.47.3, 146; 44.12.3, 151; 52.25.6, 146; 55.27.1–3, 156, 157; 56.34.1–2, 226; 61.20.2, 179; 66.23.4, 256; 66.24, 258
Ennius
   Ann. 95 Sk., 50; 156 Sk., 233

Index Locorum

Epicurus
  Epistle to Menoeceus ap. D.L.10.125, 313
Euripides
  Bacchae 918–22, 283

Hermogenes
  Progymnasmata 9, 55
Hippocrates
  On the seed 5, 103
  The nature of the child 13, 103
Homer
  Hymn to Venus 89, 119
  Iliad 5.333–80, 106; 9.158, 38; 20.254, 327
  Odyssey 6.102–9, 110, 111, 119; 113, 110; 146, 110; 24.12, 55; 11.543–64, 121
Horace
  Epistles, 11, 13; 1.1.14, 312; 1.1.59–61, 150; 1.4, 312–323; 1.4.1–11, 315; 1.4.3–5, 312; 1.4.4, 320; 1.4.5, 315; 1.4.6–13, 317; 1.4.12–14, 312; 1.4.16, 312; 1.20, 87, 311–312; 1.20.14–16: 176: 2.1.152–4, 143, 247
  Odes 1.12.46–8, 119; 1.18.15, 60; 2.13, 303; 2.14.6, 38; 3.27.37–41, 62; 3.30.6–7, 313; 3.30.7–9, 316; 3.30.10–14, 317
  Satires 1.5, 330; 1.9.1–2, 239; 1.9.2, 761.1, 242; 1.9.9–10, 240, 241; 1.9.12, 242; 1.9.12–13, 241; 1.9.20–1, 241; 1.9.76–7, 240; 2.1.30–4, 142; 2.7.4, 169
Hyginus
  Fabulae 72, 40

Inscriptionum Graecarum
  7.2713, 180

Juvenal
  Satires 4.38, 143; 6.158, 156; 11.56–9, 241

Livy
  Ab urbe condita 1.pr.6, 212
Lucan
  Bellum Ciuile, 37; 6, 43; 6.732, 43; 6.744–9, 43
Lucilius
  fr. 712 M, 143
Lucretius
  De rerum natura 1.142, 64; 2.7–13, 217; 3.832–42, 313; 4.962–1036, 62; 4.1026–36, 64; 4.1097–1100, 54; 4.1175–92, 103
Lygdamus
  3.7.47–50, 121

Macrobius
  Commentary on Somnium Scipionis, 64
  Saturnalia 2.4.12, 177
Marcus Aurelius, 9
  Meditations 10.36, 188; 1.1, 192; 1.1–5, 192; 1.5, 192; 1–16, 189, 192; 1.17, 193; 2.1–5, 197; 3.1, 198; 3.13, 191; 3.14–16, 199; 3.16, 199; 4.3, 188; 4.48, 257; 6.10, 9.39, 196; 6.26, 195; 6.30.1–2, 195; 7, 192; 9.39, 196; 10.36, 188; 12.36, 198; 14, 192; 16, 191; 16.8, 192; 17, 189; 17.6, 191; 17.8, 191
Martial
  De spectaculis 2, 174
  Epigrams 4.44, 251; 8.70, 179, 180; 10.93.3, 162; 14.208, 245
Menander
  Perikeiromene, 71
Milton
  Paradise Lost 2.648–883, 51

Octavia
  397–406, 173; 430–1, 182; 438, 182
Ovid, 15
  Amores 1.1.1–4, 95; 1.1.20, 99; 1.1.26, 89; 1.1.4, 90; 1.4.47–8, 246; 1.5, 101, 102; 1.5.17, 90; 2.7, 243; 2.8.7–16, 243; 2.13–14, 108, Ep. 3–4, 91, Ep. 4, 89
  Ars Amatoria 1.42, 106; 1.179–228, 94; 1.211, 94; 1.646, 98; 2.123–4, 95; 2.439–40, 90; 2.580, 98; 2.595, 98; 2.717, 94, 101; 2.719, 102; 2.727, 94; 2.727–8, 101; 3.37–8, 96, 99; 3.225–30, 102; 3.449–50, 104; 3.591, 98; 3.771–86, 101; 3.772, 101; 3.786, 94
  Fasti, 5, 14, 166; 1.405–6, 99; 3.637–8, 280
  Heroides 2, 96; 2.93–4, 98, 100; 2.115–6, 98; 2.141, 98; 3.3–4, 294; 4.21–3, 105; 4.165–6, 105; 4.175–6, 294; 12.205–8, 37; 15.97, 294
  Metamorphoses 7, 5; 1.168–76, 63; 1.199–206, 64; 1.689–721, 40; 2.774, 52; 2.777, 52, 53; 2.803, 53; 3.138–52, 113; 3.182, 112; 3.185, 112; 3.192, 112; 3.200, 113; 3.361, 104; 3.381–2, 108; 3.391–2, 325; 3.463, 62; 4.676, 114; 6.103–4, 63; 6.451–4, 113; 7.530–1, 94; 8.462, 107; 8.504–5, 107; 8.532, 107; 8.805–32, 53–54; 10.45, 38; 10.346, 108; 10.374–5, 100; 10.395–6, 99; 10.397, 99; 10.409–10, 99; 10.429–30, 100; 10.460–1, 100; 11.621, 55; 11.626–8, 55, 64; 11.628, 55; 11.629, 55; 11.634, 55; 11.636, 55; 11.668, 55; 12.58–65, 56; 15.249, 94; 15.252–7, 48; 15.361, 65
  Remedia Amoris 5–6, 106; 7–8, 93; 10, 93; 11–12, 94; 12, 91; 16, 194.1, 99; 17, 321.1, 100; 29–30, 105; 41, 104, 107, 108; 43, 93, 99; 44, 99; 45, 99; 46, 93; 49–52, 104; 55, 99; 55–6, 96, 98; 56, 101; 57–8, 106; 57–8, 65–6, 95; 59, 107; 63–4, 105, 107; 83, 94; 91, 109–10, 107; 93, 94; 109–10, 91; 127–8, 105; 155–7, 94, 104; 170, 93; 171, 105; 184, 105; 211, 90; 212, 94; 214, 97; 224, 94; 261–88, 105; 297, 90; 317–20, 101;

317–22, 101; 323, 93; 327–30, 101; 333–40, 101; 362, 103; 385–6, 103; 397, 101; 403, 101; 405, 101; 407, 101; 408, 101; 410, 101; 412–3, 101; 423–4, 102; 429, 102; 429–32, 104; 429–40, 104; 431–2, 102; 432, 103; 433, 250.1, 102; 436, 103; 437, 255.1, 108; 437–8, 102; 439, 102; 439–40, 104; 447, 106; 463, 106; 463–4, 106; 502, 98; 513–16, 94; 547, 106; 547–8, 106; 571, 105; 581, 97; 591, 99; 591–608, 96; 594, 222.1, 100; 597, 99; 601, 98; 603, 98, 99, 100; 606, 99; 607, 100; 608, 105; 716–24, 106; 717–34, 90; 743–5, 105; 814, 105
Tristia 1.1.13–14, 294; 2.103–5, 112; 2.354, 103; 3.14.45–6, 90; 4.1.95–6, 294; 5.5.6–7, 90; 5.7.21, 90; 5.12.57–8, 90

Paul
Sent. 5.4.15 16, 154
Persius
1.99–102, 179; 1.104, 179; 1.119–21, 167; 1.121, 179, 241; 3.7–11, 245
Petronius
Satyricon, 178; 60.1–3, 175
Philostratus
Lives of the Sophists 1.19.1, 180
Life of Apollonius 4.35–6, 168; 4.36.2, 183
Plato
Phaedo 84a, 95
Phaedrus 275d–e, 310; 276b, 310
Republic 398c–d, 29
Plautus
Amphitryon 19–20, 69, 82; 291, 69; 630, 69
Asinaria 11, 84; 91, 79; 499–501, 70; 698–710, 79; 746–809, 70
Bacchides 213–15, 83; 728–48, 69; 789–91, 69; 995–1035, 69; 35–9, 76; 442–5, 79
Casina 18–20, 87; 20, 331; 31–4, 68; 32, 67; 32–4, 84; 50, 68; 62–6, 67; 65, 82; 635–8, 67; 738–41, 79
Cistellaria 104–9, 69; 233–5, 78; 306–71, 73
Curculio 9, 78; 419–36, 69; 591, 84
Epidicus 381, 79; 508–9, 69
Menaechmi 966–9, 75; 967–8, 68
Mercator 171, 79
Mostellaria 25–8, 78; 1149–51, 78, 81
Persa 7–9, 75, 77
Poenulus 4, 82; 16, 147
Pseudolus 51–74, 69; 594–6, 70; 595–666, 70; 607, 887.1, 72; 616–18, 70; 642–4, 71; 647–8, 71; 649–50, 72; 671–2, 72; 688–92, 73; 1113, 70, 75; 1327, 79
Rudens 1389–90, 76; 1395–6, 76
Stichus 418–25, 80

Trinummus 19, 84
Truculentus 534, 244
Pliny
Epistles 1.1, 245; 2.7.2, 207; 6.16, 257; 6.16.2, 257; 6.20, 257; 8.14.3, 228
Pliny the Elder
Natural History 3.31.1, 147; 14.51, 166, 181; 16.108, 98; 28.12, 143; 36.117, 175
Plutarch
Brutus 9.5–7, 151
Iulius 62.7, 151
Moralia; 398E, 258
Polybius
6.53.10, 222
Pomponius Mela
1.58.1, 103; 2.74, 147; 3.49, 213
Procopius
Epistles 86 pp. 565–6, 99
Propertius, 294
1.11.23, 106; 2.22a.41–2, 106; 2.33b [43–4], 325; 2.7.19–20, 106; 3.1.1, 303; 3.11.13–6, 121
Prudentius, 7
Cathemerinon 11.49–52, 60
Peristephanon 10.871–5, 60; 10.874, 60
Psychomachia 47–88, 57–59; 50–1, 60; 78–9, 60; 178–82, 59
Pseudo-Heraclitus
Homeric Questions, 51
Pseudo-Longinus
On the Sublime 10.1–3, 24

Quintilian
Institutio Oratoria 3.7.25, 93; 5.12.18, 180 ; 9.1.14, 51; 9.2.27, 170; 9.2.31, 55; 9.2.64, 51; 9.2.67, 51; 9.4.28, 177; 10.1.69, 72; 12.23.1, 216

Rhetorica ad Herennium
4, 36

Sappho
fr. 16 L.–P., 119
fr. 31, 789.1, 23–26
fr. 31.7–8, 22
fr. 96, 119
fr. 168, 27
Seneca
Apocolocyntosis, 143, 166
Consolatio ad Heluiam; 9.2–3, 172
Consolatio ad Marciam 1.3, 213; 2.3–3.2, 167
Consolatio ad Polybium 17.3–6, 167
De beneficiis 3.27.1, 151; 4.36.2, 178; 6.32.2–4, 178
De breuitate uitae 18.5–6, 167
De constantia sapientis 18:

Seneca (cont.)
 De clementia, 181; 1.3.4–5, 179; 1.9–11, 167; 1.11.
  1–2, 181; 1.11.4, 179; 1.47.14, 168
 De ira 1.20.8–9, 167; 2.31.3, 168; 3.13.4, 169; 3.18.
  3–3.19.5, 167; 3.40, 167
 De prouidentia 3.10–11, 177; 3.11, 177
 Epistles 8.2, 167; 14.7, 168; 19.9, 177; 21, 167; 29.
  1–3, 170; 47, 178; 47.20, 168; 56.9, 171; 68.3–6
  , 171; 73.1, 170; 73.4, 171; 73.8, 171; 75, 169; 86,
  642.1, 172; 88.22, 175; 90.1, 183; 90.15, 173;
  90.19, 175; 90.38, 173; 90.42–3, 174; 90.44,
  183; 92.35, 177; 95.32–4, 183; 100.12, 173; 101.
  10–15, 177; 113.30, 168; 114, 172; 114.1–27, 176;
  114.4, 176; 114.5, 177; 114.6, 178; 120.19, 177;
  122, 172
 Hercules Furens 1–124, 41
 Natural Questions 1.pr.9–10, 216; 1.5.6, 179;
  6.1.1, 256
 Phaedra 987, 182
Seneca the Elder
 Controversiae 2.1.11–12, 173; 10 praef. 4–8, 156
Servius
 ad Aen. 1.135, 36
 ad Aen. 5.4, 280
 ad ecl. 5.10, 98
Servius Auctus
 ad Aen. 4.682, 280
Scriptores Historiae Augustae
 Hadrian 16.1, 185
 Marcus Aurelius 1–8, 186; 14, 194; 15–19, 187;
  20–24, 188; 28–9, 188; 8–14, 187
 Septimus Seuerus 22.1–2, 64
Sophocles
 Oedipus Tyrannus 1403–8, 108
Statius
 Achilleid 1.293–303, 113; 1.303, 114
 Siluae 1.2.265, 255; 3.5.72–80, 252; 4.4, 258; 4.4,
  259; 4.4.78–86, 253; 4.8.3–5, 254; 5.3.104–8,
  254; 5.3.205–8, 255
 Thebaid 1.3–4, 45; 3.338, 94; 3.87, 35; 4.500–18,
  43; 4.514–8, 43; 4.517, 44; 4.776–81, 44; 5.
  34–6, 45; 5.36, 45; 7.199–214, 42; 8.53–60, 38;
  12.31–2, 39; 12.299–302, 40; 12.351–2, 39; 12.
  366–7, 39; 12.382–5, 39
Suetonius
 Augustus 19.1, 156; 51.1, 157; 51.3, 160; 55, 155, 157;
  55.1, 153; 56.1, 154; 70.1, 158; 86.2, 177
 Caligula 30.1, 163
 Iulius 22.2, 149; 24.2, 145; 49.1, 144, 148, 149; 49.
  2–3, 149; 49.4, 147; 73.1, 144; 75.5, 144; 76.3,
  145; 77, 232; 80.2, 145, 147; 80.3, 151
 Nero 7.1, 165; 7.1–2, 180; 10, 181; 21.3, 180; 28–9,
  180; 31, 174; 31.1, 173; 31.2–3, 173; 34.2, 175;
  38.2, 181; 39, 174; 39.2, 143; 49, 188; 52,
  168

 Persius, 325
 Tiberius 14.4, 147; 28.1, 161; 58, 161; 59.1, 162,
  163; 59.2, 163; 66.1, 161
 Terentius 3, 85

Tacitus
 Agricola 3.2, 234; 3.3, 230; 4.3, 187; 4.5,
  216; 10.2, 213; 22, 256; 23.2, 27.1, 215; 30.3,
  215; 33.3, 215; 33.6, 216; 45.1, 230;
  46.3, 234
 Annales 13, 14; 1.1.1, 577.1, 231; 1.1.2, 231; 1.1.3,
  231; 1.2.1, 231; 1.2.2, 231; 1.3.2, 576.1, 231; 1.3.4,
  231; 1.3.6, 231; 1.3.7, 570.1, 136; 1.3.7–1.4.1,
  232; 1.4–10, 186; 1.8.6, 226; 1.8–10, 221;
  1.54.2, 181; 1.72, 157; 1.72.1, 152; 1.72.4, 162;
  1.73.4, 161; 2.24.6, 214; 3.4, 221; 3.76, 222,
  325; 4.9, 221; 4.33.3, 201; 4.34.4, 588.1, 152;
  13.3, 180; 13.3.3, 179; 14.11, 165; 14.12, 170;
  14.16.1, 179; 14.17, 256; 14.49, 170; 14.52, 170,
  180; 14.53, 166, 181; 14.56, 166, 171;
  15.22, 256; 15.38–41, 166; 15.42, 175; 15.45,
  166, 171; 15.61.1, 169; 15.65, 181;
  16.13.3, 166; 16.18, 178; 16.22,
  167; 16.35, 170
 Dialogus, 10; 1.1, 134; 1.2, 138, 139; 2.1, 136; 3.2–3,
  137; 16.2, 139; 16.3, 139; 20, 224; 24.2, 140;
  27.1, 140; 28.1, 140; 26.1, 177; 42,
  138, 139
 Germania, 9, 10; 1.1, 203; 2.2, 210; 3.3, 212; 4.1,
  201; 28, 215; 28.1, 203, 205; 28.2, 204; 28.2,
  210; 33, 207; 33.1, 210; 33.1–2, 206; 33.2, 209;
  34.2, 211; 36.1, 216; 37.1, 213; 37.2, 209;
  37.2–6, 207; 41.2, 206; 43.3, 213; 46.4, 214;
  46.6, 214
 Historiae. 1.1.1, 229; 1.1.1–3, 231; 1.1.4, 234;
  1.2, 255
Terence
 Adelphi 1, 84; 11, 84; 15–21, 85; 25, 84
 Andria 1, 84; 12, 86; 18–20, 84; 21, 83
 Eunuchus 7, 83; 36, 76
 Hecyra 13, 84
 Heauton Timoroumenos 7–9, 84; 13–15, 82; 7–12,
  82; 217–9, 73; 22–6, 85; 25, 86; 28, 86; 28–30,
  35–6, 86; 37, 76; 46, 86; 311–3, 79; 468–71,
  74; 543–58, 79
 Phormio 5, 86
Tertullian
 40.8, 256
Tibullus
 1.4.21–4, 121
Twelve Tables
 fr. 8a, 143; fr. 8b, 143

Ulpian
 1 *ad sab.*, 154; 56 *ad ed.*, 154

Index Locorum 379

Valerius Flaccus
  Argonautica 3.209, 257; 4.507–8, 257; 5.376–7, 114; 5.377, 114
Valerius Maximus, 14
Velleius Paterculus, 14
Virgil
  Aeneid 1, 374.1, 7; 1.118, 332; 1.135, 43; 1.279, 316; 1.291–3, 65; 1.314–417, 110; 1.365–68, 277; 1.421, 333; 1.453–6, 115; 1.453–95, 111; 1.454, 110, 115; 1.456, 116; 1.464, 115, 276; 1.482, 122, 275; 1.491, 277; 1.494–7, 109; 1.494–7, 115; 1.495, 114; 1.496, 109; 1.497, 109; 1.498, 111; 1.498–504, 111; 1.501, 109, 112; 1.502, 116, 117; 1.505–8, 115; 1.509–16, 109; 1.561, 121; 1.595, 110; 1.613, 121; 1.617, 327; 2.5, 327; 2.40, 118; 2.274–5, 327; 3.340, 22, 324; 3.489–90, 328; 3.623, 329; 3.658, 330; 3.659 669, 329; 3.660–1, 329; 3.661–2, 329; 3.662, 329; 3.709, 330; 4.2, 281; 4.4, 114; 4.8, 279; 4.15–27, 277; 4.23, 281; 4.83, 326; 4.117, 328; 4.124–5, 328; 4.136, 118; 4.141–50, 116; 4.211–14, 277; 4.215, 278; 4.225 235, 118; 4.234, 118; 4.259, 333; 4.300–3, 282; 4.329, 328; 4.331–2, 118; 4.346, 282; 4.369, 118; 4.384, 327; 4.384–7, 287; 4.386, 327; 4.395, 120; 4.400, 21; 4.401–7, 21; 4.404, 217; 4.421–23, 280; 4.465–73, 282; 4.466–7, 326; 4.469, 282; 4.470, 283; 4. 471, 283; 4.548–9, 279; 4.600–2, 282; 4.610, 283; 4.661–2, 118; 5.3, 118; 5.781, 41; 5.828, 117; 6.37, 116; 6.430–40, 121; 6.450–5, 117, 118; 6.450–66, 117; 6.450–76, 117; 6.451–4, 328; 6.452, 120; 6.453, 119, 120; 6.454, 120; 6.455, 120; 6.456, 117; 6.459, 121; 6.460, 121; 6.461, 121; 6.465, 121; 6.467–8, 122; 6.469, 122; 6.469–71, 275; 6.472, 122; 6.475, 121; 6.476, 121; 6.667–8, 118; 6.698, 121; 6.776, 256; 6.895–6, 62
  Eclogues 1, 171; 1.1–2, 241; 3.76, 99; 5.10, 99; 7.59, 99; 8.41, 110; 10.8, 99; 10.37, 99
  Georgics 2.227–32, 244; 4.148, 215; 4.511–15, 105
Vitruvius
  9 praef. 17, 332

For EU product safety concerns, contact us at Calle de José Abascal, 56–1°,
28003 Madrid, Spain or eugpsr@cambridge.org.

www.ingramcontent.com/pod-product-compliance
Ingram Content Group UK Ltd.
Pitfield, Milton Keynes, MK11 3LW, UK
UKHW022237220326
469255UK00015B/234